申报世界文化遗产系列丛书

William N. Brown (潘维廉) 著

潘文功 钟太福 译

老外看老鼓浪屿

[中英对照 Bilingual]

Old Gulangyu
in Foreigners' Eyes

Olde Amoy

Nanputuo Temple
Postcard Courtesy of Mr. George Yue

Farmhouse, by Montague

Gate of Amoy, by Allom, 1843
Hand-colored steel engraving

Amoy from the Outer Anchorage, Allom, 1843
Hand-colored steel engraving

Amoy Bazaar, Nov. 1908

Amoy Wind-Rocking Stone
40 ft. long, 20 ft. high, 15 ft. thick
Pushed off the mountain by German sailors, 1908

Postcard Courtesy of Mr. George Yue
Downtown Amoy, Zhenbang Rd., 1930s

路邦鎮市門廈

Chair Bearers Near Amoy, about 1900
Hand-colored postcard

Amoy Country Cottage

Amoy Tailor, about 1910
Card courtesy Mr. Ken Chan

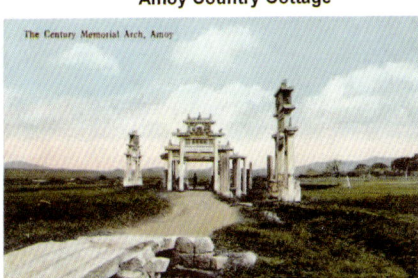
Century Memorial Arch, Amoy

Gulangyu, Signal Hill, 1930s
Hand-colored postcard, courtesy Mr. Phil Hall

Amoy, 1930s

Chinese Lady at Home

Juggler performs for U.S. fleet, 1908

Tong'an, 1948 (Hill family photo)

Japanese inspect Amoy ferry passengers

United States
Battleship Fleet's Visit

AMOY
1908

Banquet for U.S. Fleet, Amoy, 1908

Photo this page provided by Jack and Joann Hill

Tong'an Rice Paddy, 1948

Tong'an, 1948

Blauvelt Hospital, Tong'an, 1948

Sugarcane mill, Tong'an, 1948

Tong'an Street, 1948

Tong'an, 1949

Photos this page provided by Jack and Joann Hill

Plowing Tong'an kitchen garden, 1948

View from Tong'an Mission Compound, Spring, 1948

Siang-chun-thau Village, Tong'an, 1947

Playing in Tong'an, 1949

Gospel Healing Bus., Tong'an, 1948

Courtesy of Mike Bass and Jill Fowler

Photos below provided by Jack and Joann Hill

Dr. Jack Hill and Joe Esther, Tong'an, 1948

Medical Team, Tong'an, 1948

Heavenly Grandfather Day, 1948

New Church, Tong'an, 1948

Dr. Jack Hill, Tong'an, 1948

Dr. Jack Hill, Tong'an, 1948

Amoy in the Eyes of Horace Talmage Day
All images courtesy of "Tal" H. Talmage Day (Day's son)

赫拉斯·打马字·戴眼中的厦门
（本页所有图片均由塔尔·打马字·戴
【赫拉斯·打马字·戴的儿子】提供）

Amoy Gate, age 18

Amoy Temple, age 12

Horace Talmage Day in the U.S.

A Gulangyu Home, age 8

Horace Day and Siblings in Amoy

Lion Rock, Gulangyu, age 15

View from Zhangzhou City Wall, age 12

Day Family's Home, Gulangyu

Horace Talmage Day, famous American painter, was born of missionary parents on Gulangyu, on July 3, 1909, and lived in China 18 years.
　Years later, this "made in China" American artist said his unique style was influenced by both Chinese art and the lush landscapes of his childhood home, South Fujian.

美国著名画家赫拉斯·打马字·戴1909年7月3日生于鼓浪屿的一个传教士家庭。他很早就开始在厦门绘画（他的儿子，塔尔·打马字·戴收集的绘画最早可追溯到1917年。当时，赫拉斯·打马字·戴只有8岁。）
许多年以后，这位著名的艺术家解释说，他的独特的绘画风格深受中国画和闽南风景的影响。在闽南，他居住了18年。如此看来，著名的美国艺术家也有"中国制造"。

鼓浪屿申报世界文化遗产系列丛书

编委会

顾　问	郑国珍
主　任	詹沧洲
副主任	程建明　罗才福　吕参军
委　员	郑惠生　张　岩　潘力方　黄珠龙　郭俊胜
	林树枝　陈天雄　严　琪　吴振志　王伟军
	潘少銮
主　编	郑惠生
副主编	侯卫群　詹艳清　陈　娜

《老外看老鼓浪屿》编委会

主　编	郑惠生
副主编	侯卫群　詹艳清
编　委	徐晋民　林文德

鼓浪屿申报世界文化遗产系列丛书

序

碧波荡漾的厦门湾，浮现着方圆不到2平方公里的小岛，引吭鼓浪于九龙江道口，在风云百年的中国近现代苍桑岁月中，见证着社会变革，铭刻着历史的印记，这就是闻名遐迩的魅力之岛"鼓浪屿"。

和着中国近现代特殊时空的音符，鼓浪屿以其固有的地理位置、美丽的岛屿环境，承载了外来文化与本土文化的汇聚，融化了中外文化的碰撞与价值观的交流，迅速发展成为多元文化影响下具有优美环境的近代居住区，并真实而又完整地保留在现有的文化遗产中。

民族英雄郑成功在此留下的斑斑史迹，传统村落凝聚着闽南文化的积淀……体现了鼓浪屿文化的根。

五口通商，厦门开埠，鼓浪屿迎来了阵阵寒意的同时，吸纳了来自十几个发达国家的多元文化与自我更新后不断升华的本土文化，演绎出浓郁的异国风情与升华的本土文化和平共存的特殊局面。从闽南传统式建筑到外廊殖民地式建筑、西方古典复兴式建筑、早期现代风格式建筑，最终至吸纳外来及本土不同文化之元素、建筑技术与工艺特点而形成的厦门装饰风格式建筑，在鼓浪屿缤彩纷呈，是这多种文化共存局面的真实写照。中国近现代式早期城市在此萌芽、成长，道路网络与市政设施应运而生，传统社会形态受近现代建筑与公共设施等各种外来文化的融入在此向新社会形态转变……构成了鼓浪屿多元文化的源。

正是鼓浪屿这种民族的根、多元文化的源，及其在近百年间的融汇发展，产生了"鼓浪屿文化现象"，造就了一批又一批为社会做出卓越贡献的精英群体，涌现了使汉语摆脱了之乎者也进入白话时代的语言学家，将体育运动推上现代教育殿堂的体育家，"两脚踏中西文化，一心评宇宙文章"的文学家与世界知名的中西文化传播者，得以名字命名星体的天文学家，获得世界冠军的运动员，饮誉世界的医学家、科学家、音乐家……着实对中国近现代进程产生了难以估量的影响，亦为美丽的鼓浪屿留下了无数的宝藏，增添了无限的魅力。

鼓浪屿文化遗产保存状态显示出的这种真实性、完整性，赋予了其所具有的突出普遍价值。对照《实施世界遗产公约操作指南》第77段，使我们因此认识到，鼓浪屿符合世界文化遗产的第(ii)、(iii)、(iv)、(vi)共4条标准：

一、鼓浪屿在一个狭小但相对独立、完整的岛屿中保存下来的，与周边区域截然不同的整体空间结构、环境特征、风格多样的历史建筑和宅园设计，以及从中反映出当时的社会结构和文化形态，展示了从19世纪中叶到20世纪中叶100多年间，以闽南文化为代表的中国传统文化与外来多元文化，在文化、建筑、技术、园林景观方面广泛而深入地交流和融合，符合申报列入《世界文化遗产名录》的第2条标准。

二、鼓浪屿全方位地展现了一个处于封建社会晚期的传统聚落，在政治、社会、经济、文化、技术等众多层面向具有全球化初期特点的现代社区发展的变革历程，反映出这一进程中外来文化在异域寻求生存，以及本土文化传统在外来文化刺激下自我更新的特殊历史阶段；特别是进入20世纪后，活跃于当地和东南亚的华侨所表现出的强大创造力，使其成为19世纪末至20世纪中叶亚太地区本土文化传统，受到外来多元文化影响逐步向新社会形态转变，这一普遍时代变革的独特见证，符合申报列入《世界文化遗产名录》的第3条标准。

三、鼓浪屿完整且保存特别完好的城市历史景观在整体空间结构和环境、建筑类型、建筑风格形态、装饰特征方面，使其成为亚太地区甚至世界范围内，在多元文化共同影响下发展、完善的近代居住型社区的独特实例,符合申报列入《世界文化遗产名录》的第4条标准。

四、鼓浪屿与一系列影响中国文化开放和文化进步的本土精英、华侨、台胞,及其相关作品、思想的产生有着直接联系,如林语堂、卢戆章、马约翰等人。他们不仅是向西方社会介绍中国传统文化的早期尝试者,其相关作品突出地体现了东西多元文化的共同影响;而且他们还积极参与当地和东南亚的政治、社会活动,对于该区域多元文化交流与融合具有重要作用,符合申报列入《世界文化遗产名录》的第6条标准。

这些都充分体现了鼓浪屿不仅是厦门的、福建的文化瑰宝,也是中国的、世界的共同财富,理应受到全世界的认可和保护。今天,我们开始启动鼓浪屿申报列入世界文化遗产名录,正是旨在于寻找国际通用、行之有效的管理模式来保护鼓浪屿这个弥足珍贵、富于诗意的文化之岛,进一步提升鼓浪屿文化品牌,促进海峡西岸经济区建设又好又快发展。

我们深深懂得将鼓浪屿申报列入《世界文化遗产名录》的确任重道远,颇费艰辛,其间必须以务实的态度来挖掘、整理鼓浪屿文化资源,扎扎实实做好基础性工作至关重要。编辑出版"鼓浪屿申报世界文化遗产系列丛书",借以汇聚全球各地有关鼓浪屿外文资料的编译、重要史料的选辑、鼓浪屿文化研究的成果、鼓浪屿老照片的编印等,正是从这方面考虑。我们期盼着厦门各学科专家和国内外对鼓浪屿有深入研究专家的积极参与,真诚地希望有关的专家读者及关心爱护鼓浪屿的人们多提出宝贵意见、多提供有价值的线索,使我们这套系列丛书能越办越好。

勉以为序。

福建省文物局局长
2009年12月11日于福州

前言

福建人有"福"了

　　今年五月，中国国务院通过了《关于支持福建省加快建设海峡西岸经济区的若干意见》。当时，我正忙着为厦门鼓浪屿管委会编写一本宣传手册。作为鼓浪屿申报世界文化遗产的资料之一，这本书是关于老福建、老厦门、老鼓浪屿的历史，文章全部摘自1575年以来在厦门工作、生活过的外籍人士所撰写的书籍、传记、甚至私人日记，还有上千张的老照片。

　　迄今，有关福建、厦门和鼓浪屿的书籍，包括《魅力福建》、《老外看福建》、《魅力厦门》、《魅力泉州》等，我已经编写了八本，数百万字。周围的中国朋友说，我是在旧书堆里"淘金"。是的，阅读的旧书越多，我就越发觉得福建省的省名名副其实。两千多年来，福建一直是中国海上贸易的摇篮，并由此繁荣、富庶。700多年前，当马可·波罗来到中国海上丝绸之路的起点——福建泉州的时候，他盛赞泉州的对外贸易"可与埃及的亚历山大港相媲美"。

　　我是1988年举家迁居厦门的。当时，福建省的基础设施远远落后于中国的大部分省份，部分原因我想是因为福建多山，人称"八山一水一分田"嘛！1994年，我驾车四万公里，走遍中国，结果发现，中国最差的道路不在贫困的宁夏或甘肃，而在福建。1993年，我从厦门开车到武夷山，路上辛辛苦苦折腾了35小时。如今，到武夷山用不了7个钟头。最近这几年，特别是提出"海西"发展战略五年多来，福建省已经拥有了中国最好的高速公路。上等级的道路，破世界记录的隧道和桥梁，让福建的"八山"不再崎岖，福建的每个角落不再遥远。

　　1988年，福建的主要城市公共交通很落后，诸如用水、供电等基本市政服务非常欠缺，且不可靠。如今，即便在龙岩、三明、宁德或南平等偏远的山区县乡，外资企业对基础设施的需求都能得到满足，投资者信心十足。

　　2008年，福建省的国民生产总值达到1.08万亿，比2007年增长13%，居全国第12位，成功跻身"中国GDP万亿俱乐部"。我的中国朋友告诉我，"海西战略振奋人心。它意味着中央政府将给予福建更多的政策倾斜和资金支持。海峡西岸经济区不仅能够促进海峡两岸的经济发展，而且有利于加强两岸的交流与合作，为中国的统一大业作贡献。"最近，《中国日报》的报道说，福建省提出，到2020年，地区生产总值将接近或达到4万亿元。这是一个雄心勃勃的计划。我想，福建人有"福"了。在福建生活、工作21年，我们这个老外家庭应该也能分享吧！我期待着这个宏伟蓝图能够早日实现。

潘维廉博士

工商管理中心 1288 信箱，厦门大学，厦门，福建 361005

amoybill@gmail.com　　www.amoymagic.com

Contents

Introduction	Ancient Amoy Gateway to China	2	
Thanks to:		8	
Chapter 1	Ancient Amoy	14	
Chapter 2	Beautiful Amoy	22	
Chapter 3	The People of Amoy	32	
Chapter 4	Fashionable Amoy	62	
Chapter 5	Education and Government	68	
Chapter 6	Amoy Cuisine	84	
Chapter 7	Amoy Amusements, Festivals, Theater, Sports	88	
Chapter 8	Arts and Music	104	
Chapter 9	Amoy Architecture	118	
Chapter 10	Master Merchants of the Orient	128	
Chapter 11	Amoy Street Life	150	
Chapter 12	Amoy Wildlife	162	
Chapter 13	Amoy Religion	172	
Chapter 14	Amoy Military	190	
Chapter 15	Amoy Opium Trade	204	
Chapter 16	Amoy—Marco Polo's Zayton Harbor?	210	
Chapter 17	Gulangyu — International Settlement	222	
Chapter 18	Foreign Life in Amoy	248	
Chapter 19	R.I.P. in Amoy	280	
Chapter 20	Stories of Foreigners in Amoy	288	
Chapter 21	Learning the Language	298	
Chapter 22	Foreign Fun in Amoy	306	
Chapter 23	Amoy Shopping	316	
Chapter 24	Amoy Street Adventures	324	
Chapter 25	Travel in Amoy	330	
Chapter 26	Western Sports in Amoy	348	
Chapter 27	Foreign Romance in Amoy	364	
Chapter 28	Ruth Bradford's Amoy Journal (1862)	368	
Chapter 29	600 Years of Japan in Amoy	378	
Chapter 30	70 Years After Japanese Invasion of Amoy	390	
Chapter 31	Gulangyu—Cradle of Tropical Medicine	406	
Chapter 32	Amoy—Birthplace of Chinese Protestantism	420	
Chapter 33	Amoy's Pioneering Modern Education	430	
Chapter 34	The Future of China and Amoy	440	
	Stoddard Bibliography	449	

A CHINESE JUNK.

目录

前言
引言　　　　　　老厦门——中国的门户　　　　　　3
鸣谢　　　　　　　　　　　　　　　　　　　　　10
第一章　　　　　老厦门　　　　　　　　　　　　15
第二章　　　　　美丽的厦门岛　　　　　　　　　23
第三章　　　　　厦门人　　　　　　　　　　　　33
第四章　　　　　穿着打扮　　　　　　　　　　　63
第五章　　　　　教育与官府　　　　　　　　　　69
第六章　　　　　厦门饮食　　　　　　　　　　　85
第七章　　　　　厦门的娱乐、节日、戏院和体育运动　89
第八章　　　　　艺术与音乐　　　　　　　　　　105
第九章　　　　　厦门建筑　　　　　　　　　　　119
第十章　　　　　东方的商界高手　　　　　　　　129
第十一章　　　　厦门街头生活　　　　　　　　　151
第十二章　　　　厦门的野生动物　　　　　　　　163
第十三章　　　　厦门宗教　　　　　　　　　　　173
第十四章　　　　厦门军事　　　　　　　　　　　191
第十五章　　　　厦门的鸦片贸易　　　　　　　　205
第十六章　　　　厦门——马可·波罗书中的刺桐港？　211
第十七章　　　　鼓浪屿——外国租界　　　　　　223
第十八章　　　　外国人在厦门的生活　　　　　　249
第十九章　　　　厦门——"白人的墓地"　　　　281
第二十章　　　　老外在厦门的故事　　　　　　　289
第二十一章　　　学汉语　　　　　　　　　　　　299
第二十二章　　　厦门的异国乐趣　　　　　　　　307
第二十三章　　　厦门购物　　　　　　　　　　　317
第二十四章　　　厦门街头奇遇　　　　　　　　　325
第二十五章　　　行走厦门　　　　　　　　　　　331
第二十六章　　　西式运动在厦门　　　　　　　　349
第二十七章　　　外国人在厦门的浪漫史　　　　　365
第二十八章　　　露丝·布莱德福特的厦门日记（1862年）　369
第二十九章　　　日本人在厦门600年　　　　　　379
第三十章　　　　日本侵华战争爆发70年　　　　　391
第三十一章　　　鼓浪屿——热带医学的摇篮　　　407
第三十二章　　　厦门——中国新教的诞生地　　　421
第三十三章　　　厦门的现代教育　　　　　　　　431
第三十四章　　　中国和厦门的未来　　　　　　　441
参考文献　　　　　　　　　　　　　　　　　　　449

老外看老鼓浪屿 *Old Gulangyu in Foreigners' Eyes*

Introduction
Ancient Amoy Gateway to China

Across a narrow channel—then an hour-and-a-half distant by slow junk—lay Kulangsu, a place of[1] comfortable retirement for the more affluent merchants and at one period a competitor for the reputation of being the "wealthiest square-mile in the world."

Normal Goodall, 1920s

Centuries before the world had even heard of Hong Kong or Shanghai, foreigners sought their fortunes in ancient Xiamen (Amoy). Xiamen was part of the legendary port known by the Arabs as Zaiton, from which we get the word "satin." Xiamen boasted one of the deepest natural harbors on the planet, and Marco Polo, who returned to Italy from Zaiton, wrote that it rivaled Alexandria, Egypt in trade, and that "for every ship that sails from Christendom, a thousand sail from Zaiton." But this probably did not surprise Marco Polo, given that our province gave rise to China's maritime shipbuilding and exploration over 2000 years ago.

No people in China were as keen on seeking their fortune abroad as the open-minded and free-spirited Xiamen people, which is why most Overseas Chinese today trace their ancestry to this area. But those that stayed behind made a name for themselves as well, producing Fujian's famous tea, silk and porcelain. And Yankee traders met their match in Xiamen merchants—whom we can thank for American Independence. A Xiamen ship supplied the Anxi tea for the "Boston Tea Party". Had it not been for Xiamen, American lawyers would still be wearing white powdered wigs and we'd be eating French fries with vinegar instead of ketchup.

Foreigners admired their honesty and sense of fair play, as well as their uncanny business prowess, and dubbed Xiamenese as the "Yankees of China," the "Scots of China," and the "Europeans of China."

Ancient Xiamen was also known for heroes like Koxinga, the last defender of the Ming Dynasty, who made his stand in Xiamen before crossing the Straits to retake Taiwan from the Dutch. Xiamen also put up China's most spirited defense against the British during the first Opium War.

---

1 "The tea sunk in Boston harbor in 1773 came from Amoy, and all the tea grown in the island of Formosa was shipped there for reshipment…Considerable commerce is still carried on, however, the principal imports being opium, cotton, indigo and grain; the chief exports, tea, camphor, sugar, paper and earthenware." Foster, 1918, p. 238. Also see Griffis, 1913, p. 57.

引言：老厦门——中国的门户

> 穿过狭窄的水道，再乘慢船航行一个半小时，就到了鼓浪屿。对稍微富足的商人来说，鼓浪屿是一片舒适的乐土。这里还曾经是"全球最富庶平方英里"美誉的竞争者之一。
>
> ——诺缪尔·古德奥，19世纪20年代

在香港或上海闻名于世数百年前，老外就已开始到老厦门寻求财富。厦门当时就是阿拉伯人称之为神秘的刺桐港的一部分，刺桐也因此成为英文"satin"（缎子）的辞源。厦门拥有世界上最好的深水良港。马可·波罗曾经从刺桐港返回意大利。他写道，刺桐港在商贸上可与埃及的亚历山大港媲美，"如果说从基督国家驶出的是一艘商船，那么从刺桐港起锚的就是上千艘"。对马可·波罗来说，这也许不足为奇，因为中国的造船业和远洋探险就是发端于2000多年前的福建省。

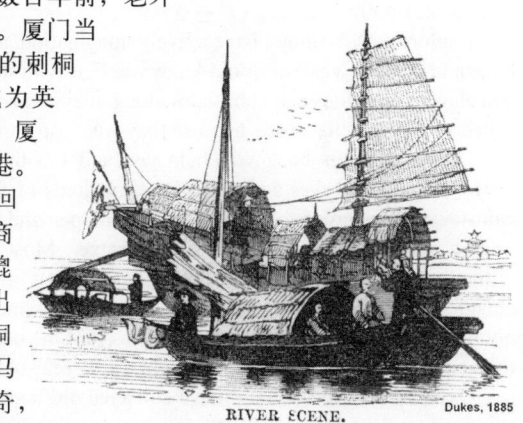

RIVER SCENE. Dukes, 1885

厦门人思想自由、开放。在中国，没有人比他们更加钟情于到海外发家致富。时至今日，大多数的华侨都在这里找到了自己祖先。坚守故土的厦门人也很争气。他们生产了福建省著名的茶叶、丝绸和陶瓷。美国商人与厦门商人惺惺相惜，并感谢他们为美国独立所作出的贡献：因为一艘厦门商船为波士顿倾茶事件提供了茶叶。外国人赞赏厦门人的诚实、公正以及他们神秘的商业力量，称赞厦门人是中国的"扬基佬"、"苏格兰人"和"欧洲人"。[1]

老厦门也因拥有像郑成功这样的英雄而闻名。作为明王朝的最后一位捍卫者，郑成功在横渡台湾海峡、从荷兰人手中收复台湾岛之前曾经在厦门安营扎寨。第一次鸦片战争期间，厦门人同仇敌忾，奋起抵抗英军入侵。

---

1 1773年美国波士顿倾茶事件中被抛入海中的茶叶是安溪茶，从厦门用船运往波士顿。要不是厦门人民的帮助，美国律师肯定现在还得戴着白色的假发上法庭，而我们美国人吃炸薯条沾的肯定还是醋，而不是番茄酱。

老外看老鼓浪屿 Old Gulangyu in Foreigners' Eyes

Xiamen may lost the battle with Britain, but it won the war. Xiamen not only accepted the invaders but absorbed them, learned from them, and by the early 20th century, Gulangyu International Settlement was the "richest square kilometer" on earth, with consulates from 14 countries, and more wealthy people than anywhere on earth except for Pasadena, California (my home before moving to Xiamen). Most of these newly rich were Chinese, and Gulangyu's hundreds of elegant old mansions are a vivid reminder of the political, economic and cultural power that our tiny island wielded a century ago.

With its unique concentration of wealth and talent, tiny Gulangyu Islet had a pivotal influence not only on Sino-foreign trade but also modern education, medicine (it was the "Cradle of Tropical Medicine"), arts, literature, music, sports, economics—even the Chinese language itself (Pinyin Romanization and Chinese punctuation were developed by a local, Lu Zhuangzhang (卢戆章).

Exploring Old Amoy I have a lively imagination, and often stroll the banyan-shaded lanes and imagine what exotic old Amoy was like, with sleek tea clippers anchored offshore, and elegant mansions and consulates along alleys so narrow that 19th century foreigners called them umbrella streets because they were too narrow to open an umbrella.

I hope that this book will help you and I both to experience life in exotic Old Amoy through the eyes and ears of the hundreds of foreigners who over the centuries painstakingly recorded their impressions with pen and ink, paintings, and photography.

These old records are increasingly scarce. Most were destroyed by time, neglect, or the frequent military and political upheavals that ravaged old Amoy. They are scarce outside of China as well, and jealously guarded. A library in New York wanted me to sign my life away and pay $175 USD for just a one-time use of an 1870s engraving of Amoy. In the end, I searched online and bought a 130-year-old book with the engraving.

Over the past few years, I have collected old books, letters and photos, engravings, paintings, and postcards, as well as journals portraying life in Old Amoy by everyone from diplomats and missionaries to a 6-year-old American girl on Gulangyu in the 1850s, and the free-spirited (but spoiled) 20-year-old daughter of the U.S. Consul in Amoy in 1862.

I interviewed retired missionaries (Jack and Joann Hill, for example) who had served in Xiamen during the 40s and early 50s, and many provided journals, letters, and old photos (Wendell and Renske Karsen loaned me 8 albums with over 1000 black and white Amoy photos). I've also received material from descendants of foreigners who lived in Amoy (Burns, Abeel, Doty, Talmage, Koeppe, and the son of Horace Day, a famous American painter born on Gulangyu). Some of this material is on our English Xiamen website, www.amoymagic.com.

At first I feared I'd not find enough material for even a slender volume on Old Amoy, but as it turned out I had far too much material. Perhaps I can compile a sequel, and I hope to eventually compile "Old China in Foreigners' Eyes."

In the meantime, please visit our website for hundreds of pages of additional material, photographs and artwork.

Enjoy Old Amoy!
Bill Brown
Xiamen (formerly Amoy)
China, Oct. 2009

引言：老厦门 —— 中国的门户 Introduction: Ancient Amoy Gateway to China

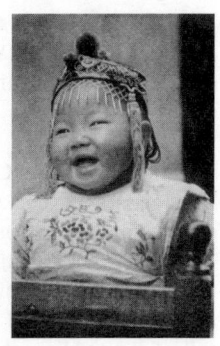

厦门抵抗英国人的战斗失败了，但最终却赢得了战争。侵略者进入厦门，厦门人同化了他们，并向他们学习。到了20世纪初，鼓浪屿国际租界已经成为全球"最富庶的平方英里"，拥有富翁的数量世界第二（美国加州帕萨迪纳市——我迁居厦门之前的老家位居第一）。14个国家在岛上设立领事馆。鼓浪屿岛上当时的新贵大多数是中国人。那里数百座典雅的旧别墅生动地再现了这个小岛100多年前所展示的政治、经济和文化魅力。

财富集中、人才聚集，小岛鼓浪屿不仅在中外贸易中发挥了至关重要的作用，而且对现代教育、医学（热带医学的摇篮）、艺术、文学、音乐、体育、经济，甚至对中文本身（罗马拼音和中文标点符号就是由厦门人卢戆章发明的）影响颇深。

漫步厦门老城区，我思绪万千。走在榕树遮阴的小巷里，我常常想象老厦门的场景：造型优美的运茶快船在岸边下锚，小巷里的别墅和使馆优美典雅。小巷很窄，窄得难以撑开一把雨伞，19世纪的老外称之为"伞街"。

100多年来，数以百计的老外亲眼目睹、亲耳所闻，并用笔墨、绘画和照片用心记录了老厦门神奇的历史。本书期望通过他们的记录，让我们得以重温那段历史。

如今，有关老厦门的记录变得越来越珍贵。随着时间的推移，加上人们的疏忽以及老厦门经常遭受的各种战争和政治动荡，大多数的记录已被损毁。中国境外有关厦门的历史资料也非常稀少，且防护严密。纽约的一家图书馆曾经为使用一次19世纪70年代的厦门版画图而向我提出了175美元的要价。这简直要我的命！最后，我上网搜索，买到了一本有130年历史的旧书，找到了这幅画。

在过去的几年里，我收集了大量有关老厦门的旧书、信件、照片、版画图、绘画、明信片，以及描绘老厦门历史生活的资料（从外交官、传教士到19世纪50年代居住在鼓浪屿的一位六岁美国小女孩，还有1862年美国驻厦门领事的一位女儿——她芳龄二十，思想开放但娇声惯养）。

我采访过诸如杰克和琼·希尔等退休传教士。他们在上个世纪四五十年代曾经在厦门传教，许多人向我提供资料、信件和旧照片。其中，温德尔和仁斯科·卡森借给我8本相册，里面有1000多张厦门的黑白照片，大多是鼓浪屿救世医院的护士们在50多年里拍摄的。我还从曾经在厦门居住过的老外的子孙后代（如本斯、阿比尔、多蒂、打马字、科皮以及在鼓浪屿出生的美国一位著名画家的孙子）那里得到了许多资料。我把其中的一部分资料上载到我们的厦门网站：www.amoymagic.com。

起初，我一直担心我找不到足够的资料来撰写一本有关老厦门的簿册。结果却发现，我的难题不是往书里填，而是删（原先的内容，我砍掉了三分之一）。也许我还可以编写续集，并最终出版"老外眼中的旧中国"。

最后，欢迎浏览我们的厦门网站。那里有数百页有关老厦门的资料、照片和艺术作品。希望您能喜欢！

老外看老鼓浪屿 Old Gulangyu in Foreigners' Eyes

The Unexplored Continent I have met only two classes of people who are able confidently to assert, 'We do!' They are newspaper reporters and globe-trotters. As for myself, I am continually discovering a continental area still unexplored.

Dr. Arthur H. Smith, in Gamewell, 1919

Two Kinds of "China Books" Two classes of books are written about China by two classes of people. There are books written by people who have spent the night in China, as it were, superficial and amusing, full of the tinkling of temple bells; and there are other books written by people who have spent years in China and who know it well,--ponderous books, full of absolute information, heavy and unreadable. Books of the first class get one nowhere. They are delightful and entertaining, but one feels their irresponsible authorship. Books of the second class get one nowhere, for one cannot read them; they are too didactic and dull. The only people who might read them do not read them, for they also are possessed of deep, fundamental knowledge of china…

This book falls into neither of these two classes, except perhaps in the irresponsibility of its author. … Take it lightly; blow off such dust as may happen to stick to you. For authentic information turn to the heavy volumes written by the acknowledged students of international politics.

…Like most Americans, you have a lurking sentimental feeling about China, a latent sympathy and interest based on colossal ignorance. … Two months ago my ignorance was fully as over-whelming as yours, but it is being rapidly dispelled. So I'll try to do the same for you…

La Motte, 1919

Painting China "China is such a vast country, and holds such wealth of beauty and interest that an artist might spend years and then only have taken the cream from each place…I venture to think that if Europeans could but see more pictures, realistically painted, of the natural and created beauties of that great Empire, they would form a better opinion, not only of the country, but of the civilization and very high artistic sense of the people… My visit to Japan was but a short one, … but I could not help comparing the two countries artistically, very much (from my point of view) in favour of China, which, with increased facilities for travelling, will become a great holiday ground for, at any rate, the wealthier traveler."

Liddell, 1909

引言：老厦门 —— 中国的门户 Introduction: Ancient Amoy Gateway to China

未开发的大陆 我只见过两种人敢自信地说"我们确实了解中国"！他们分别是记者和环球旅行家。至于我自己，只是一直在探索一个未开发的大陆。

——阿瑟·H.史密斯，在华传教45年
（1919年，于美国北卡州甘威尔，第3页）

有关中国的两种书 关于中国，有两种书，分别由两种老外撰写。其中一种是由在中国呆过几夜的外国人编写的，肤浅、有趣，书中充斥着浮躁和自大的声音；另外一种是由在中国居住多年、了解中国的外国人撰写的，有思想、信息量大、有份量、难读懂。尽管轻松、有趣，第一种书却不能给人深思，读者可以感受到作者的不负责任。第二种书也一样，太教条、枯燥，读者读不懂。潜在的读者放弃了，因为书中都是有关中国的既深奥又基本的知识……

除了作者的不负责任，本书不属于上述两种……不要信以为真，吹掉无意中落在你身上的尘埃。想了解有关中国的真实情况，请阅读国际政治专业学生撰写的鸿篇巨著。

Mountain Pass South of Amoy Johnston, 1898

跟大多数美国人一样，你对中国拥有一种潜在的情感，一种基于极度无知的隐性同情和兴趣……两个月之前，我对中国的无知跟你们一样彻底，但这种无知很快就烟消云散了。因此，我想为你们做同样的事情，消除无知……

——拉·莫特，1919年，第3页

"中国疆域辽阔。她拥有丰富的美景和情趣，足够让任何一名艺术家忙上几年，且只能在每个地方选取最精华的部位。我曾想，如果欧洲人能够多看一些在这个伟大帝国实地创作的自然风光和人工美景的绘画作品，他们对这个国家、对这个文明的印象肯定会更好一些，对这个民族人民的艺术感评价也肯定会更高一些……我对日本的访问时间很短……然而我不禁会从艺术方面来比较这两个国家，而且（从我个人的观点来看）毫无疑义站在中国的一边。交通条件一旦有所改善，中国在某种意义上一定会成为富裕的旅行者所钟爱的旅游圣地。"

——理德尔，1909

老外看老鼓浪屿 *Old Gulangyu in Foreigners' Eyes*

Acknowledgments

Thanks to:

My wife, Susan Marie, for her patience.
Gulangyu and Xiamen governments for their encouragement and support.
My editor at Xiamen University Press, Mr. Shi Gaoxiang.
Mr. Pan Wengong, of FJTV, for his painstaking translation.
Jack and Joann Hill, former 2nd-generation RCA missionaries in Amoy, for letting me interview them and providing text, images, advice, contacts and encouragement.
Wendell and Renske Karsen, for loaning me rare documents and 8 albums of over 1000 photos taken by Amoy missionaries over a 50-year period.
John Anderson, born on Gulangyu in 1939, for the chapter about his missionary parents' relief efforts during the Japanese invasion.
Tal Day, for providing the childhood Amoy paintings of his father, Horace Day, celebrated American painter who was born to missionary parents in Amoy in 1909.
Terry Bennett, author and photographer, for three photos.
Peggy Daub, Director, Special Collections Library, University of Michigan, for help with the Chater Collection.
Richard Morgan, Chief Superintendent of the Hong Kong Police, Dave Deptford, and Mike Bass and partner Jill Fowler, for into and images about the Gulangyu Police.
Michael Moorish, of the U.K. for the colored Amoy beheading photo.
Postcard Dealer Claudia Kienel, Germany, for the "Photo of Amoy Admiral Yamen"
George Yue, a Hong Kong stamp dealer whose family was from Nan'an, for 16 old postcards (scanned by his associate Rene Hout, also of Hong Kong).

引言：老厦门 —— 中国的门户 Introduction: Ancient Amoy Gateway to China

Mr. Ken Chan of Shanghai, for the Amoy Sewing Machine Postcard.
Jean Walton, Secretary, New Jersey Postal History Society, for Mary Doty's memoirs
Elwood E. Geiger, grandson of Elihu Doty's youngest daughter by his second wife, for Doty photos, and permission to use the memoirs.
Rachael Cross, of the Wellcome Library, London, for the Manson family photo, as well as an Amoy harbor photo.
Archpriest Dionisy Pozdnyaev, of Hong Kong, for info and photos of the Russian church in Amoy.
Jim Reid, of J&K Postcards (Fallbrook, California) for two Amoy cards.
Mr. Ashley Brewin, a Freemason in HK, for the Amoy Freemason postcard.
The U.S. Navy Historical Center for photos of the Navy's 1908 Amoy visit.
Mr. Tomihisa Yamashita, of Kyoto, for several old color Amoy postcards.
Dave Essing, of Bendav Postcards, for the Otte postcards.
Ms. M. Logie for photos of great, great grandfather, Robert John Hastings, Sr.
Mr. Joe McKernan, Denmark, for the "Aquatic Sports of Amoy" engraving.
And thanks to the dozens of descendants of folks who lived and served in Amoy, who visited our website, www.amoymagic.com, and provided us materials, advice, and encouragement. I have probably forgotten more people than I have thanked. My sincere apologies, and thanks to all of you.

Amoy—a British Factory
(close-up of Moll's Map of China, 1710)

Amoy Harbour in 1873, from Koolongsu. Photo by Thomson

老外看老鼓浪屿 Old Gulangyu in Foreigners' Eyes

鸣谢

苏珊·玛丽，我的妻子，我挑灯夜战写作，她耐性极好。

鼓浪屿管委会，热心资助本书的出版。

施高翔，厦门大学出版社本书编辑，在书稿截止期超过一年多之后，依然非常耐心。

潘文功，福建电视台，再次组织人员翻译本书。

杰克和琼恩·希尔，美国归正会厦门传教士子女，他们慷慨地接受我的采访，并提供了不少文字资料、图片、建议和鼓励。

温德尔和仁斯科，借我8本影集、超过1000张照片，均由厦门传教士拍摄，时间跨度超过50年（还有其他资料）。

约翰·安德森，美国加州山景城人，1939年生于鼓浪屿，提供了有关其父母作为传教士在日本入侵鼓浪屿期间参与难民救助工作的内容。

塔尔·戴，美国著名画家赫拉斯·戴（1909生于厦门，父母均为传教士）的孙子，提供了赫拉斯童年时代在厦门绘画作品的副本。

特瑞·本赖特，精美的《1853—1912日本映像》的作者和摄影者，提供了两张教堂照片和一张赛马照片。他编辑的《中国老照片》一书即将出版。

佩琪·多伯，美国密执安大学图书特藏馆馆长，帮我收集了有关切特先生的资料。

理查德·摩根，麦克·巴斯和他的伙伴，提供了有关鼓浪屿警察的图片和信息。

米歇尔·莫里斯，英国人，提供了厦门行刑的彩色照片。

克劳迪尔·吉尼尔，明信片商，提供了厦门海军衙门的照片。

叶乔治，香港邮票商，他的家族来自福建南安，提供了16张旧明信片，并由他的香港同事仁尼·豪特扫描复制。

常坤（音译）先生，上海人，提供了厦门缝纫机的明信片。

基恩·沃尔特，新泽西州邮政历史协会秘书，提供了玛丽·多蒂未出版的回忆录，可上我们的魅力厦门网站（www.amoymagic.com）阅读全文。

艾尔伍德·E.基格，耶力忽·多蒂与第二任妻子所生的小女儿的孙子，提供了多蒂的照片，并允许我使用多蒂的回忆录。

拉希尔·克劳斯，英国伦敦维尔康图书馆，提供了曼森的家庭照和一张厦门港照片。

季奥尼西·波兹尼夫，东正教香港教区主牧，提供了在厦门的俄国教堂的照片和资讯。

富久山下先生，日本东京人，提供了数张厦门的旧明信片。

感谢数十位在厦门生活、工作过的外籍人士后裔，他们浏览我们的魅力厦门网站，为我们提供了相关的信息，给我们建议和鼓励。

我可能还遗漏了十几个人。对此，我深表歉意和衷心的感谢。

希望大家喜欢老厦门！

潘维廉博士

引言：老厦门 ── 中国的门户 Introduction: Ancient Amoy Gateway to China

The Saturday Magazine.

Nº 677. JANUARY 21ST, 1843. {PRICE ONE PENNY.

THE FIVE PORTS OF CHINA OPEN TO BRITISH TRADE.

AMOY, FROM THE ANCHORAGE, SHOWING THE FORTS.

I. AMOY.

IN previous volumes of the *Saturday Magazine* we have given a historical notice of the origin and progress of the British trade in China; of the city and province of Canton; and of the manners and customs of the Chinese in general; thus presenting such interesting details respecting the remarkable inhabitants of this great empire, as the sources of information up to the present eventful period had enabled us to collect.

But our recent contest with the Celestial Empire, and the interest which has now become attached to those portions of China which have been the scene of conflict, or which are thrown open to us by the late treaty, have caused so much inquiry on the subject, and have clothed the accounts of the latest writers with so great a charm, that we proceed to place before our readers a particular notice of the towns most frequently named in connexion with late events; and especially of the five ports now opened to British enterprise and commerce; together with such additional notices of the Chinese character and condition as our increased acquaintance with their country has enabled us to obtain. A clearer idea will be gained of the subject if our readers will refer to a map of China, as they peruse these articles. They will meet with some inaccuracies in most of our maps, when compared with the latest intelligence, yet they will find it advantageous to consult them.

The five ports we shall notice in the following order—
VOL. XXII.

I. AMOY. II. FOO-CHOO. III. NING-PO.
IV. SHANG-HAI. V. CANTON.

Amoy is a celebrated sea-port in the province of Fokien, on the eastern coast of China, and it will be seen by reference to our illustration, that its scenery has somewhat of a picturesque character, although not indicative of great fertility. Amoy is seated on the left side of a bay which deeply indents the country and forms numerous islands. The importance of this place as a British trading post may be estimated by the description of the city given by the Rev. Mr. Gutzlaff.

The city is very extensive, and contains at least two hundred thousand inhabitants. All its streets are narrow, the temples numerous, and a few large houses owned by wealthy merchants. Its excellent harbour has made it from time immemorial one of the greatest emporiums of the empire, and one of the most important markets of Asia. Vessels can sail up close to the houses, load and unload with the greatest facility, have shelter from all winds, and in entering or leaving the port experience no danger of getting ashore. The whole adjacent country being sterile, forced the inhabitants to seek some means of subsistence. Endowed with an enterprising spirit and unwearied in the pursuit or gain, they visited all parts of the Chinese empire, gradually became bold sailors, and settled as merchants all along the coast. Thus they colonized Formosa, which from that period to this has been their granary; visited and settled in the Indian Archipelago, Cochin-China, and Siam. A population constantly overflowing demanded constant resources for their subsistence, and this they found in colonization.

677

老外看老鼓浪屿 *Old Gulangyu in Foreigners' Eyes*

引言：老厦门 —— 中国的门户 Introduction: Ancient Amoy Gateway to China

老外看老鼓浪屿 *Old Gulangyu in Foreigners' Eyes*

Chapter 1   Ancient Amoy

Amoy Harbor in 1575   The entrance of that port was a fine sight, for besides being so large that a great number of ships could be contained therein, it was very safe, clean and deep; and from the entrance, it is divided into three arms of the sea and so many ships were cruising under sail on each one of them that it was an amazing thing to see…

Father Martin De Rada, July, 1575

The first commerce carried on by Europeans with China was at a port called Emouy, in Fokien…

Dobell, "Counselor to Emperor of Russia," 1830

Celebrated Amoy   Both Amoy and Chinchew [Quanzhou] were celebrated even before A. D. 800 as emporia, and their traders were formerly found in the ports of the Archipelago and India, and as far as Persia…Europeans began to trade at Amoy very soon after their appearance in China.

Mayers and Dennys, 1867

View of Kulangsu, 1872   Photo Courtesy of Wellcome Library, London

第一章 老厦门

1575年的厦门港 当时厦门港的入口处视野很好,因为港湾宽阔,可容纳大量船只,而且安全、整洁、吃水深。厦门港从入口处就被分为三条航道,每条航道都挤满了数量众多的海船,实在是美不胜收……
——马丁·德·拉达神父,1575年7月

欧洲人与中国的第一次商贸活动就是在福建一个叫厦门的港口进行的……
——都贝尔,沙皇顾问,1830年

著名的厦门港 厦门和泉州在公元800年前就是著名的商业中心。来自这两个地方的商客首先出现在东南亚群岛和印度的港口,然后远至波斯……欧洲人一在中国露脸,就开始在厦门做生意。
——梅尔斯和丹尼斯,1867年,第244页

THE TOWN OF AMOY FROM KULANGSEU   Dukes, 1885

Amoy Better than Canton The island and city of Amoy will succeed to a large share of that trade, which is hourly passing away from Canton forever. The navigation of the Canton river is tedious, and often insecure,--the entrance to the cove of Amoy is short, deep, and unimpeded. Egress is equally inconvenient from the former city, while vessels may wait in the inner harbor of Amoy, under island-shelter, for favorable weather, and sail almost the moment of its return. Besides the natural advantages, all which have more than once been dwelt on in these brief notices of the great empire of the Chinese, our embassies and expeditions have uniformly found a kindlier spirit, a more generous feeling, predominant at Amoy, towards foreigners, and traders, and visitors, than at other parts of China...

Allom and Wright, 1843

Open Amoy People Amoy... unlike Canton, is quite open to foreigners, who are indeed freely permitted to enter within the walls of all the other towns and cities on the coast, or accessible from it. In visiting Amoy, the first thing that strikes a foreigner coming from the south is the feeling of delight which he experiences in rambling everywhere unmolested. After being forcibly turned back on entering within the gates of the so-uthern metropolis, as has been my experience repeatedly, it is pleasant to revel in the unrestrained luxury of rambling through the streets, and everywhere within and without the walls of Cap-Che, Amoy, Chang-Chow, &c. ... The disposition of the people throughout the whole of the province of Fuh-Keen, in which Amoy is situated, is exceedingly favourable...

Amoy   MacGowan, 191

They are candid, open, and friendly in their intercourse with foreigners. Several large and beautiful churches have been built here.

Gillespie, 1854

Amoy in 1759 Hia-men, or the island and port of Amwy, Emoy, or Amoy, is one of the most convenient and safe harbours in all India [Sic] on account of the road which is formed by that island between it and the continent; which is so deep and capacious, that it can receive 1000 ships of the largest size, which can come as near to land as they please, and ride safe from all winds; on which accounts its commerce hath increased to such a degree, that there is constantly a vast number of Chinese transports that trade from thence to other parts of India; and the emperor keeps there a garrison of 6000 or 7000 men, under the command of a Chinese general.

Sale, 1759

第一章 老厦门 Ancient Amoy

AMOY. KULANGSU.   Smith, 1900

厦门胜过广东　　鼓浪屿和厦门岛将承接中国对外贸易的一大部分,而广东的份额正在日益缩小。在广东(广州珠江)河面上的航行十分艰苦,且很不安全,而进入厦门港的航道短、水深且畅通无阻。对广州来讲,出港也很不方便,而对厦门来说,轮船可在岛屿的庇护下,在港内等待风和日丽的好天气,并且随时可以返航、出港。除了上述优越的自然条件(中国政府反复在简报中述说)外,我们的使领馆官员和探险人员一致认为,跟其他地方相比,厦门大多数市民对外国人、外国商人和外来游客更加友好、大方……

——阿罗穆和莱特,1843年

开放的厦门人　　跟广东不一样……厦门对外国人相当开放。我们可以完全自由地进出沿海所有城镇。访问厦门时,对一个来自南边的外国人来说,首先印象深刻的是他可以随意走动,没人干扰。这是怎样的一种喜悦的心情啊!在南边,我经常被强力驱出城外。在泉州、厦门、漳州等地,我走街串巷、出入城门,不受限制,实在令人感到高兴。福建省(厦门系其中一地方)全省各地人民的性格都非常友好……他们率直、开放,与外国人交谈友好。这里已经建起了几座漂亮的大教堂。

——吉勒斯俳,1854年

厦门1759年　　厦门,或称厦门港、厦门岛,在整个印度地区(原文如此。从英国人的角度上来看,可能是"英国东印度公司"开展业务地区的统称——译者注)最便捷、安全的港口之一。厦门港与中国大陆地区的交通网络畅通,港口水深、水面宽阔,可容纳上千艘最大型号的轮船,可随意驶近它们想靠近的陆地,并躲避所有的台风天气。因此,这里的贸易已经发展到相当的规模,经常有大量的中国船只从这里出发,与东印度的其他地区开展贸易。中国皇帝在这里驻扎了六七千人的兵力,有一名中国将领统帅。

——西尔,1759年,第47页

老外看老鼓浪屿 Old Gulangyu in Foreigners' Eyes

Ptolemy & Amoy? Amoy has been one of the conspicuous names in the history of the Chinese Empire. Being one of the natural entrepots of the nation, it was early brought to the notice of foreign Powers. It is quite likely that this is one of [the very places that Ptolemy "the celebrated geographer," mentions in his writings concerning places along the coast of China. Yet, it would be profitless to even attempt to verify this, or to identify satisfactorily the names mentioned in this early record. But still, there are enough undisputed facts to prove that Amoy was known to the traveler and the merchants in the very earliest centuries of the Christian era...

Pitcher, 1893

The Dutch in Amoy It was during this period [1573-1644] that the Dutch made their appearance by way of Formosa. They took possession of the Pescadores, and landed at Amoy, from whence they penetrated as far as ChangChow and Haiting. The Dutch at the time were at war with both the Spanish and Portuguese; their trading-ships went heavily armed, and sailed as much for prizes as for trade.

Dukes, 1885
Shooting the Rapids

Denby, 1900

The Old Dutch Factory Slightly to the Northward of the Amoy dock is the wall of the old Dutch factory. Another evidence of the former connection of the Dutch with Amoy is afforded by the triumphal arches, with figures of Dutchmen sculptured on them in relief, standing a short distance beyond the site of the former British Consulate (now the Taotai's yamen). No very clear history is attached to them, but it is presumed that they were erected in about 1664, when the Dutch were permitted by special edict, to trade with Chang-chow-fu.

Mayers and Dennys, 1867

Amoy—Ancient Zayton?[1] The term Ch'uanchow Lu here employed is applicable both to the city and the district, and applying it to the district, the point of debarkation might be Anhai, Amoy harbour and Haitsang, situated on the northern part of the estuary leading to Changchow, at which point the Ch'uanchow prefecture overlaps the Changchow prefecture.

On consideration of this question, it appears that the Haven of Zayton said to be frequented by all the ships of India was most probably the present harbour of Amoy, which is very easy of access, and would—owing to its splendid landmark [Nan Taiwu Pagoda]—be the first port in China steered for not only by the ships bound for Changchow, but also by all ships bound for Chuanchow and the northern ports of Wenchow, Kanpu, and Shanghai.

Phillips, 1877

---

1 Researchers eventually decided Marco Polo's Zayton was Quanzhou—but most agree that Zayton's "Great Port" was Xiamen Harbor, given its great size, and that it was part of Zayton at that time. So it is possible that Marco Polo sailed home from Xiamen.

第一章　老厦门 Ancient Amoy

托勒密和厦门？　历史上，厦门曾经是中央帝国一个著名的地标。作为中国的天然良港和贸易中心之一，厦门港很早就引起了外国势力的注意。托勒密这位"著名的地理学家"在他的著述中所提及的中国沿海地名里，厦门港很有可能就是其中的特别地点之一。当然，想要证实这种说法，或在托勒密的著述中得到满意的答案意义不大。然而，厦门早在基督纪元早期就为旅行家和商人所熟知。这一事实却是无可争辩的……

——毕腓力，1893 年

在厦门的荷兰人　就在这段时间（1573 – 1644 年），荷兰人借道台湾造访厦门。他们占领澎湖列岛，入侵厦门，并渗透到漳州和海澄等内陆地区。当时，荷兰人正在与西班牙和葡萄牙开战，他们的贸易船只全副武装，四处航行，与其说是为了贸易，倒不如说是为了获取战利品。

——丹尼，1900 年，第 113 页

旧荷兰工厂　厦门码头偏北方向耸立着旧荷兰工厂的围墙。荷兰与厦门之间关系的另一例证就是坐落于英国旧领事馆（现为道台衙门）不远处的教堂大拱门，上面有荷兰人的头像浮雕。尽管历史记录语焉不详，但据说这些拱门大致建于 1664 年。当时，御令允许荷兰人与漳州府开展贸易活动。

——梅尔斯和丹尼斯，1867 年，第 257 页

厦门=古刺桐？　本书所说的"泉州路"指的是泉州市和整个泉州地区。当它指的是泉州整个地区时，登岸点可以是安海、厦门港和海沧。其中，海沧位于漳州湾的北部，是漳州府与泉州府接壤的地方。

从这个角度上来看，印度地区商船云集的刺桐港似乎应该是现在的厦门港，因为厦门港进出方便，且拥有显著地标（南太武塔），不仅是驶往漳州商船的第一站，同时也是前往泉州、温州和上海等北方港口的必经之路。

——毕腓力，1877 年，第 118 ~ 120 页

老外看老鼓浪屿 *Old Gulangyu in Foreigners' Eyes*

Amoy, from Ko-long-soo.

Allom, 1843

Drawn by T. Allom.   Sketched on the Spot by Capt. Stoddart. R.N.   Engraved by A. Willmore.

City of Amoy, from the Tombs.

La ville d'Amoy vue prise des tombeaux.   Stadt Amoy von der Grabmählern gesehen.

第一章 老厦门 Ancient Amoy

Allom, 1840s

Amoy, from the Outer Anchorage.

NIGHT SCENE IN AMOY.

老外看老鼓浪屿 *Old Gulangyu in Foreigners' Eyes*

Chapter 2   Beautiful Amoy

The appearance of the harbour as it is approached from the sea is one of considerable beauty. The rugged islands, the rocky hills, the blue water, and the pretty island of Kulangsu with its buildings coloured as in a southern European town, combine to make an attractive picture.

Bowra, 1908

Amoy's Beautiful Bay As we advance we draw nearer still to the land. Quemoy is replaced by Little Quemoy, and then the "Great Load"[1] and the "Little Load" are passed almost within stone's-throw, whilst finally we enter the narrow channel that leads into the bay, and, with Green Island lighthouse close on our left, we pass within the chain of islands that forms the extreme barriers of the magnificent outer harbour of Amoy. The great bay across which we are now steaming is one of the most beautiful scenes on the coast of China. Nature seems to have put forth all her strength to render it as charming as possible. To the seaward stretches the chain of islands through which we have just passed, and which appeared to have been placed there as a kind of advance guard to protect this miniature inland sea from the ravages and onslaughts of the furious waves. To the right of these, as if a protecting sentinel over the whole, towers up the "Great Southern Warrior." This lofty mountain looks down upon the bay and the islands, and sends its gaze far out to sea, as if to keep an outlook against coming foes, and also to guide the approaching mariner to the beautiful harbour at its feet. The special mission, however, which seems to have been entrusted to it is to charm by its endless transformations those who live within sight of it. Its moods are infinite, and, like the kaleidoscope, surprise the onlooker by the unexpected visions that flash upon his gaze.

On the opposite side of the bay lies the island of Amoy. It is rugged and desolate-looking, and gives one the impression that Nature has abandoned it in despair as a hopeless place for the exercise of her genius…

Macgowan, 1897

---

1   Da Dan （大担） and Xiao Dan　（小担） Islands

Gulangyu, July 7, 1925   J. Nienhuis

第二章　美丽的厦门岛

从海上看厦门港美景颇为壮观。高低不平的岛屿，岩石裸露的群山，湛蓝色的海水，与充满欧洲南部小镇特色建筑的美丽小岛鼓浪屿一起，构成了一副迷人的画面。

——博拉，1908 年

厦门美丽的港湾　随着船只的行进，我们离陆地越来越近。大金门，小金门，轮船驶过近在咫尺的"大担岛"和"小担岛"，最后进入狭窄的厦门湾水道。靠近我们左边的绿岛灯塔，船只驶入一连串的海岛。这些海岛为壮观的厦门外港在地平线上构筑了一道海上屏障。我们所驶入的这个大港湾是中国沿海最漂亮的海港之一。

"Camel Rock", Gulangyu, Jan. 1931　J. Nienhuis

Amoy Boulders　Ecke, 1935

大自然似乎已经竭尽全力，把所有的迷人之处赋予了厦门港。在我们刚刚路过的海面上，横卧着一串小岛，像是造化安放在那里，作为前哨，保护这个小小的内海免受汹涌波涛的蹂躏和袭击。南太武山耸立在海港的右边，像是一名哨兵，守卫着整个港湾。高耸的南太武俯看着港湾和小岛，凝视着大海，像是在观察敌情，同时指引着往来的船只在它的脚底下进出美丽的厦门港。大自然赋予南太武山的另一项特殊使命就是用自己变幻无常的景色来吸引它视野范围内的目光。千姿百态的南太武，就像万花筒一闪而过，用突如其来的美景，震撼看客。

港湾的另一边横卧着厦门岛。小岛高低不平，一副荒凉景象，给人一种印象，似乎大自然已经绝望地放弃了这个小岛，作为打造天才的绝境……

——麦嘉湖，1897 年，第 141 页

Mrs. Jane Edkins' letter to her brother Simon   Amoy, 20th April 1860

Here we are at Amoy. A passage of ten days in the "Palmerston" brought us, if not rapidly, at least safely.

...We anchored outside, on a beautiful moonlight evening. The scenery all round was enchanting. Noble hills of rocky brown overhung the entrance, crowned by pagodas, etc. Rocky islands, the abode of wild fowl, encircled us. The sun poured his last mellow rays o'er the delightful scene as we entered, and my heart bounded with joy at the sight. Stretching on each side, peak above peak, and peak beyond that, were high rocky hills. The sunlight gave a golden tinge to their brown grassy covering, and a warmer tint to their rocky sides. At their foot a beautiful sandy beach, smooth and glittering, extended for some distance. It was a most charming scene, and one that filled the heart. I cried with joy almost to see home hills again, for so they seemed to me.

The noise of the dropping anchor, and the hearty song of the men, did not interrupt me as my thoughts went home to dearly loved Scotland. It was especially pleasant to come up on deck after tea in the soft moonlight, when all was still, save the silent tread of the watch whenever the helm was deserted, and the white sails furled, and gaze up through the tall masts and rigging to the fair heaven so beautifully blue and sparkling. The dark hills on each side, and the soft gurgle of the waters as they gently passed by, added to the impressiveness of the scene. Mr. Edkins and I sat a long time delighting in it, and felt its strangeness and beauty heightened still more as the lightning's vivid flash frequently lighted up the dark hills for a moment.

Next morning early, Mr. Edkins called me to look at the opening bay as we entered it. I was busy packing, so I had only glimpses here and there, but these were striking. High rocks, of all sorts and sizes, line one side of the bay, many of them grown over with moss. Some of them have long weird-like inscriptions, and some seemed tottering, ready to fall.

Nestling under them was the little town of Amoy, before which we cast anchor about nine A.M. We proceeded direct to the Rev. John Stronach's, where we are now staying...

In the afternoon, Jessie, her father, Mr. Edkins, and I, went over to Kolangsu, a lovely island about half a mile's run across. We landed, climbed the beach, and reached a broad graveled walk arched with trees, then we entered a garden where roses, mignonette, and many other exquisite flowers, bloomed beautifully. The rocks were on either side like a wall to it, but their bare exterior was clothed with honeysuckle and green creepers. From that we passed into another, and then, by some steps, reached a little hill. By a path that wound round it we gained the top of one height, from which we had an interesting view of Amoy. Her navy of junks, her small fishing-boats, all lay close together in a sheltered corner, while the English ships lay outside. The houses are poor, both those of the merchants and missionaries, in comparison with those at Shanghai; but from Kolangsu all looked pretty. We descended, and by paddy-fields of fresh green we reached another hill, which we slowly climbed, and the view to the other side of the island was most captivating. The broad sea, broken here and there by islets, and bounded by magnificent hills, all bursting as it did on us without expecting it, had a powerful effect. I forgot my weariness, and gazed long on this noble prospect. Hills and sea give a higher idea of the beauty of nature than any artificial cultivation, however rich. "The everlasting hills, and the ever-changing sea," are to me the noblest works of nature...

This is Monday morning; haven't I given you a fair account of our proceedings?...

Jane Edkins

第二章　美丽的厦门岛 Beautiful Amoy

简·爱德金斯女士致其兄弟西蒙的信件（1860年4月20日，厦门）

终于到了厦门。"帕麦斯顿号"海上航行十天，如果算不上快，至少算安全地把我们送到了厦门。

……一个美丽的月晚，我们在港口外下锚。周围的精致实在迷人。宏伟的棕竹色山峰横亘在港湾的入口处，一群野生禽鸟在我们头顶上盘旋。进入港湾的时候，太阳把最后几束柔和的光线泼洒在美丽的海岛上。看到这景色，我的心狂跳不已。海港的两岸，山峰高耸，群峰延绵。太阳给棕色的植被染上了一层金黄，让山上的岩石显得更加温暖。山脚下是一片美丽、平坦的沙滩，延绵数里，在阳光下熠熠生辉。这是最令人陶醉的景色，让我的内心感到充实。像是看到故乡的山，我兴奋得几乎狂叫，因为对我来说，是这样的。

我的思绪飞向了我亲爱的故乡苏格兰，轮船沉重的下锚声和船上开心的歌声都无法打断。在柔和的月光下用过茶点，走上甲板，特别令人感到愉快。当舵轮停下，白帆卷起，除了钟表的滴答声，周围一片沉寂。透过高高的桅杆和绳索，仰望晴朗的星空，它是如此的湛蓝、美丽。夜色下，两岸山峰黝黑，海水轻轻流淌、汩汩作响，增加了海港的迷人景色。爱德金斯先生和我坐在甲板上，兴奋得久久不能自已。当闪电划破月空，照亮黝黑的群山，我们更加感受到港湾的奇妙和美丽。

第二天一大早，爱德金斯先生把我叫醒，让我看看昨天进入厦门岛的宽阔港湾。忙于整理行李，我只是东看看、西瞧瞧。不过，这已经够令人震惊了。各种形状、大小不一的岩石高高地耸立在港湾的一边，上面长满了青苔。一些石头上刻着长长的、外形古怪的文字，有些石头看上去好像摇摇欲坠。

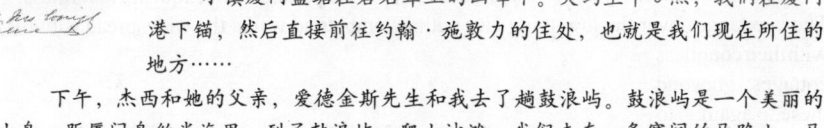

小镇厦门盘踞在岩石耸立的山峰下。大约上午9点，我们在厦门港下锚，然后直接前往约翰·施敦力的住处，也就是我们现在所住的地方……

下午，杰西和她的父亲，爱德金斯先生和我去了趟鼓浪屿。鼓浪屿是一个美丽的小岛，距厦门岛约半海里。到了鼓浪屿，爬上沙滩，我们走在一条宽阔的马路上。马路是用鹅卵石铺成的，两边绿树遮阴。走进一座花园，我们看到里面玫瑰、木樨草和其他许多美丽的鲜花争相怒放。花园两边的岩石就像一堵墙，岩石裸露的外表被金银花和爬山虎所覆盖。从这座花园，我们进入另一座花园，然后上了几级台阶，就到一座小山脚下。沿着蜿蜒小路，我们爬上了一个峰顶。在那里，我们看到了一个有趣的厦门景观：军舰和小渔船都挤在一个避风港内，而英国的船只都停泊在港外。跟上海相比，厦门岛上商人和传教士住的房子都很差。但鼓浪屿岛上的房屋看上去却很漂亮。下山，经过几片郁郁葱葱的稻田，我们来到另外一座山脚。我们缓缓爬行，小岛另一边的景色实在迷人。大大小小的岛屿横亘宽阔的海面上，两岸群山环绕。在你毫无准备的时候，宏伟的山峰映入你的眼帘。这种视觉冲击太强烈了。我忘记了疲惫，长时间凝视着这壮观的景象。群山和大海让人更多地感受到大自然的美。任何人工雕琢无论多么的精细，都难以与之媲美。在我看来，"永恒的群山"和"变化莫测的大海"是大自然最伟大的杰作……

现在是周一上午。关于我们的行程，我的描写，你还满意吗？……

简·爱德金斯

老外看老鼓浪屿 Old Gulangyu in Foreigners' Eyes

Jane Edkins' letter to her Mother-in-law   Amoy, 18th May 1860

It is nearly three weeks since we came to Amoy. We have been much benefited by its health-giving sea breezes. The scenery around greatly interests me. What with its rocks, mountains, beautiful islands, and blue sea sparkling, dashing, and foaming in all its fresh beauty around the town, I am exceedingly taken with it. … We have Chinese chapels. It was a sweet Sabbath morning when I first went to ours. For a considerable time before going, I had been seated in a low chair in our room, with a book before me; my head and heart were somehow not with it, but were drinking in the attractive beauties of the scene that presented itself from the wide open window. High, noble craggy hills, with mossy brown, still retained the warm glow of the soft embrace of the morning. A misty beauty hung around, though the sky was blue and unclouded…

Jeanie

Gulangyu's Drum Rock, 1920s   J.N.

Beautiful Gulangyu "Nothing can be imagined more pleasing, picturesque, and animated than the prospect of the vast mercantile harbor from the heights of Ko-long-soo. The deep channel, crowded with junks, is at the observer's feet; the narrow promontory, forming a chief suburb, projects beyond; further still is the second passage, backed by those noble hills of granite which separate the marine district from the mainland…

The site and scenery of this celebrated entrepot is a panorama of exquisite loveliness… The eye ranges over the low-lying city with its embattled walls; the widespread suburbs, with their countless cottages; beyond these, again, to the land-locked cove, dotted with busy merchantmen, there riding securely from every breath of wind. Above the waters of the inner bay, which closely resemble an inland lake, rises a noble chain of mountains, dentate in outline, and granite in structure. Ko-long-soo, interposed between the outward ocean and this picturesque basin, acts as a natural and most efficient breakwater, imparting such entire and constant placidity to its surface, that vessels may lie here at all seasons regardless of the weather, biding their time for unfurling the sails; and transit from shore to shore by boats of tiny tonnage, is never attended with risk or interruption."

Gulangyu, Jan. 1931   J. Neinhuis

Allom, 1843

第二章 美丽的厦门岛 *Beautiful Amoy*

简·爱德金斯致其婆婆的信件（1860年5月18日，厦门）

从我们来到厦门至今，三周已经快过去了。这里的海风轻拂，给人予健康，让我们受益匪浅。我对周围的景色感到非常兴趣。林立的石壁，起伏的山峦，美丽的岛屿，蓝色海面上波光粼粼，海浪拍岸，溅起浪花朵朵。小城周边这样鲜活的美景让我感到特别陶醉……我们拥有几处小教堂，用汉语传教。第一次上我们自己教堂是一个温馨的安息日。出发前，我久久地坐在我们房间的一张矮椅上，面前展开一本书。透过宽大的窗户，迷人的景色不招自来，我的心思无法放在书上，而是陶醉其中。岩石高耸，青苔满壁，宏伟的群山依然保留着清晨那抹柔和、温暖的阳光。天空晴朗，万里无云，一种朦胧的美丽在港湾里四处游荡。

——简·爱德金斯

美丽的鼓浪屿 从鼓浪屿最顶峰欣赏厦门商港宽阔的景色，你绝对想不出有什么比它更怡人、美妙和生动了。我脚下的这个深水港道泊满了各种船只。小岛的城郊是一片狭长的海角，向远处延伸。再远处就是另外一条航道，背后是宏伟的花岗岩山脉，把海港与大陆分开……

这个著名商业中心的位置和景色是一幅雅致、美丽的全景画……举目望去，这座小城修在低洼之地，建有城墙。城郊广阔，农舍密布。再往更远的地方看，内陆的海湾到处是商人、农夫忙碌的身影。顶着阵阵的海风，他们骑在马上，屹然不动。港湾内的水面就像内陆湖。雄伟的群山耸立在岸边，岩石裸露，重峦叠嶂。矗立在外海与这个美丽的港湾之间，鼓浪屿作为自然的防波堤，最为有效。她赋予港湾里的海面持久、全面的平静。一年四季，无论什么天气，船只都可以停泊港内，等待扬帆起航的日子，或由小船把货物转运到岸边，不会碰上任何危险或障碍。

View from Gulangyu, 1920s
Jean Nienhuis

Gulangyu, January 1931 J. Nienhuis

——阿罗姆，1843年

老外看老鼓浪屿 Old Gulangyu in Foreigners' Eyes

Gulangyu, "Beauty in Miniature" Across the harbour, which averages about a quarter of a mile in width, is the island of Kulangsu (The Drum Wave Island), so named because at certain states of the tide the waves rush through an opening in a rock on the southern side of it, and produce a sound which in the distance resembles the beating of a drum. It is exceedingly picturesque, for, though only about a mile and a half in width and three in length, it combines within itself the varied features of an extensive landscape, though of course in a miniature form. There are hills, one of two of which seem as though they would aspire to be mountains, only Nature has not given them the required space, and valleys, and plains, and sandy beaches, and high bluffs, and capes, and promontories, all producing such a diversity of scenery as makes the island one of the pleasantest on the coast of China.

Amoy, 1927
Jean Nienhuis

MacGowan, 1897

Amoy Rocking Stone[2] (1700) There are some curiosities in Amoy. One is a large stone that weights above 40 tons, that is set so dextrously on a rock, in such an equilibrium, that a youth of twelve years old can easily make it move, but an hundred men can make it move in no greater motion than that single youth can. I saw it tried with a pair of hand-screws, but to no purpose.

Hamilton, 1727

---

2 German sailors rocked the stone off its perch in 1908.

第二章　美丽的厦门岛 Beautiful Amoy

鼓浪屿＝"微缩美景"　厦门港正对面大约四分之一海里的地方就是鼓浪屿。岛上南部有一岩礁，其洞穴受海浪冲击，远听声若擂鼓，因此得名。虽然鼓浪屿大约只有1.5英里宽，3英里长，却是非常得美丽。小岛揉入了各种景观的特色，当然是以微缩景观的方式。岛上有两座小山，其中一座似乎胸怀着大山的梦想，只是造化未能给它提供足够的空间、山谷、平原、沙滩、悬崖和岬地。岛上景观的多样性使得鼓浪屿成为中国沿海最宜人的岛屿之一。

——麦嘉湖，1897年，第147～148页

厦门风动石（1700年）　厦门有几处奇观。其中一处是一块重量超过40吨的巨石，均衡、巧妙地叠在另一块岩石上，就连一个12岁的少年也能轻而易举地摇动它。不过，让100个壮年男子来摇，巨石的晃动幅度并不比一个少年来得更大。我曾看见有人用两个手动千斤顶来顶，结果也没能推动这块巨石。

——哈密尔顿，1727年，第494页

Gulangyu, 1920s　　　　Nurse Jean Nienhuis

老外看老鼓浪屿 *Old Gulangyu in Foreigners' Eyes*

Country Roads Anderson, 1920

Amoy—The Scotland of China [3] "A word about the country reached from the "door" of Amoy may not be amiss, as some people seem to fancy China is one great flat plain. I venture to call the Fokien province, the "Wales" or "Scotland" of China, so diversified is it as to natural scenery…

Joseland, Rev. Frank P., in Gaunt, 1899

Scottish Rocks The island, which is only separated from the mainland by a narrow channel, is six or eight miles long, by two or three broad, the greater part of it consisting of a succession of irregular hills, singularly barren and rugged; immense boulders piled in capricious order, one upon another, or thrown about in the wildest confusion. With the exception of Ceylon, I have not seen such rocks since I left Scotland.

Barbour, 1855

Scottish Hills of Amoy After dinner, we had a boat-excursion, in company with Mr. J. Stronach, his sister, and young Miss Stronach. This recalled the olden time in Stromness harbor [Scotland]. "We rowed and talked agreeably, though my enthusiasm about the hills…Through many an opening in the rocky hills we saw temples hid among trees, looking so picturesque, built out on jutting rocks. I wish I had my young strength again, to climb at will those mountain rocks and wild romantic paths, all in a state of nature…It is, to my taste, a delightful place, being perfectly surrounded with what I call Scotland's heathery hills. Oh, the flood of beauty tinting those hills when the sun slowly sinks to rest,—when lingeringly it leaves them, and casts its glowing mantle tenderly o'er their rugged rocky sides, softening them to melting beauty.

Jane Edkins, 1860

---

3 A disproportionate number of foreigners in China were from Scotland—perhaps explaining their love of Amoy.

老外看老鼓浪屿 *Old Gulangyu in Foreigners' Eyes*

Chapter 3 The People of Amoy

Ancient People of the Future   China is not like ancient Egypt, whose greatness has departed though she still lives on. China is a vital force whose largest possibilities of development lie before and not behind her. A new fresh life is beginning to course through the nation's veins....

Gamewell, 1919

Amoy Zest For Life   In this, our first year in China, an astonished excitement possessed us. We were confronted by a strange civilization of unparalleled richness. To unfold it was at once alarming, delightful, baffling. It radically altered the nature of my world. It was as if I had opened the smooth familiar back of my watch for the first time and discovered within the complete, complex and inexorable interaction of fine-toothed cogs—a whole self-sufficient system which had been going on all the time, and I unaware of it. It demanded, paradoxically, a jettisoning of preconceived European ideas of China and the Chinese, while requiring the best and highest of Western wisdom and culture as a yard-stick by which to measure and understand its anomalies as well as its heights. In spite of the appalling state of the country... underneath it all was China, solid and enduring...

I had felt the impact of this immense vitality the moment I first set foot in Amoy. I came upon it by no rational process, no social studies. I met the tide of lusty and abundant life full in the face, with all its primitive urges undiluted. It was a life, at times, frightening in its force.

It needed to be strong to survive such human miseries as it daily faced.

Mackenzie-Grieves, 1959

Amoy Workmen   MacGowan, 1907

A Philosophical People   To their conditions they have developed responses—frugality (nothing wasted in China), patience, industriousness, sense of humour—a philosophical approach to the realities of life. These are the qualities that make the Chinese tough and persevering and give them the will to love and fight against poverty. The Chinese enjoy few luxuries in material things. They are not an acquisitive society. The people yearn more for peace and stability—a climate for work rather than affluence or wealth for the sake of pleasure. There is a great difference in the psychology of Eastern and Western society.

Rose Talman, Amoy Missionary, 1916-1930, unpublished memoirs

第三章 厦门人

一个古老民族的未来 中国不是古埃及。尽管古埃及依然存在,但她伟大的历史已经成为过去。中国是一股充满活力的势力。最大的发展空间还没有成为历史,而是正展示在她面前。一种崭新的生活正在这个国家的血管里流淌……

——甘威尔,1919 年,第 11 页

厦门人的生活激情 在中国第一年,我们充满着惊奇和激动。我们遭遇了一种内涵丰富无比的陌生文明。一接触这种文明,你马上就会感到震惊、愉悦和困惑。它迅速地改变了我的世界观。这就像第一次打开我所熟悉的光滑表盖,发现里面精致的齿轮在运行,完整、复杂而又持续不断。这是一个完全自给自足的系统,周而复始地转动着,而我自己却从来没有留意。这就要求欧洲人抛弃他们对中国和中国人所抱有的偏见,同时用西方最精华和高级的智慧和文化作为衡量和理解不一样的中国文化及其成就。尽管这个国家的一些现象令人震惊……这些现象背后就是中国,坚固而不朽……

MacGowan, 1909

一踏上厦门,我就感受到这种巨大生命力的冲击。没有经过理智的思考,也未通过社会学的研究,我承受了这种冲击。我在这里正面遭遇了一种生机勃勃、色彩斑斓的生活,拥有所有纯净的原始冲动。这就是一种生活,能量总是惊人的。

要想在每日所面临的人间苦难中幸存下来,你必须得坚强。

——麦肯兹·格瑞芙,1959 年,第 43～44 页

达观的民族 根据实际情况,中国人作出了自己的反应——节俭(在中国,没有一样东西被浪费)、忍耐、勤劳和幽默。这是中国人应对现实生活的一种达观的策略。就是这些品质使得中国人变得坚强、忍耐,并赋予他们爱和对付贫困的意志。从物质上来说,中国人并没有享受什么奢侈的东西。一踏上厦门这块土地,我就感受到这种强大生命力的冲击。我得出这个结论并不是靠什么理性的分析,也不是通过社会学的研究。中国不是一个四处索求的国家。这个民族期盼更多的是和平与稳定。这里盛行的是劳作,而不是为享乐而拥有财富或富足。东西方社会之间的心理有着很大的差别。

——罗斯·塔尔曼,厦门传教士,1916—1930 年,摘自其未公开的笔记

Right Attitude to Life   "Fukien has taught me how to live. Material things can be acquired anywhere in this material world, but an attitude to life can only be mastered in the right environment. Fukien provided such an environment for me."

Ch'en Sze-ching, Fukien Christian University graduate, 1926 (Scott, 1954)

Life-loving Chinese   There is no doubt but that one secret of the extraordinary power that the Chinese undoubtedly have is the very large amount of genuine human nature with which as a race they are endowed. The Chinaman is a person that is full of fun. It would seem as though a sense of humour lay at the basis of his character and tinged everything with its subtle influence. A joke with the Chinaman is a solvent that disperses anger and drives away passion from the heart, and makes the broad, uncouth faces shine with a light, like sunbeams playing upon the rugged sides of a hill. If the Chinese had been a nation of sombre, gloomy people, without a gleam of humour in their natures, they would have been a positive peril to the world. As it is, the genial strain that is the woof and warp of the Celestial's being makes him a person that can win his way into the hearts of strangers, and slowly dissipate the prejudice...

MacGowan, 1907

The Kaleidoscopic Chinese   The Chinese is a person full of surprises. He is like the kaleidoscope, for you feel that whatever strange and unexpected views he may have given of himself you have not yet got the last and final one that will exhaust his character.

MacGowan, 1912

The Magnetic Chinese   The attraction lies in the people themselves, and without any effort on their side the foreigner feels himself drawn by a kind of hypnotism towards them. You cannot explain this and you cannot tell the reason why.

MacGowan, 1907

In An Amoy Village, 1933

J. Nienhuis

第三章 厦门人 The People of Amoy

热爱生活的中国人 毫无疑义,中国人肯定拥有的非凡潜能的秘诀之一就是十分丰富的真性情。作为一个民族,这种真性情是上天赐予的。中国人富有情趣,而幽默感似乎构筑了其性情的根基。在幽默感的微妙影响下,任何情趣都被感染了。跟中国人开个玩笑就像一种溶剂,它可以驱赶愤懑,消除内心的不良情绪,让可怕的臭脸焕发光芒,就像太阳的光线照射在小山粗糙的那面山坡。如果中国人是一个忧郁、沮丧的民族,天生没有一丝幽默,那他们就会变成这个世界彻头彻尾的一个威胁。因此,中国人经天纬地的天生品质使得陌生人向他们打开心扉,并慢慢地消除偏见……

——麦嘉湖,1907年,第17~18页

万花筒式的中国人 中国人是一个充满惊喜的民族。就像万花筒,他们向你展示的情景千奇百怪、变幻莫测,但你依然看不到穷尽他们性情的最后招数。

——麦嘉湖,1912年,第154页

磁铁般的中国人 迷人之处在于中国人本身。几乎不费吹灰之力,外国人感觉到自己已经被某种催眠术所控制。你无法解释这种现象,也说不出其中缘由。

——麦嘉湖,1907年

Serie III. No. 7. Photo by Dr. John Otte Koopvrouw met lekkernijen.
"Medische Zending, Nederlandsch Wilhelmina Vrouwenhospitaal te Amoy van Dr. J.A. Otte."

老外看老鼓浪屿 Old Gulangyu in Foreigners' Eyes

The Laughter-Loving Amoy People   The Chinese are a laughter-loving people… There are no people in the world that seem to have such a hypnotizing power over the men of the West as the Chinese. It is not their beauty or their eloquence, nor the fascinating way in which they talk, but in the large amount of human nature they all possess, and in the strain of humour that seems to run through them as music does through an exquisite piece of poetry…

From this it may be easily believed that they are fond of laughter and merriment and the bright and joyous side of things, and social intercourse, and plenty of company, and loud-sounding music and firing of crackers. The solitary feeling that makes an Englishman like to be alone, and shut himself up day after day in a house by himself and not care to see visitors, is something that is quite incomprehensible to a Chinaman.

… The Chinese are a humorous and jolly race of people… the position that they hold to-day in the Far East is a signal proof of the vitality and the determined pluck that have carried the Yellow race through the revolutions that during the past centuries have rent and shattered the Chinese Empire.

Tee-A With Husband and Family

MacGowan, 1907

A Noisy People   The Chinese are essentially a noisy people; all Orientals are. Spending so much time out-of-doors has doubtless something to do with their noisy way of talking; for they will shout at each other when a quiet whisper would serve their purpose as well if not better. Their music, much of it at least, is noisy what with clash of cymbals, clang of gongs, the loud-sounding drum, the harsh untuned flageolets and the shrill flutes, and the entire absence of piano effects. One must suppose that to them the constant forte and fortissimo is as entertaining as the softest and sweetest song without words is to our ears. And the crackers the firecrackers here is a perfect apotheosis of noise. A perfect carnival of uproar and deafening sound is produced, especially at New Year's time, by their almost continuous discharge, for at that joyous season a perfect pandemonium reigns rampant. Woe betide the foreigner in a native city then… Sleep is almost out of the question at night while house after house and shop after shop lets off its string of firecrackers, the rattling of the small artillery being accentuated by a louder boom every little while from a bomb of larger size.

Ball, 1856

Love Loud   …Their love for their fellow-kind is a passion with the Chinese, and they seem to be able to stand an amount of noise and loud talking and screaming babies and barking of dogs, such as would send an Englishman off his head.

MacGowan, 1907

第三章 厦门人 The People of Amoy

爱笑的厦门人 中国人是一个爱笑的民族……世界上没有任何一个地方的人民像中国人那样对西方人拥有催眠般的魔力。这不是源于他们的美貌或口才,也不是他们言谈举止极有吸引力,而很大程度上是由于他们所拥有的禀性以及他们浑身上下所散发出来的幽默气质,就像音乐渗入精美诗篇那样自然……

因此,我们有充分的理由相信,中国人喜欢笑、快乐以及一切事物的光明和欢乐面。他们喜欢社交,爱结伴而行,爱声音大的音乐,爱放鞭炮。对任何中国

A Joke　　　　　　　MacGowan, 1907

人来说,英国人所喜欢的特立独行、日复一日地闭门独居、对来客爱理不理,这样的孤独感是很难理解的。

……中国人是一个幽默、快乐的民族……他们现在在远东地区所拥有的地位是其活力和坚定决心的一种明显证据。在过去的几百年里,它推动这个黄皮肤的民族通过不断的革命斗争建立或打破了这个中央帝国。

——麦嘉湖,1907 年

爱热闹的民族 中国人从根本上来说是一个爱热闹的民族。所有的东方人都一样。他们大量的时间在户外活动。毫无疑问,这跟他们讲话大声有些关联。其实,低声耳语同样可以,如果不是要更好地达到他们交流的目的。中国人的音乐,至少绝大部分,声音很大。他们敲锣、打鼓、击钹、吹笛子,声音响亮、震耳欲聋,完全没有钢琴的调音效果。你得这样想,对他们来说,强音和极强音与最温柔、最甜美的曲子一样娱人。在这里,烟花爆竹就是声音的完美体现。特别是在农历新年期间,爆竹声声、此起彼伏、震耳欲聋,活生生一幅声音嘉年华景象,因为在这个欢乐时刻,这种混乱的场面不受管束。这个时候,苦恼降临到在那里居住的外国人头上……晚上,你无法入睡,因为家家户户、商店货铺纷纷放起了串串鞭炮。从小型枪炮般的嗒嗒声,到大型炸弹般的轰隆声,各种鞭炮声应有尽有,此起彼伏。

——伯尔,1856 年

喜欢大声 ……对自己同胞的爱是中国人天生具有的一种性情。他们似乎能够容忍噪音、大声讲话、婴儿的尖叫声和狗吠。同样的情形足以让英国人抓狂。

——麦嘉湖,1907 年

Talkative Chinese The Chinese are animated and fluent talkers. They enjoy conversation. The Western myth of the 'impassive oriental' must have sprung from the schooled restraint, the formal courtesy of the Confucian gentleman's code, for nothing could be further from it than the quips, the jokes, the laughter, the vociferous sorrow and anger of the common people.

Mackenzie-Grieves, 1959

God's Nobility ...there exists in the Chinese soul the material that heroes are made of. The Chinese can suffer and they can die for those whom they love; they can die like martyrs for a cause in which they believe, and to which they have devoted their lives. Arouse the better qualities latent in a Chinese soul, and you will discover one of God's nobility...

Davis, 1896

Oriental Spartans Take the matter of pain. He bears it with the composure of a saint. The heroic never seems to come out so grandly in him, as when he is bearing some awful suffering that only a martyr could endure. I have seen a man come into a hospital with an abscess that must have been giving him torture. His face was drawn, and its yellow hue had turned to a slightly livid colour, but there were no other signs that he was in agony. The surgeon drove his knife deep into the inflamed mass, but only the word "ai Ya," uttered with a prolonged emphasis, and the twisting up of the muscles of one side of his face, showed that he was conscious of any pain. An Occidental of the same class would most probably have howled, and perhaps a couple of assistants would have been required to hold him whilst the doctor was operating.

Amoy Women, Thomson, 1873

...It is this same absence of nerves that enables the Chinese to bear suffering of any kind with a patience and fortitude that is perfectly Spartan. He will live from one year's end to another on food that seems utterly inadequate for human use; he will slave at the severest toil, with no Sunday to break its wearisome monotony, and no change to give the mind rest; and he will go on with the duties of life with a sturdy tread and with a meditative mystic look on his face, that reminds one of those images of Buddha that one sees so frequently in the Chinese monasteries or temples... The staying power of the Chinese seems unlimited. The strong, square frames with which nature has endowed them are models of strength.

MacGowan 1907

第三章 厦门人 The People of Amoy

健谈的中国人 中国人健谈,口才极好。他们喜欢跟人交流。"冷漠的东方"是西方社会所杜撰的观点,应该发源于孔夫子关于礼的克制与教诲。嘲讽、玩笑,普通百姓的喜怒哀乐就是对经典的一种反叛。

——麦肯兹·格瑞芙,1959年,第68页

上帝般的崇高 ……在中国人的内心深处,有一种造就英雄的物质。中国人能够吃苦,愿意为他们所爱的人去死。他们愿意为自己所信仰的事业献身,直至牺牲自己的生命。唤起中国人内心深处潜在的这些优良品质,你会发现他们上帝般的崇高……

——戴维斯,1896年,第130页

东方的斯巴坦人 能够承受痛苦的事情,他们像圣人那样忍耐。在他们身上,没有轰轰烈烈的英雄气概,特别是当他们正在承受着只有勇士才能担当的某些沉重苦难。我曾经见过一个男人带着脓肿走进医院,那神情肯定是历尽了不少磨难。他的面部紧绷,黄色的皮肤已经变成了乌青,但你在他身上看不出其他痛苦的迹象。医生把手术刀伸进发炎的脓包,这个男人只发出了"哎呀"两个字,声音有些拉长,语气有

Selling Pineapple   MacGowan,1913

点加重。面上的肌肉有些紧绷,说明他能感受到疼痛。在西方,碰上类似的情况,病人极有可能会嚎叫。动刀的时候,医生肯定需要几名助手抓住病人。

……正是上述的优良品质使得中国人能够耐心、坚定地忍受任何形式的痛苦。这种忍耐是彻头彻尾的斯巴坦人。他们常年吃的食物都是那些完全不适合人类食用的东西。他们愿意承担最辛苦的劳动,没有星期天来调节疲惫和单调,没有时间让大脑休息。迈着坚定的步伐,脸上一副沉思的神秘模样,他们继续担当着生活的重任。这让人想起中国寺庙里很常见的菩萨的形象……中国人身上的潜力似乎是无限的。造化赋予他们强壮、魁梧的身躯是力量的象征。

——麦嘉湖,1907年,第112~114页

The Adaptable Chinese The strength of the Chinaman lies in his power to adapt himself to the circumstances in which he may be situated. Place him in a northern climate where the sun's rays have lost their fire, and where the snow falls thickly and the ice lays its wintry hand upon the forces of nature, and he will thrive as though he had descended from an ancestry that had always lived in a frozen region. Transport him to the torrid zone, where the sun is a great ball of molten flame, where the air is as hot as though it had crossed a volcano, and where the one thought is how to get cool in this intolerable maddening heat, and he will move about with an ease and a comfort just as if a sultry climate was the very thing that his system demanded.

He is so cosmopolitan in his nature that it seems to be a matter of indifference where he may be or what his environment. He will travel along lofty peaks, where the snows of successive winters lie unmelted, or he will sleep in a grass hut where the fever-bearing mosquitoes will feast upon him the livelong night to the sound of their own music, and he will emerge from it next morning with a face that shows that the clouds of anopheles have left him a victor on the field. He will descend into the sultry tin mines of Siam, and at night he will stretch himself on the hard, uneven ground, with a clod for his pillow, and he will rise as refreshed as though he had slept on a bed of down.

Macgowan 1907

Timeless People One advantage the Celestial has over the Occidental is what may be called his absence of nerves. The rush and race and competition of the West have never yet touched the East. The Orient is sober and measured, and never in a hurry. An Englishman, were all other signs wanting, could easily be distinguished, as he walks along the road, by his rapid stride, the jerky movements of his arms, and the nervous poise of his head, all so different from the unemotional crowd around him, who seem to think that they have an eternity before them in which to finish their walk, and so they need not hurry.

MacGowan 1907

Fruit Sellers MacGowan, 1912

第三章　厦门人　*The People of Amoy*

A Wayside Kitchen　　　　MacGowan, 1907

　　适应能力强的中国人　中国人的力量在于他们拥有能够适应各种环境的能力。把他们放在北方，那里太阳不再炎热，积雪深厚，寒冰的魔爪染指大自然，中国人照样人丁兴旺，似乎他们来自远古时代，总是生活在冰封地冻的世界里。把他们放到热带，那里太阳简直就像一团巨大的火球，空气热得跟火山岩浆没有什么两样，常人想的都是如何躲避那令人无法容忍、让人发狂的热气，找到清凉，而中国人却漫不经心、舒适无比地四处走动，好像这酷热的天气正是他们的身体所需要的。

　　从本质上来看，中国人四海为家。他们似乎不在意自己身居何处，环境如何。他们会去攀爬冰雪常年覆盖的高峰，或是在茅屋过夜，任凭身带热病的群蚊翩然起舞、彻夜叮咬，次日起来一副战场凯旋的模样。白天，他们深入暹罗闷热、潮湿的锡矿。晚上，他们以泥块为枕，凹凸不平的硬地板作床，伸足而眠。第二天起来精神十足，好像前一天是睡在羽绒床上。

　　　　　　　　　　　　　　——麦嘉湖，1907年，第112～114页

　　缺少时间观念　缺少时间概念这根弦是东方人胜过西方人的一个地方。西方人又冲又跑，竞争激烈，东方人并不为之所动。东方人冷静、从容，从不着急。英国人走路大步流星，双臂动作急促，头部姿势游移不定，与周围平静的行人大不一样，很好辨认。东方人似乎在想，有来世可以完成旅程，因此，无须匆忙。

　　　　　　　　　　　　　　——麦嘉湖，1907年，第112～114页

▶　41

老外看老鼓浪屿 Old Gulangyu in Foreigners' Eyes

Eternal China It is a noteworthy fact, that of all those ancient empires founded immediately subsequent to the deluge China alone remains. The Assyrians, Egyptians, and, in later times, the Grecians, have severally attained to a comparatively high degree of intelligence and refinement; but their star soon culminated and sank into utter darkness. China, however, has never been wrecked, her civilization has never retrograded; paradoxical though it seems, her star has remained in its zenith for at least three thousand years. Through all this long lapse of centuries the Chinese have kept up, fairly and steadily, to their original civilization; and to-day they present all the essential elements of those social, literary, and political traits which characterized them in those early epochs when the Assyrians built their magnificent cities, the Egyptians developed their subtle theory of the metempsychosis, or the Greeks were thundering at the gates of Troy.

Gulangyu, about 1930s

The permanence of Chinese institutions is worthy of notice in this connection. It is a significant and singular fact that, from the earliest period of their authentic history to the present time, the Chinese have preserved intact and inviolate every important feature and principle of their government and civilization. The successive irruptions of northern barbarians have neither abrogated nor essentially modified Chinese institutions. The conquering races who have overrun those fertile plains have stood abashed in the presence of a superior civilization; and after subduing the empire, they have invariably adopted its government, laws, civilization, and language.

Maclay 1861

The Chinese Puzzle The Chinaman's mind is a profound and inexplicable puzzle that many have vainly endeavoured to solve…Anyone who has ever studied the Chinese character must have come to the conclusion that the instincts and aims of the people of the Chinese Empire are distinctly the reverse of those that exist in the minds of the men of the West.

It may be laid down as a general and axiomatic truth that it is impossible from hearing what a Chinaman says to be quite certain of what he actually means. The reason for this no doubt arises from the fact that a speaker hardly ever in the first instance touches upon the subject that he has in his mind, but he will dwell upon two or three others that he believes have an intimate relation with it, and he concludes that this subtle line of thought ought to lead the hearer to infer what he has all the time been driving at.

Macgowan, 1907

第三章　厦门人 The People of Amoy

永恒的中国　一个值得注意的事实是,所有古代帝国建立不久就立即走向衰亡,唯独中国得以续存。亚述人、埃及人以及后来的希腊人都曾发展过相对高级的文明和修养,但他们的星光很快就触顶,并迅速地消失在茫茫的夜空中。但是,中国没有遭受过严重破坏。中华文明还未曾出现过倒退。似乎有些反常,中国这颗文明之星已经在自己的天顶保持了至少 3000 年。在过去的数百年里,中国人一直在恭俭、稳步地延续自己的文明。亚述人建过宏伟的城市,埃及人创立了灵魂转世的深奥理论,希腊人曾经在特洛伊城门外发威。这些文明古国在社会、文学和政治等领域所取得的成就,中国样样具备。

中国人的体制一直没有变化。关于这点,是值得我们注意的。一个显著而又奇特的事实是,从正史所记载的远古时代到现在,中国人完整保留了其体制和文明的任何一个重要特征和规则。北方游牧民族持续不断的骚扰也没有使中国的体制毁灭或被彻底修改。马背上的游牧民族在占领肥沃的平原之后,面对高度发展的文明局促不安。实现征服之后,他们最终选择了原来的体制、法律、文化和语言体系。

A Fruit Seller　　MacGowan, 1912

——麦考利,1861 年,第 47、123 页

谜一般的中国人　中国人的思维是一个深奥、难解的谜。很多人想揭开谜底,却徒劳无功……研究过中国人性格的人都会作出这样的结论:中国人的天性和理想与我们西方人完全不同。

一个可以自明的普遍真理是,不能根据中国人的言语来判断他们的实际想法。这个结论毫无疑义是有事实根据的。中国人很少一开始就触及自己想要谈论的话题。他们会先考虑与这个话题密切相关的其他两、三个问题,然后根据自己微妙的思路作出结论,希望引导别人从自己的言语中猜测自己的意思。

——麦嘉湖,1907 年,第 1～2 页

老外看老鼓浪屿 *Old Gulangyu in Foreigners' Eyes*

Amoy——Home of Overseas Chinese

April 7th, 1834

Today we got under way. I cannot omit to notice a few more particulars respecting this most celebrated emporium of Fuhkeen, and one of the greatest in Asia. Its harbour is excellent, and accessible to the largest men of war. The natives of this district seem to be born traders and sailors. Their barren country, which furnishes employment for only a few hands, but far more their inclination, prompts them to leave their home, either for Formosa or the principal emporium of the Chinese empire, or the Indian Archipelago, or for the fisheries along their native shores. Wherever they go, they are rarely found in a state of abject poverty; on the contrary, they are often wealthy, and command the trade of whole islands and provinces, as well by their capital as by their superior enterprise and industry. Strongly attached to their early home, they either return as soon as they have acquired a small property, or they make large remittances. Many of the merchants, settled in the north part of China, return annually with their profits. It is not surprising, therefore, that a large amount of Chinese shipping belongs to Amoy merchants, and that the greater part of capital employed in the coasting trade is their property. Hence this barren tract is one of the richest in China, from the enterprise of the inhabitants. Here is doubtless one of the best harbours for European mercantile enterprise, both for its situation, its wealth, and the stores of all Chinese exports. At an early period the Portuguese traded here; the Dutch followed them; and the Spanish have to this day a nominal right to come hither...

Loading Coolies

Literary fame is no object of their ambition; but they generally learn to count and to make up bills. Their language differs widely from the mandarin dialect, and they are obliged to learn this with the same labour as we acquire Latin. In their dealings, they have a name for honesty above all other Chinese. Though incessantly hunting for grain, they are not mean, and they are anxious to establish a fair character. Solicitous to cultivate friendship with strangers, they have always associated with them freely, whenever beyond the reach of the government. They have been frequently entrusted with high offices, by those foreign states where they have resided as colonists. One of their descendants, as late as the middle of the last century, ascended the throne of Siam. I am acquainted with his son, who became a physician instead of a king, but who, notwithstanding this degradation, possesses royal virtues, and too much sagacity to be a usurper. He is wise enough to prefer a quiet humble life, to the pageantry of royalty, with the disaffection of a nation, indignant at seeing a foreigner on the throne.

Gutzlaff, Journal of 3 Voyages, 1834

第三章 厦门人 The People of Amoy

Amoy Boat People, 1921   J. Nienhuis

厦门——华侨的故土

1834年4月7日

　　今天我们终于起航了。关于福建最著名(同时也是亚洲最伟大的商贸中心之一)的这个商贸中心——厦门,还有几个重要的细节我不能忽略。厦门港是一个深水良港,最大型的战舰能够自由出入。这个地区的人似乎是天生的商人和海员。贫瘠的土地只能容下少量的人口。无奈之余,他们只好背井离乡,要么下南洋,要么去台湾,要么迁居中国主要商业中心,要么就是在沿海打鱼谋生。无论他们去哪里,他们很少继续处于赤贫状态。相反,他们很富有。利用手中的资本或优质的企业、生意,他们控制了整个岛屿或省份的贸易。

　　怀着对故土的无限依恋,他们略有斩获就荣归故里,或向家人大量汇款。许多商人在中国北方做生意,每年都带着钱财回家。因此,厦门商人拥有中国大部分的海运业务和更大份额的沿海贸易资本就不足为奇了。厦门这块贫瘠的土地成了中国最富庶的地方之一,财富主要来自厦门人的生意。无论从地理条件,人民的富裕程度,还是中国商铺的数量来看,厦门无疑是与欧洲商人开展贸易通商的最佳港口之一。葡萄牙最早到这里做生意,随后而来的是荷兰人,现在西班牙也获得了进入厦门的权利……

　　厦门人不图虚名。不过,他们一般都懂得数钞票、赚大钱。他们讲的话跟官方语言差别很大。政府强制他们学习官话。对他们来说,这就像我们学拉丁语一样费劲。生意场上,他们以诚信著名。这一点中国其他地方的人难望其背。尽管厦门人持续不断地在追逐利润,他们并不吝啬。他们很想培养自己仁慈的性格。厦门人很注意发展与生客的友谊,经常自由地与他们交往,不受政府管制。番邦经常授予厦门人殖民地高官,委与重任。上世纪中叶,他们的后代在锡兰王国登基加冕。我认识这位国王的儿子。他没有继承王位,而变成了一名内科医生。尽管如此,在他身上,我们看到了王室的品德。他聪慧过人,但没有篡夺王位。当他发现国人不愿意看到外国人登基并开始表达不满的时候,他放弃了王室的虚荣,选择简单、平静的生活。

——古兹拉夫,三次航海日记,1834年

Amoy Dominates Fujian Trade The commercial enterprise of the people is to be seen in the fact that Amoy, though possessing only an estimated population of about 150,000, has three times as large a number of trading-junks as the important capital of the province itself. The people emigrate in large numbers to Borneo, Siam, Singapore, Malacca, Batavia, Samarang, and other places in Java; to which parts they resort in the hope of realizing fortunes by commerce, and returning to enjoy the fruits of their industry in their native land.

Smith, 1857

Amoy Emigration in 1874 Amoy has long been the centre of a large Chinese emigration, and in the year 1874, no less than 16, 500 coolies cleared for Singapore, while a few days after our arrival a large steamer left for the same port with 800 on board. They mostly go to the Malay Peninsula and Dutch Colonies an the Straits of Malacca, and are all from the Amoy district, partly mechanics and partly agriculturists…

Streetside Shoemaker   MacGowan, 1907

… Very many settle down in their adopted countries, but great numbers return home after amassing a competency; some, indeed, after death to be buried near their ancestors, for the Chinese have a deep regard for the mother country, and make a point of having their bodies embalmed, if, that is to say, they can afford it, and being sent back to their native place for burial.

Shore, 1881

Colonizing but not Conquering Paradoxical though it may seem to some of our readers, we proceed to state that the Chinese have long been a colonizing people. They have colonized along the sea-board of Asia, from the Sea of Ochotsk to the Bay of Bengal. The Japanese are an offshoot from China. The islands off the coast of China, and many of those in the East Indian Archipelago, have been colonized by the Chinese; and in early every kingdom of eastern peninsular Asia they are found in large and influential communities. It is a noticeable fact that whenever the Chinese colonize among a heathen people, their superior civilization gives them at once a decided advantage over the native population. By their intelligence, industry and capacity for business they almost monopolize all the important and highly remunerative departments of labor; commerce passes into their hands, and they become the chief factors, the leading spirits in the native communities in which they live. …Anyone familiar with the features of the North American Indian, who will look into the face of a Chinese, cannot fail to observe a striking resemblance between them.

Whence came our North American Indians? They neither dropped from the clouds, nor sprang, like the oaks, from the earth…"

Maclay 1861

第三章 厦门人 *The People of Amoy*

厦门主导福建对外贸易 据估计,厦门人口大约只有15万,却拥有三倍于福建省会的贸易船只。他们的商业冒险精神由此可见一斑。厦门人大量移居文莱、锡兰、新加坡、马六甲、巴达维亚、三宝垄和爪哇的其他地区。他们客居他乡,希望有朝一日能够通过生意积累财富,然后荣归故里、享受荣华。

——史密斯,1857年,第424页

1874年厦门人下南洋 长期以来,厦门一直是中国大规模对外移民的中心。1874年,16500名苦力离开厦门港,前往新加坡。我们抵达厦门后几天,一艘大型蒸汽船运走了800人,目的地还是新加坡。他们大多数去了马来半岛和荷兰人在马六甲海峡的殖民地。他们都来自厦门地区,一部分是工匠,一部分是农民。很多人定居在第二故乡,还有不少人在积累相当家当之后返回故土……一些人死后就埋葬在祖先的坟墓旁,因为中国人对故土有深厚的情感。也就是说,如果他们经济上能够承受得起,他们就会想方设法对尸体进行防腐处理,然后运回故乡入葬。

——肖尔,1881年,第42～43页

移民,不是占领 我们常说中国人长期以来一直就是一个对外移民的民族。对于这种说法,一些读者感到有悖常理。事实上,从鄂托斯克海到孟加拉湾,中国人一直沿着亚洲的海岸线迁徙。日本人就是从中国迁移出去的一支旁系。中国外海的岛屿以及东印度群岛(指日本列岛——译者注)都出现过中国人的身影。远古时代,亚洲东部半岛(指朝鲜半岛——译者注)的每

Contented Chinese Farmer Anderson, 1920

个王朝都有影响力极大的中国人大规模聚居区。值得注意的事实是,无论中国人什么时候移居他乡,他们所代表的先进文明赋予他们绝对优越的有利条件,让他们迅速超越本地人。

依靠自己的聪明、勤奋和生意头脑,中国人几乎垄断了所有高回报率的重要工作部门。商业在他们的掌控之中。他们成为居住社区的中间力量和领导人物……熟悉北美印第安人面孔的人看到中国人都会发现两者之间的外表极为相似。北美印第安人来自何方?他们既不是从天上掉下来的,也不是像橡树那样从地底下长出来。

——麦考利,1861年,第123页

Family in Amoy

Gulangyu Family, 1930s J. Nienhuis

China is Family There is one thing about which there can be no manner of doubt, and that is that the children never forget the home in which they were reared. The home is to the Chinese what the country is to the most devoted patriot of other nationalities. The home is larger and dearer than the nation...

If one desires to understand the Chinese, he must study the family life, for there we find the secret for much that is amusing and perplexing in their character. In all the long years of Chinese history, the ideal of the family has been an exalted one. Ancient sages have dealt with much eloquence upon it, and it has been made the model upon which the State has been built up. It is declared in books written on China that the Chinese Government is a patriarchal one, the meaning of which, put into simpler language, is that the system by which this vast and ancient Empire is ruled has been borrowed from any one of the countless homes that exist throughout the land. It has been plainly stated by Confucius, more than two thousand years ago, that a man that did not know how to rule his home was quite unfit to govern a kingdom...

...The laws of China are all based upon the assumption of the solidarity of the family, and that in its prosperity or adversity all members of it must take their share.

Macgowan, 1907

Amoy Woman Power They (the women) have been the great force which has preserved the country. I say this without fear of contradiction.

Dr. Swanson, of Amoy, in Headland, 1912

Henpecked Amoy Men Chinese women in public were always quiet, self-effacing; at home, I discovered, they were nothing of the kind. They fell into private rages which, from my window, I knew to be noisy, fierce and uncontrollable; they had great influence over their menfolk. It might well be, I often thought, that the strict family code of male superiority had been devised and upheld in sheer self-defence. But shrewd and very intelligent, the Chinese woman usually successfully wielded her power without ever usurping male privilege, that is, unless she had ambition to play a part in public life and the opportunity to fulfill it... No, the subservience of women in China has never been more than a face-saving myth...

The longer I lived in China and the more women I met, the greater became my certainty that their character and place in society differed radically in fact and flesh from fiction, convention and Confucianism. But if the men knew it, they were careful never to give themselves away.

Mackenzie-Grieves, 1959

第三章 厦门人 The People of Amoy

厦门的家庭

中国是个家 有一点毋庸置疑,那就是,中国的子孙后代从来不会忘记生养自己的家。家对中国人来说就是国对其他国家最虔诚爱国者的意义。家比国更大、更亲切……

想了解中国人,你就必须研究中国人的家庭生活,因为这样一来我们就可以发现中国人性格中复杂、有趣的秘密。在中国悠久的历史中,家的理想是崇高的。古代圣人用大量的语言论述家庭,家庭已经成为中国的立国之本。在有关中国的许多著述里,中国政府是家长制的。用更简单的话来说,就是治理这个辽阔的古国所采用的体系是从这个国家无数家庭中的任意一户借来的。2000多年前,孔子曾地说过,"一屋不扫,何以扫天下"……

……中国的所有法律都是建立在家庭团结的基础上。荣誉,或是灾难,家庭的所有成员都应该有自己的担当。

Gulangy Family, 1920s

——麦嘉湖,1907年,第28、63页

厦门妇女的力量 她们(厦门妇女)是保存这个国家(中国)的重要力量。我这么说是毫无自相矛盾之虞。

——桑逊博士在海德兰谈厦门,1912年,第76页

厦门男人怕老婆 在公共场合,中国妇女总是文静、谦逊的;在家里,我发现,她们可不一样。据我所知,私下场合她们生气时声音很大、凶悍、难以控制。她们对自己的丈夫影响很大。我常想,男人至上的严格家庭伦理很有可能已被改变,或只是为了自卫而坚持着。中国妇女非常精明、睿智。她们没有篡夺男人的特权(当然,除非她想在公共生活中扮演角色,并且有机会实现),就成功地行使自己的权力……不,中国妇女的屈从绝对不仅仅只是谜一样的面子问题……

随着我在中国居住时间越来越长,接触到了更多的女性,我越来越敢肯定,她们的性格和社会地位的现实情况与传说、传统和礼教差别很大。不过,一旦意识到这一点,男人就会非常小心。他们不会轻易放弃自己的权力。

——麦肯兹·格瑞芙,1959年,第142~144页

Lovers of Children There is no nation that is fonder of children than the Chinese. They have a perfect passion for them, and it is very rarely that a family can be found without one or more of them in it. If there are none born into it, arrangements are made to supply that deficiency by buying some for the Chinese seem to have a perfect dread of a childless home. If a man has the means, he will buy several sons, who are treated as though they were his own, and, when they grow up, they will inherit his property, and have all the privileges that are given to those that were born in the family...

The early years of a child seem on the whole to be happy ones. In the swarms of children that one sees almost anywhere, one gets the impression that on the whole they thoroughly enjoy themselves. They run about and romp and dance and gambol very much as a similar number of English children would do on the village green, or in the streets and lanes of a home city.

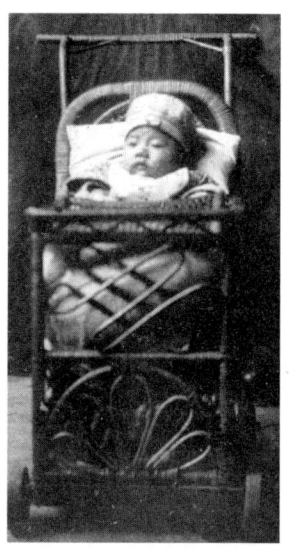

MacGowan, 1907

A Son is Born When a son is born into the family there are great rejoicings amongst every member of it...

As for the father, he walks about as proud as a turkey-cock, although according to Chinese etiquette he assumes an air of indifference as though nothing special had happened, whilst all the time under those stolid features that are as undemonstrative as a tombstone, a world of passion and joyous feeling and romantic thoughts are playing their sweet music around his heart.

MacGowan 1907

Baby Contest

第三章　厦门人 *The People of Amoy*

爱孩子　没有一个国家的人民比中国人更爱小孩了。对孩子，他们拥有一种完美的激情。不养一个或几个小孩的家庭在中国是很少见的。没生小孩，就会通过购买来弥补缺憾，因为中国人似乎很害怕自己无后。如果这个家庭有办法，他会买好几个小孩，然后就像自己的亲生孩子那样对待。长大后，养子可以继承他的财产，并享有跟亲生孩子一样的待遇……

孩子的幼年时期总体上似乎是幸福的。在中国，你随处可以看到成群的孩子，他们总体上是非常开心的。他们跟英国小孩一样在村子的草地上、街道里、小巷中四处乱跑，又唱又跳、嬉戏游乐。

——麦嘉湖，
1907 年，第 30 页

ALL ABOARD　　Anderson, 1920

儿子出生　儿子出生的时候，整个家庭都为之欣喜若狂……

至于父亲，他就像一只火鸡，骄傲地四处闲逛。当然，根据中国的礼教，他应该保持着毫不在意的样子，好像什么事也没发生。他表面上不动声色，就像墓碑那样一直毫无表情，实际上喜悦与激动之情正在他内心深处奏响甜美的乐章。

——麦嘉湖，
1907 年，第 44、45 页

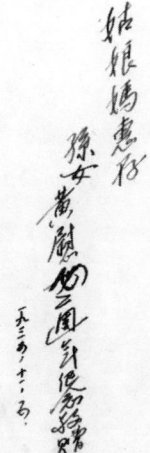

Chinese Children's Playtime The Chinese are far from being a gloomy race of people. Their hearts are full of fun and vigorous life, and this is seen in the sturdy urchins that race about with each other and that fill the air with their merry sounds of childish laughter.

With very young children this is all the more remarkable since so little is provided for their amusement. Such things as pictures or storybooks or toys in the large and profuse sense with which our nurseries are supplied in England, do not exist in this land. Childhood is left very much to its own resources to find out the means of passing the time pleasantly. It is pathetic to watch how, with the fewest and simplest materials, the little ones will pass the day, with apparently perfect contentment. The method most popular, because it involves no expense, is the making of mud pies, and the building of miniature houses with broken pieces of tiles that can be picked up from the streets.

MacGowan, 1907

Xiamen, 1920s J. Nienhuis

Children at Play   MacGowan, 1912

第三章 厦门人 *The People of Amoy*

中国儿童的游玩时间 中国人绝对不是一个悲观的民族。他们的内心充满了欢乐和激情的生活。这一切在四处追逐的强壮顽童身上得到了体现。他们爽朗的笑声响彻云霄。

幼儿的情况尤其如此,因为能够给他们提供的娱乐太少了。在英国,诸如图片、故事书籍或玩具之类的东西托儿所会慷慨地大量提供。在中国,这些东西连影子都看不到。中国儿童的童年需要在自己寻找消磨时光的快乐方法中度过。很显然,用最少和最简单的材料,小家伙们绝对心满意足地度过每一天。此情此景,实在令人同情。最流行的是做土饼,或用街上随处可见的瓦片建造小房子,因为这些玩法不花钱。

——麦嘉湖,1907 年,第 50、51 页

Make Way—Coming Through! J.N.

Amoy Boys   MacGowan,1907

53

Amoy Superstitions about Children A chain with a lock is often put about a boy's neck to make the evil spirits believe he is a girl or animal. A single ear-ring is to make think he is a girl and not worth harming. A small bag is fastened to his clothes. This contains the name of the idol which is supposed to dwell with the child, either boy or girl. At the time of the first visit to the maternal grandparents, a spot of soot is daubed on the child's forehead to give courage. On his first birthday a boy is seated in a large flat basket with twelve articles namely scissors, seeds, a garment, bread, abacus, book, money, etc. from which he indicates his future through the choice of the playthings.

Rose Talman, unpublished notes.

Inquisitive Girls Amoy, Dec.11th, 1885

It was rather a dull morning when we reached Amoy, but the sandy beach and houses of Kolong-su looked home-like, and before long Mr. McGregor and Miss Maclagan were on board, and brought us ashore for breakfast. Miss M. and I are to take possession of the Ladies' House, which has just been cleaned and painted. It has a very pretty situation, with lovely glimpses of the sea and hills beyond, and little winding paths lead up to the great grey boulders above us.

You may be sure that one of our first visits here was to the school, which compared favourably with those we visited elsewhere, and the hearty greeting we received from the children was most encouraging. I quite longed that some of those who are carrying on this work at home could have stood with us in the bright, airy schoolroom, and have heard the "Peng-an" (Peace) which echoed from every corner.

Bright Amoy Girls MacGowan, 1914

On our first visit was to the school Saturday morning, directly after breakfast, a messenger was sent to say that the whole school was coming to pay me a visit, and I had barely time to come downstairs before the tramp of feet was heard, and two by two the twenty-three girls, their matron, and teacher, filed up the approach to our house. I waited in the drawing-room to receive them as they crowded in, and felt very helpless as I smiled a reply to all their good wishes. A little quietness followed while Miss M. kindly interpreted some of their words, and told them how I hoped soon to understand and speak to them in their own language.

I was at a loss as to how such guests should be entertained, but they solved the problem themselves by beginning a tour of the room and examining each object minutely. Fortunately our furniture is but scant, as this proved a lengthy proceeding, and somewhat monotonous. However, our guests were well pleased, and proposed to visit our bedrooms; and on Miss M. consenting, the whole party trooped upstairs, and I soon heard great chattering and laughing over my boots and slippers.

Johnston, 1907

第三章　厦门人 The People of Amoy

厦门有关小孩的迷信　男孩的脖子经常戴着长命锁，让恶鬼以为他是一个女孩或动物。戴个耳环，让恶鬼以为他是一个女孩，不值得伤害。衣服上系个小袋，里面装着神仙的名字，说明小孩，无论男女，是跟神仙住在一起。首次到外公家，额头涂上一个黑点，赋予小孩勇气。周岁的时候，把小孩放在大竹匾里，摆上12件物品，包括剪刀、种子、衣服、面包、算盘、书本、钞票等，让他选择其中一件，表示他未来会从事的职业。

——罗斯·塔尔曼，《我们的中国岁月：1916—1930》，未出版的笔记

好奇的女生

——杰西·约翰斯通，1885年12月11日，厦门

我们抵达厦门那天是个沉闷的上午。不过，鼓浪屿上的沙滩和房子看上去倒是像家一样。不久，麦克格瑞高先生和麦克拉安小姐上船来把我们带到岸上吃早饭。麦小姐和我占领了刚刚修整、粉刷的女舍。宿舍位置很好，可以看到漂亮的海景和远处的群山，以及通往山顶巨石的蜿蜒小路。

毫无疑问，我们最早去访问的地方之一是学校。跟其他地方相比，这里的学校好多了。来自孩子们开心的问候最鼓舞人心。我真希望那些在老家推动这项工作的人能够与我们一起站在明亮、通风的教室里，听到"平安"的声音在学校的每个角落里回响。

"Pigtails Sticking Out All Round"
Johnston, 1907

我们第一次到学校访问是在星期六，用过早餐直接去。有人来报信说，学校师生都要过来拜访我。还来不及下楼，我就听到师生们的脚步声。23名女生排成两行，与她们的舍监、老师一起，列队走在我们房子门前的小路上。她们相拥而入，我在客厅接待她们。她们纷纷向我表达良好祝愿，我微笑应答，感到十分无助。紧接着是一会儿的寂静，麦小姐为我解释她们的一些话，然后告诉她们我希望很快能够听懂她们的话，并跟她们交流。

这么多客人如何招待，我束手无策。但她们开始参观我们的房子，仔细观察里面的每一件物品，自己解决了这个问题。幸运的是，我们的家具不多。否则的话，每件看过去，既漫长又有些无聊。不管怎样，我们的客人很满意，提出要参观我们的卧室。征得麦克拉安小姐的同意，一行人列队上楼。不久，我就听到她们在笑谈我的靴子和拖鞋。

——约翰斯通，1907年，第33～35页

老外看老鼓浪屿 Old Gulangyu in Foreigners' Eyes

Care of the Elderly In family life Chinese solidarity has its inconveniences, but it altogether prevents that painful spectacle to which people seem to have hardened their hearts in England, of sending their aged relatives to the workhouse instead of carefully tending them at the home as the Chinese do, or of one brother or sister surrounded by every luxury, another haunted by the horror of creditors and with barely the necessaries of life. If you are to help your brother, you must, of course, claim a certain amount of authority over his way of life. In China the father does so; and when he dies, the elder brother sees after and orders his younger brother about; and the younger brother, as a rule, submits.

Little, 1899

Gulangyu Granny   McGowan, 1907

Romance and Marriage in Amoy

3 Ways to Get Wives The philosopher tells us that wives are obtained in the world by one of three methods, capture, purchase, or convention. Purchase is the method most in vogue here, though high-minded fathers prefer to make a present of a daughter to some man whom they consider suitable. There is no courtship. In general, matchmaking is both a serious and tricky business. The young people must on no account act for themselves. They must accept what is given them by their parents, or guardians, whose written document makes a legal deed of marriage...

Sadler, 1897

Wedding Gifts, 1920s   J. Nienhuis

第三章　厦门人 *The People of Amoy*

照顾老人　在家庭生活中，中国的团结有其不便之处。不过，这完全可以避免发生英国人不愿意看到的情景。在英国，人们似乎只能铁了心肠，把自己年老的亲人送进救济所，而不是像中国人那样把他们小心翼翼地放在家里照顾。或是看着一个兄弟姐妹享尽荣华富贵，而另一个兄弟姐妹债务缠身、食不果腹。如果你想帮助自己的兄弟，当然，你必须对他的生活方式施加某种程度的影响。在中国，这件工作由父亲负责。父亲不在，长兄负责，并对弟弟发号施令。一般情况下，弟弟只能遵从。

——利特尔，1899年，第535页

"Aunty Velvet", Spring 1933

厦门的罗曼史与婚姻

娶妻三法　哲学家告诉我们，世界上找老婆的方法有三种：俘获、购买和契约。买卖是这里最流行的方法，尽管高傲的父亲更喜欢把女儿当作礼物送给他认为合适的男人。这里没有求爱。做媒通常是一件严肃而且需要讲究策略的事情。年轻人没有理由自己做主。他们必须接受父母或监护人指定的婚姻。只有他们指定的婚约，才能让婚姻合法……

——塞德勒，1897年，第755～758页

Bridal Chair by Otte Memorial, Gulangyu, 1920s

老外看老鼓浪屿 *Old Gulangyu in Foreigners' Eyes*

Marriage and Love With us it is an accepted axiom that to secure the happiness of the married couple, there must be love and there must be a thorough acquaintance with each other. The Chinese hold that all that is Platonic nonsense…They declare that neither of those two things are requisite, and they point to China, where marriage is the rule in social life, and where a Divorce Court does not exist in all the length and breadth of the land, as a convincing evidence that love at least is not at all a requisite for marriage. The young man and his wife then begin their married life without any knowledge of each other. They have never seen each other, and they have never dared to inquire from their parents what their future partners were like. To have done so would have filled the hearts of their fathers and mothers with a shame so intense as to be absolutely unspeakable.

Their first look into the faces of each other, after the bride has been carried with noise of music and firing of crackers in the crimson chair into the home of her husband, must be one in which is concentrated the agony and passion of two hearts, trying to read their fate for the years that are to come, from what a bashful glance at each other's faces can tell them. If either of them is disappointed, the wave of despair that flashes through the heart is hidden behind those sphinx-like faces, and no quivering of the lips and no glance of the coal-black eyes betrays the secret that has sprung up within them.

They are both conscious that their marriage is a settled fact and that there is no possibility of its ever being annulled, and so with the heroic patience that the Chinese often show in ordinary life, they both determine to make the best of things, knowing that in time love will grow, and tender affection for each other will ripen amid the trials and disciplines of life through which they will have to pass together.

The years go by, and without daring to show by word or look to the rest of the world that they love each other, the deepest and the purest affection has sprung up in their hearts. The Chinese language is full of tender epithets and phrases full of poetry to express the emotions of love, but the husband and wife may never use any of these excepting behind closed doors where none can hear them but themselves.

MacGowan, 1907

Amoy Bridal Car　　　　　　　　　J. Nienhuis

第三章 厦门人 The People of Amoy

婚姻与爱情 夫妻婚后要获得幸福,必须有爱,必须相互完全了解。对我们来说,这已经是一个人人接受的公理。中国人却认为,所有这一切都是柏拉图式的谬论……他们宣称,这两样东西并非必不可少。他们指出,在中国,婚姻是社会生活的惯例。在中国广袤的大地上,没有一家离婚法庭。这两点足以证明,爱情绝对不是婚姻的必备条件。年轻男子和他的妻子互不相识就开始婚姻生活。他们素未谋面,也不敢向他们的父母亲打听他们未来伴侣的模样。打听,就会让他们父母的内心感到非常羞耻,令人完全难以用语言形容。

在嘈杂的音乐声和鞭炮声中,新娘坐在大红的轿子里被抬进了丈夫的家。夫妻间的第一次见面必定是两颗悲喜交集的心。羞怯一瞥,他们试图从对方的脸上解读自己未来岁月的命运。任何一方不满意,涌上心头的绝望很快就会被隐藏在他们谜一般的脸上。没有嘴唇的颤动,没有乌黑双眼的对视会出卖他们内心涌起的秘密。

他们都知道,婚姻已是既成事实,婚约不可能取消。因此,以中国人日常生活中常见的英雄般的耐心,他们决定尽其所能,相信随着时间的推移,爱情会产生,彼此间的温柔情谊会在未来生活的考验和制约中成熟。

几年过去了,他们还不敢用言辞或表情向世人宣示彼此之间的爱情。但最深、最纯的爱情已经在他们的心间萌芽。汉语有很多富有诗意的温柔词句,可以表达爱的情感,但除了闭门之后无人知晓的时候,从来没有见过哪对夫妻用过这些词语。

——麦嘉湖,1907 年,第 22 页

Bridal Chair (Photo by Dr.John Otte) Draagstoel voor een Chineesche bruid.

中华民国二十三十八年结婚摄影纪念 于安妥桥西两礼拜堂举行 黄夏明与周洗兴

第三章　厦门人 *The People of Amoy*

老外看老鼓浪屿 *Old Gulangyu in Foreigners' Eyes*

Chapter 4 Fashionable Amoy

Amoy Turbans The natives of Fuhkien have always been noted for their independence. They were the last to submit to the foreign yoke of the Manchus, and when the edict went forth for the conquered people to shave the head and wear the pigtail, like their conquerors, they resisted when the rest of China had given in. Thousands lost their heads, rather than wear the queue, and when compelled to yield they wrapped a cloth round their heads to conceal their degradation, and to this day the custom is continued, though its origin is forgotten. This resistance to authority has remained a characteristic of the province.

Johnston, 1898

Blue Cotton His clothes, which are shabby and well worn, consist of the ordinary blue cotton cloth that in its dull and dingy colour helps to give a mean and uninteresting look to the wearer. If the nation would but depart from the eternal tradition that has come steadily down the ages in regard to its clothing and would take some hints from nature, whose varied moods make her look so charming, how different would these unaesthetic people appear from what they do now!

MacGowan, 1907

Fashionable Amoy Couple, 1873

Gulangyu Sunday Finery A very pretty spectacle every Sabbath morning it is to see the troops of worshippers wending their way from the large village in the central part of the island to one of these two churches [English Presbyterian or London Missionary Society]. The men have usually got on their best; and impressed with the idea that they are going to engage in a solemn service, they have made special efforts to appear as clean and as trim as the barber's art and their Sunday clothes can make them.

MacGowan, 1897

Pretty Chinese Girls' Clothing The girls, however, from the boarding schools, of which there are three, and the young married women from the various homes scattered about, carry off the palm for the picturesque appearance they present as they mingle in the throngs that crowd the main street of the village, or as they wind their way along the quieter roads that protect them from the observation and criticisms of the sterner sex.

62

第四章　穿着打扮

厦门人的头巾　长期以来，福建本地人一直以其独立的个性而闻名。他们是最后屈服于满族统治的汉人。当清朝皇帝颁发诏书，要求臣服的汉民像满洲人那样剃头蓄辫，中国其他地区的汉人遵从了，而福建人还在反抗。为此，成千上万的福建人宁肯掉头颅，而不愿意留长辫。被强制去发梳辫之后，他们戴起了头巾，隐藏自己的失落。时至今日，这种风俗依然存在，只是缘由已经被人们遗忘了。对执政当局的反抗已经成为这个省份的一个特点。

——约翰斯通，1898 年，第 30 页

蓝色棉布衫　他身上的衣服是普通的蓝色棉布衫，色彩枯燥、单一，已经陈旧不已、肮脏不堪，让人联想到穿戴者普通、无趣的外表。如果中国能够在穿着方面放弃数千年流传下来的永恒传统，从大自然中获取某些灵感，以其不一般的性情，这些缺乏美感的中国人肯定会变得更加迷人，他们的面貌也一定会比现在大为不同。

——麦嘉湖，1907 年

鼓浪屿周日华丽的服饰　安息日上午，一个壮观的景象就是信众成群结队从小岛中部的大村庄走进岛上的两个教堂（分别由英国长老派教会和伦敦差会创办）。这个时候，人们都会穿上家里最好的衣服，给人的感觉是他们即将参加一个庄严的礼拜。为此，他们特别用功，拿出礼拜天的服饰，尽量像理发师那样把自己打扮得整整齐齐、清清楚楚。

——麦嘉湖，1897 年，第 154 页

漂亮中国女孩的服饰　厦门有三所寄宿学校。当学校里的女生和散居岛上的少妇混进大街拥挤的人群，或者当她们沿着僻静的小路行走，以避开男性的目光和品评，她们同时带走了自己所代表的如画风景。

Amoy Fashion, 1921　　J. Nienhuis

Their costume is a very bright one, and thoroughly in harmony with a climate where the sun dominates everywhere and fills everything with his glory for the greater part of the year. Some are dressed in blue, with a facing that makes it stand out in striking contrast; others in pink, edged with green, whilst others again appear in black, or orange, or white, trimmed with the colours that set them off to the best advantage.

The effect is very charming, and though according to our Western ideas the harmony in colours is far from being perfect, the picture they present is perfectly idyllic, and such as one never tires of looking at.

MacGowan, 1897

Hair Ornaments   Johnston, 1907

Amoy Headdresses There is no doubt but that the head-dress has a great deal to do with the general effect that is produced on one's mind when looking at these brightly-dressed young girls. Their hair, which is very luxuriant and as black as jet—no other colour, indeed, being known throughout the empire—is done up with such art and exquisite taste that it has a very attractive and becoming look. Into this are inserted fragrant flowers, such as the jessamine or the tuberose, or other native ones which may be in season at the time, whilst gold and silver pins with imitation pearls dangling from their ends, are inserted in the hair on each side of the head, giving a finish and completeness to the toilette.

Social custom, stern and unyielding as the laws of the Medes and the Persians, demands certain things of a woman when she wishes to walk abroad. She must have flowers in her hair, and she must have her ear-rings on. To appear without these would be considered a serious breach of etiquette, but indeed no woman, not even the very poorest, ever attempts to do so. As bonnets of any kind are never worn either in summer or winter by the woman, the full effect produced by a skilful arrangement of flowers and hair-pins can be appreciated by everyone who looks upon them, especially in the case of those who have taken special care with their toilette, and who have the taste to make the best of the materials with which they adorn themselves.

MacGowan, 1897

Amoy Embroidery The women embroider very beautifully on cloth. The garments are worn by priests and officials on state occasions, and the cloths are used for decorating temples. Jewelry is used very extensively by women of all classes for the hair and for earrings. The poorest people often wear the most gorgeous head-dresses. The shops where these ornaments are made are numerous, and the implements used in their manufacture are of the rudest description. Silver wire is the principal material.

Shore 1881

第四章　穿着打扮 Fashionable Amoy

她们的服饰色彩鲜艳，与阳光普照、常年风和日丽的厦门搭配完美。一些年轻女性身着蓝色衣服，配上镶边，与她们的服装形成强烈的反差；还有一些女性的衣服是粉红色的，镶边绿色；其他还有一些人穿着或黑，或白，或橙的衣服，镶上各种颜色，把自己打扮到了极致。

这种效果的确很好。在我们西方人看来，尽管颜色方面的搭配对服装来说与完美相距甚远，但她们所展示的形象却完全是田园诗歌般的完美，令人百看不厌。

——麦嘉湖，1897 年，第 154～156 页

MacGowan, 1895
A Lady at her Toilette

厦门人的头饰　当你看到这些穿着鲜艳的厦门女孩时，她们穿着打扮给人留下的总体印象，头饰毫无疑义起了很重要的作用。她们的头发浓密、乌黑，不掺异色，在全中国都是有名的。姑娘们用艺术的眼光，精挑细梳，打理出来的发型得体、妩媚。插上茉莉、夜来香之类的几朵时令鲜花，戴上或金或银的发卡，人工珍珠悬挂在发卡的一端，女性的梳妆打扮就这样达到了完美。

顽固的社会风俗，就像难以改变的制度，对女性出门提出了苛刻的要求。她必须插鲜花、戴耳环。否则的话，就会严重违背礼仪。事实上，所有的女性，甚至包括最贫困的，都遵从了。无论是夏天，还是冬季，这里的女性都不戴帽子。相反，她们在头上巧妙地插上了鲜花和发卡。那些特别注意梳妆打扮、善于自己动手把饰品发挥到极致的女性，她们的装饰效果极佳，众人无不敬仰、欣赏。

——麦嘉湖，1897 年，第 154～156 页

厦门的刺绣　妇女在织物上所做的刺绣非常漂亮：从神父和官员在正式场合所穿着的服装，到寺庙里装饰的绣品。这里各个阶层的妇女常用首饰来装饰头发、耳根。即使最贫困的妇女也经常戴着豪华的头饰。当地有许多加工首饰的店铺，店里所用的加工工具极为粗糙，银线是最主要的原材料。

——肖尔，1881 年，第 67 页

老外看老鼓浪屿 Old Gulangyu in Foreigners' Eyes

Official's Costume Our host's [the Taotai] dress was neat and simple—characteristic of the Chinese official undress uniform-consisting of a black garment rather like an Inverness cape, over a dark blue silk skirt. The hat resembles a pork-pie with the top sides falling out, and on top is the badge of office by which the rank of the wearer is easily distinguished, consisting of a glass ball about the size of a walnut. This 'button,' as it is called, varies in colour according to grade, red being the highest, next blue, and so on, and there are different shades of each. Our host was a "blue button," while his secretary wore one of opaque white. The "tout ensemble" is pleasing to the eye, and in quite as good taste, if not better, than our custom of overlaying with buttons and lace till people look like zebras; and then the wearer [of Chinese costume] is comfortable and can eat, drink, walk or lie down without fear of his breeches splitting, the buttons flying, or of choking from the height and grandeur of his collar. On the other hand, one must admit the striking resemblance between a Chinese mandarin and the conventional toy-shop figure of Noah; and then the skirts would sadly impede a rapid flight. Perhaps the shoes are the most open to objection, being devoid of all the good qualities of a barbarian boot, and neither useful nor ornamental.

Shore 1881

Long Nails In a secluded hermitage... we found a man, who probably had seen some eighty summers— a venerable-looking priest, his beard white as driven snow. Our attention was, however, immediately distracted from all other portions of his person to that of his left hand, the examination of which, so far from being opposed to his inclination, on the contrary, afforded him infinite pleasure and pride. To use a nautical phrase, we perceived "lashed" at the back of each finger a narrow slip of bamboo, as a means of defending the nail from any casual blow; otherwise, they could not have lasted, without breaking, even for a week. At our request, he carefully removed one

Bound Feet MacGo

or two of these splints; he said he had cherished his feline weapons he knew not how many years, and through dint of great care, during this long period, without accident. It is needless to add, that this hand was totally useless to him. We had the curiosity to measure the longest nail, and found it to exceed eleven inches in length; it tapered considerably towards the point, and at the extremity much resembled a shriveled quill.

I heard of an old man, at Amoy, said to possess a nail seventeen inches in length…

Colonel Cunynghame

Pigtail-less Foreigners An old lady would scream out to her son, standing near us, to look if we wore pig-tails; a friend conveniently situated for seeing the back of our heads, would shout out that we had no pig-tails; another of an inquiring turn of mind, would at the pitch of his voice address an inquiry to the assembly as to what they thought could have become of our pig-tails; while the kindly old lady, unable to believe that barbarians who conducted themselves so decently as we were doing, could really after all be so destitute of civilization as to want a pig-talk, vociferously urges some one close by us to look carefully if our pig-tails be hanging down inside some part of our dress; and a scamp in the crowd raises a laugh, by explaining to her in an exceedingly audible tone of voice that we have had our pig-tails cut off for theft…

Letter by Rev. W.Macgregor, 1875

第四章　穿着打扮 Fashionable Amoy

Mandarin and Son　MacGowan, 1912

官服　我们主人（道台）穿的是一套典型的官员便服，整齐、简单。外面是一件黑色的外套，很像我们的披风大衣，里面是深蓝色的丝绸衬衫。他的顶子（红缨帽）像一块猪肉馅饼，顶部外翻，正中镶有一金属座，座上嵌一颗核桃大小的顶珠，用于清楚区分官员的级别。"顶珠"根据官员的品级而分质地和颜色，红色品级最高，蓝色次之，依此类推。每个品级的顶珠颜色深浅还有区别。我们的主人戴的是蓝色的顶珠，他的师爷戴的是白色、不透明的顶珠。官服给人留下赏心悦目的总体效果，品味至少跟我们国家的一样好，如果不是更好的话。国内官场的制服扣子、花边一层盖过一层，让穿着者看上去像一匹斑马。中国的官服穿戴舒服，不影响吃、喝、行、躺，也不用担心裤管开裂、纽扣掉落，更不会因为高领的奢华而令人感到窒息。另一方面，你必须承认，中国政府官员与普通百姓极为相像。还有，裙装非常不利于快速逃逸。最受非议的也许就属鞋子，丝毫没有外来民族短靴的优点，既不实用，也不漂亮。
　　——肖尔，1881年，第47～48页

长指甲　在一个偏僻的山村……我们见过一位年过八旬的老人。他是一位令人肃然起敬的道士，胡子白若飘雪。一见面，我们的注意力立即从他身体的其他部位注意到他的左手。仔细一问，发现他并不反感，相反，他表现出了无尽的乐趣与自豪。当我们看到他每个手指都带着一片狭长的竹片，以保护指甲不受任何意外伤害时，借用一个航海术语，当时我们感觉受到了"猛烈冲击"。如果没有这样的保护，指甲是无法持续生长的，不出一周就会断裂。应我们的请求，老人轻轻地取下一、两片夹板。他说，这些猫爪般的武器，他不知抚育了多少年头。由于细心呵护，这么长时间以来一直没有出现意外。不用多说，这只手对他来讲完全是没有用处的。我们非常好奇地量了一下最长的指甲，超过11英寸！指甲从手指向指尖逐渐变细，到了最尖处就像一根干枯的豪猪毛。
　　我还听说，在厦门，有一位老人，他的指甲长达17英寸……
　　——坎宁汉上校，1853年，第190～191页

不留辫子的番仔　一位老太太对站在我们身边的儿子高声叫喊，让他看看我们是否留辫子。一个朋友的站位好，能够方便地看到我们的后脑勺。他回答说，我们没有留辫子。朋友的话音未落，新一轮的问题又向围观的人群提出了。比如说，假如我们留辫子，又会怎么样等等。那位和蔼可亲的老太太无法相信我们这些行为端庄的番仔竟然如此缺乏教养，以至于没留辫子。她大声吆喝，让人仔细查看我们的辫子是否隐藏在衣服里。这时候，人群中有一流氓笑了起来。他非常大声地跟老太太解释说，因为偷东西，我们的辫子被割掉了……
　　——麦克格雷高主教的信件，1875年

老外看老鼓浪屿 *Old Gulangyu in Foreigners' Eyes*

Chapter 5   Education and Government

Pen Mightier than Sword   Far more formidable than the soldiery are the literati of China. Soldiering is despised in China; learning is esteemed.

Little, 1899

Mr. Burns, the "Book-man"   "... the Chinese are a discerning people, and they respect a 'book-man'... Mr. Burns is a favorite in Amoy. During the coolie riots of last year, he was almost the only European who dared to appear in the streets. A British soldier would not have been safe with his bayonet, but the missionary walked about unmolested with his Bible under his arm.

The Messenger

Scholars are Much Revered in China

Land of Books   China is said to have more books than any other country. I am not able to say whether this statement is true or not, but certainly the Chinese have a voluminous literature. In Peking there are several blocks of streets in the Chinese city which are devoted to books. The Hanlin Library[1] contained many thousand volumes. Among them there was one work comprising 23,633 volumes...

Denby, 1906

Fujianese Dominate Academics   "Although Chu Hsi, one of China's greatest philosophers, was a Fukienese, and, as a Foochow scholar pointed out to me, in the Chinese equivalent of the Dictionary of National Biography, one hundred and sixty-one out of the two hundred and eighty-two biographies are of Fukienese..."

Mackenzie-Grieves, 1959

Courageous Sages   There is a bravery characteristic of the sage...boldly to carry into practice his views of the doctrines of the ancient kings; in a high situation not to follow the current of a bad people; to consider that there is no poverty where there is virtue, and no wealth or honor where virtue is not; when appreciated by the world, to desire to share in all men's joys and sorrows; when unknown by the world, to stand up grandly alone between heaven and earth and have no fears—this is the bravery of the highest order.

Lewis, 1938

---

1   China's first public library was in our Fujian Provincial capital of Fuzhou.

第五章 教育与官府

文字的力量胜过武力　在中国，武士被鄙视，文人受尊敬。因此，比武士更可怕的是文人。

——利特尔，1899年，第292页

饱学之士彭斯先生　……中国人洞明世事，他们尊重有学问的人……彭斯先生在厦门颇受欢迎。1852年劳工骚乱期间，他是唯一敢在大街上露面的欧洲人。英国士兵即使带上武器也不见得安全，但这位传教士掖着圣经四处行走，没人骚扰。

Chinese Scholar in his Garden　MacGowan, 1913

——《基督信使报》，1853年

书籍之国　中国据说拥有比其他国家更多的书籍。这种说法是否真实，我无从考究。不过，说中国文学书籍浩瀚如烟海却是毋庸置疑的。在北京，好几个街区的生意与书籍有关。翰林院藏书数以千计。其中，有一部著作多达13633卷……

——丹比，1906年，第8页

福建人的学术成就独占鳌头　"朱熹，中国最伟大的理学家之一，是福建人。一位福州学者告诉我，《中国人名大词典》（相当于《英国人名词典》）里，282个名人传记中有161位是福建人……"

——麦肯兹·格丽芙，1959年，第31页

勇敢的圣人　圣人的特点是勇敢……他们敢于将古代国王的训导当作自己行动的指南：居高位而不随波逐流，行善则无贫富，作恶则财富、荣耀全无；世人赏识，则与之分享悲喜；无人喝彩，则堂而皇之地独立于天地间，无所畏惧——这就是最高等级的勇敢。

——列维斯，1938年，第111～112页

69

Faith in Education The Chinese have a profound faith in education. High and low and rich and poor are absolutely of one mind on this point, and if a boy is not sent to school, it is either because the parents are too poor, or because they have not sufficient authority over him to compel him to study. One need not be surprised at this unanimity of opinion, for education is the royal road to the honours and emoluments that the State has to bestow, and it is by means of it that the wildest ambition that ever ran riot through a young man's brain can ultimately be satisfied. In the West there are many ways by which a man may rise to eminence…In China they are all narrowed down to one, and it is the one that leads from the schoolhouse.

MacGowan, 1913

One Chinese Page=One Western Volume …the Chinese classic masters express their wisdom with such succinct clarity that a page from their works is as full of meat as a volume of Western philosophy.

Mackenzie-Grieves, 1959

Amoy Children's Education At about eight preparations are made for the lad to go to school. Terms are made with the school-master of the nearest school, a certain number of books splashed and dotted over with mysterious-looking hieroglyphics are bought, and one morning at early dawn, just as the pale grey light begins to colour the landscape, the little fellow finds his way along the silent road to the school-house. Here for six or seven years he will spend the best part of his days in the study of books that contain the ideals of the nation…

Teaching ABCs the Old Way Band, 1948

The boy begins at eight not with "Jack and Jill," or the "House that Jack built," or with any nursery rhyme that would appeal to a child's imagination, but with the solemn statements on high ethical questions that some of the greatest thinkers and teachers of China have produced. …Just imagine a boy of ten, accustomed till to-day to run as wild as a climbing plant, that creeps up trees, or over ruined walls, or down the side of a precipice, brought face to face with a statement like this, instead of the conventional one, " My dog," or "His cat," that confronts the English lad as he first enters the domain of learning.

MacGowan, 1907

The Real Rulers of China The district magistrates, so far as officials are concerned, are the real rulers of China… the first step on the ladder is open to all who can win their way by successful competition at certain literary examinations, so long as each candidate can show that none of his ancestors for three generations have been either actors, barbers and chiropodists, priests, executioners, or official servants.

第五章 教育与官府 Education and Government

重视教育 中国人对教育极为重视。在教育的问题上,无论贫富、尊卑,他们的想法是完全一致的。小孩不上学,要么是父母亲太穷,要么是他们没有足够的威信来强制孩子读书。对教育问题的一致看法,你不用感到奇怪,因为它是通往国家所赋予的荣耀和奖赏的最佳线路。通过这个办法,野心勃勃的年轻人最终能够实现自己的理想。在西方,通往成功的路径千千万……在中国,只有教育这座独木桥,它的起点就在学堂。

——麦嘉湖,1913年,第75页

中国一页＝西方一卷 ……中国古典大师善用简洁的语言表达思想。他们一页作品的信息量相当于一卷西方哲学书。

——麦肯兹·格丽芙,1959年,第33页

厦门少年儿童的教育 小孩上学,大致要做8项准备。与临近学堂的先生签约,购买一些满是笔画古怪的汉字书籍。然后,在某个黎明时刻,天刚蒙蒙亮,小家伙就开始沿着僻静的小路,走向学堂。在那里,他将度过人生最美好的六、七年光阴,学习那些充满国家理想的书籍……

小孩八岁开始读书,不是从辨认"Jack(杰克)男、Jil(吉尔)女",或练习类似"House that Jack built(杰克造房子)"这样的儿歌入手,激发他们的想象力,而是学习中国历史上最伟大的思想家、教育家关于伦理道德问题的庄严教诲……想想看,一个十岁小孩,本该像攀缘植物那样狂野地攀上树枝、翻过围墙、或爬下悬崖峭壁。在英国,初进学堂,通常都是从"My dog"(我的狗)、"His cat"(他的猫)开始,中国的少年儿童现在却已经开始在学堂接受古人的训示。

——麦嘉湖,1907年,第56～57页

中国真正的统治者 从官员的角度来看,地方官是中国真正的统治者……只要考生能够证明自己的祖先三代不是戏子、理发匠、江湖游医、道士、刽子手或官员的仆人,通向官场的第一个台阶——科举考试向所有有志参与竞争的臣民开放。

Want of means may be said to offer no obstacle in China to ambition and desire for advancement. The slightest aptitude in a boy for learning would be carefully noted, and if found to be the genuine article, would be still more carefully fostered. Not only are there plenty of free schools in China, but there are plenty of persons ready to help in so good a cause. Many a high official has risen from the furrowed fields, his educational expenses as a student, and his travelling expenses as a candidate, being paid by subscription in his native place.

Chinese Official

Giles, 1902

Ancient Chinese Democracy A missionary at Amoy, who has been trying to understand the nature of the powers that be in China, has discovered that the Chinese, so far from being petrified conservatives, are really in their own way democratic. The Emperor and Mandarins are not unchecked autocrats, but entertain a wholesome dread of a fairly effective public opinion...

Chinese Recorder, Vol. 20, August, 1889

Grassroots Chinese Democracy ...there exists among the Chinese a strong democratic element, which finds expression and scope for action in their municipal regulations. Every ward in China has its elders, its public hall, where the people meet for the transaction of business, and its placards or public manifestoes, in which the popular sentiments are boldly expressed; and both unpopular officers and offensive acts of government are sometimes criticized and denounced with irresistible logic and overwhelming ridicule. These elders are chosen by the people, either by seniority or by the sentiment of the ward, and their authority is potent and generally ultimate in adjudicating the cases brought before them... The government regards them as the patriarchs of the people, and holds them responsible for the acts of the ward in which they reside... Public meetings may be convened in the ward at any time, and notice is usually given by sounding a gong through the streets, or by written placards posted in public places. At these meetings all the people may be present and participate in the proceedings.

Maclay, 1861

Democratic Empire All the world knows that China presents to-day, as it did thousands of years ago, the only perfect specimen of a theocratic government that is now extant. The emperor is the high priest of his people. He worships Heaven, and he declares its will. His is the "Celestial Empire." He is a despot, but a patriarchal, or parental, despot. The people are his children, and the family relation is the basis of his authority. As the children owe absolute obedience to their fathers, so the people owe the same obedience to the emperor. Despotic as the emperor's rule theoretically may be, practically he governs little. He is encompassed by forms and ceremonies. Every act he does is recorded. He is the slave of precedent. Once, when a censor proposed to record an act which the emperor contemplated doing, the emperor ordered him not to record it, but the censor said that he must then record the imperial prohibition to make the record, whereupon the emperor abandoned his purpose to do the act.

Denby, 1906

第五章　教育与官府 Education and Government

可以说,对于胸怀大志、追求上进的臣民,官府想设置障碍也是缺乏手段。学习稍有悟性的小孩会得到细心的呵护。一旦被认为是天才,则宠爱有加。在中国,免费学堂数量极多,而且对于教育这样的善举,乐于资助的人比比皆是。许多政府官员从田间地头脱颖而出,他们上学堂的费用、进京赶考的盘缠都是乡亲们资助的。

——吉尔斯,1902年,第78～79页

MacGowan, 1907
A Scholar in Official Dress

古代中国的民主　厦门一位传教士一直"试图弄清中国当权执政者的本质",结果发现,中国人并非顽固不化地保守,而是拥有自己特色的民主。皇帝和官吏不是没人制约的独裁者。对于切合实际的公众舆论,他们心存敬畏……

——《中国教务杂志》,第20卷,第371～373页,1889年8月

中国的基层民主　……中国人身上存在着相当强烈的民主意识。这在他们参与市政管理时得到了表达和表现的机会。在中国,每个行政区都有自己的长老、议政厅和公告栏、告示牌。人们可以在公告栏上大胆地表达公众的意见。不得人心的官吏和官府的违法行为会被批评,有时候甚至是毫无道理、冷嘲热讽的指责。

行政区的长老由区内的民众根据长辈或民众的意见选举产生。他们的威信很高,一般能对提交给他们的案件进行最终的裁决……官府把他们当作族长,让他们负责区内的各种活动……行政区内随时可以召集民众开会,布告通常是通过敲锣在街上发布,或写在公众场所的布告栏内。上述聚会,所有民众都可以参加并参与各项议程。

——麦考利,1861年,第68～69页

民主的帝国　全世界都知道,就像它几千年前的传统那样,中国代表着现存最完美的神权政治的唯一样本。皇帝是人民的领袖。他敬仰上天,替天行道。他的国家叫"天朝",他是天朝的君主,是族长,或家长式的专制君主。人民是他的子民,家庭关系是他权威的基础。孩子完全服从父母,子民完全遵从于天子。从理论上来讲,天子的统治是专制式的,实际上他控制的东西很少。他被各种礼仪和规矩所限制。他的一举一动都会被记录下来。他是惯例的奴隶。有一次,史官想记录皇上正在谋划的一件事情,皇上命他不得记下。但史官称,他必须记录天国的禁忌,保存历史。最后,皇上放弃了他的计划。

——丹比,1906年,第2～3页

Evidences of Democracy The democracy of China is evident from the fact that the people can appeal from the lower to the higher officials, from the higher officials to Peking. The people have exerted their power to put a stop to obnoxious industries; extensive trades have been extinguished, and Imperial examinations discontinued at their demand. Representatives of the people may rise to high offices.

Local reforms are suggested and extensively carried out. There is real popular representation in China on a small scale and locally. The elders in Kwangtung and heads of clans in Fuh-kien, &c., are representatives of the people so far as liability and responsibility to the higher powers are concerned. Even the Emperor is only the 'father of his people.' He cannot go against the established code nor arbitrarily add to or take from it.

Chinese Recorder, Vol. 20, August, 1889

Law in Amoy

Ancient Chinese Law "The laws of China, " says Dr. Williams, "form an edifice, the foundations of which were laid by Li Kwei twenty centuries ago. Successive dynasties have been building thereon, adding, altering, pulling down, and building up, as circumstances seemed to require. ...The Chinese entertain a profound respect for the laws contained in their national code. " Sir George Staunton remarks that "all the Chinese seem to desire is the just and impartial execution of these laws, independent of caprice and uninfluenced by corruption…"

MacCauley, 1861

Prisoner, Gulangyu Mixed Court
MacGowan, 1897

The Cangue A very common punishment for theft or house-breaking is the wearing of the cangue, or wooden collar... ...Though the cangue appears at first sight to be a very simple mode of punishment, a very considerable amount of torture can be caused by it. As the board is broad, the man can only just manage to bend his forearm over it. He cannot reach his face with his hands. This is particularly uncomfortable at mealtimes, for it is only by manoeuvres worthy of a juggler or an acrobat, and by tilting up his board, that he can manage to get rice into his mouth. During the hot weather, when flies of all description abound, from the small, wiry kind that have such a fell purpose that nothing will divert them from it, to the huge, bloated, drum-beating kind, the cangue-bearer has no easy time of it. His face is absolutely without defence. If a fly settles on his nose, he has no resource but to call some benevolent person near by to wave it off, for a Chinese bluebottle knows when it is comfortable, and will not be frightened by a mere shake of the head.

MacGowan, 1912

第五章 教育与官府 Education and Government

民主的证据 中国民主的证据体现在，人民可向各级官员申诉，从基层官员到地方高官，从地方高官到京官。人民行使权力，要求制止某些不良行业发展、大规模贸易行为以及停止殿试。民意代表可以升迁高位。

各种改革在地方发起并广泛开展。真正的民意在中国基层小规模发展。就其对更高一层权力的责任和义务而言，广东省的长老和福建省的族长等等就是这种基层民意的代表。皇上也只是臣民的父王。他不能违背、也不能随意增减既定的礼教习俗。

——《中国教务杂志》，第20卷，第371～373页，1889年8月

厦门的法律

古代中国的法律 威廉斯博士说，"中国的法律大厦规模宏大，它的基石是由2000多年前的李斯奠定的。历代王朝根据实际情况在他的基础上删删改改，甚至推倒、重盖……中国人对隐藏在礼教习俗里的法律心存敬畏。"乔治·斯汤顿勋爵评论说，"所有中国人希望的似乎是公正无私地执行这些法律，不为变化所动，不受腐败影响……"

——麦考利，1861年，第74～75页

首枷 对付小偷或入室盗贼最常见的惩罚就是戴首枷，或枷锁……乍一看首枷似乎是一种非常简单的惩罚办法，戴上它实际上是相当大的折磨。首枷的木板很宽，受罚者的前臂只能触及木板的边缘，双手摸不着脸。吃饭的时候特别不舒服，因为受罚者要使出杂耍或杂技演员那样的动作，倾斜枷锁，才能把饭菜送进自己的嘴巴。

Native Court of Justice
MacGowan, 1897

天热的时候，蚊蝇丛生，瘦小、结实的蚊蝇叮咬目标明确、难以驱赶，硕大、肥胖的蚊蝇声若擂鼓，戴上枷锁，日子实在不太好过。受罚者的脸部无法设防。蚊蝇落在鼻尖，他毫无办法，只能求救于旁边的好人帮助驱赶。要知道，中国的青蝇可是懂得什么叫舒服，单靠摇头是赶不走的。

——麦嘉湖，1912年，第155页

老外看老鼓浪屿 *Old Gulangyu in Foreigners' Eyes*

J. Nienhuis

Gulangyu, October 10, 1921

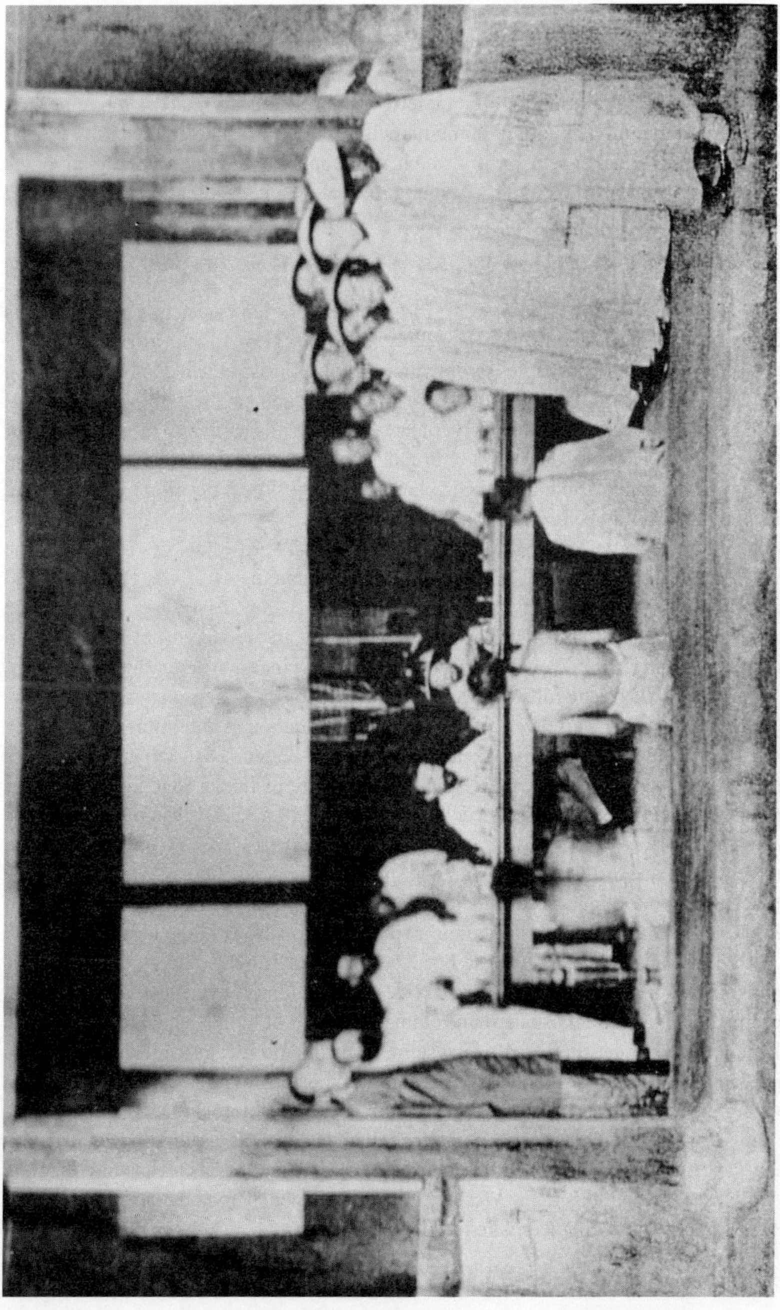

第五章　教育与官府 *Education and Government*

Gulangyu Mixed Court

MacGowan, 1897

True Story: The Mandarin's Gold Watch A mandarin, when trying a man charged with stealing some valuable things which an Englishman had left lying about, sharply rebuked the loser for his careless habits, which tempted servants to become dishonest, and added, "I sit myself sitting here in anxiety, because I left my gold watch under my pillow when I came out." On going home his wife asked him as he entered why he had sent for his watch. "I never sent for my watch, and hope you did not give it to anyone." "How could I refuse?" said the wife. "A young man came and said that you had sent him for it, and he told me that I would find it under your pillow."

Johnston, 1898

Why Chinese are not Litigious "To an American newcomer in China the laws respecting debt seem at first to be a labyrinth without a clew. Even a lawyer finds it difficult to determine the principles upon which Chinese jurisprudence is based. When, however, the student applies the touchstone of history and public policy, a system is disclosed which, thought it is at utter variance with any that prevails in countries that follow the common law or that employ a code, possesses great wisdom and practical merit. Time and space forbid a detailed account of the juridical development of China, but a brief synopsis may be of benefit to the reader.

In the first place, all Chinese law is customary law… The law books (so called) of the country are hardly commentaries. They profess to be statements of what is considered right and proper by the community at large.

In the second place, the Chinese regard litigation as an evil and try to reduce it to a minimum. There are no lawyers, no costs, fees, or allowances. There are no calendars, rules of practice, judgment rolls, nor any of the machinery which makes the attorney so prominent a feature of civilized life. A magistrate hears and determines a case very much as a father does a dispute between to children, or, better still, as an arbitrator does a difficulty between two friendly merchants. In the main, justice is done in the premises and, it must be added, is done more speedily, cheaply, and thoroughly than by the tribunals of our own race.

In the third place, litigation being an evil, public policy has increased to a very large extent the number of obligations which have no legal or binding nature except the honor of the debtor. Many of these "debts of honor" will seem monstrous to the legal mind……

…Professional services at Chinese law have in the main no legal value. In practice a physician keeps a memorandum of his services, but seldom, if ever, sends a bill. When his work is done, the patient usually hands him an amount of money equal to what would have been charged under the American system. For this no receipt is given. The same principle applies to scribes, mediums, priests, and other professionals. As a heck upon non-paying customers shrewd professional men insist upon a note, I O U, or bond before doing any work. The document, no matter what its form, is as binding as ordinary business paper. It may be well to add at this point that a creditor has means of collecting debts which seem ridiculous to the Western mind. He depends upon the profound love of peace and tranquility so characteristic of the Chinese race.

第五章 教育与官府 Education and Government

官员的金表：一个真实故事 一名官员在审讯小偷。这个小偷偷走了一个英国人放在身边的贵重物品。这位官员同时责怪失窃者粗心大意，诱使仆人偷窃。他说，"我自己坐在这里，很着急，因为早上出门的时候，我把金表忘在枕头下了。"官员回到家里，刚进家门，太太就问他为何差人取表。"我没让人回家拿呀，你没把它交给别人吧？""我怎么能不交呢？"太太回答说，"来了一个年轻人，说是你派他来拿表的。他还说，你的表就在枕头下。"
——约翰斯通，1898年，第40～41页

Dukes, 1885
A Chinese Officer

中国人为什么不喜欢打官司 对于刚到中国的美国人来说，有关债务的法律看上去像是一个没有头绪的迷宫。就连律师也难以判断中国法律的基本准则。不过，当学生采用历史和政策的标准，一个充满智慧和务实品质的体系便呼之欲出。它与许多国家盛行的普通法或判例法完全不同。由于时间和字数的限制，这里无法详细描述中国法律体系的演变。不过，简单的概述相信对读者是有裨益的。

第一，所有的中国法律都是习俗法……这个国家（所谓）的法典几乎不作任何注释。他们承认主流民众的意见。

第二，中国人认为诉讼是邪恶的，力图将案件数量降到最低限度。在中国，没有律师，也没有诉讼费、服务费或津贴。没有开庭日程、惯例规则、卷宗或其他让律师成为公民生活显著特征的机制。官吏听取案情，裁决案件，就像一名父亲解决孩子之间的争议。或者，顶多就像一名仲裁人调解两名和气商人之间的纷争。基本上，公正的裁决就在官邸内作出。必须解释的是，他们的裁决比我们的法庭速度快、成本低、干脆利落。

第三，因为诉讼是邪恶的，官府制定的公共政策已经在很大程度上增加了诉讼双方的义务。除了债主的人情，这些义务没有任何法律或制约的作用。多数情况下，这些"人情债"对有法律意识的人来说简直是极端荒谬的……

……对中国法律提供专业服务基本上没有任何法定价值。事实上，在中国，大夫会保存处方，但很少（如果有的话）给账单。看完病，病人通常像美国的做法那样用现金支付大夫开出的医药费用，没有收据。这种做法也适用于文书、中间商、道士和其他专业人员。碰上没有现金支付的顾客，精明的专业人员在提供服务之前会坚持让他写欠条。无论怎么写，欠条都跟普通商业文书一样有约束力。在这里，需要进一步说明的是，债主催债的方式在西方人看来简直荒唐可笑。他依靠的是对和谐与安宁的深爱。这是中国人典型的做法。

When a patron or client shows a disinclination toward payment, he visits the latter's house, sits upon the threshold, and weeps and harangues until his bill is paid. It seldom requires more than an hour of lamentation to collect any reasonable claim.

In cases of insolvency legal debts and those of honor are almost invariably paid by the debtor if he retrieves his position. In very many cases the obligations of bankrupt have been assumed by his children and even grandchildren. This is a legal duty when the debt is legal in character. When it is a debt of honor, its payment by a second generation is considered an act of high filial piety.

A custom, probably peculiar to China, is that of mutual forgetfulness. Business men who have advanced moneys or sold goods on credit and find it impossible to collect their capital or to obtain payment in full of the amount due them, but who are on friendly terms with their debtors, will, after several years, call upon the latter and agree to "forget everything to date." This is equivalent to a mutual release under seal and is highly favored by the great magistrates and priests of China. In conclusion, it may be stated that commercial litigation and insolvency are much rarer in China than in Europe or the United States. The number of tribunals, magistrates, and court officers is scarcely one-third, and the amount involved not a tenth, of what is at stake in the courts of Christendom.

Beyond the fear of going to law is the greater fear and disgrace of being a delinquent debtor. A Chinaman who becomes financially embarrassed will sell himself for a plantation coolie, go into exile for twenty years, or even commit suicide. It is part of his religion to pay off all he owes in the last week of the year, in order that he may begin the next one free from care and obligation…

…The matter may be summed up in the remark that the expression "a debt of honor" in China is "a debt of duty," and that one of their great maxims is "the highest good is the performance of every duty, even the humblest."

Edward Bedloe, U.S. Consul at Amoy, 1893

The Judge and the Goddess—a True Tale The Chinese judge, having nothing to control his decisions excepting his own free will, frequently settles cases after a very free and easy method. He sometimes shows great common-sense and ingenuity in the ruses adopted to elicit the truth in some disputed case. An amusing instance occurred some time ago, when the mandarin showed himself to be a man of humour and one well acquainted with the ins and outs of the Chinese mind.

A Chinese went abroad and stayed away for fifteen years, where he accumulated quite a comfortable little sum, with which he determined to return home and spend the rest of his days in comfort. Night had fallen when he reached the entrance of the village where his home was. During all the years he had been away no letter had passed between him and his wife, and no tidings had ever reached him about her or his home. Was she alive? And, if so, would she receive him kindly after the neglect of years? His mind was so agitated about the reception he was likely to receive that he took the bar of gold into which he had converted his savings, and hid it in the ashes of the incense dish in front of the village idol in the public temple, and then with beating heart he made his way to his home. He found his wife alive, and to his delight she received him without any reproaches. She was too happy to have him back again to dream of scolding him.

第五章 教育与官府 Education and Government

当客户不愿意付钱时,债主就会找到客户的家,坐在门槛上,又哭又闹,直到钱款到手。恸哭无须超过一个钟头,欠款就能收回。

即便丧失还债能力,债务和信用最终还得由借方在他具备偿债条件时偿还。通常情况下,还债的责任还可以由借方的儿子、甚至孙子来承担。如果债务本质上是合法的,则还债也属于法定责任。当债务信用由债务人的第二代偿还,则其行为会被视为一种高尚的孝道。

在中国,还有一种非常特别的做法,即双方放弃债权、债务。生意人事先垫款或赊账售货,后来发现资金无法回收或款

MacGowan, 1912

项到期无法全额收回,但与债务人关系友好,通常在若干年后会拜访债务人,申明"债权即日起一笔勾销"。这种做法相当于一种盖了章的债权、债务互相免除,中国官吏对此极为赞赏。总之,应该指出,在中国,商业诉讼及破产案件的数量比欧洲或美国少得多。法庭、官吏和司法人员的数量很少超过西方国家法院的三分之一,案件数量不足十分之一。

比起怕上法庭,欠债不还让债务人更为恐慌、更丢面子。一旦陷入金融困境,中国人可能会卖身做苦力、离家出走 20 年、甚至自杀。每年最后一星期还清当年债务,这已经成为中国人习惯的一部分。这样一来,第二年他就可以无忧无虑地开始新生活……

……总而言之,在中国,"债务信用"就是"债务责任"。他们信奉的伟大箴言之一是"最高尚的美德就是承担所有的责任,哪怕是最微不足道的。"

——爱德华·壁洛,美国驻厦领事,1893 年,第 500~503 页

判官与女神:一个真实故事 除了自己的自由意志,中国的判官没有别的东西可以控制自己的裁决。他经常用一种非常随意、简单的方法裁决案件。有时候,他在审判某些有争议的案件时,为了辨明事实,采取了各种各样的策略,以显示他非凡的常识和智谋。不久前曾发生过一起有趣的案例,证明这位审判官富有幽默感,且对中国人的详细情况非常熟悉。

有一个中国人离家出国,在海外生活了 15 年,并积累了一笔可过舒适生活的财富。带着这些财富,他决定回国舒适地度过余生。回到村口的时候,夜幕已经降临。在他离开的这些年里,他与妻子之间从未通过信,也没有有关妻子和家人的音信。她还活着吗?如果还活着,离别多年,她还会友善地对待他吗?一想到见面后妻子可能对自己采取的态度,男人焦虑不安。他把自己用全部储蓄换成的金条藏在了本村庙里供奉菩萨的香炉里,然后忐忑不安地进了家门。结果,他发现,妻子依然健在。让他高兴的是,妻子对自己没有任何责备。她对丈夫回家感到高兴,没想到要责备他。

As they sat talking he told her how much money he had made and how it was then in the incense dish in front of the Goddess of Mercy in the village temple. He tried to tell her this in a low voice, but he did not succeed. A Chinese does not seem to know how to whisper. He can shout and bawl and howl, but the art of speaking quietly into another's ear is a lost one in China. The expression "in a pig's whisper" would be utterly misunderstood in this land.

At a crack in the wall that separated his house from his neighbour's was an ear that drank in every word that was uttered by husband and wife. It seemed glued to it. It was fascinated, indeed, by the strange stories that poured into it, and when the tale of the gold bar was related it thrilled with joy, for it seemed as though some fairy had come to reveal a hidden fortune. Next morning, before the dawn of the day, the husband wound his way silently to the temple for his gold bar, but to his horror he found it was gone. He at once accused his neighbor of the theft, but the latter declared that he had not even heard of his return, and, therefore, he could not possibly have known anything about his gold.

Finding it useless to discuss the matter, he hurried to the nearest mandarin and laid his complaint before him. This official happened to be a man of humour as well as a very sagacious one. He summoned the accused before him and ordered him to restore the gold. This the man declared he could not do for the simple reason that he had never taken it. The mandarin, who was convinced of his guilt, now determined to adopt a ruse which he believed would be successful.

He ordered his policeman to go to the village temple and bring the idol in whose incense dish the gold had been concealed into his presence. When it arrived he asked the goddess who had stolen the gold. Profound silence was the only reply. "Don't you consider it your duty to tell me who the thief is, seeing that the money was practically entrusted to you care?" asked the mandarin. Still no reply. Upon this the judge became indignant and accused the idol of want of respect to him, and also of neglect in allowing a theft to take place in a temple that was her residence. The mandarin now adjourned the case for a day and in an angry tone threatened the goddess that if she did not confess then he would have her publicly beaten with rods by his policemen.

That same evening the mandarin summoned the accused into his private room, and with a look of mystery on his face and in a voice trembling with emotion he said: "The goddess has confessed that it was you who stole the gold. She is furious with you, for you have made her 'lose face' to-day when I threatened before my whole court to have her beaten, and she vows vengeance against you and your whole family. She says she will make your fields barren and send sickness into your home. Yours sons will die, and when you leave the world there will be no one to worship at your tomb, and you will wander a hungry and wretched spirit in the land of the shades. The only way in which you can avert the wrath of the goddess is by an instant confession. If you do this, I will use all my influence to get her to forgive you."

The man was so terrified at the prospect of such awful calamities awaiting him that, trembling and full of awe, he made a clean breast of it and restored the bar of gold to the rightful owner; and, though he was punished by the mandarin for his wrong, he considered he had got off lightly, since he had not to suffer the vengeance of the goddess..

MacGowan, 1912

第五章 教育与官府 Education and Government

坐下来拉家常,他告诉妻子自己赚了多少钱。钱这会儿就放在庙内菩萨的香炉里。告诉妻子的时候,丈夫试图尽量压低嗓门,但没能成功。中国人似乎不懂得怎样低声耳语。中国人懂得大喊大叫,但低声耳语的艺术在中国似乎已经失传。"低声耳语"的说法在这片土地上已经完全被误解了。

恰好,这户人家与隔壁邻居的墙上有一裂缝。夫妻之间的讲话全部被邻居给听走了。邻居的耳朵紧贴着墙壁。听到丈夫对妻子所讲述的奇妙故事,隔壁邻居实在着迷。听说丈夫把金条放在香炉里,隔壁邻居欣喜若狂,简直就像仙女下凡来向他透露财富的秘密。第二天早上,天还没亮,丈夫静静地走向寺庙,准备取回金条。结果,他大吃一惊:金条没了!他立即指控隔壁邻居偷窃。邻居却说自己连他回来的消息都没听说,因此不可能知道金条的事情。

Guanyin--Goddess of Mercy

发现隔壁邻居无法沟通,失主赶紧向离家最近的官府报案。受理的官吏恰好是一位幽默、睿智的判官。他立即传唤被告,要求他归还金条。被告称,他没拿金条,无法归还。判官认为被告肯定有罪,决定采取一个策略。他确信这个方法一定会成功。

判官命令捕快到村里去,把香炉所供奉的那尊菩萨带来过庭。菩萨到庭后,判官问她是谁偷走了金子。菩萨默不作声。判官再问,"金条放在你那边,请你照看,你不认为自己有责任告诉我谁是盗贼?"菩萨依然无语。看到这种情景,判官生气了。他指控菩萨藐视判官,并因疏忽致使盗窃案在她的住所发生。判官宣布休庭一天,并生气地威胁菩萨说,如果不老实交代,他将让捕快公开用大板惩罚她。

当晚,判官在私室里召见了被告。面带神秘,声音发抖,判官告诉被告说,"菩萨已经承认是你偷走了金条。她很生气,你今天让她'丢脸',因为我当众威胁让人打她。菩萨发誓要报复你和你的家人。她说,她将让你的田地荒芜,并给你的家室送去病灾。你的儿子即将死去。你离开人世的时候,会没人给你上坟。你将像一个可怜的恶鬼在阴间里四处游荡。要想平息菩萨的愤怒,唯一的办法就是马上认罪。如果你认罪,我将动用我的所有力量,请菩萨宽恕你。"

听说自己面临如此可怕的灾难,被告全身发抖,惊惧万分。他彻底坦白,并把金条还给了失主。最后,被告受到了判官的惩罚。但一想起不用遭受菩萨的报复,被告总觉得自己已经轻松脱身。

——麦嘉湖,1912年,第104页

Chapter 6   Amoy Cuisine

"If there is anything we are serious about, it is neither religion nor learning, but food…The French eat enthusiastically, while the English eat apologetically. The Chinese national genius decidedly leans toward the French in the matter of feeding ourselves."

Lin Yutang

Polite Hypocrisy (Keqi)   Here we were received by an official—the governor's secretary, no less! Shaking his clasped hands at us in an alarming way and chin-chining vigorously. After thus relieving his feelings, he shook hands and ushered us into the presence of his Excellency the Tao-tai, a pleasant looking elderly person who received us in the same way. In the room was a table laid out with a quantity of good things in the shape of sponge cakes, jam tarts and fruit, at which we were invited to seat ourselves, while our hats were seized and placed tenderly on stools by our side. After a short introductory gossip, the secretary commenced operations on the cake, while the Tao-tai cut up the jam tarts, and then they piled up our plates, apologizing at the same time for the humble fare—a bit of polite hypocrisy.

Shore, 1881

Chopstick Diet   They do not use knives and forks. Their food is principally rice and "chowchow" or hash, and they use two small sticks like lead pencils. These are held between the fingers, so as to bring the two ends together or separate to suit the article they are eating; and although a fast-eating Yankee would starve if compelled to eat with chopsticks, yet I do not see but the Chinese are as fat and as hearty as any people.

Coffin, 1908

Birds' Nests   I did not really like birds' nests either, and always wanted to tell my Chinese friends that, cooked in chicken broth as they invariably were, vermicelli tasted much the same and cost considerably less, but since I only ate them in their homes, courtesy kept me silent. Certainly, they were prized for their properties, and were eaten hopefully by some as an aphrodisiac. Boiled with sugar they were considered a sovereign remedy for a sore throat, and often sent as such to my bedside.

When I saw the caves whence the bulk of nests came, I wondered how anyone had ever thought of trying them as an article of food…In thick swampy jungles, many miles from the Borneo coast, concealed behind small fissures and holes in sudden limestone rocks and cliffs, reached by climbing up wooden ladders, by crawling down subterranean passages and water-courses, the great vaulting caves must have been hard to find, forbidding to explore…Would a lost man, starving in a cave, have thought of eating the nest, rather than the bird? And if he had, how would he have reached it? But there it is: Chinese for generations have paid fantastically high prices for them, though exactly when the acquired the taste, I do not know.

Mackenzie-Grieves, 1959

第六章　厦门饮食

"人世间倘有任何事情值得吾人的慎重将事者,那不是宗教,也不是学问,而是'吃'……法国人的吃是热烈地吃,而英国人的吃是歉疚地吃,中国人就其自谋口福而论,是天禀的倾向于法国人的态度的。"

——林语堂

客气　接待我们的官员是巡抚的秘书(布政使),至少是这级官员!他一边紧握双拳,不停作揖,阵势吓人,一边热情地跟我们说,"请!请!"。一番情感宣泄过后,他跟我们握手并向我们引见了道台大人,一位相貌堂堂的长者——他也以同样的热情接待,并邀请我们在屋内的小桌旁就座。桌上摆满了好多东西,有松糕、果酱馅饼和水果。我们脱下帽子,小心地放在旁边的凳子上。稍作寒暄之后,布政使开始分松糕,道台大人切馅饼。他们一边为我们装盘子,一边为食物的简单道歉——有点客气。

——肖尔,1881年,第47页

用筷子吃饭　中国人用两根像铅笔一样的细长木棍吃饭,不用刀叉。他们的食物主要是米饭、酱菜和蔬菜。他们用手指拿筷子,筷子两端根据他们所吃食物的大小分合自如。真用筷子的话,吃饭速度极快的美国人肯定得挨饿。当然,这种情况我没看到。但中国人的确跟其他国家的人民一样壮硕、开心。

——柯芬,1908年,第168页

燕窝　"他们总是用鸡汤炖燕窝,吃起来像意大利细面条,但价格贵多了。其实很想告诉我的中国朋友,我并不喜欢。不过,我只是在他们的家里吃燕窝,出于礼貌,我没说出来。当然,物有所值,有些人把燕窝当作补品、壮阳药来吃。加糖煮,燕窝是治疗喉咙痛的特效药,他们经常把它送到我的床前。

当我看到产出大量燕窝的洞穴,我一直在想,他们怎么会想到把燕窝当作食品吃……在潮湿的密林里,距婆罗洲海岸数英里,燕窝隐藏在石灰石悬崖峭壁的裂缝里、洞穴中。需要借助木梯向上爬行,然后穿过隐秘的地道和地下河,燕窝栖息的拱形圆顶洞穴肯定很难寻觅,令人望而却步……采集燕窝的人,如果在洞穴中迷路、挨饿,他想到的是吃燕窝,还是燕子?如果想到的是燕窝,他怎样才能吃得到?但事实是,尽管我不知道中国人什么时候开始爱上这种味道,他们确实世世代代在高价购买燕窝。

——麦肯兹·格丽芙,1959年,第52页

老外看老鼓浪屿 *Old Gulangyu in Foreigners' Eyes*

Chinese Food Names To the Westerner it would be preposterous to name a dish after a poet, or a stew after a playwright…But the Chinese openly name certain cuts of meat after great names in history and their various soups after great artists. They go further than this. They write poems about a certain vegetable soup and relate the details of entire menus at the crucial point of a story, for they believe that the good soup honors a man's name and that the menu, too, is crucial in the development of the story.

Spencer, 1943

Amoy Tea & Drinks

Amoy—Home of Tea The first Chinese tea imported directly into England was bought in Amoy in 1689. At that time it seemed as if Amoy would become the chief port for the European trade... But the rarest of the local teas the Chinese connoisseurs kept for themselves, making it in doll-sized red earthenware teapots, ceremoniously sipping it from minute bowls, savouring its curious after-tang on the tongue.

Mackenzie, 1959

English Tea in Amoy (1940s) The more pretentious the household, the less likely was it that Chinese tea would be served to foreigners on social visits…To me this seemed almost a betrayal of historical glory, for Amoy previously held a high reputation for its tea, and although exports to foreign markets were now negligible, it was still being produced to suit all tastes of the local market, from the raw green variety, favoured by labourers, to the highly scented flavoured with petals of jasmine, rose, chrysanthemum and other flowers. The early tea clipper races had begun from Amoy and the word for tea itself in the local vernacular was 'te'.

Sorting Tea   Stoddard, 1897

Neill, 1956

Ganbei! Sherry was presently brought round and glasses clinked as a sign of friendship; but we had reason to suspect his Excellency was inclined to press his hospitality on us rather too profusely, for the glasses were replenished again and again and no denial taken, so we expostulated mildly; whereupon the bland secretary smilingly inverted his wine glass and pointing to ours as still untouched insisted on us polishing off the contents and no heeltaps; but finding us stand out against his artful machinations, and further that we had reached the limit of our capacity for sponge cake and marmalade pastry, he ordered a beverage which you must be careful not to confound with the black decoction we drink in England; but a pale delicate fluid, without milk or sugar, and which a British housekeeper would indignantly reject as "slops." …

Shore, 1881

第六章 厦门饮食 Amoy Cuisine

中国食物的名称 对西方人来说,以诗名菜,或以戏名汤是十分荒唐的事情……但中国人公然用历史伟人的名字来命名某些肉食,并用一些伟大艺术家的名字来称呼某些羹汤。不仅如此,他们还专门为某一菜汤作诗,并在一个故事的关键章节描述整桌饭菜的全部细节。他们相信,好汤是对名人的一种敬意。饭菜对故事情节的发展至关重要。

——斯宾塞,1943年,第204~206页

厦门茶叶和饮料

厦门——茶叶的故乡 第一批直接进口到英国的茶叶是1689年在厦门采购的。当时,厦门似乎已经成为欧洲贸易的主要港口……不过,最珍贵的本地茶叶中国品茗家自己留着。他们把这些好茶放进红色小瓷壶里冲泡,煞有介事地用小杯啜饮,然后用舌头品尝。

——麦肯兹·格丽芙,1959年,第21、22页

英国茶叶在厦门(20世纪40年代) 越爱炫耀的家庭,他们用中国茶招待到访番仔的可能性就越低……在我看来,这似乎是对厦门光荣历史的一种背叛,因为厦门历史上曾经以本地茶叶为荣。尽管现在厦门茶叶出口国外的数量已经少得微不足道,但从劳工喜欢的粗糙绿茶,到加入茉莉花、玫瑰花、菊花和其他干花、香气浓烈的花茶,本地茶农依然在制作各种口味的茶叶,以满足本地市场的需求。早期欧洲运茶快船之间的比赛就是从厦门开始,tea(茶)这个单词本身源自于当地方言"te"(闽南话)。

——尼尔,1956年,第74~75页

Amoy Dinner (about 1910)

干杯! 一圈下来,雪利酒很快又倒满了。碰杯是友谊的一种象征。不过,我们有理由相信,主人非常殷勤地想对我们表示自己的好客,因为酒加了一轮又一轮,无法拒绝。我们想婉转地谢绝,这时,和蔼可亲的幕僚笑眯眯地喝完酒,酒杯倒拿,同时指着我们原封不动的酒杯,要我们喝光杯中酒,一滴不留。发现我们继续抵抗他的阴谋诡计,更重要的是在吃过松糕、果酱面包之后,我们肚子的容量已经装不下了,他叫人送来一种饮料。你千万不要把这种饮料跟我们在英国喝的那种黑汤混淆起来。这是一种灰白色的鲜美饮料,不加牛奶或白糖。在英国,管家会愤怒地称之为"脏水"……

——肖尔,1881年,第47页

Chapter 7
Amoy Amusements, Festivals, Theater, Sports

No Sabbath Now, many of the sources of amusement that are open to the people of the West have no existence in this country whatever. They have no Sunday on which they can lay aside the eternal round of work, and forget for one day that life is a treadmill which never stops its grinding. There are no stated holidays, when people rush off to the seaside or to the moors or to some fishing stream, where midst the hills they can forget the heat and pressure of the city... The school-boys, indeed, after eleven months of cramped school life have been thought worthy of a month's holidays at the end of the year, but the grown-up people have to work. Without that, large sections of the community under present conditions would starve.

MacGowan, 1907

Dukes, 1885
In a Gentleman's House

Kites, Puppets, Tops and Shuttlecocks There are tops and kites... There is also the popular game of shuttlecock, played not, however, with battledores, but with the sides of the soles of the shoes, and done so expertly that the shuttlecock will be kept flying in the air for several minutes at a time. There [are also [... puppet shows that have a fascination about them because of the ingenious and marvelous way with which the operator causes the figures to imitate the motions of actual life, simply by a deft movement of the strings attached to their limbs.

MacGowan, 1907

Dancing Dolls   Dukes, 1885

第七章
厦门的娱乐、节日、戏院和体育运动

没有星期天 对西方人来说是乐趣之源的许多东西在这个国家根本就不存在。他们没有星期天可以用来搁置没完没了的工作,或借以忘记生活是永无止境的折磨。没有定期的假日让百姓到海边或郊野休闲,或去小溪垂钓,或在群山之中,他们可以忘却城市的热浪与压力……实际上,读书郎在狭小的学堂里苦读11个月之后年底还有一个月的假期,成年人却不得不终日劳作。要不是这样,按现有的条件,这个社会很多人就得挨饿。
——麦嘉湖,1907年

风筝、木偶、陀螺和毽子 有陀螺和风筝……还有这里流行的毽子,不是用球拍打,而是用鞋帮踢。会玩的高手一次可以踢上几分钟。还有……木偶戏,挺有趣的,玩家熟练地抽动细线,木偶就会惟妙惟肖地模仿人的动作,心灵手巧,实在令人称奇。
——麦嘉湖,1907年,第146～149页

Puppet Show in the Countryside　　MacGowan, 1909

The Festival   Forgues, 1875

Kit Flying Kite-flying is a gentlemanly pastime among the Fuh-chauans [Fujianese]; and groups of men are frequently seen moving about among the graves, upon the hills, engaged in this amusement. Sometimes the kite is made to represent a flock of birds; and on one occasion we observed that they were so natural and bird-like in form and motion, that, had we not been assured to the contrary, we should have taken them for what they only appeared to be. The Chinese, in fact, are said to succeed so admirably in making and flying these bird-kites that an Englishman, on first arriving in the country, being out on a hunting excursion, fired into a flock of them before perceiving his mistake. We also saw a centipede-kite, said to be a hundred feet in length, which was flying, and in its motions was not unlike the frightfully disagreeable reptile it represented.

Williams, 1864

Amoy Festivals

Chinese New Year The most important ... is the New Year's holiday. The feasting and jollity really extend over three days...

On this day all business is suspended, and for once during the year China puts on a Sunday look, for the shops are all closed, with the exception of those that deal in shoes and stockings, which by a license that has come down from the distant past, are permitted to sell their wares, even though it is a New Year's day.

Every one is dressed in his very best, and the women put on their gayest and most attractive garments. The children, too, decked out in clothes that have been carefully folded and put away in boxes for this special occasion, appear early in the morning, with faces full of joy and eyes sparkling with delight, ready for all the fun and enjoyment that the day is going to bring them.

The male members of the household go and pay visits to their friends, whilst the ladies stay at home and entertain the neighbours or relatives that may be calling upon them. It seems to be the object of every one to be as nice and agreeable to each other as they can be. No unlucky words must be uttered, for they might bring sorrow and disaster during the coming year, and so one sees everywhere pleasant, smiling faces, whilst the air resounds with kindly greetings and with wishes for prosperity and happiness...

It is the custom on this festal day of the year to paste bright red papers on the lintel and on both side posts of the door, on which have been inscribed in large Chinese characters a wish for some form of happiness to be bestowed upon all that live within. "May the five happinesses descend upon the home." "May Heaven bestow peace and happiness, and may clouds of trade gather round the business carried on here." " May righteousness have its fullest accomplishment in this home." "May the days of Shun and the times of Yau (two ancient rulers of China, when it is believed that the country attained its greatest prosperity) be the experience of this home."

MacGowan, 1907

第七章　厦门的娱乐、节日、戏院和体育运动 Amoy Amusements, Festivals, Theater, Sports

放风筝　放风筝是福建人所喜爱的一种高雅的消遣方式。经常可以看到一群人在坟堆间、山坡上放风筝。有时候，他们做的风筝就像一群鸟。有一次，我们看到，风筝的造型像鸟一样，动作也像鸟。我们怎么也没想到它只是风筝，因为我们只从外形上看。据说，因中国人放的风筝实在太像小鸟，有一次，一位第一次到中国的英国人，外出打猎，毫不怀疑地就朝着这群风筝开枪。我们还见过一只蜈蚣风筝，据说长100英尺，在空中飞舞的时候，它的动作没有一处不像那种令人讨厌、害怕的爬虫。

——威廉斯，1864年，第286页

厦门的节日

农历新年　最重要的……是农历新年放假。美食与欢乐持续三天……

这一天，所有商业活动都暂停了。一年一度，中国终于有了周日的样子，因为所有的商店都关门歇业，只有鞋袜店铺例外。根据很早以前沿袭下来的特许，鞋袜店获准新年第一天照常营业。

Amoy Card Players (photo by Dr. John Otte)　Kaartspelers.

这一天，人人都穿上了自己最好的衣服。女性穿上了她们最鲜艳、最引人注目的服装。小孩的新衣服整齐叠好，放进箱子，就等新年的到来。他们一大早就起床，满脸欢喜，双眼发亮，期待着新年即将带给他们的欢乐和喜悦。

家中的男性成员一般会出门走亲访友，女性则待在家里招待可能到访的邻居或亲戚。每个人的目标似乎是为了尽可能让对方感到友好、愉快。不能说不吉利的话，因为这可能会给新年带来悲伤和灾难。因此，你在任何地方看到的都是和蔼可亲的笑脸，友好的问候和恭喜新年发财、快乐的声音在空气中回荡……

新年喜庆的日子里，在门槛和门框上贴鲜红的对联是一种习俗。对联用硕大的汉字写在红纸上，为住在门内的人丁、五畜祈求某种形式的幸福。

——麦嘉湖，1907年，第131、133、134页

Gravesweeping This has its serious side as well as its pleasant one, and many a heart pours out its sorrows in tears and heartrending cries over the loved ones that have vanished into the dark world, whilst others, again, gather round the graves to hold fellowship, in spirit at least, with those whom they believe are conscious of their presence, and who can in some way or other affect the fortunes of the living.

Once a year the whole population turns out to visit the family graves. The wear and tear of wind and rain during the twelve months have flattened them down and given them a neglected and disordered look. They need repairing and returfing, and so with loving hearts the relatives wend their way amongst the countless tombs that cover the hill-side to the ones that belong to them, and with their hoes they dig about and fix them up to bear the brunt of storms of rain and fierce typhoons for another year. ...

It is a very pretty and interesting sight to see the hillsides dotted with the countless figures that are moving about on them, making their offerings to the spirits, and doing up the graves that have become dilapidated during the year...

When they have done their work, and the new sods have been beaten well down on the top and sides of the grave to enable it to stand another year's wear and tear, the cakes are taken out of the basket, and laid out in front where the spirit can see them. Then a little bottle with whisky in it is brought forth, and three diminutive cups holding about a tablespoonful each are filled with it and placed beside the cakes. Finally a small piece of boiled pork that has lain snugly at the bottom of the basket is taken out and laid carefully amongst the other good things.

Everything is ready now for the offering to be presented to the old grandfather, and the family stand up, and with hands clasped bow before the grave as though the old gentleman were in the flesh standing in front of them, and could hear every word that is said to him...

After the worship has been concluded, the cakes and the pork are laid out in picnic fashion on the grass and the family gathers around them, and they laugh and chat, and the youngsters break out into boisterous mirth. Everything around them conduces to clear away the shadows from their hearts. The stifling air of the city has vanished, and the smells and the monotonous surroundings, and here the purest forces of nature combine to lift their thoughts out of the narrow ruts in which they have been running.

MacGowan, 1907

Dragon Boat Racing   MacGowan, 1907

第七章　厦门的娱乐、节日、戏院和体育运动 Amoy Amusements, Festivals, Theater, Sports

扫墓（清明节） 扫墓有其严肃的一面，也有其愉悦的一面。很多人将满腹的悲伤化作泪雨，用悲惨的哭声哀悼已经消失在黑暗世界里的亲人。另外一些人则再次聚集在坟墓前，与其他扫墓者延续交情，至少在精神上。他们认为，来扫墓会让人意识到自己的存在，并以某种方式影响生者的命运。

一年一度，中国人倾巢而出，祭扫祖坟。在过去的十二个月里，风雨的侵蚀使得坟堆变平，一副荒废、杂乱的模样，需要修整。就这样，亲人们带着爱心，绕过山坡无数的坟堆，找到属于自己家族的坟墓。他们用锄头除去坟墓四周的杂草，把坟墓修整起来，让它们能够承受未来一年风雨的冲击……

看到山坡上无数人的身影在坟堆间移动，给祖先上供品，修整过去一年被损毁的坟墓，的确很壮观、很有趣……

扫墓完毕，新长出来的杂草被整掉了，坟堆能够承受新一年的磨损。这时，扫墓者从篮子里取出糕点等祭品，摆在祖先灵魂能够看得到的地方。接下来取出的是一小瓶的酒和三个小酒杯，大约可装下一汤匙的酒，摆在供品旁。最后是放在篮底的小块熟肉，被小心翼翼地与其他供品摆在一起。

现在，敬献给老祖宗的供品一切准备就绪。参加扫墓的家人都站起来，在祖先坟前双手作揖，好像老先生就这样活生生地站在他们的面前，能够听到对他所说的每一句话……

祭扫完毕，糕点、猪肉等供品像野餐那样摆在草地上，一家人围在一起，有说有笑。年轻人突然欢笑起来，非常吵闹。周围的一切帮助他们消除了内心的阴影。令人窒息的气氛从这座城市消失了。这里的气息和单调的环境，以及这里大自然最纯正的力量一起把人们从狭窄的思维中解放出来。

——麦嘉湖，1907 年，第 138～140 页

Dragon Dance　　　　　　　　　　　　　　Anderson, 1920

老外看老鼓浪屿 Old Gulangyu in Foreigners' Eyes

Thomson, 1876

Hungry Ghosts There are several other festivals, such as the Feast of Lanterns, and the Seventh Moon Festival, when all over the Empire tables are set with abundance of food for the spirits of the dead world, who have no living friends in this. The most expensive plays, too, are performed for the enjoyment of the hungry, wandering ghosts, who have been let loose by the prince of that gloomy land for one month to try and get some recreation and comfort in this upper world.

Whilst the ravenous spirits are supposed to enjoy the food that has been so abundantly provided for them, and to look with delight upon the actors that are putting forth their best artistic talent in order to amuse them, it is the people who provide these entertainments that really enjoy this month of feasting. The food that has been provided for the troops of hungry spirits that hover invisibly in the air, is diminished neither in quality nor in quantity, and a merry time the town has in disposing of the good things which nominally they have provided for the guests from the lower regions, but which they have arranged should be eaten by friends and relatives who have been specially invited beforehand.

It is the same with the theatricals. The highest talent has been engaged, and the most amusing and comical plays have been selected from the actors' repertory, but whilst they profess to be moved by a desire to entertain the ghosts, it is their own amusement and pleasure they are thinking about all the time. "What would happen," I asked a broad-faced, jolly-looking Chinaman, "if the spirits were really to come and eat up the numerous dishes that you have laid out for their special benefit?"

"They would never have a chance of doing so again," he promptly replied, "for we should take every good care never to make any offerings to them again in the future."

MacGowan, 1907

Amoy Chinese Theater

Natural Born Actors The acting before us is first-rate, for the Chinese are natural, born actors... What specially strikes one about these actors is the coolness and ease with which they perform their parts, and the natural life-like way in which they act the characters they have taken. Two women for example are quarrelling and scolding each other. As women are not allowed to be actors, two men have assumed their dress. The looks, the gestures, the feminine toss of the head, the rising tones that grow shriller and shriller as their passions become excited, are exactly such as may be witnessed in the quarrels of women almost any day in the streets of Amoy. We forget, in the reality of the scene before us, that these persons are actors. They have impersonated an actual event in human life so realistically, that the stage seems to have vanished, and we are standing in one of the narrow streets of the city, with the crowd around us, watching two women so completely absorbed by their passions as to have become oblivious of the many eyes that are fastened upon them.

Mcgowan, 1889

第七章　厦门的娱乐、节日、戏院和体育运动　Amoy Amusements, Festivals, Theater, Sports

饿鬼（鬼节）　还有其他几个节日，如元宵节和七月半（鬼节）。到了鬼节，全中国的供桌上都为阴间没有亲朋好友的鬼魂摆满了丰盛的祭品。最昂贵的戏曲在戏台上演出，以娱乐孤魂野鬼，因为鬼节一到，阎王打开地狱之门，让他们回到人间，享受娱乐与安慰。

按理说这些饿鬼应该尽情地享用人间为他们准备的丰盛祭品，兴高采烈地观看演员倾尽演艺才能为他们演出的戏曲。但事实上，享受鬼节欢乐大餐的却是招待恶鬼的活人。

恶鬼成群结队，在空中隐形盘旋。人们为他们提供的食物，无论是数量还是品质都没有变化。这些好东西名义上是为来自阴间的客人准备的，实际上最终都被事先特别邀请的亲朋好友吃掉了。这是小镇的快乐时光。

MacGowan, 1912
Actors

戏曲也一样。请来最佳阵容，从他们的保留曲目中挑出最有趣、滑稽的戏曲。尽管他们表示，目的是为了娱乐鬼神，但实际上从头到尾享受欢笑和乐趣的还是活人。我问过一位宽脸、快乐的中国人，"如果鬼神真的来了，并吃掉你们为他们特别准备的祭品，结果会怎么样？"

他立马回答说，"他们会失去再这样做的机会，因为我们会很小心，将来不再给他们上供品。"

——麦嘉湖，1907年，第144、145页

厦门的中国戏院

天生的演员　我们眼前的表演是一流的，因为中国人是天生的演员……特别给人印象深刻的是这些演员表演时很冷静、放松，把他们自己所扮演的角色演得栩栩如生。例如，两个女旦吵架，互相指责。由于女性不能当演员，两个男演员穿上了她们的服装。那外表、神态，那种女性所特有的甩头，以及随着吵闹越来越激烈而越升越高的声音，跟平时在厦门街上可以看到的女人吵架没有什么两样。看着他们的表演，我们忘记了他们是演员。他们如此逼真地演绎现实生活中的真实故事，以至于在我们看来，舞台好像消失了。我们像是站在城市狭窄的街道里，周围挤满了人，看着两个女人完全投入到激情争吵之中，不理会身边有很多双眼睛正在盯着自己。

——麦嘉湖，1889年，第38、39页

City Temple God Play   The crowd was packed tight below the stage; sugar-cane sellers, hot dumpling and bean-cake sellers, vendors of brilliant raspberry-pink and lime-green cordials generously flecked with dead flies. The crowd was held like meat in brawn, by a thick, cloying smell of sweat, frying and cheap tobacco; glazed over by the brazen assault of the sun, of the cymbals, drums, clappers and clarionets. There had been no performance since the New Year Festival, and the troupe was playing The Monkey King (part of all repertoires) to an appreciative and certainly chiefly illiterate crowd, who, according to our Chinese companion, never missed a point. Each gesture, each movement, was symbolic, and tradition has trained the audience to interpret it. From dress, ornaments and paint, they recognize a character's profession, his goodness or badness. Even his walk and his sleep revealed his role to the onlookers. They had no need for scenery or properties; a switch was enough for a mounted man, gestures completely to furnish the stage. The audience had seen and heard it all before, they condemned the same villains, applauded the same feather-decorated patriots, laughed at the same buffoons, as generations of their ancestors had done.

But rigid as was the interpretation, it did not prevent the Monkey King himself that morning, when he saw us taking photographs, from shouting at us from the edge of the stage to take a phot ograph of him, and to pose there, with tossing beard and, we were told, broad comment, which sent the audience into paroxysms of laughter. He carried a fan, but the audience knew that he also had about him the peaches of Immortality which he had been stealing for centuries.

As we returned from the [Xiamen University] concert that evening, the players were still acting with undiminished gusto, the raucous band still lustily tearing the air with horrible discords. The children who had been sitting on the garden walls were still there, the seats for patrons on the stage were still occupied…

Mackenzie-Grieves, 1959

A Play on an Idol's Birthday   MacGowan, 1913

第七章　厦门的娱乐、节日、戏院和体育运动　Amoy Amusements, Festivals, Theater, Sports

城里的庙戏　台下挤满了人群,有卖甘蔗的、有卖热汤圆和绿豆糕的,还有小贩叫卖粉红草莓色和橙绿色的饮料,上面浮着几只死苍蝇。艳阳高照,锣鼓、长箫、拍板齐响,浓烈、令人倒胃的臭汗味和廉价的烤烟味,人群拥挤其中,就像一团腌煮的猪肉。自从春节以来,城里一直没演过戏,剧团正在为爱看戏的文盲表演《美猴王》(剧团的保留剧目之一)。按中国朋友的说法,这些戏迷从来不会错过任何一个细节。每一个姿态,每一个动作都有其象征意义。经常看戏,观众已经能够解释了。从服装、装饰和化妆,他们可以认出演员的身份,是好人,还是坏蛋。观众还可以从步态和睡姿判断演员的角色。他们无须布景,也不要道具。一转身就是骑马,各种姿势完全占据了舞台。这出戏观众已经看过或听说过,但是他们依然像他们的历代祖先那样谴责同样的坏蛋,嘲笑同样的丑角,为同样浓妆重彩的英雄喝彩。

尽管演出很古板,但那天上午,美猴王一看到我们在拍照,就跑到舞台的边缘,对我们大喊大叫,同时胡须一抛,摆出造型,满口粗话(有人告诉我们),让观众捧腹大笑。美猴王手持扇子,但观众知道他身上还有从天上偷来数百年的寿桃。

那天晚上,我们从厦门大学戏院返回时,演员们还在卖力地表演,精力旺盛的疯狂乐队还敲打乐器,喧闹声刺破夜空。坐在花园围墙上的小孩依然不动,专门为出资者在舞台上安排的位子座无虚席……

——麦肯兹·格丽芙,1959 年,第 76～78 页

MacGowan, 1913

Gathering at a Popular Festival

Long Plays Chinese plays are not such trivial things that they can be finished off in so short a time as that. The men begin the production of some popular comedy at noon. They play on till the evening is drawing near, when there is an intermission of an hour or so for the actors and the people to cook their rice. By the time this is finished, night has set in and the work of the day is over. Great flaring lamps are lighted that defy the wind, the drums are beaten, the shrill musical instruments fill the air with their weird sounds, and men and women and children, carrying their own stools with them, hurry with beaming faces towards what might be figuratively called the "Palace of Delights," and take up their position in front of the stage to enjoy the scene that is going to be acted.

The hours pass by and the great lamps flare in the night wind, and the actors, as they get more and more into the spirit of the comedy they are performing, become filled with enthusiasm, and with impassioned gestures, and with the very voices and tones of the characters they are personating, keep their audience spellbound in their attention.

The hours still move on, but the interest never flags. The rapid strokes on the drum in some of the exciting scenes, and the shrill falsetto tones of the actors, and the bursts of laughter as the crowd is convulsed by the dry humour that runs through the piece, wake the silence of the night, and people living near by, who could not leave their homes, are startled out of their first sleep by the unwonted sounds that wake up the echoes of the night.

Midnight strikes, but there is no sign that the play is near its end, or that the audience dreams of moving from the uncomfortable seats that each one has extemporized for himself. The small hours begin to lengthen and it would seem time for the women at least to be in their homes.

The stern and strict etiquette of the country forbids women to mingle with men, but when a play is being acted, etiquette is flung to the winds, and the wives and the young maidens sit on into unseemly hours, forgetful of the nation's ideals.

Roadside Theater   MacGowan, 1912

第七章　厦门的娱乐、节日、戏院和体育运动 *Amoy Amusements, Festivals, Theater, Sports*

长篇大戏　中国的戏曲演的不是平凡的故事,不可能在短时间里谢幕。演员从正午时分开始演出一些流行的曲目,一直演到傍晚。中间他们暂停一个小时左右,让观众和演员煮饭。饭熟吃饱,夜幕降临,一天的劳作终于结束。迎着海风,巨大的灯火熊熊点燃了,鼓点响起,各种乐器一起发出刺耳、古怪的声音。男女老少带着凳子,脸带笑容,匆匆忙忙地赶往被他们喻为"欢乐宫"的地方,在舞台前抢占自己的位置,观看即将上演的大戏。

几个小时过去了,灯火在夜风中闪亮。演员越来越进入状态,他们演起戏来热情高涨。充满激情的动作,各种角色的声调,让观众全神贯注。

随着时间的推移,观众的兴趣一点都没有消减。到了某些精彩的场景,鼓点密集起来了,男性演员扮演的女调刺人耳膜。观众被戏曲片段中的冷幽默所打动,人群中不时传出阵阵笑声,打破了黑夜的寂静,惊动了附近的居民。他们无法出门看戏。这些不同寻常的声音唤醒了夜空,也把他们从傍晚的第一觉中惊醒。

半夜时分,没有任何迹象表明戏已经临近尾声,观众也没有想从不太舒服的座位上离开的意思。时间开始往后推移,似乎到妇女至少应该回家的时刻了。

这个国家苛刻、严格的礼教要求男女授受不亲。但演戏的时候,这些规矩就飘然而去。妻子和少年坐在台下,直至深夜,把国家的理想抛到九天云霄之外。

Actors in Costume　　MacGowan, 1897

The wind becomes chiller and the darkness of the East deeper and denser, but still the merriment grows more fast and furious, when suddenly, as if with the wave of an enchanter's wand, a thin streak of light touches the border of the thick curtain that has fallen on the world, and ere long the dawn dyes the eastern sky with its colours and night begins to fly before the coming day.

This is the signal for the play to stop. The actors, weary with their long night's work, descend quickly from the stage, whilst the audience, with pale faces and worn looks, hurry away to their homes to cook their rice and prepare for a long sleep to make up for the loss of it during the night.

It has been a merry time for them all, and the blue feeling that had been gathering round their hearts and made them have long faces and caused them to be unpleasant in their homes, has vanished in the laughter that caused them almost to split their sides. A celebrated humorist has declared that if he could have but one laugh a month, the whole character of his life would be changed. During the pleasant hours in which the actors beguiled the time, they must have laughed scores of times, and the memory of those jokes will linger in their brains for many a week to come, and make them look on their sorry surroundings with a lighter and a more cheerful heart.

MacGowan, 1907

The People are the Props Nothing can equal the humor of a Chinese actor, who on a stage, bare of scenery, gallops across the stage floor, dismounts and passes his horse to a groom. Or, one who wanders down a street stopping at an open shop window to flirt with a pretty girl; or hides behind an embattlement to attack his enemy. Nothing is there but the man, and yet one sees it more clearly and realistically than if there were a hundred scenes and endless props. Only the costumes help him and these may be lavish.

More humorous still to the Westerner is the complete disregard of realism. At the end of their parts, dead men get up and walk off the stage. Sometimes a corpse, if the story requires that he be carried off, will act the part of his own bearers and make the motions of carrying himself away! Or at a tense moment an attendant, not part of the play, will march across the foreground with a cup of tea to clear the throat of the leading performer who is at that very instant appealing to high heaven.

Spencer, 1943

Nothing New A Chinese audience does not go to the theatre to see the play, for probably it knows the story of it and has seen it many times before. It goes to see how well the actors render it. ...

...much is left to the imagination of the actor, for the barer the framework upon which his story stands, the more garnishing he can do. Gesture, caricature, tricks of tone, and suggestion turn the work of the Chinese actor into an art differing greatly from that of the actor of the West who learns his part word for word, is supported by every conceivable device, by prompter, props, scenery, appropriate music and lights.

Spencer, 1943

第七章　厦门的娱乐、节日、戏院和体育运动 Amoy Amusements, Festivals, Theater, Sports

风变冷,夜色越来越浓。但欢乐的时光过得越来越快,越来越激烈。突然间,就像巫师挥舞的魔棒,一缕薄薄的白光抹上了黑夜的边缘。很快,黎明的霞光染红了东方的地平线,黑夜开始为白天让路。

这是大戏落幕的信号。经过长夜的劳累,演员们很快走下舞台。观众们则脸色苍白,面带倦意,匆匆忙忙赶回家里煮饭,并准备睡上一大觉,以补回夜里损失的睡眠。

对他们所有人来说,这是一个快乐的时刻。聚集在他们内心深处、让他们拉着长脸、在家里很不开心的忧伤此时随着开怀大笑而烟消云散。一位著名的幽默大师宣称,让一个人笑上一个月,就会彻底改变他的性格。演员们帮助观众轻松地消磨了几个小时,至少让他们笑了十来次。这些笑话将在观众的记忆里保留很长的一段时间,让他们以更加轻松、愉快的心情去看待周围的困境。

Thomson, 1876

——麦嘉湖,1907年,第146~149页

人就是道具　中国演员的幽默没人能比。在舞台上,没有布景,他们表演骑马、下马,然后把马交给马夫。或者,走在街上,在一家店铺的窗口停下,与漂亮姑娘打情骂俏。或者,躲在城垛后打敌人。舞台上除了演员,空无一物。但观众却能看得明白、看得真切,好像台上有上百个布景和数不清的道具。能帮助他的只有戏服,而这些戏服也是一种浪费。

对西方人来说,更加幽默的是演员完全不顾现实。自己的戏份演完后,死去的人自己站起来走下舞台。有时候,一具尸体,如果故事情节需要它被抬走,死者却扮演自己搬尸体的角色,作出一些把自己抬走的动作!或者,在某个关键时刻,不是戏中角色的仆人,会端上一杯茶,跑到前台,让正在祈天的主角润润喉。

——斯宾塞,1943年,第172、173页

没有新意　中国观众上戏院不是为了看戏,而是为了看演员表演得怎么样……也许是因为他们知道戏里所讲的故事,或者以前已经看过多次。

……演员有很大的想象空间,因为故事的框架越简单,他发挥的空间也就越大。手势、滑稽的模仿、玩笑的语调和暗示把中国演员的工作变成了与一种西方演员大相径庭的艺术。西方演员逐字逐句地背台词,还有许多有形的手段,如提示台词的设备、道具、布景、相应的音乐和灯光来帮助他们演戏。

——斯宾塞,1943年,第172、173页

老外看老鼓浪屿 Old Gulangyu in Foreigners' Eyes

Amoy—Home of Modern Chinese Sports[1]

Take Weight off—or put it on? (1940s) The Amoynese, like other Chinese, were not given to indulging in very energetic sports. Most Westerners try to keep slim or take off weight, but the Chinese invariably hope to get fat and put on weight. For them, there is something supremely serene in the sight of an old man sitting in his small shop fanning away the buzzing flies on a hot day, dressed in only a pair of silk trousers and a thin singlet emphasizing the diffused and overflowing contours of his flesh. The Greeks concentrated on statues of handsome gods and of athletic young men holding javelins or discs in perfect poise, but the Chinese prefer to mould a fat, laughing Budda.

Neill 1956

Amoy Fire Hopping. Letter by Dr. John Otte, October, 1901

I have long thought of writing you some description of a very peculiar sport I witnessed not long ago. Apropos of the many college games entered into nowadays is one Chinese sport I do not think Hope College venturesome ones would care to try, nor the most liberal among the faculty to encourage. I refer to jumping over the fire.

On the fifteenth day of the first Chinese month (generally about the middle of February) the "Feast of Lanterns" is observed. On the evening of this day you may see all over the city small bonfires, bright, cracking, and evidently pretty hot. There are little groups of men and boys standing near. Our party went a little to one side to watch with interest. After their prolonged staring at us, one after another gained courage, and then made a dash, a spring through the air, and safely landed on the other side, would come down a living figure, wiping the perspiration and dust from off his heated face. This is kept up for several hours, the waning fire being constantly replenished. Strange to say, but few accidents occur, and long after midnight you may hear the sounds of revelry.

The more dignified among the Chinese worthies indulge in other sports, such as archery. How old-fashioned that sounds to us, and yet it is still practiced, and prize examinations are held every year at the famous annual examination periods.

There is, however, much for the Chinese to learn in the way of genuine beneficial bodily exercise, and his phlegmatic temperament might be improved were he stimulated more by some of our Western ideas...

But the longer I live in China the more I am impressed with the fact that the Chinese are not only a peculiar, but an interesting people, if viewed from the right standpoint. And I believe I am about as interested in their great antiquity as in anything else.

---

1 Chinese ruffled foreign feathers by claiming to have invented golf and soccer (a claim even the FIFA has lent credence to). But for centuries, most Chinese were not into physical "sports," per se, with the exception perhaps of martial sports—archery, horsemanship, kung fu. Unlike us violent barbarians, cultured Chinese engaged in cultural pastimes—calligraphy, painting, poetry, tea. But Amoy helped change that.

The British introduced soccer to Amoy in 1898, and Xiamen's YMCA, started in April 1912, established Amoy's first sports program. Gulangyu was home to the "Father of Modern Chinese Sports," John Ma （马约翰）, and over recent decades Xiamen has produced numerous world class athletes (three Xiamen athletes alone shared a total of 19 world championships).

第七章 厦门的娱乐、节日、戏院和体育运动 Amoy Amusements, Festivals, Theater, Sports

厦门——中国现代体育的发源地[2]

减肥,还是增胖? 跟其他中国人一样,厦门人不太沉迷于激烈的运动。大多数西方人都试图保持苗条身材或者减肥,而中国人却希望变肥、增加体重。对他们来说,看到一位老者大热天身上只穿着丝绸裤子和薄背心,满身横肉,坐在小店里,手持扇子,扑赶苍蝇,这是何等的安详啊。希腊诸神和健美年轻人的雕像都是手持标枪或铁饼,姿态完美。中国人则更喜欢雕塑一个笑眯眯的胖菩萨。

——尼尔,1956年,第78~79页

厦门跳火盆

郁约翰博士的信件,1901年10月

我很早就想写信告诉你前不久我所看到的这里一种非常特别的运动项目的一些情况。关于现在许多大学开展的运动项目,有一项中国的运动,我想霍普大学胆大的人也肯定不敢一试,体育系里最开明的人士也不敢提倡。我指的是跳火盆。

中国农历正月十五(一般大约在公历二月中旬),这里庆祝元宵灯节。这天傍晚,你可以看到整座城市到处都有小型的篝火,烧得亮堂堂,噼里啪啦作响,温度显然很高。一小群男人和男孩站在火盆边。我们一伙人走到一旁,饶有兴趣地围观。他们盯住我们看了一会儿,然后不知道哪里来的勇气,一个接一个地腾空而起,跨过火盆,安全地落在火盆的另一侧。落地后,依然生龙活虎,同时他们把发热的脸上的汗水和灰尘抹掉。跳火盆连续进行几个小时,他们不断地往即将熄灭的火盆里添加柴火。很奇怪,没有发生什么事故。半夜过后很久,你还能听到他们的欢闹声。

中国比较富裕、有地位的人则纵情于诸如射箭之类的运动。这听起来对我们来说是多么的老派啊!但事实如此。每年年试期间都会举行射箭比赛。

当然,中国人需要学习的有益于身体健康的运动项目有很多。要是他们能够接受更多的西方思想的刺激,他们淡定的性格也许会有所改变……

不过,在中国待得越久,我就更多地感受到,中国人不仅奇特,而且有趣。我相信,我对中国悠久、伟大的历史与她的其他方面一样感兴趣。当然,你看问题的角度首先应该是正确的。

---

2 中国人声称自己发明了高尔夫和足球(这种说法连国际足联也相信),这让外国人相当恼火。不过,数百年来,中国人自身没有进行过什么体育运动。倒是武术运动——射箭、骑马、功夫,是个例外。不像我们这些粗暴的番仔,有教养的中国人进行的都是有文化的消遣——书法、绘画、诗歌、茶艺。但是,厦门帮助人们改变这种状况。

英国人在1898年把足球传入了厦门。厦门的基督教青年会于1912年4月在厦门举办了第一场体育赛事。鼓浪屿是"中国现代体育之父"——马约翰的故乡。最近几十年,厦门培养了许多世界级的运动员(其中,三名厦门籍运动员赢得了总计19项的世界冠军)。

老外看老鼓浪屿 *Old Gulangyu in Foreigners' Eyes*

Chapter 8 Arts and Music

Intricacy …Their patience is wonderful; their fancy carved work is wrought in the most minute and elaborate manner. To the naked eye, they appear to be a confused mass of the most delicate workmanship, but examine them through a microscope, and you will find that the human figures, with a head no larger than a pin's head, have eyes, nose, mouth and chin, all in their proper places, with an expression suited to the design.

Coffin, 1908

Chinese Cult of Beauty (Gulangyu, 1920s) Little Yi-hsing teapots, with a colour and patina that reminded me of the Etruscans, were popular in Fukien. The old ones were greatly prized. "They should be smooth and glow, and they must have good voices,"Grandfather Tan told us. He showed us how to strike the lid against the rim and listen for the proper resonance. It was typical of the subtle refinement of Chinese pleasures. That subtlety has sometimes been called the over-refined aestheticism of a decadent people, but it is far more than an aesthetic principle…It is the outcome of a two-thousand-year-old philosophy of life which determined the behaviour of Grandfather Tan's remotest ancestors, just as it determined his own attitude towards themselves, towards Heaven, earth, humanity and the little red teapot…

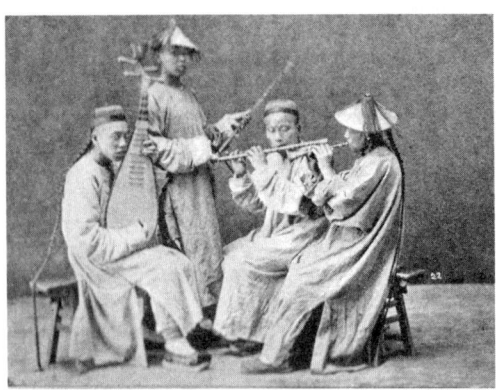

Chinese Band   MacGowan, 1897

This close attention and regard for matter was not confined to metaphysics: neither did the Chinese ever divide aesthetics from philosophy, which was—in theory—never divorced from civil administration. It was always held to be the duty of artist and craftsman to reveal the li, the tao, the peculiar character in fact, of the landscape he painted, the materials which he fashioned. But for generations, Chinese craftsmen, having absorbed the tradition, completely assimilated the superlative standards set in their remote past, have been unconscious of obedience to a moral principle; yet they have never lost the close and flawless relationship with wood, stone and clay which it engendered.

We could not help contrasting their slow and contemplative savouring of each object of sensuous pleasure with the Western habit of grasping, and discarding half-assessed, a multiplicity of objects or experiences. The Chinese cult of beauty in all forms never lacked elaboration, but it was an elaboration in depth. A spreading downwards of understanding which, like the roots of a tree, nourished and increased pleasure…

Mackenzie-Grieves, 1959

第八章　艺术与音乐

复杂的工艺　……他们的耐心非同寻常。他们的雕刻工艺品花俏、精致、工序复杂。裸眼一看，似乎只是一件杂乱的精致工艺品。放在显微镜下仔细观察，你会发现上面的人物图案脑袋不过针头大小，眼睛、鼻子、嘴巴和下巴应有尽有、各就各位，表情与图案极为相称。

——柯芬，1908年，第167、168页

中国人对美的崇拜（鼓浪屿，20世纪20年代）　宜兴小茶壶在福建很时髦。它的颜色和绿锈让我想起了伊特拉斯坎人。小茶壶年代越久远越值钱。谭爷爷告诉我们，"茶壶应该表面光滑、有光彩，能发出好听的声音"。他向我们演示了如何用壶盖敲茶壶的边缘，然后判断它的回声。赏茶壶是中国人诡秘、优雅乐趣的典型之一。那种诡秘有时候被称为过于精细的唯美主义颓废派。然而，这种诡秘不仅仅是一个审美的原则……它是中国2000多年来生活哲学的结局，决定

Amoy Lantern Shop, 1930s　J. Nienhuis

了谭爷爷远祖们的行为举止，就像它决定了谭爷爷对祖先、对天、对地、对人类以及对紫砂壶的态度那样……

中国人对物质的细心关注和照料不仅仅局限于纯粹的哲学，他们也从来没有把美学与哲学分开。从理论上来说，前者与公共管理密不可分。人们总认为，艺术家和工艺师有责任揭示自己所创作的山水画、所制作的材料的理和道，事实上就是特性。然而，长期以来，中国的手艺人一直不太在意遵从某种道德原则。他们在吸收传统的同时，完全消化了远古时代制定的那些最高标准。他们从未放弃与能够产生艺术品的木头、石头和瓷土之间亲密无间的关系。

在这里，我们不禁把中国人细细品味每件艺术品所获得的感官上的满足与西方人习惯于马上拥有，然后迅速抛弃艺术品或艺术体验的复杂性作比较。中国人对一切形式的美的膜拜从来都不缺乏精细，而且是一种有深度的精细。他们对艺术的理解向下蔓延，就像树根，培育了乐趣，增加了愉悦……

——麦肯兹·格丽芙，1959年，第22~24页

老外看老鼓浪屿 Old Gulangyu in Foreigners' Eyes

Calligraphy At Dr. Lim's we met a calligrapher of note. Persuaded to write an inscription for us, his brush almost miraculously brought to life and movement to the paper. With a superbly graceful precision, his hand seemed to be evoking beauty that was already there, rather than making a dogmatic statement. But the Chinese have, it seems, always known that truth and beauty cannot be taken by storm.

Later, in Sarawak, the Datu Imam wrote for me a sentence from the Koran in 'Stamboul' Arabic script, and again I was fascinated by the rhythmic movement of his cut quill and the elaborate beauty he created, but it was a written statement of wisdom, not the picture of it painted by the Chinese calligrapher.

Hitherto, I had written my dictations for Mr. Law with a pencil but, after this, I bought ink tablet, brushes and a large squared copy-book. Although my hands were already trained to pens, pencils, brushes and gravers, I first had to master control of the vertically held brush. It was well worth learning. There was sensuous pleasure in practising the infinite variety of pressures, the long slow sweeps, the sharp clean halt, the flicked dot, full of life and spring compared with our full-stop. It was soothing because it was harmonious, stimulating because it demanded vitality and precision. Merely to build up the character in the right order of strokes-the Seven Mysteries, as the Chinese call them-I found infinitely satisfying in itself, perhaps because it was the rhythmic practice of the poise and balance which are consciously or unconsciously the basic needs of body and spirit. Yet it was not the held poise of static beauty achieved, but the dynamic vigour of an athlete for a moment caught and arrested. Even to have written badly—and only the cultured and talented minority even among the Chinese can hope to write exquisitely—is to have been enriched.

Mackenzie-Grieves, 1959

Amoy Paintings[1] Chinese scroll paintings are usually done on long strips of rice paper which may be pasted on silk scrolls and then hung up on a wall. There is no sense of perspective, as in Western art. The effect is that of looking down on a landscape from above rather than at it from the ground. The paintings are essentially impressionistic and usually the result of an inspiration that comes to an artist, suddenly releasing an overflow of creative talent on to the paper with a few quick brush strokes. In this he is helped by a study of calligraphy and by having had to write Chinese ideographs with a brush from early school days. Calligraphy can help to bring out a wide range of aesthetic reactions. It teaches the artist to use his brush in sweeping, light or heavy strokes with a spontaneity that will stand him in good stead when he turns to painting. Some artists concentrate solely on calligraphy, and may write one large character, such as 'happiness', with such finesses that it in itself becomes a highly valued scroll.

One seldom sees a Chinese artist painting out of doors like his fellow artists with palette and easel in Montmattre. His style is different. First he goes to look at something for himself, and then retires to a room to think it over. After a moment of contemplation, the brush is taken out and with the minimum of strokes, a picture is completed of how the scene has impressed his poetic sense. Some of the greatest artists in China never even waited to look for a brush in moments of inspiration, but used whatever was at hand, from their own fingers to the stalk of a lotus flower.

The study of flowers, birds and trees excites the Chinese artistic spirit.

Neill, 1956

---

1 Today, Xiamen is one of the world's greatest producers of oil paintings.

第八章 艺术与音乐 Arts and Music

书法 在林博士家,我们遇到了一位著名的书法家。我们请他题字。只见毛笔在他手中神奇挥舞,字字栩栩如生。书法家不是在机械地写字,他的笔法庄重、优雅、精准,落笔生辉。看来,中国人深知,真理和美是不可能通过强夺豪取来获得。

后来,在沙捞越,一位清真寺官员从古兰经里挑了一个句子,用斯坦布尔体的阿拉伯字为我们题词。他手中的羽毛笔运用自如,题词优美,令人陶醉。它只是一副与智慧有关的格言,不像中国书法家创作的书法作品。

之前,我一直用铅笔给刘先生写留言。此后,我买来笔、墨和一本正方形的

FIVE CHINESE BLESSINGS Anderson, 1920

大字帖。尽管已经练过钢笔、铅笔、毛笔和雕刻笔,我首先还得掌握如何控制直立书写的毛笔。这样的学习很值得。落笔花样无穷、弯勾又长又慢、抬笔干脆利落、句号轻点,用毛笔练习汉字,与写英文字母相比,生龙活虎,乐趣无穷。写毛笔讲究协调,令人兴奋。它需要活力和精准,令人感到宽心。我发现,只是把汉字按照笔画顺序,也就是中国人称之为"七条规则"写好,本身已经是其乐无穷。作为人体和精神有意或无意中所具备的基本要求,书法也许可以有节奏地训练人们的平衡能力。只不过,这不是静止美的一种稳定平衡,而是运动员所捕捉到的充满动态活力的瞬间。只有少数受过教育、有才气的中国人才能够写得如此优美。写得不好,也是一种充实。

——麦肯兹·格丽芙,1959 年,第 33、34 页

厦门绘画 中国画一般是画在长条的宣纸上,然后再裱在丝绸的卷轴上,悬挂起来。没有西方艺术的透视感,中国画的视觉效果是俯视,而非仰视。这些画基本上属于印象派,通常都是艺术家灵感的结晶。他们灵感突发,简单、快速几笔,作品随即跃然纸上。之所以能够这样,是因为中国人从小就开始用毛笔写字,同时又研究书法。书法可以帮助他们对美作出宽泛的反应,培养艺术家用毛笔随心所欲地轻描或浓墨。这对他们从事绘画很有好处。一些艺术家只专注于书法,可以写出诸如"福"这样的大字,手法精湛,本身就是一幅高价值的画卷。人们很少看到中国的艺术家像他们的蒙马特同行那样带着调色板和画架到室外去创作。他们有自己不同的风格。首先,他们自己会到户外去观察,然后回到室内仔细思考。深思熟虑之后,他们会取出画笔,轻描淡写简单几笔,画出风景在他们脑海里留下诗意,一幅画就这样完成了。中国最伟大的一些艺术家灵感一来,从来不会费时去找画笔。从手指头,到莲花梗,他们作画手边有什么就用什么。

对花卉、鸟兽和树木的研究,激发了中国人的艺术灵感。

——尼尔,1956 年,第 64、65 页

Amoy – the Isle of Music

Chinese Music: An Acquired Taste
"Do you enjoy our music?"... Of course, we were unanimous in the opinion that it is a nerve-racking discord. "It is not strange you do not appreciate it," said the diplomat in the sing song intonation of the Chinese language. "China was the first to compose and write music and had musical conservatories while the people of Europe were still chasing rabbits in the stone age. We have the advantage of several thousands of years of musical culture."

"What sounds to you a discord is to us the sweetest harmony. I am told that in America and Europe people who are uneducated prefer simple tunes and primary harmonies to the grand music of Wagner. Musical culture is necessary to appreciate your grand opera and classical music, but you must be educated still further before you can be expected to arrive at the Chinese type of music."

Caldwell, 1906

Chinese Band, Amoy, 1908

第八章 艺术与音乐 Arts and Music

厦门——音乐岛

中国音乐，后天养成的品味 "你喜欢我们的音乐吗？"…… 当然，我们一致的看法是，中国的音乐是相当令人伤脑筋的喧闹。"你不喜欢它，并不奇怪，"这位外交家用唱歌般的语调说，"中国是世界上最早作词、作曲，并最早拥有音乐学院的国家。那时候，欧洲人还处于石器时代，四处追赶兔子。我们已经拥有数千年音乐文化的历史。"

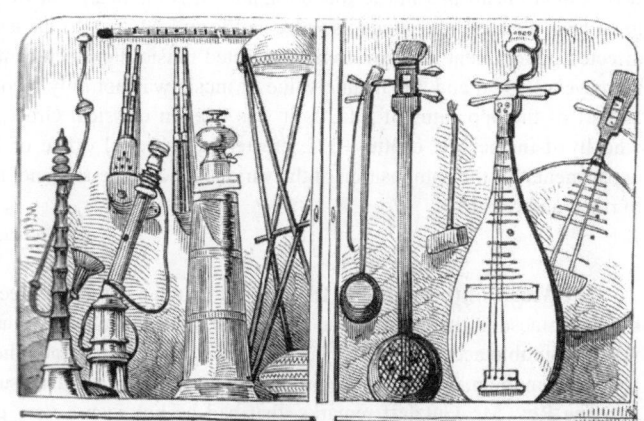

Musical Instruments　　Dukes, 1885

"对你们来说是喧闹，对我们则是最甜美的和声。有人告诉我，美国和欧洲没受过教育的人更喜欢简单、原始的乐音，而不是瓦格纳雄伟的乐章。要欣赏你们华美的歌剧和古典音乐，需要音乐素养。但要真正了解中国音乐，你的音乐素养必须进一步提升。"

——卡德威，1906 年，第 88、89 页

Singing Girls

Amoy Music (1920s) In China, music had been inextricably woven into the whole pattern of life… Music not only had the powers that the West knew through Orpheus, but was held by the Chinese to be essential to the world's equilibrium. Through his musical harmonies or disharmonies, man was responsible for the balance of the earth. The welfare of the empire depended on the correctness of the pitches and scales that he made. But it was in man's heart that music was born, and "it is the heart that works the miracles, the great heart that in music finds its voice and form". Music, the ancient Chinese believed, affected government and government affected music. Fourteen centuries before Christ, the psychological and therapeutic value of music was not only recognized but accepted as part of the apparatus of rule, as it was later in classical Greece. The Emperor Wu who lived in the first century B.C. created an imperial office of Music, with special departments for the composition of the various kinds necessary, not to entertainment, but to ritual and to rule.

Mackenzie-Grieves, 1959

The Music of the Chinese (1843) "Although a certain degree of skill is exhibited by the Chinese in the construction of musical instruments, yet we are not able to give a very favourable account of their taste, or ability to produce melodious and harmonious sounds from them. However, we propose to describe their music, such as it is…

The Rev. Mr. Gutzlaff remarks, that had he not seen a very elaborate treatise on the Music of the Chinese in the Memoires sur les Chinois, he might have asserted that this people have no music, having been so frequently deafened by the sound of their gongs and other instruments. Though he was present at marriages and funerals, and at the review of troops, he was never able to make out a single air.

"Musical notes, (he remarks), though known, are not in common use. …The principle on which a concert is played, appears to be, which of the musicians shall outdo the other in loudness of sound, in which attempt the beater of the gong generally succeeds in admiration…Some Chinamen finger the guitar tolerably well, and accompany this with a song, yet the nation has no musical ear, not are the instruments very harmonious. Like most things in China, they are the first efforts of invention, left in an imperfect and unfinished state for want of further improvement.

"Mr. Gutzlaff also states that the Chinese do not enjoy our music, nor do they even attempt to imitate it, having, apparently, none of the finer perceptions of melody and harmony, and being only susceptible of harsh tones.

"But this unfavourable report is somewhat qualified by the statements of Mr. Lay, who in his interesting work entitled "The Chinese as they are," gives a minute and excellent account of the state of musical knowledge and practice among this people. This gentleman not only made himself acquainted with the different instruments in use among them, and the amount of skill employed in their use, but became himself the pupil of their musicians, and seems to have acquired considerable facility in performing the peculiar evolutions which are the characteristics of Chinese style…

The Saturday Magazine, Nov.4th, 1843

第八章　艺术与音乐 Arts and Music

厦门音乐（20世纪20年代）（摘自《魅力鼓浪屿》）　在中国，音乐是生活不可分割的一部分。……对于中国人而言，音乐的力量已超出了西方人对俄耳甫斯神的了解范围，它还对保持万物均衡至关重要。音律的协调或不调，会影响世界的平衡；编制的音阶与音高是否精确，会关系到帝国的福祉。但是，唯有在音乐中能发现声音与形态的心灵，能创造奇迹的伟大心灵，才能产生音乐。古代中国人相信，音乐能影响社稷，反之亦然。早在公元前十四世纪，中国人就认识到音乐在心理与医疗方面的效果，并将它作为统治工具，就像后来的古希腊一样。公元前1世纪，吴王建立了宫廷音乐部门，专事谱写朝廷所需的各种曲子，并非用于娱乐，而是用于仪式和社稷统治。

——麦肯兹·格丽芙，1959年，第75～79页

中国人的音乐（1843年）　"尽管中国人在制作乐器方面展示出相当程度的技术，但是我们还是没有办法对中国人的音乐品味、或者说创作优美旋律和悦耳乐音的能力作出非常正面的评价。不过，我们还是打算描述他们的音乐，实事求是地……

"古兹拉夫主教说，中国的锣鼓和其他乐器经常让他震耳欲聋。要不是在《中国论文集》里看到一篇有关中国音乐的详细论述，他可能会认为，这个民族没有音乐。尽管经常出席婚礼、葬礼，参加阅兵仪式，他辨不出中国音乐的一个音符。

"音符，他说，中国人虽然知道，但并不常用……一场演出下来，似乎有一条原则，那就是演奏者必须比别人大声。结果，敲锣的声音一般总能获得人们的赞扬……有些中国人吉他弹得很好，配上歌曲。但这个国家没有欣赏音乐的能力，乐器配合也不协调。就像大多数东西，最初是他们发明的，然后就搁在那里，半成品，也不进一步完善。

"古兹拉夫先生还指出，中国人对和声旋和律没有更好的认识，只对刺耳的音调敏感，不喜欢、也不模仿我们的音乐。

"这份不太正面的报告被莱先生的言词所证明。莱先生在其有趣的作品——《真实的中国人》一书中，对中国人音乐知识和实践作了优美、详尽的描述。这位先生不仅熟悉中国人常用的各种乐器及其使用技巧，而且自己还向中国音乐家拜师学艺，似乎已经掌握了演奏这些具有中国特色乐器的基本技巧……"

——《周六杂志》，1843年11月4日，第180页

老外看老鼓浪屿 Old Gulangyu in Foreigners' Eyes

Amoy University Concert (1920s) The University looked quiet and purposeful in the grey afternoon. The large plain blocks were lifted from monotony by the up-curved, green-tiled roofs, an excellent blend of Eastern and Western idioms. Its situation, between the granite rocks and the sea, had an austere dignity. It was hard to associate the place and the quietly animated students, drifting about the still raw quadrangle and gardens, with riots and rabbles; with histrionics perhaps, but not with hysterics. Yet, all over China, it was the students who supplied the most ardent and fanatical agitators, as well as the political spearheads of revolution...

In one of the smaller halls we gathered to hear the se players. The first performer already sat behind the table which bore his instrument, a kind of psaltery, and was there a single orchid in a vase-or am I in another picture? He wore grey brocaded silk beneath his short black satin jacket and bent gravely over the silk strings.

'1 hope,' he eyed us solemnly, 'you, my honoured audience, will not emulate the Emperor Huang Ti who, you will remember, was so deeply moved by the Lady Su's playing of the se that he forthwith ordered the number of strings to be halved in order that he might suffer less.'

The audience was delighted.

'What are they laughing at? What did he say? Do tell me.' I, who had not been able to follow him, pestered Mrs. Lim. She told me, and added that the Emperor Huang Ti had lived a legendary four thousand five hundred years ago.

From the first, the music was between the player and his se. He seemed to be privately communing with the strings. Then I had the sensation that he and the se were one, and that their utterances were too subtle for me to understand. ...Its idiom was entirely strange, too baffling for immediate enjoyment, but it left us both with an aftermath in memory as strong and elusive as the aroma of Chinese tea on the palate.

In China, from legendary times, music was written for poetry and poetry written to be sung. Both spoke a language I could not understand, using age-old symbols, classic repetitions and allusions to which I had not been educated to respond either intellectually or emotionally. Yet this delicate, esoteric-seeming music, the Chinese told me, had been considered so potent as to be dangerous to the virtue of young women, so that the female performers were usually hetaira-like courtesans. Balinese and Javanese music I can easily accept as emotionally and erotically stimulating, but I have never heard any Chinese chamber music that I felt to be anything but cerebral. Perhaps for the Chinese, too, it had a delayed effect, for the Chinese, in spite of a culture based on the male-female concept-the Yin and Yang-and of a hearty sexuality, are one of the most sexually decorous people in the world. No open display of sexual emotion is tolerated. The twentieth-century girl entertainers, who were still a feature of Chinese banquets, were trained to charm but not seduce, and each one appeared to sing and to pour wine accompanied by her elderly woman attendant. ...

Listening to the se players, the power of Chinese music seemed to me to be by association rather than direct appeal to the senses.

Mackenzie-Grieves, 1959

第八章 艺术与音乐 Arts and Music

厦门大学的一场音乐会（20世纪20年代）（摘自《魅力鼓浪屿》） 这是一个灰蒙蒙的下午，学校显得安静又有意境。简朴的大楼因向上弯曲的琉璃瓦屋顶而不再单调，体现了东西方智慧的完美融合。它位于花岗岩石和海之间，彰显出一种简朴的高贵。活泼的学生们安静地出入于庭院和花园，很难把他们及这样一个地方与暴乱闹事联系起来，就算有大概也是演戏，而不是真的歇斯底里。然而在全中国，确实是学生们充当了革命最狂热的鼓动者和政治先锋。

我们聚在一个稍小的礼堂里准备听瑟的演奏。第一个表演者已经坐在桌子后面，桌上摆放着他的乐器，这是一种古代弦乐器，边上一朵兰花插在花瓶里——莫非我是置身在画中吗？他上身穿着黑色缎子短袄，下身着灰色锦缎马褂，神情庄严地专注于琴弦。

"我希望大家，"他说话时眼神严峻，"我尊敬的听众，不要像黄帝一样。众所周知，他被苏夫人的瑟深深打动之后，立刻命令将琴弦的数量减半来减少自己的痛苦。"

听众都笑了。

演奏一开始，音乐存在于演奏者和"瑟"之间，他似乎在和琴弦喁喁私语。后来我感觉他和"瑟"融为了一体，两者间的交谈太玄妙令我难以理解……这种语汇是全然陌生，令人困惑的，不能给人即时的愉悦，但却给我们留下一段回忆，就像中国茶留在腭间的芳香一样强烈而又难以捉摸。

在中国，从有传说的年代开始，音乐就为诗而作，诗又为了歌而作。它们都传递着我无法理解的语言。对于那些古老的符号、经典的重复和暗示，在理性上和感性上我都不知如何产生共鸣。

中国人告诉我，这种看似难懂的优美音乐很有影响力，会对年轻女性的贞操造成威胁。因此，女性演奏者通常都是官妓。巴厘和爪哇的音乐，我一听就感觉到它是刺激情色的，但我从来没听过任何中国室内音乐不是理智的东西。也许，对中国人来说，音乐有一种延迟的效应，因为中国人是世界上在性方面最讲究礼节的民族，尽管他们的文化是基于阴阳（男女）协调的理论。在中国，公开场合表达性爱是无法容忍的。20世纪的女艺人依然是中国宴会上的一个特色，但是培训的时候要求她们妩媚，而不是性感。她们出场唱歌、敬酒，身边总有老妇人陪伴……

听她们弹瑟，我觉得，中国音乐似乎是间接，而不是直接对感官形成冲击。

——麦肯兹·格丽芙，1959年，第76～78页

老外看老鼓浪屿 Old Gulangyu in Foreigners' Eyes

One-Man Band I also fell in with a nondescript individual who composed a complete band in his own person; he had somehow acquired a smattering of European taste. He had on the top of his head a branch of some kind of shrub, with a number of small bells of different tones; a shepherd's range of pipes was fastened on his chin, and a small flageolet was fixed in each nostril; a bass drum was lashed to his back and the sticks fixed on to his elbows; a hurdy-gurdy was slung in front; a pair of cymbals was attached to his knees, and other strings of bells encircled his ankles. He marched along the narrow lanes, with an air of pomposity which made the Celestial pigtails stand back to let him pass. He shook his head and the bells chimed, he slewed his mouth and the pipes whistled, he blew his nose and set the flageolets squealing, he brought his elbows back and whang went the bass drum, brought his knees together and clang went the cymbals, and as he stepped, he brought his feet down with a jerk and tinkled the ankle bells, while all the time he turned the crank of the hurdy-gurdy with one hand and managed the stops with the other. Altogether he managed to raise a discord almost equal to a modern church choir with their chromatics, diatonics and inharmonics.

Coffin, 1908

Chinese Women Musicians How delightful will be the music, for these ladies have acquired some celebrity by their acquirements; yet evil suspicion is beginning to dawn on me. Two slave girls hand their mistresses a rude, ominous-looking guitar and fiddle; the Chinese host takes possession of a wooden drum with a look of placid enjoyment, and, ah! …what a terrible yowl is uplifted! The Shanghai opera all over again, only in closer proximity. The women yell with a discord remarkable in its piercing effects; the stringed instruments shriek like a concord of field gun axles deficient in oil, and the tomtoms bang out a dropping fire of wooden shots. Loud is the applause bestowed on, great is the pride of performance evinced by, these prime donne, stimulated thereby to still more deafening results. Their flagging energies are from time to time sustained by the services of the slave girls who hold tea to their lips, sipped without any break in the melody, or the amber mouth-pieces of long pipes from which whiffs are continually drawn.

After about three-quarters of an hour of this pastime: "Let us resume dinner,"says our host…

Knollys, 1885

Amoy Gongs…   which are beaten to distraction on the arrival and departure of junks. No sooner does one of these craft appear within the limits of the harbour, than two or more of the crew instantly perch themselves on the bow with their gongs, and after a few preliminary strokes by way of taking the stiffness out of their joints, settle down to work with an earnestness and calm deliberation worthy of a better cause.. Their energy, their strength of arm, and lasting powers are truly wonderful; indeed, had I not been unfortunate enough to witness the display, I should have deemed it incredible. They beat as if their very lives depended on the result; no careless random strokes, but a steady continuous crash, now sinking into a subdued strain, and encouraging the hope that at last their strength is exhausted, and then as if in very spite they warm to it once more, till they make those gongs quiver again. …

第八章 艺术与音乐 Arts and Music

一人乐队 我偶然碰上了一个难以归类的人。他独自一人就是一个乐队。对欧洲音乐,他似乎略知一二。他头上戴着灌木树枝做成的帽子,身上带着几个不同音调的小铃铛,下巴顶着一排牧羊人用的笛子,每个鼻孔贴着一把小型的六孔竖笛,背上背着大鼓,鼓槌绑在手肘上,一把手摇风琴挂在胸前,一对铜锣摆在膝盖上,还有一串的小钟缠在脚上。他穿街走巷,相当招摇,连漂亮的小姑娘也要侧身为他让路。他一摇头,身上的铃铛就响起来了。嘴巴一扭,笛子响起。鼻孔一吹,竖笛尖叫。手肘往后一伸,大鼓轰然响起。两个膝盖一碰,铜锣铿锵。走路的时候,双腿一弯,脚上的小钟叮当作响。一路走来,他一手拨弄琴键,一手摆弄其他乐器。就这样,他所制造的喧闹在色彩、音调和不协调等方面几乎可以同一个现代教堂唱诗班相媲美。

——柯芬,1908 年,第 168、169 页

中国女音乐家 音乐令人感到非常愉快,因为这些女乐手已经颇有名气。我渐渐地开始理解那种邪恶的猜疑。两个女仆将一把粗糙、难看的吉他和提琴递给她们的女主人。男主人拿着木鼓,面带温和的笑容。啊!…… 可怕的咆哮上场了!再次充斥着整个上海戏院,让人听了感觉离得更近了。女人们高声尖叫,噪音震耳欲聋。刺耳的琴弦像没上机油的野战炮车轴一样吱吱作响。手鼓像投射木球一样轰然爆炸。观众掌声如雷,证明他们对演出感到非常满意。以这些精华的演出垫底,引发了更加喧闹的音乐。女仆们时不时将茶水端至主人唇边,主人一边啜饮、保持体力,一边继续演唱,或不断吹奏黄褐色的长笛。

吹拉弹唱,如此娱乐大约 45 分钟之后,主人说:"我们继续用餐吧"……

——诺利斯,1885 年,第 291 页

厦门的铜锣 ……铜锣是在轮船抵港或离港时敲打的,实在令人厌烦。船只一进入港口的视野,两、三个船员就马上手拿铜锣,站在船头。敲几下铜锣,活动活动关节,然后再认真、冷静地干活。这种从容完全可以让他们胜任一份更好的工作。他们的精力、臂力和耐力实在惊人。说实在的,要不是我有幸亲眼目睹他们的工作,我会认为这是令人难以置信的。他们并不是随意乱打,而是持续不断、从容冷静地敲:一会儿陷入平缓的旋律,让我们觉得他们已经筋疲力尽;一会儿又把铜锣敲得连天震响,好像他们的生活有赖于铜锣的音效。

This is one part of the performance. No sooner do the occupants of the junks in harbour hear these dulcet strains, than the spirit of music is stirred within them, and each prow is quickly manned by a pair of rival musicians, and then commences a contest of gongs which beggars description. It really is very remarkable what one can get used to in time; I believe I am correct in saying that the Chinese like it. Tastes certainly vary.

Shore, 1881

Gulangyu's First Piano[2] The young tea merchants often called at our home, and enjoyed mother's singing and playing on the piano for them. She was the only one who possessed a piano, of the entire foreign colony [Gulangyu]. It is on record that an Englishman asked father's permission, most courteously, if he might present her with one. There were a few "melodeons", but no other piano!

These young men brought pieces of music for her to play or sing for them—just new then "Lily Dale", "Wha'll Buy A Calla Herring' from a Scotchman, and "Blue Bells of Scotland", "Auld Lang Syne", " "Sweet Afton", "Annie Laurie", and others.

She often sang to other groups,—or to her own family, the old darkey songs, "Old Virginny",[3] "Rosa Lee", "Up and Down the Swanee River", "Old Kentucky Home". Also the "Last Rose of Summer", and many others whose tunes I have carried always, and which seemed old familiar ones, when transferred to the "sings" around the piano after we reached America. We children often sang with her, songs within our childish comprehension, and hymns whose words she taught us first. The Chinese women seemed spellbound at the instrument, as well as the voice, producing such sweet sounds. Men, too, wondered, as they came among us for calls now and then.

Mary Doty's Unpublished Memoirs

Foreign Pianos; Englishmen unmusical   Monday, June 2nd

This evening Pa and I went down to the beach and hunted shells and eye stones for nearly two hours. Got our pockets pretty well filled and came back. If I'm not mistaken, I'm tired for the first time. It is very hard work walking on a sandy beach. Found a Jews harp tonight in the bottom of a basket. Carried it to Pa with great delight, and he played a good while. It is all rusty. I will make my coolie scour it up tomorrow. I do so want to hear some music. All the foreign houses here have pianos; but none, or very few, of the ladies play. The English pianos are not good. I wouldn't have one as a gift, and the English are a very unmusical set. Mrs. Boyd told me she wishes I would come up every day and practice on her piano. I will go up once in awhile, I guess. We go to Mr. Brown's tomorrow night. It is very hot tonight.

Ruth Bradford's Journal

---

2   Gulangyu is today known as "Piano Islet," with 1 in 5 families owning a piano. Read more about Gulangyu at http://amoymagic.com/discovergulangyu1.htm (1850s)

3   Mary Doty's memoir was obviously failing her in her later years. She is writing of the 1850s, but "Old Virginny" was not written until 1878. But the Doty family did have the Piano Island's first piano.

第八章 艺术与音乐 Arts and Music

这只是演出的一部分。港内的船主一听到这些优美的旋律,音乐的精灵就马上在他们的内心搅动。然后,每个船头很快就站着一对乐手,与之遥相呼应,并开始了一场难以形容的敲锣比赛。人们立即就能够适应,这实在是很了不起。我说中国人喜欢这样的场面,我相信这一定错不了。品味肯定有差别。

——肖尔,1881 年,第 84 页

鼓浪屿的第一台钢琴(19 世纪 50 年代) 年轻的茶商经常造访,并欣赏母亲为他们演唱的歌曲和弹奏的钢琴。在(鼓浪屿)这个外国人聚居地,她是唯一拥有钢琴的人。有记录说,一位英国绅士非常有礼貌地问父亲,是否可以送母亲一台钢琴。当时,岛上有几台手风琴,却没有一台钢琴!

这些年轻人把曲子带过来,让母亲为他们演唱或演奏。有当时很新的曲子,如"百合谷"、"苏格兰的蓝钟"、"友谊地久天长"、"可爱的阿富顿"、"安妮罗莉"和其他曲子。

母亲还经常给其他人,或她自己的家人唱黑人老歌,如"弗吉尼亚佬"、"罗莎莉"、"天鹅河上下"、"肯塔基老家"。还有我一直带在身上、既熟悉又古老的歌曲——"夏日里的最后一朵玫瑰"和其他许多乐曲。这些曲子在我们抵达美国之后就变成了钢琴伴奏的歌曲。孩提时代,我们经常跟母亲一起唱小孩能够理解的歌曲。歌词都是母亲先教给我们的。钢琴和曲子能够产生如此甜蜜的声音,简直让这些中国女性入迷了。男人也一样着迷。他们时不时会到我们家来拜访。

——玛丽·多蒂未出版的回忆录

外国的钢琴:英国人没有音乐素养
露丝·布莱德福特的日记,星期一,6 月 2 日

这天晚上,父亲和我下到海滩,用将近两个小时的时间寻找贝壳和眼石,直到我们的口袋装满了,才往回走。如果没记错的话,这是我第一次感到累。在沙滩上走的确很辛苦。今晚在篮底发现了一把犹太琴。很兴奋,把它拿过去给父亲。父亲弹了好长一段时间。犹太琴已经锈迹斑斑。明天我要让仆人把它擦亮。我的确想听些音乐。这里所有外国人的房子里都有钢琴。但没有,或者说很少有女人在演奏。英国人的钢琴质量不好。我不想要英国钢琴作礼物。英国人是一群不懂音乐的家伙。博易德女士告诉我,她希望我能每天去她家,用她的钢琴练习。我想,我过一段时间就会去一次。今晚天气很热,我们要去布朗先生家。

老外看老鼓浪屿 *Old Gulangyu in Foreigners' Eyes*

Chapter 9   Amoy Architecture

Amoy's Arches   Triumphal arches form another object of Chinese architecture, which, from its constant recurrence in views of Chinese scenery, is almost as familiar to us as the pagoda. These are, in fact, monuments to deceased persons of distinction, generally of widows who have not married a second time, or of virgins who have died unmarried… One of the most solid examples yet published is one forming the gate, or at least spanning the entrance, of the city of Amoy.

Fergusson, 1855

Amoy Yamen Entrance   The entrance to the yamen led through a kind of porch, and was closed by four immense doors on each of which was depicted in glowing colours a repulsive featured Chinaman. Perhaps the idea of making these cartoons so ugly is to inspire awe in the minds of the people, on the same principle as an English nurse sometimes tries to frighten a naughty child into good behaviour. It was flanked by a pair of animals of a nondescript kind, half dog and half lion, cut in granite, while in front was a white screen on which an imaginative artist had depicted a dragon in startling colours, hog backed and with a bright green tail, and the ground filled in with strange birds, beasts, reptiles, &c., the offspring of a very diseased imagination.

Shore, 1881

Postcard Courtesy of Mr. George Yue

第九章　厦门建筑

厦门的牌坊　牌坊是中国建筑的另一个特色。它反复出现人们的视野里，就像塔一样让我们感到熟悉。实际上，这些牌坊是有身份的逝者的纪念碑，一般是没有再婚的寡妇或未婚逝去的老姑娘……已知最可靠的案例之一是成为厦门城门、或至少横跨城门入口的牌坊。

——福格森，1855 年，第 138 页

厦门衙门入口　走过一段门廊，就到了厦门衙门，入口处有四扇大门把关，每扇大门都用中国特色的醒目颜色粉刷，让人看了很不舒服。也许把大门画得如此丑陋的目的是想让老百姓望而生畏。这跟英国护士时不时吓唬淘气的小孩、让他们听话，原理是一样的。大门两侧站着一对花岗岩动物，半狗半狮，不知何物。大门正对面有一堵白墙。想象力丰富的艺术家用华丽的色彩在上面画了一条背部拱起、尾巴鲜绿的龙，底座挤满了奇兽怪鸟、蟒蛇等等。真是奇思怪想！

——肖尔，1881 年，第 45 页

Gateway at Amoy　　Ferguson, 1855

老外看老鼓浪屿 *Old Gulangyu in Foreigners' Eyes*

Gulangyu Architecture (1920s)   Square, stuccoed, with its solid arched verandas facing a big garden, our house was typical of the early Treaty Port architecture. The Portuguese must have been originally responsible for it, how it evolved I do not know. Although clumsy, it was yet practical for a climate which ranged from coal fires in winter to fans which hardly mitigated the sweltering summer heat. The houses, moreover, symbolized the solid dignity of the mid-nineteenth-century merchants who settled on the island to develop British trade. They were not incongruous, for they suited their purpose and possessed a character of their own.

Foreigner's Residence, Amoy   Goodrich, 1911

Mackenzie-Grieve, 1959

Anathema Cottage   One of the most curious and attractive of the artificial features of this island is unquestionably the little bungalow on Messrs. Elles and Company's property popularly known as "Anathema Cottage." Built at the summit, and almost overlapping the edges of a huge boulder which rises perpendicularly to a height of some fifty or sixty feet, this airy fairy residence is admirably adapted for catching every breath of the much-coveted summer monsoon. It was erected in the year 1876 after considerable opposition on the part of the Chinese authorities who objected to the chosen site on the score of interference with Feng-Shui—an objection which, we have reason to believe, melted like snow beneath the genial influence of some carefully applied Mexican dollars.

Giles, 1878.

Timeless Bridges (1920s)   For me, the Roman coliseum rises yawning like an empty wasps' nest; life has gone from it. Even in Lucca, whose coliseum is a teeming hive of cell-slums, built with the help of Lombardic bricks and Romanesque hewn stones, builders and users are buried in history—remembered it is true, but as a legend. But across the great stone Fukienese bridges the people swarmed, thinking, acting, writing, talking, exactly as their forebears had done for more than seven hundred years. The stream of pole-carriers, litter-bearers, pedestrians, flowed unbroken throughout the centuries, the strong tide of life undiminished, undiluted; an endurance so close-textured, so ubiquitous that, living in China, one accepted it and only afterwards was amazed…

"For me, the great granite bridges of Fukien had an indescribable fascination. …At the roofed gateway sat a massive stone figure, the twelfth-century builder himself. When we saw them, their function had not altered in any way since they had been built.

McKenzie-Grieves, 1956

第九章 厦门建筑 Amoy Architecture

鼓浪屿建筑（20世纪20年代） 四方型、灰泥粉刷、结实的拱形阳台面向大花园，我们的房子是通商口岸早期的典型建筑，最初是由葡萄牙人负责的。期间的演变，我不太清楚。房子看上去尽管笨拙，但挺适合厦门的气候条件：从需要炭火的冬天到扇子难以减轻闷热的夏天。更重要的是，这些房子象征着19世纪中叶居住在岛上开展对英贸易商人的尊严。没有什么地方不协调，因为它们适合自己的用途，拥有自己的个性。

Postcard Courtesy of Mr. George Yue

——麦肯兹·格瑞芙，1959年，第20页

咒骂小屋 岛上最令人好奇、最有吸引力的人造景观之一毫无疑问是埃黎丝女士和公司地产上的小平房，俗称"咒骂小屋"。小屋建在山顶，几乎与一块巨石的边缘叠在一起。这块巨石垂直矗立，高度大约50或60英尺。这样仙境般通风的住所可以捕捉人们所觊觎的夏季季风的每一次呼吸，令人羡慕。中国地方当局激烈反对。之后，小屋却在1876年建成。我们有理由相信，在墨西哥元的温柔影响和巧妙运用之下，当时以破坏风水为理由反对这个选址的官员不再阻拦。反对终于像雪花一样消融了。

——吉尔斯，1878年

永不过时的桥梁（20世纪20年代） 对我来说，罗马大剧场像一个空荡荡的蜂巢站在那里，裂开大口，里面了无生气。就连用伦巴第砖和罗马毛石建成的卢卡大剧场，也不过是用人工凿成的无数洞穴填满的。它的建设者和使用者都被埋进了历史。人们只记得它是真实的，但已经是一个传奇故事。在福建宏伟的石头桥上，人们在成群地移动。他们在思考、在演戏、在写作、在谈话，与他们的祖先700多年前完全一样。数百年来，挑担的、抬轿的、走路的人川流不息。强大的生活潮水没有减少、掺杂。精密编织的忍耐如此之普遍，在中国生活，人们接受它。之后又为之感到惊奇……

对我来说，福建的石桥有一种难以描述的魔力……桥头带有屋顶的关卡里，矗立着一尊巨大的石头像。它就是800多年前的造桥者本人。这些石桥自从建成之后，功能一直没有任何变化。

——麦肯兹·格瑞芙，1956年，第112、113页

老外看老鼓浪屿 *Old Gulangyu in Foreigners' Eyes*

Chinese View of Architectural "Preservation"

"Ancient" Nanputuo Monastery (1940s)   The monastery [Nan Pu Tuo] was of fairly modern construction, the only indication of its years being a plaque to commemorate the visit in 1906 of a foreign warship. Here and in other parts of China there was little opportunity to indulge in the pleasures of ruin sentimentality, as in Rome, Greece, Carthage, Syria or Egypt—countries which abounded in ancient temples, fallen palaces and crumbling walls that extended beyond the reaches of time to remind mankind of the glorious past.

Sitting Room MacGowan, 1914

This monastery was of recent structure, but even if it had been built many years ago, its architecture would have maintained the same appearance of modernity.   For the Chinese, accustomed to the ravages of war, pestilence and floods, planned their edifices so that if destroyed or injured, they could easily be rebuilt or repaired. The very frailty and transience of some buildings caused them to crumble and be resurrected, rhythmically like the death and rebirth of a Phoenix, with the same shape and outlines and with the same life. They had none of the colossal massiveness of an Egyptian pyramid or the great columns of a ruined Baalbek temple, but the eternal continuity of this and other Chinese temples was surely more awe-inspiring than the contemplation of dusty ruins. For they were reminders of the direct survival of a people and their buildings dating from a time when other fabulous ruins were in their full glory. Those stupendous temples of Syria and Chaldaea were built to last for thousands of years, and yet they and their people had soon fallen. But in China it was different. Chinese civilization and the vigour of its race had remained uninterrupted. Their architecture had remained the same. Most of the temples and palaces which they had built were flimsy structures but neither their sites nor their designs had ever been abandoned, being continuously renewed according to the same pattern. Their monasteries, founded hundreds of years ago, were not forgotten ruins covered in dust and desolation. As they had stood in the dim past, so they still stood alive and vibrant today with the same people, the same meanings and with the same purpose to which they had been dedicated so many years ago.

Nothing had changed. The roofs were the same, the vermilion pillars were of the same colour and shape, the Buddhas had suffered no alteration and the courtyards were peopled with monks in the same garb. Due to the rigid continuity of tradition and undisturbed continuity of life in this ancient land, I was in the present and yet I was in communion with the past. It seemed to make no difference and the phenomenon staggered me whenever I thought of it. These temples were not an isolated example of this unity between the present and past. There were many other buildings such as pavilions, ornamental ponds and tombs which destroyed the illusion of the abysses of time. Not only had these survived, but also the living men with whom they had been intimately associated.   The descendant in direct succession of that great sage Confucius himself lived in the same surroundings and in the same place in Shangtung as his illustrious ancestor…

Neill, 1956

第九章 厦门建筑 *Amoy Architecture*

中国人保护建筑的方法

"古"南普陀寺(20世纪40年代) 这个寺庙(南普陀)建筑相当现代。唯一能够证明其年代的是一块纪念1906年外国军舰到访的牌匾。在罗马、希腊、迦太基、叙利亚或埃及,大量的古庙、残垣断壁、废旧宫殿拥有漫长的历史,让人们想起它们辉煌的过去。在这里以及中国的其他地方,你没有机会沉溺于废墟情结的快感。

南普陀寺是最近建成的。即便是很久以前的建筑,它的建筑还是保持同样的现代风貌,因为经常遭受战争、瘟疫和水灾的侵袭,中国人在设计的时候已经考虑到,如果建筑物被毁或受创,可以不费力地重建或修复。一些建筑的脆弱和短命使得它们的崩溃和重建,就像凤凰涅槃一样富有规律:一样的外观,一样的结构,一样

Gentlemen's Country Home MacGowan, 1912

的生命力。它们没有埃及金字塔的宏伟,也没有巴尔贝克庙废墟的巨柱,但是这座庙和中国其他庙宇的永恒与持久确实比在废墟前的冥想更加令人敬畏,因为它们让人立即想起了一个民族及其建筑的遗物。当其他寓言般的废墟还处于全盛时期,这个民族和她的建筑却变成了遗物。叙利亚和迦勒底王国规模宏大的巴尔卑克神庙建筑寿命长达数千年,但是这些建筑和它们的民族很快就衰落了。中国却不同。中华文明一直生生不息,中华民族的活力从未衰败。它们的建筑风格一直得以延续。他们建造的大多数寺庙和宫殿结构都很脆弱,但建筑物的位置和设计风格从未被废弃。只是不断地根据原有的结构被更新。他们几百年前建造的寺庙都没有遗弃在尘土间、荒野外而变成废墟。它们曾经矗立在昏暗的历史里,如今,它们仍然与同样的人民、以同样的人生价值,朝着它们这么多年来所追求的同样的目标站立着,活力四射、充满生气。

没有发生任何变化。屋脊是一样的,柱子是一样的形状、一样的鲜红。佛像没有任何改变,寺庙里的和尚还是穿着同样的袈裟。在这片古老的土地上,传统被严格地传承着,生活不受惊扰地在延续着。我既是活在当今,同时也在跟过去对话。似乎没有什么差别。想起这种情况,我就有些犹豫、动摇。这些寺庙并非中国历史与现实的这种一致性的孤例。还有许多其他建筑,诸如亭榭、池塘和坟墓,它们摧毁了时间已经逝去很久的假象。不仅这些建筑物得以保存,与它们亲密相处的人们也幸存下来了。伟大圣贤孔子的直系后裔就跟他著名的祖先一样生活在山东的同一个地方、同样的环境里……

——尼尔,1956年,第133、134页

老外看老鼓浪屿 *Old Gulangyu in Foreigners' Eyes*

Gulangyu, January 1931　　　J. Nienhuis

THE ILLUSTRATED LONDON NEWS, MAY 15, 1880--477

NEW MASONIC HALL, KOOLANGSU, AMOY.

第九章 厦门建筑 *Amoy Architecture*

High tide, 22 September 1899 Native Custom House. Amoy Bund.

THE RESIDENCE OF LIM NEE KAR

Bowra, 1908

The Bund, Amoy

Postcard Courtesy of Mr. George Yue

老外看老鼓浪屿 *Old Gulangyu in Foreigners' Eyes*

AMOY.   Johnston, 1898

The Amoy Harbour

Postcard Courtesy of Mr.George Yue

第九章 厦门建筑 *Amoy Architecture*

Bank of The Hongkong and Shanghai Bank at Amoy Bowra,1908
(Acting Agent W.H.Wallace)

Gulangyu, Oct. 1937   J. Nienhuis

老外看老鼓浪屿 *Old Gulangyu in Foreigners' Eyes*

Chapter 10 Master Merchants of the Orient

Chinese Merchant Dukes, 1885

Smallest but Richest (1843)   The province of Fokien, in Amoy is situated, is the smallest of the provinces of China, is reckoned among the richest, on account of its extensive commerce.

Saturday Magazine, Jan. 21st, 1843

China's Wealthiest Merchants (1849)   The district in which this flourishing town is situated, is the most barren in all China, with the exception of Hong-Kong. In spite of these disadvantages, no spot in the empire, numbers so many wealthy and enterprising merchants as Amoy; from whence they have spread themselves all along the coast of China, and have established commercial houses in many parts of the Eastern Archipelago.

Sirr, 1849

Amoynese Outrival Cantonese (1856)   The men of Fokien are, nevertheless, considered to be the boldest and most energetic in China, and when our successes at Canton were talked of, the Chinamen only shrugged their shoulders, and said, "Wait till you go to Fokien; you will pay for it there."

Ball, 1856

Amoy Trade (1861)   The traffic is considerable. In 1847, 117 vessels entered the harbour, with an aggregate burthen of 16,494 tons; and the value of the imports, by British ships, during the same year, was 179,758L, by foreign vessels 75,975L; of the exports in British ships 7,139L., in foreign vessels 8,568L.   The principal exports are, crockery ware, umbrellas, tea, sugar, sugar-candy, paper, tobacco, camphor and grass-cloth. Population in 1847, 250,000.

King, 1861

Serie I. No. 4. **Amoy Harbor (photo by Dr. John Otte)** AMOY.

第十章　东方的商界高手

最小、但最富裕　福建省，下辖厦门，是中国最小的省份，但因其规模宏大的商业而被认为是中国最富庶的地方之一。
　　——《周六杂志》，1月21日，1843年

中国最富有的商人（1849年）　这座繁荣的小镇所在的区域是中国（香港除外）最贫瘠的地方。尽管条件不好，这个帝国没有一个地方比厦门拥有更多的富商。他们都很有魄力。从这里，他们足迹遍布中国沿海各地，并在南洋群岛的许多地方建立了商业机构。

Merchant Family　Anderson 1920

——瑟尔，1849年

厦门人胜过广东人（1856年）　不管怎么说，福建人被认为是最大胆、最精力旺盛的中国人。谈及我们在广东所取得的成绩，中国人只是耸了耸肩，说，"等到了福建，你们会为此付出代价的。"
——波尔，1856年，第170页

厦门贸易（1861年）　这里的贸易量相当可观。1847年，117艘船只进入厦门港，总载重量达16494吨。同一年，进口货物价值，英国船只带来的是179758英镑，其他外国船只，75975英镑；出口货物价值，英国船只运走的是7139英镑，其他外国船只8568英镑。主要的出口产品为陶瓷、雨伞、茶叶、蔗糖、糖果、纸张、烟草、樟脑和夏布。1847年，厦门的人口是25万。

Amoy Harbor　MacGowan, 1909

——金，1861年

老外看老鼓浪屿 Old Gulangyu in Foreigners' Eyes

Appearances Deceive The general appearance of the town of Amoy is anything but prepossessing. The houses are built irregularly, and have a frowsy, dilapidated look, that gives one the impression that the city is in anything but a flourishing condition. This would be an entirely wrong inference to draw, for the Chinese, in common with all Orientals, do not believe in beautiful business houses with magnificent fronts as essential to trade.

MacGowan, 1897

The Underrated Chinese Public opinion throughout Christendom underrates, we think, the intellectual capacity of the Chinese...the Chinese mind is eminently quick, shrewd, and practical. It has an intuitive logic of rare vigor and certainty. Admit the premises in the argument of a Chinese, and his conclusion is generally inevitable...As businessmen they are remarkably energetic, efficient, and adroit...The Yankee must rise early in the morning and keep wide awake all day if he expects to get to windward of a Chinaman before nightfall.

Maclay 1861

Why Bankruptcies Unknown ...'tis a fact that the Chinese merchant is considered absolutely reliable and honest in all business transactions. When a Chinese merchant says "Can do" after a verbal agreement, the European trader knows it will be done even if the Chinaman loses money. He drives a close bargain, but when the "Can do" is passed, his word will be kept. There are no bankruptcies...A failure would be a serious calamity, for the entire family would be held liable and probably heads would fall.

Caldwell, 1906

Business with Integrity There are honest merchants and tradesmen of high integrity. It was well known that, during the whole time that trade was carried on with China by the East India Company, there never was an instance of their losing money by the fraud or failure of a Chinese merchant; large sums of money were given to the Chinese by the Company for the purchase of tea in the interior of the country, where they were not allowed to go-often with nothing more than a verbal engagement-with perfect confidence on the one side, and with perfect fidelity on the other. Even if an individual or house of business failed, the family or friends would make up the loss. ... It was when unprincipled traders went into the China trade, after the abolition of the monopoly of the East India Company, that failures and frauds became a perplexity to the Governments of England and China, and led to recriminations, and insults, and war.

Amoy Harbor, 1934   J. Nienhuis

Johnston, 1898

第十章 东方的商界高手 Master Merchants of the Orient

表相靠不住　小城厦门的外貌相当讨人喜欢。这里的房屋建得不整齐，看上去很肮脏、破烂，让人想不到这是一个繁荣的城镇。但这种推论是完全错误的，因为，跟所有东方人一样，中国人并不相信，漂亮的商业大厦、宏伟壮观的门庭是生意的必备条件。

——麦嘉湖，1897 年，第 163 页

被低估的中国人　我们认为，整个西方世界都低估了中国人的智力……中国人的脑袋转得特别快。他们精打细算、讲究实际。他们少见的活力和确定性之间存在着必然、直观的联系。对中国人如果有先入之见，那么他的结论一般都是老一套……作为商人，他们精力特别旺盛、效率很高且机智、灵活……要在天黑前赶上中国人，美国人必须早起，并且终日不休。

——麦考利，1861 年，第 121、122 页

为何不知破产　事实是，在所有的商业交易中，中国人被视为完全可靠、诚实的。当中国商人与你达成口头协议之后说，"能做"，欧洲商人知道，生意肯定成了，哪怕中国商人赔钱。中国商人讨价还价逼得很紧，不过，"能做"一出口，他们就会信守诺言。没有破产的说法……生意失败可能会造成严重的灾难，因为整个家族都会被牵连，也许还会人头落地。

——凯德威尔，1906 年，第 96、97 页

诚实经商　中国人是高度诚信的诚实商人。众所周知，在东印度公司与中国进行贸易的整个过程中，没有发生过因中国商人欺诈、失信而造成亏本的情况。公司向中国商人支付大笔资金，请他们在公司未获许进入的内地代购茶叶，通常只有口头协议。但是，一方信心十足，另一方诚信有加。即便商业机构或某个商人生意失败，整个家族或朋友会先替他弥补损失。……只是后来东印度公司的贸易垄断权被取消之后，不讲道德的商人参与中国贸易竞争，失信、欺诈的事件开始成为困惑中英政府的事情，最终导致了相互指责、辱骂和战争。

Women Spinning　　Johnston, 1907

——约翰斯坦，1898 年，第 39、40 页

老外看老鼓浪屿 *Old Gulangyu in Foreigners' Eyes*

Amoy Money—Everything but Gold (1849) Every description of silver coin passes current in Amoy, by weight, Spanish dollars, Mexican ditto, Indian rupees, Dutch guilders, English shillings and sixpences, are taken by the natives with equal avidity. Gold the Chinese do not estimate as a circulating medium, and those parties who wish to pay for merchandise in doubloons or sovereigns, lose by the low rate given for these coins by the Chinese: nevertheless, gold is occasionally used in China as a circulating medium, as ingots, or bare of gold, of a very pure description, weighing several ounces, are given by the natives of Amoy for goods purchased of our traders.

Sirr 1849

Eight Pounds of Cash ^{Franck, 1925}

Strings of Cash In travelling, the carriage of money is a great annoyance, owing to the smallness of its value and the large number of coins or "cash" necessary to make up an amount of any size. Exchanging eighteen shillings English for brass cash, the weight of them amounted to seventy-two pounds, which had to be carried by the coolies. These cash have a square hole in the middle, and are strung together upon a piece of straw twist. Should the straw break, the loss of time in getting up the pieces is much more than the loss of the money. The Chinese are honest, very keen at a bargain, but when the bargain is made the Chinaman may be depended on to keep it.

Bishop 1900

40 Chinese Coin = One British Penny ^{MacGowan, 1914}

Millions in Pocket Change (1940s) "The market took a plunge recently," he said as he opened a green bag he was carrying, to reveal some bulging notes. "And I had to bring six million Chinese dollars to see you ashore."…

Neill, 1956

Amoy Laborers

Clever Carpenters The carpenter's tools at first sight seem rude and clumsy to a Yankee, but to see them handle them one must confess that they do not work so hard and can accomplish more than our carpenters. Take even their gimlets, for instance; instead of twisting their fingers almost out of joint, as I have sometimes done in making a small nail hole, they use a spindle drill, which they whirl rapidly round, by means of a staff and line, like a fiddle bow, and will make ten holes to my one and never split the timbers. They paint better than we do; the paint is mixed thick and one man passes along daubing on a coat of paint with a wad of tow, while another follows with a very fine and stiff brush, smoothing it over, leaving a fine polished surface.

Coffin, 1908

第十章　东方的商界高手　Master Merchants of the Orient

厦门的货币：黄金以外的任何东西（1849 年）　各种各样的银元在厦门按重量流通，西班牙银元、墨西哥银元、印度卢比、荷兰盾、英国先令和六便士银币，当地人一律热烈欢迎。中国人不使用黄金作为通货。他们给西班牙金币和英国金币的兑换率很低，那些想用金币支付货款的人遭受了损失。不过，黄金偶尔也会在中国被当作通货。厦门人会用金锭或很纯的足金，几盎司重，向我们的商人购买东西。

——瑟尔，1849 年

40 Chinese Coin = One British Penny　　MacGowan, 1914

串钱　旅行的时候，携带铜钱很麻烦，因为币值很小，要带上一笔钱，铜钱或"现金"的数量必须很大。用 18 英国先令兑换铜钱，重量达到 72 磅，必须请伙计挑着走。铜钱中央有一方孔，用绳子串起。要是绳子断了，把钱再串起来所花的时间比丢掉这些钱的损失还要多。中国人很诚实，热衷于讨价还价。一旦生意谈成了，中国人完全靠得住。

——毕夏普，1900 年

百万零花钱（20 世纪 40 年代）　"最近，市场一落千丈，"他一边说，一边打开随手携带的绿色袋子，露出一些大额钞票。"来接你上岸，我得带上六百万（中国）法币……"

——尼尔，1956 年，第 20、21 页

厦门劳力

聪明的木匠　乍一看，木匠的工具似乎很粗糙、笨拙。不过，看他们使用这些工具，你不得不承认，他们用不着那么卖命工作，完成的工作量也要比我们美国木匠多。比如说，手钻，我们快把手指的关节给扭弯，就像我挖个小洞的时候那样。中国人用的却是一把轴钻，用一条线和木轴，像提琴弓那样快速旋转。我挖一个洞，他们能钻十个，而且不会把木料搞裂。漆，他们也上得比我们好。他们把漆拌得很稠，一个师傅用一叠麻纤，边走边抹，先上一层漆。另一个师傅紧随其后，用很细密、坚硬的刷子，把漆抹匀，留下了一层光滑的表面。

——柯芬，1908 年，第 167、168 页

Mechanization or Men? The commonest criticism of the Chinese artisan is his failure to adapt machinery to his use, but where population is so enormous and the labor market so overcrowded, mass production would seem to offer only a threat to individual security. Better that many men sweat long hours at toil for small recompense than that the few prosper and the majority starve to death, argue the Chinese. Hard work holds no terrors for this industrious race, but insecurity is to be dreaded beyond all other fates. Leave a man his work and he will endure any and every calamity with fortitude; force idleness upon him and he will end in the depths of misery.

Lewis, 1938

Chinese Sawmill Anderson, 1920

Individual Industrialists If any one Chinese virtue occurs more widely and to m-ore marked degree than others, it is probably integrity in workmanship… Whether a potter struggling to perfect a glaze; an ivory carver laboring for years on a screen worth a king's ransom; or a humble housewife stitching shoe soles for her family, the same patient and painstaking attention is given to detail, the same effort poured into producing what will not only serve the immediate pursuit, but will have beauty and durability as well. Satisfaction in work well done seems to be its own reward in China; certainly no other is apparent in this land where labor, even when it becomes creative art—and only the thinnest line exists between Chinese artist and artisans—is the cheapest of all commodities.

This racial characteristic of thoroughness may be due to the Middle Kingdom's having been throughout the centuries a civilization composed of individual industrialists. The largest establishments rarely consisted of more than the proprietor and six or seven helpers; great factories and mills appeared only with the introduction of foreign methods. Any man trained in a craft could set up business for himself in his own home; doing all the work in person or being assisted by the members of his household until that day when he could afford to feed and shelter an apprentice.

Corner, 1847
Stone Cutter

Lewis, 1938

第十章　东方的商界高手　Master Merchants of the Orient

机械化，还是人工？ 对中国工匠批评最多的是他们没能机械化生产。在人口众多、劳力过剩的国度里，大规模生产似乎只会对个人的安全造成威胁。中国人认为，大家一起长时间劳作以获取微薄的报酬，好过少数人发财、多数人饿死。对于这个勤劳的民族来说，艰苦的工作并没有什么可怕，最可怕的是不稳定的生活。让中国人工作，他们能够坚强地承受所有一切灾难；强迫中国人赋闲，他们最终只能陷入悲惨的深渊。

Grinding Rice MacGowan, 1912

——列维斯，1938年，第61、62页

个人手工业者 如果说中国人有一个长处比别人更显著、更为人所知，那可能就是他们工艺方面的至善之美……陶工努力工作，让瓷器的釉面完美，象牙雕刻师可以在价值连城的屏风上用工多年，或者说纯朴的家庭主妇为自己的家人缝补鞋底，再小的细节也是给予了同样的耐心和勤勉。他们注入同样的心血，不仅是为补好鞋底，而且还要让鞋子漂亮、耐穿。在中国，对工作完美收官的满意本身似乎就是对自己的奖赏。尽管劳力有时会变成富有创造性的艺术，而且中国艺术家与艺术工匠之间只存在着一条纤细的连接线，但在中国这片土地上，没有任何一件事情比这更显而易见，那就是劳力是最便宜的商品。

Carpenter Anderson, 1920

中国人完全、彻底的民族特征也许可以归咎于数百年来中央帝国的文明是由个人手工业者构成的。在最大的商业机构，业主很少雇用超过六、七个帮工；大工厂、大作坊也仅局限于介绍国外的生产方式。受过训练的手艺人一般只在自己的家里营业，自己亲自动手，或者让家里人帮忙，直至他能供得起一个徒弟的食宿。

——列维斯，1938年，第57、58页

Amoy Coolie Trade

The notorious Coolie Trade appears to have commenced in the shipment of a hundred and fifty coolies from Amoy for South Australia in 1848; but soon afterwards grew to great proportions…In October, 1865, the ship Dea del Mare left Macao bound to Callao; on touching at Tahiti she had only 162 emigrants alive out of 550.

Thomson, 1888

Coolies Wait for Boat MacGowan, 1914

Bitter[1] Life of the Coolie For a few years past a great number of Chinese coolies have been sent from this country to Peru, to work in the mines and on the Guano islands. The poor creatures are induced to embark on these expeditions by fraudulent representations. They have not the means of paying for their passage, and are induced to bind themselves to work three years for their food and clothing, and at the expiration of that time to be free. But when once there they become slaves, and worse than slaves, for their master or owner has no inducement to keep them in good working condition when their time of service is drawing to a close. The most horrible accounts have been received from Peru within the last year, yet still the traffic is carried on, generally by foul means.

… How prone is human nature to oppression. A braggart whom the accident of birth and fortune has placed in a station above some of his fellow creatures, treats those over whom he has a temporary authority as though they were not of the same flesh and blood as himself, a sure sign of a miserable coward when brought in contact with his equals. …

Coffin, 1908

U.S. Consul Helps End Coolie Trade At the close of the year, 1866, General Le Gendre was appointed U.S. Consul to Amoy, where he at once displayed his administrative ability and rectitude of character by a thorough reform of the office, into which innumerable abuses had insensibly crept. He needed no Civil Service reform commission to instruct him to his duty. In 1867 a French coolie ship which was chartered by an American reached Amoy with her illicit cargo. The American captain was instantly arrested by consul Le Gendre, punished by fine and imprisonment, and the coolie trade definitely broken up…

Stevens, 1880

---

1 "Coolie" is from the Chinese for "bitter effort," or kuli (苦力).

第十章 东方的商界高手 Master Merchants of the Orient

厦门苦力贸易（猪仔买卖）

臭名昭著的"苦力贸易"似乎起源于1848年的厦门。当时，150名苦力从这里乘船出发，前往澳大利亚南部。很快，苦力贸易就迅速发展起来了……1865年10月，"迪德玛丽"号离开澳门，前往秘鲁西部的卡亚俄。到美国大溪地岛的时候，船上550名苦力只活下来了162人。

——汤姆逊，1888年

A Wood Carrier　Darley, 1903

苦力的苦涩生活　几年后，大批的中国苦力被送往秘鲁挖矿，或在关岛干体力活。这些可怜的劳力被不诚实的买办引诱，走上了这条不归路。由于中国苦力无法支付船票，因此被诱签约卖身三年用以支付旅费和食宿费用。契约期满，方可赎得自由身。一到目的地，他们变成了奴隶，甚至比奴隶更惨，因为契约期快满的时候，他们的主人或雇主就没有动力让他们保持良好的工作条件。去年还收到了来自秘鲁有关中国苦力最可怕的报道，但是苦力买卖还在继续，通常都是通过肮脏的手段。

Coolies　MacGowan, 1897

……人性对压迫是那么的自然。会自夸的人，他偶然的出生和财富已经凌驾于他的同胞之上。当他们暂时拥有管理权的时候，他们对自己同胞形同陌路。但是，跟自己地位相同的人接触时，他们却完完全全是一副可怜懦夫的模样……

——柯芬，1908年，第172～174页

美国领事帮助结束苦力贸易　1866年接近年关的时候，勒·琴德将军被任命为美国驻厦门领事。在厦门，他立即展示了自己的管理能力和正直的性格。他彻底改革了领事工作，清除了在不知不觉中蔓延的许多陋习。他无须内务改革委员会的指导就展开工作。1867年，一名美国商人租赁的法国苦力船载着非法的货物（苦力）抵达厦门。这位美国船长立马遭到了勒·琴德领事的逮捕，并被判罚金和监禁。苦力贸易就此宣告结束……

——史蒂文斯，1880年，第397页

Amoy Fishermen

Daring Fujian Fishermen Of all the Chinese fishermen, which is a very numerous class of people, the natives of Fuhkeen [Fujian] are the most enterprising and daring. The greater part of the Chinese coast is visited by them; they brave all dangers for a scanty livelihood, and suffer the severest hardships to return to their families with five dollars after the toils of a whole year.

Fishing with Cormorants   MacGowan, 1907

Gutzlaff, 1834

Amoy Aquaculture The excellence of the fish supply must strike the most casual observer. Both river and sea fish, salt and fresh, are conspicuous by their abundance, as is also the supply of bamboo oysters, so called because they are artificially bred on this coast, where bamboo oyster-fields are prepared more carefully than any hop-field or vineyard. Holes are bored in old oyster shells, which are then stuck into pieces of split bamboo about two feet in length. These are planted close together on sand flats between high and low water-mark, where strong tidal currents are said to bring the oyster spat. Certainly, the said spat is soon found adhering to the old shells, which in due time are covered with tiny oysters. The bamboos are then transplanted and set several inches apart; and within six months from the date when they were first planted they yield a crop of well-grown oysters ready for the market. Nor are even the shells wasted; for though Chinamen have learned to appreciate the luxury of transparent glass, a large number of oyster-shells are still scraped down till they are so thin as to be translucent, when, neatly fitted together (like the diamond panes in the casements of our ancestors), they form the ornamental windows in the inner courts of rich men's houses.

Miss Gordon-Cumming. 1888

Amoy Fishermen, 1930s   J. Nienhuis

第十章 东方的商界高手 Master Merchants of the Orient

厦门渔民

勇敢的福建渔民　中国的渔民数量庞大。在所有的中国渔民中,福建本地渔民胆子最大,最富有冒险精神。他们到过中国大部分沿海地区。他们冒着各种各样的风险,为的是获得微不足道的生计。他们经历了最艰难的困苦。一年劳累,带回家里的只有五元钱。

——古慈拉夫,1834 年,第 417 页

厦门水产　即使最漫不经心的旁观者也会对厦门上乘的鱼类供应留下深刻印象。无论是淡水鱼还是海鱼,新鲜的还是腌制的,其丰富程度是有目共睹的。竹蚝也一样。之所以被称为竹蚝,是因为它们是在沿海人工养殖的。养竹蚝的滩涂地整理得比任何牛蛙地或葡萄园更认真、仔细。把竹子劈成长约两英尺的薄片,在旧海蛎壳上钻孔,再把他们粘在竹片上,然后把粘满海蛎壳的竹片根据高低不同的水位线一片接一片地栽种在滩涂地上。据说,强大的潮汐流会把蚝苗带进来。当然,上述的蚝苗很快就会黏附

CHINESE FISHERMEN.

在旧海蛎壳上。不久,旧海蛎壳就沾满了小海蛎。这时候就要把竹片移动一下,让竹片与竹片之间有几英寸的空间。从竹片栽到海滩上那天算起,6 个月内,海蛎就长大成熟、可以上市了。甚至连壳也不会被浪费。因为,尽管中国人已经学会欣赏奢华的透明玻璃,但是他们还是愿意把大量的海蛎壳打磨,直到它们变得又薄又透明。然后,他们再将这些半透明的海蛎壳整齐地串起来(像我们祖先窗户上的钻石玻璃),为富裕人家的内院装饰窗户。

——戈登·坎明小姐,1888 年,第 314~316 页

老外看老鼓浪屿 Old Gulangyu in Foreigners' Eyes

Ancient Oyster Beds The culture of oysters is practiced in the neighbourhood of Amoy on a large scale, and very successfully... it appears that artificial oyster-beds were formed in this country long before they are known to have existed amongst the Romans; and while we in Europe are still writing essays and pamphlets on the theory of the subject, this practical people have been obtaining good results for the last 1,800 years.

Shore, 1881

Amoy Boat Life

Green Amoy Junks The junks of Amoy have this peculiarity, namely, being painted a bright green colour at the bow ; the inhabitants call their vessels green heads, to distinguish them from the Canton junks, which being painted a brilliant red, are termed red head. ...

Sirr, 1849

Boat Life, 1924   J. Nienhuis

Amoy Sampan Life
Let us step on board some of those sampans. Each is about the capacity of an average-sized Thames punt, but as light and flimsy as papier mache, and is covered with a gipsy shaped awning, beneath which an entire family, consisting of, say, father, mother, and three children, cooks, eats, sleeps, and has its being; I will not say dresses, because they wear no clothes worth mention, and I have an opportunity of observing that the funny little stomachs of the child imps are swollen to amazing protuberance. And then, oh wonder of wonders, the sampan is as clean and tidy as a new fourpenny bit...Sometimes, it is true, this virtue is rather marred by the presence of a pig on board, but he is a small, quiet, tidy, dog-like pig, and is unobtrusive, as though ashamed of his own existence. Quack! Why here is a duck tied up in the corner, so sleek and fat. Some day he will furnish a feast for the entire family in this little flesh-eating community.

Look at the bright hothouse plants ranged around the extreme edge of the sampan, they alone give an aspect of prettiness to the craft, each of which is thus decorated. And the mother sits, busy with some feminine nothingness, on boards so clean that you might eat dinner off them. Every vestige of bedding, cooking, and household apparatus is stowed neatly away in a hollow in the bows. The women's pillows are curious wooden blocks, rivaling in comfort, it may be supposed, the stones or swordhilt which is recommended in the ' Soldier's Pocketbook.' But the Chinese female's pillow merely acts as a support to the small of the neck. She dares not rest her head on it lest she should thereby disarrange that tower of starched hair which she has spent hours in erecting, and which she contrives to keep unrumpled for many days.

第十章　东方的商界高手 Master Merchants of the Orient

古代的海蛎养殖场　厦门附近地区大量养殖海蛎,而且很成功……看来,中国比罗马更早建造了人工海蛎养殖场。我们欧洲人还在写文章、发册子讨论海蛎养殖场的理论时,务实的中国人已经在 1800 年前就获得了满意的成果。

——肖尔,1881 年,第 83 页

厦门的海上生活

绿色的厦门小船　厦门的平底小船有一个特点,那就是,船头涂成翠绿色。当地居民称这种船为"绿头",以区别于涂成鲜红色的广东船——"红头"……

——瑟尔,1849 年

厦门的船家生活

让我们上几艘小船看看。每艘小船的容量与泰晤士河上的中等体积的平底船差不多,却跟用混凝纸浆做的船只一样轻便、脆弱。船上的天篷与吉普赛人的大篷车形状一样,下面住着整个家庭,包括,比如说,父亲、母亲和三个小孩,吃喝拉撒,一辈子都生活在船上。我不提服装,因为他们身上穿的几乎不值一提。有一次,我看见船上的小顽童肚子胀得圆鼓

Boat children, Amoy, 1922　　J. Nienhu

鼓,实在令人称奇。更奇怪的是,小船非常干净、整洁,就像一枚崭新的便士……有时候,说实在的,这种优点被船上圈养的猪给破坏了。小猪很安静、干净,像一条狗,非常谦虚、客气,好像对自己出现在船上感到羞愧。嘎嘎!船上的一个角落里绑着一只鸭子,油光光的,养得很肥。总有一天,它会变成船上这个小小食肉人家的一顿美餐。再看看小船四周环绕的鲜艳温室植物。每艘船上都是这样,它们给小船增添了一丝的亮丽。母亲坐在船上,忙着女人的杂事。船很干净,你可以在甲板上用餐。每一件被褥、餐具和居家用品被整齐地摆放在船头的凹陷处。女人的枕头是用木头做成的,很奇特。可以想象,它肯定跟《士兵手册》所推荐的石头或剑柄一样很舒服。但是,中国妇女的枕头只是她们纤细脖子的撑架。她不敢把头靠在枕头上,因为她们担心这样做会弄乱自己花了好几个小时才盘起来的头发。她们希望自己的发型还能继续保持一些日子。

老外看老鼓浪屿 *Old Gulangyu in Foreigners' Eyes*

The children of tender age skip about as securely as though in a large nursery ... Surely, with all the care in the world, they must sometimes topple over, or be jerked into the water? Ah, I see, you have provided for that contingency by fastening round the child's waist a long, light cord, to which a float is attached, and which, bobbing about as though a huge salmon were at the end, enables you to lug out the little amphibious animal...

Knollys, 1885

Amoy Boats Faster than English Boats In a letter addressed to the juvenile contributors to the China Mission, Mr. Johnston gives a lively account of one of his excursions in the boat which he had got built, for the purpose of paying visits to the towns and villages on the river. He named it "Hokyun Chun",[2] Good News Boat, and had found great advantage in having it, over using the ordinary passage boats. In describing it to his youthful readers, he says,

"It is not like anything you have seen in England. It is a genuine Chinese boat, and that is not to he seen anywhere but in China; so I must describe it to yon as well as I can. Suppose yourself to be looking at a wooden swan, about twenty-three feet long by ten feet wide, with a little cabin six feet by four, standing about two feet above the back, which has been made even and boarded over; and if, instead of the long neck, you put a pair of eyes on the breast, and paint the whole blue, you will have a good idea of the cut of my boat. Add to this, one tall mast, and one short one at the head, with square sails made of bamboo poles across, and a thin network of bamboo slips, lined with bamboo leaves, with the necessary ropes, and oars, and anchor, and rudder, and we are folly rigged. A strange cut and rig you will think it, and some wise youth will say, "She has too much breadth of beam for her length; and if she's round in the bottom, like the body of a swan, she won't take hold of the water;' but that is just what the Chinese wish their boats not to do; instead of making their boats to go through the water and giving them the form of a fish, as in England, they make them to skim over the water, and give them the form of a water-fowl. In this they are right; and I think there are few boats in England that could keep up with the Amoy boats; with a fair wind and tide, I have often gone from six to seven miles in half an hour.

Barbour, 1855

---

2 Hokyun Chun: Amoy Dialect of Fuyin Chuan (福音船); "Gospel Boat"

第十章 东方的商界高手 Master Merchants of the Orient

年幼的小孩在船上蹦蹦跳跳，好像在大型托儿所里……当然，即使再小心，他们有时候也会翻船，或掉入水中吧？噢，我明白了。应对这种紧急情况，他们在小孩的腰部系上了一根长长的细绳，绳子的一端绑着一个浮筒。绳子摆动的时候，好像一头巨大的三马哈鱼上钩，让你捞出水陆两栖的小动物……

——诺利斯，1885 年，第 273～275 页

厦门船快过英国船　在一封写给到中国传教的年轻人的信中，约翰逊先生生动地描述了他在船上的旅行经历。这艘船是他专门为访问河边村镇而建造的，被命名为"福音船"。　约翰逊先生生发现，比起普通的渡船，福音船优势很大。在向他的年轻读者描述时，他说：

"（福音船）不像你们在英国看到的那种船。这是一艘真正的中国船，只有在中国才看得见。因此，我必须尽可能详细地向你描述。先想象你这会儿看到的是一只木头天鹅，大约 23 英尺长，10 英尺宽，小船舱 6×4 英尺大，矗立在福音船尾部，高约 2 英尺。船的尾部已经弄平，小船舱就架在上面。假设说，天鹅的眼睛不是长在头上，而是在胸部，而且全身蓝色，那么，你完全可以想象我的福音船是怎么的一个模样。船头还有长短不一的两根桅杆，上面横挂着用竹竿做成的方帆和竹片做的薄网，用竹叶做里，加上必要的绳子、木桨、锚和舵，我们的装备就这样齐全了。你可能会以为这是一艘造型、装备奇怪的小船，一些内行的年轻人可能会说，'船的横梁太宽，超过船的长度'，如果像天鹅那样平底，那么她就无法吃水。'可是，中国人就不想让船吃水。英国人把船造得像一条鱼，让它在水里穿行；中国人却把船造得像一只水鸟，让它掠过水面。在这方面，他们非常正确。我想，风和日丽的情况下，没有几艘英国船能赶上厦门船。我的福音船经常半个小时走六、七英里。"

——巴博，1855 年，第 64～66 页

Fisherman Poles His Boat　Franck, 1925

143

Eastern Tortoise, Western Hare! (true story!). On one occasion a race had been arranged for between two cutters —one managed by an English crew and the other by ordinary Chinese boatmen. The former were men who had been selected with great care from a British man-of-war, whilst the others were men who were daily getting their living by rowing passengers across a broad river. The contest was a peculiar one, for, it was meant to be a test of the powers of endurance of the men of the East and the West, and so it was decided that the course should extend to a large village in the interior nearly twenty miles distant.

Looking at the crews as they sat in their boats waiting for the signal to start, one felt that there could not be the least doubt as to which would be the winner. The bluejackets [British] in their well-known uniform looked the very picture of strength. They were big, brawny men, with thews and muscles that seemed to be made of iron. These men could never tire, one thought, and there was a proud and confident look on their faces that made one feel that there was no doubt in their hearts as to who should gain the victory.

The Chinamen, on the other hand, with the careless, indolent way in which they are accustomed to hold themselves, gave on the impression that they could never hold out to the end of the journey.

They had never been made to sit upright, and they lounged on their seats as though the whole thing were a vast joke. There was an amused smile on their faces, and they were, no doubt, tickled at the idea that they were going to compete with the famous English, whose deeds of prowess had often been exhibited, to the detriment of their Empire.

At last the signal was given, and away the boats started on their long race. The English got away with a swing, and soon they were far ahead of their Chinese competitors, who continued to row with an even, steady pull upon their oars as though they were quite unconcerned at the rapid progress that the English were making ahead of them.

The beat and the rhythm of the sounds that came from their boat never quickened, nor was there any excitement in the faces of the men, but with a calmness and serenity typical of the East they kept on with their measured strokes, apparently indifferent whether they won or not.

By the time that they had gone ten miles the English crew began to show signs of distress. Their faces were flushed, and their clothes were wet with perspiration, whilst the vigorous swing and dip of their oars with which they had begun the race had lost their naturalness, and were not the result of a strained effort that had begun to feel the stress that was laid upon their powers. The Chinese, on the other hand, seemed absolutely unchanged from what they were when they first started. There was no sign of distress on the faces of any one of them, and their pull was steady and regular as though the men were pieces of machinery that were being moved by some invisible force that brought no fatigue upon the rowers.

In the meanwhile the boats were drawing nearer to each other, apparently without any special effort on the part of the Chinese, and finally the latter took the lead and easily came in victors without any signs of strain or fatigue such as were seen in the English crew when the long, exhaustive race was ended.

MacGowan, 1913

第十章　东方的商界高手　Master Merchants of the Orient

编者注：在海上，谁跑得快？下面的真实故事将给你拨开迷雾。

东方龟，西方兔！　　中国人总体来说是精力充沛和健康的民族。我很肯定，这主要是因为他们为了谋生而工作不息。在中国旅游时，中国人劳动不知疲倦令人惊叹，我常想他们是如何承受岁月的折磨而变得像现在这样强壮和坚毅。赖以糊口的粗陋食物，超强的日常劳动，造就了这样一个民族，他们的强健和坚韧在生活中随处可见。

一次有人安排了一场比赛——参赛的一方是英国水手，另一方是普通的中国船夫。前者是从一艘英国军舰上精心挑选出来的，而后者的工作是每天把行人摆渡到大河对岸。这是一场罕见的竞赛，因为它是东西方男人之间耐力的较量，赛道的终点定在大约20英里外的一个大村庄。

看着水手们坐在船上等待出发信号，毫无疑问英方将取胜。身穿著名蓝色水手服的英国人看起来充满力量。他们身材高大，肌肉发达，像是钢铁铸成，永远不会疲倦，脸上流露出的骄傲和自信表明，他们将赢得绝对胜利。

相反，那些中国人一如平时所表现的那样随意懒散，让人感觉他们肯定坚持不到终点。

他们从不坐直身体，而是斜靠在座位上，好像整个比赛不过是一场儿戏。在中国，经常可以见到这些赫赫有名的英国人"累累战功"的破坏痕迹，和他们比赛，着实令中国人感到讽刺，于是大家都面露笑意。

信号终于发出，两条船开始了漫长的赛程。英国人"一桨当先"，很快就把中国人远远地甩在后面。中国人则始终平稳匀速地划桨，仿佛一点也不关心英国人正在拉开距离。

他们划船的节奏一点也没有加快，脸上也看不到丝毫兴奋的表情，而是以东方人特有的平和冷静整齐地划桨，显然他们不在乎输赢。

船到10英里处，英国水手颓势初现。他们的脸变得通红，衣服被汗水浸湿，出发时有力的摆臂划桨动作也开始变形了，这可不是因为他们感到比赛压力而在故作努力。相反，那些中国人看起来和出发时没什么两样。他们脸上都看不到沮丧，划桨也是坚定有序如同机器一般，仿佛有种无形的力量将他们的疲劳一扫而光。

其间，中国人并没有特别卖力，但两条船越来越近了，最后中国人反超并轻松取胜。经过漫长艰苦的比赛，英国人看上去非常紧张疲劳，而中国人却一点事也没有。

中国人是健壮刚毅的民族，体能强大，这让他们能够年复一年地承受持续劳作带来的磨难。英国工人赖以休闲的众多假日在中国是不存在的。这里没有礼拜天，不能像英国人那样，每七天享有一天基督教的休息日。虽然一年中依照民俗，确实有几天节日可以停止工作休息一下，但除此之外的每天，人们劳动不息……

有两种现象在中国是并存的。一方面，全国人民大都健康充满活力，每个阶层的劳动者都任劳任怨，直到上了年纪才不得不干点轻活；另一方面，大量的病患存在于各个地区，但偶然经过的路人永远也不会发现这个事实。因为在忍受病痛方面，中国人堪称英雄。如果需要，他们会默默地承受痛苦和死亡，而不会将烦恼流露，否则生活对他们而言就成了一种折磨。

——麦嘉湖，1913年

Amoy Farmers

Smiling Hills and Valleys Spring brought a smile to every fertile valley and treeless hill. Like the folks who lived upon it, the soil of China seemed blessed with irrepressible hope.

MacGuire, 1946

World's Best Farmers There are no more clever farmers in the world. Their farms are exceedingly small, compared with American farms. They are kept under a high state of cultivation, and around about Amoy are expected to yield two crops each year.

Their little farms of half an acre to three or four acres, some terraced one above the other up the hillside, have more the appearance of garden spots than otherwise.

Pitcher, 1893

Three Harvests a Year A farmer has a rice field which Nature, in response to his marvelous skill in husbandry, clothes with abundant crops three times a year. It is a course of blessing to his family, which flock to it when the harvest time comes round, and gather with joy and with laughter the golden grain that is to being plenty to the home.

MacGowan, 1897

2,000 Feet of Terraces At first the hills rise abruptly from the water's edge on either side, those to the south rising to a height of two thousand feet rugged and bare, except where the indomitable energy and industry of the Chinese have planted their little crop of rice on terraced slopes, or in nooks and crannies which seemed from our point of view as inaccessible as the nest of the eagle. On other parts of these barren hills, graves, neatly kept, in the form of the last letter of the Greek alphabet, Ω, relieve the eye and suggest food for thought."

PLOWING, CHINESE FASHION

Johnston, 1898

第十章 东方的商界高手 Master Merchants of the Orient

厦门农民

"Red-Tiled Cottages amongst the Banyans."
Johnston, 1907

微笑的小山和山谷 春天给每个肥沃的山谷和每座光秃秃的山头带来了笑容。中国这片土地跟生活在它上面的人民一样似乎充满了无限的希望。
——麦克圭尔,1946 年,第 34 页

世界上最棒的农民 世界上没有(比中国农民)更聪明的农民了。与美国农场相比,他们的农田特别得小。农田的耕作水平很高,厦门及其周边地区,农作物一年可收获两次。

他们的农田从半英亩到三、四英亩,有些农田就修建在山坡上,就是一层叠一层的梯田,外表看上去更像是园艺场。
——毕腓力,1893 年,第 40 页

一年收三季 好像是大自然对他非凡耕作技术的奖赏,有一位农民的稻田一年可收获三季的农作物。这对他的家庭来说是一个欢乐的过程。收获季节一到,他们纷纷聚集到稻田里,欢声笑语收获给家庭带来富足的金黄稻谷。
——麦嘉湖,1897 年,第 176 页

2000 英尺高的梯田 山峰从小河的两岸直刺云霄。小河南岸的山峰高度 2000 英尺,层峦叠嶂、山石裸露。中国人以不屈不挠的勇气和勤奋,在梯状的山坡上和悬崖峭壁上种植水稻。在我们看来,这些地方跟鹰巢一样难以企及。在这些贫瘠山坡的另一侧,造型像希腊语最后一个字母 Ω 的坟墓整齐排列,让人们的眼睛感到很舒服,同时也想到了自己的归宿。
——约翰斯坦,1898 年,第 19 页

Amoy Irrigation, 1922   J. Neinhuis

Anxi Farms On a second visit to the North, I and Mr. Barclay accompanied Dr. Douglas and Mr. Rapalje, of the American Mission, who were a committee of Presbytery to visit Chinchew [Quanzhou], with the view of organizing it as a congregation under elders. We had by the way a mission tour in the tea country of Ankoi [Anxi] from which there are several church members in Amoy, but where hitherto no mission has undertaken work.

We entered the Ankoi region by crossing a magnificent chain of mountains (visible from Amoy), which rise almost from the sea level to a height of some thousands of feet. From the top of the pass,

Rainy Day in a Rice Paddy, 1920s   J. Nienhuis

by which we crossed, we should have seen Amoy Island, had not the day been dull. The descent on the Ankoi side is along the brink of a chasm, with an almost perpendicular descent of over a thousand feet. This is the high road (not more than five or six feet wide), between two important and populous districts. On the opposite side of the chasm the spurs of the mountain sloped down more gradually, and it was astonishing to see to what a height their sides were terraced, so that to reach the upper ones from the valley below and get back again seemed likely to be in itself good part of a day's work. The lower terraces grow rice; those above, sugar-cane, millet, wheat, &c.; those still farther up, potatoes, beans, &c., while highest of all would be grown pea-nuts, and such other things as best stand draught.

Macgregor's letter, 1875

Amoy Farmer, 1920s   J. Nienhuis

4,000 Years of Farming We had long desired to stand face to face with Chinese and Japanese farmers; to walk through their fields and to learn by seeing some of their methods, appliances and practices which centuries of stress and experience have led these oldest farmers in the world to adopt. We desired to learn how it is possible, after twenty and perhaps thirty or even forty centuries, for their soils to be made to produce sufficiently for the maintenance of such dense populations as are living now in these three countries. We have now had this opportunity and almost every day we were instructed, surprised and amazed at the conditions and practices which confronted us whichever way we turned; instructed in the ways and extent to which these nations for centuries have been and are conserving and utilizing their natural resources, surprised at the magnitude of the returns they are getting from their fields, and amazed at the amount of efficient human labor cheerfully given for a daily wage of five cents and their food, or for fifteen cents, United States currency, without food.

King, 1911

第十章　东方的商界高手　Master Merchants of the Orient

安溪农田　第二次向北旅行,巴考利先生和我是陪美国传教团道格拉斯博士和拉帕杰先生而去的。他们是长老教会委员会的成员,到泉州访问,想把泉州纳入他们的会众。我们顺路到茶乡安溪传教。这里有厦门教区的几座教堂,但传教工作一直没有开展。

Threshing, 1922　　J. Nienhuis

我们翻过无数座山峰(海拔均在上千英尺以上,可远眺厦门),进入安溪。要不是旅途单调、枯燥,我们在所翻过的山峰上肯定可以看到厦门岛。从山顶下到安溪,我们几乎行走在峡谷的边缘,悬崖峭壁的高度几乎在 1000 英尺以上。这是连接两个人口较多的重要地区的官道(宽度不过五、六英尺)。峡谷的对面是山峰的支脉,山坡平缓多了。梯状的山坡很高,从谷底到山顶,再从山顶回到谷底似乎用去了一天的大部分时间。真是惊心动魄啊! 山坡较低处的梯田种水稻,再高一些的地方种甘蔗、小米、小麦等,再往上就是土豆、豆类作物等,最高处种花生以及其他耐旱作物。

——麦克格雷高的信件,1875 年

4000 年的耕作史　很久以前,我们就希望跟中国和日本的农民面对面,到他们的田里去走一走,亲眼目睹他们的耕作方式、耕作工具和习惯,并向他们学习。数百年来的苦难和经验让世界上最古老的农民吸收了这些耕作方式和习惯。我们想知道,在 2000 多年、也许 3000 多年、甚至 4000 多年之后,他们的土地是如何生产出足

Amoy Farm Folk, 1921　　J. Nienhuis

够的粮食来养活这三(二)个国家密度如此之大的人口。现在,我们终于找到了机会。几乎每一天,无论走到哪里,我们都会碰到一些令人惊奇、意外的情况和做法。数百年来,这些国家一直、并且还在用各种方法和手段保护和利用自己的自然资源。这些做法让我们受到教诲。他们从土地上得到了巨大回报,他们高效率的劳动量换来的是,按美国货币计算,每天 5 美分(包伙食),或 15 美分(不包伙食)的报酬。这一切,都让我们感到无比惊奇。

——金,1911 年

▶ 149

老外看老鼓浪屿 *Old Gulangyu in Foreigners' Eyes*

Chapter 11   Amoy Street Life

Second Hand Bookvendor, 1934

Street Life   These main streets are capital places for seeing how the Chinese live. Everything is open to the public. What they talk about, what they eat, how they spend their time, and how hard the majority of them have to work can all be seen by a quiet walk down any of them. It is amazing in what a narrow space a Chinese family can live, and how many families can be accommodated in a house that, according to our ideas, is capable of giving room to only one…This is their home, where their lives are spent. During the summer the place is stiflingly hot, and it is a mystery to us how human beings can live and seem moderately happy in such a terrible atmosphere. I presume they have not much time to think about the heat. The great problem with them is how they shall earn enough to pay the rent, and feed and clothe the family…

The pleasures they enjoy are very few. As they know nothing of the Sunday, every day is a work-day to them…

MacGowan, 1895

An Amoy Street   MacGowan, 1907

第十一章　厦门街头生活

街头生活　主街是了解中国人生活的重要场所。在街头，所有的一切都暴露在公众视线里。悄悄地沿着任何一条街道，他们所谈论的事情，所吃的东西，他们如何消磨时光，以及他们大多数人如何努力工作都会暴露在你的眼皮底下。看到一个中国家庭挤在狭窄的空间里，还有好几个家庭共享一座房子（这样的房子在我们看来只能供一户人家使用）

Amoy Harbor Pear Seller

实在令人称奇……这就是他们的家，他们一生居住的家。夏天，房子闷热无比。人怎么能在这样恶劣的环境中生活，并似乎活得相当地快乐，这对我们来说是一个谜。我认为，他们肯定没有多少时间可以去想热的问题。对他们来说，如何赚足够的钱来支付房租，并让家人吃饱穿暖才是重要的问题……

他们享受的乐趣实在少得可怜。他们不知道安息日。对他们来说，每天都是工作日……

——麦嘉湖，1895 年，第 32 页

Walking Restaurant (1920s)

老外看老鼓浪屿 *Old Gulangyu in Foreigners' Eyes*

Lively Amoy (1920s)   Kites flew in the hot September sky: hundreds of them in different shapes, at different levels above the roofs of the city. Leaning on his oars, our boatman pressed back the water with his whole weight, driving the sampan under the painted eyes of junks, under the bows of freighters, little coastal steamers, the Japanese and French gunboats. We were among a hundred of the sampans, loaded with limp green vegetables, saffron bean-curd cakes, with squealing pigs in wicker cylinders, piping, heaving baskets of chicks, with women, with men, with coffins. Our ears were stormed by cries, shouts, laughter, hoots, steam-whistles, winches...

The granite-slabbed streets, shut off from the sea by shops, from the sun by jutting awnings, by red, gold and black suspended signboards, were full. Men in long gowns and short satin over-jackets, men naked to the waist, beggars in filthy rags, country women in black or blue cotton trousers and head cloths, city women, young and emancipated in 'Shanghai' dresses, old and hobbling on bound feet and ebony canes. And everywhere children, darting on errands, on the end of kite strings, collecting round the ambulant kitchens, the sweetmeat vendors; sick and dying infants displayed by begging mothers, and all but the babies pushing and pushed by each other, by the loaded polecarriers, the bearers of a rich citizen's sedan chair, all laughing, shouting, hawking, spitting, talking at the top of their voices.

MacGowan, 1914
Beggar

The shops displayed sacks of millet, rice, beans, pickled eggs, jars of purple and green sauces, and pork crawling with flies; cottons, brocaded silks, cloth shoes, little saucers of carved jade pieces, and jade rings, bracelets and beads. Images, baskets, birds in cages, pottery decorated with bold blue brushwork, incense, herbs, copper pots, brass ladles. Apothecaries purveyed drugs, dried beetles, tiger bones, bezoar stones, elephant dung, turtle shell, aspirin, 'Lung Tonic' and 'Tiger Balm'.

There was no bad craftsmanship, no botched job. Even the smallest presentation packet was folded with red paper, elaborately knotted in red and white string. In the pawnshops among the greasy filth of worn padded clothing-the dusty rubbish heap which was the most precious stock in trade-glowed the rich, discarded trappings of dynastic circumstance: exquisite embroidery from sleeves, from skirts, the bird and dragon symbols of rank, unparalleled lavishness of craftsmanship for a few cents.

There was a lavishness, too, of rich material-coral, crystal, enamel, rose-quartz, silver-gilt objects inlaid with shimmering kingfisher feathers, amulets intricately adorned: a tiger claw became a curving gold-finned and headed fish, a bat, a lotus, delicately elaborated in tarnished silver-gilt, and buckets, literally buckets, of cornelian beads like sunset-tinged shingle with the sea receding. Cut and polished in Amoy they were used, we were told, for the necklaces of office in Imperial days, yet I never saw a cornelian one among the still strung Mandarin necklaces. Carved ivory or bone with blue and green enameled plaque and pendants, or sometimes jade with coral, rose-quartz and amethyst, they lay gleaming in the dust, incredibly neglected for rags to cover men from the cold. Outside the shops stood huge earthenware jars of night-soil and urine, which were kept to manure the vegetable gardens on the city's outskirts. To save labour they were not emptied until they were full...

Mackenzie-Grieves, 1959

第十一章　厦门街头生活 Amoy Street Life

生动的厦门（20 世纪 20 年代）　风筝在九月灼热的天空中飞翔：数以百计，形状各异，高低不一，在小城的屋顶上飘荡。艄公荡起双桨，用尽全力划着小舢板，穿行于描着眼睛的帆船、货轮、小型海岸汽轮和日、法炮舰之间。周围还有上百条小舢板，载着被晒蔫了的绿色蔬菜、金黄色的豆腐糕、藤笼里尖叫的生猪、叽叽喳喳的小鸡、男男女女、还有棺材。我们的耳边充斥着叫声、喊声、笑声、呵斥声、汽笛声和辘轳声……

Itinerant Cook　MacGowan, 1912

店铺把花岗岩石板铺成的街道与大海隔开了。遮篷撑开了。金黄、红、黑色招牌挂满街头，遮天蔽日。整条大街到处都是人。有穿着长袍和绸缎短外套的绅士，有光着膀子的男人，有穿着肮脏、破旧衣服的乞丐，有身穿黑色或蓝色棉裤、头扎花布巾的乡下婆娘。城市女性，年轻的穿着上海时装无拘无束，年老的裹着小脚，拄着乌木拐杖步履蹒跚。小孩，有领着差使一路小跑的，有放着风筝线快放完的，有围着流动摊贩、甜食摊点拣吃的。有病奄奄、没剩两口气的婴儿被母亲当作乞讨的道具。还有幼儿在街上相互推搡，或被挑着重担的脚夫、抬着富贵人家的轿夫推来碰去。笑声、喊声、叫卖声、吐痰声以及交谈声，无一不是竭尽全力、歇斯底里。

店铺里摆满了一袋袋的粟米、大米、豆子、皮蛋，一罐罐紫色、绿色的酱汁，以及爬满苍蝇的猪肉，还有棉花、丝锦缎、布鞋、各种小浅盘里的雕刻玉件、玉耳环、玉镯和玉珠子。人头像、篮子、笼中的小鸟、饰有深蓝色绘画的陶器、神香、铜罐、黄铜长柄勺。江湖游医兜售草药、干甲虫、虎骨、牛黄石、大象的粪便、龟壳、阿司匹林、龙力（肺癌补药）和虎标清凉油。

没有不好的手艺，也没有笨拙的工作。即使是最小的礼盒也要用红纸包住，再用红线、白线精心捆扎。当铺里，这个年代被遗弃的豪华服饰在肮脏、破烂的衣服堆里（布满尘埃的垃圾堆是这个行当最值钱的存货）鲜艳夺目：袖口、裙子的精美绣花，显示社会地位的鸟兽、龙凤图案，手艺之奢华无与伦比，却不值几分钱。

还有这里盛产的奢华物品：珊瑚、水晶、珐琅、蔷薇石英、镶嵌着闪闪发光的翠鸟羽毛的镀银器皿、戴法复杂的护身符——虎爪变成一个弧形、有金黄的脚蹼和人头的鱼、蝙蝠、莲花，用失去光泽的镀银制作，还有一桶桶，或者说名义上是一桶桶的肉红玉髓，像退潮时布满海边的小圆石，被落日染上了颜色。有人告诉我们，在厦门加工、制作，这些玉髓在帝王时代是用来装饰办公场所的。但是，我从未见过任何一位政府官员项链上串着这种小圆石。

蓝绿色珐琅饰板和牌匾上的雕刻象牙或骨头，有时候是饰有珊瑚、蔷薇石英和紫水晶的玉石，在尘埃中闪闪发光。令人难以置信的是，为了让人们免受饥寒，它们被遗忘在当铺里，与破旧衣服为伍。店铺外面满街都是装大小便的大陶罐。人们把粪便挑到城郊的菜地里浇菜。为了省力，这些便罐满了才有人去清空……

——麦肯兹·格瑞芙，1959 年，第 41～43 页

老外看老鼓浪屿 Old Gulangyu in Foreigners' Eyes

The Barber (1850s) The barber had his following, too. He carried his shaving implements around from door to door, and was hailed in passing, or solicited a job of shaving heads back to the place where the queue began, in those old days where queues were commanded, to show submission from the Chinese to the Manchurian Empire. Besides shaving heads, the barber massaged the eyeballs—and … He also cleansed the ears before completing his job.

Mary Doty's Memoirs

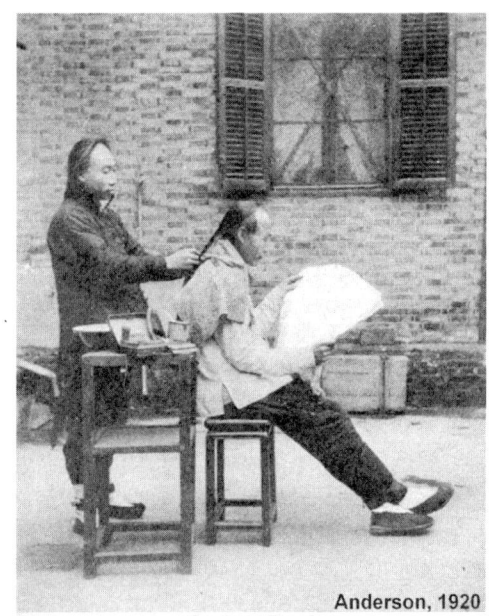

Anderson, 1920
Street Barber

Bird Seller's Shop, 1934   J. Veldman

第十一章　厦门街头生活 *Amoy Street Life*

剃头匠（19世纪50年代）　剃头匠也有他的追随者。他带着理发工具，走街串门。剃头匠路过的时候，有人跟他打招呼。在有人排队的地方，拉客剃头。在那些日子里，让人排队是为了显示中国人对满洲王朝的屈服。除了理发，剃头匠还替人按摩眼球，还有……剃完头之前，他还替人挖耳朵。

——玛丽·多蒂未出版的回忆录

Fruit Vendor　J. Veldman

Open-air Noodle Shop, 1934

Cigarette Vendor, 1934　J. Veldman

Medicine Peddlar, 1934　J. Veldman

Lollipop and Toy Maker, 1934   J. Veldman

Sweet Potato Peddler, 1934   J. Veldman

The Candy Man (1850s) Chinese peddlers, or venders, carrying cabinets hung on one end of a pole placed across the shoulders, and on the other end, either a brazier of charcoal swung, or another cabinet, according to the articles for sale, came now and then into the hall from the street, and we were called downstairs to see their wares. The candy man had fondant keeping hot, or melted over the fire, and he would blow figures after glass blowers' methods, some very ingenious, some like lollipops; and father or mother would buy them for us. I remember a rooster which was blown before our eyes, which had a bit of reed in its tail, so arranged as to cause a crowing—to our great delight. Another vender would show beautiful pieces of silk, or of embroidery, and skeins of silks of all the delicate shades which we recognize in their fine work in this day, which has found its way into our wardrobes or markets.

Mary Doty's Memoirs

Sidewalk Restaurants (1850s) Food was such a casual article with multitudes of the people that a brisk trade was carried on by these street venders, who sold a bowl of rice, or a bit of vegetable, or boiled dough, and other simple edibles, for a few cash, gladly bought by many to soothe the gnawings of hunger; or there would be better food and treats for the well-to-do.

Mary Doty's Memoirs

第十一章　厦门街头生活 *Amoy Street Life*

Splitting Firewood, 1934

Fortune Teller, 1934

Knife and Scissors Sharpener, 1934

糖果贩（19世纪50年代）　中国的商贩，或摊贩，用扁担一边挑着货箱，另一边根据自己兜售的物品要么挑着炭炉，要么是另外一个货箱。他们经常从大街走进住户的门厅，叫我们下楼看看他们的货品。糖果贩把软糖保温，或在火上融化，然后再像吹玻璃那样做出各种各样的人物造型，有些造型设计独特，有些做得像棒棒糖。父母亲经常买给我们吃。我记得有一只公鸡就在我们的眼皮底下吹成的，尾巴还插上了一点干芦苇。这样做是为了让公鸡更像在啼鸣，着实让我们非常兴奋。另外一个商贩会向我们展示漂亮的丝绸布，刺绣品以及一束束不同颜色的精美丝绸。这些丝绸现在让我们认识了中国人的精工细做，最终进入我们的市场，被我们收入衣橱。

——玛丽·多蒂未出版的回忆录

路边餐馆（19世纪50年代）　对大多数民众来说，吃是很随便的事情。街边小吃摊的生意很好。一碗饭，或一点青菜，或捞面条及其他简单、能吃的东西，只要一点钱。许多人开心地买上一点，聊解饥饿。对稍微富有的人家，还有更好的食物和招待。

——玛丽·多蒂未出版的回忆录

Beancurd Peddlar, 1934

157

The Letter Writer   We now come to a part of the road that is slightly wider than the rest. At the side of it is a man seated at a small table, on which are laid materials for writing. Two ink-slabs, one for black and the other for red ink, are placed in order before him. He is a man of about fifty years of age, with large spectacles on his nose, and he assumes a learned look, as though he would try and persuade the public that he belongs to the literary class. He is wanting, however, in that invisible something that marks the true scholar, and consequently no one is deceived by him. He is a broken-down tradesman perhaps, or a ne'er-do-weel who had been partially educated when he was young, but who had not character enough to go on with his studies. He is now picking up a very precarious living by writing letters for the very poor and uneducated classes of society.

Making Fried Cakes, 1934

But let us draw near, for a woman has just come up to his table, evidently on business, and custom will allow us to stand by and listen to what she has to say. The letter writer has now assumed a learned look, and he peers over the spectacles at her with an air of profound thought, as she tells him what she wishes him to write about. She wants him to write a letter to her son, who has gone abroad, and has not written to her for a very long time. ... After she has concluded he proceeds to write the letter. The paper is soon covered with strange hieroglyphics in perpendicular columns, written with black ink. Then the stops are all put in with red ink, and important sentences underlined with the same, and finally it is read over to her to see whether it contains all she desired to say. It is then folded up and addressed, and for all this he receives the modest sum of one penny.

MacGowan 1895

Hawker of Second-hand Items, 1934

Dry Goods Vendor, 1934

第十一章　厦门街头生活 *Amoy Street Life*

帮人写信　现在我们走到了比其他街道稍宽的地方。街道的一边有一块小桌，上面摆着书写工具，旁边坐着一位先生。他的面前整齐地排放着两块墨砚，一块放黑墨水，一块放红墨水。这位先生大约50岁，鼻尖上架着一副大眼镜，看上去很有学问的样子，好像他要试图告诉大家，他属于有文化的阶层。然而，无形中，他缺少了真正学者的某些东西。结果，没人被他所蒙蔽。也许他是一名破产的商人，或者年轻时受过一些教育，但不具备继续深造条件的失意者。现在，他操起了一份非常不稳定的营生，为社会上没有文化的穷苦人家写信。

不过，让我们走近看一下。一位妇女走到他的桌前，显然是带生意来了。根据当地的风俗，我们可以站在旁边，听听她要说的话。

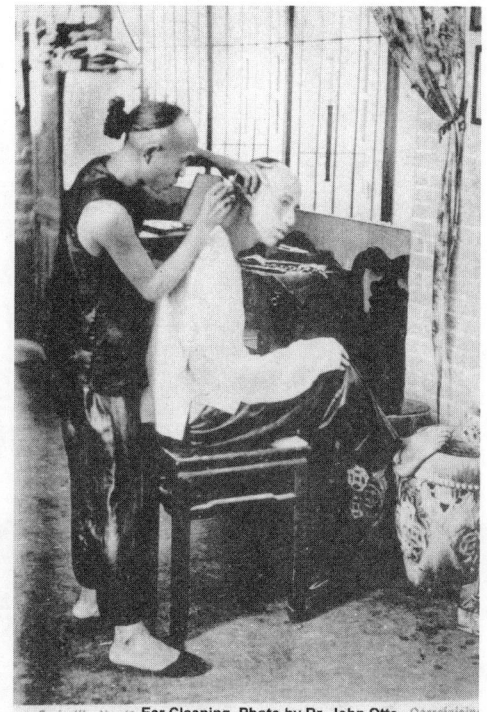

Serie III. No. 10. Ear Cleaning, Photo by Dr. John Otte
"Medische Zending, Nederlandsch Wilhelmina Vrouwenhospitaal te Amoy van Dr. J.A. Otte."

写信的人现在装出一副有学问的样子。他透过眼镜盯着她，听她想在信中诉说的内容，一副深思熟虑的神态。原来，她儿子出国了，很久没有给她写信。她想给他写封信……她一说完，写信的人就开始工作了。白纸上很快就写满了奇形怪状的汉字，一行行排下来，用黑墨水写的。然后，句号全部是用红墨水写的。还在重要的句子下面用红墨水画线。最后，读一遍给她听，看看信里是不是已经包含了她想说的所有内容。然后，折起来，写上通信地址。写这么一封信，他收到了不太高的报酬：一文钱。

Fresh Fish Market, 1934

——麦嘉湖，1895年，第29～31页

老外看老鼓浪屿 *Old Gulangyu in Foreigners' Eyes*

The Cobbler, 1934

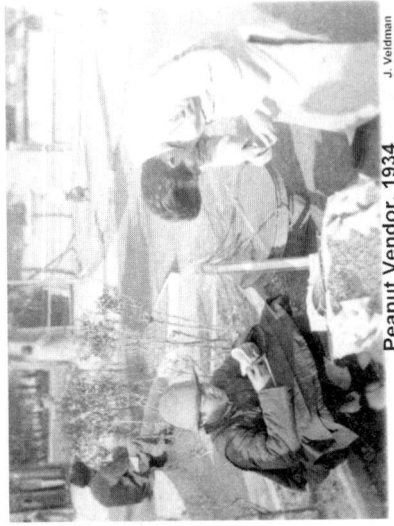
Peanut Vendor, 1934

Vegetable Vendor, 1934

Chinaware Mender, 1934

第十一章　厦门街头生活 *Amoy Street Life*

Meat Merchant, 1934

Open-air Grocery, 1934

Poultry Shop, 1934

Chinese Medicine Peddlar, 1924

Chapter 12 Amoy Wildlife

Dragon and Tiger,1640 (Dutch Engraving)

Two things in Fukien impressed Marco Polo: the beauty of the women and the size of its tigers.
Mackenzie-Grieves, 1959

9-Foot Amoy Tiger Mr. H. R. Bruce brought into Amoy the largest tiger that had ever been seen in that place, measuring over nine feet from nose to tip of tail.
September 20th, 1888. (in Chinese Recorder, Vol. 19, Nov., 1888)

Amoy Tigers[1] Fight Crime Tigers of enormous size constantly roam about the countryside in the interior, and keep the people in a perpetual state of terror. Not unfrequently they carry off a man, woman, or child, while at work in the fields, of whom nothing more is ever seen, excepting occasionally a few bones. However, they are in one way beneficial to the country, as they effectually prevent all robbers, and night prowlers from roving about after dark.
China Review, Vol. 22, No.3, 1896

Tame Amoy Tiger A gentleman took us to see a young tiger, between six and seven months old, which was so tame that it followed him about like a dog, and seemed quite pleased when we patted his head. The gentleman told us he paid ten dollars for him when he was first caught, a few months prior to the time we saw him, and that he had now sold him to the English Consul for a hundred pounds. I believe it is intended for the Zoological Gardens in London, where it will figure as the first from China ever seen there, and where we may someday renew our acquaintance with the tiger of Amoy.
D'Almeida, 1863

Tiger Hunting in Amoy "But the crowning sport with which the name of Amoy is associated is the pursuit of that king of the jungle, the wily tiger. Tigers abound more or less all along the coast of China, and native trappers declare that they are more abundant in 'Kwang Tung' province than in Fokien.

These trappers travel over several provinces in search of tiger lairs, and having discovered one they find that the tiger follows the same track in entering and leaving. They survey this track, select some point where the track dips a little below the ground on one side or the other.
Adapted from "Sport in Amoy," China Review, Vol. 22 No. 5 (1897) By H. R. Bruce
Chinese translation from "Magic Xiamen"

---

1 "All Amoy tigers are village prowlers, and man-eaters." Bruce, 1897

第十二章　厦门的野生动物

福建有两样东西给马可·波罗留下了深刻印象:女性的美丽和老虎的体型。
　　　　　　　　　——麦肯兹·格瑞芙,1959年,第69页

九英尺长的厦门虎　H.R.布鲁斯先生把那个地方未曾见过的、体型最大的老虎带进了厦门。这只老虎从鼻子到尾巴,超过9英尺。
　　　　　　——1888年9月20日(摘自《中国教务杂志》第19卷,
　　　　　　　　　　　　　　第540页,1888年11月)

厦门虎[2]打击犯罪　体型彪大的老虎总是在内地的乡下四处游荡,让人们老是处在一种恐怖的气氛里。它们经常叼走在田间劳作的男人、女人,或小孩。除了偶然发现的几块骨头,被老虎叼走之后,再也找不到他们的任何痕迹。不过,老虎对乡民来说还是有一个好处,因为它的出现有效地防止了劫犯和夜贼天黑之后四处作案。
　　　　　　　——《中国评论》第22卷,1896年第3期

Amoy Tiger　Caldwell, 1953

驯服厦门虎　一位绅士带我们去看一只虎仔,大致6、7个月大,已经被驯得服服帖帖,像狗一样跟在主人后面。轻拍它的头,似乎还挺开心的。这位绅士告诉我们,这只虎仔在我们见到之前几个月刚刚被捉住,他花十块钱就把它买下了。现在,它已经以100英镑的价格把它卖给英国领事。我想,英国领事应该是为伦敦动物园买虎。这将是来自中国的第一种动物。届时,我们在伦敦就可以再次见到我们所认识的厦门虎。
　　　　　　　　　　——德阿美达,1863年,第285页

厦门猎虎　不过,最高尚的运动就是追寻丛林之王——狡猾的老虎,这项运动总是与厦门的名字"Amoy"联系在一起。中国沿海地区是老虎活跃的地区,而据当地的捕猎者说,广东省的老虎比福建的还多。
　　这些捕猎者四处搜寻虎穴,脚步遍及好几个省。他们发现,老虎出入时总是循着同一条路线的。他们勘察这条路线,选择其一侧倾斜并低于地面的几处。
　　　　　　——(《中国评论》1897年第22卷第5期,"厦门运动",

2　"厦门虎都是夜间出动的,会吃人。"布鲁斯,1897年

On this higher ground they dig a hole like a grave and fix therein a very powerful bow with a poisoned shaft protruding through a small tunnel that connects the grave with the track. The bow is fired by a small thread fixed across the path, so as to catch a passing tiger's chest, and the poison is so effective that the wounded beast seldom gets away.

The tiger is a valuable prize, he is good medicine from his whiskers to the tip of his tail, and all who covet strength, courage or ferocity compete for a portion…there is no adulteration act to ensure that all that is sold as tiger, is really tiger, so that with the help of an ancient buffalo, or of a dead horse, a tiger of 300 pounds weight gives fully 1,000 pounds retail weight.

The natives have curious ideas about tigers occupying lairs in their neighborhood. If a man has been killed they welcome the foreign sportsman most cordially, and chin-chin him as the savior of the people, but if the tiger has not been known to take human life they are disposed to propitiate him, and condemn the folly of enraging him and perhaps converting a good dispositioned beast into a maneater. Then again they will say, 'What is the use of shooting him, two new tigers will at once occupy his den.'

"Sometimes a tiger has the character of never harming the villagers who are his neighbors; although he eats up strangers and travelers by the score, the villagers are quite sure of their own safety. If one stays in the village for a few days another reason for their immunity suggests itself. Owing to their propinquity to a permanent tiger lair they have inherited habits of early hours at night, and late hours in the morning, that give the poor tiger no chance, so he has to fall back on benighted strangers with less regular habits.

All Amoy tigers are village prowlers, and man-eaters. There is no game of any sort: goats, pigs and cows are carefully pounded at night, so that probably village dogs comprise 5/6ths of the necessary support for the tigers of this province. Their hunting ground being so much among the haunts of men, tigers, after dusk at any rate, have lost all instinctive dread of man, and the sounds and odours of humanity, and will stroll up a village street soon after bed-time, and break open a door in search of pig, or dog. It is by no means an uncommon occurrence for a tiger to take a man out of his bed, and in the hot weather many lives are lost by sleeping in the doorway, and under the eaves.

It may be asked how it comes to pass that sportsmen bag tigers in Amoy, and not at other ports. For thirty years there have been casual hunts for tigers, but it was only some ten years ago that that indefatigable sport Mr. A. L. B. Allen succeeded in proving that patience, perseverance, lots of time, and good nerves could bring a tiger to the bag. Since then the sport has been keenly pursued, and that indomitable old shikaree Mr. Frank Leyburn heads the list with about 20 'kills.'

There is not much jungle within 20 miles of Amoy. The tigers lie up in subterranean passages in the rocky nullahs common to every hill-side. To drive them out of these caves the native hunters fearlessly enter armed with spears, and torches fixed on long bamboos. If Mr. Stripes has a bolt-hole he will bolt and come under the guns outside; but if caught in a cul-de-sac the sportsman must crawl into the cave, wriggle past the hunters and shoot at 20 years or less, usually a tame performance compared to an encounter in the open.

Of course much rough work, and many discomforts attend tiger shooting, but on the other hand there are many compensations which make a trip enjoyable. If one is lucky enough to put up in one of the mountain temples, far from the madding crow, and commanding a wide view of the neighbouring valleys, with their unrivalled agriculture feeding a thousand to the square mile, the fresh air and charming scenery are enough to live on. Again to acquire a good knowledge of the country, and to study the habits of the people is always of interest, and although one cannot hope to bag a tiger every week, when the lucky day comes, there is a decided feeling that the noble sport is well worth our most ardent devotion.

第十二章　厦门的野生动物 *Amoy Wildlife*

在高一点的地方,他们挖一个像墓穴一样的洞,在里面安装上强力的弓弩,箭头涂上毒药,从连接洞穴和路线的小隧道伸出。弓弩由一根跨过此路径的细绳触发,路过的老虎触碰到此细绳便会被射出的箭刺中,烈性毒药随即发作,少有能生还的。

老虎全身都是宝,从它的虎须到尾巴都是很好的药材,是强身健体之特效药,人们为之争夺不休。而且,没有打假的法律来保证买卖老虎的真伪,因此,用一只老水牛或死马掺假,一只 300 磅重的老虎零售能卖出 1000 磅来。

当地人对在他们附近安家的老虎有种奇怪的想法。如果有人被老虎吃了,他们会热烈欢迎外国冒险家的到来,将他奉为人民的救星。但是,如果这只老虎并没有伤人的前科,他们则会劝阻这位冒险家,谴责说激怒它可能使一只脾性好的野兽变成一只食人魔。他们还会说:"为什么要杀死它?杀了它之后,马上会有两只新来的老虎占领它的洞穴的。"

有的老虎可能从来不伤害邻近的村民,尽管它可能会吃掉不少陌生人和过路人,但村民们知道自己是安全的。如果一个外人在这个村子里住上些天,他也不会遭到老虎的侵犯。这都是由于长期以来与老虎为邻,村民们养成了一种根深蒂固的习惯,每天迟出早归,可怜的老虎没有机会,所以它只好袭击那些缺少这种生活习惯的陌生人。

厦门的老虎都会频频光顾各个村子,也常吃人。夜晚时分,猪、牛、羊都被关起来,老虎只能望而兴叹,这样村里的狗就构成了老虎 5/6 的食物。老虎的猎食区域甚至包括人们常去的地方。每当黄昏降临之时,它们便会失去所有与生俱来的对人类及其声音、味道的惧怕。人们就寝之后它们便开始在村道上流窜,还会闯进猪栏捕捉猪狗。有的人还不幸从被窝里被老虎叼走,这也不是没有的事。天气热的时候,有人就睡在门口或屋檐下,却因此丧了命。

也许你会问:"为什么探险家们喜欢在厦门捕猎老虎,而不是其他港口?"三十年来,捕捉到老虎是罕见的事,直到十多年前,不知疲倦的艾伦(A. L. B. Allen)先生成功证明了:耐心、毅力、时间和勇气是捕猎老虎的关键所在。自此,这项运动开始盛行,而老猎手弗兰克·莱本(Frank Leyburn)先生百折不挠,以捕杀 20 只老虎名列榜首。

厦门岛上,20 英里内丛林并不多见,但山腰上常有岩石峡谷,老虎大多栖息于这些峡谷的地洞中。为了将它们赶出地洞,当地的猎人手持长矛,并将火把固定在很长的竹竿上,然后勇敢地钻进地洞。如果这些满身条纹的家伙有逃生的洞穴,它们肯定会逃脱。但如果被困在死胡同里,冒险家们就得爬进洞穴,越过这些猎人,在 20 码内开枪。这相当于在露天情况下遇到一只老虎,那场面就乏味得多了。

当然,捕猎老虎过程中充满了艰辛与困难,但也有许多东西令人赏心悦目的。若能幸运地碰到一座远离尘嚣的山间庙宇,在此欣赏附近峡谷间的秀丽景色,以及无与伦比的农田乡野,正是这一方水土养育着一方人。那清新的空气、迷人的风景都将让你流连忘返。另外,还可以欣赏田园山村,了解民风民俗,何乐而不为?尽管你不可能每周都捕猎到老虎,但当幸运的时刻降临时,你一定会觉得,这项高尚的运动值得我们倾注一生的热情。

作者：H.R. 布鲁斯，中文译文摘自《魅力厦门》

"A Few Remarks on the Fauna of Amoy" "…Who has not wondered at the bare hills of Amoy, at the first glimpse he obtains on entering the harbor, and, seeing the great boulders of rock rise one another in endless confusion, thought to himself with a shudder, Can animal life be there? But though animal life is there to a small extent, it is to the plains, which are inhabited and cultivated with such care by the natives, that we must look for most that will interest us in our science.

"The wily fox is … the largest of the Carnivora we possess…

"The greatest devastator among the poultry of the poor is an animal belonging to the weasel (鼬鼠) family (Mustelideae)…

"We have also heard certain stories about the sea-otter that is occasionally seen prowling about on Six Islands, seeking his finny prey at the dead hour of night, and avoiding the light of day…

"…The next quadraped… is the scaly ant-eater or pangolin (穿山甲)…

Robert Swinhoe[3] (1857)

Some of Swinhoe's 174 Amoy Birds … The peregrine falcon (*Falco peregrinus*) is a straggling visitor… An osprey is sometimes seen even in the harbour, but little is known of him… A sparrow owl (Nyctipeles, Swain.), and a small tawny Scops owl (probably Scops rufiscens of Horsfield), are seen occasionally in winter. …

…the blackbird and rock thrush (*Petrocincla violacea*) are always with us …

… The most diminutive of all stands next, the little tailor-bird (Orthotomus)…Flocks of the beautiful white egret, or paddy bird, as they are familiarly known to us (*Herodias Garzetta*), often attract our attention as they wing their way slowly through the obscure blue of a summer twilight, from the fields where they have been feeding…We have, besides, five or six other species of heron, nearly all remarkable for their elegance and beauty.

"The egret is much admired by the sentimental Chinese, and is often alluded to in poetical compositions by the style Loo-sze; and the Island of Amoy is often poetically called Loo-mun, Loo-keang, and Loo-taon, from the number of these snow-like birds that annually frequent it. Of the ninety-two species of Insessores found here, nine are British birds.   Seven species of the Grallatores, and nearly all the Natatores, with the exception of the pelicans, albatrosses, and a few gulls and terns, are identical with those found in Great Britain…

" …It is unnecessary to dilate on the beauties and delights of the study of Nature: the heart of every man naturally throbs in the contemplation of the Creator's handiwork, and thrills with joy at the discovery of some new manoeuvre in the wondrous economy which so beautifully modulates and arranges all animal and vegetable life upon the globe.

---

3   Swinhoe, Amoy Consul and celebrated naturalist, found 174 species of birds in Amoy.

第十二章　厦门的野生动物 Amoy Wildlife

关于厦门动物的几点评述　刚刚进入厦门港，第一眼便是厦门光秃秃的小山，随后却是许多巨石，峰峦叠嶂，绵延不绝。你可能心里想：这里可能有野生动物吗？虽然这里的动物规模不大，但却是属于这片土地的，当地人民在此繁衍生息，而我们就应该尽可能寻找我们在科学中感兴趣的东西。

狡猾的狐狸是……最大型的食肉动物……

狐狸是穷人家家禽最大的威胁，它属于鼬鼠科（学名 Mustelideae）动物……

我们还听说，海獭也偶尔在六岛附近游荡，深夜时分出来寻找有鳍的猎物，避开白天的阳光……

……下一个四足动物要提到穿山甲……

——罗伯特·郇和（1857 年），摘自《魅力厦门》

郇和的鸟儿们　……游隼（学名 Falco peregrinus）时不时地会光顾这里，去年就有一对游隼把巢安在南太武的高山上，这里的顶峰上矗立着一座宝塔……在这个海港有时还会见到鱼鹰（学名 Pandion），但是对它知之甚少。我亲眼见过一只鱼鹰在船舷下方附近袭击一条鱼，然后抓着鱼扬长而去……冬天偶尔也能见到雀鹰（学名 Nyctipeles, Swain）和小型茶色的角枭（学名可能是 Scops rufiscens of Horsfield）……

画眉和矶鸫（学名 Petrocincla violacea）常常与我们做伴……

最小的鸟儿要数缝叶莺（学名 Orthotomus）……

一大片美丽的白鹭（学名 Herodias Garzetta，我们比较熟悉，所以也叫稻田鸟）经常吸引我们的视线，它们慢慢地从夏季朦胧的蓝色暮色中掠过……

除此以外，还有五至六种苍鹭，大都以形态优雅美丽而闻名。

富于情感的中国人给予白鹭诸多赞美之词，常在"老子"风格的诗歌作品里提到它们。由于这种雪白的鸟儿成群结队地经常光顾厦门，厦门岛因而常被诗意地称为鹭门、鹭江或鹭岛。在厦门发现的 92 种栖木类鸟中，有 9 种来自英国。有 7 种涉禽类鸟，以及除了鹈鹕、信天翁和少数几种海鸥和燕鸥以外的几乎所有的游禽类鸟和在英国发现的确是一模一样……

……探索大自然给人带来的美好和快乐无需赘述。当人们注视着造物者的杰作时，每个人的心都会因兴奋而悸动，会因为在这个神奇的自然界里发现了新的规律而喜悦地颤抖。自然界是那么完美地控制安排着地球上所有的动植物。

"Solomon said, "There is nothing new under the sun;" so, probably, there is not; but a great deal of what passes around man is new to him, and astonishes him when brought to his notice, simply because he has not made use of those powers of observation that he has been endowed with. In conclusion, I cannot do better than quote the words that Milton puts in the mouth of the Divine Author of Nature in his address to our first parent:-- "Is not the earth With various living creatures, and the air, Replenish'd; and all these at thy command, To come and play before thee?"

Robert Swinhoe, 1857

Amoy Water Buffaloes Few animals in that strange land are more interesting yet less attractive than the cow and dog.

The… buffalo cow is more worthy a full description. Resembling an elephant in size, color, and ungainly shape, it seems to have been formed after the supply of beauty had been exhausted. The great rough horns, turned backward until they nearly rest on the neck, suggest that these are ornaments, not weapons; and ornaments only because the owner is such an ugly appearing creature. Gentle as a lamb, it is led by a rope fastened to a ring in its nose, and obeys its little boy or girl leader as faithfully as it would a giant. The people call this animal a "water cow," some a "water hog," not because of any resemblance to a milkman's pump, but on account of its fondness for water. When free, it seeks a pond or other body of water, and, if able during the warmer weather, lies submerged except its nose, and so saves itself a great amount of work when flies and other insects are about.

…The street dog, however, if stories regarding him are true, is the genius and fool in the Chinese animal world…

Davis, 1896

Foreign Ladies Eye a Water Buffalo, 1922   J. Nienhuis

第十二章　厦门的野生动物 Amoy Wildlife

　　所罗门说:"天下无新事。"很可能的确是这样。但是，发生在人们身边的事物有许多对其来说是新事物，当他们注意到时会感到惊奇，这只不过是因为人们还没运用自然所赐予他们的观察能力。最后，我想最好还是引用米尔顿（Milton）通过造物者之口对人类的始祖（亚当和夏娃）所说的几句话来做结束语:"万物生长的地球，还有充满地球的空气，和所有你支配的事物，难道不是为你而生存的吗？"

——罗伯特·郇和，1857 年

　　厦门水牛　在中国陌生的地方，有几种动物挺有趣，但不如牛和狗更吸引人。

　　……水牛就更值得详细描述了。水牛的外形、颜色及其笨拙的样子像大象，似乎造化是把美用光之后才创造了它。两只大牛角很粗糙，向后长，差点就要碰到自己的脖子，证明这对牛角是装饰品，不是武器，因为牛角的主人是个外形丑陋的家伙。温顺如绵羊，用串在鼻子上的一根绳子被小男孩或女孩牵着，水牛没有反抗，老实地跟着走，就像牵着它的是个巨人。当地人叫这种动物为"水牛"，有点像"水豚"，不是因为它像送奶工人的泵，而是因为它喜欢水。一闲下来，它就找个池塘或其他有水的地方。如果可能，天气更热的时候，整身躺进水里，只露出鼻子。这种做法在苍蝇和其他昆虫四处横飞的季节可以让水牛少做很多事。

　　……街上的狗，如果有关它们的故事属实，倒是中国动物世界里的集天才和傻瓜于一身的玩意儿……

——戴维斯，1896 年，第 146～147 页

A Coolie Airs His Bird　　Anderson, 1920

老外看老鼓浪屿 *Old Gulangyu in Foreigners' Eyes*

Amoy Dogs The dog of the street is not an unmixed evil, for he is the city scavenger. He never deserts his post unless driven away; never shirks his duty; never goes on a strike; always hungry, usually starving, he allows no food to waste, nothing eatable to decay. Without him epidemics might be far more common than now; yet his only reward comes in kicks and curses. It is said, in some places, the writer has reason to believe with truth, that the street dogs have a government of their own, and each brute knows his place and keeps it. Certainly it was almost impossible to coax, very difficult to force, a dog beyond certain limits in the city of Amoy years ago. And woe to the dog out of his beat! He must run, fight, or die; occasionally one was compelled to do each in turn. If forced a few blocks from home the brutes, bold enough before, became cowardly, and made desperate efforts to return.

Davis, 1896

Immortal Amoy Dogs [from Ruth Bradford's Amoy Journal, 1862]

Wednesday, June 11th …The dogs fairly swarm here. And such rascally looking animals I never saw before. They will come to our yard and are a perfect nuisance. Pa thought he would quietly make away with a few of them, so he got some arsenic and administered it to them in large doses. They swallowed it down, but it never fazed them. Then he got strychnine. They took that too, but it has no effect on them. I never saw or heard of anything like it. There is one white dog here which has taken a large dose of arsenic, two large doses of strychnine, and Ollie has shot him several times; but still he seems to be in perfectly good health and condition and runs around in the yard as if he had a right there. Pa has at last, in astonishment and disgust, given that dog up as a proof against death. About time, I think.

Little, 1899
British Consul's "Peking Dog"

Thursday, June 12th Immortal Amoy Dog Dies …Ollie succeeded in killing the white dog, shot him in the head and had four or five Chinamen bury him; but I believe the dog has come too again; for if I didn't see him this morning, I saw one that was his exact image. … It has cleared off and is a still night. The crickets are very musical and the mosquitoes and fleas very lively.

第十二章　厦门的野生动物　Amoy Wildlife

厦门的狗　　厦门街上的狗不是一种纯粹的坏蛋，因为它们是这座城市的食腐动物。除非有人驱赶，否则它们从不擅离职守，从不逃避责任，从不罢工。因为总是饥饿，常常快被饿死，它们决不浪费一点食物，也不让任何能吃的东西腐烂。少了街上的这些狗，瘟疫可能比现在更普遍，但是它们得到的唯一回报是脚踢和诅咒。据说，在一些地方，文人用事实证明，街狗也有自己的领地，每只街狗都知道并捍卫自己的地盘。几年前，要把街狗哄走，或把它们驱逐出城区是很困难的、几乎是不可能的。悲哀啊，把狗赶出它们的领地！它们必须奔走、打斗，否则就是死路一条。有时候，它们必须轮番上阵。被赶离家门没多远，这些先前非常胆大的畜生，变得胆小。然后，它们会不顾一切，再杀回来。

——戴维斯，1896 年，第 147～148 页

不朽的厦门狗（摘自露丝·布莱德福特的《厦门日记》，1862 年）

　　6月11日，星期三　　……狗整群地在这里移动。这是我以前未曾见过的动物，一副无赖相。它们涌进我们的院子，实在令人讨厌。父亲认为，他能不动声色地把它们弄死几只。因此，他拿了些砷，给它们下了大剂量。狗吞了下去，没有任何犹豫。然后，父亲再拿了些士的宁。狗照样吞下，没有任何反应。这样的事情，我从来没见过，也没听说过。有一只白狗，吞下了大量的砷，还有两个大剂量的士的宁，奥力还向它开了几枪，可是这条白狗还是身体贼棒，在院子里四处奔跑，好像它拥有权力在院子这样做。惊诧之下，厌恶之余，父亲终于放弃。他把那只狗当作不朽的物证。实在折腾太久了，我想。

Amoy Dogs　　MacGowan, 1914

　　6月12日，星期四，不朽的厦门狗死了　　……奥力终于成功地把那只白狗给枪杀了。子弹打在狗的头上，四、五个中国人把它埋了。不过，我相信，这只狗还会再回来，因为如果我今天早上没有看见它，我一定会看到一只跟它一模一样的……一切都过去了，夜晚很平静。蟋蟀声还是那么悦耳动听，蚊子和跳蚤还是那样的活跃。

老外看老鼓浪屿 *Old Gulangyu in Foreigners' Eyes*

Chapter 13　Amoy Religion

The Chinese have no such institution as a cemetery upon Koolangsu. Their dead are buried promiscuously all over the island.

Giles, 1878

Nation of Ancestor Veneration　If we were to search through every class of society in China for the one spiritual force that influences and dominates them all, we should find it to be ancestor worship. ... A man, for example, may worship the idols or not: he may profess a belief in them or he may express his utter scepticism about them, and no one cares a button what he thinks. Let a man, however, neglect the worship of the dead, and he is looked upon with the utmost scorn, both by his own kindred and also by his neighbours. The bitterest taunt that the Chinese can hurl against the convert to Christianity, and the one that stings him most, is the sneering statement that he has no ancestors.

Family Ancestor Worship　[PERSEY. MISSION, in MacGowan, 1914]

This worship dates back to the very earliest times of Chinese history. Confucius, in his "Record of Rites," lays down minute rules as to the etiquette that should be observed in its performance. It would seem, however, as though its character has materially changed since his time. Then, the service in the ancestral temples were simply memorial ones, in order to keep alive the recollection of the loved ones who had passed away and to prevent their memory from fading out of the minds of the living.

During the centuries that have elapsed since then, a great many accretions have been added to the original idea. Men after a time began to believe that the founders of their clans, though dead, possessed great power in the land of the spirits, and that they could control the lives and fortunes of their kindred on earth.

Gulangyu Funeral, 1930s　*J. Nienhuis*

MacGowan, 1913

第十三章　厦门宗教

在鼓浪屿岛上，除了墓地，中国人没有设立任何机构。他们先人的墓地散落在岛屿各处。

——吉尔斯，1878 年，第 18 页

举国敬奉祖先　如果想在中国各个社会阶层找到影响并主导所有中国人的一种精神力量，我们发现这种力量就是敬奉祖先……例如，一个人可以信佛，也可以不信：他可以公开表明自己的信仰或者直接表达自己的怀疑。他的想法没人会在意。但是，如果不敬奉已经逝去的祖先，他就会被族人和邻居所鄙视。对信奉基督教者，中国人最恶毒的辱骂、也是令信教者最刻骨铭心的是冷嘲热讽他们没有祖宗。

Amoy Funeral, 1930s　J. Nienhuis

这种敬奉可以追溯到中国历史的早期时代。孔子在他的《礼记》中对臣民应该遵守的礼仪做出了详尽的规定。此后，礼仪的特性似乎已经发生了实质变化。祖屋里的仪式只是纪念性质的，目的是为了追忆已经逝去的亲人，以免生者忘记了祖宗。

Amoy Funeral, 1930s　J. Nienhuis

在已经逝去的几百年里，礼教已经在原来的基础上增加了许多内容。人们开始相信，自己家族的创始人，虽然已经逝去，但在精神领域仍然拥有巨大的力量，可以操控活在人间的亲人的生死和财运。

——麦嘉湖，1913 年，第 91 页

老外看老鼓浪屿 *Old Gulangyu in Foreigners' Eyes*

U.S. Amoy Consulate Midst the Tombs (1893) The United States consulate is regarded as a very superior locality, but it is surrounded by over a hundred tombs. A score of the large blocks of granite used in and about it are old tombstones. On the hill immediately behind the residence of F. Malcampo, esq., the graves touch one another at every point and form a solid white surface of rock, brick, porcelain, and cement, covering more than a million square feet. Near the lam-paw-do Joss-house [Nanputuo Temple] 30,000 bodies are said to have been buried vertically to save space. They lie or stand in a plot of land of as many square feet. Amoy proper and its suburbs have a living population of about one million, and a dead one of four and a half times as many.

U.S. Consul Bedloe, 1893

Gulangyu Funeral, 1930s

California Chinese Coffin Trade Very many settle down in their adopted countries, but great numbers return home after amassing a competency; some, indeed, after death to be buried near their ancestors, for the Chinese have a deep regard for the mother country, and make a point of having their bodies embalmed, if, that is to say, they can afford it, and being sent back to their native place for burial.

… The coffin trade between California and Canton has on this account always been a lucrative one, and a steamer seldom returns without a fair proportion of embalmed Celestials. [The Americans are going to tax the export trade in embalmed Celestials, and make it a source of revenue.]

Shore 1881

Gulangyu Grave (1920s) — J. Nienhuis

第十三章 厦门宗教 Amoy Religion

乱坟堆中的美国驻厦门领事馆（1893年） 美国驻厦门领事馆被认为是一个风水上乘的好地点,但是它的周围有100多座坟墓。使馆里面和周围有十几块花岗岩大石条就是旧墓石。F.马尔坎珀主教住宅正背后的小山上,坟墓一个紧挨着一个,组成了一个由石头、砖头、陶瓷和水泥构成的、坚固的白色外表,面积超过100万平方英尺。靠近南普陀寺,据说有一个地方,为了节约空间,三万座坟墓几乎垂直地建在了一起。死者或躺或站,占地不过几平方英尺。厦门城区和郊外大约有100万人口,死者大约是生者的四倍半左右。

Amoy Funeral, 1930s   J.Nienhuis

美国驻厦门领事壁洛,1893年

加州的中国棺材贸易 许多中国人在他们的客居地定居下来,但在积累了一笔财富之后回到中国的人数量巨大。一些中国人死后想葬在自己祖先坟墓的边上,因为他们对自己的祖国有一种深厚的感情。如果能负担得起这笔开销,他们就会想方设法把自

Amoy Funeral, 1930s   J. Nienhuis

己的遗体进行防腐处理,然后再运回家乡入葬。

……因此,加州和广东的棺材贸易一直利润颇高。大海轮到中国很少不携带一定数量、经过防腐处理的中国人遗体(美国人将把这种遗体运输当作一种出口贸易征税,作为财政收入的一个来源)。

——肖尔,1881年,第43页

老外看老鼓浪屿 *Old Gulangyu in Foreigners' Eyes*

The Power of the Dead   Now, mighty and overwhelming though the living force of Chinese life may be, it is an undoubted fact that the dead and sleeping nation, as a religious factor, in many respects controls and dominates the living tides of men that impress us so vividly with their vast numbers. Even the casual traveler in China cannot help but be impressed with the way in which the graves of the dead thrust themselves upon the attention of the living. There is no getting away from them. The mountain sides very often are so thickly covered with them that one has to tread upon them if one would pass from one part to another. Every uncultivated spot on the lower levels has been eagerly seized upon as spaces where to bury the dead. Even the cultivated fields have been invaded by them, and mounds right in the centre of some diminutive rice or potato patches show how the little farm has been narrowed down in order to make room for some members of the family that have passed away. These graves thrust themselves up to the edge of the great roads, and seem to be prevented from grasping even them only by the incessant march of the countless feet that hurry along them from dawn till dark. The clearings and little hills outside the cities that cannot be used for cultivation are all seized upon as unprotected cemeteries for the dead, and the little mounds like tidal waves advance up to the very edge of the walls of the town, and are stayed in their progress only by these huge bulwarks.

MacGowan, 1907

Potted Ancestors   It was a curious scene, every bit of ground, as far as one could see, being thickly sprinkled with the odd-shaped erections which mark the resting-places of the Chinese, with here and there a small house containing rows of jars filled with ancestral bones, commonly called 'potted ancestors,' as well as numbers of tablets with the ancestral names cut on them, which are objects of worship. It is customary in some parts of the country, after the body has lain a certain time below ground, to disinter the bones and preserve them in jars. ... We passed a grave where the ceremony of potting was going on. The coffin-lid had been broken open, and the bones were being sorted from the earth; at one end an elderly lady was seated waving her arms and chanting a weird song broken by bursts of crying. It was a strange performance, but whether the old lady was hired for the occasion, which I understand is sometimes done, or that the sight of the dried bones called up touching memories, history does not relate.

Shore, 1881

Potten Ancestors, Amoy, 1921   J. Nienhuis

第十三章　厦门宗教 *Amoy Religion*

死者的力量　中国人口众多，给我们留下深刻印象。尽管中国人生活的有生力量可能是非常强大、势不可挡，但死者和阴间作为一种宗教因素在许多方面控制并主导着活人的生活。这是一个不容怀疑的事实。在中国，死者的坟墓总能博得活人的关注。即便是漫不经心的游客也无法忽视这个事实。坟墓无处不在。山坡上到处造满了坟墓。从山坡一侧走到另一侧，你不得不踩着坟堆。山坡较低处未被开发荒地，人们会争抢过来，给死者作为墓地。墓地甚至已经侵入了耕地。小片的稻田或地瓜地中间的坟堆证明，为了给已经逝去的家族某些成员腾点空间，小小的农田是如何被缩小的。坟墓还非常猛烈地向大路的边缘推进，似乎只有日夜不停踩在这条路上的无数脚印才能抵挡坟墓的进攻。不能用于耕作的城郊空地和小山丘都被占为死者不受保护的墓地。小坟堆已经像波浪一样推进到城墙脚下，只是巨大的城墙挡住了它们前进的脚步。

——麦嘉湖，1907 年，第 74～75 页

陶罐里的祖先　在厦门，你可以看到的一个奇特景象是：这里的每一寸土地都密集地竖放着一些奇形怪状的陶罐。这是中国人安息地的标志。四处散落的小屋里一排一排地堆放着装着祖先遗骨的陶罐，俗称"陶罐里的祖先"，以及许多刻有祖先名字的石碑。这些东西都是人们敬仰的对象。在中国的一些地方，人们习惯在尸体入葬一段时间后把骨头捡出，存放在陶罐里……有一次，我们路过一座坟墓，那里正在进行尸骨入殓仪式。棺材盖打开了，尸骨从泥土中捡出并分类。一位老太太坐着坟墓的另一侧，一会儿舞动双手、有节奏地吟唱着古怪的歌谣，一会儿号啕大哭。真是一个奇怪的表演。这位老太太是否被人雇佣出现在尸骨入殓仪式上，还是尸骨引发感人的回忆，没有人能说得清楚。

——肖尔，1881 年，第 53～54 页

Last Ferry Ride　　　　　　　　　MacGowan, 1907

老外看老鼓浪屿 Old Gulangyu in Foreigners' Eyes

Pilgrim's Progress & Tombstones The greatest service of a literary kind which Mr. Burns performed for the Church of Christ in China was his translation of the *Pilgrim's Progress* into Chinese,…The style of language is well chosen, partaking as much as possible of Bunyan's Saxon simplicity; it was a congenial work, and no pains was spared on its composition. The greatest difficulty was in finding suitable names of persons for Bunyan's quaint and expressive ones. Mr. Burns spent days on the hills around Amoy, which are covered with graves like a grand natural cemetery. From the headstones on these he found his well-chosen names. His peregrinations during his long search were called by the Missionaries Burns' "meditations among the tombs".

Johnston, 1898

MacGowan, 1914
Sacrificial Paper House and Furniture

Coffin Clubs To judge from the number of coffin shops, the undertakers drive as good a trade here as elsewhere. The coffins are strange looking articles. In shape they resemble the trunk of a tree cut close to the ground, and are very massive in construction. The lower end is closed after the body is inserted by a convex plug. In some parts of China there are burial clubs which advance money to poor people who are unable to afford the expenses of a funeral.

Shore, 1881

Koxinga's Amoy Tomb A group of monumental statues stands by the way-side, a little out of the city, in a street leading to Aming-kang (Xiamen Port; 厦门港), a large village a mile south of Amoy. It has been supposed by some to be the burial place of that renowned pirate chief, Koxinga, or, more correctly, Cheng-chin-kong [郑成功]…His old forts and watch towers and entrenchments are still pointed out. But whether he was buried here, on the spot indicated by these monumental statues, is a question not entirely settled to the satisfaction of those who have made the investigation.

These monumental statues are of colossal size—the two figures each nearly nine feet in height, and measuring over three feet across the shoulders. They are of solid granite, and although bearing the marks of time, the features are remarkably distinct and the expression most surprisingly perfect. The effigy of the horse is about five feet in length, and it is the same distance from the ground to the upper arch of his neck. The whole figure, with the curiously devised and richly wrought caparisons, is finely chiseled in stone, and exhibits a superior degree of artistic skill…

Mayers, 1867

第十三章　厦门宗教 Amoy Religion

天路历程和墓碑
彭斯先生为中国基督教堂在文学领域所作的最伟大贡献是把《天路旅程》译成中文…… 该书的语言风格尽可能地传承了班扬的萨克森式的简洁。这是一件宜人的工作,在创作方面不用花多少力气。最困难的是为班扬古怪、而又富有表现力的主人翁找到适合的名字。彭斯先生花了几天的时间在厦门周边的山头上。这里到处布满坟堆,像是一座宏伟的自然公墓。从墓碑上,他精挑细选,找到了他想要的人名。他在坟堆里的旅行被称为传教士彭斯的"坟堆冥想"。

Amoy Graves　　Johnston, 1907

——约翰斯顿, 1898 年, 第 78 页

丧葬俱乐部　　从棺材店的数量上来看,从业者的生意跟别的地方一样兴旺。棺材是一些长相奇怪的东西。从外表上来说,它们像是靠近根部的树干,体积庞大。遗体放进棺材后,棺材盖便从较低的一端盖起来。在中国的一些地方,还有丧葬俱乐部。俱乐部把钱借给那些无法支付丧葬费的穷人。

——肖尔, 1881 年, 第 64 页

郑成功在厦门的坟墓　　在厦门城区往南一英里左右,有一条通往厦门港的街道。这里有一个大村落。村道的边上矗立着一组的纪念雕像。有人认为,这是著名的海上首领郑成功的墓葬。……郑成功建造的城堡、瞭望台和战壕依然历历在目。但是,他是否葬在厦门,葬在这些纪念雕像所指引的地方,考察者至今仍无法找到完全满意的答案。

这些纪念雕像规模庞大。其中,两尊人物雕像每尊的高度都接近 9 英尺,肩宽超过 3 英尺。雕像是用坚硬的花岗岩做成的。虽然历经风霜,外部轮廓依然清晰可见,表情仍然保存完美。战马的雕像长约 5 英尺。战马到地面高度与它到脖子顶端的大致相等。整座雕像设计奇特,马饰华丽,是用一整块石头上精雕细琢而成,显示了石雕艺人高超的工艺技巧……

——梅尔斯, 1867 年, 第 256 页

Amoy Temples

Napoleon in Nanputuo!   There is still one very superb temple, by far the best specimen I had yet met with. This, as usual, was filled with gods and demons of all denominations and attributes. The entree of these figures does not appear to be exclusively restricted to Chinese deities, a clay statue of Napoleon having been found in one of their temples at Amoy, in his cocked-hat and boots; how he got there, it would be difficult to determine.

Cunynghame 1853

Beautiful Temple Sites   The early founders of Buddhism in China must have had a profound love of the beautiful in Nature, and have had at the same time the genius to transmit the same to the long line of priests and abbots that have since succeeded them throughout the empire. We are led to this conclusion by the fact that the priests of the present day show the most exquisite taste in the selection of spots where they build their temples and monasteries, wherever Nature gives them a chance to do so…set them to select some place where a future temple is to be built, and, with the instinct of the poet in their hearts and with the eye of the artist who has caught the secret of Nature's charms, they will select the very spot where the soul may spend years of solitude and retirement without being reduced to despair by its surroundings. With the mountain peaks around, the great silent valleys stretching at their feet, the musical echoes of rustling streams, and the inarticulate sounds that Nature is ever uttering, they are enabled to spend the years of a solitude that otherwise might have driven them to despair.

But let me try and describe in as vivid colours as I can one of these Buddhist temples. The time I shall begin with is the hour just before the dawn. Everything is shrouded in darkness, huge boulders that lie around the monastery in fantastic shapes seem like sleeping dragons watching over it during the night. A profound silence reigns everywhere, and the very pines that stand near by are as erect and as motionless as thought they were sentinels on guard.

All at once, as if a miracle had been wrought, the mountain ridge away in the front seems to drop its mantle of darkness, and to become dimly visible. It looks as though some conjurer were at work, for in a moment or two a delicate light that seems to belong to another world trembles shyly at its top. With another wave of his wand sunbeams like golden threads flash through the twilight and weave themselves in and out in various colours. Soon the mountain crests and peaks are crowned with sunlight that slowly travels down the sides of the hill, peers into the dim caverns, and plays around the giant boulders, under which run murmuring rills that are to grow into the rushing, foaming torrent that leaps, with a mad joy in its heart, farther down the mountain-side.

ravine on the edge of which the temple is perched. What a view it has to look upon this glorious morning! The mountains are bathed in light, the shadows chasing each other like schoolboys along their rugged sides; the sea in the distance, touched with the morning glory, gleams like a lake of gold, and the far-off peaks seem so distant that they must verily belong to another world—these are the sights upon which the priest may gaze and forget that he is alone.

MacGowan, 1912

第十三章　厦门宗教 Amoy Religion

厦门的庙宇

南普陀里的拿破仑！　在厦门，有一座很好的寺庙，是迄今为止我所见过的最好的寺庙。跟其他寺庙一样，这座寺庙里摆满了各种各样的神仙和魔鬼。寺里好像不只是供奉中国的神灵。在厦门的一个寺庙里，有人发现了一尊拿破仑泥塑。他头戴摺边帽，脚穿长筒靴。很难确定拿破仑是怎么来到厦门的。

——坎宁汉，1853 年，第 115 页

寺庙漂亮的位置　中国佛教的早期创始人应该是非常热爱大自然的美，同时又有能力把这种热爱一代又一代地传递给全国各地继承他们事业的和尚、道士。我们之所以能够得出这个结论，是因为中国的神职人员在为寺庙、宫观选址的时候会展示出极为细致的品位，一旦造化赋予他们机会。

请他们为未来的寺庙选址，他们的内心会用诗人的直觉，再用艺术家的眼光捕捉大自然美的奥秘，然后再选出恰当的地点。在那里，他们可以让自己的心灵长期处于独居和隐退的状态，而不会被周边的环境逼入绝境。四周群山环绕，空旷的大峡谷静静地在脚下延伸，淙淙的溪水发出悦耳的响声，以及大自然发出的各种难以表述的声音，所有这一切都使得中国的神职人员能够长期隐居。否则的话，他们肯定会被逼入绝境。

下面请允许我试着对其中的一个佛寺进行尽可能详尽、生动的描述，时间始于黎明前一小时。周围笼罩在一片漆黑之中，摆放在佛寺四周各种奇形怪状的巨石看上去像是一群沉睡的巨龙，守卫着夜间的寺庙。周围一片死寂，矗立在佛寺边上的松树高大挺拔、屹然不动，像是一群哨兵在站岗。

突然间，好像奇迹发生一般，正前方远处的山梁似乎已经抖掉自己身上的夜色，开始若隐若现。看上去好像魔术师在用力，因为，须臾间，一道来自天界的柔弱光线羞涩地在山峰上颤动。魔棒一舞，太阳光像金线一般闪过黎明的天空，编织成各种颜色的晨光。很快，阳光洒满了群峰，并慢慢地照耀山坡，照进昏暗的山洞，在悬崖峭壁上飞舞。岩壁下面泉水叮咚，慢慢地变成了奔腾的激流，心里充满狂喜，最后冲到远处的山脚。

紧接着，太阳越升越高。光线照进了深深的峡谷。寺庙就坐落在峡谷的危崖上。清晨，能够看到这些景象是这么得辉煌壮观啊！群山沐浴在阳光下，乌云像男生一样在崎岖不平的山腰互相追逐。远处的大海染上了清晨的霞光，像一湖金子那样闪闪发光。更远处的山峰离得更远，好像它们是非天界莫属。这就是中国神职人员每天可以凝视的景观，足以令其忘却孤独。

——麦嘉湖，1912 年，第 143 页

Gulangyu Temples Four places of worship, exclusive of Protestant missionary establishments, minister to the religious cravings of the Chinese population on this island. The most important of these is the Palace of Flourishing Virtue, situated at the corner of the cricket ground, beneath the shade of two magnificent banyans.

It is said to date back as far as the Yuan, or Mongol, dynasty, which was founded in A. D. 1206, and belongs to the Taoist faith, being inhabited and looked after by a Taoist priest whose religious designation is Wrinkled Wave. The God to whom it is dedicated is the "Lord Protector of the People;" and we are informed by a scroll hanging up within the temple that this deity's shrine was formerly in Ching-chiao [Quanzhou] of whence it was removed to Koolangsu. The corresponding scroll on the other side tells us that "holiness benefits mankind and brings about the salvation of millions."

Giles, 1878

New Temple to a Leader (1693) In anno 1693 I was at Amoy, and then the island was governed by a chungcoun, or a general of 10,000 men. He was a man of about eighty years of age, of a very agreeable aspect. He had done many singular services to his country, particularly in supressing pirates that mightily disturbed the province, and governed with much justice and moderation, but next year he died, and was succeeded by a teytock, or deputy-general of 5000. In anno 1697 I went thither again, and found a new temple built in honour to the old chungcoun, and his image placed in it, as much like his person while alive, as ever I saw anything represented in my life, with every lineament and feature in his face, and I saw many votaries worship his image. It seems the Chinese are speedier in their canonizing than the Romans are."

Hamilton, 1727

Small Gulangyu Shrine (Spring 1932)   J. Nienhuis

第十三章　厦门宗教　Amoy Religion

鼓浪屿岛上的寺庙　除了新教的几处礼拜堂，鼓浪屿岛上还有四个地方可供中国各种信徒朝拜。其中，位于板球场边上、两棵大榕树下的茂德宫是最重要的一个地方。

茂德宫的历史据说可以追溯到建立于公元1206年的元朝，也就是蒙古人的时代，属于道教，由一位名叫周波的道士照管，敬奉的神灵叫"护民君"。宫里悬挂的一幅卷轴告诉我们，这位神灵的祖殿在泉州，后来迁往鼓浪屿。与之相对应的另一幅卷轴告诉我们"神灵普度众生，造福人类"。

——吉尔斯，1878年，第15、16页

敬奉一位领袖的新庙（1693年）　1693年，我在厦门。当时，这个小岛由一位将军管辖，手下兵员一万。将军大约80岁，和蔼可亲。他为国家做出了许多杰出的贡献，特别是消除了长期困扰福建的海盗问题，并能够公正、中庸地治理地方政务。不过，第二年，他就去世了。接任的是一名提督，手下兵员五千。1697年，我再次访问厦门，发现这里建了一座新庙，用于敬奉已故的老将军。将军的遗像安放在庙内，栩栩如生。将军脸部的每一条皱纹、每一个特征都非常像。我一辈子也没见过画得这么像的。我看见许多信徒在他的遗像前祭拜。为死者封圣，中国人比罗马人神速多了。

——哈密尔顿，1727年，第494页

Roadside Shrine, Graves　MacGowan, 1913

老外看老鼓浪屿 *Old Gulangyu in Foreigners' Eyes*

White Stag Temple (1890s) At length we come to the outskirts of the town, and at the base of a low range of hills that runs along the eastern side of the island of Amoy, and which terminates rather abruptly some little distance from its north-eastern coast. These hills are distinguished for the number of Buddhist temples built on their sides and in their valleys, in the most charming and picturesque spots that men with the keenest insight into the beauties of nature could have selected. One of these is called the White Stag, from a tradition that a white deer, which was really an incarnation of a good spirit, one day fled wildly across the hills pursued by a number of infuriated dogs, when it fell down exhausted and dying on a rock, where its figure is seen reclining at the present day. ...

There is no question but that the deer was a true artist by nature. A more romantic spot where she chose to breathe her last would be difficult to find. It is on the slope of a hill that rises somewhat abruptly from the very edge of the large and populous city.

...Here we have a situation which of all others seems adapted for retirement and meditation. Great rocks and mighty boulders, that Time with her patient hand has smoothed and rounded, like thickly strewn around in that artless way with which Nature can drape these unwieldy forms into the most artistic attitudes. In the midst of these

White Stag Temple Priest

the temple of "The White Deer" lies enshrined. The beauty of the position is greatly enhanced by the natural grottos that are formed by overhanging rocks and projecting boulders, that cluster around as though the fairies had flung them with graceful hand into positions where they could serve as resting-places for the visitors after their steep climb from the city below. Stone seats have been placed within these where one can sit under the shadow of the rocks, certain that no burning sun shall send its fiery rays to interfere with the delightful coolness that always reigns within.

Macgowan, 1897, and MacGowan, 1912

Nanputuo Temple (1940s) This was the universal shrine for Overseas Chinese departing for and returning from the South Seas. The rate of contributions from successful businessmen, who in devout gratitude ascribed their financial successes to the tutelary guidance and goodwill of the temple gods, enabled the monks not only to live themselves in great comfort but to provide adequate fare and entertainment to their many visitors and friends, with special receptions reserved for regular patrons. ...

第十三章 厦门宗教 Amoy Religion

White Stag Temple

白鹿寺 终于,我们来到了城镇的郊区。在这里,一条低矮的山脉横贯厦门东部,并在距东北海岸不远的地方戛然而止。山腰间、山谷里建了不少佛寺,地点都是由那些对大自然之美有最真知灼见的人选出的,风景极佳,景致极美。其中有一座寺庙叫白鹿寺。传说,有一天,一头白鹿被一群疯狗狂追,落荒而逃。最终,筋疲力尽,卧倒并死在一块岩石上。实际上,这只白鹿是某个神灵的化身。它的图像至今仍然横卧在岩石上……

毫无疑义,白鹿是大自然创造的一位真正的艺术家。白鹿呼出她生命中最后一口气,非常浪漫。这个地方就在一座小山的山坡上。小山就是这样贸然地从这座人口稠密的大城市边缘隆起。要找到一个比它浪漫的地方非常困难。

……在这里,我们选择的地方首先似乎很适合隐居和沉思。高耸的岩壁、坚硬的岩石,时间老人用自己耐心的双手打磨,造化把这些毫无章法地四处散落、难以驾驭的东西打扮成最具艺术特色的形状。就这样,白鹿寺拔"石"而起。更让寺庙选址美上加美的是,悬崖峭壁所形成的洞穴,好像是神仙用优雅的手法把它们连接在一起。来自城里的游客从山脚爬上陡峭的山坡之后,可以把这些洞穴里作为自己的歇脚地。洞穴里安上石椅,人们可以坐在岩石的荫凉里。毫无疑问,灼热的太阳光肯定无法侵入洞中,搅乱里面怡人的清凉。
——麦嘉湖,1897年,第167、168页,及麦嘉湖,1912年,第146页

南普陀寺(20世纪40年代) 这是华侨前往南洋或从南洋归来必拜的一个寺庙。成功商人虔诚地把自己的商业成就归功于神灵的庇护和善意。来自他们的捐献不仅让寺庙里的和尚丰衣足食,许多香客和云游和尚也得到了充分的款待。对于定期捐献的香客,寺庙还有特殊的款待……

...To the side were two long bamboo chairs with a little table between them. Clad in jackets and ample trousers a couple of stout elderly men reclined on the chairs leisurely sipping tea and cracking water-melon seeds. One of them was grotesquely fat. His immense belly, trembling and shimmying, like the rising dough in a baker's vat, seemed about to drop to the floor at any moment in quivering folds. His stertorous breathing filled the aisle with a wheezing sound, and gave rise to fear of an attach of asphyxia at any moment.

I rose to walk through the temple and the abbot, who followed slowly behind me, whispered that these two men were very rich merchants, who had retired from the South Seas and had recently contributed a very large sum to the monastery. They had come for a week's stay to relax from their business cares and to improve their health by a diet of vegetarian food, specially prepared at this monastery, for the Prolongation of Longevity.

Neil, 1956

Chinese Virgin Mary Quanheim (Guanyin) has the most votaries. She is placed in state, sitting on a cushion with rich robes, and her little son standing before her, with a charged trident in his right hand, ready to throw at offenders of the laws of humanity and nature, and also at those who make no freewill-offering to his mother. The Chinese, who have seen the Roman Catholic churches and worship, say that she is the Chinese Virgin Mary.

Hamilton, 1727

Nanputuo Temple and Soldier's Graves   MacGowan, 1914

第十三章　厦门宗教 *Amoy Religion*

……边上有两张长长的竹制躺椅，中间摆放着一张小桌。两个肥胖的老先生身穿夹克和宽松的裤子，斜靠在躺椅上，悠闲地嗑着瓜子、喝着茶。其中一位先生胖得变形了。他大腹便便，像面桶里发酵的面团，微微颤抖，随时可能掉到地上。他的鼾声极大，在整条过道里回荡，让人随时担心他会窒息。

我站起来，在寺里走走。主持慢慢地跟在我后面，小声地说，这两位先生是殷富的商人，从南洋归来，刚刚向寺里捐献了一大笔的款子。他们放下生意，到寺里休息一周，并希望通过素食改善身体健康状况。素食是寺里特别准备的，有利于人们的健康长寿。

——尼尔，1956 年，第 131、132 页

Nanputuo Priest　　MacGowan, 1907

中国的圣母玛丽亚　拜观音的人最多。观音身着华贵的长袍，坐在莲花座上。童子站在她前面，右手持着三齿渔叉，随时准备掷向那些胆敢触犯人道和自然法则，以及冒犯圣母的人。见过罗马天主教堂及其礼拜的中国人说，观音就是中国的圣母玛丽亚。

——哈密尔顿，1727 年，第 502 页

Buddha's 18 Arhats (Disciples)　　MacGowan, 1912

187

Divining Rods MacGowan, 1914

Josh Sticks Sat. October 20th, 1856 —About noon, started, in company with Mr. Tait, Mr. Patten and Mr. Craig, to visit the White Stag Temple. Mr. T., who was well acquainted with the country, led us through the streets of the city, passing the White Heart Temple on our way.

We ascended the mountain by crooked flights of stone steps, passed over, and by corresponding flights of steps descended into a deep valley beyond. When part of the way down, we stopped a few minutes to look at an ancient tomb, built into the hill-side. ...Two women were chin-chinning Josh at the shrine, on which, in front of the gods', the incense, or Josh-sticks, were burning and smoking. The women tried their luck with a bunch of bamboo slips, and the casting on the floor of two pieces of dice-wood. One of the women shook the bunch of slips in a bamboo box, until one gradually worked up and fell out on the ground. This, like all, having a motto engraved on it, the woman carried to the priest, who interpreted it, and gave her a corresponding response, for which she paid a number of copper cash.

…She was not so lucky. She tried them over and over with alternate chin-chinnings; but either the two round sides came up, or the two flat. She went on, finally, with such desperation, that I really pitied her. She continued, however, to pick them up and let them fall as fast as she could, until she was really lucky; and then, with an air of satisfaction at having conquered, she gave the idol a look that seemed to say, "Well, you see I did succeed, notwithstanding;" and then she left the temple.

After they had gone we all tried our fortunes, much to the amazement of the priests. Some of us were lucky, and some unlucky: I was among the unlucky ones, but, persevering, became lucky.

Ball, 1856

Burning Incense Dukes, 1885

Buttons & the Temple (1850s) There were Navy officers with their brass buttons on caps and coats, and gold lace, and the rest of the men in pith helmets and white linen suits, and the ladies in pretty muslins.
…

Some of the party visited the Temple on a high prominence, with many steps to climb to reach it. We children held father's and mother's hands tightly, a little fearsome of priests of another faith, and a big idol with fierce countenance which faced us. We entered the Temple, when a priest stopped us, saying an offering to their god was expected. Money was offered, but he said that would not suffice; their god wanted some of those bright buttons! The officers demurred and argued, and probably were rather arrogant and insistent in refusing. They started to walk past the priest, but were as insistently held back for the buttons. Finally, not very graciously I guess, one of the officers whipped out his knife and cut off one or two and handed them to the company of priests who had gathered by this time. They blandly and suavely received them and allowed us to pass.

Mary Doty's Memoirs

第十三章　厦门宗教 Amoy Religion

上香　1856年10月20日，星期六。午晌前后，与泰特先生、帕特先生和克拉格先生做伴，出发前往白鹿寺游览。泰特先生对郊区很熟悉。他带着我们穿街过巷，途中路过了白心寺。

我们沿着蜿蜒的石头台阶路上山，又走在同样的石阶路进入一个狭长的山谷。下山谷时，我们在一座古墓前停留了一会儿。古墓建在山腰上……两个女人手持冒烟的神香，跪拜在神灵前。她们一个摇动签筒，求神问卜；一个像扔骰子那样在掷筊。抽签的女士摇动签筒，直至竹筒中的一根竹签慢慢升起并掉到地上。跟筒里的所有竹签一样，这根竹签上面刻有一段箴言。女人把竹签拿给道士，让他解读。道士给她相应的解释，女人支付了几枚铜钱。

Idol and Incense Seller MacGowan, 1914

……另一个女人就没有那么幸运了。她反复上香、反复抛掷竹筊，得到的结果要么是两块竹筊的凸面一起朝上，要么是平面一起朝上。她反复掷筊，最后有些绝望，搞得我实在有些可怜她。但是，她还是继续把竹筊捡起来，并且尽可能快地抛掷下去，直到一凸一平的圣筊出现。征服竹筊之后，她看了神灵一眼，一副满意的样子，好像在说："啊，你瞧，不管怎么说，我终于成功了。"然后，她离开了寺庙。

她们走后，我们都在神灵前试试自己的运气，令寺里的道士惊奇不已。我们当中有几个人运气很好，有的就没那么好了。我是运气差的一个。不过，我坚持了一下，圣筊就出现了。

——波尔，1856年，第328页

纽扣和寺庙（19世纪50年代）　海军军官的帽子和上衣钉着黄铜纽扣，其他男士头戴遮阳帽、身穿白色尼龙套装，女士穿着用麦斯林纱做的漂亮衣服……

团队里的一些人爬了许多台阶，造访了高处的一座寺庙。我们小孩子紧抓父亲或母亲的手，有点害怕另外一种信仰的神职人员以及我们所看到的凶神恶煞的高大神像。进入寺庙的时候，一名和尚拦住我们，说希望向他们的神灵捐献。我们捐了钱，他却说，这些还不够。神灵想要几个黄灿灿的纽扣！军官们犹豫了一下，开始讨论。拒绝的时候，他们相当地傲慢、坚决。他们从这位和尚身边走过，但和尚却坚持要求他们给些纽扣。最后，一群和尚围了过来。一位军官快速地取出他的小刀，割下了一、两个纽扣并把它们交给了和尚。做这些动作的时候，我想，他并不太和蔼。和尚和颜悦色、温文尔雅地接过纽扣，让我们进入寺庙。

——玛丽·多蒂未出版的回忆录

老外看老鼓浪屿 *Old Gulangyu in Foreigners' Eyes*

Chapter 14   Amoy Military

Soldier   MacGowan, 1909

Amoy's Famous Fighters[1]   The Amoy men make good soldiers, so at least it is said; they certainly fought well for their independence, and were the last to yield to the Tartar invaders, and they are those upon whom the conquerors seemed to have pressed most heavily. To this day they wear the turban which they assumed to hide the tonsure and queue imposed on them by the conquerors.

Thomson, 1876

Peaceable Amoy Folk   The people of this district [Amoy] are exceedingly industrious and peaceable, rowdies excepted, and have never in all the troublesome times, through which this empire has been too often called to pass, disturbed or molested the foreigner or the native Christians. While perchance their love for us is no greater than that of the natives in any other section of this empire, nevertheless they have ever treated us with fairness and commendable hospitality. And in the present calamities [Boxer Rebellion] probably there has not been up to the present time another place in China so undisturbed and so little agitated against foreigners and native Christians as Amoy.

Pitcher, Nov, 1900

Yellow No Peril   Some writers have predicted that a day may come when, inspired by a spirit of war, they [the Chinese] will flash their swords in a wild conquest of the West. This is a dream that will never be realized. Both by instinct and by ages of training, the Chinese are essentially a peace-loving people. The glory of war is something that does not appeal to them. Trade, and commerce, and moneymaking, and peaceful lives are the ideals of the race. No sooner is a clan fight begun, or a war with another nation, than the air at once resounds with the cry, "Mediate," "Mediate." Mediation is in the very blood of the nation, and the man who is a successful mediator is one that wins a golden reputation for himself.

What the West has to fear is not the warlike spirit of the Chinese, which has never been a very important factor in their past history, but their numbers. ... The Chinese are a strong race, and can live in comfort, and even luxury, on incomes that would mean starvation to American or Australian workmen. The battle of the future with the Yellow race will not be fought on any battlefield, but in the labour markets of the nations that they would invade.

MacGowan, 1907

---

1   Amoynese were known for being both the most peaceable of Chinese as well as the fiercest of Chinese fighters when their home was threatened—a paradox admired by their enemies.

第十四章　厦门军事

著名的厦门斗士　厦门人可以成为好战士，至少有人这么说过。为了国家独立，他们不懈斗争。他们最迟屈服于满清王朝，也似乎是受征服者的压迫最深重的臣民。直至今日，他们还戴头巾，以掩饰征服者强制他们蓄留的发辫。

——汤姆逊，1876 年

热爱和平的厦门人　这个地区（厦门）的人特别勤劳，而且热爱和平。他们不爱热闹。在这个帝国时常经历的困难时刻，他们从不打扰或妨碍外国人或当地的基督教徒。尽管他们对我们的爱护并不比中国其他地方的老百姓更多，但是他们对我们还是相当的公道、友善。在当前的灾难（义和团）中，迄今为止，中国没有一个地方像厦门那样不骚扰外国人和本地基督教徒，不煽动对他们的不满情绪。

——毕腓力，1900 年，第 550 页

Soldiers　MacGowan, 1909

黄色非危祸　有些作家预言，将来某一天，中国人在好战精神的鼓动下，会疯狂亮剑征服西方。这是一个永远不会实现的梦想。无论是处于本能，还是岁月的磨炼，中国人本质上是一个爱好和平的民族。战争的荣耀对他们来说没有什么吸引力。贸易、商业和赚钱，以及平静的生活是这个民族的理想。一场家族争斗，或与外国交战刚刚开始，周围的气氛立即回响着"调停"、"调停"的呼声。调停正是这个国家的品性。一个人成功地进行调停就会为自己赢得金子般的声誉。

西方人应该担心的不是中国人的好战精神，而是他们的人口总量，因为战争一直没有成为中国历史上很重要的因素……中国人是一个优秀的民族。美国或澳大利亚工人认为处于饥饿线的收入，对中国人来说，他们可以过得很舒适，甚至奢侈。未来与这个黄皮肤种族之间的战争不会发生在任何战场，而是他们可能进入的国家的劳务市场上。

——麦高文，1907 年

老外看老鼓浪屿 *Old Gulangyu in Foreigners' Eyes*

Might versus Right The soldier occupies the lowest position in the Chinese classification of society, and this arrangement, we think, is in accordance with the true sentiment of the nation on this point. The Chinese do not regard it as at all derogatory to their character to be told that they are deficient in the elements of warlike strength. "We are not a military people," say they, "we are a literary nation. With us reason, and not force, defines rights and privileges; argument, and not the sword, decides controversies."

MacCauley, 1861

Fujian Governor's Toast to America & China Amoy, 4th of July, 1891

At the celebration of the Fourth of July at Amoy, China, by the Americans, the governor of the province was invited to the banquet, and made a remarkable speech, which shows his intelligence, and suggests some things worthy of consideration.

Tsin Chin-chung was called upon to respond to the toast, "The Emperor of China." In part he said: "China, having followed its own principles of advancement during more than 5000 years, is now compelled to change and move along European channels. It has begun to own steamships and railways. Its telegraph now covers every province. It has mills, forges and foundries like those of Essen, of Sheffield and of Pittsburgh. China is to-day learning that lesson in education which Europe has obliged her to learn,—the art of killing, the science of armies and navies. Woe, then, to the world if the scholar, profiting by her lesson, should apply it in turn. With its freedom from debt, its inexhaustible resources and its teeming millions, this empire might be the menace, if not the destroyer, of Christendom. No matter what happens, it needs no prophetic gift to know that the 20th century will see at the forefront of the nations of the world,—China in the East and America in the West. Well may we pray that, for the welfare of humanity, their purposes will be as peaceful and upright as to-day."

Chinese Recorder, Vol. 23, January, 1892

Pink Ribbon on Cannons The barge carried eleven small cannon decorated with bits of pink calico tied in bows round the muzzle…

Shore, 1881

192

第十四章　厦门军事 Amoy Military

强权与权力　在中国的社会结构中，士兵处于最低层。我们认为，这样的安排与这个国家的真实情感是一致的。如果有人说中国人本质上缺乏好战的实力，他们一点也不会觉得这是对自己人格的一种诋毁。"我们不是尚武的民族，"他们会说，"我们是文明之邦。我们用理智，而不是武力来决定权力和荣誉；我们用辩论，而不是刀剑来解决争议。"

——麦考利，1861年，第31页

福建总督为美国和中国干杯　　　　　　　1891年7月4日，　厦门

7月4日美国人在厦门庆祝独立日的时候，福建总督应邀出席宴会，并进行了一次出色的演讲。讲话显示了他的才华，并暗示着值得注意的一些事情。

对于为中美友谊干杯，总督作出了回应。他在演讲中说："中国皇帝和中国在遵循自己的原则行事5000多年后，被迫作出改变并按照欧洲人设计的方向前进。我们开始拥有蒸汽船和铁路。电报已经覆盖中国所有的省份。中国的面粉厂、冶炼厂和铸造厂已经跟德国的埃森、英国的谢菲尔德和美国的匹兹堡没有什么两样。今日的中国正在接受欧洲强迫她接受的教育——杀戮的技术：陆、海军的战术。如果学生从所学课程中受益，并反过来用诸实践，那么，对这个世界来说，是一种灾难。以其取之不竭的资源和数万万的人口，一旦还清债务，中国可能成为西方基督国家的威胁，如果不是毁灭的话。无须天才的预言，我们就能看到，无论发生什么，20世纪走在世界最前列的国家——中国在东方，美国在西方。让我们祈祷，为了人类的幸福、安康，他们的意图是和平的、正直的，就像今天一样。"

——《中国教务杂志》，第23卷，第18页，1892年1月

火炮上的粉红丝带　驳船装载着11门小型火炮，粉红印花布作为装饰物扎成弓形，绑在炮口……

——肖尔，1881年，第61页

Gulangyu Cannon, 1920s　　J. Nienhuis

老外看老鼓浪屿 Old Gulangyu in Foreigners' Eyes

From Servant to Admiral The naval worthy in question began life as a ' boy' or servant in one of the Consulates at Amoy; while a brother officer, likewise of the party, boasted of equally humble antecedents. It was probably at this period of their career that they acquired a taste for malt liquors and other barbarian drinks, when imbibed at their master's expense. How suggestive this is to a thoughtful mind! What a happy land surely, where rank and wealth count for nothing in the struggle for office when pitted against talent and merit.; where intellect is not the slave of money to be petted and rewarded when it panders to the tastes of the multitude, and whipped into obedience when running counter to the stream. How pure must be its constitution, and how liberal its laws, when the humble sweeper of offices with no recommendation beyond an aptitude for business, and an acquaintance with "Pigeon English," can raise himself to the exalted position of captain in the Imperial Navy of China! What a lesson to us! But even this bright picture has its reverse, for exalted rank does not screen the holder from the sharp whacks of the bamboo; and a Chinese \writer has very sagely remarked, "that station is vanity, office is vanity, when the tide of fortune is spent, the retributions of justice begin, and remorse is without bounds."

U.S. Sailors on Gulangyu

Shore, 1881

Display of Martial Prowess On the occasion of a visit, my companion requested one of these brave but hardly-used defenders of the country to go through his pike drill for my edification, a request which he showed a praiseworthy alacrity in complying with, and seizing his trusty weapon, sprang into the arena, assumed an attitude calculated to inspire terror in his possible enemy, and for the next ten minutes amused us by going through a variety of contortions and gymnastic feats emblematic of spiking his antagonist in every conceivable position -a species of military can-can[Can-can: French dance] in fact. It would be unfair to pass over this feat of arms without acknowledging his marvelous agility, energy and resources; indeed, a foe would have to be unusually active to escape that pike. Once started, however, this misguided youth had no intention of stopping; his martial ardour was thoroughly roused, and he was becoming positively dangerous. His pike was here, there, and everywhere; so remembering that in such cases discretion is the better part of valour, we retired, immensely impressed with the pike drill, and the last thing we saw on passing out of the fort was this blood-thirsty soldier still impaling some imaginary barbarian.

Shore, 1881

第十四章 厦门军事 Amoy Military

从佣人到将军 这位海军军官曾经在厦门的一个领事馆里当过男仆或佣人,还有一位同事也同样出身贫寒。也许正是在这个阶段,有主人买单,他们学会了喝啤酒和其他野蛮人喝的饮料。对于一个有思想的人来说,这又会引起怎样的联想啊！在跟有才气和优点的人竞争官职的时候,地位和财富不起任何作用；当才智不再是被人宠爱和奖赏的金钱奴隶,而是为了迎合大众的口味,它在逆潮而动的时候已经被人收拾得服服帖帖了。这是一个多么快乐的国度啊！当办公室卑贱的清洁工在没有任何人推荐（除了拥有处理办公事务的能力）、只懂得"洋泾浜英语"的情况下,能够在中国皇家海军里坐上舰长的高位,这个国家的宪法肯定很抽象,她的法律肯定很随意！对我们来说,这是多么生动的一课啊！不过,即便是这么生动的景象也有其相反的一面,因为高位并不能让其拥有者免受舆论的鞭笞。一位中国作家很睿智地指出,"地位是虚幻的,官职也是虚幻的。当运气用完,正义惩罚开始,懊悔是无穷无尽。"

——肖尔,1881 年,第 57～58 页

展示军威 有一次到要塞去访问,陪同人员请求这个国家勇敢、但尚无用武之地的士兵为我操练长矛的套路,让我开开眼界。这个请求他们欣然同意。抓起自己所信赖的长矛,士兵跳入场地,作出一副令其潜在敌人战栗的姿势。在接下来的十分钟里,他用长矛操练了一系列的柔体表演和体操姿势,从各个可能的角度打击敌人。这些动作其实更像法国肯肯舞的一个种类,让我们感到很开心。忽视长矛的技艺,不承认这位士兵非凡的精力、体力和灵活度是不公道的。说实在,要逃避他的长矛,对手一定得非常敏捷。不过,一操练,年轻人显然被误导了。他没有停下来的意思。他的武术热情被完全调动了。很明显。他开始变得危险了。长矛左冲右突,无处不在,令人印象深刻。在这种情况下,谨慎判断比刚猛更重要。离开现场,矛操给我们留下深刻印象。走出要塞,我们所看到的最后一幕是,那位士兵还在拼命地刺杀自己想象中的某些野蛮人。

——肖尔,1881 年,第 85～86 页

The Capture of Amoy—"Unnecessary"[1]   The important seaport of Amoy was attacked and taken after what was called "a short but animated resistance... The Chinese had raised a rampart of 1,100 yards in length, and this they had armed with ninety guns, while a battery of forty-two guns protected its flank. Kulangsu was also fortified, and the Chinese had placed in all 500 guns in position. They believed in the impregnability of Amoy, and... no inconsiderable skill as well as great expense had been devoted to the strengthening of the place.

When the English fleet arrived off the port, the Chinese sent a flag of truce to demand what it wanted, and they were informed the surrender of the town. The necessity for this measure would be hard to justify, especially as we were nominally at peace with China, for the people of Amoy had inflicted no injury on our trade, and their chastisement would not bring us any nearer to Pekin. Nor was the occupation of Amoy necessary on military grounds. It was strong only for itself, and its capture had no important consequences. As the Chinese determined to resist the English, the fleet engaged the batteries, and the Chinese, standing to their guns "right manfully," only abandoned their position when they found their rear threatened by a landing party. ... some of their officers, preferring death to dishonor, committed suicide, one of them being seen to walk calmly into the sea and drown himself in face of both armies. The capture of Amoy followed.

As the authorities at Amoy refused to hold any intercourse with the English, the achievement remained barren of any useful consequence, and after leaving a small garrison on Kulangsu, and three warships in the roadstead, the English expedition continued its northern course."

Boulger, 1902

Bombardment of Amoy   The capture of Amoy was chiefly a naval operation; and for four hours did the ships pepper at those enormous batteries without a moment's cessation. The cannonade was certainly a splendid sight. The stream of fire and smoke from the sides of the liners was terrific. It never for a moment appeared to slacken. The Wellesley and Blenheim alone each fired upwards of 12,000 rounds, to say nothing of the frigates, steamers, and small craft; yet the works [Amoy fort] were as perfect when they left off as when they began, the utmost penetration of the shot being sixteen inches. From twenty to thirty people were all that were killed by this enormous expenditure of powder and shot.

Macpherson, 1843

---

1   Amoy was captured during the first Opium War (see Opium Chapter).

The Capture of Amoy, August, 1841, by Lt. R.B. Crawford,R.N., Plate I Chater Collection

第十四章　厦门军事 Amoy Military

厦门被占——占领厦门"毫无必要"　对重要的海港厦门的进攻遭遇了所谓的"短暂、但激励的抵抗"。之后，被占领……　中国人修筑了长度为1100码的防御工事，配备了90条枪，侧翼还有42条枪在支持。鼓浪屿也是固若金汤。中国人在阵地上安置了总计500条枪。他们迷信厦门牢不可破。……他们没有为强化这个地方的防务投入足够的技术准备和经费。

当英国舰队抵达厦门港外，中国人打出休战旗，质问英国人想干什么。英国人要求厦门投降。采取这种手段的必要性很难证明其有正当的理由，特别是当时我们表面上与中国并未开战，厦门人也没有伤害我们的贸易，对他们的惩罚并不会让我们更加靠近北京。从军事的角度出发，占领厦门毫无必要。厦门的强硬只是为了自己，占领厦门并没有什么重要的影响。随着中国人决心抵抗英军，舰队开始参战。面对敌人的炮火，中国人"很勇敢"。当他们发现后方被敌人的登陆部队所威胁的时候，他们才放弃阵地……　一些指挥官宁死不屈，最后殉职了。有人看见其中一位指挥官腹背受敌。他平静地走向大海，在敌人的面前自杀。接着，厦门被占。

由于厦门当局拒绝与英国人进行任何谈判，占领厦门没有取得任何实质性结果。在鼓浪屿留下少量驻军、港外锚地布置三艘战舰之后，英国舰队继续北上。

——博格勒，1902年

炮击厦门　占领厦门主要是由海军负责的一次行动。舰队连续四小时不间断向厦门巨大的防御工事发射炮弹。炮击肯定是一个壮观的场面。从炮舰两侧冒出的浓烟和火光实在吓人。看上去似乎没有一刻减弱。仅"韦尔斯利"和"布兰尼姆"两艘炮舰就各自发射了12000颗以上的炮弹，更甭提护卫舰、蒸汽船和其他小船。然而，炮轰之前与炮轰之后，厦门港的防御工事完全一样。炮弹打击最深的地方不过16英寸。总共只有20至30人在这场威力巨大的炮击中死亡。

——麦克赫森，1843年，第204页

The Capture of Amoy, August, 1841, by Lt. R.B. Crawford, R.N., Plate II Chater Collection

老外看老鼓浪屿 *Old Gulangyu in Foreigners' Eyes*

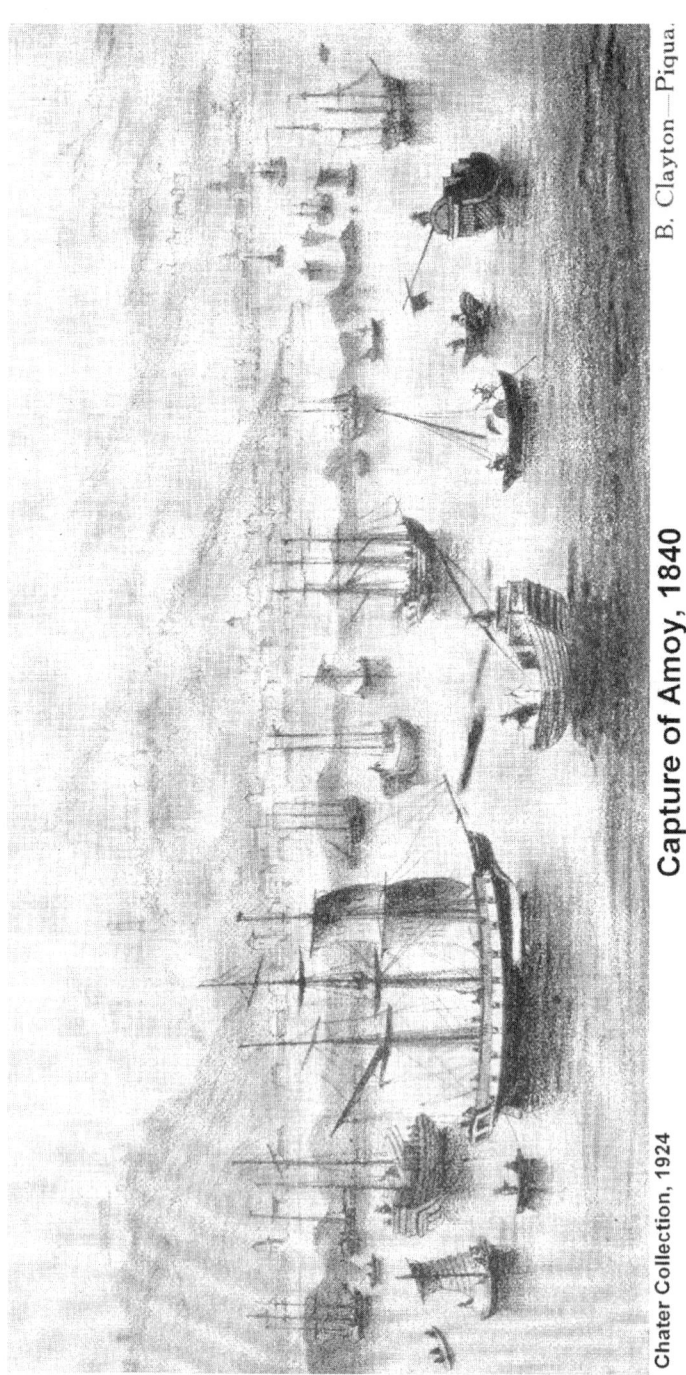

B. Clayton—Piqua.

Capture of Amoy, 1840

Chater Collection, 1924

第十四章　厦门军事　*Amoy Military*

THE ILLUSTRATED LONDON NEWS, OCT. 2, 1875--333

ENGLISH OFFICERS DRILLING CHINESE SOLDIERS AT AMOY.

老外看老鼓浪屿 Old Gulangyu in Foreigners' Eyes

The U.S.' Great White Fleet in Amoy The visit of the American fleet to the port of Amoy and the cordial reception accorded by the Chinese government through a special commission during the first days of November marked another important step in China's friendly relations with foreign powers. The arrangements at Amoy were extensive, the receptions given to officers and men most elaborate.

Chinese Recorder, Vol. 39, Dec. 1908

Chinese Reception of U.S. Navy The reception of the American fleet at Amoy and the appointment of an envoy extraordinary to convey the thanks of the Emperor to America for remitting half the Boxer indemnity are notable matters of public interest, although many others quite as interesting do not figure in the published edicts. Whether or not a closer understanding is probable between America and China, in an official sense, the sending of this embassy and the concomitant sending of many students to America, as in the days of Yung Wing, must mean much for international comity and fraternity.

Chinese Recorder, Vol. 40, Jan. 1909

U.S. Navy's "Great White Fleet," Amoy, 1908

Souvenir Post Card, Reception to the U.S. Fleet, Oct.--Nov., 1908

第十四章　厦门军事 *Amoy Military*

美国大白舰队访问厦门　11月初，美国舰队访问厦门，受到了中国政府特别指定委员会的热烈欢迎。这标志着中国与外国列强的友好关系又向前迈出了重要的一步。厦门的安排非常周到，对官员和士兵的接待也非常细心。
　　　　——《中国教务杂志》第39期，1908年12月，第711页

中国接待美国海军　在厦门接待来访的美国舰队，并特别指定陪同人员是一件事关公众利益的大事，它表达了清朝皇帝对美国政府返还一半庚子赔款的谢意。不过，很多同样有趣的事情却没有出现在公开发布的公告里。不管美国和中国能否更加亲近，本次派出代表团，和同时派出很多学生包括容闳前往美国留学，应该可以代表国际互助友爱的精神。
　　　　——《中国教务杂志》第40期，1909年1月，第34页

Thomson, 1909　　　　　　　　　　　　　　　UNDERWOOD & UNDERWOOD, N.Y.

Chinese officials at Amoy, Nov., 1908, entertaining officers and crews of American fleet. Admiral Emery proposing health of Empress Dowager

201

老外看老鼓浪屿 Old Gulangyu in Foreigners' Eyes

Banquet Held in Honor of U.S. "Great White Fleet", Nov. 1908, Amoy
Photo Courtesy U.S.Navy Historical Center

第十四章 厦门军事 *Amoy Military*

Stars and Stripes Fly Over Parade Ground, Amoy, Nov. 1908

Welcome Arches Built for Reception of U.S. Fleet, Amoy, Nov. 1908

老外看老鼓浪屿 Old Gulangyu in Foreigners' Eyes

Chapter 15   Amoy Opium Trade[1]

"Opium smoking came in through tobacco smoking.... Through the Philippines the American narcotic, tobacco, was introduced at Amoy, and thence to Formosa...the year 1620 is given as the date of the introduction, about the time of the "Counterblaste to Tobacco" of King James the Sixth of Scotland and First of England. The Chinese Emperors were animated by the same feelings as King James, and the last of the Ming Emperors (1628-1644) prohibited tobacco smoking in his dominions. The first of the Manchu Emperors [wrote in 1641]: "To smoke tobacco is a fault...As to the prohibition of tobacco smoking, it became impossible to maintain it because you princes and others smoked privately, though not publicly."

An Opium Smoker

Morse, 1919

British Opium Smuggling   The contraband trade carried on at Amoy in opium, China's curse, is very considerable, balls of it being sold publicly, in the shops; we have been informed that the mandarins received ...a bribe to close their eyes for every ball of opium they allowed to enter Amoy. To the disgrace of our [British] Government be it said, that although the clippers were ordered out of the harbour of Amoy, they are permitted to ride at anchor outside the bay; and boats devoted wholly to carrying the poisonous drug, ply openly for hire. Amoy may prove a port of considerable importance to the British merchant, who will confine his dealings in trade to honest lawful traffic...

Sirr, 1849

"Harmless" Opium   Very few quiet-going people at home have the least idea of the magnitude to which the trade in opium is carried on in China, or the daring and determined character with which it is prosecuted; this is fostered through the folly of the imperial court, in still retaining the prohibitory laws against its admission into the country. From the experience I had in constantly watching its use, I am of opinion that, taken as it almost invariably is, in great moderation, it is by no means noxious to the constitution, but quite the reverse, causing an exhilarating and pleasing sensation; and, in short, does them no more harm than a moderate quantity of wine does to us. It must always be borne in mind, that in point of food, they are generally moderate and abstemious, and they seldom drink any other thing than very weak tea. Of course, if carried to excess, opium is as bad, but I think not worse, than the immoderate use of spirits, which too frequently in our own country brings on delirium tremens, and a hundred other dreadful maladies.

Cunynghame 1853

---

1   The foreign governments that forced opium on China at gunpoint for a century claimed it was harmless, but read "Dr. Otte's Opium Refuge" on the next page, age judge for yourself. For more background, read "Lords of Opium" in "Magic Xiamen."

第十五章　厦门的鸦片贸易

吸食鸦片是与抽香烟一起进来的……菲律宾人把美国人的致幻毒品——烟草引进厦门,然后再卖到台湾…… 1620 年是烟草引进的时间,大约与苏格兰国王詹姆斯六世(同时也是英格兰国王一世)"抗击烟草"同一时期。中国皇帝的感受与詹姆斯国王完全一样。明朝的最后一个皇帝(公元 1628 – 1644 年)禁止他的臣

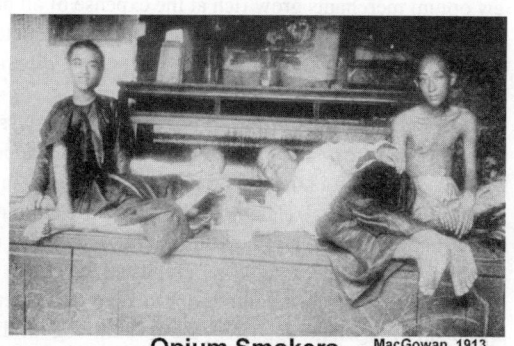

Opium Smokers　MacGowan, 1913

民抽烟。清朝的第一位皇帝于 1641 年写道:"吸烟是一种过错…… 至于禁烟令,你们王宫贵族和其他臣民虽然没有公开,但私下吸食,所以无法维持。"

——摩斯,1919 年,第 335 页

英国人走私鸦片　鸦片是中国的祸根。在厦门进行的鸦片等违禁品的贸易数量极大。鸦片球在厦门的店铺里公开出售。有人告诉我们,政府官员受贿,对鸦片球进入厦门视而不见。尽管快速帆船被赶出厦门港,它们还是被允许在厦门港湾外的海域下锚停泊,令我们(英国)的政府蒙受耻辱。这些快船完全从事毒品运输,不断地公开做买卖。对英国商人来说,厦门是一个极其重要的港口。在这里,他们的买卖仅局限于诚实、合法的贸易……

——瑟尔,1849 年

"无害"的鸦片　(英国)国内的普通民众很少会想象得到我们在中国进行的鸦片贸易规模有多大,以及进行这种贸易所需要的勇气与决心。这是皇家法院所造成的愚蠢行为。它至今仍然维持不许鸦片进入国内的禁令。我一直不断地观察鸦片食用。从经验上来看,我认为,中国人吸食鸦片总是很有节制,应该对他们的身体是有益无害的,一点儿也不会伤害国家法律。相反的,它还能给人带来轻松、愉快的感觉。简而言之,鸦片对他们的伤害并不比适量的酒对我们的伤害更大。必须牢记在心的是,从饮食的角度上来看,他们(中国人)一般是适度的、有节制的。他们很少饮用淡茶以外的东西。当然,吸食过量,鸦片也是不好的。但我想,不会比过量饮用烈酒更糟糕。在我们自己的国家,因酒精中毒引起的震颤性谵妄和其他上百种可怕的疾病这些情况并不少见。

——坎宁汉,1853 年,第 258、259 页

"Opium Paralyzes Amoy" This is the title of a leader in the *North-China Daily News*. ...This is unhappily a picture of China... Industry at Amoy is paralyzed by the opium habit. ... Facts are proving too hard for the defenders of the traffic. If industry is paralyzed, so will the power to buy imports decrease, and at last it will be seen that a few opium merchants grow rich at the expense of all other traders. Surely we are all now prepared to follow the ironical advice of the pamphleteer: "Let us all smoke opium!"

Chinese Recorder, Vol. 31, Feb. 1900

Otte's "Opium Refuge" "For the first five days these patients are considered and treated as maniacs. They are locked up, and their food is handed them through a barred window. It is only in this way that they can be kept in the hospital.

[Of five patients] "The first day all went well, but the next day they became raving maniacs. Night and day they did nothing but crawl on the ground and howl like wild beasts; their room became filthy, and, when the coolie went in to clean it, four men [were needed] at times to watch the room to keep the patients from escaping...Whenever the physician or assistant appeared, they would beg on their knees to be let out, if only for a few minutes. When reasoned with, they said they were doing their best to keep quiet, but they seemed to have lost all control. Knowing this, they were patiently and kindly treated. When left alone, they made strenuous efforts to escape, and finally succeeded in wrenching off a foreign lock from the door. This was discovered in time, and heavy iron staples were clenched on the inside, and the door secured on the outside with a padlock. But on the fifth night they bent the staples with their fingers, so as to open the door. They then jumped down from a verandah twelve feet high and made their escape."

by Dr. John Otte, Amoy

No Chinese Oppose Opium?! "There is no evidence from China of any popular desire that the import of Indian opium should he stopped."

Report of the Opium Commission, Vol. vi., P. 61.
Quoted in Chinese Recorder, Vol. 27., January, 1893.

Opium Smokers (in back)   MacGowan, 1897

第十五章　厦门的鸦片贸易　*Amoy Opium Trade*

"鸦片毁了厦门"　这是《华北日报》一篇社论的标题……很不幸，这是中国的真实写照……厦门的商业被吸食鸦片的习惯给毁了……　对支持鸦片贸易的人来说，这些事实证明是很难接受的。如果商业被毁，人们购买进口产品的能力就会下降。最终是少数鸦片商贩以牺牲所有其他贸易商为代价发财致富。想必我们大家现在都准备遵从社论作者冷嘲热讽的建议："让我们所有人都来抽鸦片吧！"

——《中国教务杂志》，第31卷，第266页，1900年2月

郁约翰的"鸦片收容所"　"前五天，这些病人被当作疯子来处理。他们被关起来，食物通过窗户送进。只有这样才能把他们留在医院。"

"第一天，（五个病人）都很好。第二天，他们开始发疯。白天、黑夜，除了像野兽那样在地上爬、对着窗外嚎，他们什么事也没做。他们的房间开始变脏。工人进去清扫，有时候需要四个大男人看守，以防病人逃跑……医生或助手来看他们的时候，这些病人就会下跪请求让他们出去，哪怕就几分钟。跟他们讲道理，他们说，自己已经尽可能保持安静，但他们似乎已经完全无法控制自己。因此，医生的救治非常耐心、体贴。没人管的时候，他们用尽全力想逃跑。最后成功地扳开门上的一把外国铁锁。被及时发现后，门内牢牢地钉上了几个重重的大铁环锁，门外用挂锁锁牢。但是，到了第五天，他们用手指扭弯了铁环锁，打开房门。然后，从12英尺高的阳台跳下，逃走了。"

——郁约翰博士，厦门

没有中国人反对鸦片？！　"没有来自中国的证据表明，民众希望印度鸦片的进口必须停止。"

——鸦片委员会的报告，第六卷，第61页，
引自《中国教务杂志》，第27卷，1893年1月

Millard, 1916
Ceremony for Destroying Opium Paraphernalia

60 Tons of British Opium Per Week (1906) Portuguese traders brought opium to China in the sixteenth century. In 1757 the Indian trade passed into the hands of the East India Company. Britain inherited the traffic from the East India Company, which had done its utmost by smuggling and bribery to increase the traffic with China.

Two bloody wars were fought before China would consent to legalize the traffic. These are popularly known as the first and second opium wars. Some defenders of British diplomacy claim that these wars were fought in consequence of China's determination to refuse ordinary trading facilities; but although there was a question of trading facilities, the facts of history show that the opium traffic was the cause of actual hostilities in both wars...

Indian opium is now pouring into this country at the rate of about sixty tons every week. This is all used as it comes, and 400 tons weekly, besides, of Chinese grown opium, are required to satisfy China's terrible craving for the drug. What a task to stop such a torrent!...

Dr. John Anderson, Amoy, 1906

Opium Smoker

Amoy—Gateway for Chinese Tobacco & Opium (1600s) The rise of the opium-smoking habit in China seems to have followed the introduction of tobacco smoking to that Empire. The tobacco plant had been transplanted by the Spaniards to the Philippine Islands. From here it appears to have been introduced by way of Formosa to Amoy and its neighborhood, in the Province of Fukien...The result was a prohibitory Edict against it. But in vain; the habit could not be checked by law.

The Manchus followed the Mings and in the year 1641 an Edict was again published which prohibited the smoking of tobacco.

The prohibitory Edicts issued by the last Ming and first Manchu seem to have been just as ineffectual against tobacco smoking as were the later Manchu Edicts against opium smoking. During the seventeenth century the spread of the tobacco habit was as rapid and as difficult to control by Edict as the spread of the opium-smoking habit in the nineteenth century. The prohibitory Edicts emanated from Emperors who it cannot be gainsaid were moved by a deep paternal interest in their people. The common sense of the better classes and the propriety of the Confucian mind were shocked by both practices.

In 1729 the Chinese Government found itself face to face with a rapidly spreading and alarming vice. Native opium was being diverted from medicinal uses to pander to an evil. The opium poppy began to flourish all over China, while imports of the Indian drug began to move upward. Alarmed, in 1729, the Emperor issued an Edict prohibiting the sale of opium and the opening of opium divans. The penalties imposed on those who disobeyed were severe, the most important being on the sellers of the drug. In 1730 another Edict was aimed at the practice amongst the Chinese colonists in Formosa.

Since these Edicts were promulgated, it may be said in truth that the ruling authorities of China have steadfastly regarded opium smoking as a crime.

1782 letter of Thomas Fitzhugh in China to Mr. Gregory in London: "The importation of opium to China is forbidden under very severe penalties; the opium on seizure is burnt, the vessel in which it is brought to port is confiscated, and the Chinese in whose possession it is found for sale is punishable with death..."

Blakeslee, 1910

第十五章 厦门的鸦片贸易 Amoy Opium Trade

每周 60 吨英国鸦片（1906 年） 16 世纪，葡萄牙商人把鸦片销往中国。1757 年，印度的贸易转到了东印度公司的手中。他们通过走私和行贿增加对中国的出口，把鸦片贸易做到了极致。

在中国准许鸦片贸易合法化之前，发生了两次的血腥战争。这就是广为人知的第一和第二次鸦片战争。一些支持英国外交政策的人声称，这两场战争均缘于中国拒绝一般贸易机构的进入。尽管贸易机构有一些问题，但历史的事实表明，鸦片贸易才是引发两次战争及其敌对行动的根源……

Davis, 1836
Mandarin Smoking Opium

如今，印度鸦片大量进入这个国家，大约每周 60 吨。货一运到，就全部被用光。中国自产的鸦片除外，每周需要 400 吨才能满足中国人对这种毒品的可怕需求。要挡住（鸦片贸易）这股洪流是多么艰难的一项工作！……

——约翰·安德森，厦门，1906 年，第 431～434 页

厦门——中国烟草和鸦片的门户（17 世纪初） 在中国，吸食鸦片的习惯似乎是伴随着烟草的引入而兴起的。烟草是西班牙人移植到菲律宾群岛的。从那里再通过台湾，最后被带入厦门及福建的周边地区……结果引来了皇上的禁烟令。禁烟令无功而废，抽烟的习惯是法律所无法禁止的。

紧跟明朝，清政府于 1641 年再次颁布禁烟令，禁止吸烟。

由明朝末代皇帝和清朝开国皇帝颁布的禁烟令似乎与后来清政府颁布的鸦片禁令一样徒劳无益。19 世纪吸食鸦片的传播速度与 17 世纪吸烟的传播速度几乎是一样的快，且难以用法令控制。皇帝颁布的禁令不容辩驳，但男性臣民对烟草的浓厚兴趣却使得禁烟令形同虚设。抽鸦片和吸烟这两种习惯冲击了小康阶层的常识和孔子的礼仪。

1729 年，中国政府发现自己面临着一个传播迅速、令人震惊的恶瘤。本土的鸦片偏离了它原有的治疗功能，被用于迎合一种罪行。罂粟在中国各地开花结果，来自印度的鸦片进口数量急剧上升。当年，皇帝发布诏令，严禁出售鸦片和开鸦片烟馆。违禁者处罚严厉，针对出售鸦片者的处罚最为严厉。1730 年，针对台湾殖民地吸食鸦片的恶习，皇上再次颁布御令。

自从这些禁令颁布以来，可以说，中国的统治当局实际上已经坚定地把吸食鸦片视为犯罪。

1782 年，身在中国的汤姆斯·菲兹休致信伦敦的格雷高里：“中国已经采取重罚严禁鸦片进口。截获的鸦片被销毁，运输鸦片的船只被没收，中国人一旦被发现私藏、出售鸦片被判极刑……"

——布莱克斯利，1910 年，第 157 页

老外看老鼓浪屿 *Old Gulangyu in Foreigners' Eyes*

Chapter 16
Amoy—Marco Polo's Zayton Harbor?[1]

Foreign Ships in Amoy Harbor (1897) The scene upon the harbour is a very pretty one. Sampans are passing and repassing in large numbers. Fishing-boats, with their mat sails, are beating out to sea, and here is a large junk that has come in from Formosa, with men standing on the bows beating gongs in response to the welcome that is sounding from those at anchor.

The objects, however, of greater interest are the foreign shipping, and especially the large steamers that lie anchored waiting for the cargoes they are to carry to the Far West.   Here is one of the famous 'Glen' line that sails tomorrow for New York. Both sides of her are lined with cargoboats, that are filling he, as rapidly as the Chinese can work,

Manson and Alcock, 1927 H.M.S. Hornet, Amoy Harbor, 1873

with chests of tea from Tamsui, in the island of Formosa. The Oolong that is produced there is a great favourite with the people of the States, as well indeed it may be, for no more fragrant tea is produced in any of the famous tea-plantations of China than that which comes from this lively island. Not far from her lies one of the famous 'Empress' steamers, bound for Vancouver, also taking in tea, as well as carrying passengers for that far-off port. What a magnificent ship she looks, as she stands high out of the water, ready for the perilous voyage she had to make across some of the stormiest seas in the world! She gives one the impresses ion great strength combined with great speed, and that she is well-fitted to cope with the fierce gales and mountain seas she will have to encounter in the North Pacific Ocean, as she is racing against time to fulfill her mail contract.

Macgowan, 1897

Ships of Many Nations (1850s) Occasionally, Charley and I accompanied our parents when they were calling on the Captains of British and American ships, and on their wives, who sometimes came with them, or on those of other nationalities; and were invited down into their staterooms—large and handsome, or small and grimy, according to the class of vessel, or the nation they belonged to. "Britannia ruled the waves" even then too, and everything on their ships was in fine order, and on ours too, though they were few and far between compared to the British ones. An East Indiaman, or Dutch or Siamese or Persian craft would be unkempt.

Mary Doty's Memoirs

---

1 Many foreign experts believed Marco Polo's great "Zayton Harbor" was Amoy Harbor, given that it is one of the best in the world, and was part of Quanzhou (Zayton).

第十六章
厦门——马可·波罗书中的刺桐港？

Chinese Trading Ship, 1793, by W. Alexander

厦门港的外轮（1897年） 港口一派繁忙。大批舢板穿梭往来，草帆渔船纷纷驶往大海。一艘来自台湾岛的大型橡皮船也停泊在港口，船头上站满了船员，他们敲锣打鼓感谢锚点的欢迎。然而，更能吸引人们注意力的是那些外轮，尤其是大型的蒸汽机轮船。它们停靠在码头，等候运往远东的货物，其中就有著名的"格伦"号，准备第二天开往纽约。轮船的两边挤满了货船，中国工人们正尽力往船上装上一柜又一柜来自台湾淡水出产的乌龙茶。那里出产的乌龙茶在美国非常受欢迎，也许是因为全中国都没有其他地方可以生产出那么香的茶叶。"格伦"号附近停靠着著名的"皇后"号蒸汽机轮船，她的目的地是温哥华，船上满载茶叶，并站满了前往遥远目的港的旅客。停靠在港口的"皇后"号看上去非常壮观。她高高地露出水面，随时准备穿越世上最多风暴的海洋，开始她危险的航程。她就是力量和速度的结合体，完全能够对付北太平洋的狂风巨浪，同时她也要和时间赛跑完成本次的邮递合同任务。

——麦嘉湖，1897年，第159、160页

万国轮船（20世纪50年代） 偶尔查理和我会陪同父母前往拜访英国和美国的船长们及其偶尔同行的夫人，或者来自其他国家的人。他们会邀请我们下去参观不同轮船的特等客舱，有些宽敞漂亮，有些狭小肮脏。那个时候，"大不列颠统治了海洋"，他们船上的一切井井有条，我们的也不错，但是比起英国来，我们的船只数量要少得多，距离也远得多。不论是东印度公司的大商船，还是荷兰，暹罗或者波斯的小轮船都是乱糟糟的。

——玛丽·多蒂未出版的回忆录

▶ 211

老外看老鼓浪屿 *Old Gulangyu in Foreigners' Eyes*

The Talma (the Calcutta-Rangoon-Penang-Singapore-Hong Kong-Amoy-Shanghai-Moji-Kobe line) J.N.

"Empress of Japan," Amoy, Sept. 4, 1930 J.V.

H.C.S. Nemesis Chater Collection

第十六章 厦门——马可·波罗书中的刺桐港？ *Amoy—Marco Polo's Zayton Harbor?*

The S.S. Tjikini in Amoy, 1920s   J. Nienhuis

The Tsikini's Officers   J.N.

Amoy Ferry, 1933   J. Veldman

Amoy Dock & 16 Foot Tides

The rise and fall of the tide at Amoy is considerable, and it thus offers peculiar facilities for the construction and use of docks, two of which are now completed and in full employment. The average rise and fall is about 14½ feet but at high tides exceeds 16 feet.

The docks of Amoy are worthy of notice. Vessels of almost any size visiting the port can here obtain everything necessary for repairs &c. The chief establishment is situated on the Amoy side, but a fine dock is in course of construction at Ku-lang-su. The Company's premises afford every facility for repairing and sparring vessels and for cleaning and painting iron and steam ships. Their large granite dock is 286 feet long on the blocks, and at average spring tides can take vessels drawing 16 to 17 feet water. The dock is fitted with a caisson gate and with a centrifugal steam pump of great power ensuring despatch in all states of the tide. For repairs an ample stock is kept on hand of timber, Oregon spars, sheathing copper and yellow metal, and of every description of material required for dock-yard use. The premises comprise an Engineer's workshop, a large Smithy and carpenter's workshops, and the works are superintended by resident Europeans, viz., a shipwright, an engineer, and a blacksmith. Dry godowns have been erected for the reception of vessels' stores &c., when requiring to discharge them.

The New Amoy Dock Company   Bowra, 1908

Mayers & Dennys, 1867

Gulangyu, 1930s   J. Nienhuis

第十六章 厦门——马可·波罗书中的刺桐港？ Amoy—Marco Polo's Zayton Harbor?

厦门码头和 16 英尺的浪高 厦门港的潮水涨得快,退得也快,需要特别的设备来建设和使用厦门码头,其中两个已经建好并交付使用。潮水涨落的平均高度是 14.5 英尺,潮水最高的时候浪高会超过 16 英尺。

厦门码头值得一看。几乎所有尺寸的船只进港后都可以在这里获得诸如维修等方面的必要补给。主码头坐落在厦门本岛一边,正在建设的另一个码头则位于鼓浪屿。码头厂房可以提供所有的设备来维修或者加壁护条,并为铁船和蒸汽轮船提供清洁和油漆服务。用大理

石建造的大码头长 286 英尺,平均大潮可以停靠吃水 16 到 17 英尺的船只。码头配备了浮坞门和大功率的离心蒸汽泵以确保在各种潮水情况下保持通讯畅通。至于需要维修的船只,仓库里储备了大量的木料、俄勒冈壁护条、铜套、黄铜以及码头需要的任何材料。码头包括工程师车间、锻冶场和木工车间,所有工作由来自欧洲的造船师傅、工程师或铁匠指挥。码头还建造了干燥的货栈,以便接收和保管船上卸下的货物。

——梅尔斯和丹尼斯 1867 年,第 255 页

The Dock, Amoy

Postcard Courtesy of Mr. George Yue

Amoy—Germany's Base in Asia Amaranth's first port of call was Amoy, a major port north of Hong Kong, which had become the unofficial center of German trade in East Asia.[2] Diederichs and his fellow crewmen worked hard, exchanging the ship's cargo, German industrial goods, for Chinese silk and Amoy's famous tea. Once their work was done, they had a brief opportunity for shore leave before moving on to the next port of call. Amoy offered sights to intrigue any European traveler, including a famous Buddhist shrine and a large but decaying fortress with stone fortifications and obsolete cannon. Although Diederichs was no stranger to the royal monuments of Berlin and Potsdam, the mysterious and novel Chinese architecture and culture impressed him greatly."...

"Lying approximately equidistant between Hong Kong and Shanghai, Amoy possessed a good harbor with a spacious anchorage. The port had become the unofficial center of German naval and mercantile operations in Chinese waters in the past twenty years. Twenty years after Luise's visit, when Diederichs returned to East Asia as commander of the Cruiser Squadron, Amoy topped the navy's list as a prospective site for an official German naval base in China...

Chinese Junk   MacGowan, 1895

Diederichs faced a potential second problem, this time involving the crew...One of the other warships present at Amoy was U.S. sloop Ranger, whose under-strength crew numbered only 114 out of a regular complement of 165. Because American ships had been known to recruit German seamen, Diederichs took extra precautions to see that none of his own crew deserted...

Gottschall, 2003

The "German's" Port Most warship commanders chose to winter in southern ports like Hong Kong or Manila. Schering decided instead to proceed south to Amoy, toward which the Germans had an almost proprietary attitude. Luise, in fact, remained there from 30 December 1879 until 17 March 1880, providing time for work, drills, and the occasional liberty ashore. The local Amoy Gazette welcomed Luise's lengthy stay and cultural contribution. When Luise's band backed up an amateur theatrical group, a reporter noted, "[The band's] efforts, in no small degree, added to the success of the evening's entertainment."

"Luise and her crew were called upon for other services at Amoy, notably an attempt to clear the harbor of a shipwreck. At the request of the Amoy authorities, Diederichs assigned a work crew to remove the navigational hazard with explosives. Diver Kaufmann spent two hours in freezing cold weather planting three explosive charges underwater. The triple blast, however, did little more than muddy the water and blow away parts of the wreck's superstructure. The surgeon forbade Kaufmann to dive again because of the cold, and other efforts had equally little effect.

Gottschall, 2003

---

2 28 Nov. 1896, Admiral Eduard Knorr wrote that he supported the "seizure of Amoy at a later time."

第十六章　厦门——马可·波罗书中的刺桐港？ Amoy—Marco Polo's Zayton Harbor?

厦门——德国的亚洲基地　　"不凋花号"停靠的第一个港口就是香港北面的大港口厦门,后来成了德国在东亚的非官方贸易中心。迪德里希斯和他的船员尽力把船上的货物德国的工业产品换成了中国的丝绸和厦门的名茶。交换货物后,他们启程前往下一个港口。之前,他们可以请短假参观海滩的风景。厦门的风景很容易吸引欧洲旅游者,其中就有著名的佛教寺庙和一个用石头筑成的堡垒,不过堡垒有些毁坏了,而且堡垒中的大炮也是过时的。尽管迪德里希斯非常熟悉柏林和波茨坦的皇家纪念碑,中国神秘奇特的建筑风格和文化还是深深吸引了他们。

"厦门港位于香港和上海之间,是个拥有宽阔的停泊所的良港。在过去的二十年里,厦门变成了德国在中国海域非正式的海军和商务活动中心。路易斯号停靠厦门二十年后,迪德里希斯作为巡洋舰中队指挥官回到了东亚,厦门就是德国海军名单上第一个可以成为德国在中国的海军基地备选港口……"

Doc Holleman Departs Amoy

迪德里希斯还要面对另外一个潜在的问题,这一次和船员有关……停靠在厦门港的另外一艘战舰是美国的"漫游者号"单桅船,正常情况下该船应该配备165位船员,但目前只有114人。众所周知,美国船只喜欢聘用德国海员,迪德里希斯只好采取额外的防范措施以防他的船员弃船而去……

——戈特沙尔,2003年

"德国"的港口　大多数战舰指挥官都会选择在南方的香港或者马尼拉港过冬。西林则选择了德国人好像有专属权的厦门港。实际上,"路易斯号"从1879年12月30日停靠到厦门港,到1880年3月17日离开,期间都在这里工作、操练,偶尔上岸度假。当地的《厦门公报》肯定了"路易斯号"在长期停靠期间所做的文化贡献。"路易斯号"的乐队曾替代当地一个业余剧团上台表演。一位记者写到,"乐队的努力很大程度上使得当晚的节目大获成功"。

"路易斯号"轮船和船员也会经常参与厦门的其他任务,最著名的就是清除港口里一处沉船的残骸。在厦门当局的要求下,迪德里希斯组织了一个工作队专门负责用爆炸的方式清除那个可能给航运带来危险的残骸。潜水员考夫曼在寒冷的海水中花了两个小时放置好三个炸药点。可惜这三个炸药点收效甚微,只是搅浑了海水并炸飞了一点点残骸。考虑到寒冷的天气状况,医生禁止考夫曼继续潜水。其他的努力同样也收效甚微。

——戈特沙尔,2003年

老外看老鼓浪屿 *Old Gulangyu in Foreigners' Eyes*

(Engraving of German ships in Amoy, German Newspaper, 1880s)

第十六章 厦门——马可·波罗书中的刺桐港？ *Amoy—Marco Polo's Zayton Harbor?*

Longtou Jetty, Gulangyu, 1920s — J. Nienhuis

Amoy Harbor, 1873 — Thomson

Amoy Harbor, 1930s — J. Nienhuis

老外看老鼓浪屿 *Old Gulangyu in Foreigners' Eyes*

Boat Carrying Sedan Chair — MacGowan, 1907

Gulangyu Pier, 1934 — J. Nienhuis

第十六章 厦门——马可·波罗书中的刺桐港? *Amoy—Marco Polo's Zayton Harbor?*

Roger, Owen, Eleanor and Ruthie Koeppe on ship (1930s) J.Nienhuis

Edna and Jessie, Hope Hospital Jetty, Oct. 22, 1930 J. Nienhuis

老外看老鼓浪屿 Old Gulangyu in Foreigners' Eyes

Chapter 17　Gulangyu – International Settlement

"There are upwards of five hundred European residents at Amoy, for the most part merchants and their families."

Lawrence, 1870

British Consulate Blows its Top　When the first British consul was appointed to Amoy in 1844, the British Concession—a block of properties on the seaside of the city owned by various trading concerns—had been open a year. Kulangsu, an island two miles long and half a mile wide, was supporting a few fisherfolk and a British garrison, left there since the end of the Opium War. Mr. Alcock, who was later to become Sir Rutherford, had the soldiers removed and, on a pink-cliffed bluff above the sea, built himself one of the square, verandad houses, or perhaps the consular residence was the prototype of all the high square houses on the island. But it did not remain so for long. A typhoon blew off the second storey and, re-roofed without it, it was left uniquely low and intimate.

It was removed from the clamour of the port, but from his garden Mr. Alcock could both look far across the great harbour to Nantai Island, with its ancient stone watch-tower, to the hills of the mainland and, although Foochow had monopolized most of them, watch the tea-clippers bearing up the roadstead between the squat brown junks, like swans among ducks.

Mackenzie-Grieve, 1959

A daily paper, The Amoy Gazette, is printed at one of the two printing-offices in Amoy and laid every evening upon the dinner-table; and during the winter an illustrated comic publication is also issued under the title of Waffles' Bimonthly. Ice and aerated waters of various kinds are manufactured upon the island, which now boasts a "company" formed with the object of supplying residents with pure un-watered milk. Add to the above the fact that Koolangsu is in direct telegraphic communication with most parts of the globe, its cheap and varied market, its salubrious climate, and beautiful surrounding scenery; and it will only remain to acknowledge that truly

"The Drum-Wave Island is a paradise on earth;
The Egret River is second to none!"

Giles, 1878

KOLONG-SU, AMOY.

第十七章　鼓浪屿——外国租界

> "厦门居住着至少 500 个欧洲人，大部分都是商人以及他们的家属。"
> ——劳伦斯，1870 年，第 250 页

英国领事馆的屋顶飞了　1844 年英国向厦门派出第一任领事的时候，英国贸易商人已经在海边拥有一个街区的不动产，租界已设置一年了。长两英里，宽半英里的鼓浪屿岛上住着一些渔民和鸦片战争之后留下来的英军。阿尔科克先生，也就是后来的阿礼国爵士撤走了那里的士兵，在海边粉红色的绝壁上给自己建造了其中一座方形、带凉台的房子，领事馆驻地也有可能成了岛上所有高大、方形房子的样板。但是没过多久，一场台风就把第二层刮跑了。没有盖上第二层只重新加了屋顶，后来就变得特别得低矮和亲切了。

房子避开了港口的喧闹。但是，从阿尔科克先生的花园可以放眼宽阔的厦门港，眺望南太武岛以及岛上古老的石灯塔，远望内陆的群山（大部分由福州管辖），观看装满茶叶的快船挺立在锚地众多的棕色小帆船之间。

——麦肯兹·格瑞芙，1959 年，第 21 页

《厦门公报和航运报道》　在厦门仅有的两家印刷厂之一印制，每天傍晚就可以放到餐桌上。冬天的时候，一份名叫《华夫饼双月刊》的也会刊登带插图的漫画。岛上生产冰块和品种繁多的汽水，现在已经成了一个"公司"提供给居民未加水的纯净牛奶。此外，鼓浪屿和世界大部分地方都保持着电信联络，这里物美价廉、气候宜人、风景优美，我们无法不承认：
"人间天堂鼓浪屿；
"鹭江风景甲天下！"

——吉尔斯，1878 年

Johnston, 19

老外看老鼓浪屿 *Old Gulangyu in Foreigners' Eyes*

Foreign Homes on Gulangyu (1888)   The large luxurious foreign houses are scattered in the most pleasing manner amongst huge madder-colored boulders and rock-masses, shaded by clumps of feathery bamboo, and the flowers or foliage of well-cultivated gardens in a semi-tropical climate. Naturally, in the scorching summer droughts the land does acquire a sickly yellow tone; but in the cooler winter season the island is comparatively green, and here and there a vividly verdant hillside shows where diligent husbandmen have laid out their terraced rice-fields. Carriages and horses are here unknown, their place being filled by chairs and human bearers—strong, patient Chinamen; and boats are ever ready to carry those whose business required their presence to the busy city, which rises so picturesquely on the further shore of the narrow blue strait. To the left lies the harbor; crowded with quaint native junks, wonderful alike in form and color; and a great assemblage of boat-houses, wherein an incredible number of human beings contrive to exist in a much more decent and cleanly way than their neighbor in the streets. On an average, about one thousand foreign vessels annually clear this port.

As seen from the houses of the foreign residents, the island of Amoy is strikingly picturesque. Though the high, steep hills are in themselves parched and barren ranges of disintegrated granite, they are strewn in every direction with gigantic boulders of the aforesaid rock, which seem as if they could only have dropped from the clouds; though here and there a rocky ridge crops up, cresting the sky-line. One such ridge divides the town itself, and is strongly fortified, heavy guns commanding the estuary where lie so many trading-vessels. Very irregular streets run in and out among the great boulders along the shore, where junks lie stranded, and fine old trees overshadow shrines and temples and nameless graves; the latter being chosen here and there, according to Chinese notions of good luck. ... One point of interest for an afternoon's expedition is a Buddhist monastery, perched on the hillside in this rock wilderness. Stately aloes seem specially to flourish in the soil of decomposing granite, and are thoroughly in keeping with their surroundings.

Miss Gordon-Cumming, 1888

THE SETTLEMENT, AMOY   Goodrich, 1911

第十七章　鼓浪屿——外国租界 Gulangyu – International Settlement

鼓浪屿外国人住宅（1888年） 宽敞豪华的外国人住宅精致地散落在茜红色大圆石和岩体之间。一丛丛茂密的竹林，以及亚热带气候条件下精美花园里的花草为他们的住宅遮阴。在炎热、干旱的夏季，大地自然地染上了病态的黄色基调；但是一到凉爽的冬季，鼓浪屿就变得绿意盎然了，到处都是翠绿的山坡，显示了勤劳男人辛勤劳作的成果。这里没有马车，到处都是轿子和强壮、耐心的中国轿夫，随时都有渡船把需要打理生意的人送到喧闹的市区。市区处在狭小的蓝色海峡对岸，从鼓浪屿看过去风景如画。左边是港口，挤满了当地离奇有趣的小帆船，它们的造型和颜色都很接近。还有一大批船屋，上面不可思议地住着一大群人。他们的居住环境比街上的邻居要好得多，干净得多。每年平均有一千艘外国船只到达这个港口。

从外国人住宅看过去，厦门岛风景如画。虽然又高又陡的小山本身就是一堆干透而且光秃秃的大理石块，到处都是巨大而又圆滚滚的大理石岩，似乎就像是天上掉下来的云朵一样。山梁冷不丁地从岩石上冒出来，直插云霄。一道山梁把小镇分成两半。山梁上工事坚固，重武器正对着停靠着很多商船的（厦门）港区。街道蜿蜒穿行在海边的大圆石之间，岸边停靠着小帆船，细细的老树树荫下是庙宇和无名墓地。这些墓地都是根据中国风水来选择的⋯⋯有个地点适合下午去参观。它是一个佛教寺庙，高高地坐落在这片岩石荒地的山腰上。高大的芦荟似乎特别容易在碎大理石的土地上生长，并完全融入了周围的环境。

——戈登·康明小姐，1888年

A European Home, Amoy　　　　　Goodrich, 1911

The Doty House (1850s) Opening on our front water, through a heavily barred window high up from the floor, was a play room and catch all. At times of typhoons, the water would rise so high that it came within a few inches of the window-level on front and side of the wharf...

Our furniture was, naturally, very simple—white, or red and white check mattings, and a good deal of rattan in chairs and settees, with some of the noted carved pieces of native make...

The piano (first drawing card) and mahogany center table, some beautiful Chinese bric-a-brac, a marbleized mantelpiece with a grate, on both sides of which were Chinese vases about two and one-half or three feet high, were the chief articles. Tall stalks of rice paper flowers, much like double magnolia blossoms, pink and white, and leaves of cloth very naturally imitated, stood about four feet high in these vases.

Mary Doty's Memoirs

International Settlement Committee A committee is elected every year that has the supervision of the taxes raised from the community, and that has power to repair the old roads and to open new ones. That these committees have acted with great wisdom is evident from the splendid condition of the highways, and also from their extent. Considering the limited area on which they have had to operate, it is very creditable to them that they have managed to make about eight miles of good serviceable roads, which can be used in nearly all weathers.

MacGowan, 1897

第十七章　鼓浪屿——外国租界 Gulangyu – International Settlement

多蒂的家(19世纪50年代)　正对我们家门口的海岸线上,透过一扇高高、厚重的落地窗,有一间娱乐室和一些打捞工具。台风到来的时候,水位涨得很高,离码头前门和两侧窗户只有几英寸……

我们的家具自然是非常简朴,白色或者是红白相间的格子床垫,椅子和沙发用很多藤条做成,当然也有一些来自国内的雕刻家具……

主要的家具包括钢琴(我们家吸引人的第一张王牌)和红木桌子,一些漂亮的中国小古董,带炉排的大理石壁炉,两边都是2.5或者3英寸高的中国花瓶。这些花瓶里放着4英寸高的宣纸花卉,就像双层的粉色和白色的玉兰花一样,用布做的树叶模仿得惟妙惟肖。

——玛丽·多蒂未出版的回忆录

国际租界委员会　每年都要选举一个委员会负责收取社区的税收,维护旧路,修建新路。委员会的聪明才智很明显可以从公路的良好状况以及长度看得出来。尽管负责的区域有限,他们还是想方设法修建了大约8英里公路,路况良好,可全天候使用,非常值得称赞。

——麦嘉湖,1897年

Postcard Courtesy Mr. Tomihisa Yamishita, Kyoto, Japan

Kyokuei-Shoin, Amoy, China. 厦门旭瀛书院本院

老外看老鼓浪屿 *Old Gulangyu in Foreigners' Eyes*

Gulangyu Scenery and Roads The beauty of the natural scenery of this island is greatly enhanced by the residences of the foreigners that are scattered over it in every direction. As a rule these are spacious and handsome buildings, and are surrounded by trees and gardens, where flowers of many kinds thrive with the greatest luxuriance and scent the air with their fragrance. There is one feature of the island that is a very striking one, and that is the excellent roads that abound throughout it. These are the result of a considerable outlay by the foreign community, who tax themselves to keep them in order. The Chinese never concern themselves about the making of roads, excepting on the great trunk lines, over which the mandarins and high officials have to travel in passing from one district or one province to another. Footpaths are quite enough for them, and Nature is left to regulate their condition, as no man feels himself called upon to spend his money in providing a pleasant way for his neighbor to travel.

Macgowan, 1897

Gulangyu Trees One special charm about these latter is the trees that have been planted along their sides. They not only add to the picturesqueness of the island and enhance the beauty of the walks, but they are also a great comfort during the hot months, when the sun, in the greatness of his strength, pours down his molten rays. The trees planted by the committee are about the very best that could have been selected for the purposes they were intended to serve. They are very umbrageous, and resist all efforts of the sun to penetrate them. They grow rapidly, so that in the course of two or three years they attain to a comparatively large size, and they are easily reproduced. A branch cut off and stuck in the ground will begin, in the course of a few days, to put out leaves, and without any care but that of Nature it begins its new life. Even the Chinese, who seem utterly regardless of the intense heat that prevails, highly appreciate the coolness that exists beneath these trees, and praise the wisdom and benevolence of the foreigners for thinking of the public in a way that would never have suggested itself to the mind of the heathen.

Macgowan, 1897

Gulangyu (Nurses Home to Left), 1930s   J. Nienhuis

第十七章　鼓浪屿——外国租界 Gulangyu – International Settlement

鼓浪屿风景和道路　外国人住宅分散在鼓浪屿岛的各个地方,大大增添了这个小岛自然风光的美景。通常情况下,这些住宅都非常宽敞,外形漂亮,绿树环绕,花园里百花怒放,空气中都充满了花草香味。小岛的另外一个显著的特色是它四通八达、路况良好的道路。这些都是外国人社区花费大笔资金建造的。他们通过税收用来维护道路。中国人除了建造那些干线方便文武官员在各地区或者省份之间来往之外,从来就没有考虑过修建道路的事情。人行小径就已经很足够了,管理这些小径就靠大自然,因为没有一个中国人觉得有义务花钱为邻居们提供方便行走的道路。

——麦嘉湖,1897年,第147、148页

鼓浪屿的树木　鼓浪屿特别的魅力之一是道路两边的树木。它们不仅为岛上增添美景,美化道路,在热天太阳喷出热焰的时候也提供舒适的树荫。委员会种植的树木是最适宜这种目的的。它们都是多荫树种,能够抵抗住太阳的穿透力。它们长得很快,两三年就相当高大了,而且再生能力非常强。砍下的树枝插入地上,过了几天就会长出新叶子,而且也只需要大自然的照料就可以开始新的生命。中国人似乎从来都不会在乎酷暑,但他们也非常喜欢在树下乘凉,赞叹外国人这种考虑公众方式的智慧和善行,而异教徒是从来不会这样考虑的。

——麦嘉湖,1897年,第147、148页

A Gulangyu Garden　　　　Little, 1902

老外看老鼓浪屿 *Old Gulangyu in Foreigners' Eyes*

Conquering Camel Rock, Gulangyu, 1920s   J. Nienhuis

Camel Rock[1] (1940s)   Walking up a sun-steeped lane, I came to the highest point and centre of the island, known as Camel Rock…

Around this sleeping motionless camel were clustered tier upon tier, rows of red and drab-white brick houses, criss-crossed by a series of narrow lanes which could not be travelled either by car, bicycle, or rickshaw. The only equipage available on Kulangsu were some old sedan chairs, but even these were sparingly used and principally by pregnant women on their way to the mission hospital when they felt their critical hour was approaching. Scattered shops lay at one end of the island in which fat shopkeepers were dozing away their siesta houses in long easy chairs, lazily fanning themselves in a state of coma…About fifty foreigners of many nationalities still lived here together with retired Chinese officials, professional men and the wealthier merchants whose interests lay on the Amoy side but who preferred the greater quiet of Kulangsu…

Foreigners were advised not to stay on Amoy Island after dusk. Nothing had ever happened, but one day it might.

Neill, 1956

Early Amoy Telecommunications   Close by this sunny spot [Ganzaihou Beach] are the offices of the Great Northern Telegraphic Company, which plays an important part in the life of the Amoy community. Here great questions in commerce are decided in a few seconds, and with the flash of the electric current tidings are sent away to far-distant lands, to bring either pain or gladness to the friends there. Every day the important news of remote countries is talked of and discussed the same day that the events themselves occurred, although they may have happened at the other extremity of the globe. It is a comfort to the foreigner to feel that, though far removed by space from those he loves, he can in any emergency, by stepping down to these offices, come speedily into touch with them, and in the course of a few hours know accurately how they are, and what they are doing.

Macgowan, 1897

---

1   Today, called Sunlight Rock, 日光岩

第十七章　鼓浪屿——外国租界 Gulangyu – International Settlement

骆驼岩（即现在的日光岩）（20世纪40年代）　走过洒满阳光的巷子，我来到了岛上最高点和中心点，也就是著名的骆驼岩……

聚集在这头纹丝不动的睡骆驼周围的是一间间红色和褐白色相间的砖房。一条条狭窄的巷子相互交错，汽车、自行车和人力车都无法通行。鼓浪屿上唯一可用的设备是种古老的轿子，但是也很少人使用，主要用于怀孕的妇女感觉快要生的时候才坐上轿子赶往传教士医院。岛屿的另一头有一些商店。胖乎乎的店主躺在长椅上睡午觉，昏睡时还慢慢地摇着手上的扇子…… 大约有50位来自世界各国的外国人和退休的中国官员住在这里，也有一些专业人士和富裕商人喜欢鼓浪屿的安静。所以，他们也选择住在鼓浪屿，虽然他们需要打理的事情都在厦门岛上…

有人建议外国人在黄昏之后都不要在厦门岛逗留。什么事都还没有发生，但是也许某一天就会。

——尼尔，1956年，第26、27页

早期的厦门电讯服务　就在这个阳光明媚的地方（港仔后海滩）附近就是大北方电讯公司的办公室。这里对于厦门人的生活起到了举足轻重的作用。很多重要的商业问题在这里几秒钟内就决定了，并通过闪电般快捷的电流发送到遥远的地方，给那里的朋友带去痛苦或者开心的消息。就在事情发生的当天，遥远国度的重要新闻每天都被谈起或者讨论，就像在国内一样，即使事情是发生地球的另一端。对于外国人来说，这是一种安慰，尽管他们在空间上远离亲人，但是在紧急情况下，他们就可以走进这里，迅速地和亲人们取得联系，几个小时之后就可以准确了解亲人们的情况，目前从事的工作等等信息。

——麦嘉湖，1897年，第153、154页

Hongkong and Shanghai Bank　Pitcher, 1912

老外看老鼓浪屿 *Old Gulangyu in Foreigners' Eyes*

Foreign Law in Amoy   The island became an international settlement under the control of the Council on May 1, 1903. There is a Mixed Court Magistrate, appointed by the Chinese authorities, who deals with charges brought by the Council or others against Chinese on the island, while foreign offenders are dealt with by their own Consuls.

The Council employs a foreign superintendent of police, who is also secretary to the Council, and a small force of Sikh police. Under this management the island has made progress in many ways, and has become the place of residence, in addition to the foreigners, of a number of wealthy Chinese, who have bought or built foreign houses there.

Like Kulangsu, the British Concession on Amoy has its Municipal Council, consisting of five members elected from the lot holders, who hold their land from the British Government, which rents the whole Concession from the Chinese Government. There is a British inspector of police and a small force of Chinese constables.

Bowra, 1908

Where is China?   An American pointed at different colored places on a map of China and said his company would work here, or there, or somewhere else, but each time he was told, "No, that belongs to Britain. No, that is French. Can't do—that is Russia's. No, this is Germany's." He finally demanded of the Chinese and European officials, "Where the hell is China!"

La Motte, 1919

Guy Bass
Chief of Police
Kulangsu Municipal Council

American Consulate

Japanese Consulate   Pitcher, 1912

第十七章 鼓浪屿——外国租界 Gulangyu – International Settlement

厦门的外国法律　1903年5月1日,厦门成了在委员会掌控之下的国际租界。这里有中国政府任命的综合治安法庭,处理委员会或者其他人对于岛上中国人提出的诉讼,对于岛上外国人的诉讼则由他们自己成立的委员会处理。

委员会聘用了一位外国警司,同时担任委员会的秘书,还有一小队由印度锡克教徒组成的警察。在这种管理体制下,鼓浪屿各个方面都取得了进步,成了不仅仅是外国人的住地,也成了一些富裕中国人的住地。他们在这里购买或者建造外国式的房子。

就像鼓浪屿一样,厦门岛上的英国租界也有市政委员会,由土地使用者中选取的5位成员构成。这些成员从英国政府中租用土地,而英国政府则从中国政府手中租用了整个租界。厦门岛上也有一位警察巡官和一小队中国警察。

Courtesy of Mike Bass and Jill Fowler

——博拉,1908年

中国在哪里?　一个美国人指着中国地图上不同颜色的地方,说他的公司分布在各地,但每一次别人都对他说:"不,那是属于英国的地方。不,那是法国的。不行,那是俄国的。不,那是德国的。"最后他只好询问中国和欧洲的官员,"中国究竟在哪里?"

——拉·莫特,1991年,第48、49页

German Consulate

British Consulate　Pitcher, 1912

老外看老鼓浪屿 *Old Gulangyu in Foreigners' Eyes*

The Kulangsu Municipal Police, Amoy. Bowra, 1908
(C. Berkeley Mitchell, Superintendent, in centre.)

第十七章 鼓浪屿——外国租界 *Gulangyu – International Settlement*

A sitting of the mixed court of the International Settlement of Kulangsoo, Amoy.

老外看老鼓浪屿 *Old Gulangyu in Foreigners' Eyes*

Foreign Consulates[2]   Amoy, the door to the Fookien Province, as its name in Chinese indicates, would be the proper residence for a Consul whose jurisdiction would extend over agents of Swatow [Shantou] and Vice Consuls for the Formosa ports.

Carles, William Le Gendre, U.S. Consul in Amoy, 1871

"The elder consuls, we found, invariably liked the Chinese, admired their former achievements, deplored their present situation…and detected the growth of a new national consciousness."

Mackenzie-Grieves, 1959

The Consul's Chinese Writer   Perhaps the most conspicuous instance of the dominating influence of the Chinaman is seen in the foreign Consulates. In each of these there is a Chinese official employed that is called a writer. He is a gentleman and a member of the literary class. His duties are to write dispatches in Chinese to the mandarins and to be the one connecting link between the native authorities and the particular foreign Consul in whose service he happens to be. All petitions or complaints from the Chinese have to go through his hands, so that his position is one of great responsibility and power.

If the Consul happens to be a man of strong, independent character he will hold his own, and the business of the Consulate will be in a large measure under his own control.

If he is, however, easy-going or of average intellectual ability, he comes at once under the hypnotizing influence of the wily self-contained Chinaman, who before long becomes the master spirit in the office. This fact is so far realized by the leading mandarin of the place that he actually subsidizes him to influence the policy of the Consul to be favourable to him. A hostile writer could so easily influence his mind against the former, and cause such strained diplomatic relations, that he would incur the resentment of his superiors and be dismissed from his office.

I have known a case where the whole policy of a Consulate was dictated by the writer, who was a clever, intriguing scamp. All Chinese documents had to pass through his hands, and it depended upon the amount of the bribes received whether any of them got a dispassionate investigation at the hands of the Consul. His reputation became so bad that he was finally asked to resign, but he did so with a very comfortable fortune that enabled him to take a commanding position amongst the leading men in his neighbourhood.

In whatever direction one likes to take the Chinaman, he seems to have an hypnotic power that secures, if not favour, at least attention.

Macgowan, 1907

---

2   Gulangyu had consulates for 14 countries.

Gulangyu (original U.S. Consulate on left)

第十七章　鼓浪屿——外国租界 Gulangyu – International Settlement

外国领事馆　厦门，就像它中文意思一样，是福建省的门户，很适合作为领事馆的驻地，管辖区域可以扩展到汕头的代办和台湾岛港口的副领事。

——李仙得，美国驻厦门领事，1871年

我们发现，年长的领事总是喜欢中国人。他们敬仰中国祖先的成就，悲叹当今的状况……并发现了新的国家意识的成长。

——麦肯兹·格瑞芙，1959年，第27页

领事的中国书记员　也许最能表现这个中国书记员影响的地方就是外国领事馆。这些外国领事馆都聘用一名中国官员，做书记员。他是一个绅士，知书达理。他的职责就是用中文给官员写快讯，保持当地政府和他所服务的外国领事馆

U.S. Consulate, Gulangyu, Summer 1930　J. Nienhuis

之间的联络。所有来自中国人的请愿和抱怨都要经过他的手。因此，他的责任和权利都很大。

如果领事是一个坚强、独立的人，他会坚持自己的观点，领事馆的事务大部分都会在他自己的掌控之下。

但是，如果他平易近人，知识水平一般，他就会立即受到这个诡计多端而又沉默寡言的中国书记员的影响。很快，这个书记员就会成为领事馆精神上的主人。当地官员也很快就意识到了这个事实，他就会贿赂这个书记员，让领事馆做出有利于官员的政策。一个充满敌意的书记员轻而易举就可以动用他的影响力反对官员，引起紧张的外交关系，当然也会引来他上司的反感以至于被革职。

我认识这么一个书记员。他是一个聪明、有趣的坏蛋，领事馆所有的政策都由他起草。所有的中文文件都要经过他的手。他是根据收到贿赂的多少来决定那些文件会受到领事馆公正的调查。他慢慢变得非常臭名远扬，最后被迫辞职。他虽辞职了，但是也积累了相当的财富，让他成为尊贵人家邻居中最能发号施令的人。

不管从哪一个角度看待这个书记员，他似乎有一种催眠的力量使他获得他人注意，如果不是喜爱的话。

——麦嘉湖，1907年，第16、17页

老外看老鼓浪屿 *Old Gulangyu in Foreigners' Eyes*

Getting to Gulangyu These sampans comfortably seat two, the rower standing in the stern of the boat with his face to the bow, whilst the passengers sit in the front. They are very safe; they cross the harbour in all kinds of weather, and very rarely indeed does an accident happen to them. Of course, when the natives hire a sampan, a great many more than two are crowded into it. Sometimes as many as twelve or fourteen will be seen packed in the bow and in the middle of the boat, until she sinks deep in the water, and it would seem as though with an extra rush of the wave she would sink with her living cargo. Experience has taught, however, that except in severe storms, or whilst the typhoon is raging, when no boat dares to look out even from the narrow creeks in which they have taken refuse, the passage can be made without any risk either to life or to property.

MacGowan, 1897

Crossing to Amoy (1897) It is now time to leave this picturesque little island, and passing over to Amoy, examine the various objects of interest that are to be found there.

Coming down to one of the jetties we find a large number of sampans grouped around it, each one with its head pointing to the landing, and kept in position by the boatman's boat-hook being inserted in the narrow spaces between the slabs of stone of which the jetty is composed, and holding it firmly in its place. No sooner do we appear than a shout is raised by the owners of every boat, each one endeavouring to pitch his voice higher than his neighbour's, and calling upon us to hire his sampan. As we walk leisurely down towards the boars, enjoying the scene suddenly presented to us, the men become more demonstrative, and strive to attract our attention. Loud stentorian voices beseech us to come into their boats, and shrill falsetto tones cut through the air as their owners point with many an impassioned gesticulation and descant on the merits of their craft. Not one of the twenty or thirty boatmen stays his cry, or resigns this good-natured contest to secure a fare, until we enter the boat we have selected. Then the uproar ceases and a sudden calm succeeds the tempest, and faces are wreathed in good-humoured smiles at their own defeat, and the lucky boatmen pushes his boat away from the jetty, leaving the rest with no feeling of ill-will or of jealousy because they failed to get us to hire them.

MacGowan, 1897

Amoy Harbor Sampan, 1924   J.Nienhuis

第十七章 鼓浪屿——外国租界 Gulangyu – International Settlement

上鼓浪屿　这些舢板坐两个人很舒服，划船人站在船尾，面对着船桨，旅客则坐在船头。舢板很安全，可以在任何天气情况下来回穿梭，而且很少会发生事故。当然，本地人租用舢板船的时候，船上就不止两个人了。有时候可以看到12或者14个旅客拥挤在船头和船身直到舢板船吃水很深了，看起来好像再来一个波浪船就会和船上的活货物一起沉入大海。但是，经验告诉他们，这样来回是不会对人或者财产带来任何危险的。除非有非常强烈的风暴，或者是在刮台风的时候，停靠在狭窄湾区避难的船只没人敢开出来。

——麦嘉湖，1897年，第159、160页

摆渡去厦门（1897年）　现在该是离开这个风景如画的小岛的时候了。摆渡去厦门，可以去看看自己在那里所发现、喜欢的物品。

从码头下来后，我们发现很多小舢板围着码头，每艘船头都对着岸边，整整齐齐排列着。船夫用钩具插入码头的石头缝中，稳稳地固定住舢板船的位置。我们才出现一会儿，每艘船上的船东就大声喊叫，每个人都试图比他邻居喊得更大声，招呼我们坐他的舢板。我们慢悠悠地走向这些小船，一边欣赏这突然出现在我们面前的景象，这些船夫更起劲了，拼命喊叫以吸引我们的注意力。洪亮的声音恳求我们到他们的船上去，激动的假声响彻云霄。船夫用夸张的手势和曲调大声说出船的优点。二三十人没有一个停止喊叫，或者放弃这种为了得到船费的愉快的比赛，直到我们走进我们选好的船里。然后，喧嚣就停止了，骚动之后突然安静下来，尽管没能吸引我们上船，船夫脸上还是充满了开心的笑容。幸运的船夫把船撑离码头和其他船夫。尽管没能吸引我们坐他们船，其他船夫的脸上也没有流露出任何的恶意和嫉妒的表情。

——麦嘉湖，1897年，第159、160页

Hope Hospital Jetty, 1930s　　　　　J. Nienhuis

老外看老鼓浪屿 *Old Gulangyu in Foreigners' Eyes*

Six Million Dollars to Cross Amoy Harbor (1940s)　At high tide, almost at the stroke of eleven, The Esteemed Positive Principle glided next to a pontoon wharf and we were tied up in Amoy. The gangplank was immediately swamped with people looking for friends, porters and smugglers' agents. Tony, already well established in Amoy for two months, fought his way through with Sheila to meet me.

"The market took a plunge recently," he said as he opened a green bag he was carrying, to reveal some bulging notes. "And I had to bring six million Chinese dollars to see you ashore…"

Crossing the narrow stretch of water involved heavy demands inflicted by different waterfront gangs. The wharf porters demanded ten Hong Kong dollars for each package carried off the steamer, and as soon as one stage in the journey had been completed, we moved into the sphere of another gang, who participated in the chain of transportation and again indulged in further financial fleecing. From the Dragon's Head jetty at Kolangsu, we walked slowly along the narrow lanes of the island to a local French pension, and were soon standing before the door of a large square two-storeyed stone house. A retinue of husky Chinese porters in shorts and singlets followed with bamboo poles balancing over their shoulders, laden down with the weight of baggage that brought out the chiseled massiveness of their leg and shoulder muscles.

"One minute," said the gang leader aggressively barring the entrance, "you never said anything about carrying the luggage upstairs. There is an extra charge for that," he added, boring into me with his flashing black eyes. I could not understand all that he said, but the meaning was clear. We were too hot and tired to argue and just nodded, handing over the last of the six million dollars.

Neill, 1956

6 Million Dollar Ferry Crossing? (U.S. Consulate in Background)　J.N.

第十七章　鼓浪屿——外国租界　Gulangyu – International Settlement

六百万法币乘船渡过厦门港（20世纪40年代）　高潮涨起的时候，就在11点左右，受人尊敬的"正向原则"号滑行到了趸船码头附近，在厦门港停靠。踏板上立即挤满了寻找朋友的人、搬运工和人口贩子的代理。托尼已经在厦门住了两个月。他带着谢拉拼命挤进人群来接我。

"最近市场大跌，"他一边说，一边打开手上拿着的一个绿色袋子，可以看到一些折皱的货币。"我得带着六百万法币来见你啊……"

乘船渡过这片狭窄的水域需要支付不少钱给码头帮派。码头搬运工从船上搬运每件行李要付10港币。刚刚支付完，我们就进入了另外一个帮派的地盘。他们帮助我们搬运行李，同时雁过拔毛，我们也要支付运费。我们从鼓浪屿的龙头码头慢慢沿着岛上一条小巷走到一家法式廉价小旅店。很快，我们就站在了一栋方形两层楼的石头房子门前。一群穿着短裤和汗衫的中国搬运工肩上挑着扁担跟来了，沉重的行李压在他们肩上，腿上和肩上的肌肉就像凿出来的一样。

"等等，"帮派头目凶狠地挡住了入口，"你没有说要我们把行李挑到楼上的，要另外付钱，"他补充说道，闪亮的黑眼睛好像要穿透我一样。我一点都不明白他说的话，但是他的意思很明确。我们太热了而且也太疲劳了，没有和他讨价还价就同意了，把六百万剩下的最后一些都给了他。

——尼尔，1956年，第20、21页

Gulangyu Signal Cannon, Spring 1932
"The gun that tells us in Kulangsu when each Sat, reaches 12 noon and incidentally shakes the hospital." Jean Nienhuis

老外看老鼓浪屿 *Old Gulangyu in Foreigners' Eyes*

No Vehicles on Gulangyu (1920s)   There was no wheeled traffic on Kulangsu: no horses, no bicycles, no rickshaws. Man provided power for sedan chairs, wheel-barrows and carrying poles. The roads, in consequence, were quiet and narrow, running steeply up and down between high-walled gardens. The noises, except in the streets stretching out from the slipways facing Amoy harbour, were the quick, flat slap of weight-carrying bare feet, the hollow drag and clop of wooden sandals, and always the sound of the sea. The Chinese, with their respect and care for the appropriate name, called it Drum Wave Island. In the small, close-packed town on the harbour, there were Chinese shops, lodgings, little one-storey dwellings, a wall-less theatre, small shrines and temples, linked by waste plots, each ruled by one or more fierce black-tongued chow who waged relentless, blood-spattering battle, until the intruder lay, throat torn out, to rot in the sun, or be gratefully eaten by a poor man's family. Up through an old graveyard and a shimmering acacia grove, one could climb huge granite boulders to the crowning Camel Rock and from it survey the whole island with its square, double-arcaded white houses set in a froth of light and dark green, its too-rare Chinese roofs, its small sandy bays. In summer the green shade was restful; opposite Amoy the mainland coast had long since been stripped of woods.

Mackenzie-Grieve, 1959

Stroll by Hope Hospital, 1920s   J. Nienhuis

第十七章　鼓浪屿——外国租界 *Gulangyu – International Settlement*

鼓浪屿没有机动车辆（20世纪20年代）　在港口边这个狭小拥挤的小镇上有中国人开的商店、旅馆、单层小房子、露天剧院、小神龛庙宇，中间还夹杂着垃圾堆，每个垃圾堆都由一条或者好几条凶猛的黑舌松狮犬控制。它们没完没了地进行血腥的抢夺战，直到入侵者喉咙被咬断，倒在太阳底下慢慢腐烂，或者被穷困人家心怀感激地当作食物吃掉。穿过一个古老的墓地和一小丛洋槐树，你就可以爬过巨大的大理圆石到最高

的骆驼岩（即日光岩，译者注）。在那里可以俯瞰整个小岛，方形而且有双层拱廊的白色房子就伫立在浅色和深绿色的泡沫之上，非常少见的中国式房顶，还有满是沙子的小海湾。夏季绿色的树荫很好让人休息，厦门的对岸靠近大陆的海岸则很长时间都没有种植树木了。

——麦肯兹·格瑞芙，1959年，第43页

Hope Hospital "Ambulance", 1920s　　J. Nienhuis

▶ 243

Gulangyu's Wealthy Chinese   Rich Chinese lived in some, like the family opposite us, but they were mostly those who had had long contact with European merchants or who had made money in the South Seas and, therefore, were not rigidly bound by tradition. Not that they preferred to live among foreigners, but in an International Concession they were better able to safeguard their hard-earned fortunes. Most of them were of humble origin, but the Tan family, whose flowery terrace overlooked our garden, preserved great dignity and a rigid conservatism through their grandfather, who had been a magistrate before the 1911 revolution. In the fine months he was always to be seen sitting among the pots of pink camellias, brush jar and ink slab before him, smoking a long pipe with a minute copper bowl. Occasionally we would meet him, in his long grey silk coat, taking his caged song-bird down to the sea for an airing. He was constantly served by the whole family; filial piety being one of the two basic Confucian principles. But the service was also a genuinely felt tribute to wisdom and experience.

Mackenzie-Grieve, 1959

A Rich Chinese' Gulangyu Garden (1920s)   Wei-ju was the richest inhabitant of the Settlement. A humble man who had, it was said, made his fortune in Javanese sugar, he owned several houses, pavilions and gardens on the island. The whole of the right-hand crescent of our bay belonged to him. The formal garden that he had laid out on the rocky point was open to the public. There was no custodian but, in spite of much great poverty, no one ever damaged or stole from the superb array of potted plants. No one left litter. But this was partly due to the shortage of fuel in a deforested land … In the little pavilion overlooking the sea, Wei-ju was keeping his mother's corpse until such time as the geomancers had declared the Feng-shui of her burial place to be favourable. Since his continuing prosperity and that of his children depended upon it, the correct aspects of wind and water were essential.

The house where Wei-ju entertained was set in another formal garden, neat and brilliant as an embroidery, with its seasonal, potted patterns of narcissi, zinnias, phoenix tail, crotons and chrysanthemums. Inside, the carved and lacquered Chinese furniture of the hall was enlivened by a complete set of white-painted European bedroom furniture, a gigantic stuffed orang-utan in a glass case, and a discreetly draped marble woman with dove in the Alma Tadema tradition. The thirty or so courses of excellent food which he always provided, the crowd of gaping sightseers, the poor relations on the marble stairs, the indescribable cacophony produced by two bands of musicians playing against each other, the good humour, the throat-clearing, the spitting, were wholly Chinese. The returned emigrant, the successful, self-made man, deserved to enjoy his success…

Mackenzie-Grieves, 1959

Gulangyu Chinese Garden of Mr. Wong (late 1940s)   Mr. Wong's house, like most of those in Amoy and on Kulangsu, was built in a foreign style of modern architecture, without the coloured tiled roofs, upturned eaves and paved central courtyards which I had anticipated in China.

第十七章　鼓浪屿——外国租界 Gulangyu – International Settlement

鼓浪屿上富裕的中国人　有些房子是富裕的中国人住的,就像我们家对面的那一家,但是他们大多数都是那些很久以前就已经和欧洲商人有联系,或者已经在南海发了财的人,因此都不是非常严格遵守传统。并不是他们喜欢和外国人住在一块,而是在国际租界里,他们可以更好地保护好来之不易的财产。他们大多数人出身卑微。不过,陈姓家族的祖父在辛亥革命之前是一名地方官员,他们保持了守旧的传统。他们家的阳台种满了花草,可以俯瞰我们的花园。天气好的时候,总是可以看到他坐在紫色山茶花盆之间,用带有一个微小铜碗的长烟斗抽烟,面前摆放着毛笔和砚台。

有时候,我们也会碰到他穿着长长的灰色真丝外套,手上提着鸟笼到海边呼吸新鲜空气。他全家人经常要照顾他,孝顺是儒家思想中最基本的两个原则之一。但是,那种照顾也是一种让人真实感觉到人们对智慧和经验的尊重。

——麦肯兹·格瑞芙,1959年,第20页

中国富绅的岛上花园　魏举黄奕住是岛上安家落户的居民中最有钱的一个。原本出身卑贱,据说在爪哇经营蔗糖发了财。他在岛上有多处房产别墅。我们海湾右手边的那块地就是他的。他曾在岩石顶上建起了花园还对外开放(此为黄仲训的标志)。虽然无人管理,而且穷人遍布,可是就没有人会去破坏或偷窃那些成排的盆花,也没人乱扔垃圾。但这也可能是因为岛上森林日稀,燃料短缺。……魏举黄奕住将母亲暂时安葬在可俯瞰大海的小亭里,直到风水先生找到风水宝地才移走。确实,他个人及其子孙的万世基业都需仰赖风水,可见风水的重要性。

魏举黄奕住娱乐消遣的处所则建在另一处花园里。园内犹如一幅刺绣,整洁鲜亮,处处点缀着当季的盆花,水仙、鱼尾菊、凤尾、巴豆,还有菊花。屋内,精雕油漆的中式家具在全套白色欧式卧室家具的映衬下,添了几分生动。玻璃柜里摆放着大猩猩,还有极具埃及风格手托鸽子的大理石雕美女。他通常会用30道左右的精美菜肴款待宾客。蜂拥而至的宾客,大理石阶上的穷亲戚,两支乐队演奏着完全不同的乐曲而产生难以描述的刺耳噪音,清喉咙的嗓音,吐痰的声音,人群混杂,颇具讽刺,这就是纯粹的中国特色。这位海外归来的华人,功成名就,有资格享受成功,那又为何与大猩猩相伴?我想,可能他想提醒自己别忘了在南洋丛林中的日子吧?

——麦肯兹·格瑞芙,1959年,第43页

鼓浪屿王家的中式花园(20世纪40年代末)　像厦门和鼓浪屿上的其他大部分房子一样,王宅是外国风格的现代建筑。没有我在中国见到的琉璃瓦屋顶、上翘的屋檐和铺上砖、石的中央庭院。

But like other wealthy businessmen with overseas connections, he had tried to turn the little garden space he had into something that approached the spirit and form of a typical Chinese garden, where small things are made to seem large and large things small—narrow paved walks, dwarf hedges and walls with ornamental openings through which small arbours and pavilions could be viewed as if through a square or vase-shaped telescope to give the illusion of a living landscape picture. Here and there were grotesque contorted rocks, draped in waves of mauve wisteria, or cascades of flowers in the coils of the green tresses of some exotic creeper. Against the flaming sheets of colour that arose from rose bushes, peonies, magnolia blossoms and lotus flowers, these rocks became the central pivot from which the eye turned to admire the riot of colour and to whose natural greyness it returned for relaxation. There were other things too in his garden, large vases with small well-trained shrubs, bird-cages, stone lions soporifically guarding some vantage point, and bowls of foppish goldfish, floating and flickering their burnished gleaming bodies before the admiring eyes of relaxes spectators. Some were of a fiery gold, some scarlet or silver and some with wasp-like stripes and spots of a velvety transparence. Circulating with an easy grace, swaying their diaphanous tails Cextended like crinoline panniers, protruding their pouchy ogling eyes, and gulphing out beaded bubbles that floated slowly to the top of the bowl, they provided an endless source of enjoyment and happiness to their proud and contemplative owner, whenever he tried to free himself from the worries of the Philippine sugar market.

..."Not a very good garden," said Mr. Wong with a customary self deprecation,"and a very poor house,"he added with a chuckle.

Neill, 1956

Mr. Lim[3] Nee Kak holds a very prominent place in the .social and commercial life of Amoy. He has gained many distinctions from the Government, and is now accounted one of the richest men in China. Born in Pangkio, Taipei, Formosa, in 1874, he was educated privately, and at an early age assisted his father, Mr. Lim See Fu, who was Chinese minister in the island, in the management of his rice estates and gold mines, and in prospecting expeditions into the interior. After the Japanese War the family came to Amoy, and here Lim Nee Kar assisted his father to establish four banks, as well as one each in Hongkong, Tientsin, and Shanghai. The death of Mr. Lim See Fu took place in 1905, after which his son took charge of all the businesses. Success followed success. He has visited the Throne at Peking, and was granted a title equal in rank to that of an ambassador, and carrying with it the privilege of petitioning the Throne in person. Amongst the many positions he has held as a prominent man of business may be mentioned the chairmanship of the Chinese Chamber of Commerce, to which he has been elected three times. In 1906 he was asked by the Government to establish the Sin Yong Corporation Bank, and, at the present time, he is a director of the Fokien Railway Company: superintendent of the Amoy Telephone Company; chairman of the Shanghai Hwatong Marine and Fire Insurance Company; and auditor of the Taiwan Bank in Amoy. At the time of writing he is using every effort to secure the construction of some efficient waterworks on the island. He is a great believer in the advantages of a European education, and his sons, who are now studying under a European governess, show every promise of developing intellectual faculties similar to those which have characterised their father and grandfather.

Mackenzie-Grieve, 1959

3　The Lin Residence is now at 11-19 Lujiao Rd.

第十七章　鼓浪屿——外国租界 Gulangyu – International Settlement

但是，跟其他拥有海外关系的富裕商人一样，他也试图把花园变成具有中国精神风貌的典型中式花园。花园里小物品被放大了，而大物品则被缩小了：铺上了砖、石小道很窄，篱障像侏儒般矮小，围墙上有几个装饰性的开口，可以看到藤架和凉亭，就像是用方形或者瓶状的望远镜看到一幅鲜活的风景画一样。到处都是奇形怪状的岩石藏在紫藤丛中，或者是瀑布般的花朵开在绿色爬山虎中。

玫瑰花、牡丹花、玉兰花、莲花竞相开放，形成了一片片燃烧的花海。岩石成了眼睛欣赏鲜花怒放的中枢，其自然的灰色变成了人们放松眼神的地方。王宅的花园里还有其他东西：种在大花盆里的小盆栽、鸟笼、石狮子巧妙地守卫着某个重要的地点、鱼缸里的俗丽金鱼忽明忽暗地摆动自己光洁、闪亮的身躯，吸引悠闲的看客羡慕的目光。有些金鱼是金黄色的，有些是鲜红色或银色的，有些金鱼身上长着黄蜂般的条纹和天鹅绒般透明的斑点。它们从容地在鱼缸里游转，摆动着像垫臀宽裙一样撑开的明亮尾巴，小袋子般的媚眼凸出。它们呼出珠子般的水泡，慢慢地从鱼缸底部冒上来。骄傲、沉思的主人试图摆脱自己对菲律宾蔗糖市场行情的担忧时，金鱼为他们提供了无穷无尽的欢乐与快感。

……"算不上什么好花园，"王先生用惯有的自谦说，"房子也很一般，"他轻轻一笑，又说了一句。

——尼尔，1956 年，第 74～75 页

林尔嘉先生[4]　在厦门社交圈和商业界，林尔嘉先生名声显赫，政府授予他很多荣誉，现在被称为中国最富有的商人之一。他于 1874 年出生于台湾台北板桥市，早年在私塾接受教育，在年少时就开始协助他父亲管理田产和金矿，并深入内陆地区从事勘探工作。他父亲名叫林时甫（即林维源），当时是岛上的神职人员。日本人占领台湾后，他们全家都搬到了厦门。在这里，林尔嘉先生协助他父亲一共开办了四家银行，另外三家分别在香港、天津和上海。林时甫先生 1905 年仙逝后，他儿子全盘接管了所有生意。成功接连不断。他去北平拜见了皇帝，得到了一个相当于大使的称号，他可以直接上书皇帝。在他所拥有的职位中，厦门商务总会会长是一个商业巨子所能拥有的最显赫的职位，他三次当选。1906 年，政府邀请他开设新永银行。目前，他担任福建铁路公司的董事长，厦门电话公司主管，上海华通海事和火灾保险公司董事长，厦门台湾银行的审计师。此时，他正在竭尽全力建设岛上的水厂。他信奉先进的欧洲教育体制，他的儿子们都在一个欧洲私人教师指导下学习，他们身上都充分展现了他们父亲和祖父身上所特有的才智。

——麦肯兹·格瑞英，1959 年

4　林宅现在的地址是鹿礁路 11—19 号。

Chapter 18   Foreign Life in Amoy

"East is East and West is West..."

Kipling

"Extremes Meet."

Chinese Proverb.

There is a subtle influence in the air of the East that puts a drag upon a man, and even the vigorous Westerner by and by feels his footstep becoming slower and a tendency to put things off creeping over him.

MacGowan, 1909

He [the foreigner] was firmly convinced that the white race was superior to the yellow, and they were equally sure of the opposite. When he demanded that they pay respect to science and invention, they countered with an invitation for him to consider the importance of art and literature in the scheme of living.

Lewis, 1938

Big-Nosed Foreigners   There was perfect freedom to stroll into every shop, to turn over the wares higgledy-piggledy, and yet to make not the smallest purchase. The traders were lost in gaping wonder at the strange aspect of the customers, at their extraordinary dress, their long hair, their, to them, grotesque features, and especially at the stupendous size of their noses...

Knollys, 1885

The Chinese Stare   Chinese stare at the foreigner, sometimes with skepticism or even thinly veiled contempt, but once they know you, "The crowd becomes sympathetic. The sneer dies out of their faces. There is nothing that touches the Chinese heart so mightily as practical benevolence. It is a virtue they highly appreciate. Their stolid, emotionless features begin to light up with genuine feeling, and the eyes of some are twinkling and flashing as their hearts are moved... [what] has just happened has been a mighty revelation. It has brought you closer to the Chinese heart than you were before, and it has revealed to you the wondrous possibilities of the future..."

Little Foreigners Draw the Crowd, 1933   J. Nienhuis

MacGowan, 1895

第十八章　外国人在厦门的生活

"东是东来，西是西……"

——吉卜林说

"物极必反"

——中国谚语

东方空气中微妙的影响会让人变得拖拉，即使是充满活力的西方人也会不知不觉地放慢脚步，倾向于把要做的事情都抛之脑后。

——麦嘉湖，1909年，第6页

外国人坚信白种人比黄种人优越，黄种人则恰恰持有相反的观点。当外国人要求黄种人尊重科学和发明的时候，黄种人则请求外国人在生活安排中多考虑文学和艺术的重要性。

——列维斯，1938年，第159页

Gulangyu Taxi　　MacGowan, 1907

大鼻子老外　　外国人可以随便走进商店，把物品翻来翻去，但是不买一点东西也没有关系。店员都忘记做生意了，只顾目瞪口呆地看着这些奇怪的顾客：不同寻常的衣服，长长的头发，以及让他们觉得非常可笑的大鼻子…… 这些都让他们觉得非常古怪的。

——诺利斯，1885年，第226页

中国人凝视的目光　　中国人有时候会带着怀疑，甚至是轻微掩饰的轻蔑眼光凝视着外国人。但是，当他们一旦认识了你，"他们就会变得非常有同情心。嘲笑就会从他们脸上消失。没有其他什么比现实的善意更能打动中国人的心。这是被他们非常遵从的一种美德。他们呆板、毫无表情的脸慢慢随着真实的感情舒展开来了。有些人的眼睛则随着心灵的感动也开始闪烁起来…… 刚刚发生的一切都成了威力巨大的心灵启示。它能让你比以前更接近中国人的心灵，而且也让你感受到未来神奇的可能……"

——麦嘉湖，1895年

老外看老鼓浪屿 Old Gulangyu in Foreigners' Eyes

Going Mad (or odd) in Amoy Anyhow, the result [of no, or slow, mail] tends to heighten the sense of isolation, which is perhaps nowhere so much felt as among Chinese. Whether it is their expressionlessness, their want of sympathy, or the whole character of their civilization being so different from ours, very few Europeans can spend more than a year amongst Chinese without suffering from it. Some go mad with it, and all are accused of growing odd...

Bradford, 1938

Little, 1899

Angry She-Devil Foreign Wives (1840s) Upon the conclusion of the war, the most friendly feelings were evinced by the Chinese of all classes, as I have often mentioned, towards us, and in no place were they more so than at Amoy. English pony-races and other sports got up by the officers of the garrison were duly attended by the mandarins, and interchanges of complimentary visits were constantly made between both parties.

Upon one occasion, a party of young Chinese gentlemen were inspecting the military barracks of the Royal Irish. Of a sudden, the harmony of their visit was interrupted by the cries and screams of one of their number, who was seen flying across the barrack-yard, loudly calling for help, pursued by no less fearful a personage than a certain Meg O' Flanagan... with an immense broomstick, and by no means contenting herself with the demonstration alone of this ugly weapon, she was applying it with extreme vigour, and screaming at the height of her voice — "I'll teach the long-tailed black-guard to spy upon the Irish girls." It appeared that, prompted by a vain curiosity to view more narrowly a Fanqui-fo (a foreign-devil wife), he had been sufficiently rash to peep through the aperture of a half-closed door, where the said Mrs. O'Flanigan was in the act of performing her toilet, when, much to her surprise, she perceived a reflection in the glass of a long-tailed gentleman looking over her shoulder.

The sequel is readily understood: to use her own expression — "Faith, I made the long-tailed blackguard get out of that." "No wonder,"said the affrighted mandarin, on recovering himself a little, "that the men are such devils, being the offspring of such she-dragons."

Colonel Cunynghame 1853

Rickshaw at Gulangyu Ferry (Amoy Side), 1934 J. Nienhuis

第十八章 外国人在厦门的生活 Foreign Life in Amoy

在厦门发疯或变得古怪　不管怎么说,没有或者迟到的邮件进一步加剧了与世隔绝的感觉。和中国人在一起的时候也许感觉得更加明显。不管是他们面无表情,缺乏同情心,还是他们的文明和我们的大相径庭,没有几个欧洲人可以和中国人待在一起超过一年还没有深受其害的。有些人发疯了,所有人据说都变古怪了……

——利特尔,1899年,第89页

愤怒的魔鬼——外国太太(19世纪40年代)　正如我经常提起,战争结束后,中国各个阶层都对我们表达了最友善的感情,特别是在厦门。驻军官兵组织的英式矮种马比赛和其他运动项目中经常可以看到中国官员的身影。双方往来频繁。

有一次,一群年轻的中国绅士正在参观爱尔兰皇家部队的营房。突然,平静的局面被其中一个绅士的大声喊叫打断了。只见他从营房花园中飞奔出来,大声喊着救命。追在他后面的是一个可怕的女人名叫梅格·奥弗拉纳根,她手里拿着一把巨大的扫把,一点都不满足于展示她手中丑陋的武器,而是使出浑身的力气挥舞着,同时尖声高喊:"我要好好地教训一下偷窥爱尔兰姑娘的长辫子无赖。"后来,我们得知,他纯粹出于好奇,非常鲁莽地透过半开的门缝,近距离地观察番鬼婆(外国鬼子的夫人)。此时,梅格·奥弗拉纳根夫人正在上厕所,在镜子上看到了一个长辫子绅士的影子从她肩头上冒出来,让她大吃了一惊。

结局很快就明了了。用她自己的话说:"上帝,我把长辫子的无赖赶走了。"而那个绅士喘口气说:"难怪外国男人都像魔鬼一样,原来都是这些女魔头的后代啊。"

——坎宁安上校,1853年,第214、215页

Seeing off Dr.Bosch and Family, 1920s　　J. Neinhuis

老外看老鼓浪屿 *Old Gulangyu in Foreigners' Eyes*

Signal Hill; Mail Ships (1850s) One daily service father gave his painstaking care to recording, was the receiving of signals of shipping through flags and colored balls, lowered and raised on a flagstaff,[1] with known meanings to the initiated, from a station far out in the harbor, seen only through a spyglass.

Whenever a vessel or "Man of War" was turning into our waters, great excitement followed, as the news was broadcast in our community. Was it an American, British, Dutch, French, or East Indiaman? All carried mail, which may have been months en route. And news of all kinds might be coming forward to meet friends—of joy or sorrow, distress or comfort. So a deep suspense seemed to hover over all the company, some of whom would gather at our house, as the place where first information could be had, and also was situated nearest to the outer harbor. As the vessels approached, first, the masts just rising above the horizon could be sighted by the naked eye; then the sails and hulls; and by this time, the spyglasses could discern to what nationality the vessel belonged, and to what class of ship.

If the "Stars and Stripes" flew at the stern, 0! the thrill to our American family! If the cross of St. George was there, our warmest friends were cheered; and all of the American Colony would be glad too, for our interests were closely entwined, and our mails often, too, found their way to us through the British ships.

Our American ships would bring the most direct letters to us, or boxes, or perhaps a friend—a missionary—to join forces with those who waited to welcome them. If a British boat, an English or Scotch friend and his wife might be returning again to China, after a visit to their homelands, or new faces to add to their colony and make friends with all.

---

1 Mr. Zhu Siming, age 85, whom I interviewed in March 2008, said flags signaled typhoons, inspections of ships for infectious diseases, and warned Xiamen University water company (Amoy's best) to prepare for ships coming to purchase their water. In addition, everyone set their clocks and watches each noon by flag, and a cannon fired from Signal Hill (photo page 243).

Bradford, 1934

第十八章　外国人在厦门的生活　*Foreign Life in Amoy*

升旗山[2],**邮轮**（19世纪50年代）　父亲每天都要认真记录的是船的旗杆上用旗帜和有色圆球升起或落下的信号。这些信号对于发起人来说都代表某种意义，在距离港口很远的地方用小望远镜才能看到。

载满士兵的轮船访问厦门港。消息传开后，我们都会兴奋一阵。是美国人，英国人，荷兰人，法国人还东印度公司的人呢？所有的船只都载有旅行了好几个月的邮件，给朋友带来开心、悲伤、苦恼，或者惬意的消息。大家的心悬得很高。我们家距外港最近，有些人就会聚集过来，了解第一手资讯。轮船驶近厦门港，首先肉眼能看到的是船上刚刚露出海平面的桅杆。接下来是船帆和船身。此时，用小望远镜就能看清船舶所属的国籍及其等级。

如果船尾飘扬着美国的"星条旗"，我们美国家庭是多么得激动！如果是英格兰国旗，我们的朋友都会热烈欢呼，所有美国人也会非常开心，因为我们的利益互相关联，而且我们的邮件经常也是由英国转递到美国船上。

我们美国轮船带来了我们的邮件、礼盒，或者是朋友——即将加入欢迎他们的传教士团队的传教士。英国轮船上则有英格兰或者苏格兰朋友以及他的夫人回家度假后又回到了中国，也有新面孔加入租界，成为所有人的朋友。

——玛丽·多蒂未出版的回忆录

2　朱思明，85岁，2008年3月接受我的采访时说，信号旗发布台风、上船检测传染病的消息，并通知厦门大学水务公司（厦门最好）为前来买水的船舶做好准备。此外，每天正午，大家还根据信号旗校对时钟和手表。与此同时，升旗山响炮一次（见第243页照片）。

THE ILLUSTRATED LONDON NEWS　　SEPT. 3, 1853

AMOY--SKETCHED FROM THE SIGNAL STATION

The Undine often brought mail (1861)

Chater Collection
J. W. Jeffreson.

老外看老鼓浪屿 *Old Gulangyu in Foreigners' Eyes*

Writing Letters Home [3](1850s)   About once a month, father would bring home from his morning's work, to mother, word that a ship carrying American mail would sail in a few days, or even less. Then intensive writing was the main occupation of both of them, to gather together what had been written through the month, with present additions; letters "home" always, and to many friends and relatives, or official reports to the "Board of Foreign Missions", or other public matters. Then we children were quite neglected, and banished to the care of the two nurses. If we ventured to steal into the room where mother sat at her Chinese lacquered desk, with pen rapidly scratching up and down, as we thought, and ventured to ask a question, her hand would go out, and her voice said, "No, children, you must not disturb me. Mother will answer after the mail leaves."

Gulangyu Home, 1930s

We knew it was final and crept away, longing for letter time to stop and we could be with her again. We never ventured into father's study, I guess. This was a frequent memory, as letters were faithfully and lovingly written through those eleven years by both father and mother, and after that, as faithfully sent by the one left, to the mother, and as loyally and affectionately replied to by grandmother.

Mary Doty's Memoirs

---

3   See Ruth Bradford's Journal (next chapter) for more on the joys and sorrows of mail

"Study." Jean Nienhuis, 1923

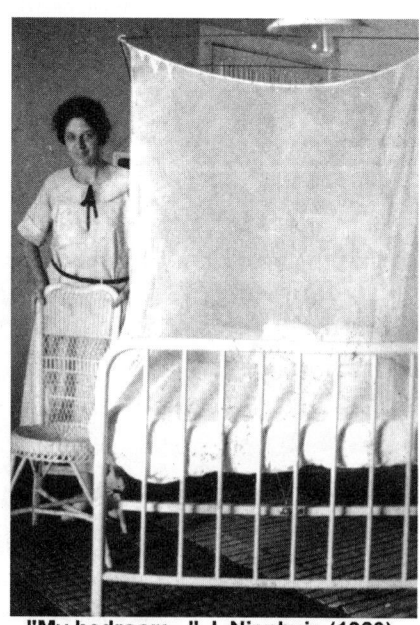

"My bedroom..." J. Nienhuis (1923)

254

第十八章　外国人在厦门的生活 *Foreign Life in Amoy*

写家信（19世纪50年代）　每个月一次，父亲早上做完礼拜后来，都带话给母亲，告诉她几天后，或更短时间内，一艘美国邮轮就要出发了。接下来，父母亲就会开始忙于写家信，收集了过去写下的东西并加上最新的发展情况；所谓"家信"包括给朋友和亲戚的私人信件，也包括给海外传道会的报告和其他的公事。我们小孩就会被扔在一边，完全交给两个仆人照料。如果我们敢偷偷跑进妈妈房间，就可以看到她坐在中式漆凳子飞速地写着东西。如果我们试图问她问题，她会挥一挥手，说道："不行，小孩，现在不能打扰我。邮件寄出后，我才会回答你。"

我们知道这就是最终的结果，只好偷偷溜出去，暗自希望她赶紧写完信，才能有时间和我们在一起。我记得我们从来不敢走进父亲的书房。我们记忆中在这11年间，都是父亲和母亲至真至诚地、满怀爱心地写完家信后寄出，随后就可以收到祖母亲切的回信。

——玛丽·多蒂未出版的回忆录

"My study". Jean Nienhuis, 1923

Amoy Mission Friends　　　　　　　J. Veldman

255

老外看老鼓浪屿 *Old Gulangyu in Foreigners' Eyes*

Inescapable Amoy[4] As everyone in China knows, at the end of his first seven years of service a Customs Assistant may apply for two years' leave on half-pay, which period he may spend anywhere usually "at home," viz. Europe his return passage to China being paid for him. But of those Assistants who may take their leave, under such favourable conditions, there are a great many who do not find themselves in a position to do so, and this in spite of having received regular and excellent pay during their period of service. At the end of his first seven years in China a man has often saved nothing, his brain having been turned by the mere possession of money, seemingly inexhaustible to one who has perhaps been brought up in narrow circumstances. Or, he has been bitten rabidly by what is known as "Sinology," and lives, speaks, thinks, and dreams of nothing but the Chinese language and literature. Or, he has been drawn into the ring of speculators, and has risked, even if he has not lost, all his savings in strange and wonderful mines and companies. Or, he is drinking himself into an untimely grave. And as it is far easier to live on nothing at all, and to die leaving your family to your friends, or to be a Chinese student, or to be a speculator, or to be a hard drinker, in the East than in the West, the man of seven years generally stays out fourteen.

Boehm, 1897

Amoy, August, 1901

Bustling Laowai Life on Amoy Foreigners are not as lonely in this part of the world as, possibly, in the days of our grandparents; for various reasons many of the European race are wending their way hither. A visitor is not such a rare occurrence as once. Of course, I refer particularly to the ports, but even in many inland places in China a foreign face is met with So it has come to pass that we in Amoy often feel that life is full of rush, and we live in a sort of whirl very much like our own brothers and sisters, not only because of much more foreign intercourse (and, by the way, we are often very glad of the change), but also because the cares and worries of household life, of school life, of hospital life, of Chinese life in general, wear heavily upon our nerves. All this, plus the severe heat and climatic changes, have caused some of us to run away for about twelve days to a small island, six miles from Amoy where we can be quite alone, with no interruptions, no one to argue or disagree with—in short, a place to vegetate and to muse and to rest.

J.N.
Harold and David Depree, 1920s
Family in Amoy from 1907-1948

---

4 After 21 years in Xiamen, I can understand why those who did escape Amoy regretted it. During Dr. Young's last days, he said, "Oh! if I were but back to Amoy!" Barbour, 1855, P. 55

第十八章　外国人在厦门的生活 Foreign Life in Amoy

无法逃脱的厦门　每个在中国的外国人都知道,结束 7 年的通关助理工作后可以申请两年的半薪假。期间,他通常会选择"回家"——欧洲,到中国的回程船费也已经预付了。但是在这样优惠的条件下选择度假的助理中,很多都无法做到,尽管工作期间他们都定期拿到了丰厚的薪水。在中国工作 7 年后,很多人都没有什么积蓄。他们的脑子里想到的都是用之不竭的钱财,至少对那些没有攒钱的人来说是这样的。或者,他深深沉醉于著名的"汉学",在他的生活、言语、思维和梦想中只有中国语言和文学。或者他加入了投机商人圈子,他把所有的积蓄都冒着风险投入了奇妙的矿山和公司。第三种可能是酗酒过度,英年早逝。和在西方相比,在东方一无所有,死后把家庭交给朋友,或者当中国学生,做个投机商人或者酗酒者好像更容易生存,7 年之后的人通常都会呆到 14 年。

Dr. Boot (Amoy 1903-1940)
Jessie Platz (Amoy 1930-1947)

——布恩,1897 年,第 7、8 页

老外在厦门的忙乱生活　厦门,1901 年 8 月。在厦门,老外已经不像我们祖辈那时候那么孤单了。原因是多方面的,很多欧洲人纷纷来到厦门。不像以前,来访的人也多了。当然,我最喜欢的地方是港口,但是即使在中国许多内陆地区也可以碰到外国人。所以,我们在厦门感觉生活节奏很快,我们和其他兄弟姐妹一样生活在漩涡之中。这不仅是因为和其他外国人越来越多的交流(当然,我们也很高兴见证这种变化),也因为对于家庭、学校、医院以及生活在中国的担心和忧虑让我们神经紧张。所有这一切,加上酷暑和多变的天气,迫使我们逃到距离厦门有六英里外的一个小岛。在那里,我们就可以很清净了,没有人打扰,也没有人和我们争论或提出不同意见。总而言之,这是一个可以让我们无所事事,沉思和休息的地方。

——郁约翰发自厦门的信件,1901 年 8 月

老外看老鼓浪屿 *Old Gulangyu in Foreigners' Eyes*

The Chinese Carpenter Makes a Bed (1940s) He promised that whatever else might be of second rate quality, he would ensure that every attention was paid by his carpenters in making my bed. This was the most important piece of furniture in a Chinese household and was sometimes a house in itself; by traditionally requirements sufficiently large for several concubines, but without anything so enervating as a spring or mattress. The old man, however, knew the weakness of foreigners for spring mattresses and prided himself on being able to provide one to complete satisfaction.

The Chinese bed usually had four posts from which hung ornate curtains that could be tactfully closed when required and were essential in a country which frowned upon closed doors. At one end was kept a suitcase with clothes, and underneath was scattered a mass of odds and ends which might one day become useful. The Chinese with their inborn thrift disliked discarding any article that could possibly ever be of use, and their reluctance to dispense with empty tins and bottles was as much a manifestation of thrift as a lack, by Western standards, of a sense of hygiene. There was never any intention that my bed should acquire the utility or the trappings of a real Chinese bed, but it was something of a shock to see such an enormous four-poster being carried down the street by half a dozen laughing carriers.

Neill, 1956

Dorothy and Bobby's Birthday Party, Gulangyu, 1920s   J.N.

第十八章　外国人在厦门的生活 *Foreign Life in Amoy*

请中国木匠做张床（20 世纪 40 年代）　他保证说其他人做的床都有可能是二等货，他会要求木匠一丝不苟地做好我的床。床是中国人家里最重要的一件家具，有时候床本身就是一个家。传统的床一般都很大，可以睡好几个小老婆，但是没有令人萎靡的弹簧或床垫。不过，那个老先生知道外国人喜欢弹簧或床垫。他非常骄傲地说，他可以做一个床垫，做出一张完美的床。

中国人的床一般都有四个柱子，上面挂着华丽的床帘，需要时可以放下。这对于一个

Two Carpenters　　MacGowan, 1913

内敛的国家是非常必要的。床的一头是装满了衣服的箱子，底下散落着有一天可以派上用场的零碎物品。中国人天生节俭，不喜欢把可能还有用的物品到处乱扔。在西方人的标准看来，他们不愿意扔掉空罐头和瓶子表示节俭，同时也表示缺乏良好的卫生习惯。我从来没有想到自己的床会和中国人的一样拥有各种各样的装备和装饰。但是，当六个搬运工把这张用四个柱子撑起来的大床沿着大街抬到我家的时候，我们真是大吃一惊。

——尼尔，1956 年，第 63、64 页

Relaxing on front porch, Tong'an, 1928　　J. Nienhuis

老外看老鼓浪屿 Old Gulangyu in Foreigners' Eyes

Never Alone in China China is a country that is distinguished for its dense population. Wherever you travel you never seem to be able to get away from the human Celestial. The great cities and market towns and public thoroughfares present a never-ending succession of Chinese forms and faces that becomes absolutely monotonous. It is natural to expect them in these great centers of population, but you go into the most out-of-the-way places, and even there you are confronted with the same perplexing problem.

You wish, for example, to be alone, absolutely alone for a time... There is a hill nearby that you believe to be entirely deserted, and you think if you could only get up there, the desire of your heart would be gratified.

You walk briskly down the street, as though you were projecting a good long constitutional, in order that no one may be mad enough to think of following you. By and by you make a sudden flank movement that takes you into a lane leading off from the main road. Casting hurried glances back on the way you have just travelled to see that no one is watching you, you make rapid strategic doubles in the direction of the hill, till you find yourself calmly and with a contented mind slowly rising higher and higher, until at last you have fairly left all traces of human life behind you, and you are actually alone.

Seating yourself on a grassy mound, you look out on the broad expanse before you, and you breathe a sigh of content. No mechanical sounds of voices, as though they were being ground out by some creaking machinery, fall upon your ears. You hear the sighing of the wind and you see the grasses waving their heads as though they would talk in dumb show with you. You look down at the river, that winds like a silver thread along the plain, and you feel that this contact with nature is a most delightful break on the eternal monotony of faces...

All at once you receive a shock. You catch the gleam of an eye through an opening in two or three bushes that you never dreamed of concealing anything human behind them. You are startled, for you feel that the Chinaman has outwitted you. You turn round and cast suspicious glances towards a hedge, where wild flowers are growing and that you thought to be the very picture of sylvan solitude, and you see several figures dodging behind it.

The delightful sense of being alone vanishes, and you realize that that is an impossibility in China. You stand up disgusted, but with the feeling of amusement predominant, and one after another comes out of his hiding-place, where the black, piercing eyes have been scanning your every movement for the last ten minutes, and at least a dozen ungainly forms creep up to you and with smiling faces try to make friends with you.

MacGowan, 1907

Friendly Crowd   J. Nienhuis

第十八章 外国人在厦门的生活 Foreign Life in Amoy

在中国从不孤单 中国举世闻名的是它密集的人口。不管你走到哪里，都似乎无法远离人群。无论是在大城市、市场，还是在大街上，到处都是穷无尽的中国人和他们的脸孔，让人感觉非常单调。在人口密集的地方很自然可以理解，但是到了偏僻的地方，你还是会碰到同样令人迷惑的问题。

例如你希望有一段时间完全与世隔绝……你知道附近有一座人迹罕至的小山，只要能爬上那里，你心灵的需要就会得到满足。

你开心地走过街道，就像在进行一次漫长的保健散步，以便没有人会疯到跟着你。你突然侧身，很快就走进一条远离主路的小巷。匆忙往身后一看，发现没有人在观察你。这时，你赶紧一路小跑，放心地往小山走去，平静而又满意地向上爬。最后，你把所有的人类迹象都抛在脑后，你终于与世隔绝了。

坐在草土墩上，看着面前宽阔的地方，你终于可以满意地呼了口气。就像刚被辗轧机碾压掉一样，一点机械噪音都听不见了。你只能听到微风的叹息声，看到绿草摇晃着脑袋好像和你进行无声的交谈一样。眼前的小河就像一条银线在平原上蜿蜒。你觉得和大自然的亲密接触是在见过没完没了无聊的脸孔后之后最惬意的休息……

突然之间，你就会大吃一惊。透过两三个灌木丛的缝隙，你可以看到微光闪烁，而那是你从来就没有想到有人会躲在那里的地方。你大为惊讶，觉得那个中国人比你聪明。你转过身来，带着怀疑的眼光地看了一眼树丛，那里长满了野花，你原来以为那只是树林，但是你却看到了几个人藏在后面。

愉快的独处感觉消失了，你也意识到在中国是不可能独处的。你厌恶地站起身来，但开心的感觉还是占了上风。他们一个又一个人走出藏身之处，用乌黑锐利的眼睛观察着你过去 10 分钟内的一举一动。最后，十几个人笨拙地爬到你身边。他们脸带笑容，想和你交朋友。

——麦嘉湖，1895 年，第 71～73 页

Amoy Outing, 1927 — J. Nienhuis

老外看老鼓浪屿 *Old Gulangyu in Foreigners' Eyes*

July 4th Celebration on Gulangyu, 1921

第十八章 外国人在厦门的生活 *Foreign Life in Amoy*

New Years Celebration, Gulangyu, 1938
Photo Courtesy of John Anderson (whose parents are the Gypsy and Snowman)

老外看老鼓浪屿 *Old Gulangyu in Foreigners' Eyes*

New Year, Gulangyu, 1936
Photo Courtesy of J. Anderson

第十八章 外国人在厦门的生活 *Foreign Life in Amoy*

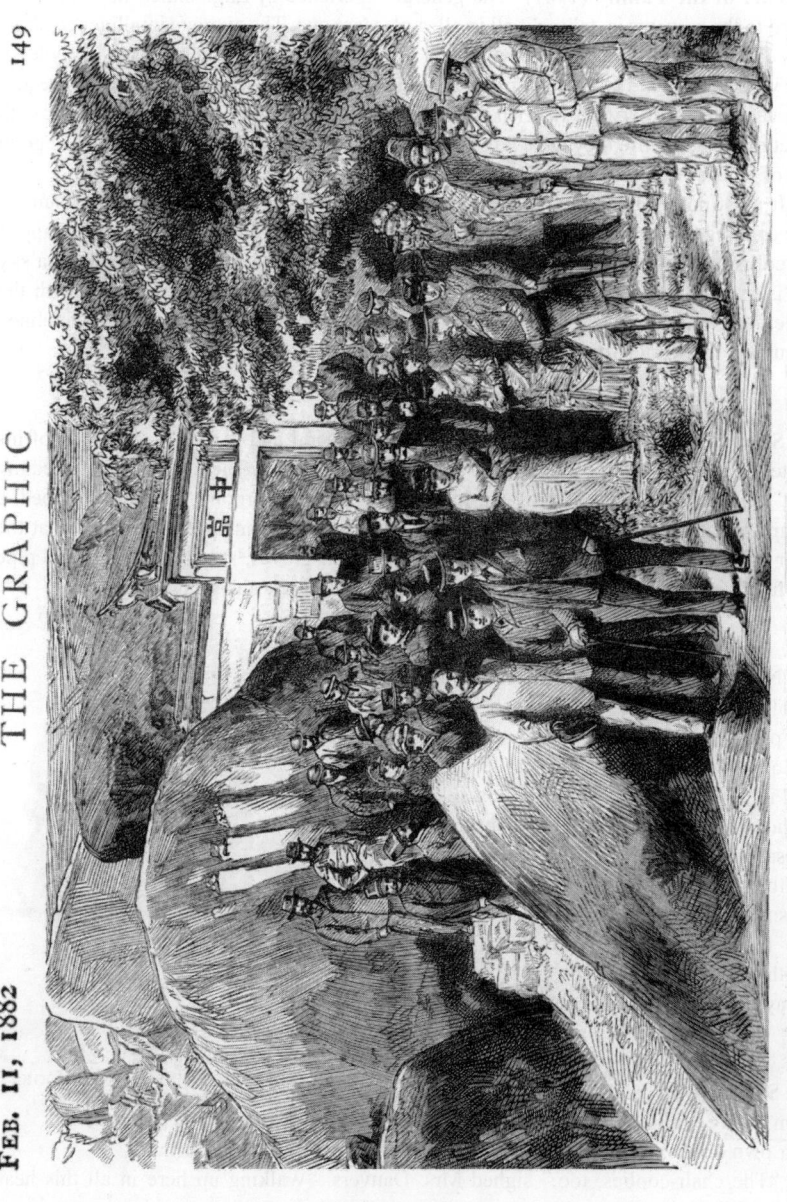

老外看老鼓浪屿 *Old Gulangyu in Foreigners' Eyes*

Amoy Servants

Part of the Family (1907) The general experience of Englishmen in China with regard to the servants is, taking it all in all, a pleasant one. The average intelligence of the class of men and women that are employed is a fairly good one. They consequently learn their work easily, and as they are industrious and moved by a sense of fidelity they render such very pleasant services that when families have to return to England, they think with regret of the home life they have left behind them in that far-off land, which owed a good deal of its charm to the cheerful and willing service rendered by the servants in it.

It must not be inferred that there never is any friction. That would be to assume a state of things that could be found nowhere in the wide world. Disagreements do happen and collisions do take place, but these are but as it were the occasional clouds in a sky that is usually sunny, and besides there is so much of the grotesque mingled with the unpleasant, that after the affair is over and the irritation has subsided one is more inclined to laugh at the whole affair than to be angry.

MacGowan, 1907

Studying the Master Each one makes the general and particular character of his master his special study sometimes to a very amusing extent. The first day I engaged my 'boy,' I had carelessly tossed my hat into one corner of the room, gloves on the bed, a stump of pencil at an acute angle with one corner of the mantelpiece, and a pipe at the other corner. For many successive days I found hat, gloves, stump of pencil and pipe carefully deposited in exactly the same spot and at precisely the same angle.

Knollys, 1885

No One's Home! The Chinese being totally unable to pronounce our English names with any proximity to accuracy, it is customary for a visitor, even though well known, to send up his card in advance, and it is quite allowable during the hot siesta hours for the 'boy' to bring back the message 'no can see.' 'Here is that stupid Mr. Smith,' says the lady to her husband. 'Oh, do not let the snob in,' is the drowsy reply. Accordingly the 'boy' thus delivers himself to the self-complacent Smith, 'No can see. Master say you snob. Missus-ee say you plenty too much fool-o.'

Knollys, 1885

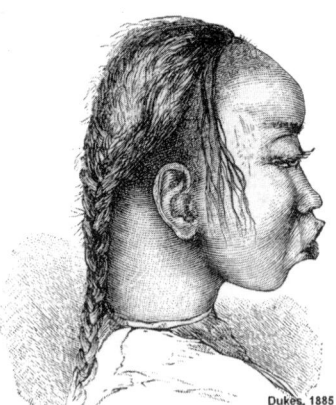

MASTER MERCY, THE COOK,

Servants on Strike (1920s) "Doesn't it seem funny without servants? I mean, getting your own drinks. Why, I'd hardly been into my kitchen till this morning..."

"The chair-coolies, too," sighed Mrs. Danvers. "Walking up here in all this heat. Frightful!"

266

第十八章　外国人在厦门的生活 *Foreign Life in Amoy*

厦门佣人

家庭中的一员（1907年）

英国人在中国与佣人相处总体说来都是比较愉快的。雇用的男女佣人都有良好的智力，因此他们学得很快。而且，由于他们非常勤劳，非常忠诚地提供各项服务，以至于当主人回到英国的时候都会非常遗憾地想念那些千里之外的家庭生活。这一切都是因为佣人们所提供的愉快且心甘情愿的各项服务。

当然不能由此推断主仆之间没有摩擦的发生。这是世上任何地方都不可能发生的事情。不同意见确实存在，摩擦也在所难免。但是，这些摩擦就像是平日阳光明媚的天空偶尔冒出的几朵乌云。这种感觉非常复杂。事情过后，不愉快消退了。大家都觉得整个事情非常可笑，而不觉得很生气。

Joseland children and Amah

——麦嘉湖，1907年，第94、95页

研究主人　每个佣人都会把主人当作特别的学习对象，有时甚至到了非常可笑的地步。雇用小男佣第一天，我无意中把我的帽子扔在房间的角落里，手套扔在床上，把一根铅笔成锐角状态摆在面对壁炉台的地方，还把烟斗放在另外一个角落。接下来的好几天，我发现手套、铅笔和烟斗都放在原来的地方，连角度都一样。

——诺利斯，1885年，第44页

没人在家！　中国人完全不能正确说出英国人的名字。因此，即使是知名人士外出拜访，通常也要提前出示名片，而且在炎热夏天午睡时间是允许小男佣和客人说"不能见"。夫人对先生说："又是那个愚蠢的史密斯先生。"昏昏欲睡的先生就说："别让那个势利小人进来。"因此，小男佣就对志满意得的史密斯先生说："不能见。主人说你是势利小人，夫人则说你太过愚蠢了。"

——诺利斯，1885年，第45页

佣人罢工（20世纪20年代）"你不觉得没有佣人很好笑吗？我是说自己拿饮料。我到今天早上为止都很少进厨房呢……"

丹弗斯太太叹息一声说："还有轿夫呢，那么大热天走路上来，还真是可怕！"

——麦肯兹·格瑞芙，1959年，第97页

Western Food in Amoy

Ruth's Amoy Cook Tuesday, June 3rd, 1862   Rained all day. The "Formosa" came in and took our mail...Put on a dirty dress and apron and went to the cook house (or rather, the room over it) to show Sooah how to make an American peach pie. Succeeded very well. Sooah imitates better than anybody ever I saw; indeed all the Chinese do. He makes the best sponge cake I ever saw. Pa thinks so too, and I just showed him once. I think him a perfect jewel, and he is a splendid cook and waiter...

The Boot Family (in Amoy from 1903-1940)

Monday, June 9th,   1862 Sooah is sick, and I am on the border of despair. If Sooah stays sick, I'll have to go right back to America; for I cannot do a thing without him...

Ruth Bradford's Amoy Journal

Frog Chicken (1870s) One day we were invited to dine at Tait & Co.'s. It is needless to add that we had a fine dinner, for the foreign merchants in all of China lived like princes, and there is no country where the variety of foods is greater or better than in China. One course Mr. Tait pronounced chicken pie. My wife and cousin thought it excellent, but after dinner was over we found it was made of frog's legs. Neither of us had ever tasted them before, but afterwards we had them often on board ship.

Captain Low, 1906

Western Feast in Amoy (1850s)   Monday, Oct. 8th. You may like to know if foreigners get enough to eat in this part of the world, and so I will tell you what we had on the dinner-table this evening. We had first soup, fish baked, roast goose, boiled mutton, stewed beef, and several kinds of vegetables; then we had puddings, marmalade, cheese and beer, plantains, five kinds of nuts, persimmons, guavas, pumaloes, four kinds of preserves, etc., and the various wines, and lastly we had coffee. It was seven in the evening when we sat down to dinner. Mr. L and I drank to the Queen, and then to the President of the United States, etc. ... When I left, which was half past twelve, the moon shone brightly overhead, lighting up the whole interior of the court. Attracted by its silvery appearance, the cool air, and the quiet and deathlike stillness, I took a seat on the stone steps, and enjoyed the tranquility of the place alone. Completely shut out from the street.—for the doors at the bottom of the court were closed—the buildings seemed like a kind of palace. I am told that it was formerly the residence of the Chinese governor of this province, and everything is laid out, handsomely arranged, befitting his station.

Ball, 1856

第十八章 外国人在厦门的生活 Foreign Life in Amoy

厦门西餐

露丝不可或缺的厦门厨师

1862年6月3日，星期二　一整天阴雨连绵。"福尔摩莎号"进港，带走了我们的邮件……穿上一件脏衣服和围裙，就去了厨房（或者说是厨房上面的房间）教苏雅如何做美国桃子馅饼。非常成功。苏雅比其他我碰到的任何人都模仿得好；确实所有的中国人都这样。他做的发糕是我见过的最好的。爸爸也这么认为。我只教过他一次。我觉得他是个完美的珠宝，是个出色的厨师和侍者……

1862年6月9日，星期一　苏雅生病了，我则处在绝望的边缘。如果苏雅继续生病，我只好直接回美国了，因为没有他我什么事都做不了……
——露丝·布莱德福特的《厦门日记》

田鸡

有一天，我们应邀请去泰特公司吃饭。不用说我们吃得很好，因为外国商人在中国过着像王子一样的生活，而且全世界没有一个国家可以像中国那样拥有那么丰富多彩的食物。有一道菜，泰特先生说是鸡肉馅饼。我夫人和堂兄都觉得很好吃。饭后，我们才发现这道菜是用田鸡腿做的。我们以前都没有尝过，但是在那之后我们就经常吃到了。
——娄船长，1906年，第152页

厦门的西餐盛宴

（19世纪50年代）10月8日，星期一　你也许想知道外国人在这里是否有足够吃的东西，那就让我现在告诉你今晚我们的餐桌上有什么吧。我们吃了第一道汤、烤鱼、烤鹅、白切羊肉、炖牛肉、好几种蔬菜；然后我们吃了布丁、果酱、奶酪、啤酒、大香蕉、五种坚果、柿子、番石榴、柚子、四种干果等等，还有各种红酒。最后，我们还喝了咖啡。我们开始吃饭的时候是傍晚7点。L先生和我还提议先为英国女王，然后为美国总统干杯……我离开的时候已经12点半了。头上是明亮的月亮，照亮了整个庭院。它银色的外观，凉爽的海风和安静死寂的情景吸引了我。我坐在石头台阶上，享受着这个地方的平静。庭院的门是关着的，完全与外面的街道隔绝。这房子就像是皇宫一样。据说这原来是这个省总督的住宅。一切都安排得井井有条，和他的职务非常相配。
——波尔，1856年

Tea Party in Tong'an, 1920s

老外看老鼓浪屿 Old Gulangyu in Foreigners' Eyes

French Consul's Chinese Feast (1920s) On my left the French Consul, Monsieur Pigoux, was frankly devoting himself to food and, having pronounced the mullet worthily cooked, expatiated on the delicacy of Chinese cookery.

"I repeat, Madame, that in all France you cannot find such dishes as the Chinese prepare-even in the houses that pay the greatest attention to the cuisine. Their boned stuffed duck; par exemple, it is absolutely hors concours."His fmger and thumb picked the duck's image from the air, held it to his lips, released it with a flourish. I could almost see it flapping.

"Our cook gives us a Chinese dinner once a week, and we find it delicious."

"Ugh, how could you! Do you mean to say you like sharks' fins and birds' nests, and …"

"Yes, sea slugs." This was just to shock Mrs. Danvers, because I found beche-de-mer well-flavoured but tough as old leather. I did not really like birds' nests[5] either…

Mackenzie-Grieves, 1959

Why Forks, Knives and Spoons? (1940s) "Why so many spoons, knives and forks?" asked Mr. Tan.

"For soup, fish, meat and dessert," I replied.

"But we have several soups, meat and fish courses," he answered incredulously,"and all we need is a pair of chopsticks and a small porcelain spoon. It seems such a waste of money."

"Why do Red-Haireds spend so much money on table cloths also?" asked Mr. Lau.

"Our dining room." Jean Nienhuis, 1923

"Eating off a well-laid table helps our appetite and sense of well-being," I replied.

"But would your appetite be better served," he asked, "by spending more money on food itself and less on how you eat it?"

"And how can you really enjoy your food," added Mr.Tan, "if you always have to think about not dirtying your expensive table cloth and napkins?"

"But surely the Chinese use napkins?" I asked. "I have often seen them at dinner parties."

"Paper ones," Mr. Lau quickly added, "and only to wipe our chopsticks or clean our bowl before we start our meal."

"Would it not be more sensible if you used a napkin to clean what you ate with, rather than your face after you have eaten…?"

"It is difficult for me to argue," I hurriedly replied, "as I know so little Hokkien and you cannot speak English," thankful that I could fall back on this face-saving though unconvincing line of retreat.

Neill, 1956

Otte, Frances Phelps, Letter from Amoy, August, 1901

5 See "Amoy Food" chapter

第十八章 外国人在厦门的生活 *Foreign Life in Amoy*

法国领事的中餐宴会(20世纪20年代) 坐在我左边的法国领事皮诺斯先生正忙着吃东西。他说鲻鱼做得真好吃,接着开始细述中国菜中的美食。

"我再和你说一遍,女士,在法国,你永远都吃不到像中国人做的美食,即使是在非常注重饮食的家庭里。比如他们带骨的填满东西的鸭,绝对是无与伦比的。"他用手指和手心比划了一下鸭子的形状,放到嘴边,然后极为夸张地把它给放飞了。我好像都可以看到鸭子的翅膀在拍动。

"我们的厨子每周做一次中餐,我们发现太好吃了。"

"呸,你们怎么可以这样!你是说你们喜欢鱼翅和燕窝,和……"

"是啊,还有海蛞蝓。"这样说就是为了吓到丹弗斯太太,因为我发现海参虽然煮得味道很好,但是硬得像老猪皮。我也不怎么喜欢燕窝……

——麦肯兹·格瑞芙,1959年,第50、51页

为什么要用叉子、刀和汤匙?(20世纪40年代) "为什么那么多刀叉和汤匙?"陈先生问。

"用来喝汤,吃鱼,吃肉和吃甜点,"我回答道。

"但是我们有好几份汤、肉和鱼呢,"他怀疑地答道,"我们要的只是一双筷子和一个小汤匙。这样好像太浪费钱了。"

"为什么红毛老外花那么多钱做桌布呢?"刘先生问。

"摆放整齐的桌子边吃饭可以有助于开胃,而且让我们感觉到生活富有啊。"我回答道。

"但是如果多花钱在食物本身,而不是餐具,不是更能让你的胃口好吗?"他问到。

"如果你总是想着不要弄脏那么昂贵的桌布和餐巾,你怎么可以真正享受食物啊?"陈先生又说道。

Story-telling Time, 1920s   J. Nienhuis

"但是中国人也用餐巾啊,我就在晚宴上看过他们用过。"我说。

"都是纸的,我们只是用来擦筷子或者吃饭前擦碗的。"刘先生很快就答道。

"如果用餐巾擦一下餐具,而不是吃完后用它擦脸不是更有意义吗?"

"我的福建话太差,而你们英语又不好,实在是太难和你们争论了,"我赶紧答道,心中想着这样退出总算不会太丢脸,尽管不能令人信服。

——尼尔,1956年

老外看老鼓浪屿 Old Gulangyu in Foreigners' Eyes

Foods from Home (1850s)　As long back as my memory can carry, boxes came from the homeland, from family and friends... there came a box with daguerreotypes, and tears of joy and brushing them away and talking softly over them—"this was ma" and "this pa"—O! so good and precious to look upon and pore over. And there were books for the children suitable for our tender age, and older ones as we grew older. Perhaps the wonderful Rollo books[Most popular fictional series for juveniles in 19th century America, by Rev. Jacob Abbott.], which we pored over with thrills all the days we lived in Amoy, or "Songs for Little Children at Home". Clothes were sometimes sent, wonderful ones we thought, and when they were for the children, we thought they looked like the ones worn by the girls and boys in the Rollo books,—like American children—the height of our ambition.

　　Dried cherries and preserved currants—so happily received by our parents—were just little hard stones and seeds to us, which we did not like! Methods of sending to the Tropics, with long months of salt sea air surrounding them, had not developed, as in our day, and many things would not bear transportation. Only dried fruits could be counted on, as apples and cherries.

　　A trial was made of sending fresh apples, wrapped thoroughly in paper and in other ways protected. I can recall mother's and father's eagerness over them, as they unwrapped one, with bated breath, to see and taste the first fresh apple since they left "home", right from one of their choicest trees! But it was a solid mass of black decay! Then another one was unwrapped—just as spoiled! I remember mother saying, "Maybe there will be one good one, so we must try every one." But, alas, to no purpose! Then there was a bit of silence, while we children wondered.

　　A quilt was sent, quite early in the years, I think. Each one of many friends had made a block—with name and sentiment in the center—out of print material that mother would recognize as worn by friends in the homeland. The blocks were joined by white strips and on these, the names of all the brothers and father, and friends among her acquaintance, had been written, some with sentiments attached. Even "old Jack" and "Granny" and other colored members of the family asked an "humble corner" written by grandmother's own hand.

Mary Doty's Memos

"Our kitchen." Jean Nienhuis, 1923

第十八章　外国人在厦门的生活 Foreign Life in Amoy

老家寄来的食物（19世纪50年代）　从我记事起，我们就会陆陆续续收到来自家乡亲人和朋友的包裹。有一次，包裹里还有银板相片。看到这些照片，欢喜的泪水不由自主就掉下来了。擦干泪水后，对着照片轻声慢语——"这是妈妈""这是爸爸"——哦！凝视着这些照片的感觉真好，真是珍贵。包裹里还有适合我们这个年龄段阅读的书籍，也还有等我们长大一点阅读的书籍。我们住在厦门的日子里，每天都非常激动看着罗洛系列丛书，或者是"小孩歌集"。有时候，他们也会寄来衣服，我们都觉得非常漂亮。穿在身上，我们就觉得看起来就像罗洛系列丛书里面的小孩一样——就像美国小孩。当时，那就是我们最大的理想了。

樱桃干和无核葡萄干是我们父母非常高兴地收到的礼物。对于我们来说，那只是一些坚硬的小石头和种子，我们一点都不喜欢！在我们那个时候，运送到热带地区的方法还是没有什么进展，沉浸在咸海水

Gulangyu Playmates, 1920s　　J.Nienhuis

空气中好几个月，很多东西都没有办法运送。只有干果还可以，比如苹果和樱桃。

也有人尝试用纸严实地包着，或者其他一些方法寄送新鲜的苹果。我还能记起父母对于这些包裹的期待之情。他们屏住呼吸，打开包裹，看着并闻着自从离开家之后那些到达的第一批新鲜苹果。这些苹果还是直接从他们最喜欢的果树上摘下来的！结果看到的是一团坚硬的黑色腐烂物！接着又打开第二个包裹－和刚才的一样也坏掉了！我记得妈妈还说，"也许总有一个好的，我们还是每个都打开吧。"但是，结果都一样！最后就是一片沉寂，我们小孩则则站在那里发呆。

我记得早些年的时候还寄过来一床被子。每个朋友都用印刷的材料在被子中间做了一个方块，写上名字和他们的祝福，母亲都可以认得出是家乡朋友们用的。这些布块都用长白布连在一起，白布上写着所有兄弟们、父亲、她熟人中的朋友的名字，有些还有祝福词。甚至"老杰克"和"奶奶"以及家庭其他黑人成员都要求奶奶亲手在一小块地方写上他们的名字。

——玛丽·多蒂未出版的回忆录，1850年代

Hogsheads of Butter from Home (1850s) Butter was a great luxury, not to be procured in Amoy, or anywhere in that region, but it was sent to her from the loved home.

Through the great labor of love of her mother, preparing the butter herself, lest all the buttermilk and water should not be absolutely extracted in the process of being made (knowing its being preserved, pure and sweet, depended on this work) it was made possible to send it to her in a well preserved condition.

Mary Louise Talman, 1920s J.N.
Talmans in Amoy from 1916-1931

And then the painstaking care of her father in packing it in small wooden kegs—previously prepared to receive the butter—sealed, and put into a hogshead covered with strong brine and headed up, completed its preparation.

This was continuously done for the beloved daughter during all her days, and after, until we all returned to this country, and by them shared with their friends. The coming of these hogsheads was another great event.

Mary Doty's Memos

Mail Order Supplies (1920s and 30s)   Our supplies which we could not locally buy or buy on Kulangsu or Amoy we ordered from America. Usually we ordered from Montgomery Ward as they did a very big shipping business with the Orient & had very good freight rates & knew how to pack for foreign shipment. We bought our White sewing machine $32.00 and had them ship also a foreign iron stove (for kitchen)

Rose Talman's Memoirs

New clothes just from home, 1920s   J. Nienhuis

家乡寄来的大桶黄油（19 世纪 50 年代）　黄油当时是非常奢侈的，在厦门以及本地区其他任何地方都买不到，只好由亲爱的家人寄来。

出于伟大的母爱，她妈妈亲自做好了黄油，确保在制作过程中酪乳和水完全挤干，因为这项工作决定了黄油是否能够保存，味道是否地道香甜。这样就可以保存完好地寄给她。

接下来就要由她父亲付出巨大心血把黄油分装到小木桶里（以前是用来收黄油的），封装后放入装满卤水的直立大木桶，准备工作就结束了。

在她还在世的时候，为了亲爱的女儿，这项工作从来都没有间断。在我们回到美国后，才和朋友们分享。这些大木桶的到来确实是个大事件。

——玛丽 · 多蒂未出版的回忆录

Casks of Butter to Amoy

(Doty Family, 1850s)

Feb. 24th

Sam has made his first effort in letter writing & begs me to send it, as it w
weigh much I have concluded to do so.

In regard to expenses of shipping the butter, I find that

The casks cost each	$6.00	=	$30.00
The freight for all	11.00		11.00
Insurance	7.25		7.25
Railroad freight each	.75		3.75
Ferry charge	1.37		1.37
			$53.37
			1.87
			$55.24

Besides this the Morris R. Road charged us 3 shillings each for bringing them up in
first place which added to the other expenses will make $55.24.

my my dear Father
this is my
first writting so pleas Excuse all mistakes
I suppose you will like to hear
from me and now I will tell you about
Uncle George He sent me a pare of verry fine
skates and I have learned to how to skate

Feb. 24th

Sam has made his first effort in letter writing & begs me to send it, as it wont weigh much I have concluded to do so.
In regard to expenses of shipping the butter I find that
the casks cost each $6,00 = $30,00
the freight for all 11.00 11.00
Insurance 7 25 7.25
Rail Road freight each .75 3.75
Ferry charge 1 37 1.37
$53.37
1.87
55.24
beside that the Morris R. Road charged us 3 shillings each for bringing them up in the first place which add to the other expenses will make $55.24

邮寄物资（20 世纪二三十年代）　当地无法买到，或者在厦门或鼓浪屿买不到的物资，我们从美国订购。通常，我们通过蒙哥马利 · 沃德公司订购。他们和东方有很大的航运生意往来，运费也公道，而且知道怎么包装运往国外的货物。我们花了 32 美金买了一台怀特牌缝纫机，还让他们寄来了厨房用的进口铁炉子。

——罗斯 · 塔尔曼未出版的回忆录

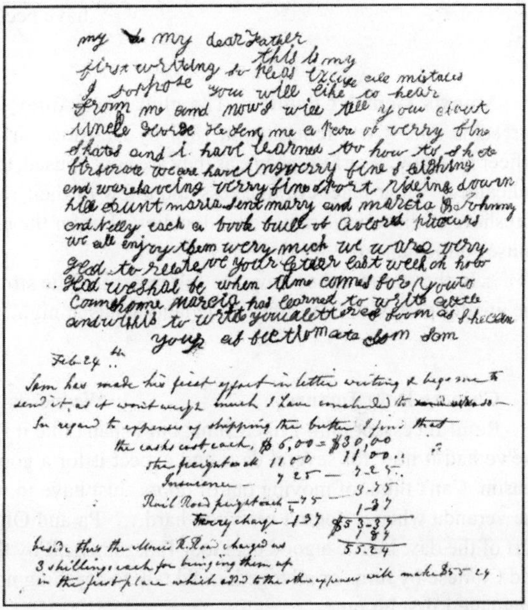

Amoy Weather

After a Typhoon, 1922 — J. Nienhuis

Feeble Foreign Brains in Chinese Weather Without common-sense, a missionary will neglect his own health and become a burden to his colleagues, his friends, and himself, as did a certain young man, who on being urged to wear a sun-hat and carry an umbrella, smiled serenely, and quoted, "The sun shall not smite thee by day." The recorder says that he is now at home with an enfeebled brain, which, one surmises, can never have been very strong.

Soothill, 1907

Amoy's Genial Climate The climate of Amoy is, for its latitude, a mild and agreeable one. It was remarked in 1871 by Dr. (now Sir) Patrick Manson, then medical officer in Amoy:"For Europeans, as they are now housed, the climate cannot be considered unhealthy. "Their places of business and a few of their residences are situated along the foreshore of the town—rather a hot locality—but for the most part they have their private houses on Kulangsu.

…In the summer they have the full benefit of the strong sea-breezes blowing during the greater part of the day, and of the land winds at night…

Bowra 1908

Chinese Rain Torture   Wednesday, June 4th, Amoy, 1862
Rain! Incessant rain! I like China, but I shan't like it if it is going to rain all the time. We've had it now for several days and expect it for a good many more as it is the rainy season. Can't think of moving out of doors. Just have to walk about in the house and on the veranda when it doesn't blow too hard… Pa and Ollie are busy writing the greater part of the day. I write a good deal too. Talk to myself by the half hour in English, French and Chinese by turns or all together. I'd talk to anything no matter what it was and in any language I first hit on.

Ruth Bradford's Journal

An Amoy Typhoon The heavens are shrouded in masses of thickest clouds, that seem to fly in absolute terror before the wind that has suddenly and ominously grown into a wild gale. The sea, too, has risen with a bound, and long rolling waves dash underneath us, and rear us upon their storm-tossed heads. The mercury is steadily falling, and the barometer with its silent, unerring finger marks to us the certainty of the approaching tempest.

The blasts become more fierce, as though each one were shot out of a cannon's mouth, and the rain is beginning to fall, a sure sign that we are within the radius of the typhoon's march.

Macgowan, 1897

第十八章　外国人在厦门的生活 Foreign Life in Amoy

厦门天气

中国天气中脆弱的外国脑袋　要是没有常识,传教士就会忽视自己的健康,成为他同事、朋友以及他本人的负担。就像有个年轻人一样,有人叫他戴上遮阳帽,并且带上雨伞的时候,非常平静地引用说:"白天的太阳伤不着你。"教务杂志报道说,这个年轻人由于脑衰已经回家了。当然,有人推测,他的脑子一直就不够坚强。

——苏西尔,1907年

Summer Sunhats, 1924　J. Ni

厦门暖和的气候　对于它的纬度来说,厦门的气候还是非常温和舒适的。1871年,当时的厦门医务官帕特里克·曼森医生(现在的帕特里克·曼森爵士)曾经说过:"对于欧洲人来说,现在都有地方住了,就不再认为这里的气候对人健康不好了。他们上班的地方以及有些人的住宅都坐落在海滩沿线上。这里还是一个相当热的地方,但是大多数人都在鼓浪屿上有私家住宅。

夏天的时候,他们白天大部分时间都在享受来自海洋的微风,晚上则是来自内陆的凉风……

——博拉,1908年

中国雨天的折磨　1862年6月4日,星期三,厦门

下雨!没完没了的雨!我喜欢中国,但是如果一直下雨,我就没办法喜欢它了。雨已经下了好几天了。由于是雨季,有可能还要继续下很多天,根本就没办法到室外去。只能在家里来回走动,或者在风不大的时候到走廊走走。爸爸和奥力一天大部分时间都忙着写东西。我也写了很多。每半小时我就轮流或者同时用英语、法语或者汉语自言自语。我不管碰上什么都要和自己说说,想到什么语言就用什么语言。

——露丝·布莱德福特的日记

一场厦门台风　天空中乌云密布。乌云以非常恐怖的速度在天上飘,然后再突然变成一阵狂风。潮水涨起来了,巨浪在我们脚下翻滚、拍岸,风暴卷起的浪尖追赶着我们。水温慢慢下降,气压无声、准确地告诉我们暴风雨即将来临。

风吹得更加猛烈了,好像加农炮口射出来一样。雨也开始下了,这就表明我们处于台风半径中。

——麦嘉湖,1897年,第139页

老外看老鼓浪屿 *Old Gulangyu in Foreigners' Eyes*

Typhoon Batters Gulangyu (1920s) The typhoon signal had been out all day. A sinister black ball on the signal-station high point. We always kept an eye on the mast. From June to September its appearance dominated the island.

The Great Wind it heralded often whirled on up the Formosa Strait leaving Amoy-with wrack and refuse-strewn beaches merely lashed by its fringes. But no one could tell when it might veer, catch up the sea and the islands, tear, twist, spew out the fragments and rage on. It did not do to be caught unprepared.

At sunset the ball had still been there, but not a breath of wind lifted the heavy heat as we dressed for our dinner-party. Then the lights went out. In Kulangsu the electricity frequently failed, sometimes because of technical faults, sometimes, it was alleged, because Harris, the lessee of the plant, a touchy man, wanted to revenge himself upon island society for an imagined slight or injury. From the Tans' terrace the click-clack of the mahjong tiles gave way to women's shrill voices and much loud laughter. In the treacly darkness mosquitoes, no longer kept bearably at bay by the lights, swarmed whining round our heads.

Mackenzie-Grieves, 1959

Amoy Rain Torture (1940s) …Sometimes the very weather seems determined to drive away the foreign intruder. No evil spirit is needed to set on edge the missioner who lives alone, in almost primitive conditions, during the rainy season. It may begin with the friendly gentleness of a freshening shower; or it may, from its first sheeted blast, scorn all pretense of good intention.

"This may not be too bad," you assure yourself. "It won't harm me to be shut in for a few days. I have correspondence to answer, and hours of study to occupy me. Maybe I'll at last get that promised article written."

To the monotonous, unending beat of the rain the typewrite clicks off belated replies to Hunan addresses, to Hankow, Shanghai, Philadelphia, New York. The pile of unanswered mail drops lower and lower—vanishes. The article is attacked, labored over, and finished. I study, eat, and sleep between Mass, Divine Office, and devotions. Day follows night, though there is little light to distinguish one from the other.

Out comes my Chinese grammar, dictionary, and doctrine books. Mass and meals, speech and sleep are measured by the hours of rain. Intricate Chinese characters are stared at until they blur. They run together mockingly. They disintegrate, dissolve, and flow down the page like drops of water. Concentration on a book is only a partial refuge, a temporary self-deception. Day crawls laggingly after day. And always—always the ears report, the bones complain, the mind repeats: "It is still raining! It has not stopped! This may go on and on. No mail, no word from the missions; and still it rains!…"

MacGuire 1945

Freezing in Amoy! (1940s)…the chilly air of January in a completely unheated home, sent some of us to bed with severe colds. That was colder to me than the zero degree weather of Michigan because of the lack of provision for heating in the relatively low temperature of the winter in the semi-tropics. It made me determined to find a pot-bellied stove somewhere so that I could give my family at least one room to get warm in.

Joe Esther, 1977

第十八章　外国人在厦门的生活 Foreign Life in Amoy

台风袭击鼓浪屿（20世纪20年代）　台风信号已经发布一天了。那是一个高高挂在信号台上不吉利的黑球。我们总是要注意一下那里的旗杆。每年六月到九月份，它的出现都会引起全岛人的注意。

预报的大风通常在台湾海峡上空旋转而成，给厦门留下不少失事船只。受到台风边缘的袭击，海滩上到处都散落着垃圾。但是没有人能知道它什么时候会转向、冲向海洋和岛屿，撕裂、扭曲、喷出碎片，并继续前行。台风是不可能让人有所准备的。

傍晚的时候，黑球还挂在那里，我们准备换装参加晚宴的时候，酷热的空气中一丝风都没有。然后灯就灭了。鼓浪屿上，电力供应经常中断，有时候是因为技术问题，有时候据说是因为电厂的承租人哈里斯脾气暴躁，会由于假象的轻视或受伤向岛上社会报复。从陈宅的阳台传来的不再是麻将牌的声音，而是女人们激动的声音以及大笑声。漆黑夜晚里，蚊子也不再继续被灯光吸引到海湾，而是集中到我们头顶上飞来飞去。

——麦肯兹·格瑞芙，1959年，第49、50页

厦门雨天的折磨（20世纪40年代）　有时候厦门的天气好像就是要把外国侵入者赶出去一样。在雨季，那些单独住在几乎是原始状况下的传教士，不用什么恶鬼就可以让他们感到非常不舒服。开始的时候可能是一阵比较友好而且温柔、令人提神的阵雨，或者有可能第一阵风就把虚情假意都刮跑了。

"这不会太糟的，"你自言自语地说。"关在这里几天不会伤害我什么的。我有很多信件要回复，而且还要花时间学习。也许我最后可以写出已经答应给别人的文章。"

伴着没完没了的单调雨声，打字机打出了寄给湖南、汉口、上海、菲律宾和纽约的已经被推迟的回复。没有回复的信件变得越来越少了，直到回信最后全部写完。文章也开始写了，修改过了，终于写完了。我在学习、吃饭以及休息之间交叉进行弥撒、日课和祈祷。日复一日，虽然日夜之间光线都很差，很难分辨。

我的中文语法、字典和教义经书都搬出来了。弥撒和吃饭，练习和休息都用下雨的时间来衡量。每天都瞪着复杂的汉字直到视线模糊为止。可笑的是，它们都形影相随。它们就像雨滴一样在每页纸上分开，溶解并流过。全神贯注读书只是逃避的一种方法，是暂时的自我欺骗。慢慢地，一天一天过去了，耳朵所报告的，骨头所抱怨的，和大脑所重复的总是："雨还在下！怎么都不停啊！难道要一直不停吗？没有信件，也没有传教士的消息，老天爷却总是在下雨！……"

——麦克圭尔，1945年，第74、75页

寒冷的厦门！（20世纪40年代）　……在完全没有暖气的家里，一月份寒冷的空气使我们有些人染上了重感冒而卧床。因为在亚热带地区，冬季相对较低的气温里是不用取暖设备的。这对我来说，比在密执安零度的天气还更寒冷。我下决心要找到一个大肚火炉，以便让家人至少可以在一间温暖的房间取暖。

——乔·艾丝特，1977年，第40页

老外看老鼓浪屿 *Old Gulangyu in Foreigners' Eyes*

Chapter 19 R.I.P. in Amoy

Gulangyu Foreign Cemeteries Some European graves on the eastern beach proved the former existence of a foreign trade at Amoy. Two gravestones, with English inscriptions, bore the respective dates of 1698 and 1700. There was also a grave-stone erected to the memory of a Spaniard. In another part were buried the remains of a former Roman Catholic bishop. ...

Near the northern village, screened from view by a little assemblage of trees, was situated the burial-ground of the missionaries. The unhealthiness of the climate had been severely felt... During the last thirteen mouths, out of twenty-five members of the missionary families, eighteen had been removed by various providential events. ... In this little retired spot of ground were interred the bodies of three female missionaries, Mrs. Boone, Mrs. Doty, and Mrs. Pohlman, with the two children of the last. They left America in the vigor of youth, to consecrate their lives to the missionary work; but were cut down, one after another, by premature death, leaving their earthly partners to sorrow not as those who have no hope.

Smith, 1857

Nurse Helen Joldersma
Arrived in Amoy 1926
Died in Amoy 1928

Buried Regiment The English burial ground is in this neighborhood ; it is a small place, and walled in. The mortality amongst the troops was very great during the occupancy of this place, and this area is said to contain over a regiment of soldiers. The American cemetery is more prepossessing in appearance. It is situated in a picturesque valley, full of beautiful trees, and did not contain many graves. From it there is a fine view of the bay and islands, and the city of Amoy.

Macaulay, 1852

Helen's Grave, Gulangyu

Graves of British Consuls Death has played sad havoc in this part of China. Out of the small community of Amoy, since 1843, we find tombs to three different British consuls. There is also one to the first chaplain. Strange that the first chaplains brought out by the foreign residents at Canton, Shanghai, and Amoy, should all have died almost immediately after their arrival.

Scarth, 1860

第十九章 厦门——"白人的墓地"

鼓浪屿外国人公墓 （厦门港）东岸有一些欧洲人的坟墓。这证明了他们曾在厦门从事贸易活动。两个墓碑用英文分别刻着1689年和1700年。另外还有一个墓碑是用来纪念西班牙人的。一个罗马天主教堂主教的尸体则埋葬在另外一个地方……

在北部村庄附近，透过一小丛树林可以看到一块传教士的墓地。这里的气候条件对人体健康很不利，导致了很多死亡。在过去的13个月里，传教士家庭25位成员中有18位遵天意辞世而去。在这一小块休眠之地还埋葬着三位女传教士的尸体：布恩夫人、多蒂夫人和波尔曼夫人，还有波尔曼夫人的两个孩子。她们离开美国的时候还是朝气蓬勃的年轻女子，准备把自己的生命都奉献给传教事业，但是一个接一个过早去世，把悲伤留给了她们在世间的父母。幸好他们都还满怀希望。

——史密斯，1857年，第338页

被埋葬的军团 英国人的墓地就在附近，地方很小，但建有围墙。占领这个地方的部队死亡率很高。据说这里安葬着一个军团的士兵。美国公墓看起来更加引人注意。它坐落在风景迷人的山谷里面，到处都是漂亮的树木，而且墓地不多。这里可以看到海湾、岛屿和厦门市区的美好风光。

——麦考利，1852年，第145页

英国领事的墓地 在中国的这个地区，死亡总是带来悲伤和破坏。自从1843年以来，在厦门这个小地方，我们就发现了三个英国领事的墓地。还有一个是第一任牧师的。非常奇怪的是，在广州、上海和厦门，外国居民选定的第一任牧师都在到达后不久就去世了。

——史咖斯，1860年，第35页

R. L. Hastings, Sr.
Photo courtesy of M. Logie
(great great granddaughter)

Darkened Sun (1940)   The Autumn was a beautiful time in Chang Chow [Zhangzhou] and we were looking for the baby's coming in early January. We went down to be with Clarence and Ruth Holleman for Christmas, 1939. Margaret[1] went into Hope and Wilhelmina Hospital with some bleeding, but things looked optimistic and we kept cheerful. On January four it was decided to do a Cesarean section for placenta previa. Margaret died on the operating table. The whole Chinese and foreign community was shocked, as were the friends in the United States. I could not believe the sun would ever shine again.

The funeral was held in Union Church with the Rev. Edwin Koeppe taking the service. Margaret was laid to rest in the Three Missions Cemetery [Gulangyu] beside her father's grave. Margaret died at age 34, her father Dr. John Otte at fifty.

Walter deVelder Memoirs

Sad Wedding for China-Bound Doty Couple   So, in course of time, they [the Doty's] were married in the church...A solemn, sad ceremony, listened to by friends and kindred from far and near, was performed. For the going into this Service [China missionary] was looked upon as about equivalent to death, certainly to all kinds of distresses; and to witness the ceremony that was to bind her to this life, was enough to fill everyone with sadness, that a beautiful young woman of their community was about to enter upon, and separate herself from them all in doing it.

Mary Doty's Memoirs

---

1   Margaret was the daughter of Dr. John Otte, founder of Hope Hospital, who died on Gulangyu in 1910 of the plague, contracted from a Muslim patient.

Margaret Develder, died of childbirth, age 34, 1940   Ed Koeppe
"I could not believe the sun would ever shine again." Walter Develder

第十九章 厦门——"白人的墓地" R.I.P. in Amoy

昏黑的太阳(1939年) 漳州的秋季是个很舒服的季节。我们期盼着小孩在一月初的时候降临。我们下来和克拉伦斯及露丝·夏礼文共度1939年的圣诞节。玛格丽特因为出血住进了救世——威廉敏娜医院。病情好像很乐观,我们也很开心。一月四日,因为胎盘前置,医院决定对玛格丽特进行剖腹产手术。玛格丽特死在手术台上。整个中国人和外国人社区都被震惊了,美国的朋友也是如此。我都不相信太阳还会再一次升起。

葬礼在协和礼拜堂举行,由艾德文·科普牧师主持。玛格丽特长眠在鼓浪屿的外国人公墓,就在她父亲的墓边。玛格丽特34岁去世,她父亲郁约翰医生50岁去世。

——沃尔特·德·维尔德未出版的回忆录

献身中国的多蒂夫妇悲伤的婚礼 最后,他们〔多蒂夫妇〕结婚了。婚礼在教堂里举行,既庄严又悲伤。朋友和亲戚,不论远近都来参加了。在中国参加传教事业就意味着随时都要面对死亡的威胁,还要面对千难万苦。参加婚礼就是见证了她要开始这样的生活,这就足够让每个人心存悲伤。社区里一个年轻漂亮的女士就要开始传教生涯。为了传教,也要和所有人都分开了。

——玛丽·多蒂未出版的回忆录

Photo Courtesy of Ms. M. Logie
Yuna, wife of Mr. Hastings

Cynthia Borgman's Grave, 1923 J.N.

Death of Mother Doty One of the events quite naturally impressing me very vividly was my sixth birthday, September, 1857, and mother died the next February, '58—so it was the last in which she partook.

…One morning in February, 1858, there seemed to be a tense atmosphere in our home, and people moving about. Mrs. Talmage was there, and mother in bed, and soon we—Charley, Sam and I with baby "Mousie", two years old—were told there was a new baby sister in bed with mother, and we were brought in to see the little head nestled on her breast, a very great wonder and delight to us children.

…then one morning, when we were quite noisy, father appeared and the sadness on his face impressed itself on me… Then later, my dear Mr. Sandeman lifted me up in his arms and carried me to the head of the bed on which mother lay… The agony on my father's face, I seem to remember plainly.

Then at once, a way to nourish the little baby had to be found. Old boa put warm milk in a blue and white teacup, with a piece of cotton soaked in it, one end of which was held by her finger to the mouth of the baby to suck. It seemed to succeed, and so the little wailing baby was fed until it died, a few months later.

Mother was beloved by the whole circle of foreigners—missionaries, merchants, and officers of American and British vessels—and all Chinese men and women with whom she came in contact. There was a large funeral. Some points I can recall. A long line of Chinese women came, in their mourning garb of white, filing in, to look on her face, with wailing and mourning.

There must have been a short service at our house, then we older children were led by someone… down on the wharf to a boat. There was a long procession of these loaned by ships in the harbor and manned by sailors. Each boat with an American flag at half mast, trailing in the water from the stern, followed the first boat which carried the coffin (no caskets in those days), wrapped in our flag, over to Kolongsu Island, where the Missionary Cemetery is located.

As we came to the Landing, the sailors on all of the boats raised their oars upright, while the American sailors in the first boat lifted the coffin to their shoulders, still wrapped in our flag, and walked, so, to the Cemetery, all following closely behind. And mother was laid in her grave by loving hands, and the familiar "I am the Resurrection and the Life", repeated over her body by Mr. Talmage, very probably, as father's closest associate. We stayed in Amoy until October, 1859.

Mary Doty's Memoirs

Dr. Vandeweg and Family, 1921
Arrived Amoy 1919, died in Amoy, 1922

第十九章 厦门——"白人的墓地" R.I.P. in Amoy

多蒂妈妈去世 其中一个让我记忆犹新的事情发生在1857年9月,我的六岁生日。妈妈在1858年2月去世了,那是她最后一次参加我的生日。

1858年2月的一个早上,我们家似乎笼罩在紧张的气氛中,人们进进出出。打马字夫人也来了。妈妈躺在床上。很快,有人告诉我们——查理,山姆,我还有两岁大的妹妹"茂茜",家里添了一个小妹妹。他们带我们进去看那个小东西,正依偎在妈妈胸前。对我们小孩来说,那真是让我们惊讶和高兴的事。

……后有一天早晨,我们都在打闹的时候,爸爸出现了。他脸上悲伤的表情深深地印在我脑海里……后来,我亲爱的桑德曼先生把我抱了起来,放到了妈妈的床头……爸爸脸上痛苦的表情,我至今都似乎还历历在目。

Dr. Vanderweg Dies, Nov. 1922   J.N.

突然之间,要找到一个办法来喂养新生婴儿。老包把温奶放进青花瓷茶杯里,用一块布浸在里面,她的手指拿着另一头给婴儿吮吸。看起来好像是成功了,就一直这样喂养这个幼小哭闹的婴儿,直到几个月后她死去为止。

妈妈深受她圈里人的喜爱,包括外国传教士、商人、美国和英国船上的官员,也包括和她有联系的中国人。我还记得起其中的一些情景。一长队的中国女人穿着白色的孝服来,哭喊着向她告别。

一个简单的仪式在我们家举行。然后,我们大一点的孩子就被带到了码头上了船。码头上排着一长列由码头租来的船只,上面站满了水手。每艘船上的美国旗都下了半旗,船尾接船头,跟着第一艘载着盖有美国国旗的中国式棺材(那时还没有美国式的棺材)的船来到了鼓浪屿,那里有传教士的公墓。

我们就要下船的时候,所有船上的水手直直地举起他们手中的船桨,与此同时,第一艘船上的美国水手把还盖着美国国旗的棺材抬到了肩上,一个紧跟一个,来到了传教士公墓。妈妈被亲人放进了墓地,打马字先生作为爸爸最亲近的同事对着妈妈的尸体重复着那句熟悉的话:"复活在我,生命也在我。"我们一直在厦门呆到1859年10月才离开。

——玛丽·多蒂未出版的回忆录

老外看老鼓浪屿 *Old Gulangyu in Foreigners' Eyes*

Dr. John Otte—Founder of Hope Hospital [救世医院] [2]

Hope & Wilhelmina Hospital
Amoy, China April 6, 1910

My dear Little Margaret:

It is Saturday afternoon, and though it is only two o'clock Papa is all through with his work for the week. It is not often that Papa is through so early, but this week there has been only a little to worry about and so I could work later than usual. So now I am just going to sit down and write to my little girl, for I know that by the time she gets this letter it will be her fifth birthday. …

…I can hardly wait to see you once more. You will be such a big girl when I get home that I will hardly know you. But we will soon get acquainted, and then we will go down town and have a real nice time. I hope that next year I will be able to go home, but I am not absolutely sure yet…

Later:

A very sick woman was brought into the hospital and I had to work with her for over two hours so after all I did not have my rest.

Affectionately yours,

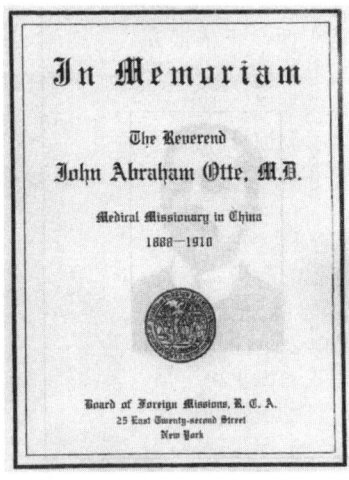

Father.

Nine days later…April 15, 1910
Dear Folks,

One of the most terrible things that has ever happened to this mission, happened yesterday. Dr. Otte died in our house yesterday of pneumonic plague. Oh, it is dreadful. It was all so sudden. He had been sick only 3 ½ days…

Anna

"The mourning of all of Amoy is far greater than any I have ever witnessed."
Dr. Warnshuis

"He [Otte] loved the Chinese, and he demonstrated it in his life as well as in his death…"

Rev. Philip Wilson Pitcher, *Christian Intelligencer, June 22, 1910*

---

2 The above letter was written two days before Dr. Otte caught the plague that killed him; it was mailed after he died, and reached Margaret on May 19th, her 5th birthday. Xiamen erected a statue to Otte's honor in 2008, in front of Jimei's #2 hospital.

第十九章 厦门——"白人的墓地" R.I.P. in Amoy

郁约翰——救世医院的创办人[3]

Dr. John Otte's Grave, 1910

救世——威廉敏娜医院
中国，厦门，1910年4月6日

我亲爱的小玛格丽特：

现在是周六下午，虽然才两点钟，爸爸已经做完了本周所有的工作。通常情况下，爸爸是很难得这么早就做完工作的。但是，本周只有一些让人担心的事情，所以我就可以比平常迟一点开始工作。现在我就可以坐下来给我的小姑娘写信，因为我知道，她收到这封信的时候就是她5岁的生日了……

我都等不及要去看你了。等我回到家时，你都成大姑娘了，我都会认不出你来。但是，我们很快就会熟悉起来，然后我们就可以进城好好享受一下生活。我希望明年我可以回家，但是我还无法确定……

后记：
一个病危的女病人送到了医院，我得工作至少两个小时。所以，最终我还是没能有机会休息一下。

爱你的，爸爸

九天后……1910年4月15日
亲爱的朋友们：
最可怕的事情之一昨天在我们传教士团队里发生了。郁约翰医生因感染肺鼠疫离开了我们。这太可怕了。那么突然。他生病才3天半呢……
——安娜

"厦门所有人的悲痛比我以前见证过的任何一次都要大。"
——沃恩舒伊斯医生

"他〔郁约翰医生〕热爱中国人，无论生前还是死后，他都表现出来了。"
——毕腓力牧师，《基督教报》，1910年6月22日

---

3 上面这封信是在奥特医生传染上致命的瘟疫之前两天写的。去世后才寄出，玛格丽特收到的时候是5月19日，她的5岁生日。为了纪念郁约翰医生，2008年，厦门在集美第二医院门口竖起了他的雕像。

老外看老鼓浪屿 *Old Gulangyu in Foreigners' Eyes*

Chapter 20 Stories of Foreigners in Amoy

Mr. C.E. Mitchell, Superintendent of Gulangyu Police   Mr. C. Berkeley Mitchell, Capt.-Superintendent of the Kulangsu Police and Secretary to the Kulangsu Municipal Council, has had an active and distinguished career. Born on February 12, 1864, he was educated at St. Olave's Grammar School, Southwark, London, S.E. He served with the Second Battalion Royal West Kent Regiment in Egypt, South Africa, Ceylon, and Hongkong, and had a full share of fighting. He was mentioned in Lord Kitchener's despatches, and among his decorations are the Queen's South Africa medal with three clasps, and the King's South Africa medal with two clasps. After twenty-two years' service he retired from the Army, having then also won the long service and good conduct medals.

Bowra, 1908

Mr. W.H. Wallace, Chairman of Municipal Council, 1908 Born in London in 1861, he was educated at Dedham Grammar School, Essex, and at the early age of seventeen accompanied an orchid-hunting expedition to South America. On his return he devoted some time to the study of botany, and one of his chief hobbies now is the cultivation of flowers. In 1882, Mr. Wallace entered the service of the Hongkong and Shanghai Bank in London, and two years later was sent to the Hongkong office. In 1890 he resigned his appointment, and for two years engaged in business in the Colony as a stock and share broker. Rejoining the bank's service in 1902, he came to Amoy, at which port and Koochow he has been since that time. Mr. Wallace is an enthusiastic sportsman, and in his younger days was a well-known figure on the football and hockey fields. He won the tennis championship of Hongkong in 1901, and even now devotes as much of his spare time to that game as to his flowers. The garden adjoining his private residence is one of the sights of Amoy, and is recognised as being one of the finest in China.

Peder and John Vandeweg, 1924

Bowra, 1908

A New Doctor in Amoy[1] (1919)   The new doctor Dr. & Mrs. Matthew VandeWeg--originally from Holland. Both or Mrs. V had studied in the U.S.; she is a nurse. Also they had served in Africa. ... He was an excellent linguist. He spoke Dutch, German, English, French, some African dialects, had studied Latin & Hebrew. He also had had a Theological education, was an M.D. & D.D. He surprised us by giving a talk in Chinese within 4 months. He made laughable mistakes but (unclear) audacity to try more than most.

---

1   Dr. Vandeweg died in Amoy in 1922, after only 3 years (see previous chapter).

第二十章　老外在厦门的故事

C.E. 米切尔先生，鼓浪屿警司　C. 伯克利·米切尔先生是鼓浪屿警察的警司队长，也是鼓浪屿市政委员会的秘书。他工作积极且成效卓著。米切尔先生生于1864年2月12日，在伦敦东南部的南华克圣奥拉夫文法学校上学，跟随皇家西肯特兵团第二营先后在埃及、南非、锡兰、香港服役。期间，参加了各种战斗。基钦纳勋爵曾在战报中提起到过他。他的军装上有三个钩扣的女王南非勋章和两个钩扣的国王南非勋章。服役22年后，他从军队退役，赢得了长期服役表现良好的勋章。

——博拉，1908年

W.H. 华莱士先生，市政委员会主席，1908年　华莱士先生1861年生于伦敦，在艾塞克斯的戴达姆文法学校接受教育。17岁时跟随一个兰花探险队到过南美洲。回到英国后，他开始学习生物学。现在，种植花草成为他主要的业余爱好。1882年，华莱士先生开始在伦敦汇丰银行上班，两年后被派驻香港。1890年，他辞去银行的工作，在香港当了两年的股票经纪人。1902年，重新加入汇丰银行，并先后到过厦门和福州。华莱士先生是一个狂热的体育迷，年轻的时候在足球场和曲棍球场上是很有名气的。1901年，他赢得香港网球锦标赛冠军。直到现在，他花在打网球上的时间与种植花草花费的时间一样多。他私人住宅边上的花园是厦门的一景，被公认为中国最好的花园之一。

——博拉，1908年

新到厦门的医生（1919年）　新来的医生马修·范得维格博士和他的太太都是荷兰人，在美国接受教育。太太是一名护士。他们都在非洲服务过。范得维格博士是个杰出的语言学家，会说荷兰语、德语、英语、法语和一些非洲语言，也学过拉丁语和希伯来语。他接受过神学教育，获得医学硕士和博士学位。到中国4个月，他就会讲中文，让我们大吃一惊。当然，他也会犯一些可笑的错误，但是他的努力给我们印象最深。

——罗斯·塔尔曼未出版的回忆录

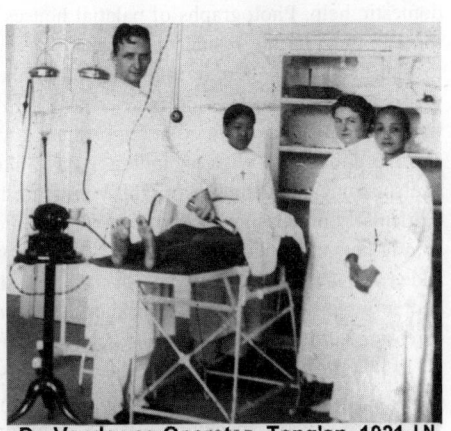

Dr. Vandeweg Operates, Tong'an, 1921 J.N.

老外看老鼓浪屿 *Old Gulangyu in Foreigners' Eyes*

Natasha and Igor (1920s)   What must it be like to be Natasha, I wondered, uncomfortably. She and Igor were White Russians, who like hundreds of others had managed to reach the Chinese coast, and were now waiting for transit visas to return to any European country that would take and support them. Living hand to mouth, they were the victims now of the West's disdain for the East, for as Europeans they could get none of the menial work which had always been left by the white men to the Chinese, yet many of them were unequipped to earn their bread in an Asiatic city in any other way. ... Natasha and Igor were living in a Chinese lodging house, haunted by the fear that their money would give out before they obtained permission to move on…Yet both she and Igor had a gay inconsequence, a resilience that I envied and admired. Natasha's reputation as a seductress had been built up, like a Tibetan mani, by the countless small stones thrown upon it by passers-by. I secretly hoped that she might find a husband, although the selection of bachelors on the island was neither large nor appealing.

Mackenzie-Grieves, 1959

Madame Veronique, owner of Neill's Pension, Gulangyu (1940s)   It started off many years ago on the banks of the Seine, where groups of foreign students gathered in small intimate cafes to meet fellow French students and friends. Her husband was one of these, a young Chinese from an inland Fukien village whose family had saved and scraped to send him to Paris. Their marriage was not unusual. Many other French girls had married Chinese students, whose infinite charm and subtly novel approach to the problems of love had exercised a strong attraction on them.

The DePaman Home, 1922

He had led her to believe that she was marrying into a rich official's family with a splendid mansion on the coast, and with an amplitude of domestic help. Photographs of palatial houses in Kulangsu were produced, which later turned out to be the residences of heads of foreign firms. It was a tremendous shock to find herself on their return to China as the only European woman in a small old-world village in the interior, married to a man of good but humble origins.   There she was plunged into an unfamiliar atmosphere governed by old-fashioned ideas on etiquette and the duties of a wife, including a slave-like submission to a mother-in-law. Never had she anticipated such firm family pressure for the immediate production of children, particularly unpleasing to a woman who counted a thorough knowledge of birth control among her many accomplishments. "Women who have children are just careless," she added with a puckered brow. "Such suffering, such loss of figure, mon cher! If only more people would consult me,"she sighed. "Of course, the sensible ones do," she added, caressing her fluffy white dog and bending down to kiss him…

…"Some of the foreigners in the old days used to enjoy an opium pie on your bed after dinner," she explained with a look of happy days at its large, lumpy uneven surface.

"Have you any special preferences. Fads or habits?" she enquired hopefully.

"Oh yes! Fresh butter and I'm a little fussy about tea—Ceylong please," I disappointingly replied, remarking with a smile that only in England did I ever ask for China tea.

Neill, 1956

第二十章 老外在厦门的故事 Stories of Foreigners in Amoy

娜塔莎和伊戈尔（20世纪20年代）　　一想起娜塔莎是个什么样的人,我就感觉不太舒服。她和伊戈尔都来自白俄罗斯。跟成百上千个白俄人一样,他们想尽办法来到中国沿海等待过境签证,前往任何可以接受他们的欧洲国家。他们过着紧巴巴的日子,成了西方人对东方人蔑视的牺牲品,因为欧洲人根本无法从事那些白人留给中国人的卑微的工作,但是这些白俄人又没有其他技能可以在亚洲国家谋一份可以养家的工作。娜塔莎和伊戈尔住在一个中国人公寓里,天天担心还没有拿到签证前身上的钱财都用光了……但是她和伊戈尔身上有一种快乐、达观的个性。这让我感到既嫉妒又敬佩。很快,有关娜塔莎是一个风尘女子的传言慢慢传开了,就像每个路过的人扔下的无数小石头垒成的西藏嘛呢堆一样。我心底希望她能够找到一个丈夫,但是岛上可供选择的单身汉数量不多,吸引力不大。

——麦肯兹·格瑞芙,1959年,第59、60页

薇罗尼卡女士,鼓浪屿尼尔养老金的主人（20世纪40年代）　　这个故事发生在好多年前的塞纳河畔。一群群外国留学生聚集在那里的小咖啡馆里,与来自祖国的同学和朋友碰头。她先生——一个来自福建内陆山村的年轻中国人就是其中的一个。家人节衣缩食把他送到巴黎。他们的婚姻非常普通。很多法国姑娘嫁给了中国留学生。这些人魅力无限,对待爱情微妙而新颖,深深地吸引了法国姑娘。

他让她相信嫁给了一个富有官员的家庭,在海边有漂亮的房子,并且有一大批的佣人。他展示了很多鼓浪屿上面宏伟房子的照片,后来才知道那些是外国公司老板们的住宅。来到中国后,她发现自己是福建内陆小山村唯一的欧洲女人,嫁给了一个教育不错但是出身卑微的男人。这对她来说是一个巨大的打击。在那里,她陷入了一个陌生的深渊：既要受制于老套的礼仪,也要承担妻子的责任,包括像奴隶一样对待婆婆。她从来也没有想到家人会如此强烈地要求她快生孩子。她原先还把计划生育知识当作自己取得的诸多成就之一。"生孩子的女人都是太不小心了,"她皱着眉头说,"多么痛苦啊,身材全变形了,亲爱的！"她叹口气又说："要是有更多人咨询我一下就好了,不过明智的人都会来咨询我。"她一边说,一边抚摸着毛茸茸的白狗,并弯下腰来亲了亲它……

Dr. Hofstra and Family in Amoy 1922-1951

"过去,有些外国人非常享受在晚饭后躺在床上吸鸦片的感觉,"她一边解释,宽大、满是皱纹的脸上显露出了过去美好时光的景象。

"你有什么特别的爱好吗？时尚,还是习惯什么？"她满怀希望地问了我一下。

"哦,对了！新鲜的奶酪,我对茶比较挑剔——锡兰茶就好了,"我非常失望,但依然笑着应答,因为我只有在英国的时候才会要中国茶。

——尼尔,1956年,第23、24页

老外看老鼓浪屿 *Old Gulangyu in Foreigners' Eyes*

The Koeppe Family (in Amoy from 1919-1951)

Stricks (Amoy 1911-24) and Hofstras (Amoy 1922-51)

第二十章　老外在厦门的故事 *Stories of Foreigners in Amoy*

Joyce and Bill Angus, 1927
Gulangyu Honeymoon
In Amoy 1925-1952

Joyce Angus, Mar. 5, 1934

Boot Kids (about 1926): Wilbur, Beatrice, Marian, Raymond, Harriet, Ethel
The Boot family was in Amoy from 1903-1940.

he Widow Barr (1920s)   She was the widow of a doctor and had a doctor son-in law in Foochow.

White-haired, small, alert, she fitted into no category. She was in China not to make money, converts, or political capital, but simply because she preferred to live there rather than anywhere else. Her house was tranquil, with a sense of stability, of the fullness of the moment. All the others in the bay were restless with time lived through, endured. Mrs. Barr had been born in Foochow, married and widowed there. She spoke both Hokkien and the Foochow dialect. English, almost ultra-English, she was yet too much part of China objectively to analyse it, but … did not divide human beings by race but by quality. In her company qualities mattered most. She it was who first made me conscious of the important part that the elderly and old play in a community… I thought, looking at Mrs. Barr that hot morning, cool in grey and white above the yellow flower-trumpets, she has both age and beauty; and I kissed my hand to her, full of gratitude.

Mackenzie-Grieves, 1959

Mr. Thomas & Mr. Morley, Standard Oil Company of New York.   A large and important business, under the direction of Mr. L. I. Thomas, the manager, and Mr. Morley, the assistant manager, is carried on at the local branch established by this Company. Their tanks are capable of holding 1,750,000 gallons. The chief trade is done in American kerosene oil, paraffin wax, mineral oils, and naphtha from America.

Bowra, 1908

Mr. F. H. Lucassen, New Amoy Hotel   One of the best little establishments of its kind to be found on the coast of China is the New Amoy Hotel, Kulangsu. The rooms are spacious and comfortably furnished. A visitor can enjoy a game of billiards and rely upon his comfort being attended to in every possible way.

Mr. F. H. Lucassen, the proprietor, was born in Emden, Germany. At the age of twelve he went to sea and served in British and American vessels trading in Chinese waters. He went through his training in the German Navy from 1876 to 1878. and then, returning to China, took his chief officer's certificate in Hongkong. Afterwards he traded up and down the coast until, in 1884, he entered the Imperial Maritime Customs service. He resigned in 1891 in order to join the Shell Transport and Trading Company, with whom he remained for nine years, at the end of which time he opened the New Amoy Hotel.

DePree Family, Spring, 1932 (in Amoy 1907 to 1948) J.N.
Henry, David "Pitts," Kate, "Harold "Pewee", and Catherine B.

Bowra, 1908

第二十章　老外在厦门的故事　Stories of Foreigners in Amoy

寡妇巴尔（20 世纪 20 年代）　她先生生前是一名医生，还有一个在福州当医生的女婿。

白头发，矮个子，行动敏捷，把她归到哪一类都不合适。她到中国来不是为了赚取金钱、教义和政治资本，只是相比其他任何地方，她更喜欢住在这里。她的房子非常安静，带着一种稳定、圆满的感觉。海湾里其他所有人呆久以后都会变得烦躁不安。巴尔夫人生于福州，在那里结婚，后来成了寡妇。她会说闽南话和福州话两种方言。她是英国人，几乎是极端的英国人，但是客观上她在中国待的时间又太长了。幸好她不以人种，而是以素质区分人。在她的朋友圈里，素质是最关键的。也就是她让我第一次意识到年长的人对于社区可以起到的重要作用……在那个炎热的早上，我看到巴尔夫人穿着凉爽的灰白相间衣服，站在黄色的喇叭花丛中。她是年龄和美的象征。我满怀感激地送了她一个飞吻。

——麦肯兹·格瑞芙，1959 年，第 61、63 页

纽约美孚石油公司的托马斯先生和莫里先生　经理 L.I. 托马斯先生和助理经理莫里先生负责为公司在当地设立分公司，从事一桩大生意。他们的油罐可以储存 175 万加仑的石油，主要的贸易产品有美国煤油、固体石蜡、矿物油以及来自美洲的石脑油。

——博拉，1908 年

新厦门旅馆的 F.H. 卢卡森先生　在中国沿海，最漂亮、最精巧的建筑当属鼓浪屿岛上的新厦门旅馆。旅馆客房空间很大，而且有令人舒服的装修。入住客人可以打弹子球，旅馆会竭尽全力确保客人住得舒服。

旅馆的业主 F.H. 卢卡森先生生于德国埃姆登市，12 岁开始出海，在中国水域的英国和美国轮船上从事贸易工作。1876 年至 1878 年，他在德国海军接受培训，然后回到中国。在香港，他获得了大副的证书。之后，他就开始在中国沿海走南闯北做贸易。1884 年，他进入帝国海关总税务司。1891 年，辞职加入壳牌运输贸易公司。在厦门工作 9 年后，他开了这家新厦门旅馆。

——博拉，1908 年

Veenschoten Family, Tong'an, 1928
In Amoy 1917-1951 (daughter returned with husband 1947-1951)

老外看老鼓浪屿 *Old Gulangyu in Foreigners' Eyes*

Veenschoten Family, Tong'an, 1928
In Amoy 1917-1951 (daughter returned with husband 1947-1951)

Back: Jean Nienhuis, Ruth Broekema, Jack and Joan Hill, Gladys Kooy
(The 3 ladies lived in the "ko'-niu-lau" (single ladies' residence).
Chinese: colleagues and workers of "Tong-An Station"
Front row: the Hill children ("Bunker"/Jack Jr., Donny, Keith), friends' kids

第二十章 老外在厦门的故事 *Stories of Foreigners in Amoy*

Lawrence John Beltman
Family in Amoy 1920-1928
Father Robert Schuller's Uncle

A. Livingston Warnshuis
In Amoy 1900-1910
Greatly influence young Lin Yutang

Gulangyu Friends, 1920s

J.N.

Chapter 21 Learning the Language

The Sweetest Language? The Chinese is the only living language in which through the phonetic element in the writing, joined with the poetry of all ages, written during 4000 years, and preserving rhymes for our examination, we have open to our investigation 4000 years of continuous linguistic development.

"The latter [Webb, 1678] says that 'if ever our Europeans shall become thoroughly studied in the Chinese tongue,' it will be found that the Chinese have very many words 'whereby they express themselves in such elegancies as neither by Hebrew or Greek, or any other language how elegant so ever can be expressed. Besides, whereas the Hebrew is harsh and rugged, the Chinese appears the most sweet and smooth language of all others throughout the whole world at this day known.' P. Premare, who was missionary and sinologist and had a right to speak with authority, becomes quite enthusiastic on the subject of this language. Chinese Grammar, he says, is for the most part free from the thorns which ours presents, but still it has its rules, and there is not in the world a richer language, nor one which has reigned so long.

Edkins, 1875

Amoy—the Original Chinese The general principles of the old Chinese pronunciation do not admit of doubt, because they are traceable in the syllabic spelling which comes down from Kwo p'u, A.D. 276 to 324...The syllabic spelling gives the standard for the language from A.D. 300 to A.D. 800...

It was about 1850 that I published my first philological essay on Chinese ... that final m in Fukien is imbedded in the phonetic characters which I studied in England in 1847 in Callery's Systema Phoneticum... when the phonetic characters were made, B.C. 2500, the final m was there. This brought with it the swift and safe conclusions that mandarin is modern... As a rule the oldest dialects are on the coast. Then follow intermediate dialects, and then comes mandarin.

Edkins, 1885

The Beautiful Language Men forgot that the Bible is an Oriental book, full of figures and similes, and teeming with illustrations from Nature that can be understood best under an Eastern sky. In coming to China it was nearer its home than it was where dreary winters and leaden skies [England] prevail. The Chinese language is one of the most beautiful in the world in which to enshrine the sacred Scriptures, and there is a flexibility and grace about it, that render it capable of expressing all the tenderness, and pathos, and poetry, and sublime thought of that most wondrous book.

MacGowan, 1895

第二十一章　学汉语

最甜美的语言？　汉语是世界上唯一保存四千多年仍在使用的语言。它字中有音、音中有形，保留了各个时代的诗歌和韵律，让我们得以考察四千年语言的持续发展。

后者（韦伯，1678 年）说，"如果我们欧洲人更加深入地去研究汉语，就会发现，中国人优雅地表达自己的词汇极为丰富，希伯来文或希腊文，或其他任何语言都无法与之媲美。"此外，希伯来文既粗犷又刺耳、难听，汉语看上去是迄今为止世界上最甜美、流畅的语言。作为一名传教士和汉学家，马若瑟的看法有一定的权威性。他相当热衷于汉语研究。他说，汉语的语法跟我们的语言相比最为零散，但仍有规律。世界上没有一种语言比汉语更丰富，使用时间更悠久。

——艾德金斯，1875 年

厦门话　汉语的始祖　古汉语音律的一般原则是不容置疑的，因为它可以追溯到公元 276 年至 324 年郭璞对《尔雅》的释诂、释训。……他的训诂学著作为汉语奠定了公元 300 年至 800 年的语言规范……

1850 年前后，我发表了第一篇有关汉语的语言学论文……福建方言中 m 的声音隐藏在汉字注音里。这是我 1847 年在英国研究卡勒瑞语音系统时发现的……公元前 2500 年注音的时候，尾音 m 依然存在。我们可以依此很快得出可靠的结论，

"Xin" ("Faith", Dukes, 1885)

那就是，汉语已经是最新的了……　一般来说，最古老的方言存在于沿海，最时新的语言是官话，两者之间还有一些半老不新的方言。

——艾德金斯，1885 年，第 251、252 页

美丽的语言　人们已经忘记《圣经》是一本充满明喻和暗喻的东方书籍，里面有大量来自自然界的插图，只有在东方世界里才能得到最好的理解。来到中国，《圣经》比拥有沉闷冬季和铅灰色天空的（英国）离家更近。汉语是世界上传播《圣经》最优美的语言之一。它拥有一种柔性和优雅。这本最神奇书籍拥有的所有温柔、情感、诗意以及崇高思想，它都能够表达。

——麦高文，1895 年，第 17 页

老外看老鼓浪屿 *Old Gulangyu in Foreigners' Eyes*

Insane Language? (Gulangyu, 1920s) "People say you get peculiar if you study Chinese too long", Mrs. Jones of Customs addressed her remark to Mrs. Theobald quite kindly. I concluded she believed the sanity of missionaries to be somehow immune.

Mrs. Weeks, the doctor's wife, said: "I knew a man who put snakes in his wife's bed; he was terribly good at Chinese."

…I should have to risk the snakes. Cyril [her husband] had to learn the language [Amoy Dialect] —that was why we were in Kulangsu. Apart from all cultural and social considerations, I, being borne in a sedan chair about the island, unable to make any sound which conveyed the least shred of meaning to the bearers, was even prepared to risk mental derangement.

Mackenzie-Grieves, 1959

Learning the Ancient Amoy Dialect Early May 1948 and the day for departure to Amoy had arrived. My[1] ship, evidently not important enough to command a berth alongside the harbor, was anchored somewhere in the Roads behind an imposing array of other steamers, billowing clouds of black smoke in preparation for their sailing. Near Clifford Pier lay a disorderly armada of small sampans, which bobbed up and down on the languid waves like discarded coconut shells, manned by Chinese who scrutinized each new arrival with an eagle's eye for a fare.

'Where are you off to?' shouted one in Malay.

'To Amoy,' I replied in my best Hokkien [Amoy Dialect]. The man looked blank. He did not understand. Those six months had been wasted.

Filled with a desire to apply my newly acquired knowledge, I made another attempt, concentrating desperately on the right pronunciation. The boatman's leathery face wreathed with a smile as a new understanding slowly dawned on him. In a flash, all the other Chinese on the pier within hearing distance had gathered around. With grinning enquiring faces they fired question … I became tongue-tied. They chuckled in amusement at my silence. I wanted terribly to explain, tell them I was going to the land of their forefathers.

'To Amoy,' I explained.

'Eee! Aiyaah!'

'To learn Hokkien [闽南语]…'

'A Red-Haired speaking Hokkien lah!' guffawed two or three in a full-throated chorus…'

[On disembarking in Amoy]… Bellowed the Captain, 'Come and see us when we return and don't go round the bend trying to learn this outlandish language.'

…There are seven distinct tones in Hokkien and several hundred monosyllabic noises which go, singly or in combination, to make up the spoken language, with nasal and aspirate variations. The nasal twang would come through with commendable mellifluousness for someone slightly adenoidal or with a cold in the head. …Correctness of tone pronunciation and tone changes was of prime importance for there was only a slight different in modulation, for instance, between returning to China and pawning a pair of long trousers.

Neil, 1956

---

1 Desmond Neil, British army officer in Asia, studied Amoy Dialect in Xiamen in the 1940s.

第二十一章 学汉语 Learning the Language

疯狂的汉语（鼓浪屿，20世纪20年代） "人们说，如果中文学得太久，你会变成怪人，"海关的琼斯女士很友善地对西奥博尔德女士说。我得出的结论是，她相信传教士健全的心智某种程度上是有免疫力的。

医生太太威克斯女士说："我认识一个男子。他把蛇放进太太的被窝里。他的汉语棒极了。"

……我应该冒冒老蛇的风险。西里尔（她的丈夫）必须学习这里的语言（厦门方言）。这是我们到鼓浪屿的原因。我出生在这个岛上的一台轿子里，却发不出任何对轿夫来说有意义的声音。除了文化和社会的因素，我甚至准备冒冒神经错乱的危险。

——麦肯兹·格瑞芙，1959年，第29、30页

学说古老的厦门方言 1948年5月初，启程前往厦门的日子终于到来。我搭乘的轮船显然不够重要，不能在港口附近找到泊位，最终在靠近大路的一个地方下锚，周围泊满了许多蒸汽船，场面非常壮观。蒸汽船冒着滚滚浓烟，准备起航。临近悬崖的码头杂乱地泊着一大排小舢板，像随意丢弃的椰子壳，慢悠悠地在波浪中上下晃动。中国人摇着这些小舢板，用鹰眼一般的目光，仔细观察每一个新上岸的旅客，希望赚点摆渡费。

"您上哪去？"有人用马来语喊道。

"去厦门，"我尽最大努力，用福建话（厦门方言）回答。听者没有反应。他没听懂。过去的六个月时间浪费了。

心里非常想用上自己新近学习的知识，于是，我再次努力，全力以赴发出正确的声音。船夫粗糙的脸庞露出了笑容，他慢慢能够理解我的话了。很快，周围能够听到我们对话的中国人都聚集了过来。他们面带笑容，好奇地连连发问……我自己说不出话来。看到我张口结舌，他们非常有趣地低声轻笑。我非常想解释，想告诉他们自己要到他们先祖的土地上。

"去厦门，"我解释道。

"咦！哎哟呀！"

"会福建话……"

"这个红毛会讲福建话啦！"两、三个中国人一起大声起哄……

（登陆厦门后）……"我们回来的时候，记得来看我们。不要在这里学什么鸟语，"船长吼道。

……福建话有七个明显的语调和几百个单音节的声音。这些单音节，单独或组合，伴随着鼻音和送气音的各种变化，就能说出这里的方言。

鼻音像稍微有些腺状肿或感冒的人发出的那种甜美流畅的声音。……正确发音和把握语调变化至关重要，因为，例如"回到中国"与"当掉长裤"之间只有语调方面的轻微变化。

——尼尔[2]，1956年

---

2 德斯蒙德·尼尔，英国驻马来亚军官，英国劳工部驻新加坡官员，20世纪40年代在厦门学习闽南话。

Incipient Insanity of Chinese Study　　The memorizing of characters was a strain largely on the memory, helped by a little ingenuity in writing every character on a blank visiting card...To help memorize a character one was tempted to draw it out on the hand or in thin air with a finger. It was on these occasions that outside observers immediately diagnosed that incipient insanity which is prognosticated for anyone learning Chinese.

Neil, 1956

Heartbreaking Language　　...the first few days rolled into weeks of heartbreaking despair as I struggled with Mr. Lim and with the tones, noises and sounds that seemed to make up no pattern, no harmony, and had little meaning for anyone. Simple sentences were understood by shopkeepers or boatmen, but in the middle of lengthier explanations and conversations, a word would slip the memory or a tone mispronounced and in my sympathetic auditor would break out into a hurried and incomprehensible suggestion of what I was perhaps endeavouring to say. At last, however, the jumbled pieces began to fit slowly together. It was like hearing an orchestral concert, prefaced first by the screeching of violins and cellos being tuned up to the right key, with Mr. Lim as the unruffled conductor. But never did an orchestra take so long to tune up.

Neill, 1956

Satanic Language! (1893)　　...the Chinese language-a language than which in the whole world there is none other so different from all others...none other acquired with so much difficulty by foreigners, or employed by them with so little facility." Whether it be supposition or fact that Satan was the author of the Chinese language or not...

Pitcher, 1893

Language, Tones, and Nervous Breakdowns　　Training in the language began under the direction of two local teachers. Since they were as eager to learn English as we were to make a beginning on Chinese, a battle of wits took place...

Teacher Chhun Hiong Siam-si and some of her pupils, Feb. 1932　J.N.
Teacher Chhun lived to over 100-years-old!
Front: Vandemeer, DePree, VanLinden, Teacher Chen, Renskers, Hofstra, Voskuil
Back: Angus, Holkeboer, Bruce Angus, Holkman, Beekman, M. Poppen, Nienhuis, Dr. Holleman, Veldman, DePree, Platz, Vandermeer, Dr. Hofstra

第二十一章　学汉语　Learning the Language

学汉语早期精神病　认汉字对记忆来说是一个很大的挑战。把汉字写在空白的访问卡上是一个小技巧，对认识汉字有帮助……为了记住一个汉字，你经常会情不自禁地用指头在另一只手的手心或者用指头在空中拼写。就这样，旁观者马上认定，这是任何汉语学习者所显示的早期精神病的症状。

——尼尔，1956 年，第 36 页

令人心碎的语言　……最初几天的悲伤变成了几星期，我与林先生和音调、语调搏斗。这些音调、语调似乎没有任何规律，也没有什么和声，对任何人都没有意义。店员或船员听得懂我说的简单句子。但是随着交流和解释的深入，我经常会忘词或发错音、用错调。富有同情心的旁听者会很快地说出一些难以理解的联想，猜测我想说的话语。最后，混乱的词语开始慢慢地拼出了规律。这就像是在听一场交响音乐会，由刺耳的小提琴拉开序曲，然后大提琴找到了合适的音调，而林先生就是沉着冷静的乐团指挥。只是没见过交响乐团花这么长时间去调音。

——尼尔，1956 年，第 38 页

撒旦般的语言！（1893 年）　……汉语——全世界找不出一个跟其他语言差别这么大的语言……也找不到一种语言外国人学起来这么困难，或者说用起来这么不方便。不管是推测，还是事实，撒旦就是汉语的创造者……

——皮切尔，1893 年

语言，语音和神经衰弱　在两名当地教师的指导下，开始学习汉语。这两位老师渴望学习英语，就像我们渴望开始学习汉语一样。因此，一场智力之战开始了……

Edna Beekman with Tutor Sui-soot Sian-si^n, 1924 (In Amoy 1914-1951)

The grammar and syntax of our adopted tongue were fairly simple. It was the limitation of all words to one syllable length that caused most of our trouble. The poverty of sound that resulted from such a one-syllable vocabulary gave rise to inflections as a method of distinguishing words…

Fortunately, nervous breakdowns are rare among the Chinese. Their calm pace and resigned attitude in life's trying circumstances are definite assets to mental health. Had they to listen to a number of foreigners practicing the "tones," I believe that the percentage of nervous disorders among them would show a marked increase."

Macguire, 1946

Tone Torture! (1907) It is not long after his commencement before he runs his head against the tones and gets hurt. They vary from five in the north to eight in the south of China. It is quite possible to talk, and make oneself generally understood, without a knowledge of the tones, for rhythm in Chinese, as in every language, is of even greater importance than strict syllabic accuracy. No man, however, can read Chinese characters aloud correctly, or in conversation lay stress on any particular word, unless he has a good knowledge of the tones. The ordinary Chinaman is quite unaware of their existence, and even amongst the literati only a small minority can accurately designate them, yet no native makes any mistake in actual usage.

We have tones in English, but they are arbitrary, and every man is a law to himself. Take, for instance, the word "What." There is the interrogatory what, the surprised what, the drawling what, the haughty what. In England, however, you may what your whats whatever way you will, and it is still a what, but in China a bing in one tone is quite a different word from a bing in another tone, as a well-known official is once said to have discovered. He was out with a party; the day was hot; so became the champagne. They were dining in a Chinese inn, and bing (ice) was demanded of the innkeeper.

"How much?" asked mine host. "A trayful" was the reply. Imagine everybody s amusement when, after waiting an unconscionable time, they saw brought in a trayful of hot native cakes, also called bing, but in a different tone.

Once upon a time I had an argument with a Christian plasterer whose conscience would not allow him to waste my money. The local whitewash possessed a yellowish tinge which did not please me, and, having a dim recollection of hearing that a little blue powder mixed with the whitening would whiten it, I said to the plasterer, "Just go and buy a little la, and mix it with this white wash."

"La! la wouldn't mix with whitewash."

"Oh yes, it would," said youthful confidence, "run off and buy some."

"It wouldn't be any good, and only waste your money."

"Never mind," I said, "I'll risk the waste, away you go."

"No," said the little man stubbornly, "it won't mix."

Becoming a trifle displeased, I looked up and wrote out the Chinese character, handed it to him, and said, "Now go at once and buy some of that."

"Oh!" said he, looking at the character, "you said la wax. It's la blue you mean." Just the difference between a rising inflection and a sort of twirl in the voice.

Even during the writing of this chapter I have heard a lady, by a slight perversion of pronunciation, read from St John's Gospel, "I am the Vine, ye are the gimlets!"

Soothill, 1907

第二十一章 学汉语 Learning the Language

我们想学的汉语语法和句法相当简单。所有的词汇只有一个音节的长度。这就是我们最主要的麻烦。单音节词汇所引起的音调短缺使得曲折变化成为辨别汉语词汇的一种方法……

幸运的是,中国人(学语言)很少患神经衰弱。面对生活最艰难的状况,他们逆来顺受、脚步不慌不乱。这对他们的精神健康肯定是一种财富。要是他们听了几个外国人练习汉语发言,我想,他们患神经错乱的几率肯定会明显提高。

——麦克格威尔,1946 年,第 24、25 页

语调折磨人!(1907 年) 开始学习汉语没多久,他就碰上了语调的问题,并因此受伤。从北方的五种,到南方的八种,汉语的语调变幻莫测。不懂汉语语调,就可以讲汉语,并让别人一般能听得懂,因为跟其他语言一样,掌握汉语的韵律比准确、严格地发好每个音节更重要。但是,除非语调把握得好,否则没人能够准确地大声朗读汉字,或者在交谈时重读某个汉字。普通的中国人并不在意语调,甚至有文化的人也很少能准确无误地驾驭语调。然而,在实际应用过程中,没人会搞错。

英语有语调,但是随意的。每个人都可以自己把握语调。比如说,"what"这个词,有提问的"what",惊奇的"what",懒洋洋的"what"和傲慢的"what"。在英国,你可以随便怎么"what","what"还是"what"。但是,在中国,一个"bing"字声调不同,意思就完全不一样。据说,这是一位知名的官员发现的。有一次,他去参加派对。天气很热。"bing"最后变成了香槟。他们在一家中国旅店里吃饭,向店家要些冰。

"要多少?"主人问。"一满盘,"回答说。等了相当长一段时间,他们看到一大盘热乎乎的当地糕点送了进来。这让大家都感到好笑。当地有些糕点也叫饼,只是音调不同。

有一次,我跟一个信基督的抹灰工争辩。这位抹灰工做事讲良心,从不浪费我的钱财。当地的白灰略带黄色,我不喜欢。印象中隐隐约约记得,掺点蓝色粉末会让白灰变白。于是,我对灰工说,"去买点 la,掺到白灰里。"

"La!La 不能跟石灰掺在一起。"

"噢,能,能掺,"我年轻气盛,"赶紧去,买一些。"

"行不通,那只会浪费你的钱。"

"不要紧,"我说,"我不怕浪费,你去买就是了。"

"不行,"这个小个子男人固执地说,"掺不到一块的。"

我有点不高兴。于是,我查了字典,写下一个汉字,把纸条交给他,然后说,"去,马上去买些回来。"

"噢!"他看到汉字,说,"你说蜡,但意思是蓝。"两个字的差别就在于升调和卷舌。

就在我撰写这个章节的时候,我还听说有一位女士,发音有些颠倒。把圣约翰的《福音》"我是藤,你是枝"读成,"我是藤,你是鸡!"

——苏特希尔,1907 年

老外看老鼓浪屿 *Old Gulangyu in Foreigners' Eyes*

Chapter 22   Foreign Fun in Amoy

Foreign Picnics in 1700   Another rarity is of five large stones, as big or bigger than the last mentioned in an hollow at the foot of a mountain (whether by nature or art I cannot tell), they are each about thirty feet long, and twelve or fourteen diameter. They lean their heads against one another, and form an alcove at their feet, wherein is placed a table and benches around it, of stone, and there is a pretty clear rivulet runs close by the table. We Europeans frequented that table on Sundays, for we often dined there.

Hamilton, 1727

The Club on Gulangyu   The spacious edifice now occupied by the members of "The Club" was erected in the year 1876, to replace some very inconvenient premises that had done duty for a number of years previously, before the community had increased to its present numerical proportions. The building contains a fair library, a reading-room supplied with all the best home and local papers, a billiard-room with two tables, a bowling-alley, a bar for drinks and oysters, and a committee-room, which last is nightly used for the table d'hote at 7:30 P.M. The latest telegraphic news of steamers dispatched to and from the various coast ports is published in the hall, where an excellent barometer is kept for the information of those interested in the changes of the weather…

Attached to the Club is a small theatre, in which a number of excellent performances are given during the winter season, many of the ladies kindly lending their assistance. The racquet-court stands alongside of the theatre, and is an inexhaustible source of health to all who can stand this severe exercise. At no great distance is the Recreation Ground, whereon some goodly cricket may be seen during the cool months. There is one annual Race Meeting, which lasts two days, and is held upon the Amoy side of the water. Extremely good shooting is to be got in the neighbourhood, where geese, duck, teal, and snipe, may be bagged in large quantities. Lawn Tennis is played both in public on the Recreation Ground and in private at the residences of those who are fortunate enough to possess available lawns. The harbor is admirably adapted for boat-sailing, and the walks round Koolangsu are pretty if somewhat monotonous.

The fine sandy beaches are devoted during the hot months to evening walks and talks, followed by a plunge in the sea as the shades of evening begin to draw…

Giles, 1878

Picnic, Amoy Water Works, Oct. 1931

第二十二章　厦门的异国乐趣

十八世纪的异国野炊　另外一个稀有的东西物是五块巨石。它和我之前提到的山脚下那个山谷里的巨石一样大,甚至更大(自然的,还是人工建造的,我不知道)。每块石头的长度大约是九米,直径大约是四米。它们一个个头靠着头,脚下形成了一个凹室,凹室里放着一张石桌,桌子周围是石凳。桌子的附近流淌着一条非常清澈的小溪。我们欧洲人周日经常去那张石桌野餐。

——哈密尔顿,1727 年,第 494 页

鼓浪屿上的俱乐部　俱乐部成员现在使用的那座宽敞大厦建于 1876 年,用来取代已经使用多年且极其不方便的旧楼。之前,社区人口也没有目前这么多。大楼里有一个不错的图书馆,一间拥有国内和当地最棒的报刊阅览室,有一间台球室,里面放着两张台球桌,一条保龄球道,一个供应饮料和生蚝的吧台和委员会的办公室。委员会办公室每晚七点三十分成了吃饭场所。来往于各个港口轮船的最新电报消息公布在大厅里。那儿还放了一支极好的晴雨表,为那些关注天气变化的人服务……

小剧院是俱乐部的附属建筑之一。冬季,那里有很多精彩的表演,许多友好热情的女士给了慷慨的资助。网球场就在剧院的旁边。对于那些能够承受如此剧烈运动的人来说,它无疑是一个取之不尽、用之不竭的健康资源。健身场距俱乐部不远。在凉爽的季节里,人们能在那儿看到精彩的板球比赛。

每年,厦门海岸边都会举行一场为期两天的赛马大会。附近还有一个非常棒的猎场,可以捕获大量的鹅、鸭、水鸭,还有沙锥鸟。有人在公共健身场上打草地网球,也可以在自家的草地上打。港口非常适合划船,绕着鼓浪屿步行,虽说有点单调,但还是很舒服的。

夏季傍晚时分,人们在美丽的沙滩上散步和闲谈。夜幕降临时,人们跳入海中……

——吉列斯,1878 年,第 32、33 页

The "Jolly Six", 1924　　　　J. Nienhuis

老外看老鼓浪屿 *Old Gulangyu in Foreigners' Eyes*

Amoy Freemasonry Close by the tennis lawn is an artistic-looking building, that has all the air and appearance of a place where scholars meet to indulge in study and to discuss the great questions that continually arise in the world of letters. There is a quietness and a scholarly look about it that impresses the onlooker. No vulgar crowd rushes in and out, but an academic calmness pervades it, such as to students who are immersed in thought love to have around them. That it must be an institution of learning is evident from the number of Chinese characters that are painted conspicuously around the main entrance. These of course intimate scholarship of a high order, and as the mercantile communities in the East are concerned about pursuits of a more agreeable character than Chinese studies can give them, there must be exceptionally studious men in Amoy, who prefer to master the intricate language and literature of China than to spend their time in the more common amusements of tennis and billiards.

On inquiry, we find that our impressions with regard to this learned-looking building were mistaken. It is not a seat of learning, but the Hall where the Freemasons assemble to carry out the secret duties of their order. It seems there are two lodges in Amoy, both of which are flourishing, and as the elite of society are amongst the leaders of them both, it may be taken for granted that the institution is a popular one with the community. That many charitable acts are performed by the members, and many a deed of mercy, is unquestionable. Since, therefore, the public acts of these men are of so pleasing a character, we may well be content to allow them to meet in secret and sedulously guard their doors from the uninitiated, in the full conviction that nothing dangerous to the welfare of society will be concocted within the walls of this attractive-looking building.

MacGowan, 1897

第二十二章　厦门的异国乐趣 *Foreign Fun in Amoy*

厦门共济会　网球场草地的附近有一栋看起来很艺术的建筑。它的外表和氛围显示学者们在此碰头埋头研究和讨论文学界不断出现的重大问题。它宁静和浓厚的学术气氛给旁观者留下深刻的印象。没有粗俗人出入，只有平静的学术氛围。这种平静是沉思的学生最向往的。大门口醒目的汉字说明，这是一处学习的场所。它自然地暗示着高层次的学问。因为东方的商贸会追求一个比中国私塾更加和蔼可亲的性格，所以厦门一定有特别勤勉的人士。比起更为大众的网球和保龄球娱乐项目，他们更愿意花时间和精力来研究中国错综复杂的语言和文学。

询问之后，我们才知道，我们对这座很有学问样子的建筑的想法是错误的。它并不是一个学习场所，而是共济会活动地点。共济会成员聚集在大厅里，执行他们的秘密使命。在厦门，它似乎有两个场所，都很生机勃勃。他们的主要成员都是社会的精英人士，共济会自然很受社区欢迎。毫无疑问，共济会成员做了很多慈善事业和仁慈之事。从此，这些人的社会行为都非常受人欢迎。我们同样也允许他们秘密集会，看住大门；以防外界干扰。我们深信，这造型美观的大楼的墙内不会有任何损害社会福利的事情发生。

——麦嘉湖，1897 年，第 152 页

Picnic, 1927　　　　　　J. Nienhuis

4th of July Party (1850s)   Above our living floor was an open verandah, well railed in fancy brick work wall, where we often went for cool breezes in the evenings. I remember a famous Fourth of July party held up there.

The guests were the American Consul, and the British and Dutch Consuls. There were English and Scotch missionaries, and the American ones, and several English and Scotch tea merchants, and their wives, who were mother's and father's warm friends,—Mr. and Mrs. Boyd of England, and Mr. and Mrs. Syme of Scotland, who formed a very congenial social group. There were officers from our own small fleet of "Men of War", as they were called in those days, and British officers of "H.M.S.'s", more numerous.

We sang National airs—"Hail Columbia", "Yankee Doodle", and "God Save The King" to our own tune of "America". I do not recall "The Star Spangled Banner", and hardly think that had drifted so far from America, or perhaps it was too near facts to be an acceptable song between Britons and Americans! There were wonderful fireworks in the Sail Yard, just opposite us (where the poor insane man had been chained). Father was ingenious in planning some of them, which Chinese skill carried out. China is the home of fireworks, as we know. One that father planned was a large illumination of "E Pluribus Unum". I should say the letters were a foot long or more. Another was a rowboat full of people, who pulled oars in unison as it ran over the ground. I do not vouch this to be a fact, but it certainly is the impression left on my mind. ...

Mary Doty's Memoirs

Nanputuo Picnic, 1925

第二十二章　厦门的异国乐趣 Foreign Fun in Amoy

七月四号的（美国）国庆聚会（19世纪50年代）　我们房子的楼上是一个露天的凉台，四周是精心设计的砖墙扶手。夜晚，我们经常去那里乘凉。我还清楚地记得，著名的七月四日国庆聚会有一次就是在那儿举行的。

宾客中有美国、英国和荷兰的领事，有来自英国、苏格兰和美国的传教士，还有几个来自英格兰和苏格兰的茶叶商人及其夫人。他们是父母的好朋友——英格兰的博伊德先生和太太、苏格兰的塞姆先生和太太，他们意气相投。来宾中还有我们国家的舰队军官，还有英国皇家海军舰艇上的军官，等等。

我们唱了国歌，我们用美国的调唱了"万岁，哥伦比亚"、"杨基歌"还有"上帝保佑吾王"。我记不起是否也唱了"星条旗之歌"，没有想到已经远离美国了，或者这首歌曲离现实太近，无法被英国人和美国人所接受。我们在我家对面的帆桁上燃放炫目璀璨的烟花，那里附近的房子里关押着可怜的疯子。我父亲精心设计了一些烟花，由中国人施放。我们都知道，中国发明了烟火。我父亲准备的其中一个烟火是一个巨大的"合众为一"的造型。那些字母至少有一英尺高。另外一个烟火则是众人在一只小船上步调一致地划桨前进。我不能保证这是事实，但这绝对是留在我脑海中的印象。

——玛丽·多蒂未出版的回忆录

After Christmas Dinner, 1930, at Vandermeer Home　　J. Nienhuis

老外看老鼓浪屿 *Old Gulangyu in Foreigners' Eyes*

Gulangyu Beach Party (1920s) On Saturdays and Sundays there would be bathing parties to which all the residents in the immediate neighbourhood were, perforce, invited, since otherwise to observe the polite conventions and preserve the privacy of the party was almost impossible… Careful timing almost obviated the risk of invasion by the Pigoux children, the state of whose bladders constantly preoccupied their Mamma…

By an unwritten code, only we of the bay assumed the rights of party-giving. Guests were exclusively European. In a temperature of rarely less than ninety degrees Fahrenheit, emerging from a lukewarm sea, it was customary for the bathers to be offered cherry-brandy on a silver salver by their hostesses' house servant…

Settlement dogs [Read about the uncultured indigenous dogs in Amoy Animals chapter] came to the parties: they were sleek, flea-less, well-fed and behaved, not to be confused, any more than their owners, with the indigenous population. Of them our own charming mongrel, Biffin, and the pointer-like Cocoa were the most engaging. The faithful attendant of an English Customs officer's four small sons, Cocoa endured at their affectionate hands a variety of uncomfortable and painful attentions anyone of which, meted out to him by a stranger, would have turned him into a snarling menace.

At Mrs. Poole's Bank Holiday picnic, the children were burying him in sand to his adoring yellow eyes, the tip of his tail still wagging until a final handful quelled its last spasmodic tremor. He did not move even when Mrs. Danvers' Pekinese stepped delicately down from her garden on silkily splayed feet to investigate the possibilities of the food. Mrs. Danvers herself eschewed all such entertainments. Keeping herself physically immune and mentally inviolate, she awaited her husband's retirement and the moment when she could return to England and resume living. "What can she do all day?"

Mackenzie-Grieves, 1959

Foreigners Learn Mahjong (1920s) Mahjong is a decorative and imaginative game. I enjoyed handling the bamboo and ivory tiles, the pondering pursuit of green dragons and of the four winds. Enjoyed it, that is, until I played with my Chinese friends. With them there was no romance; each round was as fierce and rapid as a burst of machine-gun fire. They were born gamblers and knew the ivory tiles by feel. After ten years' practice, it still left me dazed. I eventually gave up the attempt to pit my mind and fingers against their astonishing and characteristic agility.

Zhongshan Park, Amoy, 1931   J. Nienhuis

But at Mrs. Roots' we talked and ate as we played. "I'll have that three bamboos, I think," said Mrs. Danvers, the Police Superintendent's wife. She was elegant and always used a sedan chair. Her bearers bore her monogram on their white starched backs.

Mackenzie-Grieves, 1959

第二十二章　厦门的异国乐趣 Foreign Fun in Amoy

鼓浪屿沙滩派对（20世纪20年代）　每逢周末，鼓浪屿都会举行游泳派对。附近的居民必然都得到邀请，否则就是不遵守友好的传统，也不可能保护派对的隐私了。派对时间精心安排，几乎排除了被那些狼吞虎咽的孩子干扰的危险。如果他们在场，妈妈就不得不常常担心他们的屎尿。

这是一条不成文的规矩。只有我们住在港湾里的人家有权举办派对。宾客清一色都是欧洲人。在气温很少低于华氏90度的情况下，派对主人的佣人一般会把樱桃白兰地准备好，放在银盘上，送给那些刚从不冷不热的海水里游上岸的客人……

租界里的宠物狗也参加了聚会：它们被梳洗得干干净净，身上不会有跳蚤，它们被养得很好，举止也很端正。这样一来，主人就可以把它们从土狗群中分辨出来。狗群里，我们家可爱的混血儿宾菲和指示犬可可是最有魅力的。英国海关官员的四个小儿子对可可爱护有加。

Gulangyu Swimming, 1921　Nienhuis

可可忍受着他们那一双双富有爱意的手带来的不舒服、甚至是痛苦的感觉。在平时，陌生人对它喊叫常常让它狂吠不已。

在普尔太太的银行假日野餐上，孩子们把可可埋在沙子里，只剩下它那可爱的黄色眼睛和仍在摇摆的尾巴。它的尾巴一直在摆动，直到最后一把沙子压制了它痉挛的颤动。它一直都纹丝不动。即使是丹维斯太太的哈巴狗从她的花园灵敏地跳下，踩着柔软地八字脚四处觅食，可可也丝毫没有动。丹维斯太太自己拒绝所有此类的娱乐活动。她修身养性，保护自己免受身体上和精神上的侵犯。她一直等待她的丈夫退休，等待着她能回到英格兰重新生活。"她一整天能干些什么呢？"

　　　　　　　　　　　　——麦肯兹·格瑞芙，1959年，第63、64页

外国人学打麻将（20世纪20年代）　麻将是一项很艺术、且充满了想象力的游戏。我喜欢玩这些竹制和象牙做的麻将牌，喜欢思考如何得到一条青龙和东南西北风。不过，我不喜欢和我中国朋友交手。和他们打没有任何的情趣可言，每一局牌都如同机枪火力爆发一样迅速、猛烈。他们天生就是玩牌的人，他们摸一下就知道手里是什么牌。我玩了十年的麻将，还是很茫然。最后，我放弃了，不敢与他们惊人的心理和灵敏的手指继续作战。

但是，在鲁斯太太家里，我们一边聊天，一边吃饭，一边打牌。"我想我会摸到三条，"警察局局长夫人丹弗斯太太说。她气质优雅，经常坐轿子。轿夫白色的浆硬衣服后背绣着她姓名的第一个字母。

　　　　　　　　　　　　——麦肯兹·格瑞芙，1959年，第28、29页

▶ 313

老外看老鼓浪屿 *Old Gulangyu in Foreigners' Eyes*

Missionary Hobbies An interesting piece of research could be made on missionary hobbies. The E.P. Mission has contained amateur photographers, talented vocalists and musicians, skilled tennis and chess players, 'green-fingered' gardeners, and one or two Rugby and hockey internationals.

Our Hakka missionaries were attracted by the opportunity of investigating the flora of this beautiful country which abounded in wild flowers.

Band 1948

Map Making Missionaries fund Hospitals Dr. Riddel [English Presbyterian Mission] turned his attention to map-making and became an expert cartographer. In 1901 he published a series of maps of the Hakka and Swatow fields, after a careful survey of the region which they cover. 'These maps are a model of accuracy, lucidity and detail. They are indispensable to knowledge of the area in which the missionaries are engaged and are invaluable also to Chinese Government officials, who are always glad to secure copies. There are no other maps of the kind in existence, but the example of Dr. Riddel has given to some of the abler of our Hakka brethren a taste for map-drawing, particularly the Rev. Tshai Yung, who has published a reliable and detailed map of the country around the district cities of Ta-pu and of Yong-ting and Shang-hang in the North Hakka field. The profits from the sale of maps were devoted to a fund for poor patients in the hospital.

Band 1948

English Trader Plant Collecting A large number of the English connected with this Factory [in Amoy], as the company's office was then called, at Amoy and at Chusan, collected plants; in fact the earliest plants collected in south-east China, and probably for all China, which are still in existence to-day came from collections made from Fukien.

Outside Zhongshan Park, 1920s J. Nienhuis

The very first record is that of Wincheslaus Libanus who collected plants at Hamoy (Amoy), in 1685. These were apparently sent to Petiver and also to Plukenet. Jacobs Petiver and Leonard Plukenet, M. D. were two English taxonomists who wrote many books on plants and were especially interested in building up their own private herbaria. These collections were eventually acquired and incorporated in the Sloane Herbarium, and are now to be found in the British Museum of Natural History, London. I had the opportunity to see them when I was working there. I found a specimen, Petiver No. 29 from Hamoy, China, 1685 in the Sloane Herbarium (Vol. 90, p. 5) called Adiantum nigrum chinenseZ2 now known as Odontosoria chinensis\. Sm., the Toothed fern, one of the very commonest ferns of south-east China.

Metcalf, 1934

第二十二章　厦门的异国乐趣 Foreign Fun in Amoy

传教士的业余爱好　传教士的业余爱好可作为一个非常有趣的研究课题。英国长老会传教士里有业余的摄影师，多才多艺的声乐家和音乐家，有技术熟练的网球手和棋手，有能干的园丁，还有一两个国际橄榄球或者曲棍球队员。

在客家地区，我们的传教士都为遍地开满野花的美丽乡村吸引。他们都想把握机会好好研究这些植物。

——班德，1948 年，第 279、280 页

制作地图的牧师资助医院　里德博士是一名英国的长老会牧师。他把注意力转移到地图制作上，成为了一名专业的制图师。1901 年，在对客家和汕头所管辖的地区进行一系列的调查之后，他出版了客家和汕头地区的系列地图。"这些地图很准确，很清楚，很详细。要了解传教士所在的地方，这些地图是必不可少的。"这些地图对中国的政府官员也是很宝贵的。他们也很高兴得到地图的副本。世界上还没有类似的地图存在，而里德博士的事例使一些客家同胞们对地图制作产生了兴趣，特别是蔡永（音译）牧师。他已经出版了一张客家北部地区准确的、详细的地图，包括大埔、永定、上杭等周边区域。出售地图所得的利润全都捐赠给了医院里的贫困病人。

——班德，1948 年，第 280 页

英国商人"收集植物"　许多英国人都与厦门的这家公司有合作。当时，这家公司的办公室在厦门和舟山被叫做"收集植物"。事实上，中国东南部，甚至是全中国最早收集到的植物标本都是在福建收集的，至今依然保存完好。

最早的记录是温彻斯劳斯·里贝纳斯 1685 年在厦门收集植物。这些收集显然是寄给佩提夫和普拉肯内特的。雅克布斯·佩提夫和伦纳德·普拉肯内特博士是英国的

Water Fun, 1927　　　　J. Nienhuis

植物分类学者。他们撰写了很多关于植物的书籍，而且他们也很想积累自己的标本。这些标本最终收归在斯隆标本集里了，现在就在伦敦的英国自然历史博物馆里。我在那里工作时有幸见过的。我发现一个名字为佩提夫 29 号的标本是 1685 年来自中国厦门。在斯隆标本集里第 90 册第 5 页，名叫铁线蕨胡椒属，现在叫做乌蕨，别名，齿蕨，是中国东南部非常普通的一种蕨类。

——梅特卡夫，1934 年

老外看老鼓浪屿 *Old Gulangyu in Foreigners' Eyes*

Chapter 23   Amoy Shopping

No Private Shopping The natives of Amoy were very curious, and followed us about in crowds. If prices were asked or bargains attempted, everyone in the crowd had a voice in the transaction, and if money passed, they each looked at it and expressed an opinion upon its genuineness and value; but we were not long in concluding that this was due to what might be called, "good-natured inquisitiveness," rather than impertinence.

Ford, 1898

Prof. Ecke's[1] **Antique Shopping** (1920s)   Gustav Ecke, a German professor of Philosophy from Bonn, "Could be moved to a reckless ecstasy by the beauty of a Chinese plate or picture, and to incoherence when considering the unique Chinese synthesis of painting, calligraphy, poetry, philosophy, scholarship and civil administration...

Sign means "No Bargaining"

"Gustav lived on Amoy Island, near the University. When he was not lecturing or studying, he explored the alleys of the city, haunted the pawnbrokers' shops. He had very little money, but he could not bear to let a discovery go. He was the least acquisitive of men, but to allow beauty to lie disregarded in the darkness was unthinkable. In the maze of streets, packed with 220,000 citizens, he found one old Japanese dealer and connoisseur of jade and ceramics. In the dealer's little back room he was perfectly content to admire a piece of celadon, a mutton-fat jade cup, a Chang-chou [Zhangzhou] ware vase, which he knew would eventually go to Japan, but occasionally he would buy a small piece, and would arrive at our house, followed by his servant, carrying the precious object in a piece of old brocade."

---

1   Prof. Ecke wrote "Twin Pagodas of Zayton [Quanzhou]," Harvard Press, 1935.

第二十三章 厦门购物

购物没隐私 厦门当地的人对我们感到很好奇。他们一大群人跟随我们到处走。每当我们询问价格或是讨价还价时,人群中的每个人都会对这笔交易发言。等钱递过去时,他们都盯着钱看,接着就会讨论钱的真假和币值。不过,我们很快就得出结论,那是所谓的善意的好奇心,而非无礼的表现。

——福特,1898 年,第 335 页

艾克教授逛古董店(20 世纪 20 年代) 艾克·古斯塔夫是来自德国波恩的一名哲学教授。"看到美丽的中国盘子和画,他会狂喜不已;想到中国画、书法、诗歌、哲学、学问、民政的独一无二的结合,他就会语无伦次……"

"古斯塔夫住在厦门岛内的大学附近。没有讲课或研究时,他都会去逛厦门的大街小巷,而且总会去典当铺。他的钱不多,但是他不会放过任何一个发现的宝贝。他是一个最不贪心的人,但是美丽的东西无人问津,这对他而言是不可思议的。在住着 22 万市民的街道迷宫里,他遇上了一位年老的日本商人,同时也是一个玉器和瓷器的鉴定家。在商人小小的密室里,他一饱眼福,见到了一块青瓷、一块羊脂玉杯和一个漳州的花瓶。他知道,这些东西最终都会到日本去。他偶尔也买一小件东西。买来之后会到我们家,后面跟着他的仆人。仆人抱着那件用旧棉布层层包裹的贵重之物。"

Dragon Head (Longtou) Rd., Gulangyu, 1942 J. Anderson

'Ach! [Ah!] but is it not demonisch? [2] See that springing line, that harmony, that life! and feel it, feel it!' And often he would add, 'Take it.'

'Remember Lao Tzu [老子],' we would say. '"All treasures that keep their owners awake at night should be destroyed....So as to rid man's heart of the desire for possession.' That's why I give it to you."'

Mackenzie-Grieves, 1959

Seeing with Fingers (1920s) Chen taught us more about the importance of touch, demonstrating his skill with beautiful, pale-olive hands. He had an Icelandic wife: blue-eyed, fair, massive as a Viking. They had met at Edinburgh University, where both graduated before their marriage. Their child was perfectly Chinese.

Chen had inherited from his father one of the finest collections of blue and white china in the country. In his pockets he carried broken fragments of the classic K'ang Hsi [Kangxi] period.

"I feel them," he said, "and my fingers learn more than my eyes. My fingers never betray me, but sometimes my eyes will."

Mackenzie-Grieves, 1959

Shopping—Chinese Style (1920s) There was no doubt that one had to learn technical as well as aesthetic discrimination; one was not born with it.

We were gradually learning the feel and character of blanc de chine and celadon, but gained no judgment at all in blue and white while any fake bronze would deceive us.

My Chinese women friends had taught me what to look for in embroidery: to pinch up the satin-stitched motifs which, they said, should bend smoothly and look as even as the silk itself, now showing a single loop; to look for fine tight Peking know-stitch--the aristocrat of stitchery--and to examine the twist of the threads themselves. They showed me how to discover whether chopsticks were made of genuine ivory. Putting them side by side, they would lay a bamboo sliver horizontally across a drop of water placed on the sticks. If they were ivory the sliver would immediately come alive, swing round

Hawker of Second-hand Items, 1934   J.V.

vertically and stop. On any other substance it would remain motionless. But the skill by which they could infallibly distinguish carved lacquer from veneered composition, good cloisonné from pieces lifted and reassembled on modern bronzes by Japanese craftsmen, would, I knew, never be mine. It was their inheritance, compounded of discerning sight and the miraculously sensitive touch that, for them, made the incised mahjong tiles so easy to read with finger-tips alone.

---

2   Demonisch: German for demon; he meant "supernaturally beautiful".

第二十三章 厦门购物 Amoy Shopping

"哈哈,是不是超凡脱俗地漂亮?!看看这线条,看看多和谐,多有生气,你摸一下看看,摸一下看看!"经常他都会加一句:"给你,拿着。"

这时,我们就会说:"记得老子说过:'甚爱必大费,多藏必厚亡,知足不辱,知止不殆',所以,我把它送给你了。"

——麦肯兹·格瑞芙,1959年,第37页

用手指"观看"(20世纪20年代) 陈用他淡橄榄色漂亮的双手演示他的技巧,让我更加深刻地感受到触摸的重要性。他的妻子是冰岛人:蓝眼睛,白皮肤,高如海盗。他们是在爱丁堡大学认识的。大学毕业之后两人便结婚了。他们的孩子是彻底的中国人。

陈的父亲留给他一些顶级的青花瓷器。他的衣服口袋装着康熙年间瓷器的碎片。

"我感觉得到他们,"他说,"我的手指知道的比我的眼睛多。我的手指从来也不会背叛我,但是我的眼睛有时会欺骗我。"

——麦肯兹·格瑞芙,1959年,第37、38页

中式购物(20世纪20年代) 毫无疑问,一个人必须学习掌握技术上和美学上的鉴别能力。这些能力不是与生俱来的。

我们慢慢地了解了一些德化白瓷和青瓷的手感和特性,但是还不会辨别青花瓷器,随便一个假的青铜器都能把我们给蒙了。

我的中国女性朋友教我如何鉴赏刺绣品:拧一小撮针缝缎面图案,好的刺绣品有匀称的褶,看起来像丝绸,而且有一个环形的图案;其次要有北京著名贵族刺绣的精致紧密;最后还要细细地看针线本身的扭结。她们还告诉我如何鉴别筷子是不是由真的象牙制成的。把筷子一根挨一根排好,然后水平地放上一根竹片,让它横穿过筷子上的一滴水。如果筷子是真象牙,这竹片就会立刻"活起来",突然掉转方向,变成与筷子一样的垂直方向,然后停止不动。如果筷子是其他物质做成的,竹片将保持静止不动。但是尽管她们的这些技术能万无一失地辨别雕红与镶胶,能辨别景泰蓝和日本工匠制作的现代仿青铜器,但是我知道,我永远也学不会。这是她们的遗传,包括了有见识的眼界,以及神奇而敏感的手感。她们用指尖就能轻松地识别麻将牌。

Franck, 1925

For the Birds

Our Chinese friends had taught us too the rudiments of judging jade. The women showed me how to look for transparency, texture, depth of colour and so brilliant a polish that the stone looked "dipped in water". But they themselves prized only the precious emerald jade as a jewel, while I preferred the variegated stone which lent itself so perfectly to imaginative carving. This they could not understand. It was not for personal adornment any more than the white jade, which was carved into plaques, cups, bowls or figurines, and which our collector friends told us should look greasy like mutton fat. I liked too the old, grey-green, "sea-water" jade beads which had hung as pendants from the mandarins' necklaces. These, my friends despised, but they were patiently and systematically sought by Japanese dealers, so that I never succeeded in collecting enough for a necklace.

Mackenzie-Grieves, 1959

Amoy Crafts Carved peach-stones are the most remarkable productions of native industry; they are strung together as bracelets, and are wonderful specimens of minute labour. The most highly finished cost as much as a dollar apiece. The paintings on paper for decorating the walls of Chinese houses are sometimes well executed. The designs vary, but usually represent some sort of animal. The branch of a tree with birds is a very favourite subject; sometimes figures are represented. The colouring is quiet and harmonious, and generally in good taste. The artists may be watched at work, for the shops are quite open to the street. These papers are sold in sets, and are hung round the rooms in the same way as we hang pictures.

Shore, 1881

Amoy Olive-stone Bracelets Every city in China is noted for some article of manufacture peculiarly its own; and the Amoy bracelet - formed of olive-stones exquisitely carved, is a unique ornament of rare elegance. Beautiful brooches, also, carved in pseudo sandal-wood, which is of the color of the olive-stone, are made to match the bracelets. These ornaments are much in request among the foreigners visiting Amoy, and are particularly sought after by the English, who send them home, where they are said to be highly prized.

Williams, 1864

Amoy Paper Flowers Thus, in one of my many perambulations I came to a very narrow and very dark lane, where I found the humble tenants of the houses engaged in what, to me, was quite a new industry. Men, women and children were all busily occupied in the manufacture of most beautiful artificial flowers, from a pith obtained in Formosa, from the same plant (Aralia papyriferd) as that out of which the so-called ricepaper is made. I entered shop after shop, and everywhere found thousands of flowers spread out on trays, and each one so lifelike that it might almost be mistaken for nature herself. But tiny hands were at work here too, and roses, lilies, azaleas and camellias grew up with wonderful celerity beneath them.

The workshops are the dwellings, the offices and the warehouses of each firm or family; and the workers within are so closely packed that strangers not unfrequently must watch the process, or make a purchase, by taking up a position outside. I bought a great many of these flowers from a man in a very mean shop indeed. He was extremely poor, and he asked me for an advance of money, offering to furnish security if I wished.

第二十三章　厦门购物　Amoy Shopping

我们的中国朋友还向我们传授鉴别玉器的基础知识。中国的女性朋友告诉我们该如何看透明度、质感、颜色的深度以及鲜艳的抛光，它使得玉犹如浸在水中一般。但是她们自己只视翡翠玉为宝石，而我却喜欢色彩斑驳的玉。它们非常适合雕刻出各种各样的造型，这是她们所不能理解的。最适合个人装饰的是白玉。人们把白玉雕刻成牌匾、杯子、碗和小雕像。据我们的收藏家朋友说，白玉犹如羊脂玉般光滑。我也喜欢古老的、如海水般青灰色的玉珠子，就是挂在官吏项链上的坠子。我的朋友很鄙视这些玉珠子，但是日本商人却在耐心地、有系统地收藏它们，所以我永远也收集不到一条项链所需的珠子。

——麦肯兹·格瑞芙，1959年，第154、155页

厦门的工艺品　桃核雕是当地最著名的产品。把它们串成手镯，是很典型的当地小手工业。成本价最多一美元一个。中国房子有时用纸画来装修，图样各种各样，但是一般都描绘着某种动物。鸟儿高高地站在树枝上是一个很受欢迎的主题。有时候也有描绘人的画。着色很平静和谐，很有品位。人们可以看到正在作画的艺术家，因为他们店铺的门是朝街道敞开的。这么画是以成套出售的，他们也和我们挂画一样把作品挂满房间。

——肖尔，1881年，第68页

厦门的橄榄核手镯　中国的每个城市都有自己特色的产品。由橄榄核精巧地雕刻而成的厦门手镯是无与伦比的高贵饰品。用假檀香木雕刻而成的漂亮胸针，与橄榄核有着一样的色彩，是制作来搭配手镯的。来厦门旅行的外国人对这些饰品有很大的需求量，特别是英国人。他们把这些饰品寄回英国，据说收到国人的高度赞扬。

——威廉斯，1864年　第270页

厦门的纸花　不知不觉我来到一条昏暗的窄巷。在巷子里，我发现谦逊的佃户正在忙于一种全新的产业。男人、女人和孩子们都忙着制作非常漂亮的人造花。他们用来台湾的木髓和做宣纸的同一种植物（青檀树皮）制作人造花。我走进一家又一家的店铺，到处都可以看到上千朵的纸花铺在盘子上，每一朵都栩栩如生，都会被人误以为是来自大自然的真花。灵巧的手还在不停地工作着，玫瑰、百合花、杜鹃花、山茶花迅速地从敏捷的双手中"成长"。

这些作坊既是住宅又是工场，还是各个商铺或家庭的仓库。工人们挤在里面，以至于客人常常只能在店外面观看制作过程或是购买产品。我在一个极其狭小的店铺里向一个男的买了大量的纸花。他非常贫穷，请求我要是同意就预付一点定金，以保证供货。

老外看老鼓浪屿 *Old Gulangyu in Foreigners' Eyes*

I lent him a few dollars without troubling him for securities; and though I knew nothing about him, he carried out the transaction with the most scrupulous honesty."

Thomson, 1876

Copy Cat Tailors (New Patched Pants) But they are destitute of the phrenological bump of originality, but do everything from copy, and copy exactly. A tailor cannot take a man's measure and make a garment by it, but must have a coat or pantaloons to go by. A story is told of a midshipman who ordered half a dozen pairs of pantaloons, and gave the tailor an old pair as a guide. Now, Mr. Middy was just off from a long cruise and had been "hard up" for breeches, and had patched the pattern pair with a black knee piece on blue cloth. When Snip brought the new ones, they were a "facsimile" of the old, every pair being ornamented with black knees.

Coffin, 1908

Pigtail Souvenir "Pigtails, now, they make interesting souvenirs," Captain McGregor, one of the older China Coast Masters, once told me, "but they're no appreciated at home; away back in 1911, I bought a fine one, straight from a coolie's head-made him wash it and bind it with red cord as they do, all in the price. I sent it home in a nice lacquer box an' all; but did they appreciate it? No. You'd have thought I'd sent 'em a boa-constrictor, the way they carried on." It needed travel, he said, to widen one's views.

Mackenzie-Grieves, 1959

An Amoy Gate, 1920s　　　　　　　　　　　　J. Nienhuis

第二十三章 厦门购物 Amoy Shopping

Amoy Street, 1930s   J. Nienhuis

我给了他几美元,但没有把它当作定金。我根本不认识这个男人,但是他非常诚信地完成了这笔交易。
——汤姆森,1876 年

只会模仿的裁缝（新的补片长裤） 他们缺乏创意,做什么事都是模仿,完全照抄别人的。裁缝不会量体裁衣,只会照着外套或是马裤做。一位见习船员讲了一个这样的故事。他定做了六条马裤,并给了裁缝一条旧的裤子做参考。那一天,他正好巡航回来,裤子破了,就在蓝色的裤子膝盖处打了一块黑色补丁。这条裤子后来拿去给裁缝当样裤。裁缝送来的新裤子都是旧裤子的复制品。每一条膝盖部分都有一块黑色的补丁。
——柯芬,1908 年,第 167、168 页

辫子纪念品 "辫子现在成了很有趣的纪念品,"一位经常在中国沿海行走的船长格雷戈尔先生曾经这样跟我说,"但是,在国内是没人欣赏的。早在 1911 年,我也买了一个很漂亮的辫子。那辫子是刚从一名苦力头上剪下来的。我让他洗干净,用红头绳扎住。所有费用都算在辫子的价钱里。我用一个很漂亮的漆盒装好、寄回家。但是,有人欣赏它吗?没有!你可能认为我寄给他们的是蟒蛇,正如他们想的那样。"他说,人需要旅行来拓宽视野,增长见识。
——麦肯兹·格瑞芙,1959 年,第 35 页

老外看老鼓浪屿 *Old Gulangyu in Foreigners' Eyes*

Chapter 24   Amoy Street Adventures

Amoy Street Lamps   A walk through a Chinese city is sure to be amusing and instructive, if not always agreeable. There are so many strange things to be seen, while the habits and customs of the natives are always worth a study. Their methods are primitive but ingenious, and the results attained are highly creditable when we consider the limited means at their disposal.

The municipal lamps form a conspicuous feature in certain parts of Amoy; these are quaint erections in the shape of a granite shaft surmounted by a wooden box glazed with shells. I watched the manufacture of these singular contrivances. First of all the shells are well washed and scrubbed, then cut into squares, and finally slid into grooves cut to receive them in the frame of the lamp. When finished they have a neat appearance, are light, marvellously cheap, and much used amongst the poor. The shells are very thin, and somewhat resemble mica; they are more transparent than horn, and easily replaced when broken.

Shores 1881

Downtown Amoy, 1931   J. Veldman

Navigating Amoy Streets   We soon had an inkling of the difficulties and dangers in store, for at the first turn the procession came to a dead stop, my chair at the same moment collided violently with a fish stall, nearly precipitating me into a basket of crabs, while on the other side a venerable gentleman carrying home his dinner consisting of a pork chop and tea was completely wedged in; from which it may be gathered that the streets were none too wide. Patience and perseverance will overcome most things, and by dint of shoving, squeezing, shouting and finally a pull altogether the chair was at last extricated and the order of march reformed; but our progress under such circumstances was necessarily slow and dignified, affording an inquisitive but disreputable population ample opportunities for criticism which they eagerly availed themselves of. And then our chair coolies were past their prime and not to be compared with their fleet-footed and strong-backed brethren of Hong-kong: they seemed to be suffering from rheumatism or sore shoulders, for their movements were cramped and they were always stopping to rest or change the position of the shafts. Besides the difficulty in turning corners, the chairs were constantly getting violent shocks as if they had struck a curbstone. At last I found these were caused by certain black swine which dispute the right of way with passengers in the streets of Amoy.

Shore 1881

324

第二十四章　厦门街头奇遇

厦门的路灯　徒步走过中国的城市，虽然不总是让人感到愉快，但一定是有趣且有益的，因为可以看到太多奇怪的东西。本地人的生活习惯和风俗都是值得研究的。他们的方法虽然很原始，却很有独创性。考虑到能供他们选择的方法并不多，他们的效率还是相当高的。

厦门的路灯在某些地区形成了亮丽而独特的风景。这些独一无二的建筑下面是花岗岩灯柱，顶端是镶嵌着贝壳的木制小箱。我仔细地观察一番这些惟妙惟肖的发明创造。首先所有的贝壳是洗过的，而且洗得非常干净。然后再切成方块，最后沿着灯的框架放入切槽中。灯做成之后，外表很整洁，重量很轻，价格还相当得便宜，所以很受穷人的欢迎。这些贝壳很薄，有几分像云母，比牛角更透明，而且破碎后很容易更换。

——肖尔，1881年，第63页

游览厦门街道　我们很快就预感到麻烦和危险就要降临，因为在第一个转弯处，行进的列队突然完全停止了。我的轿子猛烈地撞上了一个卖鱼的摊子，几乎快把我摔进一个虾框里。另一边一位带着晚饭（一块猪排和茶水）回家的老先生被死死地堵在里面了。由此可见，这街道一点也不宽。耐心和毅力能够战胜很多事情。通过拼命地挤、推、喊，最后再使劲地一拉，我的轿子终于解脱了。队列的秩序也恢复了。但是在这样的环境下，我们的进程必然会慢下来，而且显得很威严。这给那些好管闲事的人提供了一个他们等待已久的机会来评头论足。我们的苦力又都是过了壮年期了，跟他们的那些身体强健、健步如飞的香港同胞已经不能比了。他们似乎患了风湿病和肩周炎，因为他们的动作很慢，总是停下来休息或是调整抬杠的姿势。拐过那道转弯之后，我们的轿子好像撞上了边石，不停地剧烈震动。后来，我才知道，这是因为一群黑猪在跟行人争夺厦门街道的通行权。

——肖尔，1881年，第44、45页

Amoy, Jan. 1934　J. Veldman

Dark "Umbrella" Street J. N.

Official Procession — Dukes, 1885

The Sailor and the Mandarin (Amoy, 1700)
When a mandereen [Mandarin] of any consideration passes through a street or highway, he goes in great state, either on horseback, or in close or open chairs, carried by men, and he has flags carried before him...

Yet I heard of a comical passage that happened at Amoy, between a mandereen and an English tailor. The mandereen going in his chair with his usual retinue met a sailor coming with a keg of arrack [Asian alcoholic beverage] under his arm. Everybody went off the street but the jolly sailor, who had been tasting his arrack. He was so mannerly as to walk aside, and give the mandereen the middle of the street; but one of the retinue gave the sailor a box on the ear, and had almost shoved him down, keg and all. The sailor damned him for a son of a whore, and asked what he meant by it; and at the same time gave the aggressor a box on the ear in return. The poor seaman was soon overpowered by the retinue; but the mandereen told the linguist what had happened, and bid him ask the sailor why he gave him that affront. The sailor swore that that mandereen had affronted him, in allowing his servants to beat him, while he was walking down the streets civilly, with his keg of samshew under his arm' and swore by God that he would box the mandereen, or every one of his gang, for a Spanish dollar and with that put his hand in his pocket and pulled a dollar out.

The mandereed ordered the linguist to tell him verbatim what the sailor said, and why he pulled his money out. When the linguist had told him all, the mandereen was ready to fall off his chair with laughing. And after he had composed himself, he asked if the sailor would stand to his challenge, who swore he would. The mandereen had one Tartar in his retinue famous for boxing, who had won many prizes at it, and called for him to try his skill on the Englishman. The Tartar was a lusty man, and the sailor short, but well fit. The Tartar promised an early conquest; and to the combat they went. [The Tartar lost and...] The mandereen was so pleased with the bravery and dexterity of the seaman, that he made him a present of 10 tayels of silver.

Hamilton 1727

第二十四章　厦门街头奇遇 Amoy Street Adventures

水手与官员（厦门，1700年）　任何时候官员过街或是过路，场面都是声势浩大的。他不是骑马，就是坐在封闭或是开放的轿子里。轿子由好几个人抬着，前面是浩浩荡荡的举旗队伍。

在厦门，我还亲耳听到过一名官员和一名英国水手之间的滑稽对话。一次，官员带着随从就要坐到轿子里的时候，遇上了迎面走来的水手，手臂下还抱着一壶亚力酒（亚洲烈性酒精饮料）。除了这个一直在品酒的满心欢喜的水手，大家都躲开了。他很有礼貌地走到边上给官员让道，但是一个随从却狠狠地给他甩了一个耳光。这一耳光几乎要把他连同他的酒壶都打倒在地。水手骂那个随从是婊子养的，逼问他这一耳光是什么意思，同时回了那个随从一个耳光。很快，可怜的水手就被随从打败了。官员告诉译者事情的经过，并命令译者去盘问水手为什么要冒犯他。

水手发誓说，他手里拿着一瓶酒，规规矩矩地走在街上。是官员欺负他，还让随从打他。他还以西班牙一块钱对天发誓，他一定会暴打官员和他所有的随从。说着，就真的把手伸进口袋拿出了一块钱。

官员命令译者一字不落地告诉他水手所说的话以及为什么水手要掏钱。听完之后，官员大笑起来，差点没从轿子上跌落下来。等他平静镇定之后，官员问水手是否敢与他挑战。水手勇敢应战。官员有一名随从是鞑靼人，以拳击闻名，还曾因此获得过多次奖。官员让他在这个英国人身上试试拳击技术。那个鞑靼人很强壮，而水手虽然个子不高，但是身材很好。鞑靼人信心满满，保证这场比赛必胜。他们开始比赛了，结果鞑靼人输了……官员对水手的勇敢和机敏很满意，赏了他十两银子。

——哈密尔顿，1727年，第502页

Amoy Street Scene, 1910, by Dr. John Otte

老外看老鼓浪屿 *Old Gulangyu in Foreigners' Eyes*

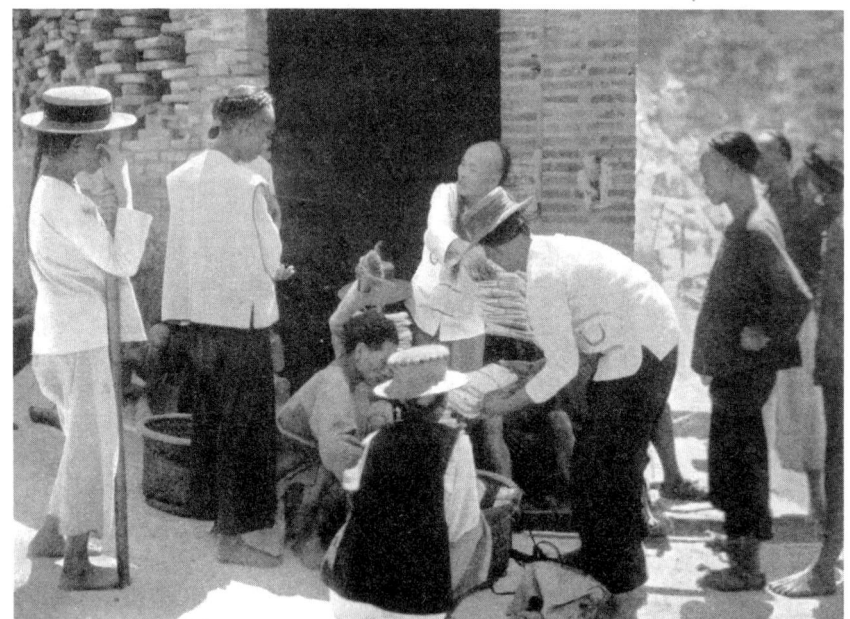

A Street Scene   MacGowan, 1907

Amoy, about 1910

第二十四章　厦门街头奇遇 *Amoy Street Adventures*

Building a New Amoy, 1931 — J. Nienhuis

"Beginnings of a new Amoy..." 1931 — J. Nienhuis

Chapter 25　Travel in Amoy

Chair Bearers　"A veteran missionary once said that the most comfortable way to travel in a Chinese cart was to pad it well with many thicknesses of quilts, put plenty of pillows at the back and sides, arrange several rugs for covering, and then—walk!"

McCasland, 2001

Tireless Chair Bearers　Traveling in the dark was not an easy matter, for we had to pick our way over narrow uneven pathways, and across broken dilapidated bridges, and over stepping-stones in a mountain brook, till finally, worn out and wearied to death, we stumbled down the dark street that led to our home, and there I threw myself into the first chair I could find, utterly exhausted by a journey that few men would undertake even in the coldest days in winter.

The chair-bearers, after a few whiffs at their bamboo pipes, started to light the furnace and cook their supper. All the weariness they had shown during the last hour or two seemed to have vanished, and they laughed and chatted about the incidents on the road and the funny sights they had seen. One chopped the wood, whilst the other washed the rice and poured it into the cauldron, and prepared the vegetables they were to eat with it.

No one looking in casually upon the scene and listening to the merry voices and to the animated conversation of these men would ever have dreamed that they had traveled fully fifty miles, carrying two hundred pounds' weight upon their shoulders, through the blazing heat of an Eastern summer day.

In one's dealing with the Chinese one is continually being reminded of the strain of dogged inflexibility that runs throughout the character of nearly every individual that one comes in contact with. It is not simply occasional instances that one runs up against. It is in the race, and there is no doubt but that it is this force that has given it such a strength that it has been able to stand the wear and tear of ages and to be as strong physically as it was a thousand years ago.

Macgowan, 1907

From Amoy to Anxi, 1924　　　　　　　　J. Nienhuis

第二十五章　行走厦门

马车夫　"一位老传教士曾经说过，乘坐中国的马车旅行最舒服的方式是在马车上铺上厚厚的被子，在背后和两侧放满枕头，再放上几张遮盖的毯子，然后出发！"

——麦卡斯兰德，2001年，第18页

不知疲倦的轿夫　在黑暗中旅行并不是一件容易的事，因为我们行走在狭窄的、坑坑洼洼的小路上，要穿过破旧不堪的废弃的桥梁，要跳过山间小溪的踏脚石，直到最后，我们都筋疲力尽，累得死去活来。我们跌跌撞撞走在昏暗的回家路上。一回到家，我就瘫坐在碰到的第一张椅子上。即使是在大冬天这样旅行，世上也没有几人会去，实在是太疲劳了。

几袋旱烟过后，轿夫开始煮饭。他们在刚刚过去的一两个小时里所流露出来的疲惫似乎都烟消云散了。他们有说有笑地谈论着路上发生的事和他们沿途看到的有趣的风景。他们一个劈柴，一个把洗净的米倒入锅中，同时准备着晚上要吃的蔬菜。

无意间看到这样的情景，听到这么欢快的声音和这么热烈的对话，人们无法想象他们已经走了整整50英里的路。他们肩上扛着两百多英镑的重量，行走在炎炎烈日的东方夏日里。

Amoy, 1931　　J. Nienhuis

和中国人的交往接触常常让人想起他们不屈不挠的血统，这是我所有接触过的中国人所共有的品质。这不是一种偶然，而是深深地扎根于民族的一种力量。毫无疑问，正是由于这股强大力量，使得他们不畏艰辛历经沧桑岁月，依然与一千多年前的祖先一样强健。

——麦嘉湖，1907年，第118页

Bus Schedules (1940s)   I had already made enquiries about the time of departure of the local bus to Longyen. Not that the official timetable was accurate, but it merely gave a general hint which was open to any interpretation. It was up to the passengers to make their final decision.

'Depart at daybreak,' said one.

'After the driver has had his breakfast,' said another.

'When he has had a bath,' suggested a third.

There was little point in wasting nervous energy about insisting on or worrying about correct times of departure. None of the other prospective passengers seemed the least concerned about such trivialities and as long as the journey was started in the morning and completed in the afternoon, there could be no complaint about having to waste time in waiting around.

In this respect rural Chinese are no different from country folk in other lands, and view with equal displeasure and amazement the complications of a modern railway guide.

…It was different in the bigger cities where life was organized to a high-pitched tempo, and the repetitive impact of the cinema, radios, automobiles, organized parties and tram timetables had sapped the mind of its natural resourcefulness and contentment. But here in the countryside, in what was still the real and true Chinese background, people were able to be satisfied with simple earthly pleasures and sit about waiting for buses to depart, talking and chattering and meditating, quite oblivious to the passage of time which was being killed only to the extent of a pull from a cigarette or a sip of almond tea or plum juice.

The driver of our bus suddenly appeared…

Amoy Bus, 1924   J. Nienhuis

第二十五章　行走厦门　Travel in Amoy

公共汽车时刻表（20世纪40年代）　我询问了从厦门开往龙岩的汽车的发车时间。不是官方的时刻表不准确，而是它只给了一个大概的时间。人人都可以有不同的理解，由乘客最终决定发车时间。

"天亮就出发吧。"一个人说道。

"还是等司机吃过早饭再走吧。"另外一个人嚷嚷着。

"我看还是等他晨浴后。"第三个人建议。

浪费宝贵的精力去坚持一定要它准时发车，或者是担心它会误点都是无济于事和毫无意义的。其他的乘客似乎一点也不在乎这些琐事，只要这车上午能够出发，下午能够到达就可以了。因此，没有人抱怨浪费大把大把的时间等车。

在这点上，中国的乡下人无异于其他国家的乡下人。他们对现代铁路管理部门的复杂性都是投以不满和惊愕的眼神。

然而，大城市的情况就大不相同了。大城市里的生活节奏很快，城市里影院、收音机、汽车、聚会以及电车的时刻表的不断冲击使得人们慢慢地动摇了自然资源丰富的想法。但是在真实的中国乡下，人们因一些简单的快乐而满足，他们或闲谈或默默地沉思，等待着汽车的启动。对于他们来说，这等待的时间在一根烟的功夫或是一杯杏仁茶一杯酸梅汁中也就消逝了。

我们的司机突然出现了……

Mountain Village, 1923　J. Nienhuis

Off to the Countryside, 1924　J. Nienhuis

333

老外看老鼓浪屿 *Old Gulangyu in Foreigners' Eyes*

...A surge of humanity made its way towards the opening. The quiet groups if impassive people who until now had been waiting with such commendable patience seemed to swell out into a yelling, screaming and scrambling mob, each jostling and pushing to secure the best seats in the square body of the bus, which had been built on top of its chassis. It was a strange vehicles, consisting of a tired-looking worn-out box structure in which the hard benches were arranged, not to provide for the passengers comfort so much as to absorb the maximum amount of humanity. Panting and scrambling and shaken from my high flown thoughts about the contemplative and quiet temperament of old China, I realized that this was only another facet to the Chinese character, the struggle for existence.

No holds were barred in the fighting, wedging and pushing of men, women and children, laden with baskets of clothing, bedding and livestock, to secure a seat. There was no question of anyone being left behind. Those who did not secure a seat, would pack themselves down the corridor until literally arms, legs and other parts of the body It was at this fateful moment that I remembered that I had left a shirt in the lodging-house, but even if I had now decided to withdraw from the fray, the pressure from behind was already too great to permit of any egress, and, what was more important, I could see that I was going to be one of the lucky passengers. A vacant seat was in view and with a considerable sense of satisfaction, I claimed my prize.

Neil, 1956

Carsickness (1940s) The sharp turns in the road and the violent swaying of the superstructure produced cases of sickness among several women passengers overcome by the motion and the heat. The onset was easily anticipated by a changing colour of the face which rapidly turned from a pleasant brownish yellow to a greenish hue. The unfortunates groaned and moaned piteously for several minutes with their heads down between their knees, and then sitting upright, preserved a rigid countenance; but again some of them without warning issued a violent and involuntary jet in any direction.

Neil, 1956

Well Loaded!   MacGowan, 1897

第二十五章　行走厦门　Travel in Amoy

……人群涌向车门。那群人虽说有点冷漠但还算安静。他们极其耐心地等到现在。顷刻之间，他们似乎就变成了一群大喊大叫、混乱的暴徒。他们横冲直撞试图抢到方形车上最舒服的位置。这是一辆奇怪的车辆：箱子状的车身破旧不堪，里面放着硬梆梆的椅子，不是为了给乘客提供舒适而是最大限度地亵渎了人道主义。喘气声、争夺声冲淡了在我脑海中闪过的旧中国那种沉默和平静的气质。我意识到，这只是中国人性格当中的另外一面——生存竞争。

提着大包小包衣服、被褥，带着牲畜的男人、女人、孩子们为了能够抢到位置，吵着，挤着，推着。没有人出来控制下这个局面，也没有人愿意落在后头。没有抢到位置的人紧紧地挤在狭窄的过道里直到手臂、腿和其他的身体部位被迫伸进这木箱子的各个缝隙和角落里。

就在这个重要的时刻，我突然想起了自己落在出租房里的衬衫。不过，即使我现在决定退出这场"战争"，也已经不允许了。后面巨大的推力使得我无法回头找出口。更重要的是，我知道我将成为一名幸运的乘客。一个空的座位映入我的眼帘，我无比满足地接受了我的战利品。

——尼尔，1956年，第46～49页

晕车（20世纪40年代）　路上的急转弯和车身的剧烈摇晃使得几个饱受颠簸和热气折磨的女乘客开始晕车。晕车的发作很容易通过脸色来觉察的，由自然的黄褐色迅速变化成青色。那些不幸的人头耷拉在膝盖之间，凄惨地呻吟几分钟之后坐直了，脸色带着很僵硬的表情，但是很快地，她们又毫无征兆地向四面八方呕吐。

——尼尔，1956年，第52页

Edna Beekman, 1934 (in Amoy from 1914-1951) J. Nienhuis

老外看老鼓浪屿 Old Gulangyu in Foreigners' Eyes

Country Roads, 1922   J. Neinhuis

Train, Feb. 1934   J. Veldman

Traveling Shoes! (1940s) "Four weeks after arrival, Mr. Poppen asked me to accompany him on one of his evangelistic tours into the country to visit the churches and mission stations in the district assigned to his supervision. Sincere there were no roads on which we could use vehicles, it was a journey on foot. It was a journey of some twenty days, traveling some 300 miles, and living on Chinese food, and spending the nights in rooms provided by the church or mission stations. We carried a small amount of food in one of our luggage baskets, and our required clothing in another basket. Each of us had two baskets weighing not over sixty pounds. These burdens were to be carried by Chinese coolies, called burden-bearers. These men traveled with us from village to village. At times we traveled as much as twenty miles per day, over hills and down into the valleys and up again to the hills. The roads were mostly two or three feet wide paths. The climbing of the hills was made easier by having granite steps placed firmly on the paths. These steps were adjusted in height and distance to the size of the Chinese. They were mostly 5 feet 2 inches or 5 feet 3 inches; we were both six feet tall. This made hill climbing and going down not too easy for us.

"Another thing I learned on this first trip was that my strong American walking shoes were no match for the Chinese grass sandals. My shoes were new when we began our trip. When we ended, the shoes were not worth repairing. My next trips were to be made in grass sandals. I had to have some extra large ones made. The price per pair of sandals was about 30 Chinese pennies. A pair of sandals would give me a minimum of 600 miles. When walking in sandals, it was easy to stop by a stream and cool one's feet and feel refreshed. I never traveled there again wearing shoes."

Beltman, 1984

Railroads (1930s)   The only Railroad in our section is a little narrow gage one 15 miles in length constructed by the Standard Oil Co.

Rose Talman Memoirs

第二十五章　行走厦门　Travel in Amoy

旅行用鞋（20 世纪 40 年代）　到达四周之后，波本先生要我和他一起去这区域内由他管理的乡下教堂和福音站去传播福音。由于路都还没有通车，所以我们只好步行。这次旅程持续了 20 天。期间，我们步行 300 英里，吃中国食物，并在教堂和福音站提供的房间里度过了一个又一个的夜晚。我们把带来的少许食物，放在我们的一个行李箱里，必需的衣服则放在另一个行李箱里。我们两个人各有两个最多六十英镑的箱子。这些重物都由中国苦力，也就是挑夫帮我们背着。他们和我们一起走过了一村又一村。有时，我们跋山涉水，一天要行走二十多英里。我们走的大多都是两三英尺宽的小路。铺有花岗石台阶的山路爬起来会轻松很多。但遗憾的是这些台阶的高度和间距是专为中国人设计的。他们的身高大多在 5.2 英尺到 5.3 英尺间，而我们两个都是 6 英尺高。因此，上山、下山我们都走得很艰难。

All Aboard! 1931　J.N.

这首次旅程还让我意识到另外一点，我那耐穿的美国徒步鞋根本没有办法与中国的草鞋相比。我们开始这次旅程时我的鞋还是崭新的，可是当旅程结束时那双鞋已经破烂不堪，不值得一补了。下一次旅程我将穿着草鞋，所以定制了几双特大号的。每双草鞋的价格大概是三块钱。一双草鞋至少能走 600 英里。穿着草鞋旅行可以很容易在路途中的小溪边停下，洗洗脚，凉快凉快。我再也不穿鞋子旅行了。

——贝特曼，1984 年，第 67、68 页

铁路（20 世纪 30 年代）　我们这边唯一的铁路是由美孚石油公司修建的长 15 英里的小窄轨。

——罗斯·塔尔曼未出版的回忆录

Village Train Stop, 1934　J. Veldman

老外看老鼓浪屿 Old Gulangyu in Foreigners' Eyes

Going Upriver, 1922　　　J. Nienhuis

Amoy Boat Excursion (1855) There were many other boats on the water, some going in one direction, some in another; and as we sailed through the fine harbour, we saw vessels of all kinds, from the British 'brig-of-war' to the clumsy junks, with their shapeless and unwieldy hulks, and boats from all the towns and villages around Amoy. Each district having a form of its own, we could tell the place from which they came, and form an opinion of the cargo of each, by knowing the commodity for which the district is famous. There were large junks with spices from Singapore, and others with the hardy production of the north. Those long boats, covered with mats, are from Chiang-Choo [Zhangzhou], laden with silks or sugar; and those with cabins, bring fruit, and vegetables, and rice from Pechuia [Baishui], or Chioh-bey [Jimei]. But we have not time to notice all; we can only glance at the hundreds as we pass and admire the busy appearance of the whole, and the gay colours of their flags, of every shape and hue. The wind was against us, but as it cooled the air, and the tide favoured us, we did not mind. Everything looked beautiful and cheerful; and as we glided on, passing many a boat more gaily painted than ours, but not so good at sailing, all seemed in good spirits, and the boatmen, who were all Christians, began to sing their Chinese hymns, in which we all heartily joined.

After a few hours' sailing, we anchored at the month of the river, and left the boat to come up at full tide; while the evangelists and I went on to visit one or two of the villages.

You cannot well understand the effect the first arrival of a foreigner in one of the towns of China produces. The excitement caused by a Lord Mayor's show in London, or the arrival of a menagerie in a country town in England, is nothing to it; and as the oldest inhabitants of this district had never seen or even heard of a foreigner being in these parts, the whole population was in commotion. As I passed along the road, the labourers in the field stood still and stared, and those who had the presence of mind shouted to their companions in the adjoining field to come and look, while some of the boys ran before to bear the news to the village, and, on reaching it, I found that every house had turned out its occupants; old and young were standing ready to receive our company; every kind of occupation and amusement was at an end, and had been relinquished so suddenly, that everything stood where it just happened to be when the strange news arrived. The blacksmith had left the red-hot iron to cool on the anvil, the shoemakers awl was sticking in the old shoe he was patching, old matrons had risen up from the spinning wheel, and boys had scarcely time to snatch up the toys they were playing with, even the beggar stood with the rice bowl in his hand, asking no alms. And it was long before any of them returned to their occupations; it was an idle time to the old, and a holiday to the young.

Barbour 1855

第二十五章　行走厦门　Travel in Amoy

厦门乘船游览(1855年)　水上漂着形状各异的船只。他们有些逆流而上，有些则顺流而下。当我们驶过港口时，我们目睹了形形色色的轮船，有英国战时的双桅横帆船，有笨重而难看的小型帆船，还有厦门周边小镇小村庄来的小船。

每个地方的船都有自己的特色。我们能从船的外形判断出他们来自哪个地方，还能根据每个地方的特产，判断出船上的货物。有些大帆船装载的是新加坡来的香料，另外一些则是装了北方来的耐寒农产品。那些用垫子盖着的长船来自漳州，里面装满了丝绸和糖，而有船舱的那些则从白水和集美运来水果、蔬菜和大米。但是我们没有时间观察所有的船只。我们只能在上百艘船驶过的时候匆匆地看上几眼，并叹赏那一片繁忙的景象和那色彩斑斓形状各异的旗帜。风阻挡了我们前进的道路，但它给我们带来了凉爽的空气。我们是顺流而下，所以我们并不在意。一切都很美好、愉快的。我们的船继续往前驶，驶过一条又一条比我们色彩更华丽的船，但是中看不中用。两只船都精神抖擞努力往前行。船上的船夫们都是基督教徒，开始唱起了他们的中国歌曲。我们也积极地参与到其中，其乐融融。

航行数个小时之后，我们的船在河的入口处下锚，等待涨潮时继续逆流而上。我和传道士一起去走访一、两个村庄。

你根本无法很好理解在中国一个小镇里第一个外国人到来所产生的巨大反响。市长大人走访伦敦，野兽出现在英格兰村镇所带来的影响远远不如它的大，因为这个地方最年长的居民大半辈子从未见过、甚至从未听说过外国人。整个村庄的人们都骚动了。在路上走的时候，地里干活的农民一动不动地站着注视我

Tracking Upriver, Spring 1932　　J. Nienhuis

们，缓过神来的还大声喊来在附近地里干活的农民一起围观。一些男孩跑在我们前面迫不及待告诉村民们这个消息。我们进村的时候，每家每户，无论年长，还是年幼都倾巢而出，迎接我们。奇怪的消息传来，他们停下手中的工作和娱乐。铁匠把烧得红通通的铁块凉在铁砧上，鞋匠把锥子穿在自己刚刚修补的旧鞋上，老妇女从手纺车旁起身，小男孩还没来得及抓住自己正玩着的玩具，甚至连手捧饭碗的乞丐也站在那里，忘记了乞讨。过了很久，他们才开始继续干活。这对于成年人是空闲时间，对于小孩则是个短暂的假期。

——巴博，1855年，第64～66页

老外看老鼓浪屿 *Old Gulangyu in Foreigners' Eyes*

Roundhouse Trip (1890s)   We walked for the first hour of our trip, and did so enjoy it—such fresh country air and real highland scenery— rivers, and burns, and rocks, and high hills hemming us in—and such lovely fern-fronds at every turn. We had about two hours of chair-ride after our walk, and had some experience of fording rivers. Twice the water was so deep as to be above the men's knees, and nearly touched the bottom of our chairs. In one place we saw some men fishing from a raft of long slender logs. It seemed to act as ferry-boat as well, as I saw some men waiting to cross on it with burdens. For the most part, however, we were alone; not even a hamlet in sight.

In a Roundhouse   This place we have reached is so strange. The village is really one huge round tower—a blank wall to the outside, with tiny slit-like prison windows and a small entrance-gate. The church is built outside, but we went in to visit some Christians, and saw the interior. Just inside the thick stone wall, and lining its lower portion, is a row of wooden stalls, where many of the inhabitants live. Another strong stone tower, just like the outer one, rises within the stalls and towers above them. We step inside, and find ourselves in a large stone-paved court, open to the sky. It is, of course, circular, and a raised pavement runs round it. Doors open into rooms the thickness of the wall—dark, gloomy-looking places; but here the people live like one large family. We just sat and watched as the women sat at the doors, one picking a goose, another smoking, another nursing her baby, and so on. In one corner was a loom, in another the stone mill for husking rice. Piles of brushwood for fuel were collected in a third corner, and in a fourth was a place where the rubbish of ages seemed stowed away. One of the girls took us upstairs to the second floor, also a ring of dwelling-houses. Another and broader flight of steps led to a third landing, where old chairs, bins of rice, etc., were kept; and one more climb led up to the attic, round which were stored the ancestral tablets and idols of the population ! Nicely out of the way! It was so strange to look down over the railing on one hand into the round court, with its busy groups of people, pigs, and hens, and on the other side to peer through the narrow windows in the thick masonry of the wall, at the natural rampart of mountains, and rivers beyond.

Touring Amoy Countryside, 1924   J. Nienhuis

第二十五章　行走厦门 Travel in Amoy

土楼之旅（19世纪90年代）　第一个小时的旅程，我们用步行，非常享受乡村新鲜的空气：真正的高山景色，河流、小溪、岩石，还有突起的小山包围着我们，处处都可以见到可爱的蕨类植物。之后，我们坐了两个小时的轿子。我们还淌过了几条河流，有两次河水都很深，没过了轿夫的膝盖，几乎要碰到轿子的底部。在一个地方，我们还看见一些男士坐在长长的木筏上钓鱼。这些木筏似乎也可以当做轮渡使用，因为我看到好些人在等待它来载他们和物品过河。然而，在旅途中更多时间我们是独行的，连一个小村庄也没看到。

关于土楼的描述　我们抵达的这个地方很奇怪。整个村庄就是一个巨大的圆塔，外面看来就是一堵空白的外墙，墙上有一些小得就像裂缝似的监狱窗户和一扇小门。教堂建在圆塔形的土楼外，但是有些基督教徒住在土楼里。因此，我们去拜访他们的时候有幸看到了它的内部。就在这厚厚的石头墙里面，在低处是住着很多居民的一排木屋。木屋里，我们看到了和外面一样的石塔。我们一进去，就看到了由大块石头铺成的露天庭院。庭院当然也是圆的，四周人行道上都有雕刻。打开门就可以走进厚厚的墙中的阴暗房间，但这儿住的人们好像是一个大家庭的人。我们坐下来就看到妇女们都坐在门槛上，有一个在抓鹅，有一个在抽烟，还有一个在照顾小孩。一个角落里放着一台织布机，另一个角落放的是碾米的石磨。一堆柴火则占满了第三个角落而第四个角落收藏的则是岁月遗留下来的垃圾。一个女孩带我们上二楼，也是一圈的住房。上了一段较宽的楼梯，我们爬到了第三层。到处放着旧椅子和米柜。再往上爬就是阁楼了，存放的是祖先的牌匾和神像。非常不寻常！一边从栏杆上往下看到圆形的庭院里忙碌的人们，猪，还有鸡，另外一边则可以从厚厚砖墙的小小窗户里窥视远处的高山——天然的城墙和河流，真是别样的感觉。

Inside Hakka Round House, 1922　J. Nienhuis

While we were talking to a woman, a man came in and examined us most thoroughly, saying finally: "What good fortune I have met with to-day to have seen these foreigners!"

We had a long talk with sonic old schoolgirls, and saw all the women church members in the place, then went home to supper. Looking up, we saw door and window packed with human heads—men's heads—watching us. They were strangers, had never seen the like of us before, and nothing would satisfy them but that we should go down and 'talk some doctrine.' They were most polite and attentive, listened for a long time, and went away praising the teaching.

The people are always pleased when we talk a little to them. I was amused to hear one of my chair-bearers—a heathen—speaking about us at a place where we rested. A man asked as usual, "Are they men or women?" "Women," "Can they speak our words?" "Oh yes! thoroughly well." "Can they read?" " Read! they read our words and their own words easily, and they read a great deal." "Are they married?" "No, they are ko-nius. They go about everywhere exhorting men to do right."

Johnston, 1907

Hike to Anxi Jan 19th, 1919—hot spell—90° in shade, 95° in the sun. Lyman & Frank Eckerson on a trip into An-khoe (Anxi) Mts, ... F.E. rode his pony. With a severed nerve in his leg where shot by a bandit, he has trouble in walking & much pain. He rode until met by a mountain chair and carriers—these we send for. They are stronger & are reliable men. Our local carriers are mostly opium smokers. Lyman walked 6 hour, 17+ miles the shorter way, 18+ miles the longer way. Our coolie brought back F.E.'s pony, of which he is caretaker. Lyman being of fair skin burns easily even though protected by a cork-sun hat and dark glasses.

Rose Talman Memoirs

Roadside Inn, 1924 — J.Nienhuis

第二十五章　行走厦门　Travel in Amoy

就在我们和一名妇女交谈时，一个男子进来了。他仔细地打量着我们，最后说："能见到这么多外国人，我今天真是走大运了！"

我们和一些年长的女信众聊了很久，并在那里见过了教堂里所有的女信徒。之后，就回家吃晚饭。我们无意间抬头一看，发现门窗塞满了男人的脑袋，一双双眼睛正在注视着我们。他们都是陌生人，从未见过我们这样的人。除非我们下去给他们讲道，不然他们是不会善罢甘休的。他们非常有礼貌也很专注地听了许久，之后就散开赞美我们的讲道了。

他们总是很开心我们能和他们说些话。在我们休息处，我听到一个异教徒轿夫的谈话后被逗笑了。一个男人一本正经地问，"她们是男的还是女的？""女的，""她们会说我们的话吗？""当然会！说得非常棒。""她们会看书吗？""会啊！我们的文字和她们自己的文字她们都会看，而且她们会看很多。""她们结婚了吗？""没有，她们是太监。她们到处去告诫男士不要误入歧途。"

——约翰斯顿，1907 年，第 52～56 页

徒步去安溪　1919 年 1 月 19 日，大热天，阴凉处 90 华氏度，太阳下 95 华氏度。莱曼和法兰克·爱克森在去安溪的途中。法兰克·爱克森骑着他的小马。由于脚上有一根神经中了土匪的枪，法兰克走路困难而且感到剧痛。他一直骑着马直到我们请来轿子和轿夫。他们很强壮，而且很可靠。我们在当地请的轿夫多数人会抽鸦片。莱曼走了 6 个小时，最少有 17 英里，最多 18 英里。我们的苦力带回了法兰克的小马，并很细心地照料它。尽管戴上了遮阳帽和太阳镜，莱曼白皙的皮肤还是很容易晒伤。

——罗斯·塔尔曼未出版的回忆录

Chairmen on Rural Plank Bridge, 1922　J.Nienhuis
("Chairman on the board")

老外看老鼓浪屿 Old Gulangyu in Foreigners' Eyes

Plank Bridge, 1924 J. Nienhuis

Hope Moncrieff, Yongchun Band, 1948

Country Stroll, Spring 1931 J. Nienhuis

第二十五章　行走厦门 *Travel in Amoy*

Memorial Arch, Quanzhou Brown, 1907

Fuqing Pagoda, Spring 1932 J.N.

Quanzhou Pagodas Brown, 1907

Fuzhou Bridge, Summer, 1931 J. Nienhuis

老外看老鼓浪屿 *Old Gulangyu in Foreigners' Eyes*

Kushan Temple, 1924

J. Nienhuis

"Fujian = 8 Parts Mountain,
1 Part Water, 1 Part Fields"
Jean Nienhuis, 1927

Fuzhou Kushan Temple, Summer 1931

第二十五章　行走厦门 *Travel in Amoy*

Kushan Temple, 1924 — J. Nienhuis

Yongchun, 1933 — J. Nienhuis

老外看老鼓浪屿 *Old Gulangyu in Foreigners' Eyes*

Chapter 26　Western Sports in Amoy

"But the crowning sport with which the name of Amoy is associated is the pursuit of that king of the jungle, the wily tiger…" (See Amoy Animals chapter)

Bruce, 1897

Amoy Sports Amoy boasts a fair race course which has been constructed on the small plain extending from the beach to the outer harbour to the hills upon which the city is situated. Races are held here annually towards the close of the year. In other respects Amoy is badly off for places of recreation. The chief amusement is boating [1], for which the port is celebrated. Boats of a first class description as whalers, gigs, and wherries are built here by the natives after foreign models and an Amoy boat will favourably compare with many turned out of our own dockyards at home. An annual regatta is held in the spring.

Mayers & Dennys, 1867

19th Century Amoy Tennis Another conspicuous feature on the island is the public lawn, where most of the outdoor recreations of certain sections of the community are carried on. Here, every afternoon when the weather is fine, the ladies and gentlemen gather for amusement. Tennis is the great institution of the place, and it is played with unfailing enthusiasm for fully nine months in the year. The practice thus obtained has developed some very fine players, who would stand high if they were placed in competition with some of the best players in the homeland. The one advantage of this game is that it can be played in the very hottest days of summer, when walking would be a burden and any other active exercise intolerable. It is a fact, that however languid one may feel after a day of intense heat, and though the thermometer may still show 90 degrees in the shade, the moment the players confront each other the feeling of weariness vanishes and the intense heat is forgotten.

Tennis Match, 1920s　　　　J.Nienhuis

MacGowan, 1897

1　See "Amoy People" chapter for boat race between British and Chinese.

348 ▶

第二十六章 西式运动在厦门

"不过,与厦门相关的顶级运动项目是追捕丛林之王——狡猾的老虎……"(详见《厦门动物》章节)

——布鲁斯,1897年

厦门的体育运动 厦门拥有一个非常不错的跑马场。跑马场建在一个小平原上,从海滩一直延伸到外港以及城镇所坐落的小山岗。每年临近年关都有赛马。从其他方面来看,厦门并不是一个休闲的好地方。主要的娱乐活动是赛船,这个港口因此而著名。诸如捕鲸船、赛艇和浅水客货船都是由当地人按照国外的模型在厦门制造的。与我们国内自己造船厂生产的许多船只相比,厦门生产的船只更有优势。每年春季,这里都要举办一场龙舟赛。

——梅尔斯和丹尼斯,1867年,第255页

19世纪的厦门网球 岛上另一个显著的特征是公共草地。某些社区的大多数户外运动都在公共草地上举行。每天下午,只要天气晴朗,男男女女都会聚集在这里开展文娱活动。网球是这个地方最为人所熟悉的重要项目,一年九个月,人们乐此不疲。这样发展起来的项目培养了一些很优秀的选手。与国内最优秀的选手比赛,他们会取得好名次。这项运动的一个优点是,你可以在夏季最酷热的日子里进行,因为这个时候走路已经是一种负担,其他激烈运动简直令人无法忍受。实际上,在一天的酷热之后,无论你会感到怎样的懒散,尽管阴凉处的温度还在华氏90度以上,选手之间的对抗一开始,疲惫的感觉消失了,酷热也被抛到九霄云外了。

——麦嘉湖,1897年,第149、150页

The Boot Children Prepare for Tennis on Gulangyu, 1920s

老外看老鼓浪屿 Old Gulangyu in Foreigners' Eyes

BOAT RACES IN THE INNER HARBOUR OF AMOY.

第二十六章 西式运动在厦门 *Western Sports in Amoy*

351

老外看老鼓浪屿 Old Gulangyu in Foreigners' Eyes

Cricket & Homesickness During the winter months the play on this lawn is varied by hockey, and football, and cricket. The last named still holds its own as the prime favourite with many of the gentlemen, and is a source of attraction to the whole community...This enthusiasm is a tribute to the game itself, but it is also a powerful witness to the strong feeling that exists in every heart for the homeland, and which the long distance from it only tends to deepen and accentuate. There is nothing that shows more distinctly how strong are the ties that bind men to their absent friends and relatives than the keenness with which anything that recalls them to their memories is appreciated. Home flowers, for example, are reared from seed and cultivated with the most loving care, whilst rare flowers, that would send people in England into raptures, are looked upon with interest, it is true, but not with the tenderness and affection that are lavished upon the more homely plants.

Macgowan, 1897

Foreign Monkey Goes Swimming (1940s) Swimming in summer and basket ball in winter were the main sources of exercise and recreation among the younger folk who took part in sport. It was only after the Japanese war that girls in any number in Amoy were to be seen exposing themselves in swimsuits on the lovely beaches of Kulangsu, to the great confusion of their elders. In the eyes of some, the display of a female figure, even in a single-piece bathing costume, was an affront to virtue and the acme of immodesty. But modern ideas were catching, and during my second year in Amoy the number of people wearing gaudy two-piece suits and trunks bought in Hong Kong had ostensibly increased. In fairness to the upholders of old-fashioned modesty, it must be conceded that what was apposite to Waikiki beach did not altogether blend with the accepted standards of a Chinese landscape.

Swimming in Amoy, 1920s J.N.

Some of the beaches were more crowded than others, and it was usual for the handful of self-conscious foreigners in Kulangsu to congregate in a secluded private bay. But bathing on the mere open crowded stretches with the rough and tumble of local life was not without its amusing and humorous side; nor indeed without its physical dangers.

"A foreigner bathing!" shouted a group of splashing ruffians in Hokkien, who had never seen me before.

"Doesn't he look just like a monkey?" yelled someone amid a roar of laughter. "So much hair on his chest!"

"Why doesn't he pluck it out?"

"Let's see if we can!"

"Now look here," I said swimming up to them, and snarling my teeth with carefully measured words, "not only do I look like a money, but I also bite like one." That was the end of that.

第二十六章　西式运动在厦门 Western Sports in Amoy

板球和思乡病　冬季那几个月，草地上的运动就变成了曲棍球、足球和板球。最后一项运动是男士最喜欢的，也是整个社区吸引力的源泉…… 这种热情本身就是对板球运动的一种赞颂，同时也有力地见证了每个人心中对家乡保留的那种深厚的情感。这种情感距故乡越远就越加浓重、明显。连接游子和亲朋好友的纽带与任何能给他们带来回忆的激情相比，后者显得更加的明显与强烈。比如说，家乡的花从种子开始培育，然后用最深情的爱来照顾。那些会令英国人陷入极度欢喜的珍稀花卉，只是随兴趣来照管，绝对不会像对家乡的花那样慷慨地投入情感和热爱。这就是实情。

——麦嘉湖，1897 年，第 150、151 页

外国猴子去游泳（20 世纪 40 年代）　对于参与运动锻炼的年轻人来说，夏天游泳、冬天打篮球是主要的运动和娱乐项目。抗战爆发后，人们开始看到不少年轻女性穿着泳衣，在鼓浪屿美丽的沙滩上暴露自己的身躯。这让她们的长者感到非常困惑。在一些老人的眼里，展示女性的身材，哪怕穿着单件泳装，也是对道德的冒犯，无礼之极。不过，现代思想开始广泛传播。我到厦门的第二年，穿两件套装和游泳裤的人数明显增加。泳装都是从香港买来的，很艳丽。为了公平对待老派的礼教支持者，必须承认，适合怀基基海滩的东西并不与中国人所能接受的情景完全混在一起。

有一些海滩比别的更拥挤。鼓浪屿岛上一小撮自我意识比较明显的外国人通常都会聚集在一个比较隐蔽的私家海湾。不过，在完全开放、拥挤的海域里让当地人窥视也不是完全没有乐趣和幽默的地方，同时还有身体方面的危险性。

Roger, Gwen, Mary Louise (Voskuil) and Ruth Koeppe
Koeppes were in Amoy from 1919-1951

"外国人在游泳！"福建一群在水中嬉戏的家伙高声叫喊。她们以前没见过我。

"他长得不像一只猴子吗？"爆笑中，有人喊道，"他胸部毛好多！"

"为什么他不拔掉？"

"看看我们是否能够帮他拔！"

"你们看着，"我一边说，一边游近他们。我龇牙咧嘴地对他们厉声说，每个词都精挑细选，"我不仅看上去像一只猴子，咬人也像一只猴子。"故事到此结束。

——尼尔，1956 年，第 78～79 页

老外看老鼓浪屿 Old Gulangyu in Foreigners' Eyes

A FOURSOME AT AMOY
BY SURGEON T. T. JEANS, R.N.
(Written about an 1887 Gulangyu Golf Game)

Rock Climbing on Gulangyu   In the centre of the island is a singular mass of granite protruding upwards to a height of some 200 feet in the form of immense rounded blocks. Several foreigners have attempted to scale this almost inaccessible knoll, but of one only is the success recorded—a commander in H.M. Naby.

Mayers and Dennys, 1867

The news of the match quickly spread through the [Hong Kong] Club, and the fact that any strangers should be confident of beating the Amoy fellows on their own links seemed to afford considerable amusement... After the race week we took one of Jardine's steamers for Amoy. Hardly had the Customs people boarded us before Rusby bounced on board and took us to Kulung-su [Gulangyu] Island-the foreign settlement.

...As we were climbing a steep incline covered with stubbly grass and strewn with boulders, I saw Calderson throw down his bag of clubs and take a look round. "What's the matter-done up [finished?] already?" I asked him jokingly. "No," he answered, diffidently, "only we've got there." "Got there!" I exclaimed; "got where?" But it was unnecessary to ask, for he was already kneeling down and scraping a little dry sand into a heap and trying to make a tee. I looked round, and dotted in among huge boulders-planked down among innumerable concrete native graves-were several familiar red flags hanging limply in the morning calm. There was not a space of clear turf within sight, and what the greens were like we could conjecture only too well.

I caught Reggy's eye; we both looked sadly at each other, and then at our numerous drivers and brasseys, both recognising simultaneously that they were practically useless here.

The first green was on the near side of a wall which apparently separated two large graveyards, and was the only spot not covered with graves or stones. "Never saw anything like this before," whispered Reggy, and I noticed that the other two were smiling at our astonishment.

There is a little hotel close by much favoured by American missionaries, and sending our coats, &c. in there, we began playing.

NOTHING BUT GRAVESTONES   Jeans, 1897

第二十六章 西式运动在厦门 Western Sports in Amoy

鼓浪屿攀岩 小岛正中央的小山是由巨大的花岗岩堆成的,向上凸起约200英尺,形成了一块圆形巨石。几个外国人试图爬上这块几乎高不可攀的巨石,但获得成功的记录只有一个。他是英国皇家海军的一名指挥官。

——梅尔斯和丹尼斯,1867年,第269页

鼓浪屿岛上的高尔夫运动(1887年)

厦门的一次四人两球高尔夫赛(T.T.瑟金,R.N.詹斯,1887年)

比赛的消息迅速传遍了(香港)俱乐部。外来选手应该有信心在厦门球场打败厦门本地选手。这种想法似乎让人觉得相当有趣…… 赛期过后,我们搭乘嘉德里的班轮前往厦门。海关人员还没放我们通关,卢斯比就跳上甲板,把我们接到鼓浪屿——这个海外殖民地。

……我们走在岛上的一条陡坡,两边长满了短硬的杂草,到处都是巨石。这时,我看见卡尔德森扔下他的球杆袋,四处观望。"怎么啦?已经打完了?"我开玩笑道。"不,"他明显缺乏自信,"我们只是到了那里。""到了那里!"我大声说,"到哪里?"其实根本没必要问,因为他已经蹲下来,刮了干土堆成一小

Jeans, 1897
MAKING TIMID LITTLE SHOTS

堆,试图做个发球座。我往四周一看,发现巨石之间,水泥墓地里,插着几面熟悉的红色小旗。它们有气无力地在安谧的晨风中飘摇。放眼望去,没有一片清楚的草地。这里原本的果岭是怎样的,我们只能尽量去猜想了。

我望了蕾吉一眼。我们彼此伤心地看着对方,以及我们无数的一号和二号木杆。我们同时意识到它们在这里基本上是派不上什么用场的。

第一片果岭靠近一堵围墙。很显然,围墙是用来分隔两块墓地的。这也是这里唯一没有坟墓或石头的地方。"以前从来没见过这样的场地,"蕾吉低声耳语。我注意到,看到我们吃惊的样子,其他两位选手笑了。

临近有一家小旅馆,是美国传教士很喜欢呆的地方。把衣物等东西寄放在旅馆里后,我们便开打了。

Calderson drove off with an iron; the hole was not more than eighty yards away, and his ball dropped dead about two yards the other side of the flag. 'That's just the place,' said Rusby, screwing his face into a comical expression of half apology, half satisfaction. 'Don't you fellows get away to the right, or you'll lose your ball.' I followed, and, using my driving cleek, of course managed to cut the ball, and away down the hill it went.

Reggy gave me a look of inexpressible scorn, and trudged after it, his long legs being very useful in negotiating graves and tombs. He called me plaintively a minute later, so down I scrambled after him, to find that he had discovered the ball nestling up to an inscription stone, and had lofted it into a dead bush about two yards away-the only vegetation, dead or alive, for thirty yards....

From the next tee we could see the flag on the shoulder of a hill about one hundred and twenty yards away, and Rusby, with a cleek, landed on the near side of the slope, clear of all obstacles.

"Just in the right space," he said, waiting for it to stop rolling, and with that same half-pitying air which he had shown before. "Don't go past it, whatever you do." Now Reggy imagines that if he is good at anything it is at judging a drive, and nothing will prevent him from using a driver. I knew perfectly well that the distance was not long enough, and, though I advised him in the most diplomatic manner, his favourite driver circled round his head, and away spun the ball over the hill, out of sight. "You won't find that ball again," the others said sympathetically; and we didn't, though Reggie insisted on us all spending a futile ten minutes searching for it.

The third green is on the edge of a cliff, the further edge overhanging the sea. Fortunately for us, Calderson did not loft his stroke sufficiently, and the ball had so much pace on after touching the ground that it rolled over the cliff, despite the ridiculous contortions of little Rusby, who was following its flight with his eyeglass tucked into his eye and his whole body bent back, as if he could thus arrest its course. ...

The fourth is the long hole-right out of sight over a sloping shoulder of rock, the hole itself being on the top of a mound surrounded by nearly vertical sand-bunkers. Our directing mark was a large boulder, and Reggy drove so carefully that he struck it, the ball rebounding and rolling downhill into a mass of loose rocks. Needless to say, we lost that, as well as the next-a short hole, situated on a very sloping green, only to be approached by dropping the ball on a small plateau immediately above it—a feat I did not accomplish, but sent it bounding downhill to the right.

Jeans, 1897

THE BALL WAS FOUND IN A BROKEN GRAVE

第二十六章　西式运动在厦门　Western Sports in Amoy

卡尔德森率先用三号铁杆开球,第一洞距离不过 80 码。开球后,球稳稳落在旗杆另一侧大约两码的地方。"那真是一个好地方,"蕾吉边说,边扮鬼脸,歉意、满意各半,全写在脸上。"你们这些家伙要是不偏向右侧打,你们就会丢球。"我听从了他们的建议,当然是用五号木杆,将球开起后,却把它打下了山坡。蕾吉非常轻蔑地看了我一眼,吃力地捡球去了。在坟堆、墓地里奔走,他的长腿非常实用。一分钟后,他伤心地喊叫。我赶紧跑下去。原来,蕾吉已经在一块墓碑上

A WAITER BROUGHT US DRINKS
Jeans, 1897

发现了小球,随后他将小球扔到两码以外的枯草丛里,这是 30 码之内仅有的植物,无论死活。

第二个开球点,我们发现小旗插在一座小山山肩,距离大约 120 码远。卢斯比用五号木杆打到斜坡的左侧,旁边没有任何障碍物。

"位置很好,"他一边说,一边等着小球停下来,表情跟先前一样:一半满意、一半遗憾。"别过去,千万别。"蕾吉一向认为,自己的长处就是对开球的判断。没有人能阻挡他用一号木杆。我完全清楚,这一洞距离不是很远。尽管我用最圆滑的方式向他建议,但他最喜爱的一号木杆还是在他头上画了一个圈后,将小球击出,只见它飞过了山坡,不见踪影。"你再也找不到那个球了,"我们的对手满脸同情地说道。我们的确没有找到,尽管蕾吉坚持我们要去找,结果花费了无用功的十分钟时间。

第三洞果岭位于悬崖的边缘,再往外走就是大海。幸运的是(对我们来说),卡尔德森的弧球打得不够高。结果,小球落地后越滚越快,最后掉下了悬崖。即使小个子的卢斯比做出各种可笑的扭曲动作也无法挽回:小球开出后,他通过眼镜一直跟随着小球的前行轨迹,不过他的身体却整个往后仰,好像这样就能阻止小球前进的步伐……

第四洞距离很远,位于岩石缓坡的背后,因而根本看不见。小洞本身就在一个土丘上,周围是几乎垂直的沙坑。我们的方向标是一块大石头。蕾吉显得非常认真,以至于真的将球击打到那块大石头上,小球反弹之后,滚到山下的一个松散的石堆里。毋庸多言,我们输掉这一洞,以及随后的一洞(第五洞)。后者是一个短洞,它位于一块非常陡的果岭上,唯一能到达这里的道路就是将球打在小洞上方的一小块平地上。我没能实现这样的壮举,反而是把球打到坡地右边,弹跳着滚下了山坡。

"I do wish you wouldn't use that idiotic iron," Reggy muttered. "If you'd only stick to your driver, we might have a chance." We did that hole in sixteen. Score: two down.

The sixth is the short hole, and Rusby implored us tragically not to go to the right, or we should lose our ball in a cow-yard about three hundred feet below. "Follow me," he said kindly, and sent his ball spinning down, right out of sight. "Just as I told you," he said, not the least perturbed. "We'll give you that hole; if you don't get in the same place."Reggy didn't, and the score was one down.

As we climbed up the rocks to the next tee, they tried to cheer us. ...The tee was on the turf-covered top of a big rock; the green on the side of a hill, the slope of which was covered with mandarins' graves. Between the two were three paddy fields, a ditch, a road-along which numerous coolies were tramping-another ditch, and a sandpit scooped out from the hill.

"Drive right past the hole, and keep to the left," was the advice Calderson gave us, as his ball, hitting the side of the hill, trickled gently down on to the green. I followed, and, though going again to the right, saw to my great relief that I had gone past the sand... the ball came rolling down nearer and nearer to the danger. A grave arrested its course for a moment, but it ran down the side, and, gaining impetus, rolled over the edge...

When I reached the ball, Reggy had just driven it further into the sand. He turned red in the face with fury in his eyes, his remarks not being fit for print...

A waiter from the hotel now brought us drinks, and also found three boys to carry our bags, so we started the second round in better spirits. We lost the first, but won the next two. At the fourth I made a very lucky drive, laying my ball dead close to the green, and ...Rusby, leading off across the valley, drove into the road, and hit one of two inoffensive coolies carrying a pig. A good drive of Reggy's won us that hole.

The match was now very exciting. Coming back over the road I got in a fair drive, and, Reggy following by a lucky niblick shot from the corner of a grave, we won that hole.

Score: eight all and one to play.

The last hole is a short cleek or iron shot downhill, but a good lie off the green is impossible. My shot landed on a big boulder, and disappeared among some graves. As luck would have it, Calderson topped his ball, and it went among a large heap of stones, my caddy, a fat boy, who took great interest in the game, giving a grunt of satisfaction. After a long search our ball was found in an open grave among crumbling bones. We shouted for instructions, and removed it, counting one, and played our third on to the green. "Not so bad," said Reggy, "they're up in the rocks." Even as he spoke there came a shout of "Fore!" and we saw Rusby's fat little figure climb rapidly to the top of a rock, screwing his glass into his eye as he followed with swaying figure the flight of his ball. Plump! it came, not two feet from the hole. Calderson, never so cool as when everything depends upon his stroke, holed out with his next, and on the match.

We had a rattling good time at the Amoy races, where we made up for our previous ill-fortune. Afterwards, at Hong Kong, if any of the fellows chaffed us at the result of our Amoy game, Reggy would burst out with, "If those... Chinese would mend their ancestors' graves, instead of fooling round joss-houses and worshipping them, we should have won." And he still considers that he has a real grievance against the whole race.

第二十六章　西式运动在厦门 Western Sports in Amoy

"我真希望你们不用那根愚蠢的铁杆,"蕾吉轻声低语,"如果你们坚持只用一号木杆,我们也许有机会。"我们在 16 洞就这么做了。目前得分:仍落后两洞。

第六洞也是一个短洞。卢斯比叫我不要往右打,否则球就会掉到山下 300 英尺的牛棚里。"看着我,"他友善地对我说,然后把球直接打到山下(右侧),看不见了。"就像我刚才告诉你们那样,"他一点儿也不烦恼地说,"这一洞我们让给你,如果你们不打到同样的地方。"蕾吉果然没有(打到同样的地方),现在(我们的)得分还落后一洞。

当我们爬上岩石到下一个发球点时,他们试图鼓励我们。……发球点位于一块草皮覆盖的大岩石上,果岭在一个小山的一侧,而山坡上到处都是中国人的坟墓。发球点与果岭之间有三块稻田、一条沟渠以及一条无数农夫行走的小路,另外一条沟渠和在山坡上挖出的一个沙坑。

"把球打过那个洞口,往左打,"这是卡尔德森给我们的建议。他自己打出去的球落到山坡上,慢慢地滚向果岭。我遵从了他的建议,开球后,小球尽管再次掉在右侧,让我放心的是,小球越过了沙坑……不过小球还在往坡下滚,越来越靠近危险区。一座坟墓稍微把它挡了一会儿,但最终还是滚了下去,速度越来越快,滚出了果岭的边缘……

我走到小球的位置时,蕾吉刚刚将它打进了沙坑的深处。他脸色涨红,眼冒怒火。他所发的牢骚看来不适合在此表述……

这时,旅馆的一个侍者给我们送来了饮料,还有三个男孩帮我们扛球袋。因此,第二轮开打时,我们的情绪好多了。第一洞我们失利了,但接下来两洞,我们都赢了。第四洞,我开球运气很好,小球稳稳落在果岭附近,与此同时……从山谷对面开打的卢斯比,将球打到路上,击中了两位抬生猪的老实苦力。而蕾吉的一击出色开球,为我们拿下这一洞。

现在,比赛进行得相当精彩激烈。回程第一洞,我开球开始进入状态。加上蕾吉从一座坟墓边用 9 号铁杆打出的幸运一击,我们拿下了那一洞。

目前得分:8 平,还剩下最后一洞。

最后一洞是一个应用使用五号短木杆或 3 号铁杆的下坡洞,可是要稳稳地落在果岭上几乎不可能。我的球落在了一块大石头上,然后消失在坟堆里。好像命中注定似的,卡尔德森把球挑高,结果落在了一堆乱石中。我的球童,一个对高尔夫球很感兴趣的胖小子,发出了咕哝的满意声。找了好久,终于在裸露的坟墓碎骨头堆里找到了我们的球。我们喊着商量对策,之后选择移动小球,当然算上一杆,随后我们用上三杆打上果岭。"不是太糟糕,"蕾吉说道,"他们也还在乱石堆上呢!"就在说话之际,有人高喊"小心前面"!我们看见卢斯比矮胖小身子飞快地爬到岩石上面,快速带上眼镜,看着小球飞行的路线。扑通!小球落在距离球洞不到两英尺的地方。轮到卡尔德森了,在关键时刻,他显示了从没有过的冷静,一杆打入,成功拿下这一洞,取得了这次比赛的胜利。

此后我们在厦门进行了多场比赛,度过了一段愉快时光,这无疑弥补了先前的这次臭运气。之后,在香港,如果有人拿我们在厦门的比赛结果开玩笑,蕾吉会回击说,"如果中国人不上寺庙求神拜鬼,而是把自己祖宗的坟墓修得好一些,我们应该会赢。"直到现在,他还在埋怨整个比赛。

Amoy Horse Races (1871) The Amoy races came off on the 9th of January, and were very good fun. They were run by ponies, some of which went capitally. Our doctor rode, and won two races, much to the delight of all our bluejackets that were present, who, of course, had backed their own officer. After the horse, or rather pony races, there were foot races, and running in sacks, which afforded great amusement.

Bax, 1875

Amoy Horse Races (1890) When the first blast of the northeast monsoon is felt ... is not our busy season at an end, to be followed by our winter sports, our shooting, our yachting, our picnics, and, chief of our delights, our horse races? Ah, those races! ridden by gentlemen riders and all on the square—the training, the betting, the sweeps, and, last but not least, the eventful race day itself...

What is your delight early some fine morning to see a dirty, nearly naked coolie walking into your veranda with a paper in his hand, which he presents with a grin, for he has already learnt from previous visits made that morning that he is the bearer of at least no unpleasant dispatch.

But let us read it:

"Amoy Races, 188—

"A meeting will be held at the club tonight at 8 o'clock sharp to make arrangements for the coming races.

"Tom Smith, Secretary."

Amoy Horse Races Outing, Volume 16, 1890

第二十六章　西式运动在厦门 *Western Sports in Amoy*

厦门赛马（1871 年）　厦门的比赛一月九日进行，很有乐趣。都是一些矮种马在跑，有些马跑得非常出色。我们的医生也参加了比赛，并且赢了两场。这让我们所有在场的水兵很开心。水兵当然支持自己的长官。赛马，或者说是矮种马比赛过后，是竞走和布袋跑，相当有趣。

——巴克斯，1875 年，第 63 页

厦门赛马（1890 年）　当人们感觉到第一波的东北季风时……我们忙碌的季节终于过去了。紧接着是我们的冬季运动，射击、赛艇、野餐，以及我们最主要的乐趣，赛马？啊，这些赛事！骑士都是些绅士，都是共济会会员。训练，下注，大获全胜，以及最后但并非最不重要的，充满变数的比赛日……

一个晴朗的清晨，看到一个肮脏、半裸的苦力走进游廊，露齿而笑，把手里拿着的那份文件递给你。从那天早上的几次探访，他已经知道自己应该承担那份至少不是那么不愉快的差使。这是多么令人感到惬意啊。

让我们看看他送来的文件：

"厦门赛马，188 —

兹定于今晚八点整在俱乐部举行会议，安排即将举办的赛马事宜。

秘书：汤姆·史密斯"

Amoy Horse Races
Photo courtesy of Terry Bennett

...Dinner over, you get into your chair, and on the shoulders of two sturdy coolies are quickly transported to the club house, where, after fortifying yourself with a very little Scotch whiskey, mixed with a good deal of soda water, you enter the large meeting room of the club, take a chair, light a fresh cheroot and proceed at once to business...

...every other preliminary settled, a gentleman (the best-looking one) is detailed to call upon the ladies-for their contribution to the "Ladies' Purse" (two sovs., Mrs. Jones, please), and everyone adjourns to the bar to take a nightcap. The bar boys are kept busy for ten minutes, the chair coolies are called, and soon the tired "sports" are being carried home, and a line of dim cheroot lights is all that indicates the course of the sleepy ones as they disappear into the quiet night.

In a few days a mat shed is erected on the sea beach near the stables, and not far from the race course, for it is on the fine soft sand that for a month to come our horses will do their training. A coolie is detailed to have hot coffee and delicious bread and butter ready for the refreshment of members of the club as they return from their early riding.

Our stables are built on the seashore on Amoy Island, to which we have to cross in the early morning by boat ; so, when the "boy" calls at 5 o'clock in the morning, "Massa, blong 5 o'clock !" you feel like heaving a brick at his head, instead of which you get into long boots, a fur-lined coat and riding trousers, and grope your way down to your gig, in which you will in five minutes, with your four stout rowers, reach the stables. Each large house or "hong" has its own stable, some of these having twelve or fourteen stalls, and it is a treat to see the anxiety of the well-groomed horses to get out for their morning gallop. How they snort and neigh and poke their noses at you, as much as to say, "My dear fellow, do take me out first."

Many of our horses are fresh importations from Mongolia, with long, matted hair, and the most uninviting material, to all appearance, over which one would wish to throw a leg...

After about a month of morning training the horses are considered ready for the track, which, like the English courses, is covered with turf and carefully watered to keep the ground soft and save the animals' legs. ...In consideration of being allowed to use the military drill ground for our races, the mandarins are invited to grace the meeting with their presence, and on one day at least they always favor us.

...And so it goes on till the third day. All the great events have come off, the Challenge Cup, two miles in 4:30 ; the Chaasze Cup, one and a half miles in 3:21 ; the Lady's Purse, half a mile in fifty-nine seconds. ...By this time everyone is tired out with excitement, exposure to the sun and the fatigue of riding or standing on foot all day. But we hear the bell for the last race—the "Native Scramble." The Chinese stable boys are to ride and we expect some fun...

John L. Anderson, Amoy, 1890

第二十六章　西式运动在厦门 Western Sports in Amoy

……用过晚餐，坐进轿子，两个强壮的轿夫迅速地把你抬到俱乐部。在那里，来点苏格兰威士忌，掺入大量的苏打水，走进俱乐部大会议室，就座，点上一个新到的方头雪茄，立即商议正事……

……所有的准备工作就绪，一位绅士（长相最佳者）被仔细要求去动员女士向"女士专款"捐钱（琼斯女士，捐两镑吧），然后大家起身到吧台喝点睡前饮料。吧台侍者忙碌十分钟，然后叫上轿夫，很快这些疲惫的运动员就被抬回家去。当昏昏欲睡的人们走进寂静的暮色中，只有微弱的雪茄烟头亮光指引着他们回家的路程。

几天后，靠近马厩的海滩上，在距离赛道不远的地方，建起了一座席棚。在松软、细腻的沙滩上，我们的马儿将在今后的一个月里接受训练、苦力被仔细吩咐备好热咖啡和美味的面包、黄油，让俱乐部的成员晨练归来能够及时恢复体力。

我们的马厩建在厦门岛的海边。每天清早，我们必须坐船前往。因此，清晨五点，当仆人叫门说"先生，五点钟了！"，你会觉得象一块砖头正举在他头上。穿上马靴、皮毛外套和马裤，摸黑走向小船，五分钟之内，四名强壮的船工就会把你送到马厩。每座大房子都有自己的马厩，有的马厩里拥有 12 至 14 个马栏。赛马得到了精心的照料。看到赛马急于出栏晨练的样子，的确是一种享受。你瞧，他们对你鼓鼻、嘶叫、伸头拨弄，好像是想说，"亲爱的，先带我出去吧。"

我们的赛马大多是刚从蒙古引进的，毛很长，象铺了席子一般，但也是外表看上去最令人讨厌的东西，真想踢它两脚……

晨练大约一个月之后，我们觉得赛马可以上场了。跟英国的赛马场一样，这里的场地铺上了草皮，并细心浇水，以确保场地松软、赛马不至受伤。……由于中方允许我们使用他们的练兵场作赛马场，我们邀请他们的官员到场，为赛会增光。通常，他们至少会在某天前来捧场。

……就这样，赛马一直持续到第三天。所有的奖项都已决出：挑战杯——4 分 30 秒，两英里；切思泽杯——3 分 21 秒，1.5 英里；"女士专款"项目——59 秒，0.5 英里。……到这个时候，一整天，大家在太阳下暴晒，或赛马劳累，或跺脚观赛，激动万分，都已经筋疲力尽了。但是，我们听到最后一场比赛的铃声响起。"本地选手争夺赛"，这是马厩里的中国仆人之间的赛马，我们期待着从中找到一些乐趣……

——约翰·L·安德森（1890 年，厦门）

老外看老鼓浪屿 Old Gulangyu in Foreigners' Eyes

Chapter 27   Foreign Romance in Amoy

Sailors and Missionary Daughters   Among the interesting incidents of our stay were the usual number of boat-races and exercises, the visit of the Tau Tai, and upon Sunday the holding of service on board the ship by one of the missionaries, whose field is at Amoy. The majority of the crew attended, influenced in no small degree probably by the presence of the two pretty daughters of the missionary. To work good among sailors, I am inclined to believe that the missionary would find it advantageous to have some pretty and attractive female to accompany him, in order to induce them to listen to him, and to fix their attention. Then he might have better hopes of being successful in his endeavors. The services were conducted after the manner of the North Dutch Church, and all seemed to be much interested, especially in the singing, in which the voices of the ladies made a great improvement."

Lawrence, 1870

Weird Wedding   Monday, August 11th, 1862   Pa had to marry a couple, Miss Fredericka Wilhelmina Prunella Funk to Mr. Harrison. The lady is half Malay, half Dutch and does not know a word of English. The gentleman is an American, who cannot speak a word of her language. They never met until within the last week. A queer wedding. It took three to marry them, Pa, an American Consul, said the words, Mr. DeGrysse, the Dutch Consul put the questions to the bride, and Mr. Doty, a missionary did the praying. Success to them I say. Mr. Kip and Mr. Rapalge had a great discussion about how Mr. Harrison popped the question but they didn't come to any definite decision.

Bradford's Journal

Marrying off the Captain's Cousin   We had a short run of three days and anchored in Amoy on August first, 1860…There were quite a number of young men in Amoy, and my cousin had numerous visitors, for young ladies were scarce in that community…

We were in Amoy for two months and during that time the ship was visited daily by many young men, and though my cousin had been in Hong Kong and Shanghai without meeting anyone who pleased her, it looked very much as though Amoy would furnish the right man. There were two who were very attentive—a Mr. Richardson and a Mr. Hancock—and it was very doubtful which was the favored one…

Then I was told that Mr. Richardson had proposed and had been accepted. He wished my cousin to stay and be married then, but I would not consent. I told him she must go home first; and they parted. We left for New York the next day.

Nothing particular happened on our voyage home, which we made in one hundred and eight days from Amoy, arriving in New York January fifteenth, 1861. We were in New York for two months and a half, a good part of which time I spent in South Danvers.

There was quite a difference of opinion in the family circle about my cousin Miss Porter's going to China to marry Mr. Richardson. Some favored it; some were very much against it, but I guaranteed his good character and carried the day, and it was resolved that she go out with me and my wife again and take the chances…

Captain Low's Recollections

第二十七章　外国人在厦门的浪漫史

Joyce Angus, 1927
In Amoy 1925-1952

船员和传教士的女儿　在厦门逗留期间，我们所碰到的趣事有司空见惯的划船比赛和操练，道台来访，以及由厦门教区一名传教士在船上主持的周日礼拜。大多数船员都参加了礼拜，很大程度上可能是受传教士所带来的两个漂亮女儿的影响。我倾向于认为，为了更好地在船员中开展工作，传教士发现带上几个漂亮、有吸引力的女性有利于他吸引信众，让他们集中注意力。这样一来，他的努力获得成功的可能性就大为增加。

礼拜是按照北荷兰教会的仪式进行的。所有人似乎对唱圣歌特别感兴趣，圣歌也因为女声的加入而增色不少。

——劳伦斯，1870年，第250页

古怪的婚姻　1862年8月11日，周一　父亲为新人——弗里德里卡·威廉敏娜·普鲁涅拉·芬克小姐和哈里森先生证婚。芬克小姐是马来人和荷兰人的混血，英语一句都不会说。哈里森先生是美国人，也不会讲新娘所说的话。他们是一周前才见的面。古怪的婚姻。三个人为他们证婚：父亲作为美国驻厦门领事做证婚词，法国领事底格里斯先生向新娘提问，传教士多迪先生祈祷。祝愿他们婚姻幸福，我说。基普先生和拉帕吉先生热烈地讨论哈里森先生突然提出的问题，但没有任何结论。

——摘自露丝·布莱德福特的个人日记

船长的表妹出嫁　我们连续三天一路小跑，终于在1860年8月1日在厦门港下锚……当时在厦门年轻人很多，来拜访我表妹的人很多，因为年轻的女士在当地极为稀缺……

我们在厦门住了两个月。期间，每天都有不少年轻人上船访问。尽管表妹在香港和上海都没遇上可心的人，但看上去厦门好像能够提供合适的人选。有两个人很殷勤，一个是理查德森先生，一个叫汉科克先生。不知道她到底喜欢哪个……

接着，我听说理查德森先生向我表妹求婚并被接受了。他希望表妹留下来，马上结婚。但我不能同意。我告诉他，表妹必须先回家，然后他们就分手了。第二天，我们启程回纽约。

从厦门回家，一路上没有发生什么特别的事情。我们走了108天，终于在1861年1月15日抵达纽约。我们在纽约呆了两个半月，大部分时间我住在南丹佛。

围绕着表妹波特小姐要到中国嫁给理查德森先生一事，家庭成员之间的意见不一致。有人赞同，有人极力反对。我向大家保证理查德森先生品质优良。当天，大家决议，表妹再次与我和妻子一起前往中国，抓住机会……

——娄船长回忆录，第152页

老外看老鼓浪屿 Old Gulangyu in Foreigners' Eyes

Lectures on Matrimony   Thursday, September 18th   Went and called on Mrs. Carnagie and Mrs. Swanson. Coming home fell in with Mr. White of course. It really does amuse me to see the patronizing, condescending way in which a gentleman who happens to be walking with me treats all the other gentlemen he happens to meet. It is a joke to watch them out of the corner of one's eye. Mrs. Carnagie read me quite a lecture on the subject of matrimony. Wonder if she imagined I stood in need of it.

Ruth Bradford's Journal

Teen Love in Old Amoy   One of my earliest passions was for the daughter of a lighthouse keeper off Amoy. She was a beautiful Eurasian girl, blending Japanese, Chinese, Scotch, American, and other bloods. Next came Sophie Novitska, daughter of a refugee Polish Count...

Caldwell, 1953

Foreigners Kissing in Public   (1940s)   My teachers went to great lengths to emphasize the importance of understanding and adopting the finer points of behavior and etiquette in social intercourse with the Chinese. Mr. Lim expressed profound horror at the sight of foreign couples kissing each other in the street. It was not so much that this was an insanitary habit, which facilitated the spread of tubercular germs, as an affront to modesty and an outrage to the sanctity of private feelings. It was essential for husbands not to display any unbecoming emotion in public, and the effusive endearments with which Western couples mutually showcased each other in public, whether sincerely or not, were highly indecorous. "Very kee-kwai," [很奇怪] he explained excitedly, entering my room one morning for a lesson. "I was passing Reverend Wheat's home this morning, just as he was coming back from one of his inland tours. Mrs. Wheat went rushing out to meet him and what do you think happened?" he added, waving his fan to and fro across his face with increasing tempo as his beady eyes flashed with surprise, anger and excitement.

She shouted "Darling" and he then embraced her in full view of all passers-by!

"It's an old Western custom," I added.

"But not in public!" exclaimed Mr. Lim with sustained shock, and, leaning over with all the air of one divulging a secret court intrigue, added, "I understand from their cook that Mrs. Wheat is expecting..."

But this was not the only type of emotional display in public which shocked the old-fashioned ideas of Chinese etiquette. Hearty handshakes or back-slapping, reminiscent of the regimental mess or the aftermath of a successful game of football, were strictly forbidden, and I was advised that the height of good manners was to shake my own hand on being introduced to a stranger, instead of his, and to continue: "Your honourable surname?"

...Most of these embellishments and pleasantries of polite etiquette were still common in the countryside and not unknown among the more leisurely and educated circles of Amoy. But the tempo of modern life and the effect of Hollywood films were helping towards their disappearance in all the coastal ports, and final evidence of their total eclipse could be seen in Hong Kong hotels where "Hiya" back slaps were exchanged with an enthusiasm that would have done justice to any Californian house party.

Neill, 1956

第二十七章　外国人在厦门的浪漫史　Foreign Romance in Amoy

婚姻课　9月18日，星期四　前往拜访卡内基夫人和桑姆森夫人。回家路上，偶然遇上怀特先生。看到跟自己同行的绅士碰到其他男士摆出一副居高临下、派头十足的样子，实在有趣。看着他们远离自己的视线，很可笑。卡内基夫人就婚姻问题不厌其烦地给我上了一堂课。不知道她是否觉得我实在需要。

——摘自露丝·布莱德福特的日记

老厦门的少年恋爱　我最早的一次恋情是厦门外海一位灯塔看守员的女儿。她是一位漂亮的欧亚混血儿，身上流淌着日本人、中国人、苏格兰人、美国人和其他国籍人士的血液。第二位是苏菲·诺维斯卡，一位波兰流亡伯爵的女儿……

——卡德威尔，1953年，第80、81页

外国人在公众场合接吻（20世纪40年代）　我的老师长篇累牍地强调在与中国人进行社交活动时必须理解和遵守的行为和礼仪要点。看到外国情侣在街上接吻，林先生表示极为惊恐。与其说接吻是一种容易传播结核病菌的不卫生习惯，倒不如说它是对谦逊的一种冒犯和对私人情感尊严的一种侮辱。（在中国）丈夫是不可以在公众面前表露任何不得体的情感，西方情侣在公开场合表现出来的过分热情的亲热，不管是否真诚，都是极端无礼的。"很奇怪，有一天，林先生激动地走进我的房间向我请教，"今天早上，我路过惠特牧师的家，看到他刚从内地传教归来。惠特女士冲出来迎接丈夫。你猜猜，到底发生了什么事？"他的扇子在脸前上下晃动，速度越来越快，又小又亮的眼睛充满了惊奇、愤怒和激动。

她大声叫"亲爱的"，然后惠特先生就在大庭广众之下拥抱她！"

"这是西方古老的习俗，"我告诉他。

Gulangyu Honeymoon, 1927

"那也不能在大庭广众之下呀！"林先生惊恐不已地大声叫嚷，然后一副泄露秘密法庭阴谋的样子向我靠过来说，"我听他们的厨子说，惠特女士一直盼望着……"

当然，这不是在公众场合展示情感的唯一案例，却足以震惊中国礼教的老派人士。（在中国）追忆团队的混乱，或足球赛赢球之后的开心握手或拍背安抚都是不允许的。有人告诉我，与人第一次见面，最高的礼仪是抱拳作揖，而不是紧握他人的双手，然后再说："请问尊姓大名？"

……大多数的礼节和寒暄现在仍然在乡下盛行，在厦门有闲、有教养的阶层里并不少见。但是，现代生活的节奏以及好莱坞电影的影响使得这些礼仪在所有的沿海港口消失殆尽。这在香港的宾馆里可以找到最后的证据。在那里，人们热情地说：你好！这跟加州的任何一次家庭宴会没有什么两样。

——尼尔，1956年，第72～74页

老外看老鼓浪屿 *Old Gulangyu in Foreigners' Eyes*

Chapter 28
Ruth Bradford's Amoy Journal [1](1862)

Monday Sept. 16th, 1861   [On Ship Julia G. Tyler]
Seasick   We have been at sea one week today…The first two days and nights we were out a heavy storm raged; and all, with three exceptions, were seasick; and in that one little sentence, "All were seasick," an unexperienced person little dreams of how much misery is contained…Words cannot express it…

Thursday, Oct. 24th   Sailing Backwards   We drifted backward toward New York 19 miles last night; that's encouraging. These calms are really very hand to undergo. Such an old tub as this ship is, I never heard of. She can't sail when she has a wind; and when she has none, she can't even lie still, but sails backwards.

Monday, April 28th, 1862   Arrive in Amoy   Came into Amoy harbor last evening; a great many boats came off to the ship. Among the rest, Ollie and Mr. Hyatt; they had been looking for us for a week. We were received with great demonstrations: the big flag run up and a general fuss made….It seems to be a very pleasant, homelike place. Nearly all the foreigners reside over here on the island, and there are some handsome residences. Think I shall like it very much indeed.

Thursday, May 1st The Only Young Girl   Have had a great many visitors. At one time the drawing room was so full we could hardly seat them all. It is a beautiful day. Took a walk this afternoon. Like the place more and more.…I am the only American lady here and the only young girl, so I suppose I am an object of some curiosity. Nearly all here are English.

---

1   The high-spirited 20-year-old daughter of U.S. Amoy Consul Bradford (Presbyterian minister appointed as Amoy Consul by Abraham Lincoln), kept a delightful Journal, which included her 7 ½ month sea voyage from New York to China, and her 8 months in Amoy. The entire journal is available online.

第二十八章
露丝·布莱德福特的厦门日记[1]（1862年）

在朱丽叶·G.泰勒号船上 1861年9月16日，星期一 晕船 到今天，我们已经在海上航行一个星期了……头两天两夜，我们碰上了暴风雨。除了三个例外，船上所有人都晕船。简短的"所有人都晕船"一句话，没有经历过的人绝对无法想象得到里面所包含的辛酸……那是言词所无法表达的……

1861年10月24日，星期四 船往回飘 昨夜我们的船往纽约方向回飘了19海里，真是振奋人心啊。这些无风带实在难走。泰勒号应该算是老家伙了。往回走这种事我前所未闻。有风暴，她不能走。风平浪静，她连静静地停泊都不行，会往回飘。

Bradford, 1938
Ruth Bradford at Eighteen

1862年4月28日，星期一 抵达厦门 昨夜进入厦门港。很多小船驶近泰勒号。其中有奥莉和凯悦先生。他们已经在这里找我们一周了。我们受到了非常热烈的欢迎。他们升起一面大旗，制造了不少的忙乱…… 这里看上去是个好地方，像老家。岛上（鼓浪屿）有不少漂亮的住所，几乎所有的外国人都住在岛上。我想我应该会喜欢这里的。

1862年5月1日，星期四 岛上唯一的年轻姑娘 来了很多客人。有一次，来客太多，客厅几乎都快坐不下了。这是美丽的一天。下午出去散步。越来越喜欢这个地方了……我是这里唯一的美国女性和年轻姑娘。因此，我想我是人们好奇的对象。这里几乎所有人都是英国人。

---

1 基督教长老会牧师布莱德福特被阿布拉罕·林肯任命为美国驻厦门领事。他有一个活泼可爱的女儿露丝·布莱德福特，年仅二十。露丝在日记里愉快地记录了她从纽约到中国7个半月的航程，以及她在厦门八个月的生活。日记全文可上网阅读。

Sunday, May 4th Church in Amoy   Went to church over in Amoy. Mr. Burns preached. He is a Scotchman and a missionary who wears the Chinese dress, shaved head, long tail and all. Have a melodeon there. Pretty good music is sung… How I wish Pa could just get up in the pulpit and show them what a sermon was. All Mr. Burns said was very good, but there was no originality about it. However, if we all practiced what he preached, we would be a good deal better than we are. There's no rubbing that out.

Bradford, 1938

Wednesday, May 7th Dislikes the English[1]   An English gun boat, the "Bustard" has come into the harbor. She coasts between here and Swatow. Her commander, Lieut. Tucker, called today. He is rather a pleasant young Englishman. I can't say I like the English generally, for I don't, but once in a while they are pleasant enough.

Friday, May 9th Six Dresses in One Day   The "Azoff" came in today bringing the mail and a letter from Mother with good news from home. Also glorious news from the war. All the Americans here in high good humor. Went out calling today. How I do hate to make formal calls. I'm played out; have done little all day but dress and undress. I've had six or seven different dresses on for different occasions since morning and am now arrayed in the most comfortable of all — my night dress; and if I don't get out of this lounging chair now, I'll have to stay here all night; for I'm going to sleep.

Wednesday, May 14th Buttons   …Wash man brought home the clothes, and I'll have to sew on buttons all day tomorrow… washing on stones is hard on the buttons, but they do things up in a very nice style, no mistake about that.

Thursday, May 15th 56 More Buttons; pretty Chinese woman   Made six buttonholes today, sewed on fifty-six buttons… Saw a very pretty China woman, so pretty that I stopped and looked at her for half an hour. She was handsomely dressed too, a lady of some rank and wealth, I suppose, but with no feet at all.

---

1 Americans mistrusted British motives during the Civil War, and Ruth's July journal entries were only six months after the Trent affair which almost led to war between Britain and the U.S. Ruth's journal offers humorous insights on some Americans' love/hate relationship with Britain.

第二十八章　露丝·布莱德福特的厦门日记　Ruth Bradford's Amoy Journal

1862年5月4日，星期天　厦门的教堂　到厦门本岛上的教堂。彭斯先生布道。他是苏格兰人，剃头蓄辫，穿着中式服装传教。教堂里有一台手风琴。唱诗班的音乐很好听……我真希望父亲能够上讲台，向他们展示什么叫布道……彭斯布道讲得都不错，但缺乏创意。不过，如果我们都像他那样布道，我们就会比现在好得多。这是毫无疑义的。

1862年5月7日，星期三　不喜欢英国人　一艘英国炮舰"大鸨号"进入厦门港。这艘炮舰在汕头和厦门之间巡航。炮舰的指挥官塔克上尉今天来访。他是一位彬彬有礼的英国年轻人。我不能说自己喜欢所有的英国人，但是，有时候他们还是挺友善的。

1862年5月9日，星期五　一天换六次衣服　"阿佐夫号"今天进港，带来了母亲寄来的邮包和信件，以及家乡的好消息。还有关于战争的好消息。这里所有美国人的兴致都很高。今天出去串门。我非常讨厌正规的拜访。把我弄得筋疲力尽的，整天什么事情也没干，就是穿衣服、换衣服。

Bradford, 1938

从早上开始，我为不同的场合已经换了六、七次服装了。我现在穿的是最舒服的晚装。如果现在不从躺椅上站起来，我整个晚上都会睡在上面，因为实在太困了。

1862年5月14日，星期三　纽扣　……洗衣工把衣服送回来了。明天一整天，我得把纽扣缝上……在石板上洗衣服对纽扣损伤很大。不过，他们做得不错，没有出过差错。

1862年5月15日，星期四　缝了56颗纽扣；漂亮的中国妇女　今天做了六个扣眼，缝了56个纽扣……遇见一位非常漂亮的中国女性。太漂亮了，我驻足看了她半个小时。她的着装也很得体。我想，应该是一位有身份、有钱人家的太太，没有裹脚。

Monday morning, May 19th Flea Fight & Sleepless! I acknowledge myself beaten, vanquished, played out, anything, everything else. I, who was always such a sound sleeper, who never found anything in America which could keep me awake nights and at sea have slept through storms that kept everybody else's hair on end -- I was kept awake nearly the whole of last night by the fleas. Talk about fleas! There isn't a flea in America, not one; even at Tristan Da Cuna, where they were as large as small mice and picked me up and carried me out of bed, I slept through it. BUT last night -- if there was one flea on me, there were a thousand. Nothing but hop, hop, crawl, crawl, bite, bite. I dropped asleep once from sheer fatigue, dreamed about them, thought we were both fleas running a race, woke up and thought it was literally true. ... Went to sleep again for a minute; dreamed I was a thousand legged worm. Woke up with a jump that nearly tore down the mosquito bar. Hope I may be forgiven for all the bad things I said and thought. Had a notion to cry but didn't, thinking it would please the fleas too much. How I lived until morning, I don't know. It is one of the mysteries. At any rate I got up without being called for the first time since I have been here.

Saturday, May 24th Queen's Birthday; Regatta Queen's birthday. Took tiffin on board H.M. gunboat "Bustard." Had a gay time. Everybody was there. Elegant tables and fine decorations. Regatta went off very well. The race was well contested. Mr. Ward's boat was winner. He is an American gentleman. Took a good stiff. Lieut. Tucker very gallant. Drank the Queen's health with a good will. Had plenty of fun. All the shipping in the harbor was gaily decorated with flags. We had the big flag on the flagstaff and another on the top of the mast. Dipped it seven times at noon in honor of the occasion...

Friday, May 30th Amoy a Party Town Been at an evening dinner party at Mr. Boyd's. Had a good time. Ollie and I went. Got home at 12. Received invitation cards to Mr. Brown's on Tuesday evening. Amoy is quite gay.

Thursday, June 5th Cold Nights Rained nearly all day. Held up awhile in the afternoon... These rainy, windy nights are quite cool ...

Friday, June 6th Beautiful Night; Moon Journey ...It is a most beautiful night. ...Would like to take a journey to the moon this evening and call in America on my way, but I wouldn't stop there long... Oh, no, of course not.

Bradford, 1938

第二十八章 露丝·布莱德福特的厦门日记 Ruth Bradford's Amoy Journal

Bradford, 1938

1862年5月19日,星期一　与跳蚤搏斗,一夜无眠!　我承认自己被打败、击溃,筋疲力尽,怎么说都行。一向以来,我睡眠极好。在美国,没有任何事情可以让我彻夜难眠。在海上,暴风雨让所有人毛骨悚然,我照样入睡。昨晚,在这里,我却被一群跳蚤弄得一夜无眠。想想这些跳蚤!美国没有跳蚤,一只都没有。即使是在特里斯坦达库纳,跳蚤大如小老鼠,把我弄醒、赶下床,我都照睡不误。但是,昨晚,我身上哪怕只有一只跳蚤,也像是千军万马。他们蹦蹦跳跳,四处爬行,到处叮咬。有一会儿,我太累了,终于睡过去了,梦里还是跳蚤,感觉自己也是跳蚤,在跟它们赛跑。醒来,发现简直太真切了……再睡了一会儿,梦见自己是一条千腿虫。把自己吓醒了,跳起来,差点拉断了蚊帐的架子。真希望自己所说和所想的坏事能够得到宽恕。真想哭,但没哭出来,因为我想那只能让跳蚤太得意。我也不知道自己是怎么熬到天亮的。这是其中的一个谜。无论怎么说,这是我到厦门来之后第一次不用别人叫就自己起床的。

1862年5月24日,星期六　女王生日,划船比赛　女王生日,带午饭上英国炮舰"大鸨号"。玩得很开心。大家都在炮舰上。桌子摆得很雅致,装饰精美。划船比赛进展顺利,竞争很激烈。伍德先生的船获胜。他是一个美国绅士。塔克上尉很勇敢。友善地为女王的健康干杯。很有趣。港内的所有船只都插满了彩旗,一片欢乐景象。我们在旗杆和桅杆上分别升起了一面大旗。为了表示庆祝,中午时分,行点旗礼七次……

1862年5月30日,星期五　派对小镇厦门　到伯易德家参加晚宴派对。玩得很开心。奥莉和我一起去,12点回到家里。接到布朗先生家的邀请,参加下周二的派对。厦门挺好玩的。

1862年6月5日,星期四　凉爽的夜晚　几乎整天下雨。下午稍稍暂停了一会儿……这种风雨交加的夜晚挺凉爽的……

1862年6月6日,星期五　美丽的夜晚,月亮之旅　……这是一个最美的夜晚……今晚真想到月球上去旅行,顺路回美国一趟。不过,不在家里停留很长时间……噢,不,当然不可能。

▶ 373

Tuesday, June 10th Angry Over No Mail; Beautiful Ships[2] Feel very much disappointed and a little angry. The mail steamer came in the morning and brought no letters from home. We did not get any last mail either. I think it is too bad. They might write. We have only had two letters since August, nearly a year; and how many dozen have we written, I wonder. I can't think what it means at all...

The Lammermuir

A large American ship came in - the "Europa." I like no better fun than to see a fine, large ship coming in under full sail with the stars and stripes floating from her monkey gaff. It is a beautiful sight. She is the only full-rigged ship now in the harbor. There are plenty of barques, brigs and schooners, but no ships but her.

Friday, June 13th Free Frog Concert; China's Perfect Fleas A very hot day! Sewed a little this morning; did nothing the rest of the time...The frogs are holding a free concert. It is full moon now and a most magnificent night. The fleas are holding a free concert, or rather a free dance over me too, but the fact is I have got so used to them now that I would feel strangely if I had not fifty or sixty about me... A person has to come to China to find fleas in perfection. If there is a vestige of me left to take back to America, I shall be thankful; but at present it seems very doubtful. Oh for some tansy![Tansy: flower plant [Tanacetum vulgare] thought to keep fleas away]

Saturday, June 21st Handling Crowds Went away out on the high cliffs overhanging the sea. Looked straight down from a tremendous height at the surf rolling up against the big rocks. Very grand sight. Saw the mail steamer going out with flying colors taking our letters home; saw some vessels coming in... in a few minutes I was surrounded by a dense crowd looking over each other's shoulders -- men, women, children and dogs chattering, gabbling and commenting on me at a great rate. They all have the same opinion of me in regard to one thing: they think I was once their color but have washed myself white... The waves sing me to sleep nights. I like it. I've got to be so fond of the sea. I don't know what I shall do when I leave it.

Tuesday, June 24th (Still angry about the mail) A dull day. The "Undine" came in from Hong Kong bringing the mail; brought us letters from France and Ireland but none from America. We have come to the conclusion that the folks at home think our ship was lost and "all on board perished," which would be a very natural conclusion as that was stated in the Hong Kong papers and word to that effect was sent to New York. Well, they are mistaken anyhow, for here we are as large as life. They will probably get our first letters from China in a week now, and then we may look for letters in about two months.

Saturday, July 5th Ruth's Birthday I'm either 20 or 21 today, but I think it is 21.

---

2 For more on Tall Ships, see Amoy Harbor chapter

第二十八章　露丝·布莱德福特的厦门日记　Ruth Bradford's Amoy Journal

1862年6月10日，星期二　没收到邮件很生气，漂亮的邮轮　感到很失望，有点生气。邮轮今天上午进港，没有为我们送来老家的信件。上次邮轮进港，我们也没有收到任何邮包。我想太糟糕了。他们应该写信来。去年八月以来，将近一年了，我们只收到两封信。我想，我们往家里写了多少封信。我无法想象这到底怎么啦……

美国巨轮"欧罗巴号"进港。看到漂亮的巨轮全速驶来，信号旗斜杆上，星条旗迎风飘扬，我觉得没有比这更有趣的了。这是一个美丽的景象。欧罗巴号是港内唯一装备齐全的船只。港内有无数的多桅帆船，横帆双桅船和多桅纵帆船，但是全装帆船只有欧罗巴号一艘。

1862年6月13日，星期五　免费的青蛙音乐会，中国的完美跳蚤　今天很热！上午做了会针线活，其余时间无所事事……青蛙在开免费的音乐会。现在，月亮很圆，夜晚真美。跳蚤也在举办免费的演奏会，或者说是在我身上免费跳舞。不过，事实是，我现在已经对跳蚤习以为常了。如果身上没有那么五六十只，我会感到奇怪的……一个人得到中国来感受一下完美的跳蚤。如果能够苟延残喘回到美国，我会感恩戴德的。不过，现在看来似乎令人非常怀疑。噢，有艾菊就好了！

1862年6月21日，星期六　对付围观者　到高耸的岩壁上看大海　从极高的地方看海浪拍打巨大的礁石，场面很壮观。看到邮轮飘着旗帜，带着我们的信件回美国，看到一些船只进港……几分钟之内，我被密密麻麻的一群人围观。他们——男女老少，还有小狗，争先恐后，七嘴八舌，喋喋不休，非常起劲地评论我。关于我，他们有一个地方意见是一致的：他们认为我曾经跟他们一样的肤色，但是自己洗白了……海浪伴着我入眠。我喜欢这样。我越来越喜欢海了。不知道一旦离开，我会怎么样。

1862年6月24日，星期二　还在生邮件的气　无聊的一天　"水女神号"

入港，从香港给我们带来邮件。信件来自法国和爱尔兰，就是没有来自美国的。我们得出的结论是，老家人以为我们的轮船失踪，"船上所有人员全部报销"。这是一个很自然的结论，因为香港的报纸就曾经这样登载，这样的言语就传回了美国。唉！不管怎么说，他们肯定搞错了，因为我们在这儿活得好好的。也许再过一星期，他们就会收到我们从中国寄出的第一封信。然后，再过大约两个月，我们有望收到家里的回信。

1862年7月5日，星期六　露丝的生日　今天是我20或21岁生日。不过，我想，应该是21岁。

Wednesday, July 9th Beautiful Night　　It is as lovely a night as ever blessed the earth, perfectly clear and moonlight. The waters of the bay are one sheet of silver, dotted over with fishing boats away out to sea, and the "seven islands" look as if they were saying "keep off", and then laughing. The night birds give us a tune once in a while, and crickets and frogs come in on the chorus, and some ambitious Chinaman at no great distance is strumming on a banjo. The Chinamen all around are keeping up a great chatter as usual. I never hear a group of Chinamen holding a spirited conversation but I envy them…

Tuesday, July 29th Pirates　　…Lieut. Tucker called today. He is going out in his gun boat to see if he can't catch them. The pirates are as thick as bees around here, and are very bold. I only wish we had some American gun boats out here. We'd teach these cowardly English a lesson…

Sunday, August 3rd Chapel and American Preaching　　Went to Chapel and heard Mr. Kip preach by far the very best sermon I have heard in China, about the thief on the cross. He's a good young fellow, is Mr. Kip, and speaks as if he felt what he said. Has a few ideas too, which is more than can be said of any of the rest of them. He is an American. I suppose that's the reason.

Wednesday, August 6th Pirates Caught　　The gun boat came in with some 20 pirates aboard, which she had taken. They are all to have their heads cut off in a day or two.

Sunday, August 17th Shocking the Englishmen again　　Went to Chapel alone all by myself in the boat. The three boatmen pulled, and I with the Stars and Stripes over my head sat in the stern, held the tiller ropes and steered. Think I'll go to Chapel alone again as I got so many compliments. Things like that astonish these English…

Saturday, August 23rd No Mail from Mom　　The Aden came in today, bringing the mail, but we got no letters from home. Very queer of them I think. Pa says he has a notion to get a divorce. I tell him he'd better.

Saturday, August 30th Only Two Objections to China　　Nearly stepped on a cockroach as big as a mouse. I have only two objections to China, the roaches, and the fleas. Don't mind lizards and centipedes for they do not swarm like the roaches and fleas. But the flea season is now nearly over. The roach season is never over.

Tuesday, September 2nd Seeking Captaincy　　Captain Cass came. He proposes that I shall go home on his ship as first mate. That is two pegs higher than Captain Ranllett, but I have concluded to accept no lower post than that of Captain, so of course I declined.

Sunday, September 14th Centipedes and Bamboo　　I wish I knew what for these centipedes have as many legs. Suppose it is none of my business though, or as Pa said about bamboo, when I wondered if it wouldn't grow in America, he said "if it would have grown there why the Lord would have planted it there", so I suppose it is about the centipede's legs. If they could have walked with less, the Lord wouldn't have given them so many.

　　Other excerpts from Ruth's Journal may be found in other chapters.

第二十八章 露丝·布莱德福特的厦门日记 Ruth Bradford's Amoy Journal

1862年7月9日，星期三 美丽的夜晚 夜空晴朗，月光明亮，这是上苍赐予人类的美好夜晚。港湾里的水面像一片白银，出外海捕鱼的小船点缀其上。"七座小岛"看上去好像在说"不准入内"，然后哈哈大笑。夜莺每隔一会儿就会给我们来一段曲子，蟋蟀和青蛙却是大合唱。不远处，某个野心勃勃的中国人在弹琵琶。周围的中国人都跟往常一样在闲聊。我从来没有听过一群中国人兴高采烈地在聊天，不过，我挺嫉妒他们的……

1862年7月29日，星期二 海盗 ……塔克上尉今天来访。他的炮舰将要出海去看是否能够抓到海盗。临近的海域海盗多如苍蝇，而且胆子特大。我只希望附近能有我们的一些军舰，教训一下这些胆小的英国人……

1862年8月3日，星期日 小教堂与美国人布道 上小教堂听基普先生布道。这是目前为止我在中国听到的最好的布道，是关于十字架上的盗贼。他是一个优秀的年轻小伙子，是基普先生。他讲道的时候好像自己能感觉到自己所说的那样。也有一些想法，比其他人更值得称道。他是一个美国人，我想这就是理由。

1862年8月6日，星期三 抓获海盗 炮舰抓获大约20名海盗，并把他们带回厦门港。再过一、两天，他们就得人头落地。

1862年8月17日，星期日 再次震惊英国人 独自一人乘船去教堂。有三个船工划船，我坐在船尾，拉着舵柄的绳子，掌握方向舵，星条旗在我头顶的上空飘扬。想想我自己再次独行上教堂，受到那么多的赞扬。这样的事情令那些英国人目瞪口呆……

1862年8月23日，星期四 妈妈没来信 "亚丁号"今天入港，带来了邮件。不过，我们没收到家里的来信。他们很奇怪，我想。父亲说，他真想离婚。我告诉他，最好离。

1862年8月30日，星期四 中国令人讨厌的东西只有两样 差一点就踩到一只大如老鼠的蟑螂。在中国，我只讨厌两样东西：蟑螂和跳蚤。我不在乎蜥蜴和蜈蚣，因为它们不会像蟑螂和跳蚤那样成群结队。不过，跳蚤的季节现在几乎结束了，而蟑螂却没完没了。

1862年9月2日，星期二 想当船长 卡斯船长来访。他建议我做大副跟他的船回家。这可比兰内特船长提供的职位高出了两个等级。不过，我决定不接受低于船长的职务。因此，我理所当然地婉言谢绝了。

1862年9月14日，星期日 蜈蚣和竹子 我希望自己知道蜈蚣长那么多只脚的理由。尽管这跟我没啥关系，或者当我为竹子是否能在美国生长而发呆的时候，父亲说："如果主想让它在美国生长，他就会把它种在美国。"因此，我想，蜈蚣的脚也应该是这样的。如果它们能用更少只的脚走路，主肯定不会给他们这么多只的脚。

露丝日记的其他摘选散见于本书其他章节

老外看老鼓浪屿 *Old Gulangyu in Foreigners' Eyes*

Chapter 29 600 Years of Japan in Amoy

The first attack by Japanese[1], was in 1369, on Chin-chew [Quanzhou] ;... In 1561, another onslaught was made upon Chin-chew, which city, from its situation, and apparent helplessness, seems to have been constantly selected for attack. Thence they fell upon Tong-an, where, this time, they seem to have met with a stout resistance, as it is stated they besieged it four months. It was taken, however, in 1562, as was Nan-an, and both cities were given to the sword, and completely pillaged. After an occupation of forty days, they were set fire to, and abandoned. About this time, the Japanese moved to, and occupied, Namoa, probably for the convenience of making unexpected irruptions on the mainland. It is stated that they built themselves houses, and remained for a year there; but most likely they occupied the Islands for a much longer period.

In 1563, they appear to have captured the wealthy and important city of Chang-chou-fu [Zhangzhou] again plundered Tungan, and to have burnt a great number of houses at Chin-kiang-hsien. In 1564, they killed many mandarins, soldiers, and of her people at Chin-chew, which place they again assaulted in 1567, slaughtering and looting for three days. After having harried the coast for 200 years... The traditions of these fierce and sanguinary descents by the Japanese, and native pirates and cutthroats, who joined them, yet live in the minds of the people here; and the Amoy matron, coerces her fractious urchin with the black bogey of Woo-jin-lai·liao, or "the Japanese have come," up to the present hour."

Hughes, 1872

1   Photos of Gulangyu Refugee Camp by Amoy Missionaries, 1938 (see next chapter)

Japanese Ships in Amoy Harbor, 1938   J.N.

第二十九章　日本人在厦门600年

日本的首次侵袭发生在1369年，对泉州……1561年，他们再次攻击泉州，这座城市显然很无助，因其地理位置常常被袭击。随后，日本人攻打同安，这次遭受了顽强的抵抗，据说同安城被整整包围了四个月。1562年，同安与南安一起被日本人攻占，两座城镇饱受战火蹂躏，被洗掠一空。在攻占40天后，日本人放火烧城，然后弃城而去。在这前后，日本人转而攻占了萨摩亚，很可能是为了方便日后对中国大陆进行偷袭。据称，他们在那自己修建了房屋并呆了一年，但实际上他们占领该岛的时间很可能更长。

1563年，他们看来已攻进了富庶、重要的漳州府，再次洗劫同安，烧毁镇江县的大量房屋。1564年，他们在泉州屠杀了很多官吏、士兵和百姓。1567年，他们再次攻打泉州，屠杀和洗劫整整持续三天。掠夺海岸200年后……日本人和他们的帮凶海盗、杀手凶狠残害后代的习俗仍深深地刻当地人的脑海里；厦门主妇们至今仍用"倭种来了"（Woo-jin-lai·liao）或"日本[倭]人来了"等话语来吓唬顽皮的小孩。

——休斯，1872年，第5、6页

Lower Half of Gulangyu Refugee Camp, 1938　J. Anderson
Matt Huts Organized by Mr. Tully, Chair of Relief Education Committee

Japanese in Amoy, October, 1901   China is not yet broken up into bits, though she has received a tremendous shaking and several crashes lately, leaving her considerably cracked and scared...

We dare not prophesy the future of China; we only know that she never again can be what she once was. There has been far too much of revolution for that......

...In our lovely little harbor, at one end, we can plainly see a huge French man-of-war, closely guarded by three Japanese smaller, but still formidable, gun boats. You may easily imagine that all this produces a peculiar impression upon the minds of the Chinese. Put yourself in his place, and what would I do? Is the question each one might ask himself before he judges too harshly.

By Dr. John Otte, Published in Hope College Anchor, December 1901.

Conditions at Amoy, August 28, 1900   I have thus far hesitated writing anything for publication on the situation here in China. There are so many unreliable rumors afloat all the time that I thought it best not to write at all, fearing that I might help to promulgate what was not true and thus cause unnecessary alarm...

You know, of course, that the Japanese are very anxious to obtain possession of this (Fuhkien) province. So they have been establishing free schools for English, etc., and they have opened many places for Shinto and Buddhist worship in this region. They also rented a house here in Amoy and converted it into a Buddhist temple. At about one o'clock in the early morning of Thursday, August 23, this temple was burned. Nearly everyone here think the Japanese priests set fire to it themselves. I myself have examined the place and am inclined to think this is true. There were two Japanese men-of-war inthis harbor, and when they saw their temple had been burnt, they immediately landed a large number of marines and two quick firing guns. They put their men on guard in some of the principal streets of the city. A placard threatening to burn the Japanese consulate was also found pasted on the walls of this building and so they also landed marines on the island of Kulangsu, where most of the foreigners live. Thus they virtually took possession of this place by this high handed and totally unnecessary act. ... So every foreigner here in Amoy is fearfully incensed at the Japanese. The result of this act by the Japs has been to cause the natives to leave Amoy by the thousands. They live in abject terror of their lives. Poor people! Yesterday our consul asked Mr. Pitcher and myself to walk through the city and tell the natives in his name that they must not fear, and he and the English consul would do all in their power to protect them. In spite of this they say one-third of the people have left the place.

...The Japanese consul has been recalled to Tokio, to report, and to explain the reasons for the disturbance he caused in this region. Still, it must be said in justice to him, that he always objected to the measures the Japanese took. It was the Japanese vice-consul, a regular fire-eater and hater of foreigners, who in connection with the captains of the Japanese men-of-war, forced the consul to allow the Japanese marines to land. But for the fact that the English got here in time to prevent it [a large English cruiser entered Amoy Harbor on August 29, and sent 50 marines ashore], the Japanese might now be in possession of Amoy, for shortly after the Iris got here a transport carrying twelve hundred Japanese troops entered the outer harbor, but seeing they were forestalled they at once returned to Formosa.

第二十九章　日本人在厦门600年　600 Years of Japan in Amoy

1901年10月日本人在厦门　近年来，尽管中国遭受了一次剧烈的震动和几次碰撞，变得伤痕累累，内心恐惧，但尚未到支离破碎的地步……

我们不敢预言中国的未来，我们只知道，她绝不会再是从前的她。为此，她已经承受太多的革命……

在我们可爱的小海港里，我们可以清楚地看见，三艘恐怖的日本小炮艇严密监视着一艘巨大的法国军舰。你可以很容易就联想到，这一切会在中国人的心中产生一种特别的印象。站在他们的角度想想，你会怎么做？每个人在匆忙做出判断前是否会问这个问题？

——郁约翰，发表于《霍普学院新闻报道》，1901年12月

1900年8月28日厦门情况
迄今，我仍然不愿就中国的情况写点东西以供发表。一直以来，有各种各样的谣言在四处传播，我想最好还是什么都不写，担心写了东西可能会加剧不真实东西的传播，造成不必要的恐慌……

毫无疑问，你知道日本人急于占领福建省。因此，他们一直在建设免费英文学校等，并在该地区开放很多地方，供大家参拜日本神道教和佛教。

Refugee Child at Work　J. Anderson

他们还在厦门租了一所房子，将之改建成佛教寺庙。8月23日，星期四，大约凌晨一点钟左右，这座寺庙被烧毁。这儿的每个人都认为是日本僧人自己放火烧的。我自己也去检查了这个地方，倾向于认为这是真的。在港口有两艘日本军舰，当他们看见他们的寺庙起火，就立即运来大量的士兵和两挺速射炮。他们在市区主要干道上驻兵把守。有人在日本领事馆的外墙上张贴大字报，威胁要烧毁领事馆。因此，他们也往鼓浪屿岛上驻扎了士兵，大多数外国人都居住在鼓浪屿岛上。日本人通过这种高压但又不必要的手段实际上占领了这个地方……在厦门的每个外国人对日本人又怕又恨。日本人此举的结果是造成成千上万的厦门人离开故土。他们生活在极端恐惧中。可怜的人民！昨天我们的领事叫皮切尔先生和我到市区走一遭，以他的名义告诉他们不要害怕，他和英国领事会尽一切能力保护他们。但是，他们说，已有三分之一的人离开了厦门。

……日本领事被召回东京，报告解释他在该地区造成混乱的原因。其实，说句公道话，他对日本人所采取的措施持反对意见，是日本副领事强迫领事允许日本军舰登陆，副领事是个玩火的人。他仇恨外国人，与日本海军上校有联系。但若不是英国人及时赶来制止（8月29日，一艘巨大的英国巡洋舰开进厦门港，运送50名水兵上岸），日本可能占领了厦门。爱丽丝抵达厦门不久，1200名日本士兵被运送到外港。发现厦门港已有军队驻扎，他们立即返回台湾。

老外看老鼓浪屿 *Old Gulangyu in Foreigners' Eyes*

During the last week we have had four Japanese, three English, one American, one German, one Russian men-of-war in this harbor. Ten in all. Quite a display, and very interesting. At present there are still seven left, viz., four Japanese, one English, one German, and one American.

Letter by Rev. J.A. Otte, M.D.

Japanese in Amoy (1920s)   "Yet when, one morning, we awoke to find Japanese naval landing parties swarming like ants all over Kulangsu, we were more angry. It was an irrational anger, compounded, I suppose, of dislike for China's hereditary enemy and indignation that the Japanese should use an International Settlement for their private show of force."

"Of all the bloody cheek," Cyril growled, as we were pushed into the gutter by a party of earnest little yellow marines, bayonets fixed, coming up from the bay at the double. A machine-gun post dominated Wei's garden, and from the top of Camel rock signals flashed. Yet the Japanese displaying their capacity thus, ostensibly in the interests of us all, appeared to differ little in intention from that British force which, even now, was sailing towards Shanghai. But we deeply distrusted the Japanese, and in later years our distrust and dislike were to be tragically justified.

"By midday, the island was thoroughly infested; Japanese were everywhere. With a professional soldier's eye, Cyril reluctantly admitted that they had executed the manoeuvre with astonishing speed and efficiency. He liked them none the better for that.

Mackenzie-Grieves

Refugees on Gulangyu   J. Anderson

第二十九章　日本人在厦门600年　600 Years of Japan in Amoy

上星期,在这个港口(厦门)出现了四艘日本军舰,三艘英国军舰,一艘美国军舰、一艘德国军舰和一艘俄国军舰,总共10艘。场景多么宏大,多么有趣。目前,厦门港内还有7艘军舰停泊,即日本四艘,英国一艘,德国一艘和美国一艘。

——郁约翰牧师(医学博士)的信件

日本人在厦门(20世纪20年代)　某天清晨,我们一觉醒来,发现日本海军先头登陆部队像蚂蚁一般涌进鼓浪屿。当时,我们非常生气。这是一种无名火,很复杂。我想,这其中可能混杂着对中国夙敌的厌恶和愤慨。日本人怎能把公共租界作为他们私人展示武力的地方呢?

西里尔抱怨道:"到处都是充满杀气的脸孔。"我们被一群凶巴巴的日本水兵推进贫民窟。他们年纪不大,身着黄色服装,背着刺刀,从海湾快步走来。一挺机关枪架在魏氏花园里。日光岩(译者注:外国人称之为"骆驼峰",即Camel Rock)上信号灯在闪烁。日本人在展示他们的实力。表面上为了我们大家的利益,但实际上与英军的意图没有多大的差别。眼下,英国海军正朝上海方向航行。我们根本就不信任日本人。后来,我们的不信任和厌恶很悲惨地被证实了。

正午时分,整个小岛完全被日本人填满了。到处都是日本人。以一个职业军人的眼光,西里尔很不情愿地承认,日本人以惊人的速度和效率完成了调动。但他并不因此而喜欢他们。

——麦肯兹·格瑞芙,1959年,第163页

Gulangyu Refugee Camp　J. Anderson

老外看老鼓浪屿 Old Gulangyu in Foreigners' Eyes

Old Lau's View on Japanese (1920s) As to the Japanese, he [Old Lau] says they have always been our enemies. But when order is once more restored in the Flowery Kingdom, the intruders will be finally driven out from the north and from Taiwan, which is part of our province… 'Your country did badly in choosing to become their ally,' he said sombrely, and spat neatly into his pink enameled spittoon.

It was true. We soon discovered that the Anglo-Japanese Alliance of 1902, which had been abrogated only at the Washington Conference two years previously, had had a disastrous effect on our relations with China.

"My grandfather is old-fashioned and conservative," said Kim Kee, "but we all hate the Japanese."

l felt that, as their allies, she was including us in the hatred. Her lips closed tightly on the indictment. We waited for the old man to speak, but he, too, was silent. Our first visit to a Chinese scholar of the old school was not turning out as we had imagined. The silence grew oppressive. "I think," I said to Kim Kee, "we'd better be going."

Refugee Mother Getting Milk

Mackenzie-Grieves, 1959

Mealtime for Refugees

Little Refugee

第二十九章　日本人在厦门600年　*600 Years of Japan in Amoy*

老刘对日本人的看法（20 世纪 20 年代）
关于日本人，他（老刘）说，他们一直都是我们的敌人。当中国再次恢复秩序时，侵略者最终必将被赶出北方和台湾。台湾是我们省的一部分……"你的国家选择他们作为盟国，这很不好，"他阴沉沉地说，同时很干脆利落地向粉红色的陶瓷痰盂吐了一口痰。

的确如此。我们很快就发现，1902 年的英日联盟给我们与中国的关系带来了灾难性的后果。这个联盟两年前在华盛顿大会上刚被解散。

"我的祖父是老派人物，很保守，"金枝（音译，Kim Kee）说，"但我们都痛恨日本人。"

我觉得，作为他们的盟军，她也把我们列入憎恨对象。她在控诉的时候，嘴唇紧闭。我们等着老人再讲，但是他也默不作声。我们首次拜访老派中国学者的情形与我们想象的完全不同。沉默开始变得很压抑。我对金枝说："我看，我们还是走吧。"

Refugee Child Working

——麦肯兹·格瑞芙，1959 年，第 46、47 页

Refugees on Gulangyu

老外看老鼓浪屿 *Old Gulangyu in Foreigners' Eyes*

J. Anderson
Received Priority Milk Ration

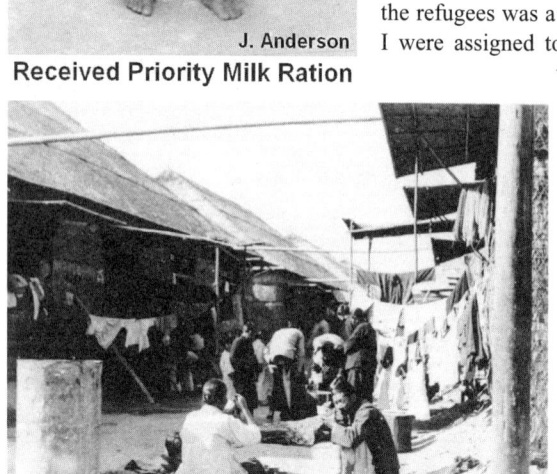

J. Anderson
Refugees Sunning Clothes

Japanese in Amoy, May, 8, 1938 May 8, 1938, a great blow came to our area, when Amoy was taken over by the Japanese. Margaret and I saw the whole debacle from the rooftop of Ioktek, Amoy Girls' High School in Kolongsu, one of the highest buildings in Kolongsu Island. We saw very sad things happening. People coming across on small rafts, some folk being held up by basketballs were trying to swim across the Harbor, but were being shot at by Japanese soldiers on the Bund.

Some 30,000 refugees came from the Island of Amoy, stretching the population to double its size in the tiny peaceful Island of Kolongsu, in international haven, run by the British and French, the US and the Japanese. Accommodation for the refugees was a huge problem. Margaret and I were assigned to the Union Church building where we took in four hundred persons. We dug a deep ditch at the back of the Church to be used as a latrine. Each person had a very limited space, just the size of a mat for sleeping on. Goldsmiths from Amoy had Chinese pillows of lacquer, and suitcases of gold pieces, and even bars. They insisted that the lights be kept on all night for protection. We fed the refugees from a central food kitchen. Men came with huge buckets of soft steaming rice at mealtimes. Everyone helped each other in very remarkable ways in the six week occupation. Finally things returned to somewhat normal conditions, but Amoy Island was cut off from the Island of Kolongsu and the mainland. As foreigners we were not restricted in our travels and on the whole the Japanese treated us well...

In 1938 Japan had pulled a tremendous hoax on the US and our government had fallen into their trap. Japan suggested we mark our property because Japan said, "We are not at war with you". We painted American flags on the tennis courts and on the flat roof tops of the houses. After Pearl Harbor we were easy targets, on the other hand, I must say that Japanese pilots did not indiscriminately bomb us, at least in Fukien Province.

Walter deVelder, Memoirs

第二十九章　日本人在厦门600年　600 Years of Japan in Amoy

1938年5月8日日本人在厦门　1938年5月8日，日本人攻占厦门。我们所在的地区遭受了巨大的打击。玛格丽特和我从鼓浪屿毓德（Ioktek）女中的屋顶（鼓浪屿岛最高点之一）亲眼目睹了溃败的全过程。我们看到悲惨的事情正在发生。有些人乘着小木筏过轮渡，有些人趴在篮球上想游过海港，但是被岸上的日本士兵开枪打死了。

大约有3万难民是来自厦门本岛，使得鼓浪屿这个平静小岛的人口翻倍。鼓浪屿是个国际性港口，由英国、法国、美国和日本共同管理。难民的食宿是一个大问题。玛格丽特和我被派往协和礼拜堂，那里收留了400名难民。我们在教堂背后挖了一条很深的沟，作为厕所使用。每个人只有一点点空间，大约只有睡觉的草席那么大。来自厦门的金匠带来不少上了油漆的中国枕头，一箱箱的金箔、甚至金条。为安全起见，他们坚持整夜灯火通明。我们在大厨房为难民准备食物。用餐时间，男人带来大桶蒸饭。在日本人占领的六个星期里，每个人都以各种不寻常的方式互相帮助。最后，事态终于回归正常。但是，厦门本岛却与鼓浪屿和内陆断绝了联系。作为外国人，我们上岛旅行并没有受到限制，日本人总体上对我们不错……

1938年，日本跟美国开了一个极大的玩笑。我们的政府落入他们的圈套。日本人建议我们将鼓浪屿岛上的财产做好标记。他们说："我们不与你们交战。"我们在网球场和屋顶平台上都打上美国国旗的标记。珍珠港事件后，我们很明显都变成了他们的攻击目标。不过，我必须说明的是，日本飞机没有不分皂白地轰炸我们，至少在福建省是这样。

——沃尔特·德·费尔德，《百年传教史》（未出版）

Gulangyu Refugees　　J. Anderson

老外看老鼓浪屿 Old Gulangyu in Foreigners' Eyes

Argument Against Partition of China (1906)   It is a pity that the framers of the Protocol of 1901 did not embody in it that, if China kept the peace, and complied with the treaties, her international rights would be respected. It would have been a splendid thing to do to guarantee that there should be no partition of her territory. It is too much to expect that the five nations which have seized her land should give it back to her. No man of affairs expects that the restitution will be made. Where the German eagle has once fastened his claws, says the German Emperor, there he will remain.

Conceding that the status quo must be preserved— what of the future? Of all the countries of the world China is least adapted to partition. No race is more homogeneous, or compact, or bound together by more ancient ties and attractions, than the Chinese. Wherever the Chinese goes he retains his national habits, customs, and solidarity. He has invaded in great numbers Hongkong, Singapore, Columbo, the Philippines, Borneo, Australia, and California, but he remains everywhere segregated in a mass secluded from the residents of the lands whose employments he has conquered. A division of China among the European powers might mean subjugation of the various portions by arms, but it would never mean absorption. The Chinese have absorbed the Mongolians, and the Manchus, and they would absorb their conquerors. Partition would bring with it incessant insurrections. Russia, perhaps, would meet the conditions by wholesale massacres, but the other powers would hesitate to adopt such bloody measures. Finally, the conquerors would quarrel among themselves. They would covet each other's territory, and a general war would break out, which would mean disaster to the beaten party.

In this day and generation it should be a sufficient answer to a proposal of partition to say that it would be wrong and unjust. No nation can afford to perpetrate a naked wrong, which the public opinion of mankind denounces. The man who soils his conscience leads a felon's life, and the nation which oppresses its weak and defenseless neighbor will inevitably pay the penalty of its wrongdoing. If China, taught by a terrible experience, executes the treaties in their letter and spirit, she should be left free to work out her own destiny. The freer she is, the more prosperous she becomes, the better will it be for the Western nations. She will become a great market for manufactured goods, and a large exporter of silks, teas, straw braid, and many other prime articles of commerce. The policy of America is to make her great, rich, and prosperous, and it is certain that the present administration apprehends to the full the expediency of this policy. We have recently acquired the Philippines. The chief argument in favour of this acquisition is the advantage that their location gives us to increase our trade with China…

No one supposes that the Chinese are less intelligent than the Japanese. I do not depreciate the latter when I repeat that the universal opinion of persons who know both races is that the Chinese are more dignified, more serious, more steadfast, than their insular rivals. What Japan has done in the way of advancement China will do if left to herself. If she is partitioned chaos will come again. You cannot make Englishmen, Russians, Austrians, Frenchmen, Germans, Italians, out of the Chinese. They are Orientals, and will so remain always. There is not much of good augury to be drawn from the domination of Eastern peoples by Western nations. No real assimilation ever takes place between the conquerors and the conquered. India to-day is held by force of arms. Tonquin, Annam, Cochin China, are held by the sword.

Denby, 1906

第二十九章　日本人在厦门600年　*600 Years of Japan in Amoy*

瓜分中国　编者按：如果说日本想占领中国似乎是野心勃勃，想想看，事实上所有西方列强都在中国争夺领地，就像他们在非洲所做的那样。毕尔士福勋爵所著的《瓜分中国》一书其实就是每个省份的一个目录。它一一列举了被外国"主人"享用的中国财产。

正如一个美国商人所言，想在中国地图上找到不属于外国势力的地方，实际情况是"中国到底在哪里啊！"

反对瓜分的意见（1906年）　很遗憾，1901年条约制定者没有在条约中注明，如果中国维持和平，遵守条约规定的话，她的国际权利应当受到尊重。保证她的领土不被瓜分是一件很了不起的事情。期待已夺走她的土地的五个国家将国土归还给中国是痴心妄想。见过大场面的人都不会期望列强归还中国土地。德国皇帝说，凡是德国鹰爪抓过的地方，都是他的盘。

退一步来说，保持现状，那将来又将是怎样？在世界上所有国家当中，中国最不适合瓜分。没有一个种族比中国人更加单纯。他们被古老的血缘关系和凝聚力紧密地捆绑在一起。无论走到哪里，中国人都保留传统习惯、风俗和团结。他们曾经大量移民香港、新加坡、科伦坡、菲律宾、婆罗洲、澳大利亚和加利福尼亚，但是无论走到哪里，他们都会从当地居民手中夺取土地使用权，并自我隔离，聚集而住。欧洲列强瓜分中国可能意味着通过武力夺取各个地区，但永远不可能是同化。中国人已经同化了蒙古人和满洲人，他们也将同化征服者。瓜分会带来没完没了的反抗。俄国可能会通过大屠杀达到目的，但其他列强不愿采用如此血腥的手段。最后，征服者们将内部发生争吵。他们相互觊觎领土，将会爆发一场世界大战。这对败者来说意味着灾难。

在当今这个年代，瓜分中国是错误和不公正的。这个回答对建议者来说理由是充分的。没有一个民族能犯得起一个明显的错误，并引起全社会的谴责。丧失良心的人过的是重罪犯的生活，压迫弱小无防御能力邻国的国家将不可避免地为自己的错误付出代价。如果中国总结以往苦难经历的经验教训，严格执行协定内容和精神，她应该能按照自己的自由意志决定自己未来的命运。越自由，她就会变得越繁荣，对西方国家好处越多。她将成为西方工业成品的大市场，成为丝绸、茶叶、稻草编织物和其他主要商品的大出口商。

美国的政策是使她变得强大、富裕和繁荣。现任政府无疑是充分理解了这一政策的精神实质。最近，我们刚刚拿下了菲律宾。占领菲律宾的主要理由是他们地理位置的优势，能增加我们与中国的贸易往来……

没有人认为中国人的智慧不如日本人。熟悉这两个种族的人都一致认为，中国人比她岛国竞争对手更有威严，而且更加严肃认真、坚定。我反复这么说，并没有贬低后者的意思。如果一切都能够自主的话，日本在发展的道路上已做过的事情，中国也会完成。如果她被分割了，则又将陷入混乱。你不可能将中国人改造成为英国人、俄国人、奥地利人、法国人、德国人或意大利人。他们是东方人，永远都是。西方国家从西方统治中无法预言什么。征服者和被征服者之间没有发生真正的同化。今天，印度是靠武力征服的。东京（Tonquin，法属殖民地时代的越南北部）、安南（Annam，法属殖民地时代的越南中部）、交趾支那（Cochin China，法属殖民地时代的越南西贡和南圻等地）是靠刀剑统治的。

——丹比，1906年，第95、96页

老外看老鼓浪屿 *Old Gulangyu in Foreigners' Eyes*

Chapter 30
70 Years After Japanese Invasion of Amoy

Gulangyu, May 1938, by John Anderson
(born on Gulangyu of missionary parents who helped in refugee work)

The Return   In October of this year, 2008, I will be coming to Kulangsu with my wife for a stay of 30 days. For me, this journey has especial resonance, for I was born on Kulangsu one year after the events of May 1938 and this is the first time that I have returned. I did not plan my return to be on the seventieth anniversary of the occupation of Amoy but it seems fitting that it should have turned out that way. I grew up with the stories told by my parents about the events of that time: "Kulangsu is a tiny island about a mile and a half long and three quarters of a mile wide. ..." Then would follow the narrative of the attack on Amoy and the resulting refugee crisis, a crisis in which my parents, along with many other missionaries, played an important part. But why should I, who left the scene at age year and a half, presume to write about these things? First it is a narrative that I lived as a child through my father's stories, and now live again through the pages of my mother's diaries, which she faithfully wrote every night, for most of her long life, even through these horrifying times. So while most of the words on the page are mine, the story is really that told by two who lived these events. I hope that this story may be of interest to you who stayed and still live on Kulangsu.

The Road to Kulangsu—my Mother in Foochow   My mother, Constance Mary Hopkinson, was born in 1895 in Tunbridge Wells in East Anglia, that most English part of England. It was not a family of great wealth, ambition, or piety, but out of her own determination and faith, she scraped together the money to study nursing and in 1925, she left England's shores to become a missionary nurse with the CMS in Foochow. There was to be one more step to bring her to Kulangsu.

Gulangyu Refugees   J. Anderson

My father in Amoy   My father, Peter Anderson, was also born in 1895 but in London, not just within the sound of Bow Bells but while they were actually ringing, so he would say. The family moved to Yorkshire where he grew up and went to school. Then he took a bachelor's degree in chemistry and worked for some years in various parts of the Yorkshire textile industry. In 1933, he felt the call and went to the English Presbyterian Amoy Mission to teach science and was promptly put to work teaching English.

390

第三十章　日本侵华战争爆发70年

1938年5月的鼓浪屿，约翰·安德森（生于鼓浪屿传教士家庭，父母均参加救济难民）撰写。

回归　我和我的妻子将于2008年10月在鼓浪屿住30天。这次鼓浪屿之行对我尤其有特殊意义，因为1938年5月事变（日本占领厦门）一年后我在鼓浪屿出生，并且这是我自幼年离开鼓浪屿后第一次回来。我并非特意选择，但我的回归似乎本来就应该发生在日本入侵厦门的第70周年。我父母对那个时期的回忆伴随着我的成长："鼓浪屿是个很小的小岛，大约1.5英里长，3/4英里宽……"接着是日本袭击厦门以及随后发生的难民危机，我父母和其他传教士是当时救济难民的重要力量之一。那么，为什么在一岁半就离开鼓浪屿的我，认为自己有必要把这些事情记录下来？因为它不仅是伴随我童年的父亲的故事，而且是伴随我现在的母亲的日记。我母亲终其一生，即使在那段恐怖的时期，都坚持每晚写日记。虽然文中大部分文字出自我笔下，但我记录的是我父母对他们亲身经历的直接叙述。我希望这个故事可以引起在鼓浪屿生活过的和现在仍然住在鼓浪屿的人们的兴趣。

鼓浪屿之前的故事——母亲在福州　我母亲叫康斯坦斯·玛丽·霍普金森，1895年生于最具英格兰典型特征的东英格兰的滕布里奇韦尔斯。我母亲的家庭并不十分富裕，没有显赫的家世，也不是非常虔诚。但凭借自己的决心和信仰，她设法筹集了完成护理学业的费用，并于1925年离开英格兰，成为英国圣公会传教团在福州的一名传教护士。这使她离鼓浪屿更接近了一步。

父亲在厦门　我父亲叫彼得·安德森，同样生于1895年，不过出生地是伦敦，但他并不认为自己是严格意义上的伦敦人。父亲随全家搬到约克郡，并在那里长大及求学。他后来获得化学学士学位，并在约克郡的纺织业工作了几年头。1933年，他作为英国长老会的传教士前往厦门，开始教授科学，很快便改为教英语。

Peter Anderson and Constance Mary Hopkinson
English Episcopal Church, Fuzhou, 10 November, 1936

Kuliang On a mountain above the city of Foochow there is a village called Kuliang. In the summer, many missionaries from many different missions would retreat there to escape the sweltering heat. It was not all holiday. Many conferences and organizational meetings would be held. Other meetings also happened; in early August 1936, Constance met Peter. Two weeks later, they were engaged to be married. The wedding duly took place on 10 Nov 1936 in the British Episcopal Church in Foochow with Bishop Hind officiating. My father returned to his teaching in Kulangsu with his bride who now joined the Amoy Mission and worked in clinics and taught nurses.

The Dark Road Far from Kulangsu, another, darker road was forming that in May of 1938 would intersect with that of my parents. It began in Mukden in 1931 with the invasion and conquest of Manchuria by Japan. It seemed clear to all that Japanese ambition would not be satisfied with its control of what it now called Manchukuo and after years of constant low-level conflict came the Battle of Luguo Bridge in July 1937 - the Marco Polo Bridge Incident as I learned to call it from my father. It also seemed clear to all that Japan would quickly conquer the rest of China. This did not happen, especially in the mountainous South, which remained throughout largely unoccupied. In an attempt to control access to the southern regions, Japan planned to establish coastal enclaves. One of the places marked for occupation was called Amoy. [SSJ][1]

Kulangsu, 1938 Domesticity and Peace: from my mother's diary

1 April[1]: Did some more to baby Defty's bibs and read *St Martins Review*. Pete read some Chemist Journals.

The Wind Rises, the Trees Begin to Bend ...
but still no-one knew what storm was to come.

10 April: Had an air raid yesterday. 3 planes each dropping about 4 bombs, at 9:30 am. I don't know what damage they have done, if any. ... and so it continued: 11th:Had 3 alarms, 8 planes came about 9 am and back later on. Don't know where they attacked. About 1:30 pm one plane dropped 2 bombs on the fort. 12th: 9 planes over dropped bombs on fort. Went to Changchow and dropped bombs there also Foochow, Yenping. 13th: Aeroplanes over but no bombs dropped. I think it must have been Changchow. ...

Respite!

16 April: Lovely day. Third day without raids. Planned a picnic to Wilson Beach.

No more picnics – invasion and occupation

第三十章　日本侵华战争爆发70年　*70 Years After Japanese Invasion of Amoy*

鼓岭　在俯瞰福州城的一座山上有个山村，叫鼓岭。每年夏天，许多不同传教团的传教士会到那里去避暑。但除了度假外，还有很多会议和组织活动。其他类型的会面还包括，1936年8月的康斯坦斯和彼得见面。两星期后，他们订婚了。婚礼于1936年11月10日按期在福州英国圣公会教堂举行，由欣德主教主持。父亲携带他的新娘回到鼓浪屿，母亲转到厦门传教团，在诊所工作并教授护理。

沉重的局势　1931年，离鼓浪屿很远的地方——奉天正在发生的一件事情，将会在1938年5月影响我父母的生活。日本入侵并占领了满洲。显然日本的野心并不满足于对它现在称为满洲国的占领，经过几年的局部冲突，1937年7月爆发了卢沟桥战争，我父亲称之为马可波罗桥事件。当时所有人都认为日本将很快占领中国的其他地区。但这并没有发生，尤其在多山的南方，绝大部分未被占领。为了获得南进通道，日本决定建立沿海飞地。一个被确定要占领的地方叫厦门。

鼓浪屿，1938，家庭生活与和平：摘自我母亲的日记
4月1日　晴……昨晚睡得很好，学习，做园艺到上午11点。[写信并邀请朋友吃晚饭] 继续缝宝宝戴夫特的口水巾，阅读《圣马丁评论》，彼得看了些化学期刊。

起风了，树被吹弯了……　但还不知道什么规模的风暴会来。

4月10日　昨天来了次空袭。上午9：30，来了3架飞机，每架投了4枚炸弹。不知道空袭到底造成了多大的损坏，如果有的话。空袭持续，11号：三次空袭警报，上午9点来了8架飞机，后来又来了两批。不知道它们的袭击目标是哪里。大约下午1：30，一架飞机对炮台扔了两枚炸弹。12号：9架以上的飞机对炮台投弹。漳州、福州、南平都遭到了空袭。13号：飞机飞过，但没有投弹。我想空袭目标大概是漳州。

喘了口气，

4月16日　晴。连续3天没有空袭。计划去威尔逊海滨野餐。

不会再有野餐了——入侵及占领

老外看老鼓浪屿 *Old Gulangyu in Foreigners' Eyes*

9 May Vice Admiral Koichi Shiozawa of the Imperial Japanese Navy steamed toward his rendezvous with the still sleeping island. He commanded the 5th fleet: an aircraft carrier with 90 planes, a heavy cruiser with ten heavy guns, three light cruisers, up to four destroyers, and assorted "gun boats". [OoB][3]

Opposing this enormous force was a rather poorly armed Chinese provincial division, the 75th, under the command of Han Wenying. There were also three coastal batteries each equipped with one or two ancient guns. [AHF][4]

May 10: At 3:45 am. A bombardment began & later leaflets were dropped informing us that the Japanese were taking Amoy over to-day. The bombardment went on until 9-30 or so & then owing to the tide the ships had to get further away. The Air raids began about 5 am & have not ceased except for a few minutes. It's now 12 am. Letter from Win took 8 days to come & one for the Bishop which I shall have to send on. Raids on until 7 p.m. A little firing since. The University Science building in flames, Chin House partially destroyed. The Refugee problem is acute. Only women girls & small children allowed to come to Kulangsu. Mr. Defty's boat is in but cannot get rid of its 300 passengers nor can he land. It is 9-15 and we are terribly weary so away to bed.

The Japanese naval bombardment concentrated on Wutung, Nichin, and Hotsu, at the eastern end of Amoy, landing sites for about 2000 Japanese marines. However, there was also heavy bombardment of bridges, roads, ferries, ships, and their support structures. [AHF] Many other buildings were also destroyed as my mother's comment on the University shows. Many refugees fled from Amoy to Kulangsu, some sources say 60,000 in 24 hr. [AHF] In agreement with this estimate, my father would say, I'm quoting from memory, that the population of Kulangsu rose from 20,000 to 80,000 in this same 24 hr.

May 11: Such a lovely day, but so cruel. Oh the life that has been needlessly lost today and the suffering everywhere. At 5:30 am Dr George Cummins rang up and asked me to be at the hospital as soon as possible. Peter and I were there by 6:30 and oh what a mess we found. Later on Dr Lin came along and several others and soon we had things a little more shipshape. It has been a day of terrible bombing and big fires and people just mowed down by the Japs and their bodies thrown in the sea, 49 in one batch seen by George and the consul and some ships officers. 200 soldiers stormed the ACC [Anglo-Chinese College] this am local militia but they have gone now. They gave up all arms and ammunition and got into civilian clothes. The Church has just been opened to the refugees, all public buildings everywhere, and yet they are sleeping in hundreds out of doors.

Refugees and Workers   J. Anderson

第三十章　日本侵华战争爆发70年　70 Years After Japanese Invasion of Amoy

5月9日　日本帝国海军舰队副司令铃木宏一率舰队抵达还在沉睡中的小岛。他指挥的第五舰队包括：一艘有90架舰载机的航空母舰，一艘有10门大炮的重巡洋舰，3艘轻巡洋舰，4艘驱逐舰，还有各种炮艇。这支强大力量的对立面是一支装备严重不足的中国地方部队，韩文英指挥的75师。还有3个装备着老旧大炮的海岸炮台。

5月10日　凌晨3:45。炮轰开始，随后空投的传单告知我们，日本自即日起接管厦门。炮轰持续至大约9:30，随后多亏退潮，舰队不得不后退。空袭从凌晨5点开始到现在中午12点，只中断了几分钟。温的信花了8天时间才送到，有一封是给主教的，我必须马上转寄。空袭持续到晚上7点。厦大的科技楼在燃烧，"Chin House"酒店部分被毁。难民的问题很严重。只允许妇女和儿童进入鼓浪屿。戴夫特先生的船靠岸了，但船上的300名乘客包括他自己都无法上岸。

厦门东海岸的五通、泥金和何厝作为2000名日本陆战队员的登陆点，受到日本海军集中炮轰。然而桥梁、道路、渡口、轮船及附属保障设施也遭到沉重轰炸。如我母亲在写到厦大时说的，很多其他建筑物也被摧毁了。许多难民从厦门涌向鼓浪屿，有人统计，在24小时内，鼓浪屿上已经有6万难民。我父亲认同这个数字，在他的记忆中，鼓浪屿的人口在那一天内，从2万增加到8万。

5月11日　晴天，不过形势严峻。无辜牺牲的生命和遍地的苦难。凌晨5：30，乔治·卡明斯医生打来电话，让我尽快去医院。彼得和我在6：30前到达医院，看到一片混乱。后来林医生和其他几个人来了，不久慢慢恢复了些秩序。一整天都是轰炸和大火，日军成批屠杀平民并把尸体扔进大海，乔治、领事和一些船长看到一批49人被集体屠杀。200个当地民兵上午冲进了英华学院，但都已经离开了。他们丢弃了武器和装备，穿上平民服装。教堂以及所有公共建筑对难民开放，然而还有成百上千人在户外过夜。

Refugee Children　　　　　　　　　　　J. Anderson

老外看老鼓浪屿 Old Gulangyu in Foreigners' Eyes

At dawn, Japanese reinforcements landed at Wutung, broke through Chinese defences, and began to sweep westward toward the city of Amoy. Other forces landed at Paishih Fort and later at both Hu Lishan and Panshi Forts. There was fierce resistance by defending Chinese troops but to little avail. The Japanese ships simply stood out of range of the coastal batteries and their ancient guns. Any troop concentrations immediately came under merciless naval bombardment. A whole battalion was killed before even setting sight on the enemy. Some local militia tried to sustain a resistance but were overwhelmed and tried to escape by jumping into the sea where they were gunned down. [AHF] Refugees continued to pour into Kulangsu. My father in his accounts gave a peak population of 120,000 for the square mile island. This number is also given in *Working His Purpose Out* by Edward Band. [WHPO][5]

May 12: Another fine day. The Japs continued bombing. Reported that the fort resisted all morning; also groups of soldiers said to be on the hills. Intervals of bombing most of the day. Back at hospital before 8:00 am. Things a little more shipshape. Amoy hospital staff turned up. Worked on store and storeroom. A good few helpers. Had a look at the Primary School, needs organizing. Chhoa hoped to go to HongKong but couldn't get on board. Gave him letter to post airmail. Apart from work for wounded and refugees, awaiting developments. (No letters or papers. Tully says Peter may be asked to be head of the Alumni School) Many refugees not enough to eat and drink. The Anking was to go out today with 3000 refugees on board, hasn't gone yet. The British Consul Fitzmaurice will not give her leaving papers.

By nightfall, the invasion was largely complete and the occupation of Amoy began. All during the attack, Amoy harbour had many Western naval ships at anchor, five US, five British, and two French. [AHF] As none of these countries were then at war with Japan, they sat out the action. Kulangsu, being an International Settlement, was not attacked. The presence of the warships was presumably to underline this special status.

Refugees—only the crisis itself can bring its own resolution

It's not clear how much pre-planning had been done by the missionaries in order to meet this crisis. After all, they knew that it was almost certain that Amoy would be occupied at some point and they would have to be responsible for coping. HJP Anderson (no relation) was not only chief of the English Presbyterian Mission but was chair of the Kulangsu Municipal Council and had been for ten years. It was expected that the hospitals would be needed for treating casualties and some restocking had taken place with a view to this expanded role [WHPO] but in the end nothing really prepares one for the magnitude of such a task and, more importantly, for the specific needs of this crisis, the one that is confronting you now. The main tasks were Housing, Feeding, Sanitation, and Schooling. How were these met? Here is a small part of that story.

Gulangyu Refugees   J. Anderson

第三十章　日本侵华战争爆发70年　*70 Years After Japanese Invasion of Amoy*

Gulangyu Refugees, 1938　J. Anderson

黎明,日军后续部队在五通登陆,突破中国防线,并开始席卷向西,进入厦门市区。其他部队先在白石炮台,随后在湖里山炮台和磐石炮台登陆。中国守军激烈抵抗但收效甚微。日军舰船在海岸炮台老旧大炮的射程之外。守军部队一集结就立刻遭到日本海军的无情炮轰。一整营的守军没看到敌人就被全部消灭。一些当地民兵试图维持抵抗但寡不敌众,跳海逃生,被射杀在海中。难民继续涌进鼓浪屿。我父亲在叙述中说这个一平方英里的小岛人口最多时达到12万。这个数字也出现在爱德华·班德著的《英国长老教会海外传教百年史1847—1947》一书中。

5月12日　又是一个晴天。日军继续轰炸。报道说炮台的抵抗持续了整个上午。据说山上也有守军。时断时续的炮轰持续了一整天。上午8:00前回到医院,秩序稍微恢复了些。厦门医院的医护人员来了。在商店和贮藏室工作。相当多的援手。去小学看了一下,发现需要人去组织。蔡想去香港,但无法上船。给了他交由航空快递寄发的信件。在为伤员和难民工作的同时,等待事态进一步发展。(没有邮件和报纸,塔利说彼得可能会被要求去担任校友学校的校长)难民太多,食物和饮用水不足。安庆号原定今天带3000名难民离开,但还没出发。英国领事菲茨莫里斯拒绝签发出航许可。

天黑前,入侵战斗基本完成,厦门沦陷。在整个攻击期间,厦门港有很多西方海军舰船抛锚停泊,5艘美国的,5艘英国的和2艘法国的。这些国家在那时候并非日本交战国,因此他们坐视了整个入侵过程,鼓浪屿,作为万国公地,未受到攻击。这些战舰的存在大概是为了特地强调它的特殊地位。

难民——只有危机本身才知道如何解决危机带来的问题

不清楚传教士们为应付这场危机是否事先做了什么准备。不过,他们知道厦门最终会被占领,他们也知道他们必须应付由此带来的问题。安德森(非亲属)不仅是英国长老会传教团的负责人,而且是鼓浪屿市政委员会的主席,并已任职达10年。事先已经考虑到医院将需要处理大量伤病员,预期将产生的补给缺口也已着手解决,但最终面对如此大规模的问题,所有的准备都显得远不足以应付当前面临的这次危机的具体需求。需要解决的主要问题是住宿、饮食、卫生和教育。这些问题都是如何解决的?以下是那段历史的一小部分。

老外看老鼓浪屿 *Old Gulangyu in Foreigners' Eyes*

Housing To begin with, all public buildings were opened to house refugees. Four thousand were crowded into the Anglo-Chinese College and its associated Girls' School, Training College and Kindergarten. Mr Tulley was in charge of the housing among other things. It was his task to organize the construction of the camps which would take the larger part of the population. These consisted of cottage-sized houses built of matting. All the materials had to be brought up from Swatow. [WHPO] Yet by the 13th May, my mother wrote: Peter and several others have gone round to the camps … " This would suggest that "camps" were already in existence within three days of the first shot being fired! These first camps can hardly have been the matting huts but rather the sizable public buildings that had been taken over on the 11th [see diary entry above] and given "camp" names, for example Gasper House Refugee Camp. Not everyone was happy with their facilities being taken over – the Japanese Consul General returned on 27 May - by 29 May my mother was writing: The poor people in the Jap club had to move today and there was nowhere to put them but the Jap school next door. That is in a terrible state and the people are terribly sad at having to go there and Mr Tully, Peter and Mr Huang nearly wept over it.

On the other hand, some noble souls even received refugees into their own house: Went for a walk in Mr. Hitchcock's garden and saw refugees everywhere. He is carrying out his communist principals [sic]. Even with all this effort, it is hard to imagine that all 100,000 extra people who were on Kulangsu at the peak of the refugee influx actually had roofs over their head and Band, in his narrative of the refugee crisis, clearly implies that they did not: Gradually numbers of refugees were got away from the island and those who remained were accommodated in camps. … At the end of the year, some 10,000 refugees remained in the camps. [WHPO]

Gulangyu Refugees   J. Anderson

第三十章　日本侵华战争爆发70年　70 Years After Japanese Invasion of Amoy

Mrs. Peter Anderson, Refugee Baby Clinic

Mrs. Peter Anderson, Refugee Baby Clinic

住宿　一开始，所有的公共建筑都开放以接纳难民。4000难民拥进英华学院及其附属女校，培训学院和幼儿园。塔利先生负责住宿和其他事务。他的任务是组织建设难民营，以接纳更多的难民。难民营主要是席子搭盖的小屋。所有的材料都得从汕头运来。但是在5月13日，我母亲写道：彼得和其他几个人参观了难民营……这说明难民营在入侵第一枪打响后三天就存在了。首批难民营并非是席子搭成的棚屋，而是在11号启用的大型公共建筑[详见上面的11号日记]，并有具体的"营名"，如Gasper House难民营。并非每个人都乐意把他们的设施让出来——日本总领事馆于5月27日回迁。29号前，我母亲写道：住在日本俱乐部的可怜的难民们今天必须搬走，但除了隔壁的日本学校，没有地方可以安置他们。那里环境很差，难民们为不得不去那里而非常难过，塔利先生、彼得和黄先生几乎难过得流泪。

另一方面，一些高尚的人甚至把难民接到他们自己的家里：在希区考克先生的花园里逛了一圈，发现到处是难民。他在实践他的共产主义者原则。即便经过如此努力，很难想象在难民潮高峰期拥进鼓浪屿的10万难民都能够有地方住宿。班德在他对这次难民危机的叙述中，明确地给出否定的暗示：逐渐地，许多难民离开鼓浪屿，留下来的都住在难民营里……到年底，大约有1万难民还留在难民营里。

Feeding The first priority was to secure a supply of rice. 15 May my mother wrote: The Japs say that they are not coming to Kulangsu. They have allowed the KMC to get rice from the godowns and water across, so that danger is averted. This seems to imply that the KMC could take rice from the Amoy godowns. Presumably this was the normal supply route for Kulangsu. Rice was cooked centrally in The Canning Factory and then carried to the camps in lots of fifty meals. When you look at the photo on the right, note the small bucket of beans that she is carrying in her hand to accompany all that rice.

On this same day, 15 May my mother wrote: Lovely day very warm 80 degrees. Had rather a hectic morning preparing for a milk kitchen [in the Girls' School] for the babies whose mother's milk is insufficient or absent. Went down to the hospital and then left early upon being phoned for by George and went to the KMC and looked for a … [illegible]. rang up various places and tried to get unsweetened tinned milk. We have some but not much when it comes to getting 3 or 4 hundred babies fed. … Went shopping and got a primus and oil stove, 2 spoons and 2 saucepans. KMC gave us 4 new kerosene oil tins for storing boiled water and supplied us with 2 tins of oil and 1 case sweetened milk. Marmite from the hospital.

Helping Refugees   J. Anderson

16 May: Peter organized teams of scouts for K.M.C. and the milk kitchen. Mrs Holleman came along and helped me get it going and Mrs HJP also came along. We had lots of mothers and babies, only a very few with no milk, but a lot with insufficient supply. It really went fairly well on the whole. On the whole, yes, but always there were things to find, to be substituted for if not found: The Ongs cannot get the alfalfa for the children's vitamin C. So I think we will use cabbage juice if I can get it made. I've begun putting marmite into the babies feeds. The work did not pass unnoticed: Mr Defty and Miriam and some of the crew of the Anking came to see us in the milk kitchen and seemed quite impressed. … Mr Isgard (?) and the Hollemans came and looked at our milk kitchen and were much impressed. Then a bath was added so that the babies could be washed. Soon there was a roster of missionary wives to do the bathing. And so it went on for all of May, June, and July. In August and September there are no more diary entries for the milk kitchen because she has handed over responsibility in order to go to Kuliang. But after her return, an entry for 18 Oct shows that she was still keeping an eye on it: Went on to the milk kitchen and saw Mrs Slater and Jessie. We had a taste of bean milk and I begged Jessie to try to get some unsweetened milk to go with the sweet. She said Mr Poppen wouldn't but I believe he would if she went the right way to work over it.

Sanitation It was always part of my parents story that my father had been inspector of latrines in this period and the official records indicate that he was assistant to Mr Tully who had responsibility for facilities including housing and sanitation.

第三十章　日本侵华战争爆发70年　70 Years After Japanese Invasion of Amoy

饮食供给　重中之重是得到大米供应。5月15日，我母亲写道：日军说他们不会登陆鼓浪屿。他们允许鼓浪屿市政委员会去粮库取米并从厦门运进饮用水，因此吃饭的问题就解决了。这似乎是说鼓浪屿市政委员会可以到厦门的粮店买米。这可能是鼓浪屿粮食的正常供应渠道。饭在罐头厂集中做，然后按每50份一批送到各难民营。当你看右边这张图的时候，请注意她挑的一小桶豆子就是配那50份饭的菜。

Gulangyu Refugee　J. Anderson

还是5月15日这天，我母亲写道：

晴天，很暖和，华氏80度。为母亲奶水不足或无奶水的婴儿设立奶水厨房[在女校]忙碌了一上午。去了趟医院，接到乔治的电话后提前离开了，去鼓浪屿市政委员会寻找一个……[看不清楚]打了几个电话找无糖罐装牛奶。我们有一些，但不够喂三四百个婴儿。去买了一个煤油汽油两用炉、两把汤勺和两个平底锅。鼓浪屿市政委员会给了4个新的煤油罐用来盛开水，还有两听油及一箱甜牛奶。从医院拿来了汤锅。

5月16日：彼得为鼓浪屿市政委员会及奶水厨房组织了志愿童军。霍莱曼太太过来帮我打理奶水厨房，安德森夫人也来帮忙。我们有许多母亲和婴儿，只有少数没有奶水，但很多奶水不足。总的来说，一切还算顺利。是的总的来说，但总有些不顺利的事，翁夫妇找不到用以给孩子们补充维生素C的紫苜蓿，因此我们打算用卷心菜汁，如果能做到的话。我已经开始给婴儿们喂汤。奶水厨房引起了人们的注意：戴夫特先生和米里亚姆以及安庆号上的一些船员到奶水厨房来看我们，看上去很受感动。伊斯加德先生和霍莱曼夫妇来看我们的奶水厨房，并认为这很了不起。随后添加了一个浴缸，用来给婴儿洗澡。很快有一群传教士的妻子来给婴儿洗澡，这样子持续了整个5月、6月和7月。在我母亲8月和9月的日记中没有再提到奶水厨房，因为她为了去鼓岭，已把奶水厨房移交给别人。但10月18日的日记显示她回来后仍然关心奶水厨房：去了趟奶水厨房，看到斯莱特和杰西太太。我们尝了一口豆浆，我请杰西兑些无糖牛奶。她说波彭先生不肯，但我相信他肯，如果她用正确的方法重做一遍的话。

卫生设备　在我父母的叙述中，我父亲在那段时期是厕所检查员，正式记录显示他是塔利先生的助手，塔利先生负责包括住房和卫生设备在内的生活设施。

老外看老鼓浪屿 Old Gulangyu in Foreigners' Eyes

The diary records for 18 May: Hot day, somewhat thundery but only a little rain for which one is thankful as there are still many homeless of the 80000 refugees on a mile square island. ... Peter was at the K.M.C. with his scouts and found the Kim Mang [?] refuge up to its neck in filth especially the latrines. 5 June: [George and Peter]talked all evening about latrines and Camps. 10 June: Peter still on Sanitary conditions. 26 June: very nice little supper at the Hollemans. He and Peter talked sanitation (and Ruth and I talked milk kitchen).

There must have been a lot to talk about: 80,000 refugees (or more), uncontrolled movement of people, crowding, lack of shelter, lack of facilities – but there was no cholera! I find that amazing.

Schooling As if just keeping people fed and sheltered was not enough, the missionaries established schools for the refugees. Band writes: The Misses Arrowsmith and Pierce, with the staffs of the two schools and the girls, organized relief, and marvellously also continued the work of the school, (except the kindergarten). ... In the autumn, in addition to taking charge of the Anglo-Chinese College and teaching a full number of hours, Mr. Tully became chairman of the Relief Education Committee. Some 16,000 children in the camps were drafted into temporary schools and taught partly by volunteers from among the refugees, partly by boys of the A.C.C. outside school hours. Band goes on to list financial support for the schools from overseas Chinese, particularly Manila and Singapore. [WHPO]

My father was also a teacher at the ACC and naturally he too was involved in this effort. In the photo above, that's him on the right-hand end of the back row. This photo is dated May 1938! No wonder that my mother writes on 28 June: HJP gave me a talking to about the amount of work Peter and I were doing and Peter and the Local Committee notes and his getting thin. I said we would see Dr Holleman and get overhauled. I can't think of anything less likely than their checking in for an overhaul. A quick checkup perhaps, then they, like the others, just kept going.

Winding down Gradually the refugees left, either to go home to Amoy or to stay with relatives on the mainland. There was great incentive to do this, despite the risks, if the relatives lived in unoccupied China. By the end of the year, only 10,000 remained in Kulangsu. The island remained under the administration of the KMC until 7 Dec 1941 but the Japanese presence was heavily felt, particularly just after the arrival of the Consul General. My mother wrote about sudden arrests of Chinese nationals. This spread great fear among everyone. The KMC was powerless to intervene and no explanations were ever given.

I was born 16 June the following year in Hope Hospital. Dr. Holleman attending...

After Pearl Harbor, the Japanese seized full control of the island and the missionaries were interned. Shortly after, HJP died of a heart attack. Most others were repatriated. The Tulleys, courageously elected to stay. They were able to continue working for a while but were eventually reinterned for the remainder of the war.

1 October, 2008 On this date we land in Amoy, an island where we have already made friends even before we arrive. In preparation for our journey, we took a brief but intensive course in Hanyu. Jintian, women dou hui shuo yidiar putonghua. Please speak slowly and wait patiently for our response: Duibuqi, qing zai shuo yi bian. We also learned a whole set of new names: Fuzhou, Xiamen, and Gulangyu. Please forgive me if I use the old names, the names that I learned as a child: Foochow, Amoy, and the one on my birth certificate, Kulangsu.

第三十章　日本侵华战争爆发70年　*70 Years After Japanese Invasion of Amoy*

5月18日的日记写道:大热天,打了几声雷,但令人欣慰的是只下了点雨,因为这个一平方英里小岛上的8万名难民中有很多人的住宿还没有解决……彼得和他的童军在鼓浪屿市政委员会工作,他发现 Kim Mang 难民营肮脏不堪,厕所尤甚。6月5日: [乔治和彼得] 整个晚上都在讨论公厕和营区。6月10日: 彼得还在设法改善卫生状况。6月26日: 霍莱曼家非常令人愉快的小晚餐。他和彼得谈论卫生(露丝和我谈论奶水厨房)。

可以谈论的东西一定很多:8万难民(或者更多),失控的人员流动,拥挤,住房不足,生活设施不足——但没有霍乱! 真令我惊讶。

教育　似乎觉得让难民有吃的有住的还不够,传教士们还设立了学校。班德写道: 阿罗史密斯和皮尔斯两所学校的教职员和女孩们,组织了这次救济,与此同时还不可思议地维持学校的正常教学秩序(幼儿园除外)……在秋天,除了负责英华学院并全职上课外,塔利先生成为救济教育委员会主席。营区大约16000名儿童被送进临时学校,教员有一部分是难民中的志愿者,另一部分由英华学院的男生在他们课余时间承担。班德还列出了海外尤其是马尼拉和新加坡的华人对学校的经济援助。我父亲也是英华学院的一名教师,很自然地也去难民学校授课。在上面这张照片中,他是后排右起第一个。照片拍摄于1938年5月! 这就不难理解为什么我母亲在6月28日写道: 安德森找我谈话,讨论彼得和我的工作负荷,彼得和地方委员会的日志以及彼得正在变瘦。我说我们会去找霍莱曼医生,做个全面体检。我想不出比他们住院接受全面体检更不可能发生的事。他们大概就做了个简单的体检,然后就像其他人一样,继续投入工作。

危机平息　难民逐渐离开,回厦门或到大陆投亲。如果有亲戚住在大陆未被日本占领的地区,投亲路途虽然不安全,但难民们还是愿意冒险。到年底,只剩下1万难民留在鼓浪屿。鼓浪屿市政委员会对这个小岛的行政权持续到1941年12月,但处于日本的阴影下,尤其在日本总领事来了以后。我母亲记下对中国人的突然搜捕。这给其他人带来极大恐慌。鼓浪屿市政委员会无法过问甚至没有收到任何解释。

次年6月16日,我生于救世医院,霍莱曼医生接生……

珍珠港事件后,日军控制了这个小岛,传教士们被拘禁。不久以后,安德森死于心脏病。其他大部分人被遣返。塔利夫妇以极大的勇气决定留下来。他们继续工作了一段时间,但最后还是被再次收押至战争结束。

2008年10月1日　这一天是我们将飞抵这个在我们到来前已经是我们的老朋友的小岛——厦门。在准备这次旅行过程中,我们参加了一个短期但课程安排集中的汉语学习班。"今天,我们都会说一点普通话。"请你们说慢点,并耐心地等待我们响应:"对不起,请再说一遍。"我们还知道了一堆新地名: 福州、厦门和鼓浪屿。请原谅我使用他们的旧名字,那些我在孩童时期知道的地名:"富抽"、"尔摩意"和在我出生证明上的这个,"库弄肃"。

老外看老鼓浪屿 *Old Gulangyu in Foreigners' Eyes*

Drill Time at School for Refugee Children   Band, 1948

Refugee Workers   J. Anderson

第三十章　日本侵华战争爆发70年　*70 Years After Japanese Invasion of Amoy*

Amoy Mission's School for Gulangyu Refugees — J. Anderson

1 SSJ: Second Sino-Japanese War, Wikipedia, http://en.wikipedia.org/wiki/Second_Sino-Japanese_War
  SSJ: 第二次中日战争，Wikipedia, http://en.wikipedia.org/wiki/Second_Sino-Japanese_War

2 Indented and italicized text are quotations from my mother's diary unless otherwise noted.
  Quotations courtesy of Hocken Library, PO Box 56, Dunedin, New Zealand.
  http://www.library.otago.ac.nz/libs/hocken/
  如果没有另外说明，缩排及斜体的文字表示摘自我母亲的日记。
  转摘许可权归 Hocken Library, PO Box 56, Dunedin, New Zealand.

3 OoB: Order of Battle for Amoy Operation, Wikipedia,
  http://en.wikipedia.org/wiki/Order_of_battle_for_Amoy_Operation
  厦门入侵战争过程，Wikipedia,http://en.wikipedia.org/wiki/Order_of_battle_for_Amoy_Operation

4 AHF: Axis History Forum, http://forum.axishistory.com/viewtopic.php?p=1054290#1054290

5 WHPO: Working His Purpose Out : the history of the English Presbyterian mission, 1847-1947. Edward Band, Cheng Wen, Taipei, 1972.
  Working His Purpose Out：英国长老会传教团历史，1847—1947

▶ 405

老外看老鼓浪屿 *Old Gulangyu in Foreigners' Eyes*

Chapter 31
Gulangyu—Cradle of Tropical Medicine

Another curious, and not altogether absurd, custom of the Chinese is to pay a physician so long as they continue in health, but if they fall ill, the doctor's salary ceases until they recover, whereupon it commences again.

Stoddard's Lectures

Gulangyu's Pivotal Role in Modern Medicine
Adapted from Discover Gulangyu 《魅力鼓浪屿》
For such a minor islet, Gulangyu has played a major role in developing modern medicine. On Gulangyu, "The Cradle of Tropical Medicine（热带医学的摇篮）," Sir Patrick Manson （帕特里克·曼森先生）made his great medical discoveries, and little Gulangyu gave birth to Lin Qiaozhi （林巧稚）, "Mother of China's Modern Obstetrics and Gynecology."

Gulangyu's trailblazing medicine began in 1842 with the arrival of Dr. Cummings, who lived with Amoy's first missionary, David Abeel (Yabili, 雅裨理), in the old home at #23 Zhonghua Rd. The two later moved to Liaozihou (寮仔后) and then to Zhushujiao (竹树脚), where in 1843 they founded a clinic that was forerunner of "Chibao (赤保) hospital" (later part of Hope Hospital).

Hope Hospital 50th Anniversary   J. Nienhuis

Gulangyu's honor roll of medical missionaries includes pioneers like Dr. J.C. Hepburn (1843-1845), Dr. James Young (English Presbyterian Mission, 1850-1854), Dr. Hirschberg (London Missionary Society, 1853-1858), and Dr. John Carnegie (1859-1862). But my favorite of the lot is Dutch-born American Dr. John Abraham Otte (Yu Yuehan, 郁约翰), of the American Reformed Mission[1] (Guizheng Jiao, 归正教).

Amoy—1st Medical Missions in China The year 1844 is a noted one in the history of medical missions. In January Drs. Hepburn and Cumming opened a hospital in the city of Amoy...

"Chinese Recorder", Volume 5, Shanghai, Volume

1　ARM, known as the Reformed Protestant Dutch Church , 1816-1826

第三十一章　鼓浪屿——热带医学的摇篮

另外，让我感到奇怪但也不完全荒唐的中国习俗是，医生身体健康、能行医的时候，就给他们支付报酬。一旦他们生病，他们的薪水就会被停发，直到康复，再开始发放。

——《斯托达德的演讲稿》，第305页

鼓浪屿在中国现代医学的重要地位（摘自《魅力鼓浪屿》）

鼓浪屿这个弹丸小岛在现代医学的发展过程中扮演了重要的角色。正是在这"热带医学的摇篮"，帕特里克·曼森先生取得了重大的医学发现；小小的鼓浪屿还诞生了"中国现代妇产科之母"林巧稚。

鼓浪屿对医学的贡献始于1842年。那年，鼓浪屿来了两个人——甘明医生和第一个进入厦门的传教士雅俾理。他俩合住于现在的中华路23号一座舒适的旧屋。这对搭档后来搬到寮仔后，之后又搬到竹树脚。在那儿，于1843年开设了一家诊所，就是"赤保医院"的前身（后来成为"救世医院"的附属医院）。

早期在鼓浪屿悬壶济世的传教士包括J.C.赫伯恩(1843—1845)医生，英国长老

Dr. Patrick Manson and Family, Amoy, 1881

会詹姆士·杨格医生(1850—1854)，伦敦差会赫希堡医生(1853—1858)，和约翰·卡内基医生(1859—1862)等先驱。不过，所有人中，我个人最为推崇的是生于荷兰的美国人——归正教的郁约翰博士。

厦门——中国最早开办教会医院的地方　1844年是教会医院历史上值得注意的一年。当年一月，赫伯恩和康明两位医生在厦门设立了第一所医院……

——《中国教务杂志》，第五卷，上海卷，第140页

老外看老鼓浪屿 *Old Gulangyu in Foreigners' Eyes*

Innoculations in Amoy, "Le Petit Parisien", February 7, 1897

第三十一章　鼓浪屿——热带医学的摇篮　*Gulangyu—Cradle of Tropical Medicine*

Hope and Wilhelmina Hospitals Staff, 1932

老外看老鼓浪屿 Old Gulangyu in Foreigners' Eyes

Patrick Manson—Father of Tropical Medicine
Adapted from Discover Gulangyu 《魅力鼓浪屿》

Sir Patrick Manson, Father of Tropical Medicine Gulangyu is known to Western doctors as the "Cradle of Tropical Medicine" because it was here that Sir Patrick Manson (1844–1922), "Father of Tropical Medicine," made discoveries that helped tackle leprosy, malaria, and other diseases that 150 years ago made Xiamen a "white man's graveyard."

Western medicine was impotent in the face of tropical disease, and Chinese medicine fared no better. In 1877, 2% of Xiamen's population died of cholera, and to Manson's frustration, traditional Chinese doctors treated the disease with alum, stimulants, hot poultices, shampooing, and "pinching." But Manson discovered that, in fact, some Chinese treatments did work.

Chinese cured a woman's anemia with pills concocted from a black chicken's dried liver. Western doctors did not learn to treat pernicious anemia with liver until 1926. Perhaps Chinese medicine's occasional successes helped spur the Scotsman on to the research that gave birth to modern tropical medicine.

Pioneer or Drunken Scotsman? In his quest to conquer China's diseases, Manson dissected everything from mosquitoes to corpses (in the dead of night, in graveyards, because Chinese frowned on carving up corpses). But it was a lonely life, and in 1877 the discouraged young pioneer wrote to a friend in London,

"I live in an out of the world place, away from libraries, out of the run of what is going on, so I do not know very well the value of my work, or if it has been done before, or better."

In fact, Manson's work was so far ahead of his time that other doctors ridiculed his discoveries. One doctor said Manson's claims represented "either the work of a genius or, more likely, the emanations of a drunken Scots doctor in far-off China, where, as everyone was aware, they drank too much whisky."

Manson was first to connect mosquitoes with elephantiasis (1878) and malaria (1894), and he discovered that only female mosquitoes suck blood (males live on fruit juices). Manson also invented new surgical techniques and instruments that even today bear his name (he had one elaborate device made by a local Chinese metal worker). He also helped introduce modern vaccination to China—ironically enough, since Taoists inoculated against smallpox almost 1,000 years ago. Ancient Chinese almost created surgery as well (see end of this chapter).

As news of Manson's medical prowess spread, patients flooded in. In 1871, Manson's first year at the Baptist Missionary Hospital, he treated 1,980 patients. His third year he treated 4,476 people. In 1877, he performed 237 elephantiasis surgeries alone. He removed over one ton of tumors from 61 of the cases and lost only two patients. He also got sued.

Suing the Surgeon! One patient had so much excess tissue that he could not move and he was carted about town in a wheelbarrow. He made a living selling lemonade and peanuts, and created a table by spreading a cloth over his massive deformities. After Manson removed eighty pounds of tumors, allowing him to move freely once again, he promptly sued Manson and sought compensation. He complained that without his convenient table of deformed flesh he had lost his livelihood!

Sir Philip Manson-Bahr, "Patrick Manson"

第三十一章 鼓浪屿——热带医学的摇篮 Gulangyu—Cradle of Tropical Medicine

帕特里克·曼森先生——热带医学之父 （摘自《魅力鼓浪屿》）

对于西洋医生来说，鼓浪屿以"热带医学的摇篮"著称。因为正是在这里，"热带医学之父"帕特里克·曼森先生（1844—1922）找到了有助于对付麻风、疟疾等疾病的办法。而这些疾病在150年前曾使厦门一度成为"白人的坟场"。

西医对于热带疾病无能为力，中医也没有更好的办法。1877年，2%的厦门人口死于霍乱。令曼森失望的是，对于这种疾病，中国医生的传统疗法是用明矾、兴奋剂等材料，采取热敷、洗头和刮痧等手法。不过，曼森发现，有些中医疗法其实是管用的。

中医拿乌鸡肝烘干后制成药丸治好了妇女的贫血病。西医直到1926年才懂得用动物肝脏来治疗恶性贫血。也许是因为中医疗法偶尔的成功激励了这位苏格兰人从事探索，才诞生出现代热带医学。

是先驱还是苏格兰醉汉？ 在探索中国疾病疗法的过程中，曼森解剖了小到蚊子大到人的尸体（解剖工作是深夜里在坟地进行的。因为中国人忌讳解剖尸体）。然而，那是一种孤独的生活。1877年，这位一时泄气的年轻的先驱者这样写给他一位在伦敦的朋友：

"我住在世界之外，远离图书馆，不知外界正在发生什么。因此我不能确定我的工作价值所在，也许这份工作以前有人做过，甚至干得比我好。"

事实上，曼森的工作远远超过了他所处的年代，以至于别的医生嘲弄他的研究成果。一名医生说："曼森的论断像是一位天才的工作成果，但更像是一个远在中国的醉酒的苏格兰医生所说的胡话。众所周知，他们在中国喝威士忌有多么凶。"

曼森是第一个把蚊子和象皮病（1878年）及疟疾（1894年）联系在一起的人，他还发现只有母蚊子才吸血（公蚊子靠吸取植物的汁液维持生命）。曼森发明了外科新技术和新仪器，至今仍沿用他的名字（他有一件由一位中国当地金属匠精心打造的疗具）。他还帮助将现代的接种疫苗技术引入中国（颇具讽刺意味的是，大约一千年前道家就曾用接种手段预防天花，古代中国人还几乎开创了外科手术。请参阅本章结尾。）。

曼森医术高超，渐渐声名远扬，病人也就纷至沓来。1871年，也就是曼森在浸会传教医院的第一年，他治疗了1980名病人，第三年他治疗病人4476名。1877年这一年，单单象皮病手术一项他就做了237例。他从61例手术中切除的肿瘤达一吨多重，仅有两位病人丧生。他还吃过官司——

控告外科医生 有个病人身上赘生的息肉过度增长导致行动不便，出门得靠别人用小板车推着走。他卖柠檬水和花生度日，用一块布铺在他巨大的畸形部位，就能搭成一个桌面。当曼森将他80磅重的瘤子切除掉，使他重又行动自如后，他马上控告曼森，并要求赔偿。他抱怨说，失去了原来畸形部位这张随身桌子，他也就失去了生计！

——菲利普·曼森·巴哈尔爵士，《帕特里克·曼森》

Manson the Tiger Hunter "Life in Amoy in those days in a mixed community of Europeans in China was far from dull. There was a gay social life, and also from time to time sporting events, such as pony races, and shooting expeditions into the surrounding countryside where excellent snipe grounds were provided by the numerous paddy-fields.

"Farther afield were the wild highlands where every now and again tigers were bagged. Manson was foremost in these adventures and soon gained the reputation of being the best snipe-shot in China.

"But, as he became more familiar with the Chinese and their ways and won their confidence, work began to accumulate.

"Sometimes he was too busy to sleep, as his services were in constant demand."

Sir Philip Manson-Bahr

Amoy Pioneering Medical Education A certain number of the young men who have been brought up under Christian influences wish to enter the hospitals to receive medical training. It is a condition of entrance that they shall have passed through our primary and secondary schools, but in cases where students are not forthcoming in sufficient numbers to give the missionary adequate assistance in his work, the rule is sometimes relaxed; boys being accepted who have not completed their High school course. The course of medical training lasts for five years, during which time the students are constantly with the doctor learning the practice of medicine and the art of surgery and receiving lectures also on medical subjects.

It would, however, be incorrect to say that Medical schools are attached to the hospitals. The number of students is strictly limited, and their training is dependent on the time and strength which the doctor can spare after the pressing claims of his medical ministry have been satisfied. Plans were recently formulated for the establishing of a Board of Examination, which might set examinations on the subjects taught in the hospitals and give diplomas to those who passed successfully. The plan, however, has not yet been carried out, owing to the refusal of one or two of the doctors to co-operate, on the ground that they could not undertake to train students up to the standard set by the Board of Examination.

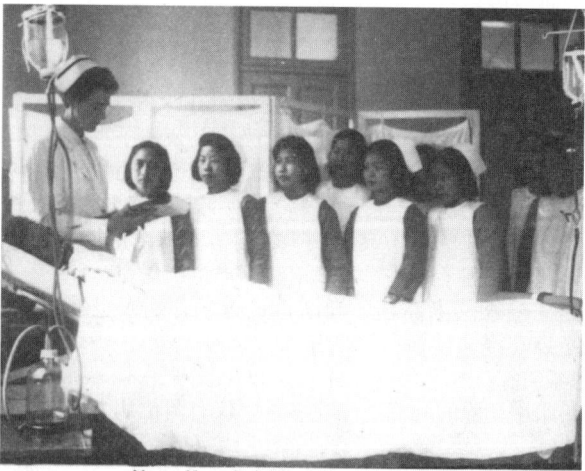
Hope Hospital Ward Teaching, 1948   J. Nienhuis

Oldham, 1908

第三十一章 鼓浪屿——热带医学的摇篮 Gulangyu—Cradle of Tropical Medicine

老虎杀手曼森 "那时候,欧洲人在中国已形成了一个混居的社群,他们在厦门的生活一点也不乏味。那儿有着五光十色的社会生活,而且还不时有体育活动,如赛马或是到附近乡下稻田遍布的区域狩猎水禽。

"再走远些则是荒山野岭,时而可以猎杀到老虎。曼森是从事这些冒险活动最为出色的人,所以他很快便被誉为中国最佳猎手。

"随着他越来越熟悉中国人及其他们的习俗,他渐渐赢得了他们的信任,他的工作也开始加重了。

"由于病人不断找他看病,有时候他忙得连睡觉都顾不上了。"

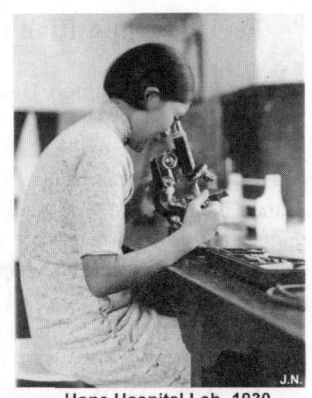
Hope Hospital Lab, 1930

——菲利普·曼森·巴哈尔爵士

厦门——医学教育的先锋 在基督教影响下成长起来的一些年轻人希望进入医院,接受医学培训。入门的条件是他们必须从我们的小学和中学毕业。不过,毕业生数量不能满足教会医院要求的时候,这条规矩有时候也可以松动。未完成中学学业的男生就可以被接受。医学培训一般持续五年。期间,学生紧跟医生,向他们学习用药知识和外科手术,并倾听医疗方面的讲座。

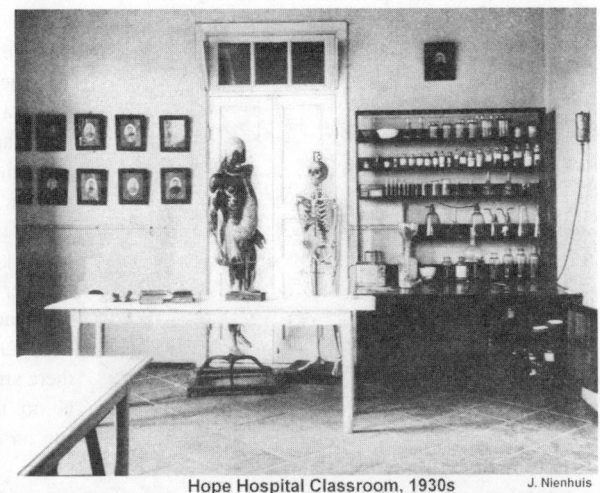
Hope Hospital Classroom, 1930s

当然,医学院是医院的附属机构这种说法并不正确。学生的数量是严格限制的。因为医生首先得完成繁重的行医任务,学生的培训学习只能依医生的时间和精力来确定。

最近,设立考试委员会的计划已经形成。委员会将对医院教授的科目进行考试,并向合格者颁发文凭。不过,这个计划尚未付诸实施,因为有一、两名医生拒绝合作,理由是,他们培训的学生难以达到考试委员会设立的标准。

——奥德姆,1908 年,第 315 页

Foreign Opposition to Hope Hospital, Gulangyu

Re: Proposed Chinese Hospital

A good deal of feeling is being aroused amongst the foreign community by the proposal of Dr. Otte to erect a hospital for Chinese on Kulangsu. The Chinese on Kulagau do not number more than 1,000, and the foreigners object to have any native hospital in their midst, whilst they would view without concern the erection of ten or a hundred on the Amoy side, where there are some 80,000 natives. On the 10th Dec., a petition, signed by 49 prominent members of the community, was addressed to the Consular Body, and a reply was received from H.B.M.'s Consul alone, referring to a proposal to establish a hospital for infectious and contagious diseases. The community, it should be point out, object to any native hospital in their midst, and they wish to know whether the other consuls have seen the petition. It may be interesting to place on record the correspondence in the matter.

A Foreign Correspondent, 17th December.

Amoy, 10th December, 1896

SIR,—We the undersigned residents and property owners on Kulangsu understand that it is the intention of one Dr. Otte to erect a hospital for Chinese on the foreshore near the late "Hauenstein Hotel."

Hope Hospital, 1924   J. Nienhuis

We consider the erection of a Chinese hospital on Kulangsu to be a grave danger to public health and also liable to seriously depreciate the value of property in its neighborhood.

We would point out that there is ample space for any number of Chinese hospitals on the Amoy side if more than the community at present maintain there are required, and that there is no need whatever to build one on Kulangsu and so import disease amongst us on that island.

Further, we would point out that previous efforts to erect hospitals for infectious diseases on Kulangsu have been relinquished in deference to public protest.

We the undersigned, beg the Consular Body to institute enquiries and to take such steps as they may deem fit for the general good of the Foreign Community in this matter.

We have the honour to be,
Sir,
Your obedient servants,.
49 signatures of Merchants, Bankers, etc. of all nationalities.
To the Doyan of the Consular Body, Amoy.

第三十一章 鼓浪屿——热带医学的摇篮 Gulangyu—Cradle of Tropical Medicine

外国人反对在鼓浪屿设立救世医院

关于：设立中国医院的提议

郁约翰博士提议为鼓浪屿的中国人建立一所医院，这在岛上的外国人社区里引起了强烈反响。鼓浪屿岛上的中国人不足一千，外国人反对在他们居住的地方建立任何为本地人服务的医院。在拥有8万人口的厦门本岛，建立十所，或者一百所，他们都无所谓。12月10日，由社区49位知名人士签名的请愿书已经递交给岛上的领事机构。目前仅收到了英国领事的回复。他建议设立一个专门收治传染病人的医院。应该指出的是，社区反对在岛上建立任何为本地人服务的医院。他们想知道其他国家的领事是否看到了请愿书。把这件事情的往来通讯记录在档很有意思。

——一名外国记者，1896年12月17日

1896年12月10日，厦门

尊敬的阁下：

我们下列签名者作为鼓浪屿住户和在岛上的物业所有者获悉，一个名叫郁约翰的医生有意在滩头靠近豪恩施泰因旅馆的地方专门为中国人设立一所医院。

我们认为，在鼓浪屿专门为中国人设立医院将严重危及岛上的公共卫生，并可能导致周边地区物业价值的严重贬值。

Dr. Otte's Wealthy Patient (Gulangyu, about 1908)

必须指出的是，如果厦门本岛社区需要，那里有足够的空间建立任何数量的中国医院。没有任何必要专门在鼓浪屿设立，并把疾病带到岛上。

必须进一步说明的是，考虑到公众的反对意见，先前在鼓浪屿岛上设立传染病医院的设想已经放弃。

我们签名者恳请岛上领事机构深入调查此事，并采取确实措施，为岛上的外国人社区谋福利。

此致

您忠诚的臣民

49名各国商人、银行家等签名，致信厦门各国领事机构的首席领事

Otte Raises the Hospital Roof "It took me two weeks of hard work, but finally it was all done and then I simply crowed. You ought to have seen me when at work. I was covered from head to foot with sticky asphalt. Even my baby, when she came with her mother one day to the hospital said, 'This is not my papa.'

"...Sometimes right in the midst of my work I would be called out on a serious case. Then I would hurriedly wash my hands in kerosene, change my clothes, and go to the case. Think of having to operate on the eye under such circumstances."

John Otte, M.D., Amoy

Otte declines (again) Consular Surgeon position (mere days before his death)

March 1910

I am sorry that the work my position entails made it necessary for me to refuse the position of Consular Surgeon, which has once more been offered to me at a fixed salary of $75.00 gold a month. The Consul, and also Dr. Foster, of the U.S. Marine Hospital Service, were very persistent in their efforts to get me to take this position, as they wanted to avoid employing a British subject. But I felt that I had reached the limit of my capacity for work...

The Tek-chhiu-kha dispensary is finished, and I feel very happy over the fact, that, with the exception of about one hundred dollars, the cost of the building ($1800.00) was earned and not begged. The building is not handsome; indeed, it is rather ugly. But the situation is such that to have spent money for adornment would have been wrong. But if it is not handsome, it is certainly very strong, and exceedingly useful. It is built of wood, best brick, steel and Portland cement. I think that my great grandchildren will still find it a great building. I believe that only an earthquake can destroy it, or, possibly, a tidal wave. There is nothing in it that the white ants can get at, except a few roof rafters which are laid in Portland cement. All our buildings ought to be built in this way. It is more expensive at first, but the repairs will be so few that in the end there will be a great saving..."

Happy Little Hope Hospital Patients, 1930s

第三十一章 鼓浪屿——热带医学的摇篮 Gulangyu—Cradle of Tropical Medicine

郁约翰亲自盖屋顶 为了确保万无一失,郁约翰亲自为医院盖屋顶。他写道:"我苦干了两个星期,终于大功告成了!我不禁畅然欢叫。你该来看我干活时的样子,我从头到脚沾满了沥青。有一天,我幼小的女儿跟她妈妈来医院,居然说,'这个人不是我爸爸。'"

"……有时候我手上活儿正好干一半,却被告知有急症候诊。于是我匆忙用煤油洗手,换衣服,出去接诊。想想看吧,这种情况下还得做眼科手术呢。"

郁约翰(再次)谢绝担任领事馆医生职务(1910年3月去世前几天)

领事馆多次以75金元的月薪请我担任医生职务。我很抱歉,我所承担的工作使我有必要予以谢绝。因为(美国驻厦门)领事,以及美国海军医院的福斯特医生都想极力避免聘任英国医生,他们非常希望我能担任此任。但我觉得,自己的工作压力已经达到了极限……

竹树脚(Tek-chhiu-kha,即保赤医院的前身)诊所已经完工。除了大约100美元,诊所楼房的费用(1800美元)都被赚回来了,没有向教会申请任何资助。楼房不太漂亮,说实在,还相当不好看。不过,如果说它不漂亮,那肯定很牢固,而且特别实用。它是用木头、最好的砖头、钢铁和波特兰水泥建成的。我想,到了我的曾孙那一代,它还是一座很棒的楼房。我想,只有地震,或者也许海浪,能够摧毁它。除了几根埋在波特兰水泥里面的椽子,楼房里面没有白蚂蚁能吃的东西。我们所有的楼房都应该这么建。最初的开销会大一些,不过维修的次数会很少。最终还是能够省下很多钱……

Joe Esther and Jack Hill, Tong'an

老外看老鼓浪屿 Old Gulangyu in Foreigners' Eyes

Chinese Medicine (1940s)   His signboard indicated that he practiced Western medicine. 'But he is also skilled in Chinese medical science,' Mr. Lim had indicated, pulling in his chin and blinking at me over the top of his spectacles. 'Dr. Lee knows all about strange brews of herbs and sea slugs, not to mention acupuncture and other ingredients, like deer-horn shavings used for the resuscitation and augmentation of virility,' he added with a twinkle.

Prepared to be offered any cure from sea slugs to acupuncture, I sat down in a queue of nursing mothers and squalling infants, one of whom left a neat puddle on the bench next to me. …

Dr. Lee looked at me with a knowing eye, expounding with prolixity on the bacteriological contents of local water. My immediate reaction was one of profound admiration for the strength of Chinese stomachs and of a suspicion that too much scientific protectiveness had robbed my own of its natural defensive lining. He shouted out to his wife to make up the mixture. Carefully she ascended a wooden ladder at the other end of the clinic to a built-in balcony, where she pounded the pills that were later lowered down in a wicker basket. The powder prescription had been placed in paper pellet bags stamped with large red Chinese characters and taken with a diet of rice gruel were soon effective on this and subsequent occasions. I suspect they were plain sulphur tablets wrapped and prepared with a touch of oriental mystery.

Neill, 1956

New Pegleg   J. Nienhuis

1st Post-War Grads (1950)
Fujian's 1st "All-High-School Grads" Class

第三十一章　鼓浪屿——热带医学的摇篮　Gulangyu—Cradle of Tropical Medicine

中医药（20世纪40年代）　招牌显示，他是西医。"不过，他也精通中医，"林先生下巴微收，脑门前倾，透过眼镜，眨着眼睛对我说。"李医生熟知所有中草药的秘方，更不用说针灸和其他验方，如鹿角粉可帮助男性恢复体力，增强性功能，"他补充说，眼睛闪闪发亮。

准备试试从海参到针灸等各种疗法，我坐下来排队，旁边有正在喂奶的母亲和哭哭啼啼的婴儿，其中有一个婴儿紧挨着我，刚尿了一泡尿。

李医生看着我，眼睛似乎洞察一切。他啰啰唆唆地向我解释了当地水质所包含的细菌。我的直接反应是对中国人肠胃的解毒能力羡慕无比，同时怀疑太多的科学防护已经剥夺了我的自然保护膜。他大声地叫喊，让他太太合成一种药物。太太慢慢地顺着诊所里面的一个木楼梯，爬上一个嵌入式阳台。在那里，她磨碾药粉，并用一个藤篮把它吊下楼来。药粉被放进几个印着红色汉字的圆纸袋里，用米粥冲服，很快就见效了。后面几次的情形也是一样。我怀疑，这些药粉是普通的硫黄片，用东方秘法包装并制作出来的。

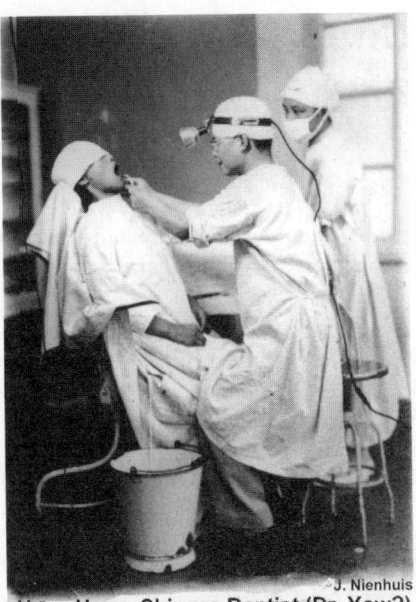

Hope Hosp. Chinese Dentist (Dr. Yow?)

——尼尔，1956年，第37页

Hope Hospital "Coolies"

419

Chapter 32
Amoy—Birthplace of Chinese Protestantism

Christians in Amoy (1700) There are about fifty Christians in Amoy, and they have a chapel served by French missionaries...

Hamilton, 1727

Why Amoy First? You will naturally be anxious to know how such good results have been brought about. I would notice, first of an, that here there is a friendly population to work upon. The foreigner is not regarded with that hatred or contempt with which he is looked upon in the south. I have visited many towns and villages in the neighbourhood, and some distant islands, some of them in a most disturbed state, at war with the mandarins and with one another, and yet could take my morning walk without any attendant, three or four miles from any friend, and twenty or thirty from Amoy, surrounded by whole villages of wondering people, many of whom had rarely if ever seen a foreigner before, without the least round of suspicion or fear...

One thing which has contributed much to induce this more liberal feeling, in this part of China, is the great intercourse which the natives of Fuh-kien have had with the outer world. The privilege of emigrating was granted to this district, when denied to other parts of China, on account of the increase of the population beyond the physical resources of the soil... Most, nearly all, the Chinese found in the Malayan Archipelago are from this neighbourhood ...and many of the wealthiest people here are men who have returned from abroad, to build themselves a nice villa in the spot from which in their youth they departed little better than beggars. The best houses, and the handsomest modern tombs, are built with money earned abroad.

Rev. David Abeel
1st Amoy Missionary

Another great advantage which Amoy bas enjoyed as a Mission station, arises from the same causes. As you are aware, the first missions to the Chinese were formed in the Straits of Malacca; and as the great mass of Chinese there were from Chang-Chow, that was the dialect learned by the missionaries. And as soon as the country was opened, there was a band of tried and trained men ready to enter upon the work here, which they could not do anywhere else, without learning an entirely new dialect, not even at Fuh-chow, which is the capital of the province. So that Amoy was not only one of the first places visited by the missionaries, after the treaty of peace, but six or seven of those who came, could preach the Gospel fully from the first, and being men of experience, no time was lost in tentative efforts; they set to work on a tried system, and went steadily on with it. How strange are the leadings of Providence!

Barbour, 1855

第三十二章 厦门——中国新教的诞生地

基督教在厦门（1700年） 厦门大约有50个基督教徒，他们有个教堂，教堂由法国传教士提供服务。

——哈密尔顿，1727年，第454页

为何首选厦门？ 你肯定会很好奇，想知道这么好的结果是如何得来的。我发现，首先是这里的人很友好。在南方，外国人常遭受仇恨、敌视或轻蔑，而在这里（厦门）却不会。我拜访过许多附近的城镇和村庄以及一些偏远的小岛，有些处于非常混乱的状态，与政府有冲突，或相互混战。在这里，我不用任何人陪同清晨仍然可以四处散步，远离朋友三、四英里，离厦门二三十英里，被全村好奇的村民包围。他们多数人之前从未见过老外，但一点都不害怕或疑惑……

在中国的这块土地上能产生这种更为自由的情感有样东西贡献很大，这就是福建本地人与外界的交往较多。该地区享有移民的特权，而中国其他地区不享有该特权，因为人口增长超出了土地能提供的物质资源……几乎所有在马来群岛的中国人都是来自这个邻近地区……这里最富裕的人大都是那些从海外归国的华侨。他们当初年轻出国的时候，只

Xinjie Church, China's Oldest Protestant Church

比乞丐稍好一点点。如今，他们都在故里为自己建造一座漂亮的别墅。最好的房子和最现代豪奢的坟墓都是用海外挣来的钱建造的。

作为一个传教点，厦门享有的另一优势也出于相同的原因。如你所知，到中国的第一个教会团体在马六甲海峡组成。那里的华人大部分来自漳州，传教士学会了他们的方言。当这个国家的国门被打开，一帮已受过培训、有经验的传教士就准备开展工作。不过，在学会另外一种新方言之前，他们是无法在其他地方传教的，即便是在福州这个省城城市。因此，在求和条约之后，厦门不仅是传教士光顾的首选地区之一，而且在到来的传教士中，有六七个可以从头传播福音。他们是有经验的人，不用在投石问路方面浪费时间，而是一开始就从很成熟的系统做起，随后稳步前进。神的领导是多么奇特啊！

——巴博，1855年，第29、30页

老外看老鼓浪屿 *Old Gulangyu in Foreigners' Eyes*

The Famous Dr. John Sung, Amoy, Nov. 1934

Band, 1948

Amoy's "Bamboo Church", 1921

J. Nienhuis

第三十二章 厦门——中国新教的诞生地 *Amoy—Birthplace of Chinese Protestantism*

Amoy Mission, 1932

First Protestant Church in China In January, 1844, two rooms were rented in the city of Amoy, one being used as a chapel for regular preaching services, and the other as a dispensary, in the charge of Dr. Cummings...The size of the audiences never diminished. but frequently they numbered two hundred eager listeners.

On March 21st, 1844, a Bible class of twelve scholars was organized, and maintained with increased interest and blessing.

Mr. Pohlman, with his wife (a sister of Dr. Jolin Scudder, of Indian fame)...arrived in Amoy in company with Mr. Doty, June 24th, 1844.

On December 16th, 1845, a special meeting for women was instituted, and has been maintained till this day with unabated zeal by the ladies of our mission...

...they had been holding services in rented quarters... Through Hok Kui-peh, the first convert, a piece of property, with four small buildings, was secured on September 16th, 1847. One of the buildings was temporarily fitted up for a chapel and occupied until 1848, when, through the solicitations of Mr. Pohlman, $3,000 having been secured, the work on the new and First Church building was begun. The building was dedicated February 11th, 1849.

The church is located in the eastern part of the city on New Street, i. e., Sin-Koe-a. [新街] It is usually spoken of as the Sin-Koe-a Church, and so reported in the Synodical Report of the Amoy Churches. The dimensions are: Height of ceiling, 19 feet and 3 inches; to top of tower, 50 feet; length: 60 feet; width, 37 feet, and portico, 10 feet. It is built of brick and after the "Etruscan style of architecture."

The front is stucco work of pure white, and on an oval slab, from the quarry of Canton, above the front entablature, there is an inscription in Chinese characters which reads as follows: "A Temple for the Worship of the True God, the Great Sovereign Ruler." On each side of the inscription are inscribed other Chinese characters meaning: "The One Thousand, Eight Hundred and Forty-eighth Year of Jesus' Advent, and To-Kong the Twenty-eighth Year," and underneath all the figures "1848." The interior is arranged after the fashion of a Quaker meeting-house, i. e., a screen separating the men from the women. And everything is as plain as those places of worship-no cushioned seats, no carpeted floors, no stained glass windows. In a majority of cases simply benches with no backs adorn the churches in the Amoy region. Tile floors always. Back of the church is a building, height 26 feet, length 40, width 14. The upper part was used as a parsonage until 1892, and the lower part as a consistory room. A new parsonage was provided in 1892.

Amoy Mission Meeting, 1921   J. Nienhuis

第三十二章　厦门——中国新教的诞生地 Amoy—Birthplace of Chinese Protestantism

中国首个新教教堂　1844年1月，在厦门市里有两个房间被租用，一个用来做日常讲道的礼拜堂，另一间作为诊所，由卡明斯博士负责……　听众人数从未减少，信徒倒是经常达到200人。

1844年3月21日，开办了一个圣经班，由12名学者组成，越来越多的人表示兴趣并表达祝福。

波罗满先生和他的妻子（卓林·斯卡德博士的姐妹，有印第安人血统）在多蒂先生的陪同下于1844年6月24日抵达厦门。

1845年12月16日，专门为妇女设立的协会创立，时至今日，教会的女士们仍饱含热情地维持着……

Some Amoy Mission Families

……他们在租界进行传教……通过福桂伯（Hok Kui-peh，即王福桂）——首位新教教徒，于1847年9月16日获得了一些财产和4座小房屋。其中一座临时装备成礼拜堂，一直用到1848年。波罗满募捐了3000美元后，第一座新教堂开始动建。1849年2月11日，教堂投入使用。

教堂位于市区中心东边的一条新大街上，即新街。人们称之为新街教堂，厦门教堂报告中也是这么记载的。大小如下：至天花板高度19英尺3英寸，至塔尖高度为50英尺；长60英尺，宽37英尺，圆柱门廊10英尺。教堂为砖石结构，仿希腊建筑风格。

教堂的前面用白灰粉刷，堂前廊台的柱子上镶嵌着一块椭圆形大理石匾。石匾来自广东，上面镌刻这鎏金的汉字："敬拜真神大主宰之堂"，两边还刻着其他汉字，意思是"耶稣诞辰1848年，道光二十八年"，下面刻着"公元1848年"。内部效仿贵格会会堂的风格，即男女由屏风隔开。所有的一切都同那些敬神的场所一样简单——没有加垫子的座位，没有铺地毯的地板，没有色彩的玻璃窗。多数情况下，厦门地区的教堂一般只配有无靠背的板凳。地面总是铺砖头。教堂后面是一座高26英尺，长40英尺，宽14英尺的房屋。一直到1892年，上部用作牧师住宅，下部作宗教法院会堂。1892年为牧师新建了住宅楼。

In the erection of this building the Reformed Church had the privilege of establishing the first Protestant church building in the Chinese Empire, as it had two centuries before of establishing the first church organization in New York (then called New Amsterdam) in 1628.

Pitcher, 1893

China's 1st Church: Simultaneous Dedication and Memorial Service   He [Pohlman] was cut off in the midst of his years and not permitted to witness this crowning act of his life in its full completion; for it was while on a voyage from Hong-Kong, whence he had gone to procure lamps for the edifice, that he lost his life at sea.

Dr. and Mrs. J.V.N. Talmage
In Amoy 1847-1892

"He set out to return to Amoy on the 2d of January (1849) in the schooner Omega. On the morning of the 5th or 6th the vessel struck, in a fearful gale, near Breakers' Point, about half way between Hong-Kong and Amoy." All on board perished save one, either at the hands of the pirates who infested those shores, or by the overwhelming waters. The people at Amoy were waiting for Pohlman's return, when they expected to dedicate the new structure. His funeral service and the dedication exercises were held at one and the same time, February 11th, 1849.

Pitcher, 1893

Unique Amoy Unity   In December, 1845, the growing congregation moved out of their small room into a more commodious and newly rented chapel.

On the 5th of January, 1846, the first Chinese monthly concert was held, consisting of a morning and evening session... It was a Union Service of all Protestant missionaries: Reformed, English Presbyterian and London Mission, and all the native converts connected with these societies.   The concert is still maintained once a month. And it is a blessed bond of union that we trust will never be broken.

Pitcher, 1893

Amoy—the Mother Church   In 1872 we find that the Mission to Amoy has expanded into three distinct centres [Xiamen, Shantou, Taiwan], independent of each other, but under the one home Committee of management. Amoy may justly claim to be the mother of them all; it was from that, as the original headquarters, that they took their departure..

Johnston, 1898

High Mortality of Missionaries   Near the northern village, screened from view by a little assemblage of trees, was situated the burial-ground of the missionaries. The unhealthiness of the climate had been severely felt by this class of the Lord's laborers, who followed in the train of earthly conquerors, to extend the bloodless conquests of their divine Savior. During the last thirteen mouths, out of twenty-five members of the missionary families, eighteen had been removed by various providential events.

Smith, 1857

第三十二章 厦门——中国新教的诞生地 Amoy—Birthplace of Chinese Protestantism

兴建新街教堂的时候,美国归正教独享在中国这个大帝国的土地上建设首个新教教堂的特权,因为它在两个世纪之前,于1628年在纽约(时称新阿姆斯特丹)设立了首个教会机构。

——毕腓力,1893年

中国首家教堂　奉献和纪念他(波罗满)英年早逝,无法亲眼目睹其生命中最辉煌的杰作完工。在为购买教堂的灯饰从香港返回途中,他不幸在海难中遇难。

Kho Seng-lan bok-su and 2 Preachers

"他于1849年1月2日搭乘欧米加号帆船返回厦门。在5日或6日清晨,大约在香港与厦门的半途中,靠近东萨摩亚,帆船被一场可怕的大风击沉"。除一人幸存外,船上其他所有人员都死了。有的死于海盗(东萨摩亚附近海域海盗横行)手中,有的则被汹涌的波涛淹没。在厦门,人们都在盼望着波罗满的归来,希望他能为新教堂题字。1849年2月11日,他的葬礼和献堂典礼同一时间举行。

——毕腓力,1893年,第73页

奇特的厦门联合会　1845年12月,基督教信徒不断增加。他们从小的集会场所搬入新租用的更宽敞的礼拜堂。

1846年1月5日,每月一次的音乐会首次举办,分为早晚两场……这是所有新教教会的联合活动:归正教、英国长老会和伦敦差会以及与这些教会有关的所有当地信众。

音乐会至今仍然每月举办一次。与主的神圣契约是我们所信赖的,它牢不可破。

——毕腓力,1893年

厦门——母教堂　1872年,厦门传教团发展扩大成三个相互独立的中心(厦门、汕头和台湾),但同归一个教会组织管理。厦门可称为他们的母亲,从那以后,他们各自作为当地的总部独立发展。

——约翰斯通,1898年,第195页

传教士高死亡率　传教士的墓地靠近北边的村子,被一小片树林挡住视线。这群上帝的苦力强烈地感受到恶劣气候的冲击。他们紧跟世俗征服者之后,和平地传递着神圣的主的福音。在最近的13个月中,传教团这个大家庭的25个成员有18人遵天意在各种事故中离我们远去了。

——史密斯,1857年,第338页

427

Self-Supporting Amoy Churches [1] The adherents of other religious societies, the Buddhists and Mohammedans, can support both worship and work, and do so, however poor they may be. Shall the believers in the one true religion do less than they? No man in this world is too poor to worship and serve the true God....

Although some of the districts about Amoy are among the poorest in China, yet most of the Churches in that region are self-supporting, and natives and foreigners rejoice together over the change which first came about through reduced appropriations. Every native Church of the Dutch Reformed Mission in China is self-supporting.

Fenn, Rev.C.H., 1898

Russian Church in Amoy In April of 1937 Fr. Dmitry Uspensky consecrated the prayer house dedicated to St. Nicholas the Miracle worker in Amoy. (Russian Ecclesiastical Mission to China). Dmitry was a priest in Beijing, sent to HK, and then Amoy. ... The divine services were celebrated in the Anglican Church until the prayer house was opened on Zhongshan Rd. #8. The church community organized Ladies' group of adherents of Church Beauty and Education, Charity Foundation, Foundation for the construction of the Church, and an amateur choir. The community intended to construct a new permanent church building in early 1940s. The drawings were prepared, but war stood in the way of these plans. Many Englishmen and Russian people became prisoners of war in the Japanese camps. Fr. Dmitry managed to keep the parish safe during that hard time.

Archpriest Dionisy Pozdnyaev, H.K., 2009

---

1 Modern China's "Three Self-Patriotic Movement" 3 principles of self-support, self-propagating and self-governing were actually developed in the Amoy Mission—in the 1850s

A Chinese Evangelist MacGowan, 1914

第三十二章 厦门——中国新教的诞生地 Amoy—Birthplace of Chinese Protestantism

自给自足的厦门教堂[2] 其他宗教的追随者,如佛教徒和伊斯兰教徒支付得起祭祀活动和劳务费用。无论多贫困,他们会这么做。其他宗教信徒做得比他们少吗?在这个世界上,没有人会穷到无法敬奉神明……

尽管厦门附近的某些地区在中国属于贫困地区,但大部分的教堂都能自立。政府拨款减少带来的变化使得当地人和老外欣喜若狂。荷兰归正教在中国的每个教堂都是自给自足的。

——C.H.费恩牧师,1898年,第51~63页

Chinese Preacher, 1922

俄罗斯东正教在厦门 1937年4月,德米特里·乌斯宾斯基神父将礼拜堂捐献给圣尼古拉斯在厦门行神迹的仆人(俄罗斯前往中国的教会)。德米特里在北京是一名牧师,曾被派往香港,后来到厦门……在中山路8号的礼拜堂启用之前,东正教的礼拜活动在英国圣公会教堂进行。教会组织了教堂装饰与教育女信徒小组,慈善基金、教堂建设基金和一个业余唱诗班。在20世纪40年代早期,教会计划建设一座新的永久性教堂。设计图也已制作好,但战争打断了建设计划。很多英国人和俄国人成了日本集中营的战俘。在那个艰苦年代里,德米特里神父竭尽全力保护教区安全。

Russian Orthodox Congregation, Amoy

——资料来源:东正教香港教区主牧季奥尼西·波兹尼夫,2009年

---

2 中国现代的"三自爱国运动"实际上发端于厦门教会在19世纪50年代提出的"自治、自养、自传"三原则。

Chapter 33
Amoy's Pioneering Modern Education

Pioneer Educators   There was no lack of congenial companionship, for this [Amoy] was the rallying point of that picket line of educational pioneers in Asia, who began the work whose fruits are seen today. In later years, in Japan, Dr. Hepburn delighted to tell about his early life at Amoy, where he was intimate with Morrison, Milne, Medhurst, Muirhead, Peter Parker, Abeel, Walter Lowrie, Bridgman and Culbertson.

Griffis, 1913

65 of Ms.Johnston's Pupils Who Became Teachers

Roots of Pinyin in Amoy (July 14, 1851) The plan is yet only an experiment, but seems perfectly feasible. We trust that, by some such means as this, much may be done towards the elevation of the great mass of this people. By the use of their present cumbersome characters, the great majority can never become intelligent readers; but by the plan thus adopted, if we can only furnish the requisite number of books, the means of learning to read will be within the reach of almost every individual.

Talmage Letter to Anderson and De Witt

Crazy English in the 1890s?   Shouting must Go![1] We need Thinking. We need a new method of studying. Here one of the greatest reforms is necessary. This bedlamian way of acquiring lessons must go. There is too much physical force expended, entirely too much lung gymnastics displayed. Under this process study becomes dangerous. Breakdowns occur at the very beginning of what promise to be useful lives. Their power has just been expended in screeching. It is all beyond reason that any group of children should shout so loud at times that you wonder the tiles do not fly off. Instead of this we must tone them down to thinking.

Shouting is not thinking. It is simply making phonographs of their tympanums, and the louder the shout the deeper the impression. Now we do not want this kind of phonograph; we want thinking men and women, we want mind development, brain enlargement and originality.

P.W. Pitcher, Letter from Kolongsu, Dec. 22nd, 1894

---

1   Chinese children traditionally learned by shouting lessons at the top of their voices.

第三十三章　厦门的现代教育

厦门——亚洲现代教育的先驱　现代教育中不缺志同道合的同伴。厦门跑在亚洲教育先驱战线上的首位，如今已见成果。后来在日本，赫伯恩博士很高兴地谈起其早年在厦门的生活。在那里，他和莫里森、米尔恩、梅德赫斯特、缪尔黑德、彼得·帕克、阿比尔、沃尔特·洛雷、布里奇曼和库伯森成为莫逆之交。

——格里费斯，1913年，第63页

厦门拼音的根（1851年7月14日）　这个计划还只是一个实验，但看起来完全可行。我们相信，通过类似的办法，提高这个民族广大人民群众的素质，可做的事情很多。他们现在使用繁琐的字符，永远不可能变成有思想的读者。采用这个计划，只要我们提供足够数量的书籍，每个人都可以学会阅读。

——塔尔米奇致安德森和德·韦特的信件

19世纪90年代的疯狂英语？　喊叫必须停止！[2] 我们需要思考。我们需要新的学习方法。必须在这里实行最伟大的改革。这种疯狂式的学习功课的方法必须停止。这种方法消耗太多的体力，肺部运动明显过多。在这种学习过程中，学习变得很危险。本来有望成为有用人才，但在培养之初就早早地夭折了。他们的能量就在大声喊叫中消耗一空。让孩子们这么大声地喊叫根本就不在情理之中。这不禁让人感到奇怪，瓦片怎么没被掀翻。相反的是，我们应该让他们静下来思考。

喊叫不是思考。只是把鼓膜当作留声机，喊得越大声，印象越深刻。如今，我们不要这种留声机。我们需要会思考的男男女女，我们想要的是思想的发展，大脑的扩充和创意。

——毕腓力，发自鼓浪屿的信件，1894年12月22日

Girls going to school, Gulangyu, 1934

2　中国的儿童传统的学习方法是高声朗读课文。

老外看老鼓浪屿 *Old Gulangyu in Foreigners' Eyes*

Amoy Dialect in Braille In the adaptation of Braille, which has been made to the Amoy Vernacular, the letters of the alphabet are full-length, thus leaving the tonal marks to be formed from upper and middle dots and the punctuation from middle and lower ones. The letters are combined phonetically —and also as initials and finals—to spell out the short monosyllabic words, which, on an average, require only three letters and a fraction to each. Of course the Braille figure-dots are kept for the use they were originally intended to serve.

Campbell, 1889

Wealthy Amoy Chinese Fund Modern Education Speaking of educational work in the Annual Trade Report of Amoy for 1909 the Commissioner uses these significant words: "The forward educational movement, which has made so much headway all over China, has at this port been continued with greater impetus than before. All the educational establishments report large increase in students; and the wealthy class continue to cooperate handsomely in this great work by giving large sums to the various institutions."

In this connection it should be mentioned that the natives of this port who reside in the Straits, Manila, and elsewhere, are manifesting the keenest interest in these educational matters. A Chinese pastor has just returned (1910) from Manila bringing a handsome contribution, in cash and promises, of $10,000 Mex. for such work. Nor does this by any means exhaust the list of similar gifts from the same sources; others have been helped in the same way by these patriotic citizens living abroad.

Annual Trade Report of Amoy, 1909

Hollister, 1932

Amoy Dialect in Braille

1890.] EDUCATION AND WORK FOR THE CHINESE BLIND.
[Chinese Recorder, Vol. 21, 1890]

c̨ k p t a e i o u n

ch kh ph th aⁿ eⁿ iⁿ oᴸ uⁿ ng

... It may be well to state that, for beginners, it is advisab[le to] have guides made that will produce dots standing slightly apart than those from the ordinary standard pattern. Failing a very good way of giving lessons on the formation of letter[s and] words is to work with short wooden pins on the octagonal [board] which the blind use for arithmetical exercises.* The pins oug[ht to] have the ends smoothly rounded, and be cut to fit the holes exa[ctly;] the readiest way of making them being from bamboo splints. [Those] whose hands have become hardened by manual labour, should lei[sure]ly wash them with soap and warm water before commencin[g]

第三十三章　厦门的现代教育　Amoy's Pioneering Modern Education

盲文的厦门方言　盲文的改写本已按厦门本地方言编制，字母是标准长度，因此声调由上方和中间的圆点构成，标点符号从中间和下方的圆点形成。文字按发音组合，同时按首字母和最后的字母组合，这样就可以拼出单音节的短词。这些短词平均只需要用三个字母和一个符号。当然，盲文中的数字点依然保留其原有的功能。

——坎佩尔，1889 年，第 450 页

厦门有钱人资助现代教育　在 1909 年厦门年度贸易报告中，谈到教育工作时，委员会委员使用了这些重要字眼："迅速发展的教育运动，在全中国取得长足发展。厦门这个港口城市比以往更大的力量继续推进这项工作。所有的教育机构都报告说，学生人数大增。富裕阶层积极参与这项伟大的工程，并慷慨地向各类教育机构投入大笔资金。

关于这一点，必须提到的是，无论是居住在海峡两岸、马尼拉，或其他地方，这个港口城市的本地人，都热衷于教育事业。有一位中国牧师刚从马尼拉回国（1910年），带来了巨额捐赠，包括现金和资助承诺，总价值 1 万墨西哥币。相同来源的类似赠品的名单很长。这些居住在海外的爱国侨民用同样的方法资助了其他事项。

Boy Scouts, Anglo-Chinese College
Amoy, 1929

Band, 1948

——《厦门贸易年度报告》，1909 年

433

Tongwen Institute
Bowra, 1908

Tung-Wen Institute was first established on Kolongsu about 1898 in a native house, and a building erected in 1902. While this is not a missionary institution, nor in anywise connected with Missions, yet to make the history of foreign educational work in this port more complete, it may be inserted here.

The founder of this Institute was Mr. A. Burlingame Johnson, then U. S. Consul at Amoy. He enlisted the cooperation and support of a number of wealthy Chinese gentlemen, from whom a Board of Trustees was chosen and by whom the Institute has ever since been successfully conducted. By constitutional authority the resident U. S. Consul is made President of the Board, and the Commissioner of Customs Vice President.

The Outlook, 1903

"The Anglo-Chinese College at Amoy" (1899) To earnest educationalists the magnificent progress made in the establishment of schools in India and Japan is highly gratifying…At the time of the Queen's Jubilee, an able gentlemen, of Chinese extraction, who had been educated at Cambridge, and held office under the British Government at Rangoon, came to Amoy, full of the educational schemes in India; and he inspired many Chinese British subjects with the desire to obtain the advantages for their children of having an Anglo-Chinese school at Amoy. This movement was specially brought before my notice by out esteemed Consul calling to inquire what part we could take in such a matter. Before long a committee was formed, consisting of the Consul, the Commissioner of Customs, and a leading English merchant, along with myself, as Westerns; while associated with us were several Chinese gentlemen. It was determined by a majority that while morality should receive strenuous attention in the school, religion should be left to outside effort. This secular movement did not succeed.

Afterwards a series of vigorous efforts were made, in the hope that Chinese non-Christian merchants might join with missionaries in founding the needed school. This scheme also fell through, [so the Christian missions funded and ran the school].

Rev. James Sadler (in Gaunt, 1899)

Amoy High School The curriculum of the Amoy High School has been approved by the three Missions concerned. In each year of the five years' course there is reading of the Old Testament, especially of the historical books and of the Psalms. Other subjects which are constant throughout the course are Chinese Literature and Composition, History, Elementary Science, Drawing, Singing, Drill, and English. In the first year Arithmetic is taught, but from that point the boys advance to Algebra and Geometry. Geography is taught in the third, fourth, and fifth years. Elementary Astronomy in the first and second years, and Mandarin in the first, second, and third years. The pupils also receive some instruction in the Art of Teaching during the last two years.

Oldham, 1908

第三十三章　厦门的现代教育　Amoy's Pioneering Modern Education

同文学院　最初大约在1898年设立在鼓浪屿的一所居民房子里。1902年，建设了自己的大楼。必须在这里说明的是，它不是一个教会机构，与教会一点关系也没有。它的存在使得这个港口城市的外国教育工作的历史更加完整。

这所学院的创始人是 A. 伯林盖姆·约翰逊，时任美国驻厦门领事。他获得了中国许多有钱人的帮助和支持，从他们中选派人员，组成了理事会，并成功地运营了这所学院。学院章程规定，常驻美国领事为理事会主席，海关关长为副主席。

——《瞭望》，1903年，第242、243页

"厦门英华学院"（1899年）　对热心的教育家来说，在印度和日本建立学校上的飞速进步是令人满意的……在女王登基50年之际，一名能干的绅士带着印度教育制度来到厦门，创办了很多中英学科，希望子孙后代能从厦门的中英学校中受益。他有中国血统，曾在剑桥接受过教育，并在仰光的英国政府部门里供过职。早在我觉察之前，这个运动就开始了。我们尊敬的领事先生找我询问我们在这件事情上应扮演什么角色，我才知道

Anglo-Chinese College, Amoy

是怎么一回事。不久，学院成立了委员会，由领事、海关关长、一位英国商人领袖组成，我作为西方人代表参加。与我们联系的是一些中国绅士。根据多数人的意见，学院决定应高度重视道德教育，而宗教事务则交由校外力量处理。这项世俗运动没有成功。

后来，学院又努力了一番，希望非基督教徒的中国商人能加入我们的行列，共同努力创建学校。这个计划也泡汤了。因此，基督教会自己出资创办学院。

——詹姆士·塞德勒牧师，（1899年，于冈特）

厦门中学　厦门中学的课程由三个相关部门审核通过。学制5年，每年的课程都设有《旧约》课，尤其是与历史和圣歌有关的部分。贯穿学业的其他常设课程有中国文学、写作、历史、初级自然科学、绘画、音乐、军训和英文。第一年教算术，然后男生升级到代数和几何。地理课设在第3、4和5年级。天文基础课设在第1、2年，中文课在第1和3年。在最后2年里，学生还要上艺术课。

——奥德姆，1908年，第310～314页

Amoy's Pioneering Women's Education

"Ten years ago," writes Miss M.E. Talmage, of Amoy, "there were comparatively few Christian women in this region who could read the Scriptures, and the pupils in girls' schools were but a few score. This year (1902) there are seven hundred girls under instruction, while there are over a thousand women who can read."

The Outlook, August 1, 1903

The Girls' School Round the school there is a veranda closed in with lattice-work, and doors lead into the different class-rooms, which, with their varnished forms and desks, maps and pictures, look a very cheery edition of an English school The teacher at her table quietly reading and the girls in their forms softly repeating their lessons are, however, very different, though in many ways as nice. All wear trousers, wide, loose, coloured ones, embroidered or trimmed at the foot, and over them a long wide jacket buttoned down one side and embroidered round the neck. The sleeves are so long and loose that at first sight you would imagine the people had no arms. The little girls are the funniest mites. I would give a good deal to be able to put one or two in a box to send you. I can only laugh at them when they come dancing round with their queer little pigtails sticking out all round. They usually wear their hair in a plait; not at the back of their heads, however, but at one side and sticking straight out. Then, above their foreheads, they sometimes have a narrow band of coloured cloth tied under their hair behind and waving in two long tails. The women often wear a black band in winter to keep them warm. I can't see how it answers! The older girls wear long plaits or have their hair smoothly brushed buck and rolled into a flat ' bun' with pins and combs and bunches of gay artificial flowers. Everyone has exactly the same glossy black shade. Such nice faces some have, the bigger ones sweet and gentle-looking, the tiniest rosy and mischievous.

Amoy Girls' Middle School Basketball Game

Johnston, 1907

Girls' Curriculum   Other lessons naturally followed, such as geography and history. Arithmetic was carried to its utmost limits, the older girls being led to understand the why and wherefore of a cube-root rule, and to think a problem in the comparative rates at which the planets revolve—a fascinating riddle! Chinese girls have good heads, and yet are so apt to rely on memory that great stress was laid on this study, so as to teach them to think and reason. Classes in very elementary astronomy, geology, and physiology were as great a pleasure to the teacher as to the taught, and the lessons were enlivened with quaint and ingenious illustrations.

Johnston, 1907

第三十三章　厦门的现代教育 Amoy's Pioneering Modern Education

厦门女子教育的先锋

打马字·马利亚小姐梅奇曾这样描述过厦门："十年前，在这个地区，只有少数几个基督教妇女能读基督教经文，女子学校有女生，但只有一二十个。今年（1902年）有100个女生接受教育，一千多妇女能阅读。"

——《瞭望》，1903年8月1日，第802页

Girls' Middle School, 1924 Class J. Nienhuis

女子学校　学校由走廊环绕着，走廊的围栏成格状，教室的门都朝着走廊开，涂漆的窗户和课桌，地图和图画，看起来像是英国学校的快乐版本。老师站在讲台边轻声朗读，女生们精神抖擞地轻轻跟读。两者之间似乎存在极大的差异，但从多方面来说非常好。大家都穿着宽松肥大的裤子，有各种颜色，裤脚上镶有花边或其他饰品。上衣又宽又长，纽扣整整齐齐地钉在一侧，衣领上镶着花边。袖子又长又宽，乍看上去还以为她们没有手臂。小女孩们是最有趣的小东西。如果能将一两个小女孩装进盒子送给你，我倒情愿花一大笔的钱。跳舞时，她们古怪的小辫子四处伸展。这时，我只能冲着她们发笑。她们一般将头发梳成辫子，但不放在后脑勺，而是在头部的一侧，很突兀地伸出来。额头上有时还系着一条窄窄的花布，花布系在头发下，长长的两端布条时时飘动。冬天的时候，女生一般都扎块头巾保暖。我不知道这样扎怎么保暖！年纪大的女生留长辫子或把头发梳得光滑油亮，在脑后卷成一个扁平的小馒头状，用发卡、梳子和漂亮的人造花固定。每个人的背影都是这么的油黑发亮。如此漂亮的脸蛋，有些还会绽放出甜美的微笑，有些则文静，脸色红润，淘气地笑着。

——约翰斯通，1907年，第66～68页

女生的课程　有些课程正常上，如地理和历史。算术则学到极致，高年级的女生须掌握立方根规则的来龙去脉，按行星运转的速度思考问题——多么奇妙的一个谜啊！中国女孩脑子聪明，记忆力好，重视学习。因此，对老师和学生来说，在天文学、地质和生理学课上教她们思考和推理都是一件很愉快的事。课堂上使用精美有趣的图片，显得生动活泼。

——约翰斯通，1907年，第74、75页

老外看老鼓浪屿 *Old Gulangyu in Foreigners' Eyes*

HOAI-TEK KINDERGARTEN TEACHERS' TRAINING DEPARTMENT, AMOY, 1936.
(Miss Pearce)　　　　(Miss Fraser)

Band, 1948

Amoy Women's School　　Johnston, 1907

第三十三章　厦门的现代教育　*Amoy's Pioneering Modern Education*

Girl Students, Gulangyu, 1921

All-Xiamen Girls' Volleyball Champions, 1932

Chapter 34 The Future of China and Amoy

Justice to China—an American's View Being an American, and having been honoured by four administrations of different political parties to a degree far beyond my deserts, I speak and write what I believe is for the interest of my own country solely. I am glad that from the President down to this humble writer all Americans are united on one subject — and that is, that justice should be done to China. Let us have no cant about this question.

Denby 1906

Amoy University--Window on the Future

China's Miracle No one, of whatever political colour, can understand or truly assess the achievement of the Chinese Communists who does not know what wholesale political, social and economic chaos they overcame. To me, having seen that chaos, even without the added havoc of the Japanese invasion, Communist China today, however much—like her own native critics—I dislike aspects of her government, is nothing short of a miracle.

"When China is united," Cyril used to say, every time we had fresh proof of the astonishing ability of the Chinese in every field they entered, "nothing will stop her becoming a world power, and none will deserve to more." But even he always added "when", on the tail end of a sigh.

Mackenzie-Grieves, 1959

China a Teacher, but not a Pupil? (1892) From time immemorial China has been the recognized teacher of all the nations around her and the pupil of none. She may well be excused for claiming a respect which for centuries all her neighbors have accorded to her. In this respect she stands in striking contrast to Japan. Japan is accustomed to take the place of learner, having largely derived her literary culture and even her language from China…It is not strange that China clings tenaciously to institutions which have stood the test of millenniums and given to her such a marvelous degree of national prosperity. Can we wonder that she listens with suspicion to any suggestion of change, especially that she should regard with apprehension a new teaching confessedly exclusive and revolutionary? Serious as the obstacles above presented are, it should be added, by way of encouragement, that the Chinese are by no means unimpressible....The fact that Japan is undergoing a rapid and complete transformation, while China as a whole is yet unmoved, though due partly, no doubt, to difference of race, is to be referred, I believe, principally to the tenfold resistance of a tenfold greater population, and also to the peculiar historical precedents and traditions alluded to above.

Dr, John L. Nevius, 1892

第三十四章　中国和厦门的未来

还中国正义——一位美国人的观点　作为一名美国人,我讲述并撰写我所相信的东西,主要是为了国家利益。由不同政治派别担纲的四届政府授予我极高的荣誉。这远远超过我应得的。让我深感欣慰的是,上至总统下至我这个卑微的作家,每个美国人在下面这个问题上高度一致——那就是,必须还中国正义。让我们在这个问题上不偏不倚。

——丹比,1906,第69~70页

中国奇迹　任何政治派别的人都不能理解或真正评估中国共产党的成就,也无法了解中共战胜了多大的政治、社会和经济混乱。对我而言,亲眼目睹了这些混乱,即使不算上日本侵略造成的浩劫,正如其本国评论家所言,我厌恶政府的方方面面。中共的今天完全是一个奇迹。

中国人所进入的任何领域中都有出色的表现。每当我们发现新证据来证明这个观点的时候时,西里尔经常说,"当中国人民团结起来的时候,任何力量都无法阻挡其成为世界强国,其他任何一个国家都无法比拟。"不过,他总是在"当"这个词后面加上深深的感叹。

——麦肯兹·格丽芙,1959年,第192、193页

中国是老师,不是学生?
(1892年)　自古以来,中国一直是邻邦的老师,从未做过他们的学生。几百年来,她要求邻邦向其朝贡情有可原。在这方面,中国与日本截然相反。日本总是将自己当作学生,文学发展的大部分来自中国,甚至连语言也是……这种制度已经受上千年的考验,给中国带来了超常的繁荣。他们坚持这种制度

Xiamen University Students at the Beach, 1950s

也就不足为奇了。中国带着疑问听取任何有关变革的建议,你难道不会感到惊讶吗?特别是要她理解并尊重一种全新的、革命性的教义。如上所述,尽管困难重重,应补充说明的是,稍加鼓励,中国人并不是冥顽不化的。日本正经历快速、彻底的变革,而中国总体上却还纹丝不动,这无疑部分源自于种族的差别。我个人认为,这主要是来自十倍多人口的十倍的抵制,以及其特殊的历史和传统。

——约翰·L.倪维思,1892年,第513、514页

老外看老鼓浪屿 Old Gulangyu in Foreigners' Eyes

The Triumph of New China (1950s) The Chinese people were involved in an enormous struggle for freedom—freedom from colonial control by western nations, and freedom from the underdevelopment which kept them poor and weak and open to aggression.

The men of the West fell in love with the beauty of China when first they beheld it, and they are in love with it still. Pottery, and sculpture, and painting, and poetry and philosophy all spoke, and the men of the West heard the sound but could not fully comprehend it. For China was speaking of the wisdom of life, and no other people had lived long enough, or were philosophical enough, or imperishable enough, or brave enough to be able to accept it—had they understood. For to men of the West bravery was every the bravery of conquest and victory by the sword and by machines which their brains conceived and their hands learned to make. To be defeated was to these to perish from the earth…

MacGowan, 1914
Fortune Teller--China's Future?

Now China finds a new expression and this expression the West can understand. For its terms are revolution against tyranny of the white man, expulsion of the invader; and its means are armies and guerrillas and planes; and its spirit is the spirit of hatred. China speaks now in terms understandable to militarism and progress in their Western sense, but she scorns the speaking even while her voice is heard. For she knows with her age-old wisdom that though man may be forced to undertake that which is despicable in order not to be wiped from the barbarous earth, the enduring things are not to be gotten by the sword. To her the things which endure are the things of the soul.

Now the loud, rasping voice of China at war rings out as she rushes into battle. But China knows that what the world hears now is not herself but only the voice of her necessity. When this is past, her true voice will speak again. Will what she has to say then be understood better than before? She wonders. For she will speak of beauty and morality and peace and democracy. She will condemn war and say quietly, as she has through many ages, "All under heaven are brothers."

Spencer, 1952

第三十四章 中国和厦门的未来 The Future of China and Amoy

中国的胜利(20世纪50年代) 中国人民为争取自由而艰苦奋战。这种自由是为了摆脱西方国家的殖民统治和落后的经济。经济的落后使得中国人民贫困、积弱,备受侵略。

西方人对中国的美一见钟情而且至今仍深爱着她。陶瓷、雕塑、绘画、诗歌和哲学都在诉说着美。西方人听到了美的诉说,却不能完全理解。因为中国诉说的是人生的智慧,而其他民族历史不够悠久,抑或哲理不够深,或不够坚强,或不够勇敢,因此不能接受这些人生智慧。要是他们能理解,历史将重新改写! 对西方人而言,真正的勇敢不过是他们用脑子想象和双手制造的刀剑与机械所带来的征服和胜利,而失败者属于那些将从地球消失的人……

现在,中国找到了新的表达方式。这种方式西方能够理解,因为它的术语是反对白人的暴政和驱逐侵略者,手段是军队、游击队和飞机,精神是仇恨。如今,中国用军事实力和进步等西方国家所能理解的术语讲话,但是她不屑去说,即使她的声音能被听到。因为随着岁月而增长的智慧,她知道,为了避免从野蛮的地球上消失,人类可能会被迫从事卑劣的行径。永恒的事物是不可能用刀剑获取的。对她来说,能经久不衰的东西只有事物的灵魂。

如今,中国冲入新的战斗,战争喧闹嘈杂的声音渐渐消逝。但中国知道,世界听到的不是自己,而是她的需求的声音。但这过去以后,真正的声音会出现。到那时,她所说的会比以前更准确地被理解吗?她不得而知。因为她将诉说的是美、道德、和平和民主。她谴责战争,她将像以往一样,轻轻地说:"普天之下皆兄弟。"

——斯宾塞,1952年,第255~257页

East and West on Gulangyu (around 1900) Jim Cummings

老外看老鼓浪屿 Old Gulangyu in Foreigners' Eyes

Goodbye Amoy (1920s)   From Camel Rock, I looked regretfully at the island we were to leave. Up on the great pile of boulders the edgeless wind stroked our faces, its gentle pawing impossible to relate to the typhoon's tearing buffets. Below us, the feathery acacias, the false peppers threw up their green spray into the steamy air. In the Chinese gardens, countless pots of neatly-trained chrysanthemums replaced the alignment of poinsettias. Everywhere the crotons flaunted their bayadere yellow and crimson, brilliantly hideous against its native green. The sea made a pewter setting in which the off-shore fishermen seemed caught and fixed, and the sea itself caught and kept still by the faint, encircling hills…

…when the Chinese get united, they'll put paid to the Japs and anyone else who comes up against them out here. And I'm not at all sure that in the long run they wouldn't be the best people to control Asia. Once they get going…

Mackenzie-Grieves, 1959

Afterword   When I recall the backwardness of China in the year 1866, and …then when I note the tremendous strides the Chinese have made during a decade or so, it seems as if the charge of inertia must be withdrawn…never again will it be possible to renew the charge of inertia; because the motion which will have been imparted is to endure for all time. But will it go on to self-destructive acceleration; or will it be wisely controlled by the rulers and leaders of the Coming China, so at to benefit the Chinese themselves and contribute to the welfare of the whole world?"

Goodrich, 1911

"Oh! if I were but back to Amoy!"

Dr. Young in his last days (Barbour, 1855)

第三十四章　中国和厦门的未来　*The Future of China and Amoy*

再见，厦门（20世纪20年代）　从骆驼峰（即现在的日光岩），我充满遗憾地看着我们即将离开的小岛。站在岩石的最高峰，微风轻拂。我们无法把它的温柔与台风季节的猛烈联系在一起。在我们的脚下，毛茸茸的金合欢像火红的辣椒在湿热的空气中长出了嫩绿的新枝。在中国人的花园里，无数精心培育的菊花盆栽换下了排成直线的一品红。放眼望去，变叶木正在炫耀自己舞女般的红黄色彩，在当地的一片绿色中显得特别丑陋。

大海好像用白锡制作了一个场景：海边的渔民入景、凝固了，灰暗的群山把大海围住，让它肃静……

……当中国人民团结起来的时候，他们将打败日本以及其他任何反对的人。他们最终将成为最合适控制亚洲的民族，这一点我深信不疑。一旦他们开始行动……

——麦肯兹·格丽芙，1959年，第176、177页

后记　当我回想起1866年中国的落后情形、然后再看看最近十几年来她所取得的巨大进步时，如果能收回指责，则似乎应该收回对中国人懒惰的指责，因为她将透露出来的动向是能够经受时间考验的。但是，中国是将加速走向自我毁灭，或者是由未来中国的领袖和统治者用智慧来掌控，让中国人自己受益，并对整个世界的福利作出贡献？

戈德里奇，1911年

"噢！要是我能再回到厦门！"

——杨格博士（临终前在巴伯尔说），1855年，第55页

445

老外看老鼓浪屿 *Old Gulangyu in Foreigners' Eyes*

FAR AMOY.

From "The Drum Wave Island and other Tales." by B.N., Hong Kong. 1904

In far Amoy—where they use their noses
    To wing the words that they wish to utter——,
Life isn't always a Bed of Roses,
    You may have the Bread and not the Butter,
        For the Gold of living has some alloy
            In far Amoy!

In far Amoy—where the Pigtail shiny
    More often circles the coolie's head,
Where the cult of Honesty's less than tiny
    And no one's silent unless he's dead——,
        The sights, the odours, the sounds annoy
            In far Amoy!

In far Amoy, of a summer morning
    The sun glares down and your eyesight dazes,
Your frame with Prickly Heat adorning;
    In early autumn (what more amazes)
        Your peace is broken by Dengue coy
            In far Amoy.

In far Amoy, when the nights are stifling,
    (No slightest whisper of cooling breeze),
Mosquitoes revel in airy trifling
    And Crickets chatter among the trees,
        So night-time gives but a little joy
            In far Amoy.

In far Amoy in the winter weather
    The perfect season of all begins,
You love her shores and her hills together
    And grant forgiveness for all the sins
        You daily suffer from Cook and Boy
            In far Amoy!

第三十四章 中国和厦门的未来 *The Future of China and Amoy*

57 GOOD-BYE!
From "The Drum Wave Island and other Tales." by B.N., Hong Kong, 1904

Passing away, the smoke behind us drifting,
    The engine's thud suggests the loss we rue—
Measured and slow, in strain like this unplifting:
    Good-bye,—and best of luck—to Kolongsu!

Gazing behind, dim grows the shore and dimmer,
    And thoughts we foster creep into the gaze,
For something makes the fleeting scene to glimmer
    With-long-drawn-memories-of happy days.

The rest has vanished, Lam Tai Bu still lingers,
    Yet it too flickers, falters, out of sight,
Like the last tingle fading from the fingers
    When one—clasped hands—and bade a last—Good-Night.

Good-bye the path that never seemed to tire
    Along the beaches of that little isle,
When the sun set, a shining ball of fire,
    Leaving the West sky—crimson—for a while!

Good-bye our strayings on Amoy's old island
    Toward Tiger-Temple, 'neath a kindly sun,
And Koan Jit Tai, o'er rocky path and byland—
    Dear idle wanderings!—All of them—are done.

Good-bye the friends, the staunch, the true and trusty,
    Those we once loved and those who love us still,
In these hot climes even Friendship may grow rusty,
    Now clear—distinct,—now faded—like yon hill!

But never mind. A difference comes at parting,
    And many praises to Yourself are due,
Just now the thought 'to return no more' is smarting :—
    Good-night,—and best of luck—to Kolongsu!

FINALE.

From "The Drum Wave Island and other Tales." by B.N., Hong Kong, 1904

When the last Amoy pumelo's eaten
    And the last Amoy oyster is sped,
When the last Amoy tiger is beaten
    From out of his cavern, and dead;
When the last Amoy sugar-cane's vanished
    And the last of the Oolong is drunk,
When the Tan and the Ng clans are banished,
    And the great Amoy joss-rock is sunk;

When each coolie, at work and at leisure,
    Lets his pigtail hang down on his back,
When the horrible music they treasure
    Has ceased to put sleep on the rack;
When they've learnt not to speak through their noses,
    And they've no longer Eight Tones but One,
When each house smells of attar of roses
    And not—as they always have done!

When Typhoid is never more heard of
    And water is drinkably pure,
When there's not any Plague to be scared of,
    And Dengue has also a cure;
When hushed is the humming mosquito
    And crickets no longer annoy,
This place may be 'perfectly sweet,'—oh,
    But 'twill be no longer Amoy!

参考文献 Bibliography

Bibliography

Abend, Hallett, "*Treaty Ports*," Doubleday, Doran and Company, Inc, New York, 1944

Allom, Thomas and Wright, the Reverend G.N., "*China in a Series of Views, Displaying the Scenery, Architecture, and Social Habits of that Ancient Empire*," Fisher, London and Paris, 1843.

"*The Amoy Gazette*" (厦门钞报)

"Amoy General Geographical Description, &c." *China Review*, Vol. 22, No.3, 1896

Anderson, John L., "Our Horse Races in China," in *Outing*, Vol. XVI, Issue 5, 5 August, 1890

Anderson, John A., M.D., "The Opium Question: A New Opportunity," in *Chinese Recorder*, Vol. 37, August, 1906.

Anti-Cobweb Society, "*Fukien Arts and Industries: Papers by Members of the Anti-Cobweb Society, Foochow, Fukien, China*," Christian Herald Industrial Press, Foochow 1933.

"*Greetings from Amoy; Amoy Mission, 1842—1907*," Pamphlet by Reformed Church of America.

"Asia Journal and Monthly Register for British India and its Dependencies," in *Supplementary Intelligence*, Vol. XXVI, July to December 1828, London, 1828

Baldwin, Rev. S.L.D.D., "Lieutenant Wood on Missionaries in China," in *Chinese Recorder*, Vol. 20, Nov. 1889.

Ball, Benjamin Lincoln, "*Rambles in Eastern Asia: Including China and Manila, During Several Years Residence*," James French and Company, Boston, 1856

Ball, J. Dyer, "*Things Chinese; or Notes Connected with China*," Kelly & Walsh, Hong Kong, 1903

Ball, J. Dyer, "*The Celestial and his Religions: or, the religious aspect in China. Being a series of lectures on the religions of the Chinese*," Kelly and Walsh, Hong Kong, 1906

Band, Edward, "*Working His Purpose Out: The History of the English Presbyterian Mission*," Presbyterian Church of England, London, 1948

Barbour, George F., "*China and the Missions at Amoy, with Notice of the Opium Trade,*" William P. Kennedy, Edinburgh, 1855.

Bax, Captain B.W., R.N, "*The Eastern Seas; Being a Narrative of the "Dwarf" in China, Japan, and Formosa,*" John Murray, London, 1875

Beach, Harlan P., "*Dawn on the Hills of T'ang, or, Missions in China,*" in Student Volunteer Movement for Foreign Missions," New York, 1905

Bedloe, Edward, M.D., U.S. Consul, reporting in "*Weekly Abstract of Sanitary Reports,*" Supervising Surgeon-General M.H,S., Government Printing Office, Washington, 1893

Bedloe, Edward, M.D., U.S. Consul in Amoy, :"*Public Health Reports*, Vol. 2, January 1, 1881

Beltman, Henry, "*90 Years with Uncle Henry,*" Robert Schuller Ministries, Garden Grove, California, 1984

Bishop, Mrs. J.F., "*Chinese Pictures; Notes on Photographs Made in China,*" Cassell and Company Limited, London, 1900

Blakeslee, George H., Editor, "*China and the Far East: Clark University Lectures,*" Thomay Y. Crowell and Co., New York, 1910

B.N., "*The Drum Wave Island and other Verses of the China Coast,*" Kelly & Walsh, Ltd., 1904

Boehm, Lise, "*China Coast Tales,*" Kelly and Walsh Limited, Shanghai, 1897. "In the Sixties."

Bonar, Rev. Andrew A., "*Memoir of the Life and Brief Ministry of Rev. David Sandeman,*" James Nisbet & Co., London, 1861.

Boulger, Demetrius Charles, "*China—Nations of the World Series,*" Peter Fenelon Collier, New York, 1902

Bowra, Cecil A.V., Commissioner of Customs, "Amoy," in *Wright*, 1908

Bradford, Ruth P., "*The Journal and Letters of Ruth Bradford, 1861—1872,*" Prospect Press, Hartford, Connecticut, 1938.

Breck, Samuel, "*Descendants of Aaron and Mary (Church) Magoun, of Pembroke, Massachusetts, Third Edition,*" Washington, D.C., 1891.

Breuer, Hans, "*Columbus was Chinese, Discoveries and Inventions of the Far East,*" Herder and Herder, New York, 1972

参考文献 *Bibliography*

Brown, C. Campbell, *"China in Legend and Story,"* Fleming H. Revell Company, NY, 1907

Bruce, C.D., Colonel, *"The Provinces of China"*; Reprinted from *The National Review (China)* as *"The National Review Annual,"* The National Review Office, Shanghai, 1910

Caldwell, George W., M.D., *"Oriental Rambles,"* G.W. Caldwell, Poughkeepsie, N.Y., 1906.

Caldwell, *"China Coast Family,"* Henry Regnery Company, Chicago, 1953

Campbell, Rev.W., F.R.G.S., "Education and Work for the Chinese Blind," *in Chinese Recorder*, Vol. 21, p. 450, October, 1889

Carles, William Le Gendre, U.S. Consul in Amoy, *"How to Deal with China. A Letter to de B. Rand. Kiem,"* in *Esquire*, Agent of the United States, Amoy, 1871.

Chater, Paul Cachik; Orange, James, *"The Chater Collection: Pictures Relating to China, Hongkong, Macao, 1655—1860; with Historical and Descriptive Letterpress by James Orange,"* London, Thornton Butterworth Limited, 1924

"Chinese Recorder", Vol. 5, American Presbyterian Mission Press, Shanghai, May

Clarke, Basil, *"Chinese Science and the West,"* Nile & MacKenzie, Ltd. London, 1980.

Close, Upton, *"In the Land of the Laughing Buddha; the Adventures of an American Barbarian in China,"* G.P. Putnam and Sons, New York & London, 1924.

Coffin, George, *"A Pioneer Voyage to California and Round the World, 1849 to 1852"* Gorham B. Coffin, Illinois, June, 1908.

Cope, Captain, *"A New History of the East-Indies: With Brief Observations on the Religion, Customs, Manners and Trade of the Inhabitants...",* M. Cooper, London, 1754.

Corwin, Edward Tanjore, D.D. *"A Manual of the Reformed Church in America (Formerly Reformed Dutch Church), 1628—1902,"* New Brunswick, New Jersey, 1902.

Cressy-Marcks, Violet, *"Journey into China,"* E.P. Dutton & Co., Inc., New York, 1942

Gordon-Cumming, Miss, *"The Explosion at Amoy,"* St. James' Gazette, *in Littell's Living Age*, Feb. 4, 1888.

Cunynghame, Colonel Arthur Augustus Thurlow, *"An Aide-De-Camp's Recollections of Service in China, A Residence in Hong-Kong, and Visits to Other Islands in the Chinese Seas,"* London, 1853

Curtis, Benjamin Robbins, "*Dottings Round the Circle*," James R. Osgood & Company, Boston, 1876

D'Almeida, Anna, "*A Lady's Visit to Manilla and Japan*," Hurst and Blackett, London, 1863.

Darley, Mary, "*Cameos of a Chinese City*," [Jian 'Ou] Church of England Zenana Missionary Society, Missionary Society, 27 Chancery Lane, London, 1917

Darley, Mary, "*The Light of the Morning*," Church of England Zenana Missionary Society, Missionary Society, 27 Chancery Lane, London, 1903

Davis, John Francis, "*The Chinese: General Description of the Empire of China and its Inhabitants*," Vol. 2, Charles Knight & Company, London, 1836

Davis, Rev. J.A., "*The Young Mandarin; a Story of Chinese Life*", Congregational Sunday-School and Publishing Society, Boston and Chicago, 1896

Dean, William, "*The China Mission: Embracing a History of the Various Missions of All Denominations Among the Chinese, with Biographical Sketches of Deceased Missionaries*," Sheldon & Co., New York, 1859

De Jong, Gerald F., "*The Reformed Church in China 1842—1951*," Wm. B. Eerdmans Publishing Co., Michigan, 1992

Denby, Hon. Charles, LL.D., [Thirteen Years United States Minister to China], "*China and Her People: Being the Observations, Reminiscences, and Conclusions of an American Diplomat,* "Vol. II, L.C. Page and Company, Boston, 1906

Denby, Hon. Charles, LL.D., "*China's Open Door*," Lothrop Publishing, Boston, 1900

Dennis, Rev. James S., "*Christian Missions and Social Progress: A Sociological Study of Foreign Missions*," Vol. III, Fleming H. Revell Company, NY, 1906

DeVelder, Walter, "A Missionary Journey Over Nine Decades" (unpublished).

Dobell, Peter, "*Travels in Kamtchatka and Siberia, with a Narrative of a Residence in China,* "Vol. II, London, 1830. Dobell: Counselor of the Court of His Imperial Majesty the Emperor of Russia".

Du Halde, P., " *The General History of China*," (4 vols: London, 1741), vol.1 p.169.

Dukes, Edwin Joshua, "*Everyday Life in China; or, Scenes Along River and Road in Fuh-Kien*," London Missionary Society's Edition, The Religious Tract Society, 56, Paternoster Row; 65, St. Paul's Churchyard; and 164, Piccadilly, 1885

Duryea, Rev. William Rankin Duryea, D.D., *"The Amoy Mission,"* Excerpted from *"A Manual of the Missions of the Reformed (Dutch) Church in America,"* by Sangster, Mrs. Margaret E., Ed.; Board of Publication of the Reformed Church in America, New York, 1877, pp.170-209

Ecke, Gustav, and Demieville, P., *"The Twin Pagodas of Zayton,"* Harvard University Press, Massachusetts, 1935.

Edkins, Jane Rowbotham Stobbs, *"Chinese Scenes and People: With Notices of Christian Missions and Missionary Life in a Series of Letters from Various Parts of China,"* James Nisbit and Company, London, 1863

Edkins, Joseph, D.D., *"Introduction to the Study of the Chinese Characters,"* Trubner and Company, London, 1875

Edkins, Rev. J., D.D., "Early Forms of Chinese," in *Chinese Recorder and Missionary Journal*, Vol. 16, No. 2, March-April, 1885.

English Presbyterian Messenger, Vol 1. 1st May 1845 to 31st December 1847, Hamilton, Adams, and Co., Paternoster-Row, London, 1847

Esther. Joe, *"This Is The Way, Walk Ye In It,"* Privately printed, Redlands, Ca. 1977

Eve, Paul F. M.D. and Garvin, I.P. M.D. *"The Southern Medical and Surgical Journal Vol. 1, 1845 New Series,"* P.C. Guieu Publisher, Augusta, Jan. 1845

Fagg, John Gerardus, *Chinese Recorder*,Vol. 23,Nov.1892.

Fagg, John Gerardus, *"Forty Years in China, the Life of Rev.John van Nest Talmage,"* Brooklyn, 1894

Fenn, C.H. Rev., "Methods of Self Support," in *Chinese Recorder*, Vol. 29, No. 2, Feb. 1898

Fergusson, James, *"The Illustrated Handbook of Architecture,"* John Murray, London, 1855

Fisher, Lena Leonard, *"The River Dragon's Bride,"* Abingdon Press, New York, 1922

Ford, John D., *"An American Cruiser in the East, Travels and Studies in the Far East,"* 2nd Edition, With an Account of the Battle of Manila, April 30, 1898, A.S. Barnes and Ford Company, New York, 1898, was First Engineer of the Pacific Station, United States Navy.

Forgues-Daurand, Paul-Emile, *"La Chinese Ouverte, Adventures d'un Fan-Kouei dans le*

▶ 453

pays de Tsin," H. Fournier, Paris, 1845

Foster, John W., "*American Diplomacy in the Orient,*" 1903.

Foster, Ellsworth, D. Ed., "*The World Book,*" Vol. 1, The World Book Inc., Chicago, 1918.

Franck, Harry A., "*Wandering in Northern China,*" The Century Co., New York, 1923

Franck, Harry A., "*Roving Through Southern China,*" The Century Co., New York, 1925.

Fullerton, W.Y., and Wilson, C.E., "*New China—A Story of Modern Travel,*" Morgan and Scott, Ltd., (Office of the Christian), 12 Paternoster Buildings, London, 1910.

Gamewell, Mary Ninde, "*New Life Currents in China,*" Interchurch Press, New York, 1919

Gaunt, Rev. L.H., Ed., "*The Chronicle of the London Missionary Society,*" Vol. VIII, No. 85 New Series, London, 1899

Giles, Herbert Allan, L.L.D., "*A Short History of Koolangsu,*" Amoy, 1878.

Giles, Herbert Allen, L.L.D., "*China and the Chinese,*" Columbia University Press, N.Y., 1902.

Gillespie, Rev. William, "*The Land of Sinim, or, China and Chinese Missions,*" Myles Macphail, London, 1854 [Gillespie was "For seven years agent of the London Missionary Society at Hong-Kong and Canton, and now minister of the United Presbyterian Church, Shiels, Aberdeen."]

Goodrich, Joseph King, "*The Coming China,*" A.C. McClure Co., Chicago, 1911

Gordon-Cumming, Miss, in "*Littell's Living Age,*" Fifth Series, Volume LXL, No. Feb. 4, 1888.

Gottschall, Terrell D., "*By order of the Kaiser,*" Naval Institute Press, Annapolis, Maryland, 2003

Graves, Rev. Rosewell Hobart, "*Forty Years in China,*" R.H. Woodward Company, Baltimore, 1895.

Griffis, William Elliot Griffis, D.D., L.H.D., "*Hepburn of Japan, and His Wife and Helpmates; a Life Story of Toil for Christ,*" Westminster Press, Philadelphia, 1913

Groot, J.J.M., "*The Religious System of China, its ancient forms, evolution, history and present aspect. Manners, customs and social institutions connected therewith,"* Vol. 1, 1892. Book 1. Disposal of the Dead. Vol. 1, Part. 1 Funeral Rites, Chapter 1, The Decease.

Gutzlaff, Karl F. A., *"Journal of Three Voyages Along the Coast of China in 1831, 1832, and 1833,"* Frederick Westley and A.H. Davis, London, 1834.

Gutzlaff, Charles, Rev. by Rev. Andrew Reed, D.D., *"China Opened; or, A Display of the Topography, History, Customs, Manners, Arts, Manufactures, Commerce, Literature, Religion, Jurisprudence, etc. of the Chinese Empire,"* Vol. II Smith, Elder & Co., London, 1838.

Haffner, Christopher, *"Amoy—The Port and the Lodge,"* The Corinthian Lodge of Amoy, No. 1806 EC, Hong Kong, 1997

Hamilton, Alexander, *"New Account of the East Indies, Being the Observations and Remarks of Captain Alexander Hamilton, 1688—1723,"* King's Printing House, printed by John Mosman, Edinburgh, 1727

Hart, Robert, *"These from the Land of Sinim: Essays on the Chinese Questions,"* Chapman and Hall, London, 1901.

Headland, Isaac Taylor, *"China's New Day,"* Frank Wood Printer, Boston, Massachusetts, 1912.

Hewlett, Sir Meyrick, *"Forty Years in China,"* Macmillan & Co., Ltd., 1943.

Hobson, John M.,*"The Eastern Origins of Western Civilization,"* Cambridge Univ. Press, U.K. 2004.

Holkeboer, Tena, *"God's Bridge, or the Story of Jin-Gi,"* Wm. B. Eerdmans Publishing Company, Grand Rapids, MI, 1944

Hollister, Mary Brewster, *"Lady Fourth Daughter of China,"* The Central Committee on the United Study of Foreign Missions, Cambridge, Massachusetts, 1932

Hughes, George, [Commissioner of Imperial Maritime Customs at Amoy] *"Amoy and Surrounding Districts,"* De Souza and Company, Hong Kong, 1872

Hurlbut, Floy, *"The Fukienese: a Study in Human Geography,"* Doctoral dissertation for University of Nebraska, 1939

Johnston, Rev. James., *"China and Formosa; The Story of a Successful Mission,"* Hazell, Watson, & Viney, Ld. London, 1898

Johnston, Meta and Lena, Jin Ko-Niu, *"A Brief Sketch of the Life of Jessie M. Johnston*

For Eighteen Years W.M.A. Missionary in Amoy, China," T. French Downie 21 Warwick Lane, London, E.C. 1907

Joseland, Rev. Frank P. *"Our Missionary Districts, Amoy and Chiang-Chiu"*, in *Gaunt*, 1899.

Keith, Marian, *"The Black Bearded Barbarian: The Life of George Leslie Mackay of Formosa,"* The Missionary Society of the Methodist Church, The Young People's Forward Movement Department, Toronto, 1912.

Kesson, John (of the British Museum),*"The Cross and the Dragon, or, The Fortunes of Christianity in China, with Notices of the Christian Missions and Missionaries, and some Accounts of the Chinese Secret Societies,"*Smith, Elder & Co., London, 1854.

King, F. H. , D. Sc., *"Farmers of Forty Centuries, or, Permanent Agriculture in China, Korea and Japan,"* University of Wisconsin, 1911

King, John W., Master, R.N., *"The China Pilot, Comprising the Coasts of China, Korea, and Tartary; The Sea of Japan, Gulfs of Tartary and Amur, and Sea of Okhotsk; and the …"* 3rd Edition, Hydrographic Office, Admiralty, London, 1861.

Knollys, Major Henry, *"English Life in China,"* Smith, Elder & Company, London, 1885

Kwantes, Helen, *"She has done a Beautiful Thing for me; Portraits of Christian Women in Asia."* OMF Books.

LaMotte, Ellen N., *"Peking Dust,"* The Century Company, New York, 1919.

Lawrence, James B., U.S.M.C. *"China and Japan, and a Voyage Thither: An Account of a Cruise in the Waters of the East Indies, China and Japan,"* Press of Case, Lockwood & Brainard, Hartford, Connecticut, 1870.

Lawrence, Una Roberts, *"Lottie Moon,"* Sunday School Board of the Southern Baptist Convention, Nashville, 1927

Lewis, Elizabeth Foreman, *"Portraits from a Chinese Scroll,"* the John C. Winston Company, Chicago, 1938

Liddell, T. Hodgson, *"China, it's Marvel and Mystery,"* John Lane, New York, 1909

Lin, Yutang, *"My Country and My People,"* Foreign Language and Teaching Press, Beijing, 1998.

Little, Archibald, Mrs. *"Intimate China: The Chinese as I Have Seen Them,"* Hutchinson & Co., London, 1899

参考文献 Bibliography

Lockhart, William, "*The Medical Missionary in China: A Narrative of Twenty Years' Experience*," Hurst and Blackett, Publishers, Spottiswoode and Company, London, 1861

Low, Captain Charles Porter, "Some Recollections by Captain Charles P. Low: Commanding the Clipper Ships "Houqua," "Jacob Bell," "Samuel Russell," and "N. B. Palmer," in *The China Trade 1847-1873*, George H. Ellis Company, Boston, 1906

Lowrie, Rev. Walter M., "*Memoirs,*" Board of Foreign Missions of the Presbyterian Church, New York, 1850.

Lu, C.C., of Ningpo, China "*China and England: A Lecture Delivered at Sheffield University*," Sheffield Independent Press, Sheffield, U.K., 1904

Macaulay, Hastings, "*A Cruise in the China Seas*," G.P. Putnam & Company, New York, 1852.

MacCauley, Hastings, "*Life Among the Chinese*", Carlton and Porter, New York, 1861.

MacGowan, John, "*The History of Self-Support in the London Mission*," *Chinese Recorder*, Vol. 18, December, 1887.

Macgowan, Rev. John, "*Christ or Confucius, Which?, or, The Story of the Amoy Mission*," London Missionary Society, 14 Blomfield Street, E.C.; John Snow & Co., 2 Ivy Lane, Paternoster Row, E.C. 1895

Macgowan, Rev. John, "*Pictures of Southern China*," The Religious Tract Society, London, 1897

Macgowan, Rev. John, "*Sidelights on Chinese Life*," Kegan Paul, Trench, Trubner & Co., Limited, London, 1907

Macgowan, Rev. John, "Lights and Shadows of Chinese Life," North China Daily News & Herald Ltd., Shanghai, 1909

Macgowan, Rev. John, "*Men and Manners of Modern China*," T. Fisher Unwin, London, 1912.

Macgowan, John, "*How England Saved China*," T. Fisher Unwin, London, 1913.

Macgowan, John, "*Beside the Bamboo*," London Missionary Society, 16 New Bridge Street, London, 1914.

Macgregor, Rev. W. Letter dated January 14, 1875, in *The Messenger and Missionary Record of the Presbyterian Church in England*, London, April 1, 1875

Macguire, Theophane, C.P., "*Hunan Harvest*, "Bruce Publishing Company, Milwaukee, 1946.

Mackenzie-Grieve, Averil, "*A Race of Green Ginger*," Putnam, London, 1959

Maclay, Rev. R. S., "*Life Among the Chinese: With Characteristic Sketches and incidents of Missionary Operations and Prospects in China*," Carlton & Porter, New York, 1861.

MacPherson, D., M.D., "*Two Years in China: Narrative of the Chinese Expedition, from its formation in April, 1840, to the treaty of peace in August, 1842*," Saunders and Otley, London, 1843.

Manson-Bahr, Sir Philip, "*Patrick Manson, The Father of Tropical Medicine*," Thomas Nelson and Sons, Ltd., Edinburgh, 1962

Martin, Robert Montgomery, "*China; political, commercial, and social; in an official report to her Majesty's Government*," Vol. II, James Madden, London, 1847

Matheson, Donald, Esq., "Narrative of the Mission to China of the English Presbyterian Church, with Remarks on the Social Life and Religious Ideas of the Chinese, by the Rev. James MacGowan (London Missionary Society of Amoy), and Notes on Climate, Health and Outfit, By John Carnegie, Esq., M.D. of Amoy", James Nisbet and Company, London, 1866.

Matheson, Mrs., Ed., Memorials of Hugh M. Matheson [1921-1898] Edited by his wife with a prefatory note by the Rev. J. Oswald Dykes, M.A., D.D. Principal of Westminster College, Cambridge. London: Hodder and Stoughton. 1899

Mathews, Basil, and Southon, Arthur E., "*Torchbearers in China, Missionary Education Movement of the United States and Canada*," New York, 1924

Mayers, Wm. Fred, and Dennys, N.B., "*The Treaty Ports of China and Japan*," Trubner & Company, London, 1867

McCasland, David, "*Eric Liddell-Pure Gold*," Discovery House Publishers, Michigan, 2001.

Menpes, Mortimer, and Blake, Sir Arthur Henry, "*China*," Adam and Charles Black, London, 1909.

"*Messenger and Missionary Record of the Presbyterian Church in England*," London, April 1, 1875

Metcalf, Franklin P., "*Travellers and Explorers in Fukien before 1700*," The Hong Kong Naturalist, December, 1934

参考文献 Bibliography

Methodist Episcopal Church Missionary Society, "*The Gospel in All Lands Illustrated*," Eugene R. Smith, Publisher, New York, Jan.-June, 1881

Michie, Alexander, "The Englishman in China During the Victorian Period, as Illustrated by the Career of Sir Rutherford Alcock, K.C.B., D.C.L., Many Years Consul and Minister in China and Japan, Vol. I", William Blackwood and Sons, Edinburgh and London, 1900

Millard, Thomas E., "*Our Eastern Question: America's Contact with the Orient and the Trend of Relations with China and Japan*," The Century Company, NY, 1916

Miller, Basil, "*Twenty Four Missionary Stories from China*," Beacon Hill Press, Kansas City, Missouri, 1948

Miller, J.Martin, "*China Ancient and Modern*," Sanderson-Whitten Publishing Co. Los Angeles, 1900

Morse, Hosea Ballou, "*The Trade and Administration of China*," Green and Company, London, 1919. Ballou was "Sometime Commissioner of Customs and Statistical Secretary, Inspectorate General of Customs."

Murray, Lieutenant Alexander,[18th Royal Irish] "Doings in China—Being the Personal Narrative of an Officer Engaged in the Late Chinese Expedition, From the Recapture of Chusan in 1841 to the Peace in Nankin in 1842." Richard Bentley, London, 1843

Nautical Magazine and Naval Chronicle for 1852, A Journal of Papers on Subjects Connected with Maritime Affairs, Notes on a Voyage to China in Her Majesty's Late Screw Steamer Reynard.—P. Cracroft, Commander. Simpkin, Marshall and Co., Ltd.

Needham, Joseph, "*Science in Traditional China*," Harvard University Press, Cambridge, 1981.

Neill, Desmond, "*Elegant Flower—First Steps in China*," John Murray, Albemarle St., London, 1956

Nevius, Helen S.C., "*Our Life in China*," Robert Carter and Brothers, New York, 1869.

Nevius, Dr. John L., Chinese Recorder, Vol. 23, Nov. 1892.

Ng, Chin-Keong, "*Trade and Society—The Amoy Network on the China Coast 1683—1735*," Singapore University Press, Singapore, 1983

Oldham, Rev. H.W., "Educational Mission Work in and near Amoy," Changpu, in *Chinese Recorder*, June 1908.

Orange, James.*The Chater Collection; Pictures Relating to China, Hongkong, Macao,*

▶ 459

1865-1860, Thornton Butterworth, Limited, London, 1924

Otte, Frances Phelps, "The Christian Intelligencer," Dec. 4, 1901 (from Taitan, Amoy, letter, August 1901).

Phillips, George, "Zaitun Researches," *Chinese Recorder and Missionary Journal,* Vol. 8, No. 2, March-April, 1877.

Pinkerton, J., "*A General Collection of Voyages and Travels, digested by J. Pinkerton,*" 1811, Vol. 8. London, 1812

Pitcher, Philip Wilson, "*Fifty Years in Amoy, a History of the Amoy Mission,*" Reformed Church of America Board of Publication, NY, 1893

Pitcher, Rev. P.W., Letter from Amoy Boy's Academy, Kolongsu, Dec. 22nd, 1894, in *Chinese Recorder,* Vol.26, February.

Pitcher, Rev. P.W., "The Native Pastorate at Amoy; or Another Object-Lesson in Self-Support," Amoy, July 26th, 1900; in *Chinese Recorder,* Vol. 31, October, 1900 pp. 503-509, and Nov., pp. 550- "The Amoy Plan."

Pitcher, Philip Wilson, "*In and About Amoy,*" Methodist Publishing House, Shanghai, 1912

Regnault, Elias, and Doane, Augustus Sidney, "*The Criminal History of the English Government: From the First Massacre of the Irish, to the Poisoning of the Chinese,*" translated from the French, J.S. Redfield, New York, 1843

Richard, Timothy, "*Forty Five Years in China; Reminiscences,*" Frederick A. Stokes Company, New York, 1916

Ross, Frank, Jr., "*Oracle Bones, Stars, and Wheelbarrows, Ancient Chinese Science and Technology,*" Houghton Mifflin Company, Boston, 1982

Rudy, Stella M., "*Children of China,*" Rand McNally and Company, Chicago, 1937

Sadler, Rev. James F., "Chinese Customs and Superstitions, or, What They do at Amoy," *China Review,* XXII, No. 6, 1897.

Sadler, Rev. James F., "*The Anglo-Chinese College at Amoy,*" in *Gaunt,* 1899.

Sale, George, and others, "*The Modern Part of an Universal History: From the Earliest Account of Time,*" VoL. VIII, Compiled from Original Writers, Printed for Richardson, S., et al., London, 1759.

Sangster, Mrs. Margaret E., Ed.; "*A Manual of the Missions of the Reformed (Dutch) Church in America,*" Board of Publication of the Reformed Church in America, New

York, 1877.

Scarth, John, "*Twelve Years in China*," Thomas Constable and Company, Edinburgh, 1860

Scott, Roderick, "*Fukien Christian University*," United Board for Christian Colleges in China, NY, 1954.

Selby, Thomas Gunn, "*As the Chinese See Us*," Fisher Unwin, London, 1901

Shore, Hon. Henry Noel, R.N., "*The Flight of the Lapwing, A Naval Officer's Jottings in China, Formosa and Japan*," Longmans, Green and Company, London, 1881

Singleton, Esther, "*China: Described by Great Writers*," Dodd, Mead and Company, New York, 1912

Sirr, Henry Charles, "*China and the Chinese: Their Religion, Character, Customs, and Manufacturers; the Evils Arising from the Opium Trade*," Vol. I, Wm. S. Orr and Company, London 1849

Smith, D. Warres, "*European Settlements in the Far East*," Sampson, Low, Marston & Company, London, 1900

Smith, Mary Augusta Doty, "*The China Story: Recollections of a Little Girl's Life in Amoy, China*," unpublished memoir. [Daughter of Elihu Doty, RCA Missionary to China, 1844—1864]

Smith, Rev. J.N.B., "Money and Missions," in *Chinese Recorder*, Vol. 29, No. 2, Feb. 1898

Smith, George, "*A Narrative of an Exploratory Visit to Each of the Consular Cities of China, on behalf of the Church Missionary Society, in the Years 1844, 1845, 1846*," Harper and Brothers Publishers, New York, 1857.

Soothill, William E., "*A Mission in China*," Young People's Missionary Movement, New York, 1907

Spencer, Cornelia "*Made in China*," Alfred A. Knopf, New York, 1952.

Stevens, John Austin, "*The Magazine of American History with Notes and Queries, vol. IV*", A.S. Barnes and Company, New York, 1880.

Stock, Eugene, "*The History of the Church Missionary Society; its Environment, its Men and its Work, Vol. III*," Church Missionary Society, London, 1890.

Stoddard, John L., "*Stoddard's Lectures*," Stationer's Hall, London, 1897

Surgeon T.T. Jeans, R.N., "*Badminton Magazine of Sports and Pastimes*", Vol. V, July to Dec. 1897

Tai, En Sai, "*Treaty Ports in China: a Study in Diplomacy*," Columbia University Printing Office, New York, 1918

Talman, Rose H., "*Our China Years, 1916—1930*," unpublished notes, provided by Sarah Koeppe.

Temple, Robert, "*The Genius of China; 3,000 Years of Science, Discovery and Invention*," Prion Books Limited, London, 1998.

Teresi, Dick, "*Lost Discoveries, The Ancient Roots of Modern Science—from the Babylonians to the Maya*," Simon & Schuster, New York, 2002.

Thomson, John, "*The Land and the People of China*," Society for Promoting Christian Knowledge, London, 1876.

Thomson, Rev. J.C., M.D., "*Historical Landmarks of Macao*," in *Chinese Recorder*, Vol.19, August, 1888

Thomson, John, "*The Chinese*," Bobbs-Merrill Company, Indianapolis, Indiana, 1909

Timothy, Richard, "*Forty-Five Years in China—Reminiscences by Timothy Richard, D.D., Litt.D.*," Frederick A. Stokes Company, New York, 1916

Warnshuis, Rev. A.L., M.A., "*A Brief Sketch of the Life and Work of Dr. John A. Otte*," Amoy Mission, China, 1911

Watson, Alfred T., "*Badminton Magazine of Sports and Pastimes, Vol. V, July to Dec. 1897*", Longmans, Green and Company, London, 1907

Webb, John, "The Antiquity of China, Or An Historical Essay Endeavoring a Probability that the language of the Empire of China is the Primitive Language spoken through the whole world before the Confusion of Babel. Wherein the Customes and Manners of ye Chineans are presented, and ancient and modern Authors consulted. With a large Map of the Countrey," Obadiah Blagrave, &c., London, 1678

Werner, E.T.C., "*Myths & Legends of China*," George G. Harrap & Co. Ltd., London, 1922.

White, Francis Sellon, "*A History of Inventions and Discoveries*," C. & J. Rivington, London, 1827

Williams, Dwight, Mrs., "A Year in China, and a Narrative of Capture and Imprisonment, when Homeward Bound, on Board the Rebel Pirate Florida; with an Introductory Note by William Cullen Bryant," Hurd and Houghton, New York, 1864. [Williams was the Commissioner of Customs at Swatow, employed by the Chinese].

Williams, Edward Thomas, "*China—Yesterday and Today*," George G. Harrap & co., Ltd., London, 1923

Williamson, Rev. G.R., "*Memoir of the Rev. David Abeel, D.D.*" Robert Carter, New York, 1848

Wright, Arnold, Editor-in-Chief, "*Twentieth Century Impressions of Hongkong, Shanghai, and other Treaty Ports of China*," Lloyd's Greater Britain Publishing Company, Ltd., London, 1908

Variations on Romanization of Chinese Names
Even into the 20th century, there was no standardized Romanized spelling of most Chinese names. Amoy was complicated further by the fact that place names were rendered in both Mandarin Chinese and, primarily, Amoy Dialect Romanizations.

厦门：Xiamen: Amoy, E'meng, Hsiamen, Emwy, Hemouy, Hiamen,

鼓浪屿：Gulangyu: Kulongsu, Koolangsoo, Koolangsu, Cullemshoe

泉州：Quanzhou: Chinchew, Chwanchow, Tsuen-tcheou-foo

福州：Fuzhou: Fu-cheuo-foo, Fuchow, Foochow

台湾：Taiwan: Teywon, Formosa

郑成功：Koxinga: Cocksing

A New Chinese University in Amoy

图书在版编目(CIP)数据

老外看老鼓浪屿:汉英对照/(美)潘维廉著;潘文功,钟太福译.
—厦门:厦门大学出版社,2010.1(2019.2重印)
(魅力·老潘)
书名原文:Old Gulangyu in Foreigners' Eyes
ISBN 978-7-5615-3421-2

Ⅰ.①老… Ⅱ.①潘… ②潘… ③钟… Ⅲ.①厦门市-概况-汉、英
Ⅳ.①K925.73

中国版本图书馆 CIP 数据核字(2009)第 205948 号

出 版 人	郑文礼
责任编辑	施高翔

出版发行　厦门大学出版社
社　　址　厦门市软件园二期望海路 39 号
邮政编码　361008
总 编 办　0592-2182177　0592-2181406(传真)
营销中心　0592-2184458　0592-2181365
网　　址　http://www.xmupress.com
邮　　箱　xmup@xmupress.com
印　　刷　厦门集大印刷厂

开本	889 mm×1 194 mm　1/32
印张	14.75
插页	6
字数	600 千字
版次	2010 年 1 月第 1 版
印次	2019 年 2 月第 2 次印刷
定价	38.00 元

本书如有印装质量问题请直接寄承印厂调换

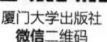

厦门大学出版社
微信二维码

厦门大学出版社
微博二维码